Urbanization and Sustainability in Asia

Urbanization and Sustainability in Asia

Case Studies of Good Practice

Edited by Brian Roberts and Trevor Kanaley

© 2006 Asian Development Bank

All rights reserved. Published 2006.
Printed in the Philippines.

Library of Congress Cataloging-in-Publication Data Available

Publication Stock No. 051206

Asian Development Bank
Case studies on urban development
    1. Asian Development Bank. 2. Urban development.

The views expressed in this book are those of the authors and do not necessarilyreflect the views and policies of the Asian Development Bank or its Board of Governors or the governments they represent.

The Asian Development Bank does not guarantee the accuracy of the data included in this publication and accepts no responsibility for any consequence oftheir use.

Use of the term "country" does not imply any judgment by the authors or the Asian Development Bank as to the legal or other status of any territorial entity.

Table of Contents

1. **Overview** 1
   Urbanization and Sustainable Development 1
   Good Practice Approaches to Urban Development 5
   Framework for Analyzing Good Practice in Asia 6
   Global Good Practice Case Studies 8
   Conclusion.. 8

2. **Urbanization and Sustainabilityin Asia**................ 13
   The Scale and Scope of Urbanization 13
   Urbanization Issues...................................... 16
   Conclusion... 40

3. **Bangladesh** 43
   Introduction 43
   Country Context 43
   Good Practice Case Studies 56
      Chittagong City Corporation:
      Dynamic and Innovative Leadership.................... 58
      Urban Credit Program of the Shakti Foundation 61
      Bangladesh Poribesh Andolon
      (Bangladesh Environment Movement).................... 63
   Strategies to Enhance Sustainable Urban Development 65
   Conclusion... 68

4. **Cambodia** 71
   Introduction 71
   Country Context 71
   Urbanization and Sustainable Development 74
   Good Practice Case Studies 80
      Phnom Penh City: Planning for All 80
      Battambang Town 86
      Growth Pole Strategy for Kratie 90

Lessons Learned from the Case Studies 94
Strategies to Enhance Sustainable
Urban Region Development 96
Conclusion... 97

5. People's Republic of China 101
Introduction 101
Country Context 104
Good Practice Case Studies......................... 115
   Nanjing: Revitalizing the Inner City 118
   Shenzhen: Building a City from Scratch........... 121
   Liaodong Peninsula: Reviving Rust-belt Industries 127
Conclusion.. 133

6. India 135
Introduction 135
Country Context 135
Good Practice Case Studies......................... 140
   Issuance of Municipal Bonds, Ahmedabad............ 141
   Reform of Property Taxation in Andhra Pradesh........ 147
   The National Urban Renewal Mission............... 151
Key Lessons 153
Sustaining Urban Development...................... 154

7. Indonesia 155
Introduction 155
Country Context 155
Urbanization Issues................................ 159
Good Practice Case Studies........................ 171
   Balanced Development in Tarakan, East Kalimantan 173
   Institutional Reform............................. 177
   Managing Rapid Urbanization in Sleman,
   the Special Region of Yogyakarta................. 178
   Community Improvement Program, Jembrana, Bali...... 181
Key Lessons Learned 183
Strategies to Enhance Sustainable
Urban Region Development 184
Conclusion... 185

8. Lao People's Democratic Republic ... 189
Introduction ... 189
Country Context ... 189
Urbanization Issues ... 191
Good Practice Case Studies ... 198
    Vientiane Urban Region Village improvements ... 198
    Luang Prabang Urban Improvements and
    Heritage Conservation ... 206
    Savannakhet and the East-West Economic Corridor ... 212
Lessons Learned ... 217
Strategies to Enhance Sustainable
Urban Region Development ... 220

9. Malaysia ... 223
Introduction ... 223
Country Context ... 224
Good Practice Case Studies ... 224
    Petaling Jaya: Local Agenda 21 Implementation ... 227
    Putrajaya, Model City of Sustainable Development ... 232
    Cyberjaya Multimedia Super Corridor,
    Innovation and Change ... 237
Strategies to Enhance Sustainable Urban Development ... 241

10. Pakistan ... 245
Introduction ... 245
Country Context ... 245
Good Practice Case Studies ... 253
    Lodhran Pilot Project ... 255
    Community-based Water Supply and
    Sanitation Services in Faisalabad ... 259
    Solid Waste Management in Lahore ... 263
Key Lessons Learned ... 266
Strategies to Enhance Sustainable
Urban Region Development ... 268

11. The Philippines ... 273
Introduction ... 273
Country Context ... 274

Good Practice Case Studies 288
   Bacolod City 290
   Naga City 295
   Iloilo City. 300
   Key Lessons Learned 303
Enhancing Sustainable Urban Region Development 304

12. Sri Lanka. 309
Introduction 309
Country Context 309
Good Practice Case Studies 321
   Community-based Solid Waste Management in
   Low-income Settlements in Dehiwala
   Mount Lavinia Municipality 323
   The Integrated Program of Action to Improve
   Health and Environment Management in the
   Colombo Municipal Area (Green Star Homes Project) . . . 326
   Clean Settlements Program in the
   Colombo Municipal Council Area. 328
   Lessons from the Case Studies. 329
Strategies for Enhancing Sustainable Urban Development. . 331
Conclusion. 340

13. Thailand 341
Introduction 341
Country Context 341
Good Practice Case Studies 355
   Muang Klaeng Municipality: Sustainable City Initiative. . . . 355
   Phichit Municipality: Waste Recycling 358
   Songkhla Municipality: Waste Management
   and Education 361
   Key Lessons Learned. 363
Strategies to Enhance Sustainable
Urban Region Development. 364
Conclusion. 366

14. Viet Nam. 369
Introduction 369
Country Context 370

Good Practice Case Studies 381
  Institutional Building in Urban Upgrading in
  Phu Thuong Ward, Hanoi. 383
  Environmental Improvement of
  Nhieu Loc-Thi Nghe Basin, Ho Chi Minh City 388
  Urban Upgrading, Environmental Impact Assessment
  in Van Mieu Ward, Nam Dinh City, Nam Dinh Province . . 393
  Lessons Learned from the Case Studies 397
  Strategies to Enhance Sustainable Urban Development . . . 398
  Conclusion. 401

**15. Global Good Practices in Sustainable
  Urban Region Development**. 403
  Curitiba, Brazil: An Unlikely but Striking Success
  of Urban Revitalization 404
  Greater Vancouver Regional District Sustainable Region
  Initiative: Turning Ideas into Action. 408
  Innovation: Key to Sustainable Urban Development
  in Singapore 414
  Brisbane: Sustainability through Improved
  City Management 418
  Greater Manchester, UK: Post-industrial Sustainability? . . . 426
  Lessons for Urban Sustainability 433

16. Lessons and Strategies for Sustainable Urban Futures . . . 437
  Common Themes. 439
  The Enabling Environment and the Performance of Cities . . 451
  Strengthening Local Government 455
  The Role of International Development Institutions. 458
  Pathways to Sustainable Urban Futures. 462

References. 467

Index 487

Foreword

Development in Asia is tied to the growth of sustainable cities. Economically dynamic cities are central to future economic growth and continuing reduction in poverty. Cities are the main locations of production, trade, and productivity growth, which provide the basis for rising standards of living. Perhaps, for too long, the discussion of development in Asia has ignored its spatial dimensions.

Over the next 25 years, Asia's urban population will grow by around 70% to more than 2.6 billion people. An additional billion people will have urban habitats. This transformation will involve major change for Asian societies with new forms of housing, employment, consumption, and social interaction for individuals and communities.

In view of this situation, the Asian Development Bank is preparing a new urban services initiative. However, little literature has been published on good practice sustainable urban development in Asia. Most studies focus on specific case studies with little reference to cross-country lessons. Therefore, it was decided to commission a book with the primary objective of disseminating knowledge about good practices in sustainable urban region development in Asia.

The Cities Alliance, a global coalition of cities and their development partners committed to scaling-up successful approaches to poverty reduction, was a natural partner for the book, and has cofinanced its production. The Asian Development Bank is an active member of the Cities Alliance, working with other members to support cities implementing financially sustainable strategies to upgrade slums and promoting inclusive long-term development strategies.

The book provides an overview of urban region development in Asia and considers how it might be made more sustainable. It examines urban development policies and "good practice" case studies in 12 countries: Bangladesh, Cambodia, People's Republic of China, India, Indonesia, Lao People's Democratic Republic, Malaysia, Pakistan, Philippines, Sri Lanka, Thailand, and Viet Nam.

We hope the book will encourage discussion on the development of Asian cities and help in the development of policies and more sustainable practices.

BINDU N. LOHANI
Director General and Special Advisor to the
President on Clean Energy and Environment
Regional and Sustainable Development Department
Asian Development Bank

Preface

Urbanization in Asia is associated with social, economic, political, and environmental transformations of unprecedented proportions. These transformations are affecting the two most populous countries in the world, the People's Republic of China (PRC) and India, and are redefining the global economy, global environmental issues, and the geopolitical landscape. Economic growth and the rapid growth of cities have brought enormous change to most Asian countries, raising living standards and reducing poverty, but at considerable social and environmental costs. The projected continuation of the urbanization process will further strain the sustainability of Asia's cities unless major improvements in city governance and management, and massive programs of infrastructure investment are implemented. The continuation of present practices and levels of investment could well see the sustainability of many Asian cities undermined, periodic urban environmental crises, and the gradual erosion of quality of life for the majority of urban populations.

This book considers urbanization in Asia and presents case studies of sustainable development "good practice" from 12 Asian countries: Bangladesh, Cambodia, PRC, India, Indonesia, Lao People's Democratic Republic (Lao PDR), Malaysia, Pakistan, Philippines, Sri Lanka, Thailand, and Viet Nam.

Each country chapter starts with a fact sheet on urbanization and economic development for the country. This country profile was derived from the databases of international agencies and provides a consistent basis for comparisons between countries. Importantly, data within the country chapters are often from internal country sources and may differ for definitional or other reasons from the country profile.

The country chapter provides an overview of issues related to urbanization and sustainability in the country concerned. Authors then present three case studies that are considered good practice. The case studies are presented under seven basic themes of sustainable urban region development. Lessons from the case studies are identified and strategies to improve the sustainability of urban development suggested.

A chapter has also been included to give examples, small vignettes, of global best practice in sustainable urban development. These case studies may not be transferable to many cities in Asia now, but provide a guide to future directions and approaches.

The final chapter presents common themes and lessons drawn from the country and case studies. The chapter then focuses on approaches for improving the enabling environment for urban governance and for strengthening local government performance. The book concludes with some thoughts on a way forward to achieve more sustainable urban region development in Asian cities.

The coeditors of the book are **Professor Brian Roberts** and **Trevor Kanaley**. Brian Roberts is Director of the Centre for Developing Cities at the University of Canberra, Australia. He chairs the Australian Capital Territory Government Sustainability Expert Reference Group. Trevor Kanaley is an Adjunct Professor of Development Studies at the University of Canberra, attached to the Centre for Developing Cities. He is an economist and planner and the former Director-General of the Australian Agency for International Development (AusAID).

The coeditors wish to acknowledge the substantial contributions made by the following authors in preparing chapters or parts of chapters in the book.

Professor Nazrul Islam, Department of Geography and Environment, University of Dhaka, and Honorary Chairman, Centre for Urban Studies, Dhaka, authored the chapter on Bangladesh.

Dr. Beng Hong Socheat Khemro, Deputy Director General, Department of Land Management and Urban Planning, Ministry of Land Management, Urban Planning and Construction, Cambodia, authored the chapter on Cambodia.

Professor Aprodicio A. Laquian, Professor Emeritus of Community and Regional Planning at the University of British Columbia, Vancouver, Canada, authored the chapter on the PRC. He was Country Representative of the United Nations Population Fund in the PRC in 1984–1990 and is the author of *Beyond Metropolis: the Planning and Governance of Asia's Mega-Urban Regions* (2005), which included studies of Shanghai; Beijing; Tianjin; Guangzhou; and Hong Kong, China.

Professor Om Prakash Mathur, National Institute of Public Finance and Policy, India, authored the chapter on India.

Dr. Wicaksono Sarosa, Executive Director, Urban and Regional Development Institute, Jakarta, Indonesia, authored the Indonesian chapter.

Richard Mabbitt, an international urban development specialist, who has been involved in urban development projects over many years, authored the chapter on the Lao PDR. He has worked on several projects in the three case study areas and other urban centers, and conducted many interviews in late 2005 to update information for this chapter.

Associate Professor Belinda Yuen, School of Design and Environment, National University of Singapore, who has worked extensively in Asia on urban planning and development projects, coauthored the chapter on Malaysia with **Professors Supian Ahmad** and **Chin Siong Ho**, Fakulti Alam Bina,

University of Technology, Malaysia. She also wrote the case study on Singapore on the global best practice case studies.

Dr. Murtaza Haider, Assistant Professor, School of Urban Planning, McGill University, Montreal, coauthored the Pakistan chapter with **Irteza Haider**. Murtza Haider was born and educated in Pakistan and has undertaken studies related to the urban sector there. Irteza Haider is a senior program officer with the National Rural Support Program in Islamabad where he is currently monitoring rehabilitation of housing and public infrastructure in the earthquake-hit areas in Northern Pakistan.

Dr. Joel Mangahas, Professor and Director, Center for Policy and Executive Development, National College of Public Administration and Governance, University of the Philippines, authored the chapter on the Philippines.

Dr. Basil Van Horen, Head of the Development Planning Program, School of Geography, Planning and Architecture, University of Queensland, Australia, coauthored the paper on Sri Lanka with **Sisira Tinnawala**, Head of the Sociology Department, University of Teradeniya, Sri Lanka.

Dr. Chamniern Vorratnchaiphan, Thailand Environment Institute, Bangkok, coauthored the chapter on Thailand with **David Villeneuve**, freelance consultant working with the Thailand Environment Institute.

Dr. Nguyen To Lang, Dean of the Faculty of Urban Management, Hanoi Architectural University, authored the chapter on Viet Nam.

Professor Hugh Swhartz, Visiting Professor of Economics at the University of the Republic in Uruguay, wrote the global good practice case study on Curitiba, Brazil. He is the author of the book *Urban Renewal, Municipal Revitalization: The Case Study of Curitiba, Brazil*.

Johnny Carline, Commissioner and Chief Administrative Officer of the Greater Vancouver Regional District, and **Lynda King**, Division Manager, Corporate Strategies, Greater Vancouver Regional District, coauthored the global good practice case study on Greater Vancouver.

John Orange, Chief Executive Officer, Brisbane City Enterprises and former Manager of Regional Collaboration, Brisbane City Council, Australia, and **Peter Cumming**, the former Chief Planner of the City of Brisbane, wrote the case study on Brisbane for the global good practice case studies with Brian Roberts.

Joe Ravetz, Deputy Director, Centre for Urban and Regional Ecology, School of Environment and Development, Manchester University, United Kingdom, wrote the case study on Manchester for the global good practice case studies and recently published a book on integrated planning for sustainable development at the city-region scale.

The coeditors also acknowledge the support of Charles Gazabon, Karen Fisher, Jenny Morris, Aine Dowling, and Associate Professor Kath Wellman from the Centre for Developing Cities, at the University of Canberra, for assistance with the editing and production of the book.

We also thank the following peer reviewers from the Asian Development Bank (ADB) who provided insights: Gulfer Cezayirli, Rudolf Frauendorfer, Tatiana Gallego-Lizon, Robert Guild, Januar Hakim, Eri Honda, Anupma Jain, Hubert Jenny, Alex Jorgensen, Amy Leung, Shakeel Khan, Michael Lindfield, Alfredo Perdiguero, Shane Rosenthal, Florian Steinberg, Martin Tornberg, Tomoo Ueda, and Robert Wihtol.

Our deep appreciation goes to WooChong Um, Director, for his strong support. In addition, special thanks to Carolyn Dedolph for publication advice; Jay Maclean and Ma. Priscila P. del Rosario for copyediting; Cecilia C. Caparas, Vicente M. Angeles, and Ronnie Elefano for layout and typesetting; and Raveendranath Rajan, Vic Lo, and Ana Maria Juico for printing.

We also thank William Cobbett, Manager, Cities Alliance; and Kevin Milroy, Sr. Operations Officer, Cities Alliance, for their insights and support.

Kallidaikurichi Easwaran Seetharam, supported by Ma. Virginita A. Capulong, coordinated the publication of the book. Kristine San Juan and Dennis Palillo also provided administrative support.

The preparation of this book would not have been possible without the funding support of ADB and the Cities Alliance.

The book is intended to help national and local governments in Asia, urban development practitioners, international development agencies, and academics and students—anyone with an interest in sustainable urban development—looking for information and examples to assist them in their work. We hope readers find the book useful in applying best practice ideas and initiatives and that it makes a modest contribution to the growth of more sustainable cities in the Asian region.

Brian Roberts and Trevor Kanaley
Centre for Developing Cities
University of Canberra
cities@canberra.edu.au
November 2006

1. Overview

BRIAN ROBERTS AND TREVOR KANALEY

URBANIZATION AND SUSTAINABLE DEVELOPMENT

Urbanization—the spatial concentration of people and economic activity—is arguably the most important social transformation in the history of civilization since man changed from being a nomadic hunter-gatherer and adopted a settled, subsistence agricultural way of life. While the timing and speed of urbanization have varied and are varying between countries, regions, and continents, the urbanization process has taken hold everywhere. It has proven to be an unstoppable and a mostly desirable phenomenon. Cities are the foundation of modern civilization; they are the engine room of economic growth and the centers of culture, entertainment, innovation, education, knowledge, and political power.

While the antecedents of urbanization are long, contemporary urbanization is now predominantly a developing-country phenomenon, centered largely in Asia. Urbanization in Asia involves around 44 million people being added to the population of cities every year. To put this in perspective, each day a further 120,000 people are added to the populations of Asian cities, requiring the construction of more than 20,000 new dwellings, 250 kilometers (km) of new roads, and additional infrastructure to supply more than six megaliters of potable water.

Urbanization has bought enormous economic and social change and benefits to most Asian countries. It has been pivotal to economic development and the growing wealth of nations in the Asian region. Urbanization has been associated with the creation of jobs for millions of people and with reductions in absolute levels of poverty. Equally important, urbanization is changing the social fabric and culture of nations. It is redefining peoples' lifestyles, employment, welfare, social structures, and institutions and creating new power relationships in households, organizations, and government. It is changing peoples' lives.

Urbanization in Asia, however, is coming at a price. More than 12 km^2 of mainly productive agricultural land and foreshores are lost daily to generally poor-quality forms of urban development. Traffic congestion and pollution continue to grow, reducing the quality of life in many urban environments. Overcrowding has become endemic in many cities. Urban poverty, associated with unemployment and the lack of access to adequate housing and services, is an increasing social problem. Urban governance—the institutions and arrangements for the planning, provision, and financing of urban infrastructure and services—has been swamped by the speed and magnitude of urbanization. There are major backlogs in the provision and maintenance of urban infrastructure and services and, if existing policy responses continue, these will worsen as urbanization continues.

Urbanization in Asia is associated with social, economic, political, and environmental transformations of unprecedented proportions. By necessity, it has elements of unpredictability and chaos. Nevertheless, as a matter of public policy, urban growth has been implemented haphazardly and inefficiently.

At best, such problems are slowing improvements in living standards and reducing the potential benefits of urbanization; at worst, they are undermining the economic, social, and environmental sustainability of Asian cities.

The urbanization process in Asia should and could be executed more efficiently and effectively. This would increase the benefits of urbanization by diminishing constraints on economic productivity and improving living standards and urban amenity. It would also reduce the human, economic, and environmental costs. Central to achieving this end is improvement in governance.

Improvements to the sustainability of Asian cities and the quality of life of their inhabitants will require nothing less than massive programs of public and private sector investments. The scale of such investments will dwarf those carried out through the Marshall Plan in the late 1940s and early 1950s or the urban public infrastructure projects in Europe in the 19th century. Central to undertaking these investments successfully is the capacity of urban governments and management to plan, implement, and finance infrastructure provision and service delivery both directly and through partnerships with the private sector. This will require political leadership and commitment to bold plans, as well as technical capacity and financial prudence. The continuation of present levels and systems of investment will see the sustainability of many Asian cities deteriorate and the gradual erosion of the quality of life for the urban population who are unable to insulate themselves from environmental problems through the private purchase of environmental goods.

In the absence of large-scale urban environmental improvement programs, the outlook for Asian cities is stark; many are reaching crisis points, as the Songhua River chemical spill in the northern People's Republic of China (PRC) in November 2005 demonstrated. While most cities will struggle to muddle through, history suggests that urban environmental crises are likely to eventuate before governments provide the leadership and focus necessary to address urban environmental degradation. The cholera outbreak in London in 1846 initiated the building of the world's first and largest urban sewer system, involving more than 2,000 km of sewers, which were constructed between 1858 and 1865. The London Great Smog of 1952 was the precursor to the switch to cleaner fuels. In the late 1980s, the Han River, Republic of Korea, became so polluted that the city of Seoul was unable to maintain a potable water supply, forcing authorities to embark on one of the biggest environmental clean-up programs in Asia. While generalizations are hard to make and conditions vary between countries and cities, urban environmental crises are likely to continue to occur in Asia until large-scale urban environmental improvement programs are implemented.

Managing the urbanization process and its consequences has not, to date, gained a central position in national policy debate in Asian countries. Concerns about the costs of urbanization and the sustainability of Asian cities receive relatively little comment in public discussion compared to national economic, political, and security concerns. National governments have concentrated on growth, international competitiveness, the attraction of foreign investment, and the creation of jobs for the growing number of unemployed or underemployed persons in Asian cities. The deteriorating urban environment appears to have been viewed as the inevitable cost of international competitiveness and economic growth. There is also a tendency to look at particular sectors rather than at the totality of what is happening in cities. This is reinforced by the sectoral structure of the administration of national governments and local government boundaries that rarely facilitate citywide analysis. Whatever the reasons, the economic, social, and environmental costs of urban development in Asia are now reaching critical thresholds.

The focus on urban issues has also waxed and waned in international institutions like the Asian Development Bank (ADB), United Nations (UN) agencies, and World Bank. Urban issues have generally had a relatively low priority in country program strategies, which tend to focus on economic development and poverty reduction without considering its spatial dimension. This is puzzling because urbanization has been associated with the largest reductions in poverty in history and is an area where strengthening policy development and program implementation would result in major improvements in economic productivity and welfare. It is particularly ironic in the light of the otherwise rapidly expanding agenda for international development. The focus on urban issues appears to have been lost in the complex web of interrelationships that make up the urbanization process, such that priorities are difficult to determine. Also, international development agencies are most comfortable dealing with national governments and agencies, which tend to focus their attention on sectoral frameworks.

The result has been that national governments and international development agencies have made only a relatively modest effort in regard to urban issues. Such efforts have usually involved tinkering with urban policies and programs; too little effort has been put into developing the enabling environment in countries for effective local government operation and into strengthening urban governance and local capacity building. As a result, few pilot urban programs demonstrate sustainability in terms of financing and affordability, size and capacity of local government, scaling-up capability, and provision for ongoing operations and maintenance. Many urban projects have been abandoned or have fallen well short of expected performance targets once support has ceased.

Recent years have seen a renewed interest in Asia in urbanization and the spatial dimensions of development. Two interrelated factors have brought this about. First, it has become increasingly difficult to ignore the social, economic, and environmental challenges associated with cities, which can only be efficiently addressed through local policies and programs. Second, national governments in Asia have increasingly recognized the political and financial benefits of decentralizing service provision to local governments and institutions. Decentralization policies of Asian governments are increasingly placing urbanization issues at the local government level with the expectation that these governments will play a more active role in managing urban development and financing urban services.

Across developing Asia, there is now an increasingly urgent need for large-scale urban environmental improvement programs and for strengthening urban governance and the capacity of local institutions to plan, implement, and finance infrastructure provision and service delivery. This is a potent mix. Both need to be achieved in concert, as one depends on the other, and the scale of the problem is continually increasing as urbanization continues. Time is critical. Probably at no time in history has so much infrastructure been required in such a short period.

There is no easy solution to this dilemma and approaches will vary between countries and cities, but there is probably no alternative to concerted, incremental efforts to strengthen urban governance and management. Within such an approach is an important role for central governments and international development agencies. Central government is particularly important in setting the enabling environment for local governments. Local governments will only be capable of meeting the challenges of urbanization if appropriate national administrative and financial arrangements enable them to match their service obligations with their financial resources. Much also needs to be done through institutional development and management and staff training to strengthen local authorities and institutions so they can fulfill their tasks more efficiently and effectively. There is also the need for increased research on urbanization and urban management, including that dealing with the interrelationships between infrastructure and service provision, capacity to pay, and the relative competitiveness and economic performance of cities.

GOOD PRACTICE APPROACHES TO URBAN DEVELOPMENT

How to address the many issues associated with the growth of Asian cities is a difficult question. The answer of strengthening city governance and improving local resource mobilization is deceptively simple but involves many complex problems and will be very difficult to achieve in a timely manner. There is no alternative.

Vast amounts of capital, along with improved city planning and management, are required to address the health, sanitation, water supply, shelter, and transportation needs of cities. National governments in Asia are increasingly recognizing that they do not have the ability or the resources to efficiently provide the infrastructure and services necessary to make Asian cities more sustainable and livable. Development partners will play only a very modest role in addressing these problems: aid from developed countries to all developing countries totals only $79 billion per annum, around one quarter of Asia's annual infrastructure requirements—and there are many other competing priorities.

Increasingly across Asia, decentralization of urbanization issues from national to provincial and local governments is the approach being taken. Cities, if they are to become more competitive and able to provide necessary infrastructure and services in this decentralized environment, will need to become much smarter and more efficient. This will not simply evolve. It will require substantial investment in strategic planning, institutional development and capacity building, and management and financial systems development. The importance of human resource development in all areas of urban governance and across the various levels of management and staff cannot be overemphasized. It will involve city governments partnering with community groups and leveraging capital and resources with the private and international sectors to deliver the services that increasingly affluent urban communities have come to expect. It will also involve paying greater attention to environmental and social development issues.

Developing and applying "good practice" is one modest, relatively inexpensive, and effective approach to strengthening urban governance and management. City management needs timely information on approaches that have been successful elsewhere and can be applied locally. The success of adopting good practice as a strategy to achieve more sustainable development in Asian cities will depend upon the creation and building of networks and information systems to disseminate and share knowledge and ideas about how good practices in fields of urban management and infrastructure and service provision can be applied more broadly.

The nature of urban development with its multiple stakeholders and complexity of issues mean that no strict blueprint for "good practice" can be identified. Good practice is relative to the cultural, administrative, economic, and environmental contexts. A general definition of best practice developed by the UN that adequately covers its key attributes is "Planning and/or operational practices that have proven successful in particular circumstances. Best practices are used to demonstrate what works and what does not and to accumulate and apply knowledge about how and why they work in different situations and contexts" (United Nations Development Program [UNDP] 2006).

Not all good or best practices will, by themselves, necessarily contribute to sustainability. A good practice measure aimed at increasing economic growth, for example, may come with significant environmental and social costs. In suggesting good practice for sustainable urban development, there is a need to consider the economic, environmental, and social dimensions. The wide variations between urban areas in these dimensions mean that it is often not possible to simply transfer, without adaptation or modification, approaches from one urban area to another. Some good practices may not be transferable at all and we are often not aware of the impacts some practices may have over time.

A further problem in considering the transferability of good practice is that there will always be inconsistencies in the data on urban areas and between regions and countries, which can influence the appropriateness of policies and programs. Also, data on most urban areas in Asia suitable for policy and planning are generally lacking, such that predicting the impact of policy changes becomes difficult. There is a critical need in Asian countries for increased investment in research and data on urbanization and urban management.

Despite the problems and limitations of the good practice approach, sharing knowledge is a fundamental tool for promoting improved approaches to sustainable urban development. This approach, however, must be applied prudently. The stamp of good practice is no substitute for critical assessment.

FRAMEWORK FOR ANALYZING GOOD PRACTICE IN ASIA

This book presents case studies of "good practice" urban region development from 12 countries in Asia. The aim is to highlight examples of urban development good practice that demonstrate elements of sustainability and that may be transferable in part, or as a whole, to other cities and countries. The book presents 36 case studies from Bangladesh, Cambodia, PRC, India,

Indonesia, Lao People's Democratic Republic (Lao PDR), Malaysia, Pakistan, Philippines, Sri Lanka, Thailand, and Viet Nam.

The case studies are classified under broad fields or headings. This provides the framework for systematically documenting, comparing, and deriving lessons of good practice for sustainable urban development. Each good practice is assessed on how it contributes to one or more of

- good governance,
- improved urban management,
- effective and efficient infrastructure and service provision,
- financing and cost recovery,
- social and environmental sustainability,
- innovation and change, and
- leveraging international development assistance.

The case studies were chosen by the authors of the country chapters. They were asked to select case studies that demonstrate innovative and successful approaches to urban issues and problems and that can be replicated in other urban areas. The authors were also asked to pick examples at different levels of urban development to avoid focusing only on large metropolitan centers. Unfortunately, time, resources, and the need to limit the length of the book meant that case studies from other Asian nations could not be included.

Many good practices cited in the case studies were developed under projects and programs involving assistance from ADB, World Bank, UN agencies, other international development assistance agencies, nongovernment organizations, and private sector organizations.

A large body of literature and numerous websites describe examples of good practice used to support sustainable urban development.[1] Their quality varies widely and some are little more than project descriptions attached to a search engine. The relevance and usefulness of information on good practices are questionable in the absence of analytical and contextual content.

In preparing the case studies for this book, the authors have responded to this problem by placing the good practice examples within an analysis of the countries' decentralization policies and programs. While the central subject is good practice, a large part of each chapter is devoted to exploring the country context. Lessons learned from each good practice example are then identified and their relevance discussed in relation to improving the overall development of the region concerned. In conclusion, the authors draw together the information on national decentralization policies and lessons learned to identify any key strategies that the country concerned could implement to improve urban development.

GLOBAL GOOD PRACTICE CASE STUDIES

To balance the discussion on the Asian case studies, a chapter on global good practice case studies of urban development has been included. The global case studies are presented as small vignettes. Five cities have been selected from five continents—Curitiba, Brazil; Vancouver, Canada; Brisbane, Australia; Singapore; and Manchester, United Kingdom. These cities have all won international awards or are recognized as leaders in developing and applying sustainable urban management practices. While other cities could have been selected for inclusion, the case studies provide a broad cross-section of good practice approaches to good governance, urban management, infrastructure provision, sustainability, innovation and change, and leveraging of capital and other resources.

Caution is necessary when comparing the global and Asian case studies presented. The former are generally set in the context of more advanced economies where governance systems are more highly developed, resource constraints are of a much lower order of magnitude, well-developed instruments of resource mobilization and urban infrastructure exist, and housing is of a much higher quality. Also, these cities are not generally facing the pressures of very rapid urbanization. Although these global case studies may not be transferable now, they provide a guide to future directions and approaches in Asian cities.

CONCLUSION

The case studies presented in this book draw upon a wide range of urban development experiences. Table 1.1 provides a quick summary of the 36 good practice case studies for the 12 Asian countries and of the 5 global good practice case studies. It is recognized that many Asian city case studies are not global good practice. They are, however, considered national good practice. The content and scope of the case studies vary significantly from modest examples of local government leadership and community action to major reforms of tax bases.

Table 1.1: Summary of Asian and Global Good Practice Case Studies

Urban and Heritage Conservation, Luang Prabang, Lao PDR

Asian Case Studies	Good Governance	Urban Management	Infrastructure and Service Provision	Financing and Cost Recovery	Social and Environmental Sustainability	Innovation and Change	Leveraging ODA
Bangladesh							
Chittagong: Dynamic and Innovative Leadership	✓	✓					
Shakti Foundation: Microcredit Program				✓			
Bangladesh Environment Movement (BAPA)		✓				✓	
Cambodia							
Phnom Penh: "Planning for All"	✓	✓	✓	✓	✓	✓	
Battambang Town Study	✓	✓	✓	✓	✓	✓	
Growth Pole Strategy for Kratie	✓	✓	✓	✓	✓	✓	✓
People's Republic of China							
Nanjing: Revitalizing the Inner City	✓	✓	✓		✓		
Shenzhen: Building a City from Scratch	✓	✓	✓	✓	✓	✓	
Liaodong Peninsula: Reviving Rustbelt Industries	✓	✓	✓		✓	✓	
India							
Ahmedabad: Issuance of Municipal Bonds	✓	✓	✓	✓		✓	
Andhra Pradesh: Reform of Property Taxation	✓	✓		✓		✓	
The National Urban Renewal Mission (NURM)					✓	✓	
Indonesia							
Tarakan: East Kalimantan: Balanced Development	✓	✓	✓	✓	✓	✓	
Sleman: Managing Rapid Urbanization	✓	✓	✓	✓	✓	✓	✓
Jembrana, Bali: Community Improvement Program	✓			✓	✓	✓	
Lao PDR							
Vientiane: Urban Region Village Area Improvements		✓	✓	✓	✓		
Luang Prabang: Urban Improvements and Heritage Conservation	✓	✓				✓	
Savannakhet: East-West Economic Corridor	✓		✓			✓	✓

Nhieu Loc – Thi Nghe Canal Improvement Project, Viet Nam

Asian Case Studies	Good Governance	Urban Management	Infrastructure and Service Provision	Finance and Cost Recovery	Social and Environmental Sustainability	Innovation and Change	Leveraging ODA
Malaysia							
Petaling Jaya: Local Agenda 21 Implementation	✓	✓			✓	✓	
Putrajaya: Model City					✓	✓	
Cyberjaya: Multimedia Super Corridor	✓				✓	✓	
Pakistan							
Lodhran: Community-based Sanitation Pilot Project		✓	✓	✓			✓
Faisalabad: Community-based Water and Sanitation Project		✓	✓	✓		✓	
Lahore: Solid Waste Management		✓	✓	✓	✓		
Philippines							
Bacolod City Study		✓	✓	✓		✓	
Naga City Study		✓	✓	✓	✓	✓	✓
Iloilo City Study		✓	✓	✓		✓	✓
Sri Lanka							
Colombo: Community-based Solid Waste Management		✓	✓	✓		✓	✓
Colombo: Health and Environment Management		✓	✓	✓			✓
Colombo: Clean Settlements Program		✓	✓	✓	✓		
Thailand							
Muang Klaeng Municipality: Sustainable City Initiative		✓	✓			✓	
Phichit Municipality: Waste Recycling		✓	✓			✓	✓
Songkhla Municipality: Waste Management and Education		✓	✓			✓	
Viet Nam							
Phu Thuong, Hanoi: Institutional Building in Urban Upgrading	✓	✓	✓			✓	✓
Nhieu Loc-Thi Nghe Basin: Environmental Improvement	✓	✓	✓			✓	✓
Nam Dinh City: Urban Upgrading		✓	✓	✓		✓	

Global Case Studies	Good Governance	Urban Management	Infrastructure and Service Provision	Finance and Cost Recovery	Social and Environmental Sustainability	Innovation and Change	Leveraging ODA
City of Brisbane, Australia							
Curitiba Brazil: Sustainable Transport and Environment	✓	✓	✓	✓	✓	✓	
Vancouver Canada: Regional and Environmental Management	✓	✓				✓	
Brisbane Australia: Management Model and Infrastructure Plans	✓	✓	✓	✓		✓	
Singapore Housing, Logistics and Environmental Management	✓	✓				✓	✓
Manchester United Kingdom: Environmental Management	✓	✓	✓			✓	✓

ODA = official development assistance.

Notes

[1] Websites on sustainable regional development and best practice include Sustainable Regions: www.sustainableregions.net/site/index.php?article=1; Asia Foundation: www.asiafoundation.org/Locations/taiwan.html; Good Practices UNDP: www.undp.org/rbap/BestPrac/surf_guidlines.htm; United Nations Centre for Human Settlements: www.bestpractices.org/ and sustainabledevelopment.org/; UN Center for Regional Development: www.uncrd.or.jp; and Institute for Management Development: www02.imd.ch/wcy/fundamentals.

2. Urbanization and Sustainability in Asia

BRIAN ROBERTS AND
TREVOR KANALEY

THE SCALE AND SCOPE OF URBANIZATION

Urbanization in Asia is proceeding at a scale that is unprecedented in human history. This creates many challenges, especially about how—in a sustainable way—to feed, shelter, and generate employment for an estimated 1.1 billion people projected to be added to the population of Asian cities in the next 25 years. Given the weakness of governance structures, the appalling environmental conditions that already exist in many cities, and existing infrastructure and service shortfalls, meeting the needs of these people appears an almost impossible task for many nations in Asia.

Urbanization is also causing problems for rural development. There is a growing loss of productive agricultural land to peri-urban development and urbanization is increasing pressures for structural reform in agriculture. The benefits that larger cities offer in opportunities for higher education, health services, employment, and higher wages are making it difficult for rural areas to compete and attract skilled persons to support development. The challenges in achieving more balanced and sustainable urban and rural development in Asian countries are enormous, but they are not insurmountable.

In 1950, some 733 million people, or 29% of the world's population, lived in urban areas. By 2005, the urban population had grown to an estimated 3,172 million or 49% of the population. By 2030, it is estimated that 4,945 million people—almost 61% of the world's population—will be urban. The urban population is set to increase by more than 55%, or 1,770 million, in the next 25 years while the rural population is estimated to decline by 3% or 96 million. Between 1950 and 2030, the population of the world will change from about 70% rural to 60% urban (Table 2.1).[1]

Developed countries are already highly urbanized. Their most rapid urban growth took place over a century ago. Population and economic dynamics in developing countries and particularly in Asia are now driving the process of urbanization. While in some respects urbanization today is not much different to urbanization in the past, what is unprecedented is the absolute size of the change—the number of countries undergoing rapid urbanization, the number of cities that are growing rapidly, and the sheer number of people involved (World Resources Institute 1996).

In Asia in 1950, some 232 million people, or 17% of the population, lived in urban areas.[2] Over the following 55 years to 2005, the urban population grew nearly sevenfold to an estimated 1,562 million, 40% of the population. By 2030, it is estimated that 2,664 million people, or almost 55% of the population in the Asia region, will be urban, representing an increase of over 70% or 1,100 million in the next 25 years (Table 2.1). Over this same period, the rural population is expected to decline by 6%, or 133 million. Almost all future population growth in Asia will be in towns and cities.

While the urbanization process is occurring in virtually all developing countries, it is now centered on Asia. Less-developed regions of the world are projected to account for 1,664 million or over 90% of world urban popu-

Table 2.1: Urbanization Trends in Asia, 1950–2030

	GDP per capita (PPP, $) 2003	Population (million) 2005	Urban Population (million) 2005	Proportion Urban			Estimated Increase in Urban Population	
				(%) 1950	(%) 2005	(%) 2030	(million) 2005–2030	(%) 2005–2030
World		6,453.6	3,172.0	29	49	61	1,772.7	56
Asia		3,917.5	1,562.1	17	40	55	1,102.2	71
Malaysia	9,512	25.3	16.5	20	65	78	10.8	66
Thailand	7,595	64.1	20.8	17	33	47	14.6	70
PRC	5,003	1,322.3	536.0	13	41	61	341.6	64
Philippines	4,321	82.8	51.8	27	63	76	34.8	67
Sri Lanka	3,778	19.4	4.1	14	21	30	2.4	59
Indonesia	3,361	225.3	107.9	12	48	68	80.0	74
India	2,892	1,096.9	315.3	17	29	41	270.8	86
Viet Nam	2,490	83.6	22.3	12	27	43	24.5	110
Pakistan	2,097	161.2	56.1	18	35	50	79.3	141
Cambodia	2,078	14.8	2.9	10	20	37	5.8	197
Bangladesh	1,770	152.6	38.1	4	25	39	48.4	127
Lao PDR	1,759	5.9	1.3	7	22	38	2.3	177

GDP = gross domestic product, Lao PDR = Lao People's Democratic Republic, PPP = purchasing power parity, PRC = People's Republic of China.
Sources: United Nations, *World Population Prospects: The 2002 Revision*; *World Urbanization Prospects: The 2003 Revision*; and United Nations Development Programme, *Human Development Report 2005*.

lation growth in the next 25 years to 2030.³ Some 66% of this urban population growth in less-developed regions will occur in Asia.

Aggregate population data are dominated by the impact of the two largest countries, the People's Republic of China (PRC) and India. These countries account for 19% and 15%, respectively, of projected total world urban population growth during 2006–2030 and for 31% and 25%, respectively, in Asia. The 12 countries in Asia considered in this book—Bangladesh, Cambodia, PRC, India, Indonesia, Lao People's Democratic Republic (Lao PDR), Malaysia, Pakistan, Philippines, Sri Lanka, Thailand, and Viet Nam—together account for 915 million, or over 50% of projected total world urban population growth to 2030, and for over 80% of urban population growth in Asia.

In Asia, there are wide differences in the urbanization experience both between and within countries. This is illustrated by the differences in the extent of urbanization and projections for the future between the 12 countries considered in this book. In general, there is a strong relationship between urbanization and economic development. Higher-income countries are generally more urbanized than lower-income countries, and urbanization increases more rapidly with economic growth in lower-income countries than in higher-income countries. Of the countries considered, Malaysia has the highest gross domestic product (GDP) per capita and the highest percentage of urban population. Bangladesh, Cambodia, Lao PDR, Pakistan, and Viet Nam are at an earlier stage of the urbanization process but are projected to have the largest increases in their urban populations (more than 100%) over the 25 years to 2030.

For all countries considered here, but particularly for the most populous countries—PRC, India, and Indonesia—country data hide large regional variations; there are regions that are very heavily urbanized and other regions still predominantly rural. Also, within countries, population growth rates of cities vary widely (Table 2.2). Growth rates of the largest cities are often relatively modest. It is the smaller and intermediate-sized cities that are frequently experiencing rapid population growth and these are also often the most poorly resourced to accommodate this growth. Even within cities, growth is not uniform: it is often on the periphery, sprawling into neighboring areas, and/or in spontaneous and unintended squatter settlements.

The evidence on the population growth of urban centers suggests that medium-sized cities in the order of 500,000 to 2 million will experience the highest urbanization rates in the future. Growth rates in larger cities can be expected to be slow both as a natural outcome of the arithmetic of growth—as city size expands, increasingly larger additional numbers are required to maintain the growth rate—and as congestion and environmental conditions make very large cities less attractive places to live. Also, as cities grow, most of the growth will occur in the peri-urban areas due to easier availability of

Table 2.2: City Size and Population Growth
(For Capital Cities and Urban Agglomerations with 750,000
Persons or More in 2000)

City Size	PRC			INDIA			INDONESIA		
	Cities	Av. Annual Growth		Cities	Av. Annual Growth		Cities	Av. Annual Growth	
	(No.)	(%) 2005–2010	(%) 2010–2015	(No.)	(%) 2005–2010	(%) 2010–2015	(No.)	(%) 2005–2010	(%) 2010–2015
0–0.5 million	126	1.80	1.91	157	2.04	2.18	14	2.38	2.47
0.5–1 million	127	2.03	2.08	45	2.45	2.36	10	2.78	2.54
1–5 million	93	1.25	1.45	33	2.79	2.52	5	2.78	2.45
Over 5 million	4	0.77	1.04	7	2.30	2.12	1	3.19	2.46

Av. = average, no. = number.
Source: UN, *World Population Prospects: The 2002 Revision and World Urbanization Prospects: The 2003 Revision.*

land and to price and land tenure arrangements acting to restrict redevelopment of older inner city areas.

URBANIZATION ISSUES

Urbanization and the Economy

The tremendous growth of urban areas has been brought about by complex technological and economic interrelationships that have redefined the spatial landscape. Urbanization has been driven by an ongoing technological revolution that has seen the rapid growth of industrial and service industries whose productivity is enhanced by agglomeration economies and economies of scale found only in a concentrated spatial environment and, conversely, by increasing agricultural productivity that has reduced the demand for rural labor. The predominant market-based economic system provides the drive and direction to urbanization and the main means of distributing benefits and costs.

A deep well of agglomeration benefits accrue to governments, businesses, households, and individuals in a spatially concentrated, urban environment that cannot be captured in a rural setting. Those who have tried to reverse or restrict the urbanization process have consistently underestimated these.

Urban environments provide high density, spatial proximity, which has led to

- growing markets;
- access to information, capital, and research and development;
- labor markets with deep pools of talent;

- high value-added productivity;
- high and more secure wages and incomes;
- low unit costs for infrastructure and public services;
- an increase in taxable capacity, from which additional public resources can be mobilized and infrastructure services paid for; and
- increased competition and, paradoxically, reduced risk.

The competitiveness of different urban locations varies greatly and is always in flux; the relative costs and benefits for any particular enterprise of a particular location are almost constantly changing. Importantly, the choice of locations of industrial enterprises, which were central to much urban growth in the past, was much less flexible than for more modern, service-based industries. A steel or textile firm is costly to move and tends to stay. Knowledge-based service businesses, such as accountancy or information technology firms, are far more mobile.

Increasingly, economic globalization is changing the relative competitiveness and growth prospects of different urban locations. Economic activity tends to concentrate where integration into the global economy is easiest—where there is access to communications technology, international capital markets, globally integrated value chains of production and distribution, and information-based industries in such areas as accountancy, law, and research and development.

Globalization has resulted in both less regulation of industry and, in such areas as trade, investment, and intellectual property, more universal standards of regulation. As a result, location decisions depend less on the particular country and more on the comparative advantages of different cities. This creates a unique juggling act for city management. Less-affluent cities tend to compete on the basis of cheap labor costs and the low costs of environmental regulation, which are important for attracting manufacturing and resource-based industries. As cities become more affluent, the availability and quality of environmental goods become increasingly significant, particularly as means to attract urban professionals in the service sector. Reconciling this tension is important if cities are to develop a broad economic base and have rising levels of productivity and income.

A consequence of the relentless pursuit of location competitiveness is a shift from a focus on national development to a focus on the development of subnational urban region economies. This is changing the role and culture of urban governance. The role of urban governance is shifting from service delivery to strengthening location competitiveness by fostering production, investment, and growth of the private sector. Urban regions that offer the greatest competitive advantage have continued to develop, increasing in size and income. They have evolved into often very large conurbations and attract the greatest share of national and foreign investments. The less competitive parts of countries have been left struggling to catch up, especially in more remote secondary city regions that have generally poor infrastructure and limited skilled persons and resources.

Studies on the flow of investment show large disparities in the levels of investment in regions of the developing countries of Asia. Many poorer urban regions lack the basic infrastructure and support services necessary for them to attract business and investment and create new industries. They have been unable to compete for investment and business nationally and globally. These regions have become poverty traps with very limited development prospects. A major challenge facing the rapidly urbanizing developing countries of Asia is to ensure that the benefits of urbanization are sufficiently widespread.

Urbanization in Asia is both driven by and supports economic growth. Asia, with the exception of 1998, has been the fastest-growing economic region in the world for several decades and this has been underpinned by large-scale urbanization. There is every reason to believe that these interrelated trends will continue. During 2006–2015, real GDP per capita in the East Asia and the Pacific and South Asia subregions is projected to grow at an average annual rate of 5.3% and 4.2%, respectively.[4] Over the same period, the urban population in Asia is expected to increase by 27% (or 428 million) to 1,990 million.

Economically dynamic urban areas are central to the economies of nation states and to future economic growth. They are the production houses of wealth and the cradle for innovation, trade, and productivity growth. As a result, urban areas account for a disproportionate share of national economic production (Table 2.3). Agriculture's share of GDP is relatively small and has been in long-term decline; the predominantly urban share of GDP—comprising industry and services—is relatively large and rising. In the 12 countries considered in this book, the urban share of GDP accounts for 50–90% of total GDP. Moreover, while city per capita output ("city product") for selected cities varies widely, it is generally much higher than the country's per capita gross national product. It is over 342% higher in Bangkok and 236% higher in Jakarta. The ability of urban areas to continue to improve productivity holds the key to growing urban populations with higher wages and incomes and improving living standards.

Global Sustainability

Urbanization and economic growth in Asia are important at the global level because their scale has global consequences.

Table 2.3: Urbanization and Economic Output

Country	Urban Share of GDP 2004 (%)	City	City Product Per Capita 1998 ($)	GNP Per Capita 1998 ($)	Increase in City Product Per Capita over GNP Per Capita 1998 (%)
Bangladesh	79	Dhaka	500	255	96
Cambodia	64	Phnom Penh	699	260	169
PRC	85				
India	78	Chennai	547	341	60
Indonesia	83	Jakarta	1,932	575	236
Lao PDR	51	Vientiane	340	320	6
Malaysia	90	Penang	4,237	3,093	37
Pakistan	77				
Philippines	86	Cebu	1,277	1,050	22
Sri Lanka	83	Colombo	43	823	-95
Thailand	90	Bangkok	9,553	2,160	342
Viet Nam	78	Ho Chi Minh	898	310	190

GDP = gross domestic product, GNP = gross national product.
Source: United Nations Human Settlements Program and World Bank databases.

Asia comprises 60% of the world's population. The PRC and India, the world's most populous countries, account for about 34% and 28% of Asia's population and 20% and 17% of total world population, respectively. Rapid economic growth affecting such large countries and huge numbers of people inevitably alters the geopolitical landscape and existing bilateral power relationships. It also affects the global economy by increasing aggregate demand, international trade, and capital flows, and causing structural adjustments in both developing and developed economies. A good example is manufacturing, with Asia increasingly—and developed countries decreasingly—the source of global manufactured goods. Growth in Asia is, to a significant extent, underpinning growth in the world economy and has improved global standards of living overall.

The global environmental consequences of this spectacular growth in Asia are less benign. Increased production and consumption are driving energy usage, carbon dioxide emissions and other forms of pollution, and the degradation of scarce resources, such as water supplies, forests, and agricultural land. While there is much debate, there is real doubt whether the earth's ecological systems can accommodate the developing world's drive toward developed countries' production and consumption patterns using existing resource-intensive technologies.

One example is energy usage and carbon dioxide emissions. In 1990, Emerging Asia[5] was estimated to contribute 15% to total world energy consumption.[6] By 2002, this had increased to 22% and is projected to increase to 31% by 2025. Overall energy consumption in Asia is projected to increase about threefold between 1990 and 2025 and will contribute almost 50% of the growth in total world energy consumption. The PRC alone will contribute about 30% of this growth. The major energy sources in Asia are coal, oil, and natural gas and demand from Asia is affecting the availability of supplies and prices paid.

Energy consumption and carbon dioxide emissions are closely related because of Asia's reliance on fossil fuels. As a consequence, carbon dioxide emissions in Emerging Asia are projected to increase from 18% of total world carbon dioxide emissions in 1990 to 35% in 2025. Emissions of carbon dioxide—one of the most prevalent greenhouse gases and at the center of climate change negotiations—are projected to increase by about 250% in Emerging Asia between 1990 and 2025. Asia will contribute about 56% of the growth in total world carbon dioxide emissions over this period; the PRC will contribute 34%.

Another rapidly emerging global problem is access to water: "even without climate change, the number of people impacted by water scarcity is projected to increase from 1.7 billion today to 5 billion by 2025" (World Resources Institute, 2005).

Issues of ecological sustainability and climate change do not respect national borders and have impacts regionally and globally. Left unaddressed, they have the potential to undermine the world economy and global security and, ultimately, human habitat. Bringing many issues of global sustainability to a head is the rapid growth of developing Asia. For example, total primary energy consumption in 2002–2025 is estimated to increase at 3.5% per annum in Emerging Asia, but only 1.1% per annum in the mature market economies. Developed countries' share of total energy consumption will decline from 52% to 42% over the period while Emerging Asia's share will increase from 21% to 31%. Nevertheless, total energy consumption is and will remain heavily concentrated in the developed countries both in total and per capita because of their high-consumption patterns and relatively small share (15%) of world population.

Maintaining ecological sustainability requires global initiatives and changes in technology, policies, and consumption patterns. Such initiatives should also provide for economic growth, rising standards of living, and reductions in poverty in Asia and the rest of the developing world.

Problems of ecological sustainability, at least initially, will often have greater impact on developing nations because developed countries are buffered by their more robust and sophisticated infrastructure and services, including emergency relief services. Developing countries tend to be highly exposed, particularly among the poor, because of their high dependence on natural resources and more limited capacity to adapt to environmental change. For example, climate change effects are projected to include rising average temperatures, rising sea levels, and more extreme weather patterns and events. Among other things, these will exacerbate flooding and problems in housing, drainage, water supply, and sewerage already prevalent in Asian cities, with negative impacts for public health and particularly the poor.

Problems of urbanization and economic development in Asia are bringing to a head global issues of ecological sustainability. If projected rapid development is realized over the next 25 years, these issues will be pushed further to the fore on the international agenda. While at the country level, issues of urbanization and economic development are the responsibility of national governments, their international ramifications will ensure that the global community has a strong self- interest in more sustainable development. Priorities and practices will have to change in Asia and elsewhere in the developed and developing world to accommodate sustainability considerations; however, where the costs of adjustment will fall and who will pay is less clear. The international architecture to address these issues is still being developed. Nevertheless, one can confidently predict it will result in increased funding from international development institutions for ecologically sustainable development activities, driven by the strong national interest of developed countries.

Land[7]

The extent of land used for urban purposes in Asia is unknown, but is in the vicinity of 100,000 square kilometers (km^2). The land needed to accommodate the 1.1 billion people expected to be added to Asian cities by 2030 as a result of population growth and declining average population densities in Asian cities will be enormous. The decline in urban densities is brought about by rising incomes and increasing willingness and ability to pay for "space," and by changing demographics and reductions in average household size.

Data on land used for urban purposes are poor, and there is frequently conflicting information based on different definitions of urban area and urban land. A particular problem is the urban boundary and the extent to which semi- or peri-urban areas, which include expanded villages and towns, constitute parts of cities and urban metropolises. Many peri-urban areas are transition zones in the process of conversion into intensive urban use. Such problems result in significant differences in the literature, with varying statistics on urban population, densities, and extent of urban areas.

Estimating likely land requirements is further complicated by poor data on land conversion rates, especially for secondary cities, and by inadequate information on the likely impact of increasing incomes on demand for land. Any average figures hide large variations between countries and cities.

There are significant variations in urban densities between Asian cities. Some differences are attributable to such factors as differences in income levels, transport infrastructure, government intervention, culture, geography, and the methods used to measure urban density.

Urban densities calculated on municipal areas for the countries considered in this book range from 39 people per hectare (pph) in Coimbatore, India, to 378 pph for Mumbai (Table 2.4). However, Angel et al. (2005) note that densities based on municipal areas can be misleading because terrain and other factors related to land use result in significant differences in calculating and reporting urban densities.

Urban densities based on the measurement of built-up areas are a more accurate measure of land used for intensive urban purposes and "compactness" of cities. Under this measure also there are significant differences in the built-up area population densities for large cities in Asia. The built-up area population density in Asian cities ranges from 24 square meters (m^2) per person in Mumbai to 148 m^2 in Fukuoka, Japan. These measurements, however, can also be misleading because the urban footprint of cities includes open spaces not suitable for or designated for urban purposes (e.g., hills, floodplains, military areas, and airports) and the treatment of peri-urban areas remains a problem.

Annual growth rates in the area of land used in Asian cities from 1990 to 2000 ranged between 1.9% for cities like Cebu in the Philippines and 14.7% for Yigang in the PRC. Average annual urban area growth rates appear to be around 5.5%. However, there are significant methodological issues in calculating growth rates of urban areas and there are wide differences between cities. The average annual urban area growth rate for cities with less than one million people appears to be around 5.3%. The urban growth rates of megacities of more than 5 million are in the order of 4%. Between 1990–2000, the urban area of Mumbai expanded annually at 3.1% and Manila, 4.5%; however, the urban area of Guangzhou grew at 8.1%. The growth rates in urban areas of medium-size cities with populations of 1–5 million are around 5.7%. Kuala Lumpur urban area grew by 6.2% and Bandung 5.4% between 1990–2000.

The population and housing densities in Asian cities are continuing to decline, as in most other cities around the world. Angel et al. (2005) estimate that global urban densities are declining at an annual rate of 1.7%, suggesting that total urban areas globally will increase from 200,000 km^2 to 600,000 km^2 by 2025. Asian urban densities are falling at a faster rate, 2–5% per annum, depending on the country and the size of cities. The density in Bandung, Indonesia

**Table 2.4: Urban Densities in Selected Asian Cities
(Person per Hectare Gross)**

City	Country	Population ('000)			Built-up Area (km^2)			Average Density (person/ha)		
		1990	2000	Increase (% pa)	1990	2000	Increase (% pa)	1990	2000	Increase (% pa)
Cities in selected Asian countries										
Anging	PRC	1,003	1,055	0.5	54	78	3.6	186	135	-3.0
Bacolod	Philippines	462	510	1.3	13	33	12.3	343	155	-9.8
Bandung	Indonesia	2,942	3,628	2.2	109	182	5.4	271	199	-3.1
Cebu	Philippines	1,118	1,524	3.0	54	66	1.9	206	231	1.1
Changzhi	PRC	1,160	1,254	1.2	104	156	6.4	111	104	-1.1
Coimbatore	India	552	613	1.1	99	156	4.7	56	39	-3.4
Guangzhou	PRC	7,712	13,156	5.5	452	979	8.1	171	134	-2.4
Hyderabad	India	4,888	5,708	1.3	167	302	5.1	293	189	-3.6
Jaipur	India	2,116	2,779	2.5	59	141	8.3	360	197	-5.4
Jalna	India	445	556	2.1	11	25	7.5	395	223	-5.0
Kanpur	India	1,124	1,442	2.3	34	60	5.4	110	79	-2.9
Kolkota	India	6,646	7,834	1.7	288	484	5.3	231	162	-3.5
Kuala Lumpur	Malaysia	2,733	4,959	5.0	383	805	6.2	71	62	-1.2
Leshan	PRC	608	670	0.9	75	146	6.4	81	46	-5.1
Manila	Philippines	14,044	17,335	2.4	444	660	4.5	316	263	-2.0
Mumbai	India	14,224	17,070	2.1	344	451	3.1	413	378	-1.0
Puna	India	3,510	4,042	2.1	93	191	11.0	379	211	-8.1
Rajshahi	Bangladesh	491	600	1.8	11	20	5.8	452	296	-3.8
Saidpur	India	503	596	1.4	9	16	5.5	564	366	-3.9
Songkhla	Thailand	220	244	1.0	14	19	3.0	159	129	-1.9
Vijayawada	India	981	1,117	1.3	40	62	4.5	244	179	-3.0
Yigang	PRC	1,108	1,135	0.5	49	100	14.7	227	114	-12.4
Summary results for all selected Asian cities										
Maximum				5.5			14.7	564	378	1.1
Minimum				-1.2			1.6	47	38	-12.4
Average				1.7			5.5	218	153	-3.4
Median				1.5			5.1	185	153	-3.0

ha = hectare, km^2 = square kilometer, pa = per annum, PRC = People's Republic of China.
Source: Angel et al. 2005.

fell from 271 pph in 1990 to 199 pph in 2000 or 3.1% per annum. Urban densities appear to be falling most rapidly in cities in India, at annual rates exceeding 4%. In the PRC, the rates appear to be about 3%. The lack of good urban data on Asian cities precludes more reliable estimates of these changes.

Falling urban densities and the increase in the urban population will mean a much greater demand for urban land in Asian cities in the future.

Growth rates for land will increase and an additional 175,000 km² of land for urban purposes may be necessary by 2030 (if average densities fall to 100 pph, close to those of Singapore). This more than doubling—and possibly almost tripling—of urban land for cities in Asia over the next 25 years poses very significant environmental, economic, and social challenges, not least of which are the protection, where possible, of prime agricultural land and the very large investment required in infrastructure and services. Other problems include inefficiencies and distortions in land markets, often unclear land tenure arrangements, and often poorly developed land-use planning policies and practices of local government authorities.

For each city, there are two key questions for urban government and public policy: what is likely to be the scale of future land requirements, and what actions can be taken now to best ensure that urban land is supplied efficiently and effectively?

Arguments that maintaining the compactness of Asian cities is necessary to achieve more sustainable development outcomes may not hold true. By itself, stabilizing urban densities will not reduce the high levels of overcrowding, pollution, traffic congestion, and environmental health problems prevalent in many cities. Also, seeking to create more compact cities will most likely increase land costs. This would decrease the affordability of housing and minimize levels of public open space, while having little impact on speculative and lifestyle use of land in peri-urban areas that is reducing agriculture production (Clark and Tsai 2005).

Uncertainty over land tenure and urban planning and management compounds the problem of land development in Asian cities. Most Asian countries have failed to manage urban land development. Speculation and uncertainties over development and building approvals and tenure add to the unpredictability of urban development in Asian cities. The failure of land tenure and administration systems has led to uncertainty over land rights, coupled with high levels of ownership disputes and illegal occupation of land. This results in the inefficient operation of land and property markets, excessive speculation, and high levels of litigation, especially in countries like the Philippines.

Issues of urban land development, urban density, compactness, and the efficiency of land use present very significant challenges for the management and sustainability of Asian cities. The preference for lower density lifestyles, as incomes rise and opportunities for choice grow, will not change. The way urban governments in Asia plan and manage the future form of their cities and regulate land and property markets will have a profound impact on the sustainability of development outcomes. Good-practice solutions are emerging and sharing these will be important to improving the sustainability of urban development in the region.

Shelter

Housing, like land supply and management, has important sustainability issues for Asian cities. The total housing stock of Asian cities is unknown, but is in the order of 300 million permanent and temporary structures used for habitation. More than 40% of the urban population in Asia live in substandard housing. Most dwelling units are overcrowded with little more than 6 m^2 of floor space per person. Sanitation, access, and lack of reliable water and electricity supply are acute problems facing many urban areas.

With the exception of Singapore, no country in Asia has solved its housing problems. Public housing programs have failed to deliver adequate low-income housing and are not affordable on the scale required from the public purse. In many cases, the elite, armed forces, police, and senior public servants have been the main beneficiaries of public housing programs. Promising low-cost housing schemes funded by development partners have not been sustainable. Cooperative housing has worked in some countries, but by and large has not been widely adopted by urban communities to meet housing needs.

Housing maintenance is another major problem for Asian cities. Many houses are built without a permit, with substandard materials, often on land without secure title, and with problems such as periodic flooding. Houses remain vulnerable to risks associated with natural hazards, political vendettas, and protection racketeering. These conditions create enormous uncertainties in housing markets. They undermine the possibility of homeowners using land and housing as collateral to support investments in business enterprises and reduce the incentive to undertake maintenance of dwellings to increase their longevity and habitability.

The demand for housing in Asia will continue to grow with rising incomes and population growth. The expected fall in average household size—from 4.8 to below 3.5 persons per house—will exacerbate this demand. Household size is falling as a result of declining fertility rates and average family size, an aging urban population, and with the increasing ability of young couples, with rising incomes, to purchase or rent a dwelling independent of the family home.

The implication of these socioeconomic changes is that an additional 400 million dwellings will be needed in Asia by 2030, requiring large and increasing investments in housing and ancillary infrastructure and services. There will also be a need to upgrade or replace more than 150 million dwellings of the existing housing stock.

Infrastructure

Perhaps the most challenging problem facing Asian cities is meeting the demand for urban infrastructure to provide access to good quality, affordable, and reliable services. The current demand for infrastructure and services far outstrips supply in most Asian cities; governments are investing far too little in infrastructure, and this is undermining economic growth, private sector development, and the achievement of social and poverty reduction goals.

One example of the demand for infrastructure is for electricity generation and distribution capacity. Electricity consumption in Emerging Asia was 1,259 billion kilowatt-hours (kWh) in 1990. This increased by 131% to 2,914 billion kWh in 2002. Electricity consumption is projected to increase by a further 159% to 7,552 billion kWh by 2025, with 60% of this growth from the PRC and 18% from India (Energy Information Administration 2005). There are also major existing shortfalls in supply. The World Bank has noted that the high-growth coastal provinces of the PRC have recently begun to experience power shortages and that business surveys in India show that shortcomings in electricity service are identified as the greatest obstacle to business operation. The World Bank estimates that Indonesia alone will need 2,000–2,500 megawatts of new installed capacity annually to sustain a 6% growth rate (World Bank 2005a).

Meeting this demand for electricity in Asia will require massive, ongoing expansion of electricity infrastructure. It will also have important global and domestic environmental consequences and will be a major contributor to the projected growth in world greenhouse gas emissions. However, failure to meet this demand will slow economic growth and associated employment growth and could potentially stall improvements in standards of living and the reduction of poverty.

Numerous World Bank and Asian Development Bank (ADB) reports detail the shortfall in Asia in infrastructure needed for services, such as road access, sanitation, water supply, solid waste management, electricity, and telecommunications. The World Bank estimated that the infrastructure investment needed to keep up with projected growth in the developing world is equivalent to about 5.5% of developing countries' GDP annually and that the public sector in developing countries, which on average provides about 75% of all infrastructure investments in their countries, is spending only 2–4% of GDP on infrastructure investment (World Bank/IMF 2005).

The current demand for infrastructure and maintenance in East Asia has been estimated in a recent ADB/World Bank/Japanese Development Bank study (ADB 2005) at $165 billion per year in 2006–2010, compared with an estimated $147 billion per year in 2000–2005 (Table 2.5). The study considers the infrastructure sectors—electricity, telecommunications, major paved interurban roads, rail routes, and water and sanitation. According to the study, "this amounts to nearly 6.2% of the GDP for the region, comprising 4.0% for investment and 2.2% for maintenance. Furthermore, the PRC alone

Table 2.5: Infrastructure Investment and Maintenance in
East Asia, 2006–2010

	Investment ($ million)	Maintenance ($ million)	Total ($ million)	Investment (% GDP)	Maintenance (% GDP)	Total (% GDP)
Electricity	63,446	25,744	89,190	2.4	1.0	3.4
Telecom	13,800	10,371	24,171	0.5	0.4	0.9
Roads	23,175	10,926	34,102	0.9	0.4	1.3
Rail	1,170	1,598	2,768	0.0	0.1	0.1
Water	2,571	5,228	7,799	0.1	0.2	0.3
Sanitation	2,887	4,131	7,017	0.1	0.2	0.3
Total	107,049	57,998	165,047	4.0	2.3	6.3

GDP = gross domestic product.
Source: Yepes 2004.

is expected to account for 80% of infrastructure expenditures in the region. Among the sectors, electricity in the PRC has the largest share (44%) of total annual expenditure in infrastructure in the region."

When the demand for infrastructure for the rest of Asia is also considered, the total requirement for infrastructure investments in 2006–2010 may well be in the order of $250–300 billion per annum. None of these estimates include provision of infrastructure for private investment purposes. While the breakup of future investments into urban and nonurban infrastructure has not been attempted, most of these investments will play a role in supporting cities and towns. Many large-scale "urban" infrastructure projects, such as electricity generation plants and dams for water supply, are usually constructed in nonurban areas, while road and rail investments connect cities and are vital to urban growth by improving the flow of goods and services.

The reasons for underinvestment in infrastructure in Asia and elsewhere in developing countries are complex. Infrastructure investments are often large and unevenly spaced, and have long-term benefit flows and financial and maintenance implications. Their planning, financing, tendering, construction, and maintenance require relatively sophisticated, well-coordinated governance arrangements and technical capabilities. While economic rates of return are often high, such large investments are difficult for governments—like many local and regional governments in Asia—whose fiscal position is stretched by poorly controlled expenditures and underperforming tax bases and user charges. Affordability of services is also an important issue along with appropriate tariffs/user charges and, where necessary, subsidies for the poor. Ultimately, however, if infrastructure were to be successfully provided and maintained, projects must be technically and financially viable, with user charges that, in aggregate, cover the cost of service provision.

The failure to plan and invest in urban transport infrastructure has created significant traffic management and logistic problems for Asian cities. The following quote shows the importance of planning and protecting infrastructure corridors from development to ensure that future transportation needs of cities can be met.

> *Bangkok, the capital of Thailand, provides an important lesson for cities the world over. In the mid-1980s, Bangkok was a model of a well-functioning land and housing market with minimal, if any, public regulation. Affordable and minimally serviced land was brought into the market by the efficient creation of a minimal number of narrow tertiary roads that connected building plots to the existing road system; mortgages became widely available; and private developers went down-market in large numbers, selling land-and-house packages that were affordable for more than half the urban households. But public sector plans, investments, and regulations did not keep up with the private sector, with the result that no adequate system of secondary roads was put in place. As a result, Bangkok quickly became one of the most congested (and polluted) cities in the world. The cost of reducing congestion in Bangkok is now higher—by one or two orders of magnitude—from what it would have been had adequate rights-of-way been secured earlier (Angel et al. 2005, 102).*

Another problem is access to investment funds. The problem is not so much the availability of finance—although the total amounts for infrastructure, housing, land development, etc., are enormous—but the ability of local governments to mobilize resources and access these funds successfully. This problem is closely linked to the financial performance of both the projects and governments noted above. Central governments frequently regulate the access of local and regional authorities and special-purpose authorities to loan funds and capital markets, both for macroeconomic and local authority financial capacity reasons. Unsurprisingly, central governments are particularly wary when the provision of such funds involves any form of central government guarantee of repayment. Capital markets also act to inject some financial prudence by normal requirements for risk management through credit ratings of the entity seeking to raise capital. Overall, the ability of governments in Asia to access investment funds and provide infrastructure will only be improved by strengthening their capacity and financial performance, along with improvements in regulatory frameworks.

Investments by the private sector in urban infrastructure and service provision are part of an effort to help fill the investment gap and reduce the financial pressures on city governments, while achieving improved project financial (and on occasion technical) performance. The private sector accounts for about 20% of total annual infrastructure investment in developing countries, primarily in the communication and energy sectors (World Bank/IMF 2005). Private sector investment in infrastructure in developing countries is particularly strong in Asia. While there are various modalities of public/private partnerships for infrastructure and service provision, such arrangements are proving increasingly popular because they can increase access to investment funds and distance governments from the fiscal discipline and sometimes from political problems of cost recovery, operation, and maintenance. Their successful operation, however, still requires that governments have the technical and financial expertise to negotiate and monitor appropriate contractual arrangements successfully.

One of the greatest challenges facing infrastructure in Asia is the lack of maintenance. There is a propensity for governments and private service providers to build infrastructure, but to give inadequate attention to maintenance and repairs. Consequently, infrastructure systems incur high losses, which add to the cost of services. Compounding the problem is the lack of "as-built" plan records, showing the location of urban infrastructure services. Damage to services as a consequence is high, with services frequently damaged when new utility services are laid over or under other services.

A further problem affecting the efficiency of infrastructure provision in many Asian countries is corruption and the lack of transparent processes across the project chain. The scale of corruption can vary from major abnormalities in tendering processes, to inadequate supervision of construction standards, to small- scale omissions in billing and collecting user charges. Corruption can occur throughout the project chain, raising costs, affecting the affordability of services, and undermining community support for government. It also acts to undermine the investment climate by reducing access to both domestic and international funds.

Social Change

It is important to reflect on urbanization as more than a technological or economic process. It is also a social transformation.

The growth of cities occurs through both migration and the natural increase of the urban population. Migration to cities mainly reflects economic disparities among regions and countless separate decisions by individuals and families to take action to change their way of life to better their position and prospects. Urban areas offer the prospect of an improved standard of living. The advantages to rural people include better employment prospects through broader labor markets, often higher and more reliable wages even in the informal sector, and greater access to education, health care, water supply and sanitation, and entertainment. This is reflected in usually higher life expectancy and lower infant mortality. Even the urban poor often have more opportunity and less risk than their rural cousins. People are making more or less rational decisions to improve their lot. Increasingly, with the growth of cities, the major source of population increase inevitably shifts to the natural increase of the urban population.

Rapid economic growth and urbanization have seen a remarkable transformation in Asian societies. Large urban agglomerations are increasingly the centers of social and economic activity: the places where people live. In the 12 countries considered in this book, there are now 9 megacities with populations of 10 million or more, 9 urban agglomerations with populations of 5–10 million, 144 with populations of 1–5 million, and 197 urban agglomerations of 500,000–1 million.

Adjustments for individuals and families have been immense: migration, new labor market and skills requirements, problems in accessing housing, on occasion new language requirements and the need to adapt to culturally foreign and more liberal religious customs, and the ongoing rapid evolution of the social and cultural milieu. Urbanization is testament to the optimism, flexibility, and adaptability of mankind. Inevitably, some people have been better able to adjust and take advantage of the new opportunities in urban areas than others. While overall and over time the welfare impacts for most individuals and households have been overwhelmingly positive, Asia remains a region of enormous disparity in income levels, living standards, and socioeconomic conditions.

Poverty

Economic growth and urbanization have made major inroads into the incidence of poverty in Asia. The number of people living on less than $1 a day in Asia declined from more than 930 million to about 650 million during 1990–2002 (World Bank 2006) (Table 2.6). Moreover, if current projections of economic growth and urbanization are realized, further reductions will follow. By 2015, the number of people living in absolute poverty on less than $1 a day in Asia is estimated to decline to 246 million, mostly living in South Asia. Poverty, however, will still remain a major social problem with large aggregate numbers still in absolute poverty and more than 1,200 million people in 2015 living on less than $2 a day.

While poverty in Asia will tend to remain worse in rural areas, urban poverty is becoming an increasingly critical issue, with some different attri-

Table 2.6: Estimates of Regional Poverty in Asia

	People Living on Less Than $1 Per Day (million)			People Living on Less Than $2 Per Day (million)		
	1990	2002	2015	1990	2002	2015
East Asia and the Pacific	472	214	14	1,116	748	260
PRC	375	180	11	825	533	181
Rest of East Asia and the Pacific	97	34	2	292	215	78
South Asia	462	437	232	958	1,091	955
	Percentage of people living on Less than $1 per day			Percentage of people living on Less than $2 per day		
	1990	2002	2015	1990	2002	2015
East Asia and the Pacific	29.6	14.9	0.9	69.9	40.7	12.7
PRC	33.0	16.6	1.2	72.6	41.6	13.1
Rest of East Asia and the Pacific	21.1	10.8	0.4	63.2	38.6	11.9
South Asia	41.3	31.3	12.8	85.5	77.8	56.7

Source: World Bank. 2006. *Global Economic Prospects - Economic Implications of Remittances and Migration.* Washington, DC. Table 1.3, and p. 9.

butes to rural poverty. Urban poverty is characterized by unemployment, lack of skills, and unequal access to infrastructure services. As demonstrated in the Asian financial crisis, it is particularly sensitive to movements in economic conditions. The urban poor live predominantly in low-quality housing without legal land tenure in squatter settlements on the periphery of cities and within cities in concentrated, overcrowded slums. Sites are often subject to flooding, landslides, and pollution. The urban poor are subject to forcible eviction, have poorer health, and inadequate access to electricity, health services, clean water, and sanitation.

In many urban areas, aggregate numbers of people living in poverty are increasing, along with the gap between rich and poor. Regional equity is also becoming an important issue, with large variations in wealth and services between subnational urban economies. Poverty is a potentially explosive social and political issue. Economic growth and urbanization have been and will continue to be central to reducing deprivation in Asia, but increasingly there will be the need for targeted poverty reduction policies and programs within and between urban areas.

Environmental Issues

In Asia, the combination of economic growth, the very rapid spatial concentration of people and economic activity in urban areas, and the inability of governance to provide the necessary regulatory environment and infrastructure services have resulted in the deterioration of the environment. Many environmental problems do not confine themselves to the administrative boundary of the urban area or of the city and have detrimental consequences for adjacent rural areas and further afield. Table 2.7 shows a range of environmental indicators for selected Asian countries.

Problems of the urban environment are the result of

- *consumption patterns*: rising incomes have resulted in growing demand for all types of goods and services. Problems relate to issues as diverse as the demand for potable water and the use of agricultural land for urban water catchments; to urban land requirements and threats to forests and biodiversity; to the explosion in demand in Asia for motor vehicles, resulting in unacceptably high levels of suspended particulate matter and traffic noise and congestion; to rapidly increasing electricity consumption and global problems of greenhouse gas emissions;

Table 2.7: Environmental Indicators

Countries Ranked by Descending GDP per Capita (PPP $, 2003)	Percent of Urban Population			Electric Power Consumption	Total Energy Use from all Sources (Kg of Oil Equivalent)	Carbon Dioxide Emissions
	Living in Slum Conditions	Using Improved Water Source	Using Improved Sanitation			
	2001	2002	2002	2002	2002	1991-2001	2000
	%	%	%	Kwh per capita	Kgoe per capita	% Change	Metric tons per capita
Malaysia	2	96	n.a.	2,832	2,129	97	5.4
Thailand	2	95	97	1,626	1,353	63	2.8
PRC	38	92	69	987	960	30	2.7
Philippines	44	90	81	459	525	49	1.0
Sri Lanka	14	99	98	297	430	41	0.6
Indonesia	23	89	71	411	737	52	1.4
India	56	96	58	380	513	40	1.0
Viet Nam	47	93	84	374	530	59	0.6
Pakistan	74	95	92	363	454	44	0.7
Cambodia	72	58	53	n.a.	n.a.	n.a.	0.0
Bangladesh	85	82	75	100	155	62	0.2
Lao PDR	66	66	61	n.a.	n.a.	n.a.	0.1

n.a. = data not available, GDP = gross domestic product, kg = kilogram, kWh = kilowatt-hour, kgoe = kilogram of oil equivalent, Lao PDR = Lao People's Democratic Republic, PPP = purchasing power parity, PRC = People's Republic of China.
Sources: World Bank. 2005. *World Development Indicators 2005*. Washington, DC; and World Resources Institute. 2005. *World Resources 2005: The Wealth of the Poor—Managing Ecosystems to Fight Poverty*.

- *resource-intensive technologies*: expanding industrial output relies on high resource inputs, including for energy from coal, oil, and natural gas;
- *governance and institutional weaknesses*: these inhibit the development of effective environmental regulations and their enforcement, and the generation of adequate revenues to fund environmental services; and
- *rapid spatial concentration of people and economic activity*: the supply of environmental services, such as water supply, drainage, sanitation, and solid waste management, has been unable to keep up with the pace of urbanization.

Most cities in Asia have in common environmental problems related to

- safe drinking water and sanitation and associated health problems from waterborne diseases;
- solid waste collection and management, contributing to blocked drains and flooding and, in some cases, leaching of toxic chemicals;
- drainage of low-lying areas;
- endemic traffic congestion;
- air pollution from industry and vehicles and from burning coal and biomass for domestic cooking and heating, causing respiratory and other health problems; and
- waterways polluted by domestic and industrial effluents with minimal or no treatment.

With further expansion, environmental conditions in Asian cities will worsen if infrastructure shortfalls widen. The technical solutions to provision of most environmental services are well known, but can only be implemented through increased infrastructure investment and better maintenance. This requires effective urban governance.

Table 2.7 lists the countries considered in this book by descending order of income per capita. In general, countries with high per capita income, such as Malaysia and Thailand, have high levels of housing, water, and sanitation services, while poorer countries are less well-served. Conversely, the countries with higher per capita incomes have high levels of consumption of environmental resources, as shown in high energy use and carbon dioxide emissions, compared with poorer countries, such as Bangladesh and Pakistan. As the incomes of countries increase, environmental problems resulting from resource consumption increase, while environmental problems resulting from a lack of environmental services and weak institutional capacity decline.

Cities not only provide jobs for their inhabitants, they also provide their habitats. Environmental problems result in increased morbidity and impaired health, increased financial costs for urban residents—such as lengthy travel times to work—and reduced urban amenity. They also impose significant costs on businesses and overall economic activity due to impaired productivity. These costs range from employee work absences due to illness, to congestion costs in moving goods and services, to the impairment of whole industries such as fisheries—caused by overfishing and the reduction or contamination of fish stocks.

Public health is the leading indicator of the urban environment. The incidence of waterborne diseases, pneumonia, chronic respiratory disease, lung cancer, and heart attack is directly related to the success of urban governance in providing the infrastructure and regulatory framework for successful environmental management. Other health issues, such as death and injuries from road accidents, are also directly related to the success of urban governance in creating a safe urban environment.

Environmental problems are closely linked to poverty. For individuals and households in most Asian cities, money buys location and land tenure, better-quality housing, access to reticulated water and bottled water, sewerage and drainage, solid waste collection, connection to the electricity supply and, for some, a backup generator. Even if local government cannot provide all these services, at a price they can be provided, albeit inefficiently, on a domestic scale. At the other extreme, absence of money results in poor-quality squatter housing on low-lying land or close to major roads and associated high levels of pollution, uncertain tenure and the risk of eviction, illegal and often dangerous connection to the electricity supply, unclean sometimes intermittent water supply from a community standpipe, stagnant pools of wastewater, access to a community latrine at best, and high risks of storm water flooding and other climatic damage. The health and other costs of environmental degradation overwhelmingly and disproportionately fall on the urban poor.

Urban Finance

Urban finance is critical to addressing the broad range of problems of urban growth and to achieving more sustainable development outcomes for Asian cities. There are two main and closely interrelated issues of urban finance: first is the enormous amount of money required to finance infrastructure and service provision; and second are the financial systems and arrangements required to mobilize these funds and ensure their effective use.

As noted in the Infrastructure section, the total requirement for infrastructure and maintenance in Asia may well be $250–300 billion per annum or more than 6% of GDP. Urban governance has to capture an adequate share of economic activity to finance this investment. There is little evidence that present funding shortfalls are the result of demand factors, such as unwillingness in urban areas to pay for services, or of the failure of capital markets. Rather, the inability to mobilize adequate resources reflects structural weaknesses in the enabling environment for urban governance, and institutional weaknesses and capacity constraints in the local governments and special-purpose authorities responsible for urban governance.

Access to loan funds and capital markets by local government depends on the assets and financial viability of the local authority and the ability of potential lenders and investors to assess risk confidently. These issues have largely been avoided to date in Asian countries. Access to finance by local authorities has mainly come through loans directly from central governments and through various forms of central government-sponsored financial intermediaries, with inevitable real and implicit subsidies and administrative restrictions on borrowings. Such arrangements have sheltered local authorities, but their long-term impact has been to isolate these authorities from normal market disciplines and to allow authorities to operate in a financially semi-viable form. The end result has been the growing backlog in infrastructure and services in Asia.

Efforts to increase the role of the private sector in infrastructure and service provision are, at least in part, recognition of the failure of central and local governments over many years to address structural and viability problems of local government authorities. Poor local government financial capacities and capabilities will not be overcome quickly and the move in Asia for the decentralization of functions from central to local governments can only bring these problems more to the fore.

Urban financial management in Asia is generally weak and the responsibility for it varies between countries and cities. In countries with federated government structures, such as Malaysia and India, there has historically been greater decentralization and local control of urban financial matters. In unitary-governed nations, such as Indonesia, the Philippines, and Viet Nam, there has been more central control and management of local government finance, especially in funding urban development. Most Asian countries have, or are moving toward, more decentralized government, with provincial and local governments having greater responsibility for the financing, planning, delivery, and management of land development and urban services.

A major problem of urban finance in Asian countries is the weakness of the revenue base of local governments. Local government is usually heavily dependent on fiscal transfers from central government and has a poor record of exploiting its limited tax base and user charges. Reforms to broaden the revenue base, to align local government responsibilities with the revenue base, and to introduce systems and processes to exploit the revenue base more effectively are urgently required.

Cost recovery and tariffs are related issues. In many cases, urban public utilities are performing poorly and services are heavily subsidized. The problem is not only the pricing structure but also the failure of systems for assessing usage and for billing and collections. Also, the poor standard of service can reduce willingness to pay. There is a strong reluctance on the part of local authorities to close or sell underperforming, loss-making public utilities for fear of creating unemployment and reducing already inadequate services. While issues of community affordability have to be addressed, loss-making public utilities erode the capital and financial base of cities, leading to the neglect or underfunding of other public services. Also, in many cases, poor accounting by local governments means that they have only a limited understanding of the financial performance of public utilities.

Asset management of local authorities is also poor, resulting in substantial underperformance of public assets. Most cities do not have or maintain a register of assets, such as public land. Many local governments have no idea of the holdings they own or their market value. Also in many Asian cities, the valuation of property does not indicate its market value. This is one factor contributing to the substantial undercollection of local government land taxes. In some urban areas in Asia, less than 5% of real property taxes collected are based on market value. Moreover, if public assets are not known or appropriately valued, they cannot be leveraged to provide access to loan funds and capital markets for financing infrastructure and service provision.

Most local governments in Asia do not use modern financial management practices, such as performance-based budgeting and accrual accounting methods. Consequently, cash flow and financial mismanagement problems are a common occurrence. Many projects and programs undergo delays because of poor cash flow management, increasing the overall costs. These problems are compounded by the lack of transparency and accountability in public sector financial management systems, which provide opportunities for corruption in local government.

Governance

The success of urban governance is central to the performance of cities in Asia. Urban governance affects the economic performance of cities through its impact on location competitiveness and the investment climate of cities. It also plays a central role in the sustainability and amenity of cities through the provision, either directly or indirectly, of infrastructure and services and the management of the social, environmental, and spatial effects of urban development. Importantly, urban governance and, in particular, local government, are at the center of participatory mechanisms to allow the involvement of local communities and civil society in local decision making.

Several major problems confront the governance of cities in Asia.

- *The complexity of governance*: cities are usually governed by complex, often poorly coordinated arrangements comprising local governments, national and sometimes regional governments, and special-purpose authorities. This complexity encourages boundary disputes and the shifting of responsibilities. There is often no city government that considers the city as a whole.
- *The capacity of governments and agencies*: local government is usually the weakest link in urban governance; there are major discrepancies between the nominal functions of local governments and their revenue-raising systems and technical capacities. Local governments often possess only a weak capacity to design, finance, and implement policies and programs. There are also major capacity problems in special-purpose authorities, such as electricity supply and water supply utilities.
- *The systems and processes of governance*: these are often poorly developed, with problems of representation, coordination, transparency, accountability, and corruption.

These problems affect the effectiveness and efficiency of urban governance. Their impacts have been accentuated by the very rapid rate of growth in Asian cities. Since 1950, the urban population in Asia has grown nearly sevenfold—from 232 million to 1,562 million. Unless actions are taken quickly to simplify and clarify the arrangements for urban governance and to strengthen government capacities, these problems will be accentuated even further by the sheer scale of future urban growth. If the performance of urban governance does not improve, there will be growing backlogs in the provision of infrastructure and services, worsening environmental conditions, periodic urban crises as environmental thresholds are crossed, and the sustainability of many Asian cities will deteriorate. At the extreme, this has the potential to stifle economic development and cut living standards in some cities.

Rapid economic and population growth has inevitably resulted in strains on urban governance and on the systems and processes of urban administration and service provision. Governance by its nature involves politics, processes, and the mobilization of resources. These can be inflexible in rapidly changing circumstances. One barrier to change in governance systems and arrangements at the local and city levels is that change often involves people and institutions at different levels of government. Change can be slow, particularly when the capacity of local organizations to develop and implement policy is starting from a low base, and national politicians and institutions do not give priority to local issues. City governance in Asia over the last 50 years has generally been swamped by urban growth. It has been too slow to develop and adjust. Local governments have been left with little alternative but to attempt to muddle through.

In general, urbanization and economic growth in Asia have increased the political and administrative pressures to decentralize government decision making and service delivery from central government to subnational, more local government. There has been an increased emphasis on regional development and on the decentralization of service provision over the last 2 decades and particularly since the Asian financial crisis. Subnational governments are increasingly being asked to take on greater responsibility for raising public money and for providing infrastructure and services. The performance of Asian countries is increasingly dependent on the capacity and performance of local governments.

Three pressures are at work in Asia, encouraging a renewed look at urban governance and particularly local government. First is the increased demand and growing backlog for services and infrastructure in rapidly growing cities, which threatens to stifle both urban productivity and national economic performance. These can often be prioritized and provided more effectively and efficiently at the local level. Second is the need for fiscal discipline in national governments, which has increased the political attractiveness of devolving responsibilities to lower levels of government and toward local resource mobilization. Third is the desire of local people, institutions, and community organizations to have a greater say in public investments and trade-offs in urban planning, which affect both the economic performance and amenity of their city.

Even with decentralization, the role of national governments in setting the enabling environment for urban governance and in facilitating coordination between the various levels of government and with special-purpose authorities will remain critical. National governments can also be expected to, on occasion, override other levels of government on matters considered of national importance or where local governments are considered to have failed.

There are always tensions in the political dynamics between national and subnational governments. This is as true in the countries of Asia as elsewhere in the world. There is often a reluctance on the part of national governments to see cities with a strong economic base develop further as important political entities in their own right and in national politics. This can be a factor militating against the creation of citywide local governments. Decentralization of governance and local government boundaries are necessarily a political compromise.

Politics, history, issues of capacity and financial resources, and inertia have all played a role leading to the weak, fragmented governance arrangements of most cities in Asia. Financial arrangements are a particular issue, with the reluctance of national governments to cede taxation powers to local authorities commensurate with their service-delivery functions, restrictive borrowing arrangements for local authorities, and their reliance on both general and specific-purpose fiscal transfers from the national level. National governments have endeavored to, more or less, maintain overall control and align the impacts of local government expenditures and borrowings with national economic policy and priorities. From a central government perspective, this may be no bad thing but it has prevented the development of local government as an independent, financially viable institution. Central controls need to be balanced with some real local-level decision-making responsibilities and appropriate resources if the benefits of decentralization are to be achieved.

In all countries considered in this book, there are at least two levels of subnational government and in some, such as the PRC and the Philippines, four. In all these countries, there is increasing focus on decentralization, although this ranges from modest decentralization of some service provision in Cambodia and Viet Nam, to major institutional and administrative change in Indonesia and the Philippines.[8] Also, local government—its finances and functions and relationship to national government—remains a work in progress.

There is a considerable amount of information on urban development and local government in Asian countries, but much less attention appears to have been paid to analyzing the enabling environment of urban governance—the institutional, administrative, and financial architecture of urban governance—and its impact on city performance. This enabling environment is largely the product of national government and comprises the legislation, policies, and directives guiding urban governance and local government operations. The national government framework for urban governance and its associated incentives structure are key factors in the performance of local governments and of urban areas.

While the legal, financial, and administrative arrangements surrounding urban governance are important, outcomes on the ground in cities vary widely even within the same national structure. In each Asian country considered here, there are urban communities and local governments that are better than others in developing and implementing programs and mobilizing resources;

that understand better the complexities of intergovernment arrangements; and that know how, when, and whom to consult to achieve effective outcomes. Others lag behind, seemingly lacking direction and resources, sometimes beset by internal political divisions, and lacking the ability to plan, prioritize, and implement programs. Some of these differences are attributable to the wealth, history, and/or stage of development of the particular city or urban area. Others reflect leadership, dynamism, and the development of a proactive culture in some urban communities at local government, community, and nongovernment organization levels.

CONCLUSION

There is much doom and gloom written about the future sustainability of Asian cities associated with the need to accommodate an additional 1,100 million people over the next 25 years. There is a sense that the magnitude of the problem is too great and that inevitably some cities will experience crises and collapse. The same was said of London and Rome in their past.

While the problems are daunting, the authors of this book are optimistic. Some Asian cities will inevitably experience crises but they are changing. There is vibrancy and vitality in Asian cities, and some have taken major steps to improve the quality of their urban services and environments. Many promising initiatives that are improving the appalling conditions in some cities and putting them on a path to a more sustainable future are being undertaken at the local levels.

Decentralization policies of national governments in Asia are increasingly placing urbanization issues at the local level. Much still needs to be done by national governments in setting the enabling environment for local government to operate. Much also needs to be done to strengthen the capacity of local governments and utility agencies so they can fulfill their functions. The need for effective citywide governance and coordination between the various levels of government and between local governments and special-purpose authorities is another important issue.

Achieving more sustainable forms of urban development for Asian cities is a challenge not only for governments but also for communities and private sector organizations. Successful urban development requires the development of partnerships between all parties involved.

While there are many ways of improving the performance of local government through assistance with strategic planning, institutional strengthening, and management and staff training, one complementary approach is by disseminating information on good practices for sustainable urban development. The following chapters of this book show how countries in Asia are developing and applying good practice to achieve more sustainable urban development outcomes.

Notes

[1] Source for population data: Population Division, Department of Economic and Social Affairs, United Nations Secretariat. 2005. *World Population Prospects: The 2002 Revision* and *World Urbanization Prospects: The 2003 Revision.* October. Available: http://esa.un.org/unup.

[2] Definitions of Asia vary depending on sources. In this book we have not attempted to reconcile data to a single definition but rather to note the source. The issues raised by urbanization in "Asia" (and "Developing Asia" and "Emerging Asia") are generally applicable to the 12 developing countries considered in this book and to very broad definitions of developing countries in the region. Asia in this population data is defined as East Asia: People's Republic of China (PRC); Hong Kong, China; Macau, China; Democratic People's Republic of Korea, Japan, Mongolia, Republic of Korea. South-central Asia: Afghanistan, Bangladesh, Bhutan, India, Iran (Islamic Republic of), Kazakhstan, Kyrgyz Republic, Maldives, Nepal, Pakistan, Sri Lanka, Tajikistan, Turkmenistan, Uzbekistan. Southeast Asia: Brunei Darussalam, Cambodia, Democratic Republic of Timor-Leste, Indonesia, Lao People's Democratic Republic, Malaysia, Myanmar, Philippines, Singapore, Thailand, Viet Nam. Western Asia: Armenia, Azerbaijan, Bahrain, Cyprus, Georgia, Iraq, Israel, Jordan, Kuwait, Lebanon, Occupied Palestinian Territory, Oman, Qatar, Saudi Arabia, Syrian Arab Republic, Turkey, United Arab Emirates, Yemen.

[3] Less-developed regions are defined as all regions of Africa, Asia (excluding Japan), Latin America, and the Caribbean plus Melanesia, Micronesia, and Polynesia.

[4] For details and projections, see World Bank. 2006. *Global Economic Prospects - Economic Implications of Remittances and Migration.* Washington, DC.

[5] The International Monetary Fund defines Emerging Asia as the PRC; India; Hong Kong, China; Republic of Korea; Singapore; Taipei,China; Indonesia; Malaysia; Philippines; and Thailand.

[6] These energy data were derived from information in Energy Information Administration, Office of Integrated Analysis and Forecasting, US Department of Energy. International Energy Outlook 2005, July 2005. Tables A1, A2, A9, and A10.

[7] This section on land draws heavily on Angel, S, S.C. Sheppard, and D.L. Civco. 2005. *The Dynamics of Global Urban Expansion.* Washington, DC: World Bank.

[8] A full analysis of the issues involved in the decentralization of government is contained in World Bank. 2005. *East Asia Decentralizes—Making Local Government Work.* Washington, DC. While the World Bank study only considers Cambodia, PRC, Indonesia, Philippines, Thailand, and Viet Nam, the issues raised and trends identified are relevant to the other six countries considered in this book.

3. Bangladesh
NAZRUL ISLAM

INTRODUCTION

Bangladesh is one of the most densely populated countries on earth. Much of the country is also prone to flooding. The Government recognizes that space should be meticulously planned, developed, and managed in a sustainable way. Rapid urban growth, which plays an increasingly significant role in the development economy, is challenging local governments in devising ways to develop and implement appropriate strategies to ensure sustainable urban development. Relevant statistics on the country are presented in Table 3.1.

This chapter provides an overview of issues affecting the planning and management of urban region development in Bangladesh. It also presents three good practice case studies related to governance and urban management in Chittagong, microcredit for the urban poor in Dhaka and other cities, and a civil society movement for the protection of the environment. The final section of the chapter presents strategies to enhance sustainable urban development, addressing the national urban pattern and individual urban centers.

COUNTRY CONTEXT

Bangladesh is a small country with an area of 147,000 km². It is predominantly an agrarian country experiencing rapid urbanization and economic transformation. In 1974, only 8.8% of the country's 76 million people lived in urban areas; agriculture provided over half the national gross domestic product (GDP) and accounted for about three quarters of the labor force. By 2004, the level of urbanization had increased to nearly 25% and the contribution of the agricultural sector to GDP had decreased to less than 20% (BBS 2005, p. 286). The share of agricultural workers as a proportion of the total labor force, however, had not fallen significantly, remaining at over 60%. The contribution of the urban sector to national GDP grew to nearly 42% in 1998–1999 from only 26% in 1972–1973 (CPD 2001). This share is probably close to 50% at present.

Table 3.1: Country Development Profile, Bangladesh

Human Development Index rank of 177 countries (2003)^	139
GDP growth (annual %, 2004)	5.52
GNI per capita, Atlas method (current $, 2004)	440
GNI, Atlas method (current $ billion, 2004)	61.2
GDP per capita PPP ($, 2003)^	1,770
GDP PPP ($ billion, 2003)^	244.4
Population growth (annual 2005-2010, %) #	1.82
Population, total (million, 2005)#	152.59
Urban population, total (million, 2005)#	38.13
Urban population percent of total population (2005)#	25
Population largest city: Dhaka (2005, million)	12.56
Population growth: 36 capital cities or agglomerations >750,000 inhabitants 2000#	
- Est. average growth of capital cities or urban agglomerations 2005–2015 (%)	34
- Number of capital cities or urban agglomerations with growth >50%, 2005–2015	3
- Number of capital cities or urban agglomerations with growth >30%, 2005–2015	20
Sanitation, % of urban population with access to improved sanitation (2002)**	75
Water, % of urban population with access to improved water sources (2002)**	82
Slum population, % of urban population (2001)**	85
Slum population in urban areas (million, 2001)**	30.40
Poverty, % of urban population below national poverty line (2000)**	36.6
Aid (Net ODA received; $ million, 2003)^	1,393.4
Aid as share of country income (Net ODA/GNI, 2003, %)*	2.6
Aid per capita (current $, 2003)^	10.10

GDP = gross domestic product, GNI = gross national income, ODA = official development assistance, PPP = purchasing power parity.
Sources: World Bank, World Development Indicators 2005; *OECD, DAC, Recipient Aid Charts, 2003; **United Nations Millennium Indicators Database; #UN World Population Prospects: The 2002 Revision and World Urbanization Prospects: The 2003 Revision; ^UNDP, Human Development Report, 2005.

Population

The population of Bangladesh in 2005 was estimated at more than 152 million. Since 1990, the national population growth rate has declined from 2.6% to 2.1% in 2005. It is projected to fall to 1.2% by 2025. Urban population growth rate was extremely high in the 1980s and 1990s, at over 7% annually (Table 3.2). It has fallen significantly since then, but still remains at over 4% per year (United Nations [UN] 2004).[1] It is expected to fall to around 3% by 2050. The total urban population in 2001 was nearly 29 million. The current urban population is estimated at 38 million and is expected to reach 74 million by 2035 (Figure 3.1).

Table 3.2: Growth of Urban Population in Bangladesh, 1951–2001

Census year	Total national population (million)	Annual growth rate of national population (%)	Total urban population (million)	Urban population as percentage of total population (i.e., level of urbanization)	Decadal increase of urban population (%)	Annual exponential growth rate of urban population (%)
1951	44.17	0.50	1.83	4.34	18.38	1.58
1961	55.22	2.26	2.64	5.19	45.11	3.72
1974	76.37	2.48	6.00	8.87	137.57	6.62
1981	89.91	2.32	13.56	15.54	110.68	10.03
1991	111.45	2.17	22.45	20.15	69.75	5.43
2001	123.10	1.47	28.81	23.40	27.38	3.25

Source: Government of Bangladesh Population Census 1981, Report on Urban Areas 1987 and Preliminary Report, Population Census 1991; and BBS 2005.

Viewed in terms of population density rather than percentage of population living in urban areas, the entire country will become a megalopolis or an urbanized country in the next 3–4 decades. Few places in the country, even in the remotest areas, will be within easy commuting distance of an urban center of reasonable size and function. Rural areas will also be urbanized with the penetration of urban services into rural households.

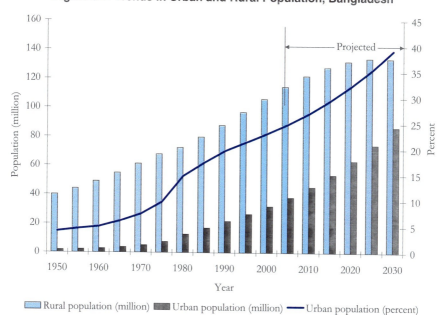

Figure 3.1: Trends in Urban and Rural Population, Bangladesh

Components of Urban Growth

The urban population in the country has grown much faster than the rural population—that is, nearly three times as much during the past 3 decades. Rapid urbanization has occurred because of such factors as (a) a high natural increase in urban population; (b) territorial extension of existing urban areas and a change in the definition of urban areas; and (c) rural-to-urban migration. The last factor mentioned has been the dominant component of urban population growth, contributing 40% of national urban population change in 1974–1981. For some large cities, this share could be even higher, up to 70% (Khan 1982). The pattern has not changed much in the subsequent period.

Spatial Imbalance in Urbanization

At present, in spite of the overall low level of urbanization in the country, there is considerable spatial imbalance in both "meso regions" (i.e., divisions, former or "greater" districts and present districts) and microregions (subdistricts). There are 64 districts with varying levels of urbanization ranging from 60% to under 10%. The district of Dhaka is over 90% urban.

In terms of distribution or spacing of urban centers, each of the 64 districts has an urban center of reasonable size, primarily because of the administrative function of such centers. For the same reason, more than 60% of the 507 subdistricts (known as *upazila* or *thana*) have urban centers of municipal status with a population of over 15,000.

The distribution of urban centers according to population size is less uniform. Dhaka, the capital and largest city with over 12 million people, has about 38% of the total urban population. Dhaka is centrally located and the most accessible city from different parts of the country.

Chittagong, with four million people, is the second largest city. It is a port city located in the southeastern region. Khulna, with about 1.2 million people, is the third largest city and is located in the southwestern region of the country. Rajshahi, located in the mid-western zone, is the fourth largest city with a population of 0.7 million. These four large cities are the headquarters of divisional administration. Two other cities, Sylhet and Barisal, were given the status of a city corporation like the other larger cities. These two are also divisional headquarters and are located in the northeastern and southern regions of the country, respectively.

Two other secondary cities of reasonable size are Rangpur in the northwest and Mymensingh in the north central region. These are yet to attain metropolitan status. The northwest, northeast, and central south regions, therefore, do not yet enjoy the services of a large metropolitan city with substantial economic strength. There are 305 *pourashavas* (or municipalities) besides the six city corporations plus another 211 small urban centers made up of 5,000–15,000 inhabitants. These small centers are distributed all over the country.

Urban Concentration

Bangladesh's urban centers are widely distributed and its urban situation is basically one of primacy and concentration. As indicated earlier, Dhaka has a very distinctive single city primacy comprising 38% of the total urban population (Table 3.3). Dhaka's status as a primary city is historical and is likely to continue into the future.

The four largest metropolitan areas—Dhaka, Chittagong, Khulna, and Rajshahi—together contain over 56% of the total urban population of the country. The concentration is also lopsided in terms of economic activities. Dhaka City alone consumes about 50% of the total power consumption

Dhaka has a disproportionately large concentration of industrial and various public sector investments, despite the Government's declared policy of decentralization. For instance, more than 75% of the 4,107 export-oriented garment industries in the country are located in Dhaka. Concentration is also obvious in the social service, trade, commerce, and finance sectors. For example, 48 of the country's 54 private universities established in the last decade are located in Dhaka City. The situation is similar with respect to medical facilities. Nonetheless, some degree of industrial concentration is also taking place in the second largest city, Chittagong, because of its port.

In Bangladesh, all nonmetropolitan cities and towns having a district headquarters status may be considered secondary cities. These generally have populations of 50,000–500,000. In most urban project documents, however, metropolitan areas other than the capital or the primary city are considered secondary cities. Urban centers with populations of less than 50,000 are considered rural towns, as in the European Commission-supported Rural Towns Project.

Table 3.3: Primacy of Dhaka in the National and National Urban Context

Year	Population (million)	Percent of National Population	Percent of National Urban Population
1974	1.77	3.0	28.2
1981	3.45	3.8	26.0
1991	6.84	5.8	30.5
2001	10.71	8.0	37.4
2005	12.00	8.6	37.5

Source: Calculated from BBS 1994, and estimate for 2005.

Administrative Regional Structure in Bangladesh

Bangladesh has a unitary form of government. For administrative purposes and convenience, the country is divided into six administrative divisions, each placed under a divisional commissioner. Each division is further subdivided into districts, with a district commissioner as the chief administrator. After the administrative reorganization in 1982, the country was divided into 64 districts. Twenty of these districts have existed for a very long period, while the rest were upgraded from subdivisions. The 20 old districts are now popularly known as greater districts. Below the district level are the upazilas/thanas (police stations) which currently number 507. In 1982, 460 of the thanas were upgraded to upazilas or subdistricts. With the abolition of the upazila system in 1991, the upazila regional administrative system reverted to the earlier thana structure. All divisional and district headquarters and most of the thana/upazilas headquarters are urban centers. Below the level of *thana* are 4,484 rural microareas known as unions and 59,990 villages. (BBS 2005:3).

The divisional level is the highest tier of administration after the national level and is headed by a divisional commissioner (popularly known as the commissioner). And since the division level office of each department is linked directly to its national office, the commissioner has only a supervisory role over all departments and agencies. With the establishment of regional (divisional) development boards in 1976, the commissioner also coordinates the development functions of all the district administrations. The regional development boards take on district board projects but do not finance them, as they lack the required expertise.

The district is the focal point in the administrative system of Bangladesh. The head of the district administration is known as the deputy commissioner. In addition to the administrative offices at the district level, which are linked to their respective higher offices, the office of the deputy commissioner is divided into several divisions and sections. Within its planning and implementation section, the annual and mid-term plans are prepared. The physical infrastructure section is responsible for construction throughout the district. If the construction is very small in nature, then it is under the jurisdiction of the thana administration. The rural development section administers rural development programs. The district and thana executives are assisted by a large number of officials and professional and technical personnel appointed by the central Government.

Besides the macro-, meso-, and microregions, there are special-purpose regions—macro in geographical coverage—and metropolitan or urban regions and urban areas. While large metropolitan regions such as the

Dhaka region can be larger than today's district, secondary city regions are usually microregions.

Local governments in urban and rural areas are entrusted to bodies elected by the people. Such bodies in the urban areas are called municipalities or *pourashavas* and currently number about 305. Rural elected bodies are called union *parishads*, or union councils, and number 4,484 (BBS 2005, p. 3).

For many years, the four metropolitan cities of Dhaka, Chittagong, Khulna, and Rajshahi nominated rather than elected mayors (heads of the municipal/city corporations). Members of the city corporation council, known as ward commissioners, were, however, elected from their respective wards. Since March 1994 though, the four largest metropolitan cities have had mayors directly elected. Two more pourashavas (Sylhet and Barisal) were upgraded to city corporation status and elected their respective mayors in 2005.

Efforts at Decentralization of Political Administrative Functions

Since its independence in 1971, Bangladesh attempted several times to develop an acceptable local government structure to decentralize political power, administrative authority, and financial autonomy. The first major attempt was the creation of the district governor system in 1975. However, it could not be implemented because the government that designed it was overthrown after a bloody coup. Another major exercise was the introduction of the upazila (subdistrict) system in 1982, which created a regional hierarchy between the district and the union. Elected union parishads (councils) had earlier been an important tier of local government, and being numerous and small, they remained close to the people. With the establishment of the upazila system, the role of the union was diminished; the union regained importance after the upazila system was abolished in 1991. Between then and now, several attempts have been made to reform local government but inconclusive debates linger on the issue of the number of tiers—varying between two to five—and on the revival of the upazila system.

At present, four tiers of local government are recognized in the rural-regional context: the zila parishad, upazila parishad, union parishad, and gram sarkar. Of these, only union parishads exist as truly elected bodies, while gram sarkars (introduced in 2004) are composed of selected representatives. Theoretically, there could be some 22 zila (district) parishads and 460 upazila parishads, but these do not exist at present. There exist 4,484 union parishads, while the number of gram sarkars is over 40,000. The average population size of a union in Bangladesh is 31,000 and of gram sarkar jurisdictions, about 3,500. The upazila parishad, whose average population was 300,000, was also physically accessible to the people as the average geographical area was only 320 km^2.

The upazila seems to be an ideal area size and demographic unit of local government in Bangladesh and the demand for its revival is fairly strong. However, its practicality is questioned in view of a possible conflict of interests between the upazila parishad leadership and the local members of parliament.

The urban local government structure has basically remained unchanged for a long time. It is a two-tier structure with city corporations for the largest six cities, and *paurashavas*/municipalities for the 305 municipal cities and towns. Very small urban centers are administered as nonmunicipal rural entities under the union parishad system. Urban local governments, as well as the rural union parishads, are formed through a democratic election process, with the mayor/chairperson also elected by direct vote of the citizens. Urban local government elections are very well attended. Women may also be elected by direct vote, both in common seats and reserved constituencies, unlike under the previous system when they were nominated by directly-elected members, almost all of whom were men. At least one large municipality (Narayanganj, which has a population of about 500,000) has a woman chairperson elected directly—the first time in the history of municipal governance in Bangladesh.

Although urban local governments are elected through a democratic process, they do not enjoy any significant autonomy. Neither do they enjoy political, administrative nor financial power. Central government control and intervention or interference occur at various stages of governance. Urban local governments cannot even appoint a junior-level employee without approval from the Ministry of Local Government, Rural Development, and Cooperatives. However, despite such limitations, some urban local authorities have tried to find ways and means to introduce programs for better service delivery in their respective cities. (One such city, Chittagong, has been selected as a good practice case study in this chapter).

While city governments are controlled by the central Government, there is also lack of devolution of authority within the city government's structure. Conceiving a very large city, such as Dhaka, as a city corporation and as a single local government unit does not conform to the concept of decentralization because its population is as large as, or even larger than, a district. Although such cities are subdivided into smaller wards, such units seldom have any functional or financial power, or human resource capacity. The quality of local leadership may also be questionable, along with their commitment to the economic and social development of their constituencies.

The National Development Planning Process

Bangladesh has a tradition of centrally-planned development. The Planning Commission, headed by the Prime Minister, is the central planning agency entrusted with the responsibility of national development planning activities. The Planning Commission acts under the general guidance and control of the National Economic Council (NEC), which is the highest policy-making body in matters of socioeconomic development.

The NEC is chaired by the Prime Minister, and all cabinet ministers are members of the NEC. The council provides overall guidance to the Planning Commission at different stages of formulation of 5-year plans, Annual Development Program (ADP), and economic policies. The NEC also finalizes and approves development plans, programs, and policies recommended by the Planning Commission. NEC reviews ADP performance and the implementation of plans, and deliberates on important economic problems and issues. There is also the executive committee of the NEC, headed by the finance minister. It meets more frequently to approve major development projects and to consider economic issues. It coordinates all major development and planning activities.

The Bangladesh Planning Commission was set up immediately after Independence in 1971. The first Five-Year Plan covered 1973–1978. This was followed by an interim Two-Year Plan (for 1978–1980). The second Five-Year Plan covered 1980–1985, and the third Five-Year Plan, 1985–1990. The fourth Five-Year Plan covered 1990–1995, and was essentially prepared in keeping with the objectives of a Perspective Plan (1990–2010). The fifth Five-Year Plan covered 1996–2001. Five-year development planning was discontinued after 2001. Instead, a poverty reduction strategy paper or PRSP was prepared and adopted in October 2005 for 2005–2015, to be implemented as a series of 3-year rolling plans during that period.

Development planning in Bangladesh has traditionally taken a sectoral rather than a regional or spatial approach. However, regional development thinking has not been totally absent; sectoral allocations to regional entities, such as divisions and districts, have been made to a certain extent. In addition, special-purpose regions are recognized and some resources allocated accordingly. The concept of planning and development of metropolitan regions also exists, such as in the four largest cities. For all other urban areas, development approaches are in terms of urban centers (pourashavas or municipalities) or urban areas.

Regional Planning and Development

Regions have been identified for administrative, economic, physical planning, and development purposes. The special-purpose regions were identified for planned development on a priority basis during the late 1970s.[2] They were the (a) Chittagong Hill Tracts (in the southeastern region), (b) Haor Basin (in northeastern region), (c) Barind (in the northwestern region), and (d) Offshore Islands Region in the south. Separate development boards were created to implement development programs in these four special regions, which had been identified as lagging socioeconomically. In addition, development boards were also formed for the four administrative regions or divisions of the country. These approaches provided some scope for regional development planning.

After creating the upazilas (or subdistricts) over the former thanas in 1982, special allocations were made for the planned development of the upazilas. In the draft fourth Five-Year Plan, upazila development received a separate allocation—a "block allocation"—forming 4.7% of the total allocation and 7.7% of the public sector allocation. These allocations were made to the upazila parishads; the local government authority at that level. Thus, upazilas received the benefits of both sectoral as well as upazila allocations. Allocations made to upazilas redirected sectoral investments in favor of smaller projects taken within the upazilas. With the shift from the upazila system to the thana system in 1991, the allocations of development funds at that level have been somewhat reduced. Allocations were also made in the Five-Year Plan for large metropolitan city authorities and municipal towns and cities, which have been kept out of the upazila system.

The fourth Five-Year Plan referred to decentralized participatory planning as the most critical input and output for planning, and identified a hierarchical order of spatial/territorial organization in terms of planning and implementation. This consisted of village development programs, union development plans, thana (former upazila) plans, district/regional plans, and the national plan.

Unlike the Five-Year Plans, the PRSP does not make any provision for urban and regional planning and development nor does it place any emphasis on comprehensive development of cities. There is no section on urban development or housing as there had been in previous Five-Year Plans. However, in the section on the environment, improving the lives of slum dwellers is mentioned (following Millennium Development Goal [MDG] Goal 7 and Target 11). This section of the PRSP refers to the adoption of a national policy on urban development (GED, Planning Commission 2005, p. 284).

Whether the PRSP considers metropolitan planning or not, it will be put into practice there because the four largest cities have their own planning and development authorities. The total area covered by the four metropolitan planning regions does not exceed 2,500 km^2, the largest being the Rajuk

Region for the Dhaka metropolitan region of about 1,530 km^2. The secondary cities (district and upazila towns) are to be offered urban planning services by the Urban Development Directorate (UDD) of the Ministry of Housing and Public Works (MHPW) and the Local Government Engineering Department (LGED) of the Ministry of Local Government, Rural Development and Cooperatives (MLGRD&C).

Urban Development and Governance

Bangladesh has only a recent record of planned urban development. Efforts were made in the 1960s and the 1970s for a national urban planning system, which would have taken into consideration such aspects as location, size, spacing, and function of urban centers; however, this remained a "paper plan." Instead, planned development was considered on an individual city basis. The four largest cities were brought under master plans in the late 1950s and early 1960s. Each city was given an urban planning and development authority to prepare master plans and to develop the cities in keeping with such plans. These authorities, RAJUK for Dhaka, Chittagong Development Authority for Chittagong, Khulna Development Authority for Khulna, and Rajshahi Development Authority for Rajshahi, prepared plans through support either from the United Nations (UN) or local private consulting groups as their own in-house planning capability was very limited. Development authorities are now able to prepare some local area plans.

Development authorities undertake schemes as recommended in the master plans and are under the jurisdiction of the Ministry of Housing and Public Works. By contrast, urban local governments, referred to as city corporations, are under the jurisdiction of the MLGRD&C. City corporations are responsible for carrying out a variety of functions, including conservation, maintenance of roads, street lighting, maintenance of parks and playgrounds, lakes, and delivering various social services. Several other agencies are also responsible for different urban services, such as water, sewerage and drainage, transportation, gas, telephone, security, education, health, and other services. In Dhaka, 41 different government organizations are involved in the city's planning and development activities (Islam 2005). Such a multiplicity of organizations creates problems in coordination and good governance. In Dhaka, the problem has been so serious that a separate committee for good governance and development for the city was established under the Office of the Prime Minister.

For other large cities, coordination and governance problems are generally settled through the initiative of their respective city mayors. For the other secondary cities and towns, which do not have separate urban planning and development bodies, responsibility for initiating urban plans rests with the city government, that is, the pourashavas. However, since pourashavas lack their own urban planners, master plans are normally prepared for them by either the UDD, LGED, or private consultancy firms under their supervision. Some support is now being given to 22 secondary cities in setting up urban planning departments or cells within their offices under the ADB-financed Urban Governance and Infrastructure Improvement Project (UGIIP).

Problems of Urban Development

Urbanization in Bangladesh poses two kinds of challenges: addressing the unbalanced structure of urbanization in the country and marshalling the efforts needed to solve the problems of individual urban areas or cities. At the national level, there is yet no policy on urbanization although efforts have been made to formulate one. Currently, a review of the status of urbanization in the country is being carried out through the Committee for Urban Local Governments headed by the minister for LGRD&C. This committee is expected to recommend a more balanced pattern of urban development as well as better governance of individual cities.

At the individual city level, there are innumerable problems not only in the large urban areas but also in small urban centers. Their problems vary in dimension. These include

- a weak economic base in most towns and cities. Poverty and inequality are common problems. Urban poverty reduction has not been a priority in public policy;
- inadequate urban utility services (water, sanitation and sewerage, electricity, gas, fuel, telephone, solid waste management, etc.);
- insufficient transport facilities and poor management of traffic. This situation leads to traffic congestion in most cities and towns, particularly in Dhaka City. Congestion causes huge financial losses in terms of time wasted as well as air pollution, which in turn has economic and health implications;
- inadequate education, health, and recreation services, both in quantitative and qualitative terms;
- housing problems, which are particularly serious for those in the lower-income strata. The problem manifests itself in the proliferation of slums and squatter settlements, especially in large cities;
- deteriorating environmental conditions in cities and towns. Air pollution, water pollution, and even sound pollution in cities and towns

are emerging as major concerns. In Dhaka City, environmental problems have reached serious proportions. Moreover, illegal occupation of open spaces, parks, gardens, lakes, rivers, and other water bodies, and the irrational leveling off of hills and cutting down of trees have further degraded the urban environment;
- deteriorating law and order situation, manifested in the escalation of crime and violence and the feeling of insecurity among the urban population. Suicide bomb blasts and other forms of religiously motivated terrorist attacks are a more recent worrying phenomenon;
- social problems, especially child abuse and oppression of women, are prevalent. Prostitution is a serious social problem. Drug addiction among the youth is a recent problem. Begging on city streets is also a problem; and
- problems related to the preservation of sociocultural heritage.

The Root Cause of Urban Problems: Poor Governance

The root of these problems can be traced to one or more major concerns. The absence of urban planning, lack of financial resources, and the weak implementation of plans, if any, aggravate the above crises.

However, ineffectual urban governance is probably the single most serious cause of such problems—lack of accountability or transparency and inefficiency on the part of those responsible for governance, and the lack of awareness and the absence of organized movements among ordinary people. There is lack of adequate devolution of power and authority to urban local bodies from the central government and similarly within the city authority to devolve power and responsibility to the lower-level hierarchy, such as the wards. Inadequacy of qualified professionals is also a major limitation in establishing good governance. Absence of good leadership at the city level is a very major concern.

External Support to the Urban Sector

Despite the absence of a comprehensive policy, the urban sector has received attention from the Government and various development agencies. The many donor agencies active in the sector include ADB, European Commission, Japan International Cooperation Agency (JICA), United Kingdom Department for International Development, United Nations Children's Fund (UNICEF), United Nations Capital Development Fund (UNCDF), United Nations Development Programme (UNDP), United States Agency for International Development (USAID), World Bank, and other bilateral donors. ADB has been the leading donor agency in the urban sector in recent years.

Early support from external agencies came from UN organizations. UNDP and the United Nations Centre for Human Settlements – Habitat offered assistance on situation analysis and urban policy formulation. UNCDF extended support in squatter rehabilitation. UNDP assisted with funding and the provision of technical personnel in preparing master/structural plans for Dhaka and Chittagong. UNDP also supported an urban poverty alleviation project and a small environmental project. The World Bank offered assistance in upgrading slums and improving the environment in Dhaka and low-income housing in Chittagong. Later, it also provided support to municipal service improvement through the Municipal Service Project and is currently supporting the Municipal Development Fund. The World Bank has also extended assistance for the Saidabad Water Treatment Plant for Dhaka Water Supply and Sewerage Authority, as well as the Dhaka Urban Transport Project.

UNICEF was a pioneer in slum improvement assistance, covering more than 25 cities around the country. The project has undergone a series of transformations. JICA has supported environmental improvement and flood control studies, and assisted Dhaka City Corporation in preparing the Solid Waste Management Master Plan.

ADB has provided assistance in both service deliveries, such as in primary health care, institutional development, and urban governance improvement. Its support to UGIIP covers 22 secondary cities and should have a significant impact on urban development. ADB's interest in supporting the improvement of the housing sector, land management, and urban poverty reduction could not be adopted as a realistic project for various reasons. ADB has also supported an urban sector review, the recommendations of which may be utilized by the government-appointed Committee for Urban Local Governments.

USAID's recent contribution has been its support to the improvement of urban institutional reforms, especially in organizing municipal representatives. This support resulted in the formation of the Municipal Association of Bangladesh in 2004. The Association is actively engaged in articulating its demands for greater authority for urban local bodies.

Notable among the international nongovernment organizations (NGOs) that have been extending support to the urban sector are CARE Bangladesh and Plan Bangladesh. However, external support received by Bangladeshi NGOs for economic and social improvements for the urban poor is probably on the wane.

GOOD PRACTICE CASE STUDIES

Three case studies have been selected as examples of sustainable development in Bangladesh:

Figure 3.2: Map Showing Location of the Case Studies

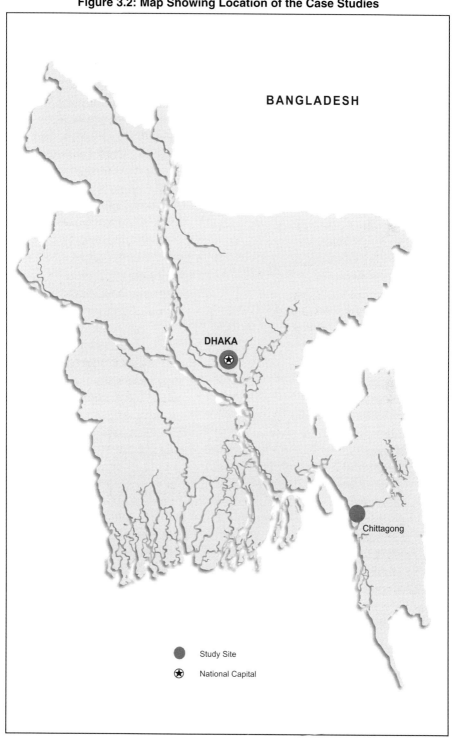

Chittagong City Corporation initiatives, a study on service delivery and resource mobilization, illustrates how a local government works for the benefit of its citizens in spite of central government controls and restrictions. The importance of good governance and the leadership role of the mayor are particularly exemplary for Bangladesh.

Shakti Foundation Microcredit Program for poor urban women was started 12 years ago in Dhaka. It has been replicated in 11 secondary cities involving 140,000 households. Shakti is a pioneer urban finance program developed after the Grameen Bank model. It focused on large NGOs working on poverty alleviation.

The Bangladesh Environment Movement or *Bangladesh Paribesh Andolon* (BAPA), a nationwide environment movement that has distinguished itself as a significant civil society movement, is fully funded by local or expatriate Bangladeshis. The program has been important in improving public knowledge about the environment and sustainability.

Chittagong City Corporation: Dynamic and Innovative Leadership

Chittagong is the second largest city in Bangladesh, with a current population of about 4 million. The population is growing rapidly at nearly the same pace as Dhaka. Chittagong is the principal seaport of the country and the second most important industrial center, with more than 40% of the country's heavy industries located there. Chittagong also accommodates 20% of the export-oriented garment industries.

GOOD PRACTICE	
Good Governance	✓
Urban Management	
Infrastructure/Service Provision	✓
Financing and Cost Recovery	
Sustainability	
Innovation and Change	
Leveraging ODA	

Chittagong is an old port city but its history of development as a planned city began only in the 1960s with the establishment of the Chittagong Development Authority. Chittagong City Corporation (CCC) is the urban local government unit responsible for overall governance. Its municipal governance, however, dates back to 1863. Constrained by the limitations set by the City Corporation Ordinance or the Pourashava Ordinance, city corporations and pourashavas in Bangladesh normally do not enjoy any significant power or authority to mobilize resources on their own nor to undertake major development programs of commercial interest. They generally depend on the central Government to bring such programs to their cities. However, they can propose such programs or projects to the Government. Chittagong, under the dynamic and innovative leadership of its mayor, ABM Mohiuddin Chowdhury, broke through the system and initiated sustainable social, economic, and environmental projects.

Due to sound leadership, Mayor Chowdhury was recently elected mayor for the third consecutive time. This is a rare occurrence in contemporary Bangladesh politics, particularly since the mayor is from the opposition party. His uniqueness lies in his pro-people approach, which takes up socially beneficial projects. He also tries to make his projects financially self-sustaining. CCC has regularly mandated programs on civic infrastructure development, garbage disposal, maintenance of parks and playgrounds, etc., but has extended its services to such other areas as education, health, environmental protection, preservation of hill areas, disaster management, establishing a compressed natural gas (CNG) plant, supplying water to poor communities, power plant installation, a pharmaceutical factory, garbage recycling plant, and shopping complexes.

City corporations normally are not expected to run institutions of higher education, such as colleges or universities, nor operate higher-level medical facilities or medical schools. However, Mayor Mohiuddin Chowdhury has led CCC to shoulder such responsibilities which, he says, are merely responses to the needs of the citizens that at the same time help the city corporation strengthen its financial position. Examples of some such initiatives in Chittagong follow.

Garbage Disposal and Activities of Shebok

The CCC has produced an example of efficient garbage disposal and city cleaning activities through the input of its manual workers (around 1,800 staff and officials) named "Shebok"—friends who help keep the city clean— and who have been operating since 1994. Chittagong City is well known as the "clean and green city" of the country, a model for other cities. Chittagong won the honorable Prime Minister's award, first prize, as the "Clean and Green City" in 2002–2003.

Environmental Protection and Improvement

A tree-planting program has been undertaken throughout the city for the last decade to beautify and protect the quality of its urban environment. The road islands, footpaths, medians, parks/gardens, and others, are decorated with different types of trees, plants, shrubs, and bushes. Many persons are employed for the maintenance of this planting activity. CCC recently took adequate measures to mitigate air pollution caused by a range of vehicles in the city through the establishment of a CNG plant. This is the biggest CNG plant of its kind so far in the country. In Dhaka City, private sector enterprises had set up CNG plants on lands leased from the government.

Educational Institutions

In the words of the CCC mayor, "We know that education is the backbone of a nation, but we have around 50% of our population who are still illiterate. So, we have undertaken programs to encourage all people to send their children to primary schools" (Chowdhury 2005). The Education Department of CCC operates 6 kindergarten schools, 2 primary schools, 41 secondary schools, 8 girls' colleges, 5 computer institutes/colleges, 1 health technology institute, 1 midwifery institute, and a university named Premier University. Many young people leave these institutions every year with adequate academic knowledge and professional skills to serve the country.

Health Service

To reduce the high maternal and child mortality and morbidity rates, CCC established six maternity hospitals and 60 health-care centers in different parts of the city. The aim is to ensure accessibility for underprivileged and deprived people to cheap health-care services, especially for female garment workers living in the city who have limited access to good urban services. CCC also started six health centers in the evening shift for this group of people to provide health services with nominal fees. Besides these, the Health Department of CCC operates a TB Clinic, Expanded Program on Immunization, leprosy program, HIV/AIDS program, school health program, adolescent health education, disaster management program, orphanage, and other services. CCC is planning to establish a referral hospital, medical college, HIV/AIDS screening hospital, cancer hospital, and a home for the aged in the city.

Disaster Management

Cyclones, storm surges, floods, and earthquakes are the major natural hazards in the Chittagong region. CCC is trying to develop necessary awareness programs as well as infrastructure to cope with such events. The city is under threat from earthquakes. In response, the CCC has held motivational programs on various occasions to generate awareness among the public and to develop adequate preparedness regarding earthquake disaster risk mitigation.

City Pharmaceuticals Factory

Chittagong City Corporation recently inaugurated the establishment of a pharmaceutical factory to support its hospitals and health-care centers by providing cheap, good quality medicines and supplies. The factory is undertaking regular production of some essential medicines and should be able to generate income for the CCC.

Water for the Poor

Supplying drinking water for the people of Chittagong is the responsibility of the Chittagong Water and Sewerage Authority (C-WASA). C-WASA is unable to provide water to all, especially the poor in low-income areas and slums. CCC has taken the initiative of supplying water to such areas in mobile tankers at fixed water points. The water tankers distribute water at over 130 points in the 41 wards of the city. This has helped the poor immensely.

Lessons Learned

The innovative ventures of the mayor of Chittagong have shown that drive and dynamism often help overcome limitations. Municipal services are meant for the people. If people need and demand such services, and if the city can come forward with positive responses, the people will welcome such initiatives. The mayor of Chittagong has earned enough credibility to muster such responses even if he belongs to the opposition. All CCC projects are designed not only to serve the people but also to be financially viable. Many projects are also complementary and are run as socially-oriented commercial ventures.

Urban Credit Program of the Shakti Foundation

GOOD PRACTICE	
Good Governance	
Urban Management	
Infrastructure/Service Provision	
Financing and Cost Recovery	✓
Sustainability	
Innovation and Change	
Leveraging ODA	

As Bangladesh is one of the poorest countries in the world, eradicating poverty has been a major concern for many in the country. Through Professor Mohammad Yunus and microcredit, the country is a great pioneer in poverty alleviation. Bangladesh now leads the world in microfinance operations. In 2000, the number of microcredit borrowers throughout the world was 9 million, of which more than 5 million were from Bangladesh (Azad, *Banglapedia 2003*, Vol. 6, p. 479). Most borrower families have been able to move out of poverty. More than 90% of the microcredit borrowers in Bangladesh are women. The credit program has not only pulled millions of households out of poverty, but has also made a tremendous impact on social emancipation by empowering women and encouraging them to send their children to school, to seek better health care, and to demand greater domestic and political rights.

Most NGOs providing microcredit do so in rural areas, where the majority of the poor live. Professor Yunus began his Grameen Bank operations in 1976. Grameen is yet to extend a credit program in urban areas but in the 3 decades since the Grameen Bank began, poverty in urban areas in Bangladesh has assumed massive proportions. Nearly 37% of 35 million urban dwellers live in poverty. The number of urban poor is rising sharply with the migration of the rural poor to urban areas. The need and demand for access to microcredit facilities have grown in equal proportion.

The first major initiative in providing microfinance in urban areas began in 1992, when the Shakti Foundation for Disadvantaged Women introduced its scheme in Dhaka. The urban credit program of Shakti Foundation is based on the Grameen Bank model of group organization and financial transaction. The major activity is financial assistance to poor women. Over the years, in response to the needs of the members, some nonfinancial services have been added as supplementary to the main program. Thus, it has gradually become an integrated scheme reaching disadvantaged women and empowering them.

Within 5 years of its initiation in Dhaka, the success of the program encouraged its replication in Chittagong. Currently, the program is being implemented in 12 cities and covers over 159,000 families. The Shakti Foundation has so far disbursed about TK5,500 million ($76 million) in the broad categories of trading, processing, manufacturing, and services (Islam, H. 2005).

The main thrust of the urban credit program is focused on the general loan scheme. Microcredit ranging from TK4,000 to TK5,000 is called a general loan. This loan is given to most people in the organization to support income-generating activities. All members of the Shakti Foundation are eligible for this loan, provided that they meet the membership criteria and utilize their loans for income-generating activities. Larger loans are given for microenterprises. As an organization, the Shakti Foundation follows a very modern management system that is fully decentralized to the city and branch levels, even in the recruitment of personnel and financial decision making.

In Dhaka, where Shakti has over 105,000 borrowers, at least one third have crossed the poverty line (Parveen 2004) and many have improved their economic condition substantially, graduating from microfinance borrowers to microenterprise borrowers to profitably utilize amounts 20–50 times greater than their initial loans of only TK5,000. At least 10% of the borrowers have moved to the lower-middle income category. Many have become able entrepreneurs and run microenterprises employing 10–30 workers. Many borrowers have moved to better shelters, regularly send their children to school, and seek modern allopathic treatment instead of going to "quack doctors."

In short, there has been significant achievement in poverty alleviation through urban microcredit. It is no longer Shakti or a few NGOs offering the service. In Dhaka City alone, nearly 100 NGOs are engaged in the activity and they are also spreading to other cities.

Poverty in urban areas is a harsh reality. Most of the poor live in city slums; MDGs aim to reduce poverty and improve the lives of the slum dwellers. Microcredit programs like that of the Shakti Foundation in Bangladesh can play a significant role in achieving the MDGs. A concerted effort by the government, NGOs, and donors is recommended.

Bangladesh Poribesh Andolon (Bangladesh Environment Movement)

Tremendous population pressures, poverty, greed, unwise planning, and poor governance in general have all worked together in causing serious degradation of the environment in Bangladesh. In addition to natural hazards like flooding, cyclones, and riverbank erosion, there are also many human-induced problems like deforestation, the filling in of water bodies, and leveling of hills. Rural habitats also suffer from massive contamination of underground water from arsenic. In the urban areas too, there is large-scale degradation of the environment.

GOOD PRACTICE	
Good Governance	
Urban Management	✓
Infrastructure/Service Provision	
Financing and Cost Recovery	✓
Sustainability	
Innovation and Change	
Leveraging ODA	

Being an alluvial deltaic plain, most cities in Bangladesh are located along rivers, with numerous water bodies in and around the cities. But with an increasing population, poor or no urban planning, and poor management, water systems have been seriously affected. Most water bodies in the cities have been unwisely filled up and canals and rivers grossly encroached on, resulting in inadequate drainage and causing serious problems of waterlogging after every major downpour. The rivers and canals in and around the cities are also becoming heavily polluted due to the uncontrolled emission of untreated effluents from factories. Untreated sewage is also being directly discharged into the rivers. Most water bodies are polluted in varying degrees. In the large cities, like Dhaka and Chittagong, the number of motorized vehicles has greatly increased. Combined with poor enforcement of legal instruments, increasing vehicular traffic has caused serious air pollution. Poor governance and greed have provided scope for encroachment into parks and lakes of cities, sometimes totally destroying such essential recreational spaces.

BAPA was established in 2000 by a number of concerned citizens of Dhaka to address environmental degradation (BAPA 2005). In 1997, the same group of people had formed an environmental organization named POROSH (Commitment to Environmental Protection); the name was changed to BAPA after an International Conference on Environment in January 2000 in Dhaka. BAPA later held two more international conferences; one on environment in general in 2002 and the second on the proposed Indian River Linking Project in 2004. Within a span of only 5 years, BAPA has become almost a household name, not because of organizing international conferences and seminars but because of its continuing strong activist programs, protesting against any type of action detrimental to a healthy environment. BAPA has also spoken out against projects undertaken, or being proposed or planned outside the borders of Bangladesh that have serious negative implications for the country.

At the city level, BAPA takes a very active role in monitoring projects that have the potential to have an impact on the environment, irrespective of size. Dhaka used to be a city with an extremely high level of air pollution, especially in lead and carbon contamination. BAPA campaigned against leaded petrol and the presence of two-stroke engines in three-wheeler taxis. After a series of dialogues with the city government, motor vehicle pollution reduction measures were introduced to phase out leaded petrol, ban two-stroke engine taxis and replace them with four-stroke engine taxis, and introduce catalytic converters for motor vehicles. The result has been a substantial reduction in vehicle emission pollution levels.[3] Similar measures were introduced in Delhi, India (Bell et al. 2004).

BAPA has also successfully campaigned against the rampant use of nonrecyclable thin plastic bags. The production and sale of such bags has been declared illegal. The organization has been persistent in its fight against encroachers into the River Burhiganga, the lifeline of Dhaka City, but with only partial success because the interest groups are too powerful and unscrupulous for BAPA and the concerned government authority. BAPA has been successful in stopping some government departments from converting playgrounds into housing projects or from parks into commercial complexes. As yet, achievements in other areas of environmental degradation have been modest.

BAPA's success is to be found in the spirit of making people more aware of the problems of environmental degradation and convincing them to organize to fight against careless members of the populace. The impacts of this effort are now clearly visible. Within the span of only half a decade, many environmental groups were established and have expanded in Dhaka, Chittagong, and other large and medium-sized cities. Citizens' environment action groups have been developed in the neighborhood as well as at the city level. On occasions, many of these organizations get together with BAPA.

In recognizing BAPA's commitment to the cause of environmental protection, the Dhaka City Corporation, Ministry of Environment, MHPW, the MLGRD, and the Office of the Prime Minister have invited BAPA to participate actively in the decision-making process in matters of environmental development activities.

It is useful to note that BAPA is a civil society organization run completely with the members' own funding and has so far avoided taking any funds from external donors, and even the Government. Expatriate Bangladeshis have, however, supported BAPA on a regular basis both with funds and technical expertise. But local expertise, professional inputs, and financial support essentially keep BAPA going. The organization is managed by a national committee, an elected executive committee, and a very small office staff. The membership of BAPA can rightly claim to have an assembly of some of the finest dedicated professionals, environmental and social scientists, intellectuals, and other activists of the country. They include former ministers, advisors, vice-chancellors, professors, engineers, doctors, architects, planners, social activists, and media people.

Lessons Learned

The organizational structure, objectives, and style of activities of BAPA and its success or limitations indicate the need for such a civil society movement in a society that is highly vulnerable to both natural disasters and human-induced environmental crises. In a situation where political or bureaucratic leadership is either insensitive or inefficient, and where the private sector or even some individual citizens are highly antienvironment or antisocial, it is absolutely essential that civil society and professional groups take a strong position for sustainable development. BAPA has shown that committed and concerted action can yield results. Environmental activist organizations should network with each other across cities and across international borders.

STRATEGIES TO ENHANCE SUSTAINABLE URBAN DEVELOPMENT

Bangladesh is struggling to develop and implement sustainable policies and approaches to urban development. There are many priority matters requiring attention. The following four policy areas are considered priority if the country is to improve its approach to and achieve more sustainable urban development in the future.

A National Urban Policy for Balanced Urban Development

Policy makers and planners at the national level, such as in the Bangladesh Planning Commission or in the Ministry of Planning, need to sit together to formulate a national urban policy. Although the Planning Commission could be the ideal host for this task, a committee has been formed in the Ministry of Local Government and Rural Development under the chair of the minister in charge of framing such a policy. The policy should aim at guiding the pace of urbanization (especially in reference to rural-urban migration), and moderating population density by encouraging decentralized development and growth of secondary cities. Geographical imbalances in urbanization can partly be reduced by providing greater incentives and development support to lagging regions. Regional planning may be considered a viable alternative or at least a strong complement to sector-based economic planning. As the Government has adopted a poverty reduction approach to national development, the spatial dimension in poverty reduction is expected to be given more attention. Otherwise, pockets of poverty will continue to push the poor into metropolitan areas.

Promoting Planned Urban Region Development

In the context of enhancing sustainability of individual urban regions or centers, the most appropriate strategy is to promote good governance. This should ensure good and effective leadership (like that of the mayor of Chittagong City Corporation), transparency and accountability, efficiency and integrity, qualified professionals, and a skilled workforce. However, most importantly, urban local bodies should be given greater power and authority to run their cities. Real devolution of power is essential. At the same time, local urban bodies should be sufficiently self-reliant in financial terms. But financial support from the central Government and development partners may be needed until local bodies acquire adequate strength.

One of the major challenges in the urban sector is the promotion of planned growth of individual towns and cities, big and small. It is necessary to create an institutional arrangement to undertake planning exercises in each city. The physical development of each city or town should be planned to embody efficiency, productivity, equity, beauty, and environmental sustainability. Efficiency is related to the functional aspects of towns and cities, to be achieved through physical planning and providing basic urban services, with emphasis on equity. Productivity is related to the economy of urban areas, while beauty is related to the aesthetic aspects of the city. Environmental sustainability is of paramount importance and can be achieved through realistic planning and governance.

The above-mentioned components of urban planning can be achieved by deploying a planning team in each big and medium-sized town. Creating such teams for each city will be time consuming, but the process should be started without delay (one example of such a planning team is the one working in the Dhaka City Corporation). Fortunately, the process has begun in 22 secondary cities of UGIIP, supported by the Asian Development Bank (ADB).

Planning activities for each city should be entrusted to the local municipality. If it is not strong enough, the central Government, through its UDD or through nongovernment consultants, should undertake such responsibilities.

In Bangladesh, people are more or less familiar with the "master plan" concept. Very recently, however, the concepts of structural and strategic plans were introduced. The point of departure from earlier master planning is that these plans are undertaken with the participation of stakeholders. In particular, people of various social strata can take part in the planning. In such participatory urban planning, importance must be attached to the local or neighborhood plan.

Whatever the process of planning may be, the plan should be strictly adhered to by all concerned. A plan prepared by a participatory process and adopted by the authority (with the agreement of all major stakeholders) should be honored. Any violation of the plan should be a punishable act. Planning personnel capacity should be increased and adequate planners trained. To this end, necessary infrastructure at the university and college levels should be created. The importance of a research institute on planning aspects also needs to be realized.

There should be a broad-based planning act for the country that municipalities and city corporations can follow as a planning guide. All urban planning activities and their implementation should be brought under this act.

Land-use Control Legislation

Enacting appropriate legislation for land-use control is also necessary. Such legislation should consider the objective conditions and the reality that majority of the urban and rural population is poor. The role of the informal sector should be appreciated and recognized in urban legislation and planning.

Urban Development-related Human Resource Development

Proper urban development requires adequate urban development personnel (i.e., urban planners and other professionals and para-professionals), and to undertake research activities on urbanization, including housing and infrastructure development. Urban regional/rural planning should be introduced as a subject in all universities and major colleges and be part of high school curricula. Urban and regional planning is a discipline—like business studies, information technology, biotechnology, and environmental science—that needs to be taught and applied in the future in Bangladesh.

CONCLUSION

The strategies for achieving sustainable urban development demand institutional and structural reforms. Municipal governments throughout the country are the main agents of urban governance. For them it is a challenge to create efficient, transparent, accountable, and people-oriented development institutions. Therefore, strengthening the capacity of municipal governments is necessary. Preference should be given to quality, rather than quantity, of personnel.

In all city corporations, including Dhaka, reform and restructuring will be necessary. To initiate such reform, legal frameworks and ordinances have to be amended. Similarly, other autonomous bodies, such as Rajdhani Unnayan Kartripakkhya (RAJUK-Capital Development Authority), DESA, and WASA, should undertake reforms to bring about qualitative changes.

A strong but accountable private sector is helpful in promoting urban development. The private sector is, therefore, to be given preference and/or supported wherever necessary. The development of partnerships between public and private sectors may well promote the rapid development of the urban sector. Adequate institutional arrangements and reform may be necessary to develop such partnerships. Similar partnerships may be forged between the public sector and NGOs, and the private sector and NGOs.

The role of civil society is also important in mobilizing public opinion and creating pressure on public agencies and the private sector to perform their duties and responsibilities more effectively. Public authorities should formulate urban development plans with community participation and implement them with sincerity and transparency. This may be possible with proper participation and partnerships. Such initiatives by civil society have already started.

Finally, international and bilateral development partners should be encouraged to continue their support for the urban sector. They should assist in poverty reduction, infrastructure development, housing provision, institutional development, and human resource development. It is hoped that the three good practice case studies have demonstrated the great potential in Bangladesh for progress in the urban sector. There are many constraints but committed efforts can overcome them. The future of Bangladesh rests very much on how its urban sector is organized and steered.

Notes

[1] The Bangladesh census estimated the 1991–2001 urban growth rate at 3.25% (BBS).

[2] The special-purpose regional development approach was subsequently withdrawn, except for the Haor Development Board which, since 2001, is called the Bangladesh Haor and Wetland Development Board.

[3] PM Is Decreasing In Dhaka. 2003. Available : www.cleanairnet.org/caiasia/1412/article-58241.html.

4. Cambodia
BENG HONG SOCHEAT KHEMRO

INTRODUCTION

Cambodia is one of the three countries of former French Indochina and a member country of the Association of Southeast Asian Nations (ASEAN). The population of Cambodia in 2005 was 14.8 million, 20% of whom lived in urban areas. Throughout the 1970s and 1980s, the country was ravaged by civil war under the Khmer Rouge, whose policies resulted in the near total depopulation of urban centers and the genocide of more than 3 million people. Cambodia is now on the road to recovery, but the destruction of its urban infrastructure, institutions, and human capital has severely constrained the capacity of the country to develop. Table 4.1 shows relevant national statistics.

This chapter examines the re-urbanization of Cambodia and the many challenges this has created for the country. Three case studies are presented: Phnom Penh Municipality Planning for All, Battambang Town Decentralization Program, and Kratie Growth Pole Study. Lessons from the case studies are then presented followed by suggested strategies Cambodia could pursue to ensure more sustainable urban development outcomes in the future.

COUNTRY CONTEXT[1]

Cambodia has an area of 181,035 square kilometers (km^2) and borders Viet Nam, Lao People's Democratic Republic (Lao PDR), and Thailand. The longest river in Asia, the Mekong River, runs through the country from north to south, breaking to the west to form the famous Tonle Sap Lake. The country is divided into 24 provinces and municipalities. Geographically, Cambodia is surrounded by mountains in the north and west along the border with Thailand and Lao PDR, and in the east with Viet Nam. In the south, Cambodia borders the Gulf of Thailand. The middle of the country is flat and mainly used for rice production. Phnom Penh is the capital city.

Cambodia is a signatory member country to most United Nations treaties and accords, and has adopted the Millennium Development Goals (MDGs),

Table 4.1: Country Development Profile, Cambodia

Human Development Index rank of 177 countries (2003)^	130
GDP growth (annual %, 2004)	6.00
GNI per capita, Atlas method (current $, 2004)	320
GNI, Atlas method (current $ billion, 2004)	4.4
GDP per capita PPP ($, 2003)^	2,078
GDP PPP ($ billion, 2003)^	27.9
Population growth (annual 2005–2010 %) #	2.28
Population, total (million, 2005)#	14.83
Urban population, total (million, 2005)#	2.93
Urban population, % of total population (2005)#	20
Population largest city: Phnom Penh (2005, million)	1.17
Population growth: 2 capital cities or agglomerations > 750,000 inhabitants 2000#	
- Est. average growth of capital cities or urban agglomerations 2005–2015 (%)	41
- Number of capital cities or urban agglomerations with growth > 50%, 2005–2015	1
- Number of capital cities or urban agglomerations with growth > 30%, 2005–2015	1
Sanitation, % of urban population with access to improved sanitation (2002)**	53
Water, % of urban population with access to improved water sources (2002)**	58
Slum population, % of urban population (2001)**	72
Slum population in urban areas (2001, million)**	1.70
Poverty, % of urban population below national poverty line (1997)**	21.1
Aid (Net ODA received, $ million, 2003)^	508.0
Aid as a share of country income (Net ODA/GNI, 2003 %)*	12.5
Aid per capita (current $, 2003)^	37.9

GDP = gross domestic product, GNI = gross national income, ODA = official development assistance, PPP = purchasing power parity.
Sources: See Footnote Table 3.1, World Bank (2005); OECD (2003); United Nations (2004, 2005).

the first and most important of which is the eradication of extreme poverty and hunger. In terms of the Human Development Index (HDI), Cambodia is a poor developing country that ranked 130 among 177 countries in 2003.

Since the early 1990s, the Cambodian economy has achieved growth of about 7% per annum, albeit from a low base. Over this period, the country has slowly transited from civil war to peace, toward democracy and multiparty elections and to a more liberalized market-based economy. Economic growth has been associated with significant structural changes in the economy. Agriculture declined from 46% of gross domestic product (GDP) in 1993 to 31% in 2003 while industry's share increased from 13% to 29%, led by the growth of the garment industry and tourism. The share of services remained at about one third of GDP. Development has seen a significant fall in poverty but to still high levels. Thirty-five percent of Cambodians lived below the national poverty line in 2004 compared to an estimated 47% in 1994. While these trends are encouraging, Cambodia remains at the early stages of urbanization and economic development. Cambodia and the Lao PDR are the poorest countries in Southeast Asia.

Cambodia relies heavily on agriculture. Poverty in Cambodia is predominantly a rural phenomenon, with some 90% of poor Cambodians living in rural areas. Agriculture employs 70% of the labor force while industry employs only 8%. As the main drivers of economic growth have been urban-focused industries with limited urban-rural linkages—export-oriented garment manufacturing and tourism—the benefits of growth have flowed disproportionately to urban areas. Between 1994 and 2004, poverty in Phnom Penh fell by more than half to 20% of the city's population and by 44% in other urban areas to about 25% of their population. Poverty in rural areas also declined but not to the same extent—it declined by more than 20% to 39% but is markedly higher in remote rural areas with limited access to roads, markets, and basic services.

Cambodia has a relatively low rural population density and rural productivity, which suggests that it still has the opportunity of improving the living condition of its rural population through agricultural upgrading and land reform. However, landlessness is rising—exacerbated by unclear property rights and rising prices of land. These problems will not be easily overcome. A study carried out by Oxfam in 2000 found that about 12% of rural Cambodia's population is landless. Data from the second 5-year socioeconomic plan similarly showed that 14.4% of rural households are landless. Rural land prices are lower than those in urban areas, but they are still often beyond the financial ability of the rural population.

Rural populations urgently need convenient access to urban settlements for supplies, services, information, and technologies that will help them increase their productivity and improve their living conditions. Most importantly, rural people need access to urban markets to sell their produce and increase their incomes. Therefore, transportation, communications, and energy systems have to be planned and installed to bring rural populations within affordable reach of towns and into the orbit of social and economic development. Small and medium-sized towns, such as the provincial capitals of Cambodia, are the first and vital point of contact for rural populations. They also form the most viable network through which a variety of key inputs for rural development can be channeled to the villages.

Cambodia has a relatively low level of urbanization and is still in the early stages of the urbanization process. Even with agricultural reform, improved agricultural productivity and profitability, and focused efforts to reduce rural poverty, urban areas can be expected to grow rapidly in the future with rural-urban migration, as Cambodia develops a more broadly based economy and investment and economic opportunities increase in urban areas. Cambodia faces a major policy and resource allocation dilemma: the existing population and poverty are concentrated in rural areas but development will inevitably see rapid urban expansion, and planning and infrastructure provision for this growth needs to commence now.

URBANIZATION AND SUSTAINABLE DEVELOPMENT

Urbanization and Population Change

The pace and direction of urbanization in Cambodia have varied, depending on the political regime. During the period after independence from France (1954–1969) and in recent years (since 1990), the country has experienced fast urbanization. During the Khmer Rouge regime (1975–1979) urbanization in Cambodia totally stopped. Instead, an agrarian state was introduced in which the urban populations were forcefully evicted to rural areas. Urban areas were left to die and be destroyed by nature and neglect. Cities were considered by the Khmer Rouge regime as the symbol of capitalism, which was against the so-called revolution.

After decades of civil war and destruction, Cambodia is currently at a relatively early phase of redevelopment. This redevelopment has not been evenly distributed; urbanization is largely a result of rural-urban migration. While the current level of urbanization stands at about 20% (in 2005), in the future the country is likely to have one of the highest rates of urban increases in Asia at about 3.5% per annum. A comparison of population changes in the urban centers over the last 4 decades shows two patterns:

(i) The old, established precolonial and then colonial centers, such as Kampong Cham, Pousat, and Kampong Chhnang or Kampot, and all other old market towns have decreased in relative size.

(ii) The fast-growing "newcomers" are all linked with foreign economic influences, or have global-local linkages: above all, Siem Reap, the prime tourist destination of the country, has exploded in size due to tourism-related investments; Sihanoukville, the port city, has grown because of foreign trade; and formerly unknown urban centers, such as Mongkol Borei, Poipet, and Suong—for this reason selected as one of the case study centers—have grown rapidly because of the border trade (Asian Development Bank [ADB], Final Report 2005).

Figure 4.1 shows that the urban population is expected to rise from 20% of the population of Cambodia in 2005 to 35% in 2030, causing urban populations to rise from 2.9 million in 2005 to 8.0 million in 2030, more than doubling the current urban population. There is much pressure for urban development, especially on the outskirts of Phnom Penh and increasingly in several border towns.

Figure 4.1: Trends in Urban and Rural Population, Cambodia

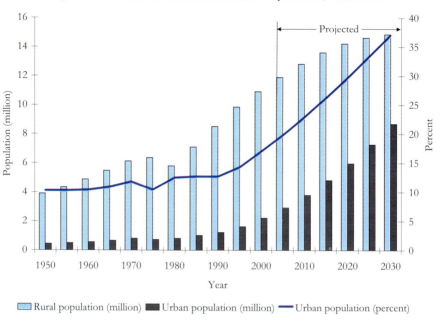

All cities in Cambodia are expanding rapidly, often before infrastructure and services can be put in place. Consequently, the number of squatter settlements has increased. In addition, most town districts are growing very rapidly. For example, in 1994, Phnom Penh recorded 10.3% annual growth; Battambang, 11.0%; and Takhmau (virtually a satellite of Phnom Penh), 13.9%. This high rate is partially explained by the rapid return of many people to urban centers after the fall of the Khmer Rouge.

To accommodate urbanization of this magnitude, the country requires key policies and management structures to be put in place in the very near future. Although urbanization in Cambodia has brought development, the Government has been unable to minimize negative impacts of expansion because of limited human, technical, and financial resources, leading to growing incidences of urban deficiencies and problems. These include disputes regarding land tenure, lack of urban infrastructure and services, degraded living environments—including contaminated water—as a consequence of solid waste, air pollution, congestion, and urban sprawl development, and the creation of slum and squatter settlements. These negative impacts of urbanization, coupled with increases in land prices and limited financial resources for investment, present alarming difficulties for managing urban development and growth.

Understanding these challenges, the Government has introduced and pilot-tested decentralization and deconcentration policies. These policies give local authorities increased responsibility for managing urban growth and accommodating the growing demand for urban infrastructure and services from the population. Assistance and intervention from the central Government is minimal, with local authorities receiving only technical assistance to help formulate and implement their plans in an efficient and effective manner.

Good Governance

Governance and public institutions in Cambodia had to be reestablished at the end of the Khmer Rouge period with very limited human and financial resources. This has proven difficult, and problems of government effectiveness and responsiveness are still inhibiting development and the provision of infrastructure and services. Governance problems are widespread in such areas as appropriate laws and regulations and their consistent implementation, public participation, and economic and financial management. There is a limited and poorly exploited revenue base and poorly functioning expenditure controls, and weak transparency and accountability. Development and investment in Cambodia are being constrained by insecure property rights, time-consuming and unproductive regulations, and widespread corruption in contracting processes. These problems are compounded by inadequate infrastructure and services. The Government's National Strategic Development Plan 2006–2010 will attempt to address these problems and has a focus on strengthening governance at all levels, economic management, the provision of necessary infrastructure, development of the agriculture sector, private sector growth, and national capacity building through improved education and health.

The Government has begun implementing a program of reforms in an effort to promote and improve governance in all government agencies. Decentralization and deconcentration programs are two ambitious policies toward good governance emanating from the central to the local governments. As a result, nationwide commune elections were conducted in 2002—for the first time in the history of Cambodia—to elect representatives of the local population. Moreover, in an attempt to spread development at the grassroots levels, two key development reforms have also been introduced: the Social Fund program and the SEILA[2] program. The aims of these programs include coordinating all overseas assistance and aid to support the decentralization and deconcentration policies.

In the 2005 SEILA program, 25% of the total budget of about $10.5 million was used for strengthening local governance (SEILA 2005). Key activities included strengthening the legal framework and regulations; working out systems and principles; capacity building; integration of management data; monitoring and auditing; and strengthening partnerships among national, provincial, municipal, and communal levels (SEILA 2005). To further delegate decision-making power to the local level, the Prime Minister has in recent years proposed that responsibility for making decisions concerning financial investments below $2 million will be decided at the provincial and municipal levels. Such decentralized decision making, although not yet fully implemented, will undoubtedly provide local government with further power to manage its own businesses.

Urban Management

Since the Government implemented its administrative reforms, greater responsibility and decision-making powers have been delegated to the provincial and municipal governments. The first commune council elections in 2002 fully began the decentralization and deconcentration policies, while the recent declaration by the Prime Minister to delegate decision-making powers on investments valued below $2 million to provincial and municipal governments put the decentralization process into full swing. The Government has pilot-tested a new "one-window service" policy, which has also contributed to the implementation of the decentralization policy.

Urban development planning and management have been delegated step-by-step to local authorities as a result of the reform policies above. Participatory planning has been introduced at the grassroots level—the village level. People are making plans themselves, with professionals and government staff acting only as trainers, facilitators, or coordinators. Provincial and municipal line departments, although under direct command from national line ministries, have carried out work in close cooperation with local authorities. Further reform is expected to include incorporation of line department payroll and budget in that of the provincial and municipal authorities. If this is implemented, local governments will plan and manage all budgets for urban development projects.

Decentralization and increased levels of public participation culminated in recent commune-level elections. Under this framework, commune authorities are responsible for preparing and implementing commune development plans along with the transfer of limited resources from the central Government. Therefore, local planning efforts should now reflect the aspirations and main concerns of the local population. As a result, a new way of planning with direct participation of the local population has been introduced to provide an effective response to a rapidly changing urban situation.

Effective and Efficient Infrastructure and Service Provision

Infrastructure, especially roads and bridges, is the responsibility of three institutions: the Ministry of Public Works and Transport, the Ministry of Rural Development, and the Engineering Corps of the Ministry of Defense. In rural areas, infrastructure projects and programs funded with financial support from overseas have been carried out by the Government, nongovernment organizations (NGOs), and international organizations. Such projects are often small and work with village committees and/or commune councils. The International Labour Organization, for example, has been working with the Ministry of Rural Development on integrated rural accessibility planning. Many NGOs, such as World Vision, have also been involved in infrastructure and service provision.

Social and Environmental Sustainability

New measures have been introduced in social and environmental management by the Government as part of its overall reforms. Four explicit programs have been implemented—the Commune and Communal Base-Natural Resource and Environmental Management, Social Fund, SEILA Program, and Natural Resource Management in the Coastal Zone Plan. Besides these major programs are many projects carried out by both the Government and international organizations in different parts of the country. Each program has been designed to provide local authorities with sound sustainable land use and natural resource management planning.

The Land for Social Concession subdecree was enacted in 2003 in an attempt to provide land for the landless poor. At the same time, it aimed to uphold sustainable natural resource management where only appropriate vacant land was used to ensure maximum benefit to the public. It also helped reduce land grabbing by providing land to members of the population in need. Two other important subdecrees are underway—the Sub-decree on Land for Economic Concession and the Sub-decree on State Land Management. Both are expected to be approved in 2006. These two subdecrees, coupled with the earlier subdecree, will provide a complete set of legal instruments for sustainable land and natural resource management.

Innovation and Change

Participatory land-use planning (PLUP) is one of the new techniques introduced to guide land-use planning in Cambodia. Full grassroot involvement is now the main driver for its planning process. PLUP is a planning process initiated at the village level in which villagers, commune councilors, and other stakeholders jointly decide on the future use and land tenure regime of all land units under their jurisdiction, and on sustainable management schemes as well as protective measures for important natural resources in their village or commune area (PLUP Manual 2004).

Commune and community-based natural resources management (CCB-NRM) focuses on strengthening communities in the management of natural resources in their localities, especially those resources used as common property assets by a large number of villagers (e.g., forest areas, fishery areas, and grazing areas). The CCB-NRM approach includes capacity building of communities and their representatives to strengthen their capacities to manage designated community forestry or community fishery areas.

District strategic development planning (DSDP) is another new change for the country. For the first time in its history of physical design, a planning manual was published in a local language. DSDP aims to delegate responsibility for local land-use planning to the district level in accordance with the Government's overall decentralization and deconcentration policies. So far, five districts have received the services of DSDP and five more are at the investigation stage.

Leveraging International Development Assistance

Cambodia is still in the process of recovering financially from the previous upheavals; therefore, it relies heavily on international development assistance. All international development assistance to Cambodia is required to go through the country's Council for the Development of Cambodia (CDC). CDC was set up by the Government to coordinate effectively all foreign development assistance in a transparent and evenly distributed manner. CDC works with line ministries to channel the appropriate development assistance to relevant areas of concern. In some cases, especially development assistance channeled through NGOs, funding has come directly from donors without going through CDC, although most of this assistance has been for relatively small development projects. The development assistance, after approval by CDC, is channeled to relevant development agencies at the national and local levels for implementation.

The process of leveraging international development assistance is performed through the government priorities set in its national development plans, such as the Socio-Economic Development Plan, Cambodian MDG, and National Poverty Reduction Strategy. At present, the priorities are education, health, and agriculture. Since most of the Cambodian population is in the rural areas where poverty is a problem, the Government accordingly channels majority of development assistance to these areas. Improvement and construction of agricultural irrigation are the main priorities in the agriculture sector.

Relevant line ministries at the national level, line departments at the provincial and municipal levels, and relevant line offices at the district level take up allocated development assistance for coordination, implementation, and monitoring. At the national level, development assistance takes the form of policy creation, strategic planning, and project and program designs undertaken by line ministries. At the provincial and district levels, development assistance manifests itself through the implementation of development projects and programs.

GOOD PRACTICE CASE STUDIES

The following case studies consider urbanization and sustainability in three different regions, which have been classified for this study based on the level and distribution of development and geographical location. These are Phnom Penh in the central region, Battambang town in the western region, and Kratie in the northeastern region. The case studies selected demonstrate important elements of good practice thinking emerging in Cambodia.

Phnom Penh City: Planning for All

Phnom Penh, the capital, had a population of about 1.3 million people in 2003,[3] almost 10 times bigger than the rest of the cities in the country put together. The second largest town is Poi Pet, which, with a population of about 150,000, is larger than the formally classified second town, Battambang (population of about 130,000). Administratively, however, Battambang is a more important center than Poi Pet.

GOOD PRACTICE	
Good Governance	✓
Urban Management	✓
Infrastructure/Service Provision	✓
Financing and Cost Recovery	✓
Sustainability	✓
Innovation and Change	✓
Leveraging ODA	

An estimated 20% of the Phnom Penh City population is considered poor.[4] About 569 squatter and slum communities are established in Phnom Penh,[5] many of which are in poor living environments. The average population density for the whole area of Phnom Penh is 2,986 people/km^2. The population density for the four central districts is 23,168 people/km^2. For rural Phnom Penh—composed of three districts with an area of 346.65 km^2—the average population density is 1,385 people/km^2.

Historically, Phnom Penh emerged from a village to a city over a 100-year period. Population explosions occurred in three stages: 1900–1940, 1950–1970, and post-1990s. Initially, this growth developed without an

Figure 4.2: Map Showing Location of the Case Studies

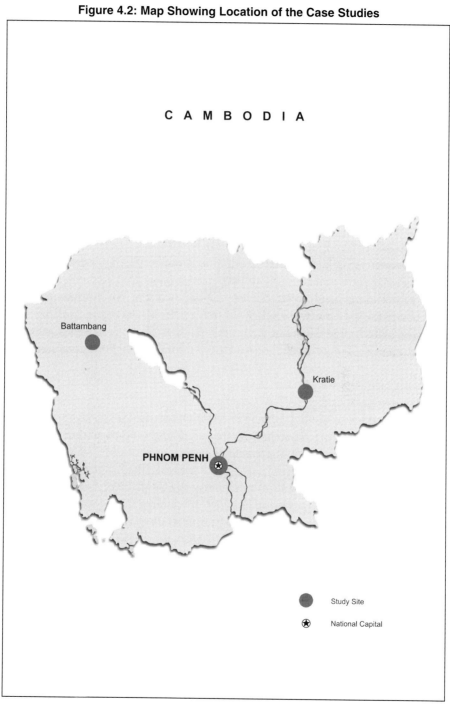

industrial base, relying on agriculture, then forming a "service" economy. Since the mid-1990s, the city has moved toward an industrial market. From 1900 to the 1930s, the population doubled every 10 years. After each growth period, informal or unplanned housing emerged on the periphery of the city.

The population in Phnom Penh shows erratic changes since 1960. In 1976, the population of Phnom Penh fell from nearly 2 million to about 4,000 as the Khmer Rouge ruthlessly imposed its de-urbanization policy. In 1979, the population of Phnom Penh began to grow following the defeat of the Khmer Rouge. The 1990s saw a second wave of growth, taking the population to more than a million for the first time since the 1970s. The only period of population decline during the 1990s coincided with the national elections.

The average population growth rate per annum is currently 3.5%. Since the 1990s, Phnom Penh has witnessed its third phase of growth, reconstructing itself and building beyond the parameters set in the 1970s. Infill is occurring in the city center. Higher-quality housing is replacing the old structures; however, height restrictions limit the size of new developments and, therefore, only marginally alter the city center density. What remains of open space in the city center is being built on. Underutilized space such as school playgrounds or inefficient housing configurations have been transformed into apartment blocks with predominately retail units at the bottom.

Good Governance

The principles of good governance overarch the districts, communes, neighborhoods, and villages comprising the larger agglomeration of Phnom Penh, enabling it to function and grow. The existing territory of 375 km^2 is divided into 76 communes, with 637 neighborhoods and villages requiring coordination and management. The municipality of Phnom Penh has about 15,000 employees (World Leadership Awards 2005) and must also coordinate its work with 28 government line ministries in its day-to-day operations. Armed only with good governance, the city has been able to respond to the enormous demand for public services with very limited resources.

According to interviews conducted in 2005, the municipal government of Phnom Penh has a regimen of meeting every week to listen to and discuss general issues arising in all administrative districts and communes of the city. During the weekly meetings, the governors for each of the city's districts have the opportunity to raise issues of concern to the board of governors of the municipality for appropriate action and solutions. The meetings have also been used as a public open forum since not only are local authorities in Phnom Penh invited to the meeting but also all other relevant stakeholders according to the proposed agenda of the meetings. Despite the regular weekly meeting regimen, extraordinary meetings have been held for urgent cases, such as issues related to security and disaster responses.

Development and strategic planning for the city has been conducted through public participation and the organization of workshops or forums. For example, in the case of squatter and slum settlements, solutions were sought through a series of discussions and workshops before appropriate and acceptable solutions were finalized.

Improved Urban Management

Like many urban centers in Cambodia, Phnom Penh is implementing the Government's administrative reform policies of decentralization and deconcentration. However, the pace of implementation is slower than in the pilot-tested secondary cities of Battambang and Siem Reap. Adoption of the decentralization policy has been channeled through the SEILA program, where local development plans are prepared by local communities and authorities at the district, commune, and neighborhood levels. Such a bottom-up approach to planning better represents local needs; therefore, the municipal and national governments are better able to respond.

To improve city management further, the municipal government has also established other operational mechanisms, such as the Municipal Development Committee to oversee city development more transparently. In addition, the city Poverty Reduction and Community Improvement Committee has been set up to work closely and effectively with urban poor. A more decentralized body, the Urban Poverty Reduction Unit, was set up under the committee above and is responsible for implementing municipal government programs and projects relevant to the urban poor, such as land sharing and slum upgrading.

At the district level, a Community Development Management Committee was set up to coordinate all work related to local communities with the district and municipal governments in an efficient manner. This committee is composed of members from the district authority, line development agencies, and representatives of the local community themselves. At the commune level, a communications office coordinates issues related to the public with the local authority. So far, the office has provided support in organizing about 600 poor communities, consisting of more than 46,000 underprivileged families living in the city of Phnom Penh. It also has mobilized poor inhabitants to save money for their communities' development. Through this grassroots initiative, communications between office staff of the municipal government and poor communities have improved, transforming the relationship from one characterized by suspicion and hostility to one of "no violence but negotiation." The success of many slum and squatter settlement projects has been attributed to the transformation in trust and increased participation by local communities.

Effective and Efficient Infrastructure and Service Provision

Since 1993, the city has been characterized predominantly by the renewal of urban facilities, reconstructing what was destroyed after almost 20 years of civil war. Rehabilitation of electricity, water supply, and sewage and drainage facilities has been financed by development partners, such as the World Bank and the Asian Development Bank (ADB). The privatization policy mentioned earlier as part of the municipal government's attempt to improve its management and service provision has contributed to the increased coverage in waste services across the city, especially to suburban areas. As a result, about 95% of the urban city area and 50% of the rural city area are covered by waste collection services.

The success is even more pronounced for water supply service provision. For example, in 2005, it was reported that 80% of the city's population was connected to the water supply system, which provides residents with good quality water (World Leadership Awards 2005). As a result, the public municipal enterprise, Phnom Penh Water Supply Authority, was recognized as the best water supply company in Asia, and received the "Water Prize-Water For All" award by ADB in 2004. In addition to reconstruction, Phnom Penh allowed private developers during the 1990s to expand the city beyond the boundaries established in the 1950s–1970s.

Financing and Cost Recovery

Phnom Penh is the first city in Cambodia to receive and implement the 50-50 shared cost policy of the Government. This formula has been very successful in motivating the public to share the responsibility for public service and infrastructure provision. Between September 2004 and September 2005, the 50-50 formula was employed to improve about 17,040 meters of city road, with a total contribution from the community of about $420,500 (SEILA 2005).

Private and public partnership in development has been one of the sources of financing and cost recovery for most local development projects. A noticeable example is the city waste collection and disposal service, where a private company (CINTRI, Canada) was awarded the contract to manage the city waste service after negotiations over the price charged to the city population. The service management in the Phnom Penh International Airport has also been awarded to a private company (SCA France and Malaysia).

The city has set up a microfinance scheme to help poor urban communities improve their living conditions through a community savings system. The microcredit scheme set up by the municipal government (Urban Poverty Development Fund) covers five important areas: housing, land, fish paste (food reserves), job creation, water supply, and urban agriculture. So far, more than $1.4 million of microcredit has benefited 12,000 families in 300 communities. The repayment rate for the scheme has been impressive at 100%. For the urban poor housing sector alone, the municipality has disbursed more than $600,000 as housing loans to more than 1,500 poor families (SEILA 2005).

Social and Environmental Sustainability

The draft master plan of Phnom Penh, which has a planning horizon extending until 2020, should, when approved and enforced, contribute to ensuring the city's social and environmental sustainability through proper land-use planning. The city's green and open spaces are protected and preserved in the draft master plan. The master plan identifies the establishment of four small satellite towns in order to cope with urban sprawl as the result of the city's economic growth. If the four small towns are built successfully, the core historical inner center of the city will be preserved. The small towns would also reduce the pressure on the city's remaining open spaces by distributing new development therein. The draft master plan also provides adequate public social facilities such as schools, hospital, markets, and other services for future population growth.

Innovation and Change

One of the most noticeable innovations and changes is in the management of poor settlements. In recent years, the municipality of Phnom Penh has moved away from the policy of forceful eviction and resettlement to upgrading and voluntarily resettlement, which has garnered international recognition. In 2003, the Prime Minister declared that the Government would no longer force squatter and slum settlers to move from their existing locations. Instead they will be reorganized and upgraded on existing sites. This concession excluded those settlements located in areas classified as public state land, such as public parks and road pavements.

The newly introduced 50-50 method for financing infrastructure development projects in Phnom Penh has been hailed as a huge success for city authorities. The success of this approach is such that the people themselves now request to be included in the program and no longer need convincing by the municipal government to take part in the program as was the case during the introductory phase. The Cambodian population as a whole is untrusting of government authorities as a consequence of past horrific government regimes, especially the Khmer Rouge genocidal regime (1975–1979); therefore, it is notable that the local population is eager to engage with the Government.

Battambang Town[6]

Battambang is a province situated in the west of the country bordering Thailand. It has one international and a number of regional border check points with Thailand. The province is considered as having the most fertile soil in Cambodia, and is the largest rice-producing area. Battambang is also the name of its urban district, the capital town of the province.

GOOD PRACTICE	
Good Governance	✓
Urban Management	✓
Infrastructure/Service Provision	✓
Financing and Cost Recovery	✓
Sustainability	✓
Innovation and Change	✓
Leveraging ODA	

In 2004, the city had a population of about 130,000 people. As with many other cities in Cambodia, the city straddles a river—in this case, the province's main river. It has its own airport and is connected to Phnom Penh and Thailand by railway as well as by national road. It is also connected to Cambodia's famous Angkor Wat complex, about 100 km away, by boat, air, and land.

Good Governance

Battambang was chosen along with Siem Reap to be one of the provinces in which the Government's "one-window service" was piloted. This service is part of the overall administrative reforms guided by decentralization and deconcentration policies. Decision-making power and responsibility have incrementally been delegated to the local authority in all fields. The one-window service aims to bring all public services closer to the local population. According to its terms of reference, all services are to be provided in the district office. As such, representatives of all line offices in the district will sit and work together in the district office. Therefore, local people no longer need to go to different offices to obtain required services.

For example, obtaining permission for motor vehicle number plates can now be acquired at the district office whereas in the past, property owners had to go to the office of transportation, the police, and local authority, then to the provincial department of transportation, and the provincial authority. The one-window service has not only greatly cut down on administrative red tape but also on time consumption and many formal and informal costs. The reforms also aim to provide the district with its own semiautonomous income and budget.

To make sure that the one-window service policy was moving in the right direction, the central Government established committees at the national and provincial levels. The national and provincial committees assist and support the district team in implementing the one-window service. The two committees comprise representatives from relevant government line agencies in a manner similar to the district one-window service team as summarized in Figure 4.3. The national committee is chaired by the Ministry of Interior, while the provincial committee is chaired by the provincial governor. The committee holds regular monthly meetings to view the performance of the pilot project and to receive complaints or proposals from the one-window service regarding delegation of decision-making power.

Improved Urban Management

As part of the pilot project on the government decentralization and deconcentration policies, Battambang has simultaneously prepared two different master plans. These are the Battambang provincial master plan and the Battambang town master plan. Although the two plans differ in scale, they are

Figure 4.3: Structure of the One-window Service Chain of Procedures

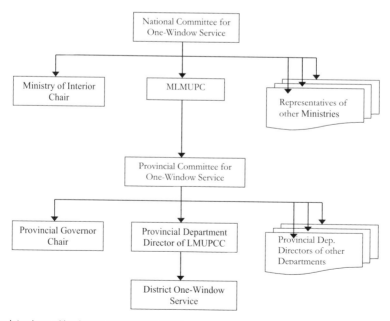

Source: Interviews with relevant stakeholders, 2005.

LMUPCC = Land Management, Urban Planning, Construction and Cadastral; MLMUPC = Ministry of Land Management, Urban Planning and Construction.

similar in the sense that the provincial master plan is based on the Battambang town master plan because of its significance as the provincial capital and also because it is many times larger than any other town in the province.

The participatory, consultative, and democratic approach adopted during the planning process is a notable example of good practice. From the start of the projects, all relevant stakeholders in the Battambang District and the province were consulted by the project teams, including government line departments, district line offices, NGOs and international organizations, the private sector, local authorities, and local communities.

Effective and Efficient Infrastructure and Service Provision

Since its introduction, the one-window service has been successful in reducing the gap between the public and public infrastructure and service provision. Similarly, the administrative shortcut from the central Government and provincial authorities to the district authority and its line agencies allows more effective service provision than before.[7] The positive effects of effective service provision are extensive. In the case of motor vehicle number plates, the local population has requested that the company which won the contract with the central Government to produce number plates should open a production branch in Battambang town so that it could produce locally and more effectively meet demand through the Battambang one-window service (One Window Service Report 2005).

To bring service closer to the people, the Office for the Population was established in Battambang District to create a new mechanism to receive all complaints directly from the population. The office then acts on behalf of the local population in bringing complaints to the appropriate government agency or agencies involved. The office works as the legal representative of the local people who are unhappy with the work of government agencies, and negotiates with government agencies to find appropriate and acceptable solutions to complaints. The service provided to the population by this office is free of charge.

Financing and Cost Recovery

The one-window service team has already been in discussion with the national and provincial authorities and line agencies regarding proposed financial incentives for good performance. If approved, the incentives would facilitate better tax collection and revenue-raising from businesses in the town. According to the interviews, the proposed approach is to take a small percentage of the revenues collected through businesses taxation and reinvest this in the team as an incentive for further improved performance.

In the future, all staff working for the one-window service will be paid in line with the new government payroll system called the Priority Cluster. This is another component of the Government's overall reform program that aims to improve the performance of government staff by introducing salary based on commitment, performance, and work results. In this regard, the team of cross-sectoral staff working for the one-window service should be included in the Priority Cluster group.

Social and Environmental Sustainability

The preparation of the Battambang master plan, with cooperation and funding from the European Union, along with a United Nations Economic and Social Commission for Asia and the Pacific (UNESCAP)-assisted project for improving urban poor settlements in Battambang town should, if successfully implemented, provide long-term sustainable approaches for all relevant government agencies and authorities. A preliminary land-use zoning was proposed by the Provincial Department of Land Management, Urban Planning, Construction and Cadastral. This was the first example of urban planning in Battambang to contribute to social and environmental sustainability in the sense that it provided decision makers with the appropriate base on which to decide what type of investment should be built and where to ensure sustainable and long-term benefits.

The ongoing UNESCAP project on Housing the Urban Poor in Battambang town should also support further efforts aimed at having sound development policy encompassing social and environmental sustainability. The project has the advantage of allowing the eventual transfer of project ownership to the master plan task force of Battambang District. This is important for ensuring the project's success because all the master plan task force personnel already have experience in collecting data and information, data analysis, and other skills developed in the course of the master plan project.

Innovation and Change

The one-window service is one of the Government's innovations as part of its decentralization and deconcentration policies, delegating decision-making power to local authorities and government line agencies. Improvements in local capacity will enable more government line agencies to delegate all local decision-making power to local authorities and line agencies.

The Office for the Population is another innovation, which has changed the relationship between government and society by making services more accessible. Never before has the local population had a government representative working for them as their true representative. This office is innovative in that the local population already has local representatives in the form of commune councils, all of whom were elected by the local population. However, employees working for the Office for the Population are not elected representatives but are personnel employed by the Government working for the population in negotiating and finding solutions for complaints and disputes between government line agencies, local authorities, and civil society.

Growth Pole Strategy for Kratie

Kratie is located in the northeast of Cambodia and has been the region's economic and political center for many years because of its geographical location and good access to Phnom Penh as well as the provinces of Steung Treng, Ratanak Kiri, and Mondulkiri. The three provinces, however, are not as well connected to Phnom Penh as Kratie because

GOOD PRACTICE	
Good Governance	✓
Urban Management	✓
Infrastructure/Service Provision	✓
Financing and Cost Recovery	✓
Sustainability	✓
Innovation and Change	✓
Leveraging ODA	✓

of longer traveling distances and poor road systems. Kratie, therefore, has an important role to play in the development in the northeast. Continual improvement of the road infrastructure from Phnom Penh to Kratie Province will further elevate its role, especially with respect to the economic development of the other three provinces mentioned.

Kratie is the capital town and district of the Kratie Province. Its main economic activities are trade, tourism, and agriculture. In 2003, Kratie District had a population of 84,642. The total population of the four provinces in the northern region—Kratie, Steung Treng, Ratanak Kiri, and Mondulkiri—was about 500,000 in 2004. The region shares similar characteristics. Population density is low. A variety of ethnic communities inhabit the region, predominantly in highland areas. Physical characteristics are also similar, with mountainous areas, forested land cover, red fertile soil, and the potential for agro-industrial development; however, at this time, the region remains underdeveloped.

Good Governance

Like other urban centers in Cambodia, Kratie first implemented the policy of decentralization through the 2002 election of commune councils. However, decentralization in Kratie has progressed in a different manner to Battambang, with Kratie implementing other forms of decentralization through planning at the local level. PLUP has been conducted in villages where the prospect of new development is likely to affect the interest and natural resources of the local communities.

In its effort to take full advantage of the Government's decentralization policy, Kratie, with its limited resources, has sought to begin designing its own town master plan to make it attractive to investors while at the same time preserving its unique resources and identity. A draft master plan for the town, which has been under discussion and consultation with stakeholders, seeks to provide a framework to develop Kratie as a growth pole to support the development of the northeastern area of Cambodia.

Good governance was at the forefront of the study, whereby all stakeholders were consulted and engaged through public open discussions and workshops. Local authorities, local communities, line department and offices, NGOs, and international organizations as well as the private sector were involved during the planning process. In design preparation of the town master plan, the master plan team also considered all local plans, such as village action plans, the communal integrated plan, and the district plan.

Improved Urban Management

PLUP and the draft master plan of Kratie have contributed greatly to the management of the town, despite not being legally implemented at this time. Since the 1979 collapse of the Khmer Rouge regime, Kratie town, like other towns and cities in Cambodia, lacked planning documents and up-to-date maps. All development approval given to both public and private investors for economic, social, or physical development projects was based on the personal judgment of decision makers.

The town economy has converted from forestry dependency into tourism and trade. This would not have been possible without better natural resource management and planning facilitated by the central Government's decentralization policy. Part of the responsibilities of the elected commune councils is to formulate commune development plans that define a longer-term development vision and goals in a policy framework. This represents a significant step toward greater local autonomy to address basic local development needs. Delegation of planning and management ownership to local communities encourages full participation of the local population, which is the key requirement for success.

Effective and Efficient Infrastructure and Service Provision

The Government's policy of privatization in public service provision has increased the involvement of private businesses in areas once solely public responsibility. Kratie town has experienced an increase in private services, including private schools that range from kindergarten to faculties and technical institutes. Many such services would probably not have been provided without involvement from the private sector due to the Government's budgetary constraints.

The entire infrastructure and services provided through both public and private finance have had rapid appraisals conducted as part of the local planning process. The Village Development Plan is the annual assessment plan conducted by the local community in order to prioritize their demands and needs which are to be met by the local authority, NGOs or international organizations, and government. The plan is also conducted at the commune and district levels.

Financing and Cost Recovery

Aside from government finance for public service and infrastructure provision mentioned above, other forms of financing are also practiced in Kratie. For example, the World Bank has financed an infrastructure project in the northwestern region, which covers Kratie. To take part in the World Bank's project, local communities are required to make partner contributions in-kind and in cash. The total contribution from the community is 12%, of which 9% is in-kind and the remaining 3% is paid in cash (NVDP and World Bank 2003). The project includes such activities as land clearance, grass planting, digging holes, transporting materials, and guarding construction sites (Table 4.2). In some projects, the local communities are required to contribute cash, but in the long term and in an affordable manner. The money obtained is used for maintenance.

Table 4.2: In-kind Community Contributions to Projects

Type of Subproject	Type of Contribution				
	Land Clearance	Grass Planting	Digging Holes	Transporting Materials	Guarding Construction Sites
Bridge	Y	Y	N	Y	Y
Roads	Y	Y	N	N	Y/N
Irrigation	Y	Y	N	N	Y/N
Water supply	Y	Y	Y	Y	Y
Sanitation (latrines)	Y	Y	Y	Y	Y

Y = yes, N = no.
Source: Abstracted from author's own field survey for the World Bank project in 2003, Northwestern Village Development Project.

Social and Environmental Sustainability

The concept of the community contribution to the project was aimed at increasing community commitment and responsibility for the life of projects as well as the maintenance period after project completion. Without local community commitment, ownership, and responsibility, projects risk failure, especially after project completion. By making local communities contribute financially and technically to their local development projects and assisting them in understanding who the project beneficiaries are, they are more likely to feel a sense of ownership. As a result, some infrastructure projects in Kratie prohibit or restrict overloaded vehicles from using bridges or roads. On occasion, local communities have created wooden or cement barriers along the edges of the roads or on bridges to protect the infrastructure from unwanted vehicles.

The town draft master plan study is still in the consultation phase and discussions are ongoing. The aims are to protect the social and environmental character of the town, and to attract investments while at the same time protecting the town's natural resources through appropriate land-use planning. Green and other public spaces are allocated to provide enough places for social activities. The plan is the result of many long discussions and consultations (through meetings and interviews) with local communities and all relevant stakeholders.

Innovation and Change

Participatory planning processes, such as those being practiced in preparing the town master plan and village plans, are innovative changes in the provincial as well as local government work procedures. It has opened up government to wider public participation. Kratie Province was one of Cambodia's remote provinces in past decades because of accessibility difficulties, which hindered reform. Most plans were top-down in their approach, not because the Government adopted a central command policy but because of Kratie's remoteness and lack of human resources to design and prepare plans. It was not until the Government initiated the mass infrastructure improvement program, especially to remote provinces such as Kratie, that the flow of information, resources, technology, and skills between large cities and small cities made it possible for administrative reforms in small urban agglomerations to be introduced.

Innovations and changes in government working and planning procedures in these small or secondary towns have been possible because human resources there have also been improved. More and more well-trained personnel have emerged as a consequence of better education, and are willing to work in secondary urban areas with better connection to the rest of the country. More well-educated people are entering the labor market; however, only a small proportion of new graduates are able to find work in the capital city. This lack of employment opportunities has led many to accept work in secondary and small urban areas, such as in Kratie town. These newly recruited personnel have helped contribute to the overall government administrative reform.

LESSONS LEARNED FROM THE CASE STUDIES

For Cambodia as a whole, the key to success has been the delegation of decision-making power from the central Government to the local government, as witnessed in the Government's overall administrative reform. These reforms have been tested and implemented through many programs, with the Social Fund and SEILA programs as obvious examples in which project design and planning are locally undertaken with local participation and involvement. Explicit bodies for tackling specific issues set up by the Government, such as the Council for Land Policy, Provincial Land Use and Allocation Committee, and National Cadastral Commission, have also been effective in dealing with their respective problems. In summary, local ownership is the key to success for all policy and program implementation.

The commitment made by the Prime Minister in 2003 to change the attitude of the Government toward squatter and slum settlements, from forceful eviction to upgrading and voluntary resettlement, is unique to Phnom Penh. NGOs and international organizations in and outside the country have welcomed this change in policy. Community participation in and ownership of projects are undoubtedly important and necessary ingredients for project success. They also help minimize unwanted opportunism from external groups wanting to skew the target of the housing projects from the urban poor to higher-income groups.

The 50-50 road infrastructure improvement and upgrading formula initiated by the city government and strongly supported by the Prime Minister is also successful, although it has been acknowledged by the municipal government that more effort is needed to make the policy more effective and sustainable. The main challenge for the policy is the quality of the road improvement as the result of inconsistent quality of contractors' work. According to an interview with Phnom Penh governor on local TV station CTN in December 2005, another challenge is the time needed at the Ministry of Economy and Finance for funds to be released because of administrative processes. Lack of independence in the project monitoring team was also raised by the governor as contributing to the challenges of the project.

Regular meetings, established by the municipal government and aimed to promote dialogue with its local authorities and communities, produced fruitful results in effectively dealing with issues. Local bodies, such as the District Community Development Management Committee, Urban Poverty Development Fund, and Solidarity for the Urban Poor Federation, were set up and supported by the municipal government, NGOs, international organizations, and development partners, and are good platforms to connect and communicate between government and civil society in working for the same goal of reducing urban poverty. These bodies bring stakeholders together in a consultative manner and provide an opportunity for dialogue, compromise, and negotiation in determining solutions to issues of concern.

The pilot-testing of decentralization and deconcentration policies in the western region towns and cities, although still in its early stage, has so far been welcomed by the local population. The key factor contributing to the success of this is the delegation of decision-making power and ownership to local authorities and communities. By doing this, local authorities as well as communities feel and see the benefits of commitment and hard work for the development of their local areas.

The capacity of current staff in local authorities could lead to ineffectiveness and mismanagement without strong support from the provincial and central governments. The one-window service program and the full decentralization and deconcentration policies might not be the appropriate approaches for other small and remote secondary towns and cities in Cambodia because the implementation of the program and the policies requires skilled employees, who may not be available. Another constraint to the success of the policy is the reported lack of incentive for the one-window service working team.

The eagerness and determination of the local government in Kratie town as well as for the province to implement the government decentralization policy and not to wait until everything is provided, especially skilled human resources, is an encouraging and good example of goodwill. This good practice has been illustrated through its willingness to allow PLUP and the draft master plan with a participatory and consultative approach for the town and the province as a whole. The concepts of participatory and consultative planning are rather new in the history of the country, which has been governed by more or less top-down systems from the glorious ancient civilization dating back a thousand years—from feudalism, to French protectorate (colonization), to capitalism, to communism (Khmer Rouge), to a central command economy and, in recent years, striving to stand as a democratic and free market economy.

Community participation in the World Bank-sponsored project in the region (the Northeastern Village Development Project, NVDP) is another good example and provides lessons about community participation from which other regions can learn valuable lessons. The introduction of different kinds of involvement and contribution, such as in-kind and in cash, according to the assessment of the community capacity to commit, encourages and enforces local ownership and responsibility, and is well taken and welcomed by the communities. Simple reasons for the communities' appreciation are that contributions required by the project were affordable in terms of time, labor, and money. However,[8] according to the assessment from the NVDP project external audit, the community participation and contribution were highest in areas where the community organization (Village Development Committee, VDC) was most competent.

STRATEGIES TO ENHANCE SUSTAINABLE URBAN REGION DEVELOPMENT

Experience shows that willingness and political will to carry out reform programs or policies are not enough for the reform to take place. It also needs to be accompanied by adequate resources and competent implementers and, to some extent, the wider public need to be able to understand the benefits so that they will be more accepting of the reform. As summarized in Table 4.3, from the author's own observation of the current situation and assessment about the future, a lot of work has to be done to ensure sustainable urban development.

There is no guarantee, of course, of achieving the requirements indicated in Table 4.3. Additionally, it is unlikely that improvements can be achieved overnight, but continuous political stability coupled with determination and capacity building of implementers and facilitators will steadily contribute to sustainable urban development. Exchange of experiences through regular meetings and study tours in cities and municipalities on all issues will also strengthen the capacity of decision makers and implementers of cities that lack experience and resources. For example, a drug rehabilitation program for youth has been working well in those places where the program was started and initiated by the local authority, such as Banteay Meanchey. The success of the program has led authorities in other provinces and municipalities to learn how to establish their own rehabilitation centers in order to tackle the growing issue of drug addiction.

Public information dissemination and accessibility are also necessary for successful sustainable urban development. The flow and exchange of information and data among cities and municipalities should be promoted, especially on good practice in governance, better urban management, and accountability. Public education on urban issues should also be considered

Table 4.3: Requirements for Enhancing Sustainable Urban Development

Factors required to enhance sustainable urban development	Contribution from Stakeholders for Sustainable Urban Development									
	Central Government		Local Government		Community		Civil Society		Development Partners	
	Now	Fut.	Now	Fut.	Now	Fut.	Now	Fut.	Now	Fut.
Political will and commitment	Yes	Re.	Yes	Re.	Re.	Re.	Yes	Re.	Yes	Re.
Resources (technical, financial, and human)	Re.	Re.	Re.	Re.	Re.	Re.	Yes	Re.	Yes	Yes
Ownership and responsibility	Yes	Yes	Re.	Re.	Re.	Re.	Yes	Re.	Yes	Yes
Participation	Yes	Yes	Re.	Re.	Re.	Re.	Yes	Re.	Yes	Yes
Consultation	Yes	Yes	Re.	Re.	Re.	Re.	Yes	Re.	Yes	Yes
Transparency	Re.	Re.	Re.	Re.	Re.	Re.	Yes	Re.	Yes	yes
Capacity (competency)	Re.	Re.	Re.	Re.	Re.	Re.	Yes	Re.	Yes	Yes

Note: Yes implies that the factor is currently in place. Re. means "requirements" and implies that, in the future, this factor will be required and needs to be provided, or requires continued improvement. Fut. = future.
Source: Author's own observation and assessment.

because urban poverty is often considered secondary to rural poverty, which leads unintentionally to negligence or poor investments, especially in secondary cities and towns.

Rural-urban linkages are gaining renewed interest from ADB and UNESCAP.[9] The exploitation of such linkages has the potential to spread the development benefits of large cities or towns to surrounding smaller ones. The role that smaller towns should aim to play is to complement nearby large cities and not waste investment by competing for the same role.

CONCLUSION

The Government acknowledges that it is only through reform in all areas that the country and its population will overcome poverty and insecurity, especially in light of the country's increasing population growth rate. Many reforms and innovations implemented that the Government implemented have been achieved with outstanding success and applauded by both the international community and its own people. These include the SEILA program, the 50-50 formula (one of the key components contributing to

Phnom Penh receiving the World Leadership Awards for 2005), the one-window service pilot program, and the PLUP approach.

All these reform programs and policies have the shared objective of bringing public services closer to the local population and motivating the public to fully participate in designing, planning, implementing, and monitoring programs and projects. As a result, the society feels that it is part of the program and, thus, has full responsibility and commitment to work for its success and sustainability. Never before in the recent history of Cambodia has the provision of public services received contributions in-kind and in cash—equivalent to 50% of total contributions—from the local communities, especially after the Khmer Rouge regime when the state was popularly perceived with suspicion and mistrust.

The reforms should be accompanied by three important factors: true commitment, affordability, and the capacity to implement the reforms. Good and sufficient laws and regulations alone, as mentioned earlier, will not be enough to overcome the problems challenging Cambodia. There is also the need for strong and constant political commitment from all leaders. The commitment made by the Prime Minister and implemented by the government line ministries and authorities to continue to eradicate corruption, nepotism, and anarchic activities, such as state land grabbing, logging, and antisocial activities, is vital for Cambodia to overcome its historic problems. However, commitment alone is not sufficient to deal with the enormous problems facing Cambodia.

To mobilize the Government's large labor force and thereby act on its commitment, stable and secure financial inputs are required. At present, majority of the Government's employees are significantly underpaid, which, if allowed to continue, will hinder efforts to meet the commitments that the Government made. Moreover, capacity of the implementers, along with commitment and affordability, is needed to transform policies and programs into practice with fruitful results. As it stands today, most government personnel need further capacity upgrading to better understand and implement these policies and programs. This is even more crucial for the staff at the local level, where many are given the responsibility to implement tasks for which they are not qualified.

It seems inevitable that Cambodia will continue to face challenges as a result of continued urban population growth. Urban challenges will be effectively and efficiently dealt with not only through reforms, but also with appropriate and comprehensive strategies and policies. Efforts made by the Government in close cooperation with international donors, such as in creating economic corridors rather than economic growth poles, along with the newly initiated ADB and UNESCAP project on Rural-Urban Linkages, should be replicated in other regions of the country. These will promote the growth of more small and secondary towns and cities in Cambodia.

Promoting the growth of small and medium-sized towns and cities through an economic corridors policy has the potential to transform past patterns of rural-to-urban migration, in which migrants from rural areas were drawn to only a few economic poles, such as Phnom Penh, Siem Reap, and Sihanoukville. Instead, through steady development in small and medium-sized towns and cities located along economic corridors, the rural population will find places to work closer to home.

The challenge in rebuilding a country so devastated by war is enormous. Despite limited resources and the destruction of much of the country's urban system, Cambodia has made significant progress toward rebuilding and planning for the future development and management of its cities. The rapid increase in urbanization is placing enormous pressure on the capabilities of national and local governments to provide infrastructure, housing, and other essential services. The case studies presented in this chapter demonstrate, in a small way, important initiatives being undertaken to improve the sustainability of urban development in one of Asia's poorest countries.

Notes

[1] The information and data in this section draws heavily on the World Bank Report, February 2006, *Cambodia Halving Poverty by 2015, Poverty Assessment 2006*. Washington, DC.

[2] SEILA is a Khmer word meaning "stone," which implies "sustainable."

[3] Statistical Year Book 2003.

[4] According to the survey carried out by Solidarity for Urban Poor Federation (SUPF), this figure differs considerably from the national poverty line data noted earlier. Such inconsistencies are very common in urban data, which usually arise from different definitions of urban terms.

[5] SUPF survey for urban poor communities in 2004.

[6] Almost all of the account provided here is based on the author's own experience as one of the participants in Battambang's urban and infrastructure planning, and conservation of the town's historical buildings, 2002–2004, as team leader and supervisor. At present, the author continues to be involved with the UNESCAP project on Housing the Urban Poor in Battambang as Team Leader for the Ministry of Land Management, Urban Planning and Construction's Task Force for the Draft National Housing Policy.

[7] Much of the information presented here arises from interviews with personnel from Battambang district authorities and provincial line departments who have worked with the author on various projects until the present. The author is indebted to all for their insights and contributions.

[8] The author worked as a national consultant with international consultants to conduct project implementation assessment in 2003; all accounts mentioned here were derived from the author's own work experience.

[9] In recent years, two similar projects of different scales have been conducted in Cambodia, Indonesia, Lao PDR, Nepal, and Viet Nam, and perhaps in a few other countries in the region. The author is closely associated with are the ADB-sponsored study project on Regional Study on Rural, Urban and Subregional Linkages in the Greater Mekong Subregion (Viet Nam, Lao PDR, and Cambodia) 2004–2006, and the UNESCAP-sponsored project on Poverty Reduction through Rural-urban Linkages of Secondary Towns in Least Developed Countries.

5. People's Republic of China

APRODICIO A. LAQUIAN

INTRODUCTION

The People's Republic of China (PRC) is the most populated country in the world and is undergoing rapid economic development and urbanization. Relevant statistics on the country's development are presented in Table 5.1. Most of the population still live in rural areas. However, by 2030, urban populations are expected to grow by more than 300 million, with 60% of the population living in urban areas. The ability to manage this expected level of urban development will be a major challenge. Significant social and environmental problems are already arising from 20 years of rapid growth.

This chapter examines some issues facing urbanization in the PRC and introduces three case studies: Revitalizing the Inner City—Case Study of Nanjing, Shenzhen; Building a City from Scratch; and Reviving Rust-belt Industries in the Liaodong Peninsula. The case studies provide examples of the application of good practice in support of sustainable urban development. The final part of the chapter reflects on what has been learned.

The PRC's commitment to sustainable development can be traced to its participation at the 1992 United Nations Conference on Environment and Development. Two years later, the State Council approved the "White Paper on China's Population, Environment and Development in the 21st Century." In that document, sustainability as "development that meets the needs of the present without compromising the ability of future generations to meet theirs" (WCED 1987) was taken as official policy. The PRC also approved Agenda 21 that spelled out its developmental policies and programs.

The PRC's Agenda 21 program set as a target the quadrupling of the country's gross national product (GNP) (1980 as the base) and increasing its per capita GNP to the level of "moderately developed countries" by the year 2000. Aside from this economic objective, the PRC's commitment to sustainability included (a) safeguarding ecological balance, (b) protecting the environment, (c) ensuring the people's social and cultural well-being, and (d) controlling population growth and distribution (People's Republic of China 1994).

It is worth noting that all the sustainability objectives included in the PRC's Agenda 21 program are directly linked to the country's urbanization policy. This is interesting because for 3 decades after the Communist victory in 1949, the PRC pursued policies favoring rural areas and strictly controlled the growth of towns and cities. Not until the launching of economic reforms and the PRC's opening to the outside world in 1978 did the country encourage more rapid urbanization. As a result, the PRC's urbanization level increased from 18% in 1978 to 41% in 2005. By 2020, the PRC projects that

Table 5.1: Country Development Profile, PRC

Human Development Index (HDI) Rank of 177 countries (2003)^	85
GDP growth (annual %, 2004)	9.50
GNI per capita, Atlas method (current $, 2004)	1,290
GNI, Atlas method (current $ billion, 2004)	1,676.8
GDP per capita PPP ($, 2003)^	5,003
GDP PPP ($ billion, 2003)^	6,445.9
Population growth (annual 2005–2010) (%)#	0.63
Population, total (million, 2005)#	1,322.27
Urban population, total (million, 2005)#	535.98
Urban population percent of total population (2005)#	41
Population largest city: Shanghai (2005, million)	12.67
Population growth (350) capital cities or agglomerations > 750,000 inhabitants 2000#	
- Est. average growth of capital cities or urban agglomerations 2005–2015 (%)	21
- Number of capital cities or urban agglomerations with growth >50%, 2005–2015	24
- Number of capital cities or urban agglomerations with growth > 30%, 2005–2015	63
Sanitation, percentage of urban population with access to improved sanitation (2002)**	69
Water, % of urban population with access to improved water sources (2002)**	92
Slum population, % of urban (households with access to secure tenure) (2001)**	38
Slum population in urban areas (2001, million)**	178
Poverty, % of urban population below national poverty line (1998)**	2.0
Aid (Net ODA received; $ million; 2003)^	1,324
Aid as a share of country income (Net ODA/GNI; 2003)*	0.1
Aid per capita (current US$, 2003)^	1.0

GDP = gross domestic product, GNI = gross national income, ODA = official development assistance, PPP = purchasing power parity.
Note: Data for the PRC do not include those for Hong Kong, China; or Macau, China.
Sources: See footnote Chapter 2 World Bank (2005); OECD (2003); United Nations (2004, 2005).

the country will be 54% urban, with an urban population of about 800 million (United Nations 2004). Figure 5.1 shows the expected change in urban and rural populations to 2030. The urban population is expected to grow by 340 million by 2030.

The main challenge to the PRC's pursuit of sustainability is its huge population. While the country has been able to reduce its annual population growth rate from 1.2% in 1975–2003 to a projected 0.63% in 2005–2010, about 12.9 million people are still added to its population every year because of the large population base. Drastically cutting down the PRC's population growth rate has also created other problems. The rapid decline in the PRC's population growth has reduced the number of people in the productive age groups. It has also increased the proportion of people aged 65 years and above from 5.9% in 2003 to a projected 9.6% by 2015, thereby increasing the country's dependency ratio (United Nations Development Programs 2005).

Aside from the size of its population, the PRC is faced with the problem of spatial imbalance. The bulk of the population is concentrated in the economically prosperous and highly urbanized coastal areas, while the interior regions have remained underdeveloped. At present, about 786.2 million or 59% of the PRC's 1,322.3 million people live in rural areas. Since agricultural land is extremely limited (the average farm size in the PRC is about 1 *mu* or 0.06 hectare), more people cannot be absorbed on farms. A significant number of

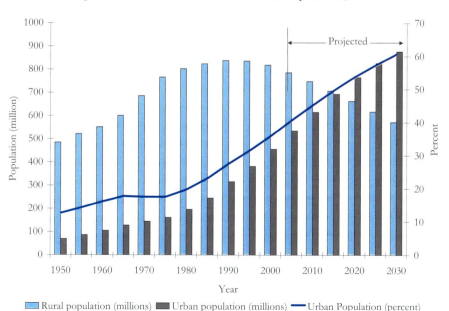

Figure 5.1: Trends in Urban and Rural Population, PRC

rural dwellers, estimated at more than 150 million, are considered redundant for efficient agricultural productivity. The authorities, therefore, have called for an acceleration of urbanization with the result that about 75 million farmers are expected to move to cities and towns by 2010 (*New York Times,* 16 October 2005). If, as expected, the PRC becomes more than half-urban by 2020, about 12–15 million nonfarm jobs each year will be needed to absorb the overflow of people from the countryside (*People's Daily Online*, 30 October 2003).

COUNTRY CONTEXT

In the PRC, urbanization is considered not just a demographic variable but also a potent instrument for policy intervention. Ideologically, Chinese development policy has traditionally focused on the rural areas, in recognition of the fact that contrary to orthodox communist theory, the peasantry and not the urban proletariat won the 1949 Chinese Revolution. Under Chairman Mao Zedong, the Chinese communists redistributed land to peasants in a vigorous agrarian reform program, confiscated farms from landlords, set up rural communes, established state farms, and pursued a farm mechanization program. Backyard furnaces and other rural industrialization schemes were pursued during the Great Leap Forward (1958–1959) with markedly disastrous results. The size and number of towns and cities were kept artificially low by strictly controlling internal migration with the use of the household registration or *hukou* system. During the Great Cultural Revolution (1966–1976), there were even efforts to decongest the cities by forcibly sending urban residents to rural areas through the "rustication" or *xia fang* movement. The results of these antiurban policies can be seen in the fact that the proportion of citizens classified as urban went from only about 13% in 1950 to 18% in 1978.

After the launching of economic reforms and opening up to the outside world in 1978, the PRC aggressively pursued urban development policies. Pursuant to Deng Xiaoping's declaration that "to get rich is glorious" and that "it is all right for some people to get rich first," the pace of urbanization rapidly accelerated. Interestingly, the economic reforms first started in rural areas with the introduction of the production responsibility system, which encouraged farmers to cultivate private plots and engage in money-making nonagricultural activities. Eventually, the newly rich farmers could not be contained in the villages so the *hukou* system was relaxed around 1980, allowing rural dwellers to leave their farms provided they moved only to small towns. Township and village enterprises were also encouraged and became the initial drivers of the PRC's rapid rate of economic growth, which has averaged more than 9% per year for nearly 3 decades.

Urbanization Issues

Despite the economic achievements since 1978, the country's leaders have been concerned with the environmental and social problems associated with the rapid growth of cities and towns. In 1980, the PRC adopted a policy "to strictly control the development of large cities, rationally develop medium-sized cities, and encourage the growth of small towns." In pursuit of this policy, rural dwellers were permitted to leave villages and move to towns provided they did not rely on urban governments for their grain supply and other benefits. This decision encouraged massive rural-urban migration as evidenced by the increase in the number of towns in the PRC from 2,786 in 1983 to 20,358 in 2005 (China in Brief 2005).

As the PRC's economic boom required more laborers and skilled workers in big cities, keeping migrants in towns became more difficult. At present, about 80 million people (known as the *liudong renkou* or "floating population") are living in cities without official nonagricultural worker status. About 20% of the population of big cities like Shanghai, Tianjin, and Guangzhou are not officially registered in those cities. These "temporary" migrants, many of whom have lived in the cities for many years, are often denied urban benefits, such as permanent jobs, standardized wages, affordable housing, health services, and education for children. They are fast becoming an impoverished underclass in a country officially committed to a policy of egalitarianism.

A serious consequence of the PRC's economic progress since 1979 has been the widening gap between rich and poor. In 2004, about 50% of the total income in the PRC went to the top 25% of the population while the bottom 20% received only 4.7% (*New York Times*, 16 October 2005). In terms of consumption, the bottom 10% of the population is estimated to consume only 2.4% of the country's output while the richest 10% consumes 30.4%. The PRC's Gini coefficient in 2003 was a high 40 (*The World Fact Book* 2003).

Another manifestation of inequality in the PRC is the widening rural-urban gap. In 2005, it was estimated that urban residents took home more than three times the income of the average rural dweller (*New York Times*, 10 October 2005). Furthermore, following Deng Xiaoping's advice, some people became richer much faster than did others. In 2003, *Forbes Magazine* came up with a list of "China's Richest," which showed that the 400 richest individuals in the PRC had a net worth of $36.6 billion. The richest person on the list had a net worth of $780 million and at least 20 persons had incomes in excess of $290 million (Liang 2003). Meanwhile, about 178 million people in urban areas lived in slum conditions and the average per capita gross domestic product (GDP) was only $5,003 per year (World Bank 2005).

Rapid urbanization has exerted strong demand for urban services. In 2002, the Government claimed that about 69% of the urban population had access to improved sanitation. The Government also indicated that 92% of urban households had access to improved drinking water sources. However, the demand for services in rapidly expanding cities has reached dangerous proportions. The national capital, Beijing, draws about 85% of its water from ground sources, causing sinkholes in some areas. In Shenyang City, the demand for water was set at 3.2 million cubic meters per day (m^3/day). It was revealed, however, that in 1995, there was already a shortage of 416,700 m^3/day of water; the city will face more serious shortages in the future (Economic and Social Commission for Asia and the Pacific [ESCAP] 1995).

Urbanization has exacerbated air, water, soil, and noise pollution. According to the World Health Organization (WHO), 7 of the 10 most polluted cities in the world are in the PRC. The largest cities have been the most affected by pollution. For example, in the largest city, Shanghai, heavy and light industries contributed 90% of gaseous emissions and 60% of liquid discharges into the environment in 1995. PRC industries relying mainly on coal for energy, contributed 81% of total sulfur dioxide and 78% of particulate emissions. The Huangpu River that cuts across Shanghai is essentially dead because about 3.4 million m^3 of industrial and domestic waste are dumped into it every day. Less than 5% of the wastewater that flows into the Huangpu and Suzhou creeks is treated (Lam and Tao 1996).

In Beijing and Tianjin, a study of water quality revealed that half of the water samples drawn from the Hai and Luan rivers did not meet the lowest quality standards set by the WHO (World Bank 1995). The Government estimated that to meet the environmental objectives of the 10th Five-Year Plan (2001–2005), it would need to spend roughly $85 billion during the plan period, about 1.3% of the country's GDP. Of this amount, about $33.8 billion would be needed for controlling air pollution, $32.6 billion for water pollution, $10.8 billion for solid waste treatment, and $7.8 billion for other types of pollution (Mayfield 2005).

The urban housing situation is a major issue. The average floor space of rural family houses is generally twice as big as that in urban family dwellings. Rural homes are also predominantly privately owned. The main problem in rural housing is lack of such basic services as water, sanitation, electricity, and solid waste collection and disposal.

The 1988 housing reform program introduced market mechanisms in urban housing provision. Instead of the Government providing housing through work units and housing bureaus, the reform program sold the houses to individual households. Traditionally, work units spent 40% of their funds for housing construction, maintenance, repair, and administration, a social burden that made them inefficient and unproductive. By encouraging people to use their savings to buy housing units instead of consumer items like television sets, furniture, and other durable goods, the Government was able to dampen inflationary pressures on the economy (Tolley 1991).

Although the PRC has invested heavily in urban housing, the huge backlog in residential construction is proving to be a heavy burden on the country's economy. In 2005 alone, the country planned to build 436.6 million m^2 of housing, up from 185.8 million m^2 in 1998. However, housing loans from commercial banks, which increased from $2.3 billion in 1997 to $99.8 billion in 2002, have strained the resources of the banking system. By February 2005, the Central Bank reported that outstanding residential mortgages had reached $199 billion, about 23% of all the medium-term lending and 9% of total lending in the whole country. The Bank raised some cautions about the inflationary pressures of such a large volume of housing loans, especially in the light of a significant proportion of bad loans in the portfolios of many banks. Cautions were also raised about some malpractices in the housing market. In April 2005, a Beijing real estate developer was reported to have defrauded the Central Bank of $78 million in forged housing contracts (Asia Focus 2005).

Regional Development Policies

PRC authorities are aware that to maintain high economic development growth, they have to make cities and towns more efficient engines of growth by concentrating investments in these settlements. With the urban population growing at 4.08% per year, the Government is pursuing policies to make urbanization a positive contributor to sustainable development. PRC authorities are keenly aware of the dangers of uncontrolled urban growth (inadequate urban services, slums, environmental pollution) especially in very large cities. To solve this dilemma, the authorities have adopted three urban policy approaches: (a) concentrate development in high-density urban nodes to take advantage of economies of scale, location, and agglomeration, as well as larger markets, availability of skilled labor, and accumulation of capital; (b) redevelop inner city areas to cope with urban decay; and (c) link inner city development with planned growth on the urban periphery to encourage the emergence of compact mega-urban regions.

Concentrated Urban Development

When the PRC decided to open its economy and society to the outside world after 1978, it concentrated development efforts in priority development areas, which included special economic zones (SEZs), coastal open cities, and open economic regions. SEZs were production enclaves where foreign and economic investors were allowed to set up their enterprises under favorable terms, provided they sold the bulk of their products in international markets. Within each zone, the Government offered economic incentives, such as duty exemption on importation of production machinery and material inputs, assured supply of reliable energy, good housing, efficient infrastructure, information and communication linkages, access to professionally trained and disciplined work force, free repatriation of profits, and full security for personnel and staff. Investors in SEZs brought in capital, technical know-how, new product designs and prototypes, raw materials, and new technology. The SEZ provided land, energy, labor, housing, social services, management, and logistical services. The most widely known SEZs in the PRC are Shantou, Shenzhen, and Zhuhai in Guangdong Province, Xiamen in Fujian Province, and the island-province of Hainan.

In 1984, the PRC opened 14 coastal cities for foreign investments (Dalian, Qinhuangdao, Tianjin, Yantai, Qingdao, Lianyungang, Nantong, Shanghai, Ningbo, Wenzhou, Fuzhou, Guangzhou, Zhanjiang, and Beihai). The following year, the state expanded the open coastal areas and extended the open economic zones to create open coastal belts in the Yangtze River Delta region, Pearl River Delta region, Xiamen-Zhangzhou-Quanzhou triangle in south Fujian, Shandong Peninsula-Liaodong Peninsula region in the northeast, and Hebei and Guangxi region in the south. Since 1992, the State Council has opened all the capital cities of inland provinces and autonomous regions to foreign investments and established 15 free trade zones, 32 state-level economic and technological development zones, and 53 new and high-tech industrial development zones located in medium-sized cities (China in Brief 2005).

One of the most dramatic urban programs has been the development of the Pudong New Zone in Shanghai. Founded in 1992, Pudong was extended preferential policies not allowed in other SEZs. In addition to policies allowing reduction or elimination of customs duties and income taxes, Pudong authorities were allowed to grant foreign investors the right to open financial institutions and run tertiary industries. Shanghai has also been permitted to set up a stock exchange and to allow foreign banks to engage in business using the local currency (renminbi).

Inner City Redevelopment

Unlike many North American cities where the downtown area becomes dark and abandoned after offices are closed and people drive back to their suburban homes, those in the PRC have vibrant and densely populated urban cores. However, basic urban services in the PRC's inner city areas (water, sanitation, and solid waste collection and disposal) are often inadequate. Housing is usually congested and some residents live in "dangerous and dilapidated" structures. Nevertheless, inner city residents are generally able to cope with these problems because they possess a strong community spirit. They extend mutual aid to each other and enjoy life in inner city lanes, in courtyard houses, and in tiny well-maintained parks. Often, they close small streets for periodic markets and celebrate traditional fairs and festivals. Since many cities trace their origins to ancient times, their inner cores usually feature heritage structures, such as temples, villas, clustered apartments (*lilong*), and courtyard houses (*siheyuan*). Specific programs to redevelop and rehabilitate these structures are now being pursued in most PRC cities.

With the high level of economic growth achieved by the PRC since 1978, considerable pressures are now being exerted on poor conditions in inner city areas. As market mechanisms have taken over from central planning, the real value of urban land has become an important element in governmental decision making. Planners and developers want to convert inner city areas from residential, governmental, and cultural functions into higher-value uses (office towers, entertainment complexes, and shopping centers). As a result, in big cities like Shanghai, Beijing, and Guangzhou, old residential areas are being cleared and offices, shopping malls, and luxury condominiums are being constructed in the central business district. Even the Ming Dynasty courtyard houses in central Beijing and the lilong apartments in Shanghai are being razed, with their occupants resettled to suburban areas.

The high level of economic growth since 1978 has revitalized urban areas. A random citing of GDP growth rates in cities attests to their rapid development. The GDP of Shenyang City in Liaoning Province, for example, grew at an annual rate of 19% in 1986–1995. The per capita GDP of Shenzhen City in the Pearl River Delta during 2000–2005 increased at a rate 5.5 times higher than the average for the whole country.

Aside from its rapid rate of economic growth, the PRC has achieved significant social advances. Unlike many developing countries, the country has been able to provide adequate housing for most of its urban residents through a massive housing reform program. Before 1988, 30% of urban households in the PRC had less than 4 square meters (m^2) of livable housing space per person. Work units and housing bureaus provided 83% of all housing units. Each household paid about 1% of cash income for housing, which was clearly not sustainable because it barely paid for maintenance costs. The housing improvements have been achieved by redeveloping inner city areas and resettling people in new houses in the suburbs.

Many Chinese cities have also redeveloped inner city areas by combining cultural conservation efforts with tourism-oriented projects. In big cities like Shanghai, Beijing, Chengdu, and Xi'an, areas adjacent to temples, historic places, and cultural shrines have been transformed into shopping and entertainment complexes that are enjoyed by local and foreign visitors alike. Traditional housing structures, with stores on the ground floor and residences in upper floors, have been restored. Streets and lanes in the vicinity of cultural and historical centers are often closed to traffic and lined with small eateries, shops, and service providers. These inner city areas, therefore, integrate employment, residence, entertainment, and services in a holistic development scheme, thereby ensuring that they continue to thrive.

The city of Nanjing, capital of Jiangsu Province, is noted for a successful program of redevelopment of its inner city areas. Founded in 495 BC as the city of Yecheng and made a provincial capital in 229 AD during the period of the Three Kingdoms, Nanjing has served as the capital of 10 dynasties. While the city walls of Beijing were torn down as symbols of the PRC's feudal past, those of Nanjing, 19 miles long and 39 feet high, have been preserved. The Ming Dynasty tombs in the city have been declared a World Heritage Site. Aside from these imperial historical sites, Nanjing also has the Sun Yat-Sen mausoleum, Art World of Red Mansions, the Presidential Palace during the Republican Period, and a famed temple of Confucius.

Development of City-regions

While inner city areas in the PRC are being revitalized, outlying regions are also planned to form viable city-regions. The main instruments that the PRC uses in fostering regional development include (a) establishment of innovation centers and high technology parks, (b) creation of special economic zones; (c) designation of coastal open cities; and (d) setting up of open economic regions. The key idea behind these regional development schemes was to concentrate population, employment, infrastructure, social services, and governance structures in designated urban places. At the same time, the economic and social linkages between urban and rural areas were not forgotten. Food production was encouraged not too far from the cities to reduce transport costs. The conversion of agricultural land into urban uses was controlled to prevent urban sprawl. Nonagricultural economic activities were encouraged in accordance with the slogan "leaving the land but not the village." Most important of all, the functional linkages between urban and rural settlements were strengthened by such schemes as "letting out" contractual jobs by urban entrepreneurs to rural dwellers, capital investments from cities in township and village enterprises, urban marketing of rural products, and extension of technical assistance and training services by urban enterprises to rural producers.

In the planned development of innovation centers, three types of high-tech parks were created. *Spark parks* were located in remote and lagging areas to stimulate growth by the introduction of high-tech innovations. *Torch parks* were set up in small and medium-sized cities to enhance growth in surrounding hinterlands. *Comprehensive high-tech parks* were established in large cities and metropolitan areas, especially in districts where universities, research institutes, industrial enclaves, export-processing zones, and special economic zones were located (Laquian 2005, p. 335).

As Chinese cities expand, they increasingly demand conversion of rich agricultural land into urban uses, putting at risk the country's objective of food self-sufficiency. The loss of agricultural land has been most serious in rapidly urbanizing regions, such as the Pearl River Delta and the Yangtze River Delta. A study in 1996 revealed that about 35% of the cropland in Dongguan City, close to Guangzhou, had been converted into urban uses (Yeh and Li 1996). Furthermore, the development plan for Guangzhou requires expanding the metropolitan territory from 335 square kilometers (km^2) in 2000 to 555 km^2 in 2010, and most of the land would be taken from croplands (Taubman 2002).

The results of the regional development policies in the PRC are seen in the relatively smooth urban hierarchy of the country. Although the country has a very large territory (9,596,960 km^2), no one mega city dominates the urban scene. Of the 666 cities, only 2 (Shanghai and Beijing) have populations in excess of 10 million. Nine cities have populations between 2 and 9 million and 23 cities with populations between 1 and 2 million. The rest of the cities (632) have populations of less than 200,000 to 1 million (People's Daily Online, 16 September 2004).

Decentralization Issues

People not familiar with the PRC's development have the common impression that it is a highly centralized authoritarian state. The reality, however, is that local governments in the country enjoyed considerable influence and power even before 1978. Strictly speaking, of course, the central Government had mainly delegated administrative authority to local units without politically devolving power to them. The center appointed top provincial and city officials. Provinces and cities are mainly held responsible for local development plans, economic administration, and management of local enterprises, and their decisions in these fields have to conform to national policies and performance standards.

Despite the legal-structural limits of central-local government relations, the demands of rapid economic development have endowed local officials with considerable influence and power. The practical demands for quick action have forced the central Government to give more leeway to local officials in decision making. The country is so large and the pressures to pursue local development so strong that local officials, like their ancient mandarin counterparts, adopted the slogan "the mountains are high and the emperor is far away." Many local officials nowadays usually decide local issues without clearing these with Beijing. Besides, such officials can rely on informal power relationships with key Beijing leaders, relying on the age-old traditions of *guanxi* (personal networks of influence) and *houmen* (back door connections) to enable them make local decisions independently. Because local officials are held responsible for results, they often assume powers without waiting for formal decentralization edicts.

The actual decentralization of authority to local officials, of course, differs from region to region. As the economic power of richer urban regions increased, the central Government delegated more authority to officials in these areas. For example, city-regions have been reorganized to form unified governance structures, with local cities and municipalities placed under the authority of regional governors and mayors. The mayors of cities like Shanghai have been authorized to approve financing for very large projects without clearing the decisions with Beijing. The Constitution has been revised to allow local officials to sell land or lease it to foreign investors. Local executives have been given powers to deal with loss-ridden state-owned enterprises, giving them direct authority to hire and fire personnel and to sell, privatize, or close down bankrupt enterprises. Local governments have even been allowed to borrow funds from local and international sources to finance infrastructure projects, with the sovereign guarantee of the central Government (Laquian 2002).

An interesting trend is the decision to decentralize authority and power at the grassroots level. Officials at the village level are already directly elected by the people. Unlike in the past when the Communist Party nominated local candidates, multiple candidates can now contest village elections. In the address of President Hu Jintao to the Politburo on the eve of the PRC's National Day in October 2003, he said that: "We must enrich the forms of democracy, make democratic procedures complete, expand citizens' orderly political participation, and ensure that the people can exercise democratic elections, democratic decision making, democratic administration, and democratic scrutiny" (*New York Times,* 1 October 2003). Based on these statements, "China watchers" are expecting that the PRC will allow open election of officials at the township, county, and higher levels of local government.

Regional Economic Governance and Intergovernmental Financial Relations

The main problem in regional economic governance in the PRC is the proliferation of government agencies, which creates administrative and political fragmentation. There is functional fragmentation where agencies in charge of water, transport, energy, solid waste management, and other urban services pursue their policies and programs independently. There is also vertical fragmentation where central government ministries and bureaus as well as local authorities at the provincial, prefectural, metropolitan, city, town, district, municipal, and neighborhood levels exercise their own authority and power. Governance is complicated further by the presence of special authorities responsible for specific functions (water boards, electric companies) as well as agencies with exclusive authority over affairs in designated geographic areas (port authorities, SEZ authorities).

As in other countries, the primary instrument that the central Government uses in intergovernmental economic relations is control over budgetary and expenditure functions. Traditionally, the bulk of central Government income came from operations of state-owned enterprises, customs duties, and the center's share in local tax proceeds. These resources were allocated to local governments on the basis of need. Central government allocation of funds, of course, did not encourage local units to raise their own local revenue.

After 1978, most state-owned enterprises ran into economic difficulties, reducing the income of the central Government. Township and village enterprises, on the other hand, thrived thereby increasing the income of local bodies. In addition, tax reforms launched in 1994 included the imposition of value-added taxes, with the proceeds from these taxes shared between central and local governments (75% to the former and 25% to the latter). Even with this adoption of a tax-sharing scheme, the portion of tax revenue going to the central Government has declined since 1995. In contrast, rich local governments have become much richer.

Before 1978, the fiscal system in the PRC was heavily redistributive, with richer local units transferring a high proportion of their GDP to poorer regions. Decentralization, however, encouraged richer local units to keep a higher portion of their GDP for themselves. For example, in 1970–1980, Shanghai gave 50% of its GDP to poorer provinces but gave only 8.5% in 1993. Similarly, the wealthy province of Guangdong gives only 0.4% of its GDP to poorer regions (Riskin 2000).

Because housing demands huge financial resources, supporting housing programs plays a prominent role in intergovernmental financial relations. Before 1984, individual work units all over the PRC provided 84% of urban housing. The housing reform program in 1988 introduced market mechanisms, setting up programs to encourage families to save funds for down payments, increasing rents, increasing wages, and encouraging the sale of housing units to individuals. The World Bank helped set up the Housing Loans Bank in 1987. In 1994, the Government required work units to create "housing accumulation funds." Under this system, employees deposited 5% of their monthly incomes into the fund and employers matched these with another 5%. The accumulated funds were then used as down payment for the purchase of a house. In 1997, the Government stopped the work units and housing bureaus from providing subsidized housing to workers. By 2002, some 65 million citizens had accumulated about $49.9 billion in the funds. About $18.3 billion of those funds had been used to purchase 20 million houses. More than 3.4 billion m^2 of housing floor space had been constructed and 500 million m^2 of older buildings had been rebuilt or renovated. Citizens had purchased about 94% of the houses in the open market (*Peoples' Daily*, 21 August 2003).

Leveraging International Assistance for Sustainable Urban Development

Unlike other developing countries, the PRC, with its huge population and robust economy, has not been overly dependent on international assistance for its development efforts. Total official development assistance (ODA) to the PRC in 2003 was only about $1,324.6 million (roughly $1.00 per capita), which is barely 0.1% of total national income. With its strong commitment to national self-reliance, the PRC initially tended to be wary of international loans as a way of financing development projects. Even after the PRC started tapping international financing, it preferred to invest in profit-generating projects and "hard" infrastructure, such as roads, railways, ports, harbors, energy generation, and water and sewerage projects. Social development projects, such as health, education, and poverty reduction schemes are given low priority in foreign borrowing schemes, especially when loans are made in hard currency that would have to be paid at set foreign exchange rates. The authorities believe that the country has enough resources to pay for these projects.

With economic profitability as a principal criterion, the PRC has tended to focus international financing on projects located in highly urbanized areas. Thus, most internationally funded projects are concentrated in the coastal regions. This tendency to favor the highly developed coastal regions has prompted the Asian Development Bank (ADB) to give higher priority to projects in the central and western provinces. In the update of the country strategy and program for the PRC for 2006–2008, ADB is allocating 85%

of its projected lending of $4.5 billion to these lagging regions. Leveraging ADB resources in this way conforms to the objective of reducing poverty and promoting more equitable development between richer and poorer individuals as well as residents of urban and rural areas.

The bulk of ADB lending to the PRC is devoted to projects with strong multiplier effects, such as infrastructure (roads, railways, power generating plants), and town-based urbanization. Recognizing the country's reluctance to borrow for social projects, ADB has allocated $11 million from the 2006–2008 country program funds for technical assistance grants to encourage the country to consider support for such projects. The Government has also contributed to the Technical Assistance Special Fund. Furthermore, funds from the Poverty Reduction Cooperation Fund from the United Kingdom have been used to encourage the PRC to invest not only in "single projects" to build additions to the National Trunk Highway System, but also to encourage area-wide approaches that link smaller roads in a regional transport network (People's Daily Online, 25 March 2005).

GOOD PRACTICE CASE STUDIES

The rapid economic growth achieved since 1978 and the country's accelerating rate of urbanization have raised the issue of whether such growth is sustainable in an economic, social, and ecological sense. Economic sustainability addresses the proper and full valuation of natural resources, maintenance of capital stock, promotion of growth with equity, and internalization of the impact of economic activities that most economists treat as externalities. Social sustainability requires consideration of "social capital," which includes factors that enhance the capabilities of human beings (education, health, skills training). It also includes consideration of social mobility, the empowerment of disadvantaged groups, poverty reduction, and the prevention of the disintegration of societies. Ecological sustainability addresses ecosystem integrity, habitat conservation, the interaction of species and their preservation, and consideration of the "carrying capacity" of ecological systems (Serageldin 1995).

A quick look at economic growth in the PRC shows its close association with the opening of the country's economy to the outside world. Globalization effects— such as foreign direct investments, trade liberalization, expansion of exports and imports—and the PRC's acceptance of foreign trade regimes by its membership in the World Trade Organization have greatly assisted economic progress. Opening-up to the outside world has brought in new ideas, technological innovations, and tradable products. It has also

Figure 5.2: Map Showing Location of the Case Studies

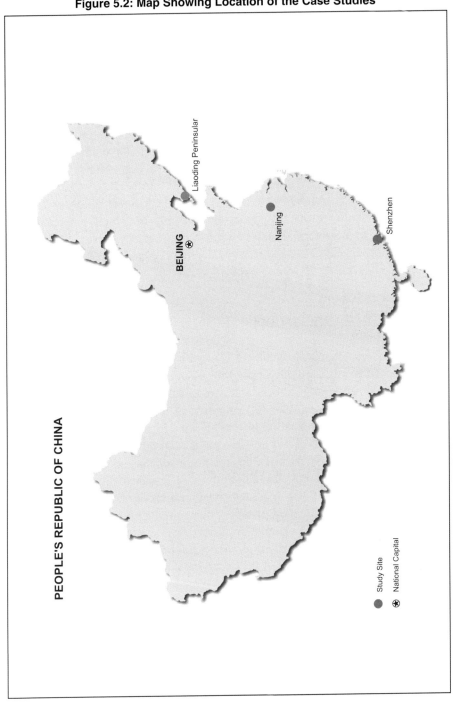

forced the PRC to abide by requirements of global trade regimes, such as respect for intellectual property rights and adherence to fair trade practices.

As far as social sustainability is concerned, economic progress has been essentially built on human development efforts that were pursued during the country's socialist period when the Government invested heavily in education, health, housing, and public welfare. Endowed with a disciplined and highly motivated work force, the PRC has been able to compete successfully in the world economy since 1978. At the same time, the country needs to be conscious of the dangers of inequality, especially the widening gap between rural and urban areas and the ultra rich and the very poor.

As the PRC has progressed economically, the environmental costs of development have become a serious problem. Many cities suffer from environmental pollution because of the heavy dependence on coal for energy. Urban areas lack an adequate water supply and suffer from poor sanitation. Surface and ground water sources have become heavily polluted. In some ways, the PRC is still paying for the environmental costs of misguided programs, such as reliance on Soviet-style planning that favored heavy industries, use of communes for agricultural production, lack of investments in urban infrastructure, and failure to enact environmental control laws and standards.

Many good practices in urban and regional development have been used in the PRC as it pursues sustainability. In this chapter, three case studies are presented to highlight the three main problems facing the country in its pursuit of sustainable development: (a) how to deal with inner city decay, especially in ancient cities (Nanjing); (b) how to create new urban settlements to serve as alternatives to existing ones (Shenzhen); and (c) how to revitalize aging industries, make regional development more efficient, and balance regional growth by effectively linking urban and rural development schemes (Liaodong Peninsula). Location of the areas is shown in the map.

The first case study—revitalizing the inner city section of Nanjing—shows the importance of economic, social, and cultural interventions in a program that attempts to deal with inner city decay. Nanjing planners, noting that many North American cities often have deteriorating inner cores, want to prevent this from happening in their own city. They realize that inner city decay is the result of factors that contribute to suburbanization and urban sprawl such as (a) a transport policy based on the use of private automobiles; (b) land policies that make the value of land the primary basis for public decisions; (c) housing programs that result in "hollowing out" the inner city by locating people in suburban housing projects; and (d) taxation policies that favor growth in rapidly growing suburban areas.

The second case study focused on Shenzhen illustrates how building a city from scratch can be achieved through careful urban and regional planning. Of the PRC's five SEZs, Shenzhen is easily the most successful, having grown from a small town of 30,000 residents before 1980 to a metropolis of more than 9 million at present. The Shenzhen story reveals the importance of urban and regional planning tools. It also shows how strategic and iterative planning can be used to deal with problems that arise from unexpected and unanticipated developments.

The third case study of how the Liaodong Peninsula has been able to revitalize its rust-belt industries and backward technological base through urban and regional planning illustrates good practices that can be adapted to conditions in other developing countries. The case study reveals how mobilizing domestic capital and infusing foreign funds and technology were used to revitalize aging industries. It highlights the importance of basic urban infrastructure as a necessary first step in achieving economic development. It shows the importance of linking urban and rural sectors of the economy in a comprehensive regional development plan. Like the case studies of Nanjing and Shenzhen, it also illustrates the importance of creating a polycentric urban form in urban and regional development.

Nanjing: Revitalizing the Inner City

The city of Nanjing, capital of Jiangsu Province, is noted for a successful program of redevelopment of its inner city areas. Founded in 495 BC as the city of Yecheng and made a provincial capital in 229 AD during the period of the Three Kingdoms, Nanjing has served as the capital of 10 dynasties. While the city walls of Beijing were torn down as symbols of the PRC's feudal past, those of Nanjing, 19 miles long and 39 feet high, have been preserved. The Ming Dynasty tombs in the city have been declared a World Heritage Site. Aside from these imperial historical sites, Nanjing also has the Sun Yat-Sen mausoleum, Art World of Red Mansions, the Presidential Palace during the Republican Period, and a famed temple of Confucius.

GOOD PRACTICE	
Good Governance	✓
Urban Management	✓
Infrastructure/Service Provision	✓
Financing and Cost Recovery	
Sustainability	✓
Innovation and Change	
Leveraging ODA	

While maintaining its cultural heritage, Nanjing aspires to transform itself into an international metropolis to rival neighboring cities like Shanghai and Hangzhou. By 2050, city authorities project that their city will reach a population of 10 million or more. The present population is about 6.4 million, occupying a territory of 6,516 km^2. About 91% of the population are classified urban and 9% rural, the latter being mostly residents of areas around 12 satellite towns and 14 organic towns in the metropolitan area. Politically, the People's Government of Nanjing City is under the authority of the Communist Party and the Nanjing Communist Party Committee secretary is the de facto governor of the city. An appointed mayor heads the executive branch of the government.

Nanjing has jurisdiction over 12 districts (Xuanwu, Baixia, Qinhuai, Jianye, Gulou, Xiaguan, Pukou, Luhe, Qixia, Yuhuatai, Jiangning, and Jiangpu) and two counties (Lishui and Gauchun). Suburban development is being pursued with the establishment of high-density urban settlements, such as those in Hexi, where the future central business district is being transferred. The cores of suburban development are usually large industrial parks, such as those in Gaoxin, Xingang, Huagong, and Jingning. Foreign financing of these parks has been encouraged and Nanjing has been able to attract electronics, petrochemical, and iron and steel enterprises such as Panda Electronics, Jincheng Motors, and Nanjing Steel. Foreign firms such as Fiat, Iveco, and Sharp have set up plants in Nanjing.

Examples of Good Practices

To revitalize its inner city areas, ensure environmental conservation, encourage economic growth, and enhance social equity and reduce poverty, government authorities and local citizens in Nanjing have set up programs and projects that reflect a number of good practices. Some noteworthy examples of such practices include (a) redeveloping inner city areas, (b) using a regional approach to achieve metropolitan development, and (c) pursuing housing reforms and poverty reduction schemes.

Redeveloping Inner City Areas. The most important feature of the Nanjing master plan is the redevelopment of the inner city. Within the downtown area of Nanjing, well-defined zones have been devoted to specific types of development: information centers, administrative centers, shopping centers, cultural institutions, and areas for production and sale of scientific and technological products.

For historical and cultural purposes, the development plan of Nanjing has demarcated 13 "protected zones" exclusively devoted to cultural structures, relics, and heritage sites. These include important structures, such as the Chaotian Palace, the Presidential Palace of the Republic of China, and buildings that date back to previous dynasties. Also protected are the Zhongshan Scenic Area and the Stone City Scenic Area, as well as ancient traditional houses, such as Mendong, Menxi, and Nanbuting. Within the historical and cultural zone are located seven major museums on ancient and modern history and a number of buildings holding historical relics.

The inner city development scheme combines cultural conservation with tourism and entertainment. For example, the Fuzimiao area focused on the ancient temple of Confucius is a noisy, rowdy, and brightly lit center for shopping, eating, and entertainment. In contrast, an area formerly occupied by squatters adjacent to the city walls in Xiaotaoyuan has been cleared and transformed into a nicely landscaped park. Part of the future plan for the area is the construction of high-end luxury housing on the other side of the river, the earnings from which would cross-subsidize the maintenance and management of the park.

To provide economic vitality to the inner city, the Nanjing authorities have converted areas formerly occupied by rundown structures into commercial, service, and entertainment centers. The 1912 development scheme located behind the Presidential Palace of the Republican era now serves as the entertainment enclave for Nanjing. There are more than 70 enterprises, such as nightclubs (Red Club), restaurants, boutiques, a spa, coffee shops (Starbucks, the Coffee Beanery), teahouses, and fast-food places. The area is well connected to the city's public transport system and currently has parking for about 180 vehicles.

Although urban redevelopment has required the relocation of some inner city families to suburban housing projects, the inner city redevelopment plan for Nanjing gives a great deal of importance to people actually living in the city center. To this end, a wide range of housing types, ranging from high-end luxury condominiums to densely inhabited courtyards where people share water facilities, toilets, and kitchens are provided in the plan. Slum upgrading programs have been pursued in a number of informal and uncontrolled settlements. Mini-parks and open spaces have been created for the enjoyment of local residents. In some areas, streets are periodically closed to make way for night markets. Conscious community development programs are pursued in inner city areas to mobilize people through social campaigns, such as neighborhood beautification, vaccination, maternal and child health, and family planning.

Using a Regional Approach to Achieve Metropolitan Development. The Overall City Plan for Nanjing (1991–2010) features not only the redevelopment of the inner city area encompassed by its ancient walls, but "clustered settlements" or urban nodes formed along the banks of the Yangtze River. The suburban settlements are connected to the central city by a system of arterial expressways (spokes) and to each other by a system of circumferential roads (rings). Unfortunately, the transport system is mainly focused on the use of road-based conveyances, especially private cars. Nanjing has constructed a rail-based metro system with a 17-km north-south line made up of 13 stations and an east-west line that started operations in 2005. To date, the metro system does not yet reach key urban nodes in the metropolitan area.

To control urban sprawl, Nanjing has concentrated high-density development in specific zones. The most important of these development schemes is located in Hexi, southwest of the city, where an ambitious development program designed to transfer the central business district from inside the city walls has been pursued. Industrial and technological development has also been concentrated in suburban areas, such as the high-tech enclave located near the international airport. It is noteworthy that the Nanjing metropolitan region has been planned as a totality, with specific functions allocated to designated areas. The areas between the nodes are also preserved as green spaces and agricultural production sites. The suburban regions of Nanjing have traditionally produced vegetables, fruits, freshwater fish, and other food items for the city. The current city master plan continues to stress urban agriculture as a major thrust in the total development scheme.

Housing Reform and Community Development Schemes. Like other ancient Chinese cities, Nanjing has densely occupied inner city zones where "dangerous and dilapidated" housing structures are found. Typical of these zones is the Menxi area located west of one of the main gates of Nanjing's city walls. Menxi is occupied by more than 40,000 people living in extremely crowded housing enclaves with multiple courtyards. With technical assistance from the American Planning Association, the Nanjing city authorities have adopted a redevelopment scheme that includes a landscaped park, high-rise condominiums, affordable housing units, local community service centers, and provision of water and sanitation.

Instead of proposing wholesale destruction of traditional houses, the redevelopment plan for Menxi will use a "slum upgrading" approach where the physical structures that can be saved will be retained. Courtyard walls will be cleaned and improved, adequate water supply and sanitation facilities provided, and people organized and directly involved in the improvement of their community. The upgrading scheme may involve the resettlement of about a quarter of the original residents. Resettlement to apartments in the suburbs will be done on a voluntary basis, with families that agree to be relocated compensated with cash awards as well as provided with apartments that have more than twice the floor space occupied in Menxi. Suburban apartments will also have private kitchens, toilets, and baths instead of shared facilities as in the old neighborhood.

Shenzhen: Building a City from Scratch

In 1978, the Third Plenary Session of the Eleventh Central Committee of the Chinese Communist Party approved the "Open Door" and "Economic

Reform" policies. Pursuant to these policies, Shenzhen was declared the first SEZ in the PRC in August 1980. Shenzhen was a small town with an area of 3 km² and a population of 30,000. When it was made an SEZ, it absorbed Baoan county and Shenzhen municipality, increasing its population to 70,000 and expanding its territory to 1,800 km².

GOOD PRACTICE	
Good Governance	✓
Urban Management	✓
Infrastructure/Service Provision	✓
Financing and Cost Recovery	✓
Sustainability	✓
Innovation and Change	✓
Leveraging ODA	

By 1988, Shenzhen's population had increased to 800,000 and its territory expanded to 2,020 km². The 2000 census set Shenzhen's population at 7 million, despite the reduction of the territory to 1,948 km² in 1995. Current estimates set Shenzhen's population at 9 million, making the city-region one of the largest (and certainly the fastest-growing settlement) in the PRC.

The years 1979–1999 were the boom periods for Shenzhen's development, with its population increasing by 13.6% per year. People migrating to Shenzhen increased from 1,500 in 1979 to 4 million by 1999, among them some of the best trained professionals in the country, attracted by high salaries, better housing, and educational opportunities for their children. GDP per capita increased by a factor of more than 60. By 2000, Shenzhen's GDP ranked it sixth among the PRC's large and medium-sized cities. The structure of Shenzhen's GDP also changed drastically, with primary sector industries making up 1%, secondary sector 52%, and tertiary sector 46% (Shiu and Yang 2002).

Examples of Good Practices

The comprehensive and strategic planning of the Shenzhen city-region illustrates a number of good practice policies and programs: (a) locating the SEZ close to the city of Hong Kong to facilitate foreign investments, technical assistance, and access to foreign markets; (b) linking the SEZ to urban nodes in the city-region instead of isolating it and limiting the spread effects of its development; (c) placing the development of the Shenzhen city-region in the context of the whole Pearl River Delta region; and (d) shifting the transport infrastructure from a road-based to a rail-based system.

Locating Shenzhen Close to Hong Kong. The location of Shenzhen was no accident: the SEZ's proximity to Hong Kong was a key factor in its establishment. Even when the city was a British colony separated from the PRC, it obtained its water, fresh food, and human resources from Guangdong Province. Shenzhen's location made for a ready source of capital, technical assistance, and managerial expertise. In effect, the Pearl River Delta served as Hong Kong's hinterland, despite the then presence of an international border. The status of Hong Kong as an international tax free port also gave the PRC good access to trade information and foreign markets.

Shenzhen's linkages to Hong Kong, China, have passed through three stages since 1978. The first stage (1979–1987) mainly involved "cross-border" manufacturing arrangements between Hong Kong enterprises and small businesses in the Pearl River Delta. These arrangements included subcontracting of manufacturing operations in which partial production of certain goods was done by small-scale Shenzhen companies.

The second stage in Hong Kong-Pearl River Delta relations (1988–1992) focused on direct investment of Hong Kong manufacturing firms, mainly in SEZs like Shenzhen. Exorbitant land costs, high salaries and wages, expensive housing, and high rentals in Hong Kong encouraged firms to have these operations done in the mainland. During this period, Hong Kong investments made up 80–90% of foreign direct investments in the Pearl River Delta, the largest portions of which went into SEZs. As manufacturing was moved to the Delta region, the role of Hong Kong shifted to transshipment of Pearl River Delta products, facilitating opening up of foreign markets to Chinese goods, serving as a source of capital, providing high-level management and technical assistance, and easing global information and communication.

The third stage, which started in 1993, involved complete plant relocations and outward service processing for mainland goods and services. The division of labor between headquarters' functions in Hong Kong and production facilities in the Pearl River Delta became more defined. Hong Kong continued to play a dominant role in capital financing, high-level management, product design, research and development, and global marketing but the bulk of manufacturing was now done in the Pearl River Delta. A 1998 survey of 37,724 foreign enterprises in the Delta found that 82% of these were manufacturing firms and 90% of these manufacturing firms were linked to Hong Kong (by then a part of the PRC) mainly as joint ventures. Half of these joint ventures were located in the SEZs (Tuan and Ng 2002).

Chinese jurisdiction under the "one country, two systems" policy in 1997 has accelerated the integration of the Hong Kong Special Administrative Region with the Pearl River Delta. In fact, one can now view Hong Kong as a mega city with the Pearl River Delta as its hinterland. One indicator of this close relationship is the cross-border traffic through Lowu that increased from 10 million persons in 1983 to 40 million in 1994 and 86 million in 2000. Vehicles crossing the border increased from 0.7 million in 1983 to 11 million in 2000.

Sharing and Spreading the Fruits of Development. A common mistake in the setting up of SEZs is the strict isolation of these production enclaves from surrounding areas. In the Philippines, Sri Lanka, and other countries, for example, SEZs are designed to be completely separated from nearby areas. Within the SEZ, foreign investors are provided with serviced land, energy, housing, technical and professional staff, and security. Products from the SEZ cannot be sold locally and are mainly exported. Access to the SEZ is strictly controlled, the zone is surrounded by barbed wire, and armed guards control the entry and exit of people and goods.

The main effect of separating the SEZ from its hinterland is to inhibit the spread of the beneficial development in the zone. In Clark and Subic Bay in the Philippines, for example, people working in the SEZ are allowed to enter in the morning and then leave in the late afternoon. These workers have to find their own housing, which means that they often live in slum and squatter areas. The cities of Olongapo near Subic and Angeles in Clark have to provide water, sewerage, electricity, solid waste collection and disposal, and other services but they do not profit from the fruits of development in the SEZs, which mainly go to the central Government. These cities are saddled with problems created by the concentration of development in the zones, including crime, prostitution, drugs, vagrancy, and juvenile delinquency.

Early in the development of Shenzhen, the negative effects mentioned above were also felt in Baoan, Dongguan and other adjacent areas. Tens of thousands of migrant workers were attracted to the SEZ and lived in makeshift dwellings near the gates, along the railroad tracks and other vacant lands under squalid conditions. To deal with the problems, the boundaries of Shenzhen Municipality were gradually expanded so that housing and other urban services were made available to all citizens. Although the boundaries of the SEZ continued to be manned, movement of people and goods was facilitated. More importantly, by expanding the boundaries of Shenzhen Municipality, the urban authorities extended urban services to all residents.

One of the most important decisions made by Shenzhen authorities was the abolition of rural *hukou* or household registration in the municipality. By erasing the distinction between rural and urban hukou, all urban services became accessible to all residents of Shenzhen. In the past, workers in Shenzhen who did not have an urban hukou did not have access to good housing, good salaries, permanent employment, education of their children, and other benefits. Despite the fact that many of these "temporary" migrants had lived in the municipality for many years, they were still discriminated against. Making Shenzhen the first city in the PRC to be completely urban, therefore, has resulted in enhancing social sustainability in the city-region.

Integrating Shenzhen into the Pearl River Delta Region. A noteworthy aspect of the planning of Shenzhen as a city-region is its integration into the whole Pearl River Delta region. Although designed as an exclusive special economic zone, Shenzhen's linkages with its hinterland and with other urban nodes in the Delta region were carefully considered in planning for its development. The all-important link of Shenzhen with Hong Kong has already been noted. In formulating Shenzhen's transportation system, energy requirements, residential enclaves, and industrial and commercial sectors, the future relationships of the city-region with other urban nodes in the Delta were carefully worked out.

Administratively, Shenzhen is made up of six districts of which four (Yantian, Luohu, Futian, and Nanshan) are in the SEZ and two (Baoan and Longgang) are outside it. The SEZ occupies only 391 km^2, roughly one fifth of Shenzhen's total area. Checkpoints in nine cross-boundary zones used to isolate the SEZ from the rest of Shenzhen but these have become unimportant and people and goods now come in and out of the SEZ regularly. Shenzhen's CBD is in Luohu, which is the main gateway for "foot passengers" to Hong Kong. A new city center is emerging in Futian, which is the locus for government offices, community services, and commercial activities. West of the city center is Nanshan on the Shekou Peninsula, the site of high-tech industries and recreation facilities. Also in the peninsula are Shenzhen's three major seaports: Shekou, Chiwan, and Mawan. To the east of the city is Yantian, Shenzhen's major deepwater port. Immediately south of Yantian is Shatoujiao, a major residential and manufacturing center.

The comprehensive plan for Shenzhen envisions a "polycentric metropolis" that connects the SEZ to a number of urban nodes through efficient transport modes. Four fifths of Shenzhen's territory lie outside the SEZ. Most of the land in the two districts of Baoan and Longgang is still undeveloped, made up of open country and farmland. The plan seeks to develop high-density settlements in the towns of Baoan and Longgang while preserving the green spaces between those towns and the SEZ center. The Shenzhen International Airport is located in Baoan and expressways connect it not only to the SEZ but also to other parts of Guangdong Province. Longgang is being developed as an important regional center despite being located some distance from its closest urban neighbors.

The development of Shenzhen is an integral part of the Pearl River Delta Regional Plan adopted by the Guangdong provincial government in 1995. Three major strategic goals were embodied in that plan: (a) to develop the Delta region as a whole; (b) to develop an urban system with an improved rank-size distribution of different types of cities, a clear division of labor with complementary functions, and a functional and balanced distribution of transportation and communication networks; and (c) to enhance rural-urban integration (Campanella et al. 2002).

As conceived, the Delta settlement pattern is made up of three city-region clusters that form a pyramid. At the apex of the pyramid is the Guangzhou-Foshan cluster. In the southeast, about 120 km from Guangzhou is the Hong Kong-Shenzhen cluster. The third part is the Macao-Zhuhai cluster in the southwest. The three urban clusters are linked together by efficient transport systems. The clustering of development in high-density urban nodes is designed to avoid urban sprawl and encroachment of development into agricultural areas.

Shenzhen's Transport Strategy. The original transport system for Shenzhen was heavily focused on roads. Expressways connect the SEZ with Hong Kong and other urban nodes. The construction of these road networks created a huge boom in car ownership in Shenzhen. In 2003, about 60,000 new cars were licensed in Shenzhen during the first 6 months of the year alone. It is worth noting that about 320,000 cars were already operating in the city during that period.

To deal with the transport problems in Shenzhen, the city authorities proposed a shift from road-based to rail-based transport. In 1988, a light rail transit (LRT) system was proposed to be set up in the city. The scheme to link the SEZ to the international airport was approved in 1992. A complete network of 272 km—composed of six heavy rail and light rail routes, three commuter rail services, and a monorail line—was approved in 1999. By 2002, the Shenzhen municipal government endorsed a Railway Development Plan to 2010 made up of eight new extensions and four additional LRT lines, covering a total of 249 km.

Aside from the rail-based system, Shenzhen operates a bus system that had 3,495 buses in 2001. Within the SEZ, 16 bus operators provided transport services while 16 operators served Baoan and Longgang districts. Bus patronage in Shenzhen, however, has been relatively low, with each bus carrying 369 passengers each way on average per day. In Hong Kong, this average is 597 passengers. Patronage of more affordable minibuses, of which there were 3,057 in 2001, was relatively heavy because of the lower fares. In addition, people also patronized about 9,000 licensed taxis in Shenzhen (Atkins China Ltd. 2003).

In 2005, a proposal to set up a bus rapid transit (BRT) system was formulated with World Bank support. It was argued that a BRT would cost much less than a heavy rail or light rail system. Some Shenzhen officials, however, were of the opinion that a BRT system was not "modern" enough and they preferred an expanded rail-based metro system. These officials were also against another World Bank proposal to expand the use of the bicycle by providing more exclusive bicycle lanes, bicycle parking facilities, and repair shops. They viewed the bicycle as a backward technology and expressed their determination to ban the bicycle from most major streets.

Despite some problems related to its transport system, Shenzhen still leads most cities in the PRC in linking land-use control by a comprehensive transport network. The city government has officially adopted sustainable development in transport planning. The strong role of the Transport Bureau in formulating transport and land-use plans and in enforcing transport regulations is very important in Shenzhen's development. Having noted these advantages, a number of issues still need to be resolved if Shenzhen is to achieve its sustainability goals.

A serious issue is the competition among various agencies and local governments in the Pearl River Delta in setting up airports, maritime ports, and other transport facilities that cause duplication and harmful competition. The growth of private automobiles has been extremely rapid, leading to serious road congestion. The rail-based transport system is just starting and Phase I of the whole metro system is not expected to be operational until 2010. The bus system is heavily used, leading to traffic congestion. With the city government authorities strongly against the use of bicycles, this environmentally friendly mode of transport will probably not flourish in Shenzhen.

Liaodong Peninsula: Reviving Rust-belt Industries

One of the most successful efforts to achieve urban sustainability in the PRC has been the planned development of the Liaodong Peninsula. This region in the northeastern PRC is made up of 8 cities and 16 counties. Shenyang, the capital of Liaoning Province, is at the northern end of the region and the port city of Dalian at the southern tip. The peninsula is strategically located because of its proximity to the Korean peninsula and Japan.

GOOD PRACTICE	
Good Governance	✓
Urban Management	✓
Infrastructure/Service Provision	✓
Financing and Cost Recovery	
Sustainability	✓
Innovation and Change	✓
Leveraging ODA	

The Shenyang city-region's population in 1995 was 6,668,000 inhabiting 12,980 km² of territory. It is made up of five urban districts (Heping, Shenhe, Dadong, Huanggu, and Tiexi), four suburban districts (Dongling, Yuhong, Xinchengzi, and Sujiatun), and four counties with the rank of cities (Xinmin, Liaozhong, Kangping, and Faku). About 81% of the region's population was classified as urban. The city of Dalian is the second largest seaport in the PRC with an area of 13,800 km² and a population of 5.9 million. It was declared an open coastal city in 1984 and became a successful economic-technological zone soon afterward. In 2000, the Government set up the Dalian export processing zone that attracted massive investments from Hong Kong, China; Japan; Republic of Korea; Taipei,China; and the United States.

Shenyang started as a border outpost of the Chinese empire around 300 BC. It was the capital of the Manchu dynasty in 1625–1644 before the capital was moved to Beijing. In 1861, Shenyang was invaded and taken over by Russia. After Russia's defeat in the Russo-Japanese War in 1905, the region was occupied by Japan. Taking advantage of the rich deposits of coal, iron, and other mineral resources, Japan started heavy industries in the region. The PRC regained jurisdiction over the region in 1911, only to be ousted again by the Japanese in 1931. Shenyang and Dalian were liberated from Japanese control in 1945.

After the Communist victory in 1949, the PRC took over the heavy industries in the Liaodong Peninsula. During the first 5-year plan (1956–1960), Shenyang was allocated the largest amounts of investments in industrial technology, especially in coal, metallurgy, and machinery production. The movement of rural dwellers to urban areas was allowed so that by 1957, 66.4% of Shenyang's population was classified as nonagricultural. The city's territory also expanded from 116.8 km^2 in 1956 to 157.7 km^2 in 1976.

Before economic reforms in 1979, the Liaodong Peninsula economy was depressed because state-owned enterprises used outmoded machinery, inefficient processes, and backward technology. Industrialization had resulted in serious environmental problems. The most serious was lack of water, especially for industrial use. Liaoning Province drew its water from eight large reservoirs, most of which were designed to support agriculture. Industrial demand had increased so rapidly that the water earmarked for agriculture decreased significantly. Adding to the problem was the discharge of wastewater, both from industrial and domestic sources. For the six industrialized cities of Shenyang, Anshan, Fushun, Benxi, Liaoyang, and Tieling, the proportion of wastewater from industry was projected to increase from 79.7% in 2000 to 80.3% in 2010 and 84.8% in 2020. Industrial solid waste was also expected to increase from 98,823 million tons per year in 2000 to 99,940 in 2010 and 100,112 in 2020 (ESCAP 1995).

A principal reason for the difficulties in controlling environmental pollution in the Liaodong Peninsula is the lack of coordination among government agencies. There are at least eight agencies concerned with environmental issues in the region. The Land Planning and Land Management Bureau is charged with land use and urban planning. Construction activities are the responsibility of the Urban Construction Bureau. The Industry and Commerce Administration examines and approves construction projects. Other agencies whose functions are linked to the environment are the Health Bureau, charged with urban sanitation and public health; Water Conservation Bureau, which manages water resources; Agriculture Bureau, which is responsible for rural environmental management; Forestry Bureau, which protects forested areas; and Environmental Protection Bureau, which has general responsibility for controlling pollution. In theory, all these agencies are supposed to be coordinated through the Shenyang Planning Committee and the Construction Committee, but each agency exercises a great deal of autonomy and coordination depends heavily on the personality of officials. Coordination is also made difficult by the fact that most direct measures for environmental protection are carried out by officials at the district and county levels. Most district and county level officials are more interested in expanding industrial production than environmental protection, so the central and provincial agencies are often thwarted in their efforts.

Examples of Good Practices

Since 1978, the provincial and regional authorities in the Liaodong Peninsula have been pursuing policies and programs to solve the main problems in the region. Some of these policies and programs that constitute good practice are (a) taking a regional rather than a single city approach in urban development, (b) urban densification and revitalization of inner city areas, (c) conservation of agricultural areas, and (d) controlling environmental pollution.

Coordinated Regional Planning. Many earlier problems in the Liaodong Peninsula could be traced to the unplanned location of various urban functions. For example, the bulk of heavy industries such as iron and steel, vehicle manufacturing, and chemical production were located in the central districts of cities. Since state-owned enterprises were also responsible for housing, education, training, and other welfare services for their workers, intense overcrowding occurred in the inner city areas. Saddled with old and antiquated physical plants and machinery, the industries created a great deal of pollution, endangering the health and lives of inner city residents.

The first innovation made by authorities was the formulation of coordinated regional plans. In 1988, the entire peninsula was named an "open economic region." Instead of focusing attention on individual cities, the regional scheme was a network of urban centers. In the northern part of the peninsula, a plan was formulated for the so-called "middle city group." This included the larger cities of Shenyang, Fushun, and Anshan, two medium-sized cities (Liaoyang and Benxi), and four small cities (Tiering, Xinmin, Tiefa, and Haicheng). This group contained 36.6% of the population of Liaoning Province. Because of the concentration of industries in the subregion, it accounted for more than half of the provincial GDP. It also anchored the northern end of a major transportation corridor known as the Shenyang-Dalian Expressway.

In the southern end of the peninsula, development was focused on the port city of Dalian. Dalian is the PRC's second largest seaport (after Shanghai), a major industrial and shipbuilding center, a busy communication hub, and a popular tourist destination. It was declared an "open coastal city" in 1984 and soon became a successful "economic-technological development zone." Unlike Shenyang, with its aged "rust-belt" industries, Dalian concentrated on electronics, finance, textiles and garments, processing of agricultural products (especially seafood), and tourism. It has also been very successful in safeguarding its physical environment, having been awarded the "Habitat Scroll of Honor" award in 1999, and the "Global 500 in Environment" award by the United Nations Environment Programme in 2001. The Government gave Dalian the first "Outstanding Cities in Tourism Attraction" award.

Densification and Inner City Redevelopment. Shenyang was the capital of the Manchu emperors from 1625 to 1644. The Manchus later ruled all the country as the Qing Dynasty. The Shenyang Imperial Palace, a smaller version of Beijing's Forbidden City, was built in 1636. The Mukden Palace, a former Qing Dynasty palatial complex, is now listed as a United Nations Educational, Scientific and Cultural Organization World Heritage site. Several tombs of Qing emperors are found in the Huanggu District of the city. The city also has ancient temples, parks, gardens, and palatial homes of prominent officials and warlords that have been converted into museums and cultural centers.

The need to preserve some cultural heritage sites has complicated the redevelopment of the inner city of Shenyang. Also, like other old cities in the PRC, Shenyang has tens of thousands of densely inhabited communities where people have lived for centuries. To improve living conditions in these inner city communities, old and dilapidated housing structures had to be torn down. Buildings that were still in good shape were renovated at great expense. While plumbing, electricity lines, and other modern facilities were introduced, the facades of old structures were kept. People who had lived in the inner city communities for generations also resisted being moved to other places. They had to be compensated for the destruction of their old homes, and offered much better housing elsewhere.

A particularly vexing problem in Shenyang was the dismantling of old factories and associated workers' housing that used to be located in the inner city. As Shenyang modernized its rust-belt industries, the city moved the factories to the suburbs. The workers and managers were also moved out, freeing the inner city land for commercial and other purposes but requiring massive resources for alternative housing.

Before 1978, almost all families in Shenyang rented their homes from their employers or from the Housing Bureau. Housing reforms were introduced in 1988 increasing rents significantly. However, wages did not rise accordingly so most people resisted the housing reforms. Later, market housing was introduced and many families started buying their own homes.

In recent years, the housing market has become so overheated that the Government has started to worry about the inflationary effects of housing. During 2005, housing prices in major cities in the PRC rose by 10%. Shenyang recorded the highest rate of increase in housing prices, about 19.2% in the last quarter of 2005. The price of land in the city rose 10.2% by the end of the year (China Daily Online, 1 January 2006).

Despite many problems, Shenyang has been able to improve the inner city by conserving historical landmarks, providing adequate housing both in the inner city and the suburbs, removing factories and heavy industries from the inner city, and providing tourist-oriented shopping and entertainment complexes downtown. Employment and housing for former inner city residents have been provided in special development areas, such as the Shenyang Economic and Technological Development Area in Tiexi District. This area covering 126,000 km^2 has been designed as a new urban node in Shenyang with a projected population of 1 million in 10 years.

Protection and Conservation of Agricultural Areas. Heavy industrialization in the Liaodong Peninsula created uncontrolled urban sprawl. The cultivated land in Shenyang City, for example, decreased from 598,300 hectares (ha) in 1980 to 567,400 ha in 1995, a decline of some 2,060 ha per year. To counter the loss of agricultural land, the Shenyang municipal government passed strict regulations on land conversion and land use. Strict standards were set up governing the use of land. Thus, if a local government sets up an industrial estate or high-tech zone on agricultural land, actual development should occur within 1 year. If no development occurs, the land is seized and returned to crop cultivation.

Because northeastern PRC has long winters and a very short growing season, technological innovations have been applied to expand greenhouse production around Shenyang. On 1 January 2006, the Shenyang municipal government announced plans for the construction of a large garden and tourism complex on the outskirts of the city. The 5.3 km^2 complex will feature 66 gardens devoted to growing vegetables, potted plants, and flowers. The garden complex will be the site of a World Horticultural Exposition in 2006 in which hundreds of foreign producers are expected to participate. The Exposition will become permanent and will be maintained both as a food production complex and a tourism and recreation area.

Controlling Environmental Pollution. In 1988, the WHO identified Shenyang as one of the 10 most polluted cities in the world. The city burned about 11 million tons of coal a year, resulting in sulfur dioxide and particulate pollution. Hundreds of metallurgical, chemical, paper, automotive, and industrial plants simply dumped their waste into the Liao River, turning it into a dead body of water.

The Environmental Protection Bureau of Liaoning ordered the enterprises to meet pollution standards within 1 year or face closure. By 2000, 700 factories were closed. However, many of these enterprises were very small inefficient units. The larger enterprises, such as Anshan Iron and Steel that employed more than 220,000 people, could not be shut down because it would cause massive unemployment and end housing, welfare, and other benefits of the workers.

In 2003, the Shenyang municipal government allocated $181 million for an environmental cleanup in the city. More than 500 heavy industries responsible for environmental pollution were shut down. Among these were paper mills, cement factories, and steel plants. Another 300 industries were ordered to improve their technologies to make them less polluting. Heavy use of coal was curtailed and buildings were required to shift to natural gas for central heating systems. These measures succeeded in controlling pollution and Shenyang has now been taken off of the WHO list of most heavily polluted cities (China Daily Online, 31 December 2004).

To complement the Shenyang municipal government's efforts, the Liaoning provincial government adopted a number of measures to control pollution. These included (a) closing polluting enterprises, (b) relocating polluting industries from urban to suburban areas, and (c) setting up strictly enforced pollution standards. The central Government, through the State Environmental Protection Administration, pursuant to a 1996 decision of the State Council, set up emission standards to be complied with by all enterprises in accordance with a national timetable. Enterprises that failed to comply were shut down. Some cities such as Shenyang posted "countdown clocks" in a number of factories indicating how many more days were left before they must meet the pollution standards.

After a great deal of effort, Shenyang achieved considerable progress in controlling environmental pollution. By 2000, Shenyang was not only off the list of the 10 most polluted cities in the world; it also ranked 12th best in environmental quality among 47 cities in the PRC. Some measures used to achieve this progress were (a) shifting from coal to natural gas or liquefied petroleum gas for household cooking and heating, (b) prohibiting the use of coal with more than 1.5% sulfur content, (c) installing water membrane dust and sulfur removers in power plants generating electricity for the city, (d) strict enforcement of automobile emission standards by annual inspections, (e) washing coal and using "desulfurizing" additives to raw coal, and (f) treating 1.5 million tons of sewage daily.

Dalian matched its annual GDP growth of more than 12% with investments in environmental improvement. In the past, the city mainly depended on soft coal for energy. By 2004, 98% of households used piped coal gas for cooking and water heating. The city's water supply was expanded and 70% of the sewage was treated before being pumped into Bohai Gulf. Vehicle emissions were strictly controlled. Harmful emissions from enterprises were also controlled: in 1998, of 519 industries that formerly violated emission standards, 385 achieved compliance, 44 were relocated or restructured, and 90 were shut down.

More important, Dalian used region-wide planning to control environmental pollution. Strict zoning ordinances were passed, requiring polluting industries to move out of the central city. The city bought vast land tracts and turned these into parks and open spaces (about 40% of the central city area is now devoted to parks and open spaces). In 1997, Dalian was designated as one of the five Chinese "model environmental cities" along with Shenzhen, Zhuhai, Xiamen, and Shantou. The city received the highest rating among 47 cities in the country in a 1999 evaluation by the National Environment Committee that used 36 environmental criteria.

CONCLUSION

Since launching economic reforms and opening-up to the outside world in 1978, the PRC has pursued policies and programs to accelerate the rate of urbanization. After 1994, the PRC formally committed itself to achieve economic, social, and environmental sustainability. The three case studies discussed in this chapter illustrate the importance given by the PRC to sustainable development. As far as good practices are concerned, the case studies highlight the following policy interventions:

1. All three case studies show the effects and impact of the adoption of a comprehensive regional approach to planning. Aside from developing the inner city area, the regional plans include suburban nodes and areas of high density that are more or less self-contained in terms of sources of employment, residences, service centers, shopping, and entertainment. Some of these urban nodes are devoted to high-tech and industrial parks and SEZs. They are not designed as new towns or residence communities but are planned and managed as complete communities in themselves.
2. All three case studies illustrate the importance of linking the urban nodes to the central city and to each other through a comprehensive transport system. These transport systems are mainly road-based at present but there are extensive plans to use rail-based systems in the future. An important good practice is the direct linking of land-use planning with transport planning. The adoption of a hierarchical transport

system that improves mobility for people and goods and access to all types of travelers is an important intervention in all case studies.
3. Preservation of agricultural land and conservation of open spaces are key interventions in all three case studies. The planned development and management of watershed areas follows a regional approach. Urban agriculture is fast becoming an important means not only for producing food close to the city but also of using the waste of the city as an input to food production.
4. The redevelopment of inner city areas is a very important element in all three case studies. Interventions and good practices in this field include (a) provision of economic opportunities in the inner city, (b) ensuring affordable housing in inner city areas, (c) creating entertainment and commercial enclaves, (d) enhancing cultural conservation by combining it with tourism and entertainment, and (e) fostering environmental sustainability by the provision of parks and open spaces.
5. The three case studies show the importance of adopting intergovernmental political and administrative mechanisms to make metropolitan and regional governance more efficient and effective. Unified metropolitan governance is used in all case studies to coordinate the delivery of urban services, with special concentration of key urban functions that are region-wide, such as water and sewerage, transport, and solid waste disposal. Financial mechanisms are also important, illustrating how a regional approach can improve the financial viability of metropolitan governments, improve sharing of tax revenues, and bring about more equity among local governments in a metropolitan area.
6. Compared to other countries, the PRC lags behind in the use of people's participation in urban governance. Essentially, urban management in PRC cities is vested in Communist Party officials although increasingly, highly trained professional planners and managers are taking over urban management functions. Even here, however, the uniqueness of the PRC situation is quite apparent. While NGOs and community-based organizations may not be active in the PRC, many structural mechanisms elicit people's participation in decision making. At the most basic level, the neighborhood associations serve as excellent mechanisms for local decision making. They are also efficient transport channels for disseminating information on urban policies and programs. In the performance of key functions, such as maintaining cleanliness and hygiene, community beautification, control of crime and juvenile delinquency, and maintenance of local road and community facilities, these neighborhood associations work very effectively by mobilizing local human and financial resources.

6. India
OM PRAKASH MATHUR

INTRODUCTION

Urban infrastructure and services in India have historically been financed by direct budgetary support. Few, if any, of the institutions responsible for infrastructure provision have been able to generate surpluses for financing them. Faced with resource compression and growing economy-wide demands on urban infrastructure and services, important initiatives have been taken in recent years, which, on the one hand, have introduced new modes and instruments of financing infrastructure and, on the other hand, focused on creating an environment for enhancing efficiency and equity in managing urban development. This chapter provides case studies of three such initiatives. Table 6.1 provides relevant national statistics.

The first case study is concerned with the issuance of bonds by municipal governments, using the strength of the potential revenue streams. The second looks at substituting the rental basis of assessing property values by area characteristics, assumed to be closer to the market prices; and the third considers wide-ranging structural and systemic reforms, with the purpose of eliminating those impediments that have constrained the functioning of land and housing markets and the flow of private investments into urban infrastructure.

COUNTRY CONTEXT

India is a union of 28 states and seven centrally administered territories. In this Union, the functions, subjects, and powers of the center and states are laid out in the seventh schedule of the Constitution of India, in what are known as the union list, state list, and concurrent list. The functions of the central Government, laid out in the union list, are generally those required to maintain macroeconomic stability, and those assigned on grounds of the economies of scale and cost-efficient provision of public services. Currency and coinage, operation of the central bank of the country, foreign relations, international trade, defense, railways and airports, core and strategic industries,

Table 6.1: Country Urban Development Profile, India

Human Development Index rank of 177 countries (2003)^	127
GDP growth (annual %, 2004)	6.91
GNI per capita, Atlas method (current $, 2004)	620
GNI, Atlas method (current $ billion, 2004)	674.6
GDP per capita PPP ($, 2003)^	2,892
GDP PPP ($ billion, 2003)^	3,078.2
Population growth (annual 2005–2010 %) #	1.35
Population, total (million, 2005)#	1,096.92
Urban population, total (million, 2005)#	315.28
Urban population percent of total population (2005)#	29
Population largest city: Mumbai (2005, million)	18.34
Population growth: 242 capital cities or agglomerations > 750,000 inhabitants 2000#	
- Est. average growth of capital cities or urban agglomerations 2005–2015 (%)	25
- Number of capital cities or urban agglomerations with growth > 50%, 2005–2015	6
- Number of capital cities or urban agglomerations with growth > 30%, 2005–2015	67
Sanitation, % urban population with access to improved sanitation (2002)**	58
Water, % of urban population with access to improved water sources (2002)**	96
Slum population, % of urban population (2001)**	56
Slum population in urban areas (2001, million)**	158.42
Poverty, % of urban population below national poverty line (2000)**	24.7
Aid (Net ODA received; $ million, 2003)^	942.2
Aid as a share of Country Income (Net ODA/GNI, 2003 %)*	0.2
Aid per capita (current $, 2003)^	0.9

GDP = gross domestic product, GNI = gross national income, ODA = official development assistance, PPP = purchasing power parity.
Sources: See Footnote Table 3.1, World Bank (2005); OECD (2003); United Nations (2004, 2005).

and operation of the stock exchanges are some of the key functions of the central Government.

The state governments are responsible for public order, police, public health, education, agriculture, irrigation, land rights, and industries and minerals other than those that are in the central Government (union) list. The state governments also have jurisdiction over functions provided in the concurrent list; however, in the event of a conflict, the central Government has overriding powers in respect of such subjects.

The distribution of tax powers between the center and state government is based on the principle of "separation," in that the tax objects are either assigned to the center or the states. Most of the broad-based and productive taxes—comprising taxes on income and wealth from nonagricultural sources, corporation tax, excise duty on manufactured goods (excluding those on alcoholic liquors, opium, hemp, and other narcotics), and custom duty—fall within the tax powers of the central Government. Tax powers assigned to states comprise tax on sale and purchase of goods, land revenue, taxes on agricultural income, taxes on land and buildings, excise duties on alcoholic liquor, taxes on vehicles, taxes on goods and passengers carried by road or inland waterways, taxes on luxuries and entertainment, stamp duties, and taxes on trades, professions, and callings.

Recognizing that the assignment of functions and tax power could result in imbalances between revenue capacities and expenditure needs of states, and that the extent of imbalances could vary between them because of the differences in their capacities and needs, the Constitution provides for a mandatory sharing of the net proceeds from noncorporate income tax, and optional sharing of the proceeds of the union excise duty. In addition, Article 275 of the Constitution recognizes the need for grant-in-aid to the states. Intergovernmental transfers are an accepted and integral component in India's multi-tiered governmental finance.

The powers to constitute local governments, both rural local bodies and municipalities (urban local bodies), rest with the state governments. They derive their powers from the state rural local bodies and municipal acts. The Constitution does not lay down either the functions or powers of the local governments. Thus, out of the state list of subjects, state municipal acts assign such functions as public health and sanitation, and functions relating to water, land, prevention of diseases, and many others to municipalities.

Similarly, they also assign the tax powers enjoyed by them under the seventh schedule, such as taxes on land and buildings, the entry of goods into a local area for consumption, and use or sale therein to municipal governments. The entire subject falls within the state government's domain. Each state government has its own act (or acts). Thus, local government roles, responsibilities, and economic functions differ in several respects between states. One state may devolve a large number of functions and responsibilities to local governments, and may decide either to give them adequate tax powers or mete out the expenditure responsibilities via a system of transfers. Another state may opt to take a different route. The discretion and autonomy of states in determining the powers and functions of municipal bodies explain the existence of very large differences in the role that transfers play in different states.

While management of cities and towns, urban development, and provision of urban services are direct concerns and responsibilities of state governments, the central Government undertakes, from time to time, policy and program initiatives in matters that it considers important from a national perspective. The central Government provides financial aid to state-level agencies for urban poverty reduction programs, including housing for low-income urban households, as well as support for the development of urban infrastructure.

Table 6.2: Urban Population and Annual Growth Rates in India

Year	Urban Population		Growth Rate (%)	
	Total (million)	% to Total Population	Change Over Previous Decade	Average Annual
1961	78.9	18.0	26.4	2.3
1971	109.1	19.9	38.2	3.2
1981	159.5	23.3	46.1	3.8
1991	217.2	25.7	36.2	3.1
2001	285.5	27.8	31.1	2.7

Source: Census of India 2001 and earlier censuses.

Table 6.2 shows the changes and projected profile of urban and rural populations in India. In 1961, the urban population of India was 78.9 million or 18.0% of total population. By 2001, it had reached 285.5 million or 27.8% of the total population. Urban populations are predicted to rise to 550 million by 2030 or 42.0% of total population (Figure 6.1). Since 1961, the rates of growth in urban populations to the present have varied between 2.3% and 3.8% per annum. This level of urbanization is significantly lower than those in other Asian nations, such as the People's Republic of China and Indonesia. While the level of urbanization may be lower, cities in India are among the most densely populated in Asia, with Mumbai having a density of 378 persons per hectare (Angel 2005). Table 6.3 gives the population and growth rates of the 15 largest metropolitan cities in India.

Figure 6.1: Trends in Urban and Rural Population, India

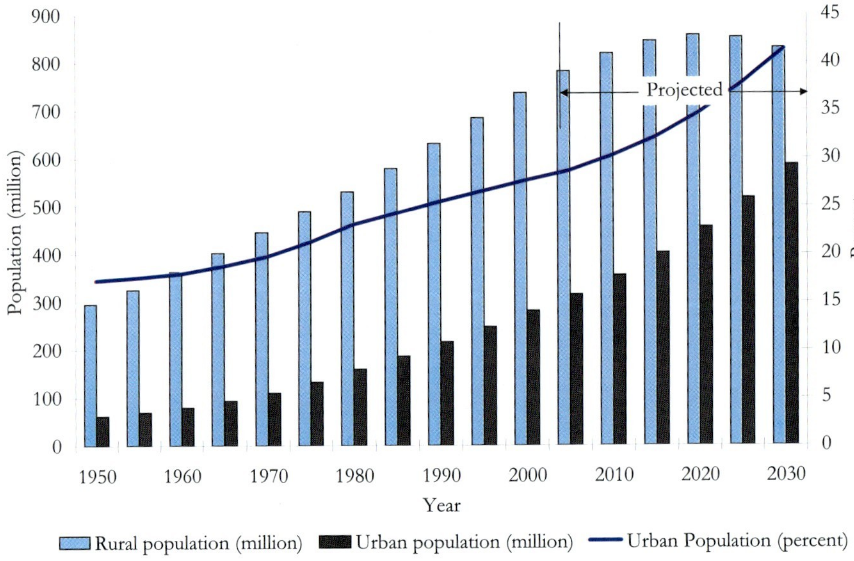

Urban growth in India, combined with rapid growth in the economy as a whole, has placed immense strain on infrastructure and services and the institutions responsible for their provision. The Census of India (2001) reported that approximately 50% of urban households did not have access to tap water at their premises, and 43% lacked toilet facilities. Land and housing markets have come under severe pressure, with the result that a substantial proportion of the urban population lives in slums and unauthorized settlements. Even with a marginal decline in urban poverty, nearly 24% of the urban population lives under conditions of absolute poverty, which is a source of serious concern. Most cities are exposed to air and water pollution, problems posed by inadequate solid and liquid waste management, large-scale use of low-grade domestic fuels, and occupation of environmentally sensitive lands.

The finances of municipal governments—the key institutions responsible for urban development and growth and development of cities and towns—are in bad condition. For reasons attributable to the narrow and inelastic tax base and its indifferent application, municipalities in India are not able to generate sufficient resources to meet even the operating and maintenance costs of services they provide. Only a few municipal administrations can apply such principles as user-pays for recovering the costs of services. Effectively, it has meant large-scale subsidization of civic services, which has increased the dependence of city administrations on the higher tiers of government.

Table 6.3: Growth Rates of Metropolitan Cities in India

State	Population 1991	Population 2001	Average Annual Growth Rate (1991–2001)
Greater Mumbai	9,925,891	11,978,450	1.9
Calcutta	4,399,819	4,572,876	0.4
Delhi	8,471,625	12,696,367	4.1
Chennai	3,841,396	4,343,645	1.2
Bangalore	3,302,296	4,301,326	2.6
Hyderabad	3,058,093	3,637,483	1.7
Ahmedabad	2,954,526	3,520,085	1.8
Pune	1,566,651	2,538,473	4.8
Surat	1,505,872	2,433,835	4.8
Kanpur	1,879,420	2,551,337	3.1
Jaipur	1,458,483	2,322,575	4.7
Lucknow	1,619,115	2,185,927	3.0
Nagpur	1,624,752	2,052,066	2.3
Patna	956,417	1,366,444	3.6
Indore	1,109,056	1,474,968	2.9
Vadodara	1,061,598	1,306,227	2.1

Source: Census of India, 1991–2001.

A recent study has estimated that financial transfers from higher tiers account for 35–50% of the total resources of city governments. Based on these characteristics, it is often contended that cities in India are unsustainable.

Given that infrastructure constraints in cities, insufficiency of urban lands and housing, and continuing fluctuations in the land market could hurt the prospect of achieving the national growth and poverty reduction targets, different tiers of government have undertaken initiatives to improve the functioning and fiscal base of municipalities. In 1992, the central Government introduced a broad-based amendment to the Constitution that aimed at providing constitutional recognition and legitimacy to municipal governments and strengthening and empowering them with new responsibilities and powers. This was followed by amendments to the Income Tax Act to allow municipalities to issue tax-free bonds for financing their infrastructure.

As late as 2005, the central Government released an urban renewal mission, which by all accounts, may be the most ambitious such intervention in urban development. Under this mission, the central Government proposes to extend grant assistance to municipalities for improving urban infrastructure and governance, requiring them to undertake structural reforms that would eliminate constraints to the land and housing market, align infrastructure prices with the cost of provision, and bring greater transparency and accountability in local decision making. Many state governments have initiated steps to shift from cash-based, single-entry to an accrual-based, double-entry accounting system to obtain a better assessment of the finances of municipalities. With limited potential for securing financial assistance from state governments, a few city governments have begun to tap into the capital market for financing urban infrastructural services. A summary of the shifts noted in recent years is illustrated in Table 6.4.

Although too few to make any sustainable impact on urban development, these initiatives signal a recognition on the part of the central, state, and municipal governments of the contribution of cities to national growth and poverty reduction objectives.

GOOD PRACTICE CASE STUDIES

The following describes three initiatives that have the potential for making the most impact on cities and urban development: (i) issuance of bonds by the Ahmedabad Municipal Corporation (AMC), an initiative to tap into the capital market, which apart from raising finances was meant to open up a new channel for infrastructure financing; (ii) property tax reform initiatives taken

Table 6.4: Local Government Finance - A Paradigm Shift

From	To
Rents to form the principal basis for estimating annual rateable value and property taxation	Area characteristics or capital valuation to form the basis for property taxation
Grant financing of local/municipal infrastructure	Debt financing of local/municipal infrastructure
Finances and functioning of municipalities based on directions of the higher tier of government	Incentive funds for municipal governments to undertake reforms for improving finances and functioning
Municipal provision of services	Public-private partnership in the provision of municipal services and infrastructure
Land treated as fixed assets	Sale of land-use rights for raising recourses
Other municipal assets held on books	Assets to be leveraged for mobilizing resources
Negotiated intergovernmental transfers	Rule or formulae based intergovernmental transfer to allow financial stability and predictability to local governments
Subsidized prices of basic municipal infrastructure and services on grounds of externality	Application of the principle of cost recovery for pricing municipal infrastructure and services

by the State Government of Andhra Pradesh, an across-the-state initiative to put property taxation on a sound footing; and (iii) a broad-based program of structural and system reforms put out by the central Government to eliminate the bottlenecks that have impeded investment in urban infrastructure and make municipalities efficient, equitable, and accountable.

Issuance of Municipal Bonds, Ahmedabad

One of the critical issues in recent years is how to finance and maintain municipal infrastructure and services. Municipal infrastructure and services have been financed out of grants and loans from the state governments. Institutional financing has also made inroads into selected municipal infrastructure. The role of municipal bodies in creating infrastructure capital has been marginal or even nonexistent, principally due to their inability to generate revenues beyond those necessary to operate and maintain such services as water supply, sewerage, roads, primary health, and street lighting. Indeed, most municipal bodies in the country have large revenue deficits, which are met out of the existing system of intergovernmental transfers.

GOOD PRACTICE	
Good Governance	✓
Urban Management	✓
Infrastructure/Service Provision	✓
Financing and Cost Recovery	✓
Sustainability	
Innovation and Change	✓
Leveraging ODA	

Figure 6.2: Map Showing Location of the Case Studies

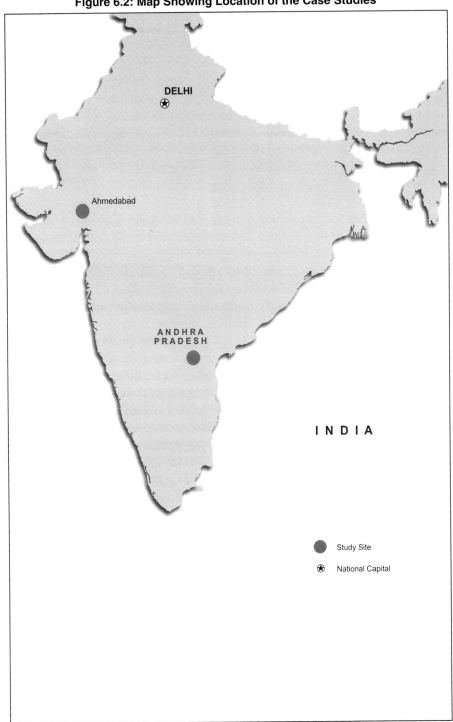

The statutory framework, which lays down the powers of municipal bodies, does not provide them with any major role in capital financing of infrastructure and services. Their borrowing powers are restricted, evidently for the reason that unlimited municipal borrowing could have serious repercussions on macroeconomic fiscal balance and stability. In most states, municipal corporations are permitted to borrow only within certain limits, which are defined in terms of a percentage of the annual rateable value (ARV) of properties or of the value of municipal physical assets. Moreover, they can borrow only with the permission of the state governments. There also exist detailed requirements for the creation of sinking funds, control on investments, and monitoring by state governments. The key point is that the municipal corporations have not made use of even these limited powers for augmenting their infrastructure and services. Debt financing of municipal infrastructure remains uncommon in Indian cities.

In 1996, AMC decided to raise a loan of Indian rupees (Rs)1,000 million ($28 million) from the market by issuing bonds. This was the first issuance of its kind in the country, and constituted an extremely important fiscal initiative on the part of a local body. This example shows a major initiative by a medium-sized municipal corporation, faced with deteriorating finances and declining levels of services, and with bleak prospects of raising loans from the traditional sources. Initially, the tax system and procedures were reformed and later the improved revenue streams were used to enter the capital market.

Located in the state of Gujarat, Ahmedabad is a large metropolis with a population of 3.5 million, growing at an annual rate of approximately 3.0–3.5%. In the post-1991 period, Ahmedabad received substantial industrial investments due to the generally progressive and forward-looking policies of the state. Ahmedabad's economic contribution to the state's GDP is substantial, and is reflected in the rapid development of its industrial base and construction activity.

Ahmedabad City is run by AMC, which was established in 1950 under the Bombay Provincial Municipal Corporation (BPMC) Act, 1949. AMC's main functions under the Act are to provide water, sewerage, solid waste management, street cleaning, street lighting, and public health. Although not obliged under the Act, AMC runs hospitals, medical colleges, and local transport. The main sources of AMC's revenues are the taxes on property and *octroi* (a tax on the entry of goods into the city) levies, which account for 80% of its total revenues. Octroi is the main tax and contributes 72–75% of the tax income. AMC can borrow in the market in accordance with the provisions of the BPMC Act, which lay down the borrowing powers and the procedure by which it can raise, deploy, and service the loans. The clarity of expression in regard to the borrowing powers and debt-servicing arrangements are a positive feature of the BPMC Act.

AMC had a sound financial base until the early 1980s. However, its financial condition started deteriorating in the late 1980s (Table 6.5); at the close of the fiscal year 1993–1994, AMC had accumulated a deficit of approximately Rs60 million (about $1.5 million) in the revenue account alone. The growth rate in the revenue yields of the two main taxes—property taxes and octroi—hardly reflected the rate at which construction and other activities were expanding in the city. The nontax component of AMC was not performing, and the administration and enforcement of municipal taxes were lax. Low levels of education, poor working conditions, and inadequate training and support of AMC's staff contributed to the deficiencies in performance.

The administrative leadership and management of AMC changed in 1994, and the new leadership was immediately confronted with a host of questions: what should be done to stem the financial deterioration? Did the problems lie in tax structures, assessment, or their administration and enforcement? What should be done to raise additional resources to meet the burgeoning financial requirements of city infrastructure? The leadership fixed for itself the following priorities:

- restore the financial balance and stability of AMC;
- build confidence in the public with respect to AMC's capacity to deliver services efficiently and equitably;
- assess the creditworthiness and risk level of AMC finances; and
- put to effective use the existing statutory provisions for mobilizing additional resources.

AMC next undertook bold measures to improve the administration and enforcement procedures with respect to property taxes and octroi, and simultaneously to project an image of the corporation as a body that was sensitive to people's needs, aspirations, and priorities. The collection of property tax

Table 6.5: Revenue Income and Expenditure of Ahmedabad Municipal Corporation (Rs million, $ million)

Year	Revenue Income	Revenue Expenditure	Cumulative Balance (– or +)
1989–90	1,354.5 ($75.2)	1,420.5 ($78.9)	–178.7
1990–91	1,486.6 ($82.6)	1,604.4 ($89.1)	–296.5
1991–92	1,746.6 ($67.7)	1,748.5 ($67.7)	–298.4
1992–93	1,988.8 ($75.9)	1,998.2 ($76.3)	–308.8
1993–94	2,197.6 ($70.9)	2,248.9 ($72.5)	–359.1

Note. The outstanding balance at the commencement of the fiscal year 1989–1990 was Rs112.8 million.

in Ahmedabad had been extremely tardy, with the collection being less than 30% of the tax demanded. A primary reason for this was lack of transparency in the valuation of ARV, which almost invariably was contested in courts, leading to delays, deferment, and reassessment. In 1994, AMC introduced a series of measures to improve property tax collection, which included

- disconnection of water supply and drainage lines on nonpayment of property tax;
- advertising names of major property tax defaulters in newspapers;
- attachment of property of major defaulters;
- restructuring and strengthening of the property tax administration;
- reorganization of the data bank on property taxes, particularly with respect to tax demand and collection from individual properties; and
- regular monitoring of tax collection.

AMC also prepared a valuation manual for the levy of octroi and a series of steps to locate and prevent leakage of funds:

- formation of vigilance squads to monitor the octroi check posts,
- creation of a data bank on the prices of goods subject to octroi levy,
- establishment of a market research wing to continually update the data bank on prices, and
- induction of professionals for checking the valuation of goods at major octroi collection points.

The impact of these measures was immediate: collection-to-demand ratio with respect to property taxes rose from 28.3% in 1993–1994 to 32.9% in 1994–1995, and in the subsequent year to 44.6%. In the aggregate, property tax revenues increased from Rs442 million ($13.4 million) in 1993–1994 to Rs800 million ($22.7 million) in 1995–1996—an increase of nearly 80% in 2 years. Revenue from octroi levies increased from Rs1,296 million ($41.3 million) in 1993–1994 to Rs2,030 million ($57.7 million) in 1995–1996. The result of the different measures, including those that covered the nontax component of AMC's revenues, was that AMC's continuing deficit in the revenue account turned into a surplus by 1994–1995 (Table 6.6). This helped restore citizens' confidence in AMC's capacity to effectively administer the local tax structure and prevent leakages and corruption.

The changed financial situation enabled AMC to undertake small capital projects of high priority to both meet people's needs and aspirations and to instill confidence among its clientele that it could deliver. However, Ahmedabad City's capital requirements were large. The new administrative leadership

Table 6.6: Revenue Income and Revenue Expenditure of the
Ahmedabad Municipal Corporation (Rs million, $ million)

Year	Revenue Income	Revenue Expenditure	Surplus/Deficit (+/−)
1993–94	2,197.6 ($70.0)	2,248.9 ($71.6)	−359.1
1994–95	2,854.6 ($90.9)	2,476.7 ($78.9)	+18.7
1995–96	3,748.1 ($106.5)	3,248.9 ($92.3)	+517.9

also needed further evidence of the fiscal strength of AMC, particularly as to whether the increase in revenues was a short-term phenomenon or sustainable.

AMC's leadership was also aware of the expansion that had taken place in the country's capital market, offering an important potential source of resources. The issue was whether, given the surpluses generated over a 2-year period and the initiatives that it had taken to reform its main revenue sources, AMC could put to use such innovative instruments as municipal bonds. India had no tradition of municipal bonds but was aware of municipal bonds as one of the most important revenue sources for municipal and local governments in the United States. Securing long-term financing like bonds, however, was essentially a function of faith in the system responsible for spending and management. Did AMC possess this faith?

A useful instrument for assessing the creditworthiness of a body corporate, such as a municipal corporation, or of a specific debt obligation is credit rating. Credit rating considers factors on the creditworthiness of the borrowing municipal government—the economic base of the city, current financial position of the city government, debt-related factors, legal and administrative issues, and project-specific issues. AMC proposed to raise Rs1,000 million ($28 million) from the capital market. It entrusted this task to CRISIL, a credit-rating agency in India, which, after detailed investigation into the finances, liabilities, and future prospects, gave an A+ rating for the issuance of a bond—meaning that there is adequate safety for the timely payment of interest and principal. This process has been of particular interest: it makes the evaluation of credit risk public, and it is also a public announcement to investors that the state government will not bear any losses on the investment.

AMC issued municipal bonds in 1997. These were general obligation bonds; for their redemption, a portion of the revenue receipts, mainly the receipts from octroi, was pledged and earmarked. AMC opened an account to ensure that the dedicated funds were set aside exclusively for paying back the bond amount. Although the public was not involved directly in decision making on the issuance of bonds, a survey conducted to ascertain the attitude of citizens revealed a high degree of willingness on their part to invest in bonds. The willingness to invest in such bonds, which were fixed obligations and could constrain local fiscal flexibility, demonstrated that the funds so raised would be invested for meeting the citizens' infrastructure priorities and needs. The bonds were oversubscribed.

The steps taken by AMC on the governance of the city were visible. The entire relationship between the Corporation and its citizens changed. The latter began to look upon the Corporation as a body that could deliver the goods and services for which it was responsible. A sense of partnership and participation among citizen groups developed. Since then, AMC has gone to the market on two additional occasions to raise funds for financing infrastructure.

Reform of Property Taxation in Andhra Pradesh

Property taxation is perhaps the most widely used source of revenue for local governments throughout the developing and developed world. It has been long favored as the principal source of revenue for local governments, mainly due to the perception that it possesses the characteristics of a benefit tax. Unlike other forms of taxation, property tax is said to be particularly suitable as a local tax because of its immobility.

GOOD PRACTICE	
Good Governance	✓
Urban Management	✓
Infrastructure/Service Provision	
Financing and Cost Recovery	✓
Sustainability	
Innovation and Change	✓
Leveraging ODA	

Property tax is used solely to raise revenues for providing municipal services and has the following advantages:

- the object of taxation, i.e., the property, is immobile, at least in the short run and, therefore, taxation of property is difficult to avoid or even shift;
- the tax provides no direct competition with other taxes that are typically imposed by the central and state governments;
- it allows the application of the benefit principle because local services are, to some extent, capitalized into property values. Property taxes are a means of allowing owners and occupants to contribute to the cost of local services;
- it is relatively stable in times of economic slowdown. Also, the effects of price movements on property taxes are minimal;
- it can be responsive to economic growth if accompanied by good property tax policy and administration; and
- it causes only minor distortions in resource allocation.

Given these theoretical and practical advantages, it is surprising that property taxes in India have not been adequately mobilized for raising resources.

Indeed, these do not form a part of the country's tax policy, nor has the reform of these taxes been considered an integral part of the ongoing tax reform process. The result is that property taxes, despite being the primary source of revenue for municipal governments, remain minor in terms of revenue yields. In 1997–1998, property taxes in India are estimated to have generated only about Rs27,640 million ($703.3 million), forming 0.18% of national GDP (Table 6.7). This share has changed little over the years, notwithstanding an extraordinarily large increase in land and property values and a dramatic increase in the share of the construction sector in the country's GDP.

Property taxes in Andhra Pradesh—the state dealt with in this case study—constitute the principal source of revenue for the municipal governments. In 1991–1992, the total yield from property taxes amounted to Rs400.7 million ($15.5 million) or 50.9% of the total internal resources generated by municipal governments. It formed 0.1% of the state's GDP. The profitability of property taxes in the state as measured in terms of yield per capita (Rs55 or $2.13) was lower than the All-India average.

Before the property tax system in Andhra Pradesh was changed in 1993, assessment of properties for tax purposes was based on ARV of land and buildings. ARV was defined as the gross annual rent at which a property may reasonably be expected to be let out from year to year. In this sense, ARV was a hypothetical or a notional rent, held as a proxy for market rent of the concerned property. In the case of rented properties, ARV was assessed on the basis of the actual rent except for those properties where a "fair rent" had been fixed under the Andhra Pradesh (Lease, Rent and Eviction) Control Act, 1960.

The Andhra Pradesh Municipalities Act of 1965, which contains procedures for levying this tax, provided for a revaluation of properties and, consequently, of tax liabilities, approximately once every 5 years. Similarly, the Act provided that ARV of properties was subject to different kinds of deductions and rebates, these being rebates to owner-occupied houses, rebates for repairs and maintenance, depreciation for the age of buildings, rebates on early payment, and vacancy remissions. Properties used for public worship, educational purposes, charitable hospitals, and buildings whose ARV was below a threshold were also exempted from payment of property taxes.

Table 6.7: Revenue Significance of Property Taxes (1997–1998)

Estimated yield from property taxes (Rs million)	27,640
Property tax yield (% of GDP)	0.18
Property tax yield (% of total tax revenues)	15.5
Property tax yield (% of total municipal revenues)	12.9
Per capita property tax yield (Rs)	105.7

Source: NIPFP. 2000. Options for Closing the Revenue Gap of Municipalities, 2000/01 to 2004/05.

The underlying considerations in granting exemptions were social justice, compensation to those properties that provided, directly or indirectly, services of merit or the public good, and high administrative cost in tax collection, particularly from low tax-yielding properties.

The property tax system in Andhra Pradesh as in other states of the country, however, was choked in each of its components and subcomponents. The method of assessing property values on the basis of ARV, i.e., rent at which a property may reasonably be expected to be let out from year to year, proved to be ad hoc, discretionary, and subject to varying interpretation. Similarly, serious problems were noted in using the "actual rents" for assessing property values because in practice actual rents were made up of a number of components (a lump-sum payment, a monthly rent, and monthly rent divided into rent for space and rent for fixtures), making assessment on that basis an extremely difficult exercise. The properties under rent control hardly yielded any tax revenue. The problem was compounded further as, notwithstanding the provision in the Andhra Pradesh Municipalities Act, only a few municipalities undertook periodic revaluation of properties, which resulted in large-scale inequities in the system, retarding the yield from property taxes. Field evidence showed that as a result, the differences between the assessed value and market value of properties widened and led to large-scale stagnation in the revenues from property taxes.

The various types of exemptions and rebates further constricted the tax base. The system of door-to-door tax collection promoted collusion between the assessor, tax collector, and taxpayer resulting in massive leakages and corruption.

Assessing the lost income due to all these infirmities of the system is difficult because (i) assessment-to-market-rent ratios were 50–60%, (ii) only about 30–35% of the total number of properties constituted the tax base, (iii) rebates were substantial, and (iv) rent control acts significantly limited ARV. The loss to the total property tax yields could be as high as 150–175% of the actual collections on this account.

The Government of Andhra Pradesh undertook to reform the property tax system, clearly with the objective of better tapping this source of revenue and eliminating the deficiencies of the system. Significantly, the initiative for the reform emanated from the chief political executive of the state, who found the entire system inefficient, stagnant, discretionary, and administratively loose.

The key to the reform process lay, at the outset, in identifying a method of assessment that would best reflect the value of a property. Three main methods of valuation—rental value, capital value, and site area—are generally used in different parts of the world. The issue was which of the three would yield better results? For the state, the issue was: Should the existing method of using a "hypothetical rent," or "actual rent," or "fair rent" be continued for assessing the value of a property? Or, should it be jettisoned in favor of using the capital value? Or should it be done on some other basis, such as the site or area valuation using characteristics of the site/area? The primary concern of the government was that the preferred method should be such that

- it is able to incorporate into assessment of property taxation the principles of equity, objectivity, fairness, and simplicity;
- property taxes are uniform with respect to buildings similarly situated;
- the new system is able to "de-link" the operation of the Rent Control Act from the assessment of property tax and reduce the discretion of the assessor and avoid arbitrariness in assessment;
- it is able to make tax administration efficient, transparent, and effective in the levy of property tax; and
- it will improve buoyancy in property tax revenues.

The state government considered their feasibility in the light of (i) political acceptance, (ii) compatibility with the legal framework, and (iii) the revenue-generating goals. The choice was made in favor of the site/area-based system under which ARV of properties could be fixed with reference to the characteristics of the area, using indicators such as location, type of construction, plinth area, age of the building, and nature of use. The area-based method constitutes the most important initiative taken in the country in recent times to eliminate the arbitrariness from which the system of estimating ARV has historically suffered. The approach is effectively a formula for property valuation, where a property is defined by a vector of six attributes:

$V = f$ (plinth area, land area, location, type of construction, type of use, age)

where f is a linear combination of these attributes.

The Government of Andhra Pradesh adopted this method because, prima facie, it seemed to possess such advantages as objectivity in assessment, procedural simplicity, standardized methodology, and better clientele appreciation and cooperation.

The new method of property assessment involved several interconnected steps:

- division of the city into convenient, contiguous, and largely homogeneous areas/zones, based on three factors: (a) availability of services, (b) nature of construction of properties, and (c) the nature of use of properties;

- a sample survey of 20% of all properties in each zone to determine the prevalent rental values and to fix the rental ranges for each zone/area;
- issuance of a draft public notification showing the division of the city into zones and the rental ranges, for inviting objections from the public: it marked a significant departure from the earlier practices when no such consultations were considered essential; and
- issuance of a final notification giving the maximum and minimum rental values for each zone/area.

The reform process also included decisions with respect to the rebates and exemptions, and tax payment procedures. Considering that the process had to be gradual, issues pertaining to rebates and exemptions were left untouched, meaning that the rebates extended earlier on account of owner-occupancy, age of the building, and repairs continued in the new system. Similarly, exemptions were not only maintained but their scope was expanded to cover owner-occupied residential buildings whose property tax burden was below a threshold level. Also, the increase in property taxes was capped so as not to exceed 75–100% of the previous tax level.

The new system incorporated two other innovative features. The first related to the procedure for property tax payment. Unlike in the past, where a door-to-door collection was prevalent, the new system brought the banking sector into the local tax system. As an incentive to the banking sector, arrangements were made with the banks so they could retain and use—for limited periods—the property tax deposits. A second feature of the new system was the introduction of an incentive grant wherein municipal bodies were given fixed amounts ranging between Rs1.5 million and Rs4.0 million (about $50,000–130,000 in 1993) if they were able to raise tax collection efficiency to 85% of tax demanded.

Several municipal bodies passed resolutions to adopt the new system and set up committees to suggest strategies for putting it into practice. Other municipal bodies communicated extensively with taxpayers about the new system, which came into effect on 1 April 1993. As a result, property tax yields have risen dramatically in a number of municipalities, often registering an increase of over 20–25% annually.

The National Urban Renewal Mission

On 28 February 2005, the central government announced the launch of the National Urban Renewal Mission (NURM), with a proposed outlay of Rs500 billion ($11.5 billion), arguing that India was faced with the challenge of urbanization that had to be met by providing "urban facilities of satisfactory standards." NURM aims to respond directly to the myriad problems that cities and towns in India had faced in recent decades. The urban transition—even in early stages—has not been accompanied by a corresponding increase in the supply of basic urban services, such as water supply, sewerage and drainage network, garbage disposal facilities, city-wide roads, public safety systems, and pedestrian pathways. Nor has the

GOOD PRACTICE	
Good Governance	
Urban Management	
Infrastructure/Service Provision	
Financing and Cost Recovery	✓
Sustainability	
Innovation and Change	✓
Leveraging ODA	

supply of land and housing kept pace with the increase in urban population. The result of this unbalanced growth is a familiar one: households without services, slums, and widespread poverty.

Until the end of the 1980s, the approach to responding to such problems centered on programs and projects that aimed at providing support for infrastructure development in small- and medium-sized cities, environmental improvement of urban slums, and basic services for the urban poor. Almost the entire direction of such support was based on the perception that the nature of urban infrastructure and services—characterized as they were with externalities—was such that it needed public policy interventions; it was claimed that only the public sector had the wherewithal to bridge the gap between the demand for and supply of urban services of communities that could not afford them. Such interventions proved to be limited in impact and inadequate to deal with the scale of the problem. The project-based approach ignored the importance of sustainable delivery of services.

Following the country's transition toward a market-based economy and the spirit of decentralization embodied in the Constitution (74th) Amendment Act, 1992, the urban sector in India has begun to change. There is a growing recognition that statutes concerned with urban development need to be reviewed and changed because they do not permit expansion of the land and housing markets. It is evident that the Urban Land (Ceilings and Regulation) Act, 1976, and rent control laws are major impediments to the development of land and property markets, and constitute a deterrent to economic growth. Similarly, the pricing system of urban services requires major overhauling because services, when sold below cost, cannot be sustained. The premise that subsidies are essential for the poor to access services has proved to be wrong, with a greater part of the subsidies leaking out to the better-off households, and the poor having to rely on poor quality, high-cost services.

NURM has grown out of the above factors and a serious examination and appraisal of experiences of past efforts for improving service delivery and management. The objective of NURM is to encourage city governments to initiate measures to improve the existing service levels in a financially sustainable manner. The Mission believes that to make cities work as well as contribute substantially to India's economic growth, it is essential to create incentives and support for urban reforms both at the state and city levels, develop appropriate enabling and regulatory frameworks, enhance the creditworthiness of urban local bodies, and incorporate the poor in the service delivery systems.

The Mission encourages states/cities to undertake fiscal, financial, and institutional changes required to create efficient and equitable urban centers. It intends to free land and housing markets from the constraints of age-old statutes, adjust infrastructure tariffs and prices to the cost of service provision in conjunction with local tax reform to meet the cost of joint services, and introduce accountability and responsiveness in municipal governments. NURM seeks to make fuller use of the energy and initiative of the private sector in implementing its reform agenda. It rests on the premise that sustainable improvements can take place only when investments are accompanied by wide-ranging statutory, institutional, and pricing reforms. The Mission entitles 63 cities to receive financial aid from the central Government for infrastructure projects and to simultaneously initiate the process of reforms.

KEY LESSONS

The first two case studies—the issuance of bonds by AMC and property tax reform in Andhra Pradesh—provide the following interesting propositions and insights into the connections between fiscal innovations and governance.

(i) A simple and transparent tax system has a greater possibility of securing citizens' acceptance and of being sustained, even if it entails a higher tax burden. The Andhra Pradesh initiative with respect to property tax reform suggests that, notwithstanding the general reluctance on the part of municipal councils to increase the tax burden on their constituencies, a system that is (a) simple and comprehensible; (b) standardized and designed to eliminate discretion in estimating ARVs or the property tax burden; and (c) transparent in that the tax rate ranges are known to the taxpayers, will be widely acceptable.

(ii) Efficient administration and enforcement of tax systems are crucial for securing public support on issues, such as raising resources in the market and pledging revenue streams for redemption of loans. The Ahmedabad case on the issuance of bonds shows that efficient administration and enforcement of a tax system, development of a data bank that updates information on the market prices of goods subject to tax levies, and taking steps to prevent leakages and corruption are necessary to restore the confidence of the citizens and tax-payers in the functioning of a local body. Public cooperation and good governance cannot be expected to follow in the absence of an efficient and equitable tax administration.

(iii) Public sharing of credit-rating information is important for building alliances and partnerships with the nongovernment sector and other interest groups. The credit rating of a corporate body like AMC has shown that it is an extremely useful instrument not only for determining the creditworthiness and risk-taking capacity of a local body, but for demonstrating to the citizens where the potentials lie, what potential is currently being tapped or not tapped, and the financial strengths and weaknesses of the local body.

(iv) Commitment and leadership are critical for initiating changes in the local fiscal arrangements. In Andhra Pradesh, initiative for change in the property tax system emerged from the highest political executive of the state who found the earlier system discriminatory and constraining in terms of its revenue-generating capacity. He opted for a system that was simple, open, and nondiscriminatory.

NURM is a testimony to the fact that sustainable urban development is a complex activity and a function of several factors related to statutory, institutional, fiscal, and pricing spheres. For India—currently in the throes of an urban transition in which its urban population base is poised to add more than 250 million persons during 2005–2030—the impediments to sustainable growth should be identified and adequately addressed, not by taking up isolated projects but by effecting structural and systemic improvements.

SUSTAINING URBAN DEVELOPMENT

India faces an enormous challenge in having to meet the requirements of a large and growing urban population base. The two initiatives discussed in this chapter— the issuance of municipal bonds and reform of property taxation—demonstrate how city governments can improve their revenue base and utilize the nascent but growing capital market for infrastructure financing. NURM aims to eliminate the numerous impediments that have blocked investments in cities and city-based infrastructure. The long-term task, however, lies in coming to grips with the urban phenomenon as it is likely to develop in the face of open borders and external influences. How to absorb them, ensuring that their gains are spread equitably among the different civil society groups, is the challenge that needs to be recognized.

7. Indonesia
WICAKSONO SAROSA

INTRODUCTION

Indonesia is the most populous country in Southeast Asia. From the 1970s until the mid-1990s, the country experienced a period of rapid economic development and urban growth. However, the 1997 Asian financial crisis had a major impact on the economy, and a period of civil and regional unrest followed shortly thereafter. These events led to pressure for greater democratization and decentralization. The national Government has introduced a series of laws since 1999 to begin a rapid multifaceted process that is dramatically changing the way the country is governed. Relevant statistics on the development of Indonesia are presented in Table 7.1.

This chapter examines trends and issues related to urbanization in Indonesia prior to and following decentralization. Three case studies are presented: balanced development in Tarakan, East Kalimantan; management of rapid urbanization and good governance in Sleman, the Special Region of Yogyakarta; and combining long-term goals with short-term improvement in Jembrana, Bali. Lessons from the case studies and strategies to improve approaches to sustainable urbanization are presented in the final part of the chapter.

COUNTRY CONTEXT

Indonesia is a 5,000 kilometer (km) long archipelago of more than 17,600 islands.[1] This sprawling country had a population of around 225 million in 2005, the fourth most populous country in the world. The population is culturally very diverse with over 300 local languages.[2] Interestingly, the remarkable diversity of this huge nation has become the *raison d'être* for two opposing approaches to governing the country: the heavily centralized system of government during the first 4 decades after independence, under the presidencies of Sukarno and Suharto (who thought the diverse nation needed a strong unifying national government), as well as the much more decentralized system of government in contemporary Indonesia, which is based on the notion that empowered local governments can understand better the various aspirations of their

Table 7.1: Country Development Profile, Indonesia

Human Development Index rank of 177 countries (2003)^	110
GDP growth (annual %, 2004)	5.13
GNI per capita, Atlas method (current $, 2004)	1,140
GNI, Atlas method (current $ billion, 2004)	248.0
GDP per capita PPP ($, 2003)^	3,361
GDP PPP ($ billion, 2003)^	721.5
Population growth (annual, 2005-2010, %)#	1.13
Population, total (million, 2005)#	225.31
Urban population, total (million, 2005)#	107.88
Urban population, % of total population (2005)#	48
Population of Largest City: Jakarta (million, 2005)	13.19
Population growth: 30 capital cities or agglomerations > 750,000 inhabitants 2000#	
- Est. average growth of capital cities or urban agglomerations 2005–2015 (%)	29
- Number of capital cities or urban agglomerations with growth >50%, 2005–2015	0
- Number of capital cities or urban agglomerations with growth > 30%, 2005–2015	15
Sanitation, % urban population with access to improved sanitation (2002)**	71
Water, % of urban population with access to improved water sources (2002)**	89
Slum population, % of urban population (2001)**	23
Slum population in urban areas (million, 2001)**	20.88
Poverty, % of urban population below national poverty line (2001)**	n.a.
Aid (Net ODA received; $ million, 2003)	1,743.5
Aid as share of country income (Net ODA/GNI, 2003 %)	0.9
Aid per capita (current $, 2003)	8.10

GDP = gross domestic product, GNI = gross national income, ODA = official development assistance, PPP = purchasing power parity.
Sources: See Footnote Table 3.1, World Bank (2005); OECD (2003); United Nations (2004, 2005).

people. While debates over centralized versus decentralized systems of government in Indonesia have been around since its independence in 1945, the current shift encompasses more than the substance of the original debate and is much more wide-ranging, embracing various aspects of governance (Vickers 2005).

Indonesia is undergoing four major transformations: decentralization; a drastic progression toward democratization of the political and governance system; rapid urbanization; and, perhaps least apparent, the privatization of various socioeconomic activities. Although these transformations are not independent of each other,[3] it is remarkable that such radical processes are occurring almost simultaneously. Despite the resulting problems, there are promising indications that such changes—especially those of decentralization and democratization—will provide stronger and more sustainable bases for the development of Indonesia as a whole. Several examples of good practices in local governance have arisen as a result of these transformations, of which three are presented in this chapter.

In the late 1990s, Indonesia embarked on the process of the so-called "big-bang"[4] decentralization (World Bank 2003) and subsequent democratization, after decades of a very centralized and, to some extent, authoritarian government. The aim of decentralization was to move public decision-making processes closer to the people most affected by those decisions. Similarly, but not in spatial terms, the democratization process aimed to provide civil society with a greater role in developing and governing the country while at the same time improving the "checks and balances" mechanisms in the country's governance system. After decades of debate and delay in implementing decentralization and democratization, the Government eventually hurriedly adopted the concepts following instances of regional unrest, as well as the emergence of widespread demands from civil society for radical political reforms. In particular, the 1997 financial crisis—followed by economic as well as political crises, including the downfall of the New Order regime in 1998—was the initial trigger for sweeping governance reforms in Indonesia.

Decentralization was initiated through the enactment of Law 22/1999 on Local Governance (which has been amended by Law 32/2004) and Law 25/1999 on Fiscal Balance between National and Local Governments (which has been amended by Law 33/2004). The law on local governance (known as the decentralization law) transfers a large number of the Government's obligatory functions from the national Government to local governments, leaving only matters related to national defense and security, foreign affairs, the judicial system, fiscal and monetary affairs, macro-economic planning, judicial system, standardization, and a few others as the prerogative of the national Government. Additionally, the accompanying fiscal decentralization law (the law on fiscal balance) aims to provide the necessary financial resources for local governments to carry out their newly expanded responsibilities. Along with the transfer of functions and financial resources, the decentralization drive also included the reassignment of 2.3 million staff from 4,000 departmental offices and the assets of 20,000 public facilities to local governments, all implemented in 1 year (Turner et al. 2003). While many related problems remain unresolved, this drastic drive to decentralize conducted within a very short period of political and economic volatility, has been applauded by the international community and various domestic stakeholders.

Concurrent with decentralization, democratization was initiated through various amendments to the country's Constitution and related laws, which fundamentally reorganized the governing structure; reformed state institutions; introduced direct elections for the heads of national, provincial, and district governments; simplified the formation of political parties (while at the same time increasing the political parties' roles in channeling the people's aspirations); and many other changes. On the surface, democratization was articulated by the increase of civil society's participation—quantitatively as well as qualitatively—in governance. This was essentially an acknowledgment of the ownership by the people of public processes, in contrast to the previous paradigm where the processes were seen as owned by government, with possible participation by the people.

Indonesia's decentralization and democratization efforts have been so dramatic that they effectively changed the way the country is governed at all levels. New institutions were created and old ones terminated. Numerous existing laws and by-laws currently require modification, amendment, or even replacement, some of them urgently. Government officials and stakeholders at all levels need to learn what their roles are in the new system of development and governance. Members of civil society have become more vocal about their role in the development processes. Members of civil society have established various urban forums to provide an additional vehicle for participation in development. Even private enterprises—domestic as well as international—find themselves needing to adjust to the new environment, not only in the form of more transparent ways of doing business or working with local governments more than ever before but also in responding to the increasing demand to assume corporate social responsibilities.

Rapid urbanization in Indonesia is compounding the pressures identified above. The proportion of people living in urban areas is predicted to exceed 50% by 2010 and to reach 60% by 2025. Most city governments—and also *kabupaten* (county) governments that cover a significant proportion of urbanized areas—have been overwhelmed by the ever-increasing demand for urban services, infrastructure, housing and facilities, and employment. The urban informal sector, within which most rural-to-urban migrants find refuge, has become ubiquitous in Indonesian urban landscapes but has not been seriously or strategically addressed by many city governments (ILO URDI 2005, UNDP URDI 2004). The urbanization trend and attendant consequences have intensified debates over balancing rural-urban development and other related issues, discussed below.

The private sector—which has practically recovered from the late 1990s crisis—has taken an increasing role in development, including in areas traditionally handled by the Government. Privately developed, large housing complexes or even new towns around such metropolitan areas as Jakarta and Surabaya have become more common—to some extent contributing to the creation of urban sprawl. Private enterprises (including foreign ones) have also undertaken to provide public services, such as water supply, waste processing management, and toll roads.

Private enterprise has demonstrated that it is more efficient and client-oriented than government agencies. However, such (formal) private sector-led development cannot be expected to always resonate with the needs of the urban poor, which by 1999 constituted about 40% of the Indonesian urban population (World Bank 2003). This is especially so if Government (national or local) cannot create the necessary conditions for (formal) private sector involvement. While privatization indeed provides solutions to some urban problems, it is certainly not a panacea. Private developers, for example, have not been able to provide affordable housing for the poor in the inner city areas where land prices are high.[5] As a result, most of the urban poor are given a choice of either residing in inner-city informal settlements or in low-cost housing areas located far from the city center.

Privatization is becoming an attractive option in Indonesia to provide basic infrastructure and public services because national and local government's economic and financial resources are limited. Public finance capacity is relatively lower now than during the 3 decades prior to the 1997 financial crisis. This is partly because of slower economic growth (from more than 7% to less than 6% annually), increasing debt service obligation, increasing domestic demand for public services from the growing and increasingly more demanding population, greater sharing of resources with local governments, and diminishing utilizable natural resources. Further, there are increasing calls for the government to reduce its dependency on loans to fill budget gaps and instead pay for necessary development.

In addition to these complex transformations, Indonesia has witnessed three presidential successions in 6 years. The successful first direct presidential election in 2004, which brought in the current administration of President Susilo Bambang Yodhoyono, is expected to provide some stability to the country. The years to come may not be as volatile as the past several years, but the multidimensional metamorphosis of this diverse nation is far from complete.

URBANIZATION ISSUES

Sustainability of Urban Population Growth

During the period of relatively rapid economic growth in the 3 decades prior to the 1997 financial crisis, and also in the recent years of economic recovery, Indonesia experienced accelerated urbanization.

Figure 7.1 shows that, until 1980 or thereabouts, the urban and rural populations increased in unison. Thereafter, growth in the rural population began to fall. Indonesia is at the point where rural and urban populations are about equal. Urban population is expected to exceed 65% by 2030 (United Nations Secretariat 2002). The implication of these demographic changes is

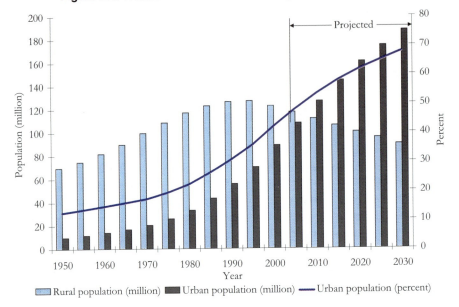

Figure 7.1: Trends in Urban and Rural Population, Indonesia

that urban population will increase by 70% from 108 million at present to 187 million over the next 25 years. In excess of 5,000 square kilometers (km²) of mainly productive farmland is likely to be converted into urban use during this period.

A key factor in rapid urbanization is the concentration of industrialization and economic growth in some major urban areas, while employment in rural areas has become less attractive to the younger members of the population. Urban migration—especially to the national capital, Jakarta—started in the 1950s and 1960s after unrest broke out in parts of the country.[6] Even after the rebellions subsided, however, the streams of people moving to urban centers continued through the 1990s, primarily because of rapid industrialization in a small number of urban centers. In the 1990s, the urban population grew at a rate of 4.4% per year, while the national population growth rate over the same period was 1.7% per year (World Bank 2003).

Cities and towns have been expanding through conversion and subdivision of nonurban areas on the periphery of major cities and along the main roads. However, it is clearly visible to anyone traveling on roads between major cities that the conversion of land tends to be disorderly rather than carefully planned. Industrial factories built on what used to be ricefields are very common along the major roads, although better planned industrial estates do exist in some metropolitan regions, such as Jakarta, Surabaya, and Makassar. Moreover, much of the land conversion is based on speculative rather than calculated considerations (Firman 1997). Such a phenomenon has occurred despite the fact that most districts in Indonesia have spatial plans that should direct physical development better.[7] Urban service improvement and urban infrastructure development generally lagged behind the ever-increasing demand brought about by the urbanization processes outlined above. As discussed below, the Government has become much more resolute about addressing such land-use practices and urban infrastructure issues. However, concrete results of specific policies remain to be seen, while many other urbanization-related issues linger.

Critical issues related to urbanization include the dire need for urban employment opportunities (including more attractive conditions for private investment as well as more appropriate and strategic treatment of the urban informal economy); adequate urban infrastructure and services (including energy, water supply, and waste management); affordable decent housing and settlements (especially for the urban poor); urban poverty and slum improvement; affordable land for urban development; security of tenure; land-use planning and development control; financing for urban development; urban economic development; urban environment regulation (including air, water, and soil pollution); safety; and many other issues (including those specific to women, youth, and the disabled) that city governments need to address internally.

From a more regional perspective, critical issues include those around rural-urban linkages—different issues faced by metropolitan areas, secondary cities, small towns, and urban fringe areas. Another key concern is the lack of balance in development between rural and urban areas and also nationally, where development has been concentrated in the Java-Bali region. Even within this large region, development has been concentrated in the Jabodetabek (Jakarta-Bogor-Depok-Tangerang-Bekasi) metropolitan area, which had a population in 2000 of more than 13.2 million people, encompassing the total population of the five cities, but excluding three kabupaten in the metropolitan region with significant urban areas. While population concentration cannot always be equated with development, Table 7.2 below helps illustrate the unevenness of urban development in Indonesia, represented by the fact that 5 out of the 12 largest cities in Indonesia are in the Jabodetabek metropolitan region.

It is important to note that in the Indonesian context, urbanization cannot be represented solely by cities (*kota*). At the district level, there are two types of administrative unit: kota or city and kabupaten, which is probably equivalent to a county in the United States. Both administrative units are autonomous under the decentralization policy. Kabupaten are not necessarily entirely rural. Often, significant urbanized areas are within kabupaten—as represented by Sleman in this chapter.

Table 7.2: 12 Largest Cities in Indonesia[8]

No	City	Population in 2000 (rounded figures)	Average Growth 1990–2000 (%)
1	Jakarta*	8,347,000	0.17
2	Surabaya	2,600,000	1.75
3	Bandung	2,136,000	3.48
4	Medan	1,904,000	1.17
5	Bekasi**	1,638,000	5.19
6	Palembang	1,452,000	2.45
7	Semarang	1,351,000	1.67
8	Tangerang**	1,312,000	4.29
9	Depok***	1,143,000	2.03
10	Makassar	1,113,000	1.64
11	Malang	757,000	not available
12	Bogor**	751,000	1.47

Notes:
* The Special Capital City (DKI) of Jakarta actually consists of five municipalities and one sparsely populated kabupaten, Thousand Islands.
** The cities of Bekasi, Tangerang, and Bogor do not cover the kabupaten of Bekasi, Tangerang, and Bogor, which are separate districts with the same names.
***Formerly part of Kabupaten Bogor, Depok but is now a separate city (and, unlike Bogor, Tangerang or Bekasi, there is no such thing as Kabupaten Depok).

There is also what the urban geographer Terry McGee[9] calls the *desakota* phenomenon (a complex mix of urban and rural physical as well as sociocultural conditions but that may not necessarily be a transitory stage of urbanization) that usually but not necessarily occurs along major regional roads and in the urban fringe areas. The poverty mapping study conducted in 1999 (PODES) calculated that the number of villages with desakota characteristics increased from around 10.9% in 1980 to 18.0% in 1999 (SMERU 2005). It is believed that the trend is continuing. Such a phenomenon is especially common in the densely populated islands of Java and Bali (McGee 1989). The Indonesian urbanization "pattern" is further obscured by the existence of circular migration, by which rural people move temporarily but regularly to urban areas while waiting for harvest time. Most circular migrants live in affordable rented shelters in urban slums and prefer to send remittances to their villages rather than help improve the physical conditions of the areas where they live in the cities.

Poverty[10]

One of the main factors contributing to poverty in Indonesia is the disparity of regional income and investment, which is heavily biased toward the larger urban regions and regions endowed with natural resources. The gross domestic product (GDP) per capita in 2003 ranged from $7,666 in Jakarta to $863 in

East Nusa Tenggara. Urban poverty is becoming a significant issue as more people migrate to the cities in search of employment.

In the context of addressing urban and rural poverty, the current administration under President Susilo Bambang Yudhoyono, has completed a draft poverty reduction strategy (PRS) *Strategi Pengentasan Kemiskinan*. The strategy outlines various poverty-target programs. It is part of the *Rencana Pembangunan Jangka Menengah* and is a government strategy and action plan that aims to attain the goals and objectives of poverty reduction over the 5-year period 2004–2009.

The strategy acknowledges poverty as a multidimensional problem. It is not just a problem of inadequate income but also embraces the deprivation of human dignity encompassing a lack of voice, power, and choices. It is characterized by poor health; lack of basic education and skills; insecurity; inadequate access to land and other assets; and vulnerability to economic shocks, natural disasters, social conflicts, and other risks. To address the multidimensional nature of poverty, the policies and programs outlined in the national PRS use a rights-based approach, defining poverty as the nonfulfillment of certain basic rights. The rights-based approach also emphasizes the state's responsibility (executive and legislative branches at all levels, and other state institutions, including the army and the police) to strive for the progressive realization of basic rights of the poor. It provides a framework for the prioritization of limited resources, at the same time making the fulfillment of these basic rights the Government's overriding priority.[11]

The national poverty reduction strategy provides a clear framework for the Government, the private sector, the general public, and other stakeholders to build a national movement for poverty reduction. The strategy's aim is to strengthen the commitment of all stakeholders to address the underlying causes of poverty, to build a consensus to support the rights-based approach, and to strengthen Indonesia's commitment to meet the Millennium Development Goals.

National Regional Development and Decentralization Policies

The central Government still plays a major role in monitoring and evaluating the decentralization process. A significant problem that has emerged recently is the increased number of district and provincial units to be monitored since decentralization. Provincial government units have risen from 26 prior to decentralization to 33, and the number of district/municipal governments, from 290 in 2000 to 440.

Unbalanced urban development poses serious problems in a vast country with a diverse population like Indonesia. It is widely understood that an urban primacy— with Jabodetabek region as a dominant urban center—emerged as the result of a heavily centralized governance system in the decades prior to the introduction of the decentralization laws. The current decentralized system of governance has, therefore, been expected to spread development more widely around the sprawling archipelago. The process will certainly be long and gradual. Cities in provinces with rich natural resources, such as East Kalimantan, South Sumatra, and Riau, have been relatively quick in seizing the opportunity provided by the decentralization laws, giving them many more financial resources (especially from revenue-sharing of natural resources utilization) than ever in the past. Other cities have to rely on whatever resources or advantages they have—relatively good infrastructure, a better-educated population, or others—to support their development and improve the welfare of their people. But many cities (and kabupaten) greatly need external support to cope with the various challenges, at least in the beginning of decentralization. Fiscal transfers alone—discussed below—cannot be expected to help reduce uneven urban development.

It is with such a background that a national urban development strategy is needed in addition to the decentralization laws. Indonesia initially issued the National Urban Development Strategy (NUDS) in 1985, which was then followed by the implementation of the Integrated Urban Infrastructure Development Strategy as a means to help stimulate planned and nationwide urban development through integrated infrastructure improvement. However, it became apparent that these national policies, strategies, and programs alone could not cope with the rapidity and dynamics of urbanization. Ownership of such efforts needs to be actively shared with appropriate local governments. It is, therefore, plausible to expect that decentralization will help increase awareness among local governments of the need for better urban strategies.

However, decentralization also has its own challenge with regard to developing a more coherent urban strategy. In their "euphoria" for having more powers of their own, many city governments have found it difficult to work in cooperation with their neighboring local governments. The capital city of Jakarta, for example, has been facing the challenging issue of finding suitable places to serve as the final dumping ground for its solid waste. In this regard, what Kabupaten Sleman has done with the "Kartamantul" joint secretariat (to be described later in this chapter) can be seen as a good example of intergovernmental cooperation in the decentralization era.

Since NUDS was formulated long before the introduction of the decentralization policy, it has been seen as pertinent to have a new and more contemporary one. Efforts have been made in that direction, the most recent being the introduction of the Ministerial Decree of Public Works[12] No. 494/PRT/M/2005 on the Policy and Strategy for National Urban Development

(KSNPP – *Kebijakan dan Strategy Nasional Pengembangan Perkotaan*), which, among other things, puts forward the following three main policies and their corresponding strategies:

> **Policy 1:** To clarify and strengthen the roles and functions of cities in national development, for which the following strategies are recommended: (i) development of national urban infrastructure and facilities to support national, regional, and local economic development; (ii) development of cities as centers for urban services as well as collection and distribution of goods within the related regions; (iii) support for cities with significant national or international roles; (iv) support for cities with special characteristics (such as fast-growing cities, cities near international borders, cities within special international cooperation regions, and underdeveloped cities); and (v) formulation of the necessary guidelines for city governments.
>
> **Policy 2:** To develop livable, prosperous, culturally rich and socially just settlements, for which the following strategies are proposed: (i) development of basic urban infrastructure that is socially just; (ii) development of livable and affordable housing and settlements; (iii) improvement in financing mechanisms and provision of land for participatory housing development; (iv) development of globally competitive urban economies; and (v) creation of socially and culturally conducive urban living.
>
> **Policy 3:** To strengthen the institutional capacity and human resources in urban management, for which the following strategies have been suggested: (i) human resource and institutional capacity building at the national, provincial, and local levels; (ii) improvement in the mechanisms to involve stakeholders; and (iii) creation of an urban information system at the national, provincial, and local levels.

The ministerial decree also outlines the vision of national urban development: "the creation of urban areas that are safe, livable, socially just, prosperous, culturally rich, productive, and progressive in sustainable ways through participatory, responsive, transparent, and accountable processes that involve all stakeholders."

To further bolster the central Government's role in managing urban development, the Directorate General of Spatial Planning of the Ministry of Public Works recently announced the creation of technical implementation units (UPT – *Unit Pelaksana Teknis*) in all provinces—except Jakarta—to assist local governments closely in dealing with spatial planning and land-use management (including development control and law enforcement). To provide a stronger legal basis for land-use management, the central Government is working on a draft law on spatial planning. This law is expected to be passed by Parliament before the end of 2006.

As for the decentralization policy, as mentioned earlier, Law 22/1999 on Local Governance was amended by Law 32/2004. While the basic concept of transferring a wide-range set of government functions to provincial as well as local governments remains intact, the latter law was deemed necessary to clarify the earlier law, especially on the roles of provinces (which principally perform dual roles: the "deconcentration" function as the representatives of the central Government in their particular regions and the decentralized function as autonomous regions), and specific responsibilities of the local governments.

The new decentralization law also attempts to rectify what were seen as fallacies, such as the statement of nonhierarchical relationship between provinces and districts, which was thought to be an obstacle to necessary regional cooperation. The new law was also intended to correspond better with the democratization process. For example, while Law 22/1999 still stated that district heads (mayors and *bupatis*—the heads of kabupaten) were elected by their respective local councils, the new Law 32/2004 dictates that the heads of districts are to be directly elected by the citizens.

By devolving almost all government functions, except those related to national defense and security, foreign affairs, the judicial system, fiscal and monetary affairs, macroeconomic planning, standardization, and a few others, it is expected that the development processes will be much closer to the people and their aspirations will be better heard by the decision makers. In some districts, decentralization goes even further than required under Law 32/2004 by transferring some of the Government's functions from the district to the lower levels of governments (*kecamatan*, *kelurahan* or villages) along with block grants to enable the transfer of functions to proceed effectively.

With regard to the relationship between urbanization and decentralization, it is important to note that both Law 32/2004 on Local Governance and the accompanying Law 33/2004 on Fiscal Balance between National and Local Governments do not differentiate between districts with an administrative status of *kota* (cities) and those of kabupaten. There has not yet been any in-depth study on the impact of such an approach, but it is widely understood that urban areas (both in the cities as well as in kabupaten) demand more infrastructure and services as a consequence of population concentration and corresponding socioeconomic and other characteristics.

The rapid growth in the number of district and provincial government units mentioned previously, which occurred in just 4 years, has caused problems in their financing, monitoring, and evaluation. It has led to reduced per capita allocation of national grants and transfers to established local governments. Larger urban governments have been affected most. The national shortage of public sector administrative skills is affecting the performance of local governments, especially in remote urban centers in eastern Indonesia. These remote urban centers have weak health, education, and community facilities, making it extremely difficult to attract professionals away from larger urban centers. This is a significant challenge in endeavoring to improve the efficiency and effectiveness of local government.

Regional Economic Governance and Intergovernmental Financial Relations

As stated earlier, Law 25/1999 on Fiscal Balance between the National and Local Governments was amended by Law 33/2004. This amendment essentially conforms to the amendment of the decentralization law. In general, it is intended to provide the financial resources for local governments to undertake their new responsibilities. Under the fiscal decentralization law, local government revenue consists of fiscal transfer from central Government to local governments, local governments' own revenue, and other revenues. The main mode of fiscal transfer is known as the General Allocation Fund (DAU – *Dana Alokasi Umum*), which comes from the national Government budget, amounting to at least 25% of the central Government's revenue after tax and distributed as block grants to all provincial and local governments according to a transparent formula. Another and much smaller mode of fiscal transfer is Special Purpose Transfers (DAK – *Dana Alokasi Khusus*), which also comes from the national Government budget for its predetermined purposes (such as for environmental protection). In addition to these two modes of fiscal transfer, local governments also receive revenue sharing of taxes (property taxes, property transfer taxes, income taxes) and revenues from the utilization of natural resources (forestry, general mining, fisheries, and oil and gas, including geothermal energy).

Local governments' own revenue consists of local taxes, local charges, profits from local government-owned enterprises, and other sources (such as sales of assets, bank interest, and grants). In their efforts to enhance their own revenues, many local governments introduced new local taxes during decentralization. However, the business community has tended to see such taxes as economic disincentives, jeopardizing longer-term, local economic development. In response, the central Government has attempted to regulate local taxes. Local governments can also borrow money from the central Government, other local governments, banks, nonbank financial institutions, and the general population (through local government bonds) to support their budget, but this is subject to central Government regulations and limitations.

Some studies (World Bank 2003) have indicated that with all these fiscal transfers and arrangements, local governments still find it difficult to carry out their new as well as old responsibilities, especially to provide basic services and infrastructure to their citizens. Much of the block grants is spent for routine expenditure, including government operational costs, building maintenance, and salaries of civil servants. The number of civil servants has increased because of the transfer of school teachers and medical doctors previously funded by central Government. City governments have been facing much greater challenges than their counterparts in less urbanized kabupaten due to: (i) higher demand for urban services and infrastructure as the results of rapid urbanization; and (ii) the need to encourage increasingly competitive industrialization and information economies.

Local governments are not allowed to borrow money directly from foreign sources except through a "two-step mechanism," in which they borrow from the central Government, which borrows from foreign sources. The local governments bear all costs, including cost of foreign exchange risk, a condition that deters most local governments (except for those few considered credit worthy). All of the above exemplifies the challenges facing local governments, especially city governments, in Indonesia in their efforts to develop their economies in more sustainable ways.

Infrastructure

The lack of infrastructure, especially roads, has hampered efforts to develop and diversify local economies and attract new private and foreign investments to regions outside Java. The central Government's approach to the development of infrastructure divides Indonesia into three zones: the developed regions of Java, located in the western part of Indonesia; the developing regions (e.g., Sumatra, Sulawesi, and Bali); and the newly developing regions (e.g., Papua) in the eastern part of the country. The difference between the three zones is that the developing regions are seen by the development sector to have low investment attractiveness due to the geography, the narrowness of the resource base, ethnic problems, logistics, and high servicing costs. These are significant barriers to regional development that must be overcome if the current disparities in investment, poverty, and income are to be reduced.

Indonesia has one of the lowest investment levels in infrastructure as a proportion of GDP, especially that of private participation in infrastructure development (Infrastructure Summit 2005). Since the early 1990s, expenditure on infrastructure as a proportion of GDP has continued to decline. Infrastructure investment in 1993–1994 was 5.3% of GDP. By 2001, it had fallen to 2.3%, but has subsequently risen to about 3% of GDP.

In all sectors there are significant infrastructure deficiencies. Only 39% of urban areas are serviced by reticulated water supplies; road density levels are 1.6 km per 1,000 people; electricity consumption is just 319 kilowatt-hours (kWh) per capita, with 45% of households not connected to electricity; only 3% of urban areas are served with fixed-line telephones, with only 27 lines per 1,000 people (Coordinating Minister of Economic Affairs 2005). It is not only the lack of services that is a problem; the quality of services is poor, maintenance is minimal, there is a lack of equity and transparency in tariff policies, there is a biased and inconsistent regulatory framework, and there is limited infrastructure-funding capacity.

The Asian financial crisis slowed down the construction of infrastructure and had a serious impact on the country's economic development. At the beginning of the crisis in mid-1997, many infrastructure projects were postponed or scaled back under a presidential decree *Keputusan Presiden* 39/1997. In an attempt to address the rapid decline in infrastructure investment, the Government issued regulations, such as Keputusan Presiden[13] 7/1998 and Keputusan Presiden 81/2001, in an attempt to accelerate the development of new infrastructure projects, albeit with limited success. Demand for infrastructure still far outpaces the ability of the public and private sectors to meet supply.

There are also significant problems with asset management and valuation. Many city governments have no idea of the value of private or public sector assets under their jurisdiction. Under decentralization, over 20 thousand public facilities have been transferred from the central to the regional government. The inventory and valuation records for these assets are poor. Subsequently, most cities own a large pool of public assets, or dead capital (De Soto 2000), that are generating limited or no returns. These are assets that are not taxed or used for public and private sector investment and revenue generation. Many regional governments find themselves in the position of being asset-rich and cash-poor. They need capacity building to manage their assets better and to reduce the dependency on debt financing, especially to fund salaries.

Several organizations are involved in overseeing improved management and financing of infrastructure. Public Private Infrastructure Advisory Facilities[14] is a World Bank agency that assists local governments improve their ability to involve and partner with formal, small-scale, water providers in urban areas. This activity aims to establish a quantitative and qualitative framework to assess the financial, technical, and organizational performance of regional water utilities in Indonesia on urban water service delivery. There is also the *Komite Kebijakan Percepatan Pembangunan Infrastruktur* (KKPPI – Committee on Policies for the Acceleration of Infrastructure Development), an interdepartmental agency established through *Keputusan Presiden* 81/2001, with the aim to foster, synchronize, and oversee infrastructure development in the country.

The Role of International Aid in Supporting Regional Development

Understanding that successful decentralization is crucial for Indonesia, many international agencies and their Indonesian Government counterparts have, since 2001, undertaken supporting programs to enhance local governments' performance, in the following areas: (i) role and functions of local councils, (ii) supervisory mechanism between levels of government, (iii) public service delivery at the local level, (iv) local development planning, (v) local public finance, (vi) local economic development and employment promotion policies, (vii) local government organizational development, (viii) human resources development, (ix) interregional cooperation, and (x) other types of support.[15] Some projects involve activities covering more than one category.

The partners in these international aid-supported capacity-building projects are not limited to local/city governments, but also provincial governments and even the national departments/agencies (which can be in the form of capacity building for national government officials to perform their new roles in the decentralized government system, or in the form of a nationwide project to support local governments or communities carried out by national government departments/agencies). Some programs/projects involve direct assistance to urban poor communities, such as in the World Bank's Urban Poverty Program, the Asian Development Bank's Neighborhood Upgrading and Shelter Sector Project, and UN HABITAT's Slum Upgrading Facility.

The types of international support include technical assistance, program loans (involving financing for specific local support programs), and investment loans (involving financing for specific local infrastructure or other development projects). Large projects, such as ADB's Community Empowerment and Local Government Support Project and the World Bank's Urban Sector Development Reform Project and Initiatives for Local Government Reform, involve loans and additional technical assistance. This involves providing support to local government reform prior to, during, and after their commitment to loans in the areas of participation, transparency, accountability, sustainability, and other principles of good governance—which are seen as measures to improve the effectiveness of the loans.

ADB's Sustainable Capacity Building for Decentralization can be seen as an innovative and comprehensive approach to support the improvement of local capacity. It provides more local-based capacity building, including local-based training providers than was the case in the top-down design of many previous local capacity-building programs implemented by national and international training institutions. The activities are no longer limited to conducting conventional training or dispatching traditional in-house experts (to work out the reform from within the local government agencies and on some occasions perform "gap-filling" work), but involve various other capacity-building exercises.

An inventory study of initiatives for strengthening local government capacity in Indonesia indicates that the majority of the capacity-building assistance is still concentrated in provinces with large populations on Java and Sumatra, which in absolute terms have a larger number of poor people than do the other islands. However, there are capacity-building programs in the islands of Kalimantan, Sulawesi, Bali, Nusa Tenggara, Maluku, and Papua. In fact, there are programs specifically for one or more of these regions, such as the German Agency for Technical Cooperation (GTZ) recently concluded Promis-NT, which focused on community-based poverty reduction in the Nusa Tenggara islands.

GOOD PRACTICE CASE STUDIES

Clearly, there is considerable need for local capacity building in order for local governments and other stakeholders to carry out their new responsibilities. While arguing that local governments and other local stakeholders need capacity building to make decentralization successful, the central Government also needs further structural reforms to make decentralization successful. Such reforms may not be in the form of "conventional capacity building"—central government officials and organizations now tend to have "overcapacity"—but more in the form of streamlining the organizations and developing better understanding and skills for their new roles as a consequence of the transfer of many obligatory functions to local governments.

Despite these problems, a number of good practices in local development offer the promise for a more sustainable development in Indonesia than provided under the centralized system. The following sections summarize case studies on the island-city of Tarakan in East Kalimantan Province, the regency of Sleman in the Special Region of Yogyakarta, and the Regency of Jembrana in Bali Province.

The three cases were selected from a number of examples of good local development practices in Indonesia after decentralization. Others include the city of Blitar in East Java Province (especially in its community economic empowerment policy), the city of Medan in North Sumatra Province (and its acknowledgement of the importance of the informal economy), the city of Mataram in Lombok Province (and its participatory development planning and budgeting), the city of Balikpapan in East Kalimantan Province (and its comprehensive local poverty reduction efforts), and the Kabupaten of Kebumen

Figure 7.2: Map Showing Location of the Case Studies

in Central Java (and its transparency and participation in local governance). The three selected cases stood out because the innovations in the three districts are not limited to one or two particular sectors or parts of the district, but balanced across sectors—a factor considered to be a prerequisite for sustainable local development.

Note that only one of the three cases bears an administrative status of a city (Tarakan), while the other two are kabupaten. However, Sleman is very urbanized because it provides space to most of the overspill from adjacent Yogyakarta, the special region's capital. The kabupaten of Jembrana, with the town of Negara as its administration center, is on a major regional road connecting Bali and Java islands. As stated earlier, rural-to-urban land-use conversion is particularly common along main roads connecting major urban centers.

Balanced Development in Tarakan, East Kalimantan

Tarakan is a 251-km² island-city in East Kalimantan with a population in 2004 of 155,000 people. Traditionally, Tarakan has been a trading center and a stopover or transit place for travelers in the East Kalimantan–Sulawesi–Sabah area.[16] During the Dutch occupation, Tarakan was one of the oil exploration centers, attracting many people to live there.

GOOD PRACTICE	
Good Governance	✓
Urban Management	✓
Infrastructure/Service Provision	✓
Financing and Cost Recovery	✓
Sustainability	✓
Innovation and Change	✓
Leveraging ODA	

However, the oil sector now only contributes around 6% ($7.7 million[17]) of the total annual Tarakan economy (around $120 million) (Panolih 2003, p. 458).

Nevertheless, the city maintains its role as a trading center for fishery and forest products and domestic goods. While Tarakan can be considered rich compared to the average district in Indonesia, its economy is the smallest among districts in resource-rich East Kalimantan Province.

After Law No. 22/1999 took effect in 2001, and under the strong leadership of Mayor Yusuf Serang Kasim (first elected in 1999 then reelected in 2004), Tarakan has undergone significant changes, especially in the areas of good governance, urban management, financing, and cost recovery as well as environmental sustainability. The innovations and changes have led to a development approach in which economic growth is balanced with environmental protection and social development.

Prior to the introduction of various initiatives, Tarakan was faced with

- A rapid population growth at 7.19% annually from 1999–2004, largely as the result of in-migration from other areas;

- threats to the environment from rapid population and economic growth, in particular the chronic problems of flooding and landslides;
- problems with energy supply, with the monopolistic state power company failing to provide an adequate supply of electricity, thereby discouraging potential investors;
- lack of infrastructure and facilities in general; and
- lack of local government financial reserves, especially to anticipate unprecedented expenses, such as unexpected natural disasters.

In general, Tarakan's administrative status as a town under a kabupaten in East Kalimantan prior to decentralization provides a partial explanation for the "backwardness" in its physical development and in the development of its human resources amid the rapid growth of its economy and population. This overall situation was the background against which Mayor Yusuf had to make the best out of Law 22/1999 and 25/1999 by launching various local initiatives.

To guide the development of the newly autonomous island-city, Mayor Yusuf outlined five main missions: (i) provide good public services, (ii) create a more conducive environment for Tarakan to become a regional trading center, (iii) improve people's welfare on the basis of fairness and justice, (iv) develop a healthy and sustainable city, and (v) cultivate a "civilized" or "cultured" local society. In addition, the new local administration also established the so-called "three pillars" of Tarakan development: (i) human resource development, (ii) rule of law and law enforcement, and (iii) economic development in the broadest sense (not only economic growth but also the development of its people's welfare (Kasim 2005). The island city-state of Singapore was considered by the mayor as an appropriate model and source of inspiration for Tarakan. Interviews with the mayor revealed that Singapore provided inspiration not only because it is similarly an island-city but also because it has been able to provide good services to the people, and educate its citizens on how to live in a densely populated urban environment as well as create a livable and green urban environment. All these references were made with a full understanding that Tarakan is much smaller than Singapore in most respects.

In its drive for development, Tarakan also applied Law No. 23/1997 on Environmental Conservation and Management, which calls for integrated efforts to manage and conserve the environment through development involving all stakeholders (Kasim 2005). For this reason, the local government and the local people have rejected an investment proposal to exploit coal in the island despite potentially generating annually around $1.2 million to the local government, on the basis that such exploitation could damage the environment. The city is eager to invite private investors as long as the investment projects do not harm the environment.

Conservation of the Environment

Besides making environmental considerations a part of every major decision-making process, Tarakan has also achieved something more visible in terms of protecting the natural environment. Adjacent to the island's ever-expanding commercial center, in which new stores, hotels, and offices constructed in the last few years are an indication of economic vitality, there is a natural mangrove forest that is set to remain untouched by economic growth. When the idea of protecting the mangrove forest first surfaced in Tarakan's early years as an autonomous administration unit, a large proportion of the mangrove forest had already gone to provide space for the physical development of the city. It was almost too late, but the decision saved the remainder of the mangrove forest.

It is remarkable for many visitors to the island city to see a relatively dense mangrove forest, which is the habitat for a number of Kalimantan's endangered proboscis monkeys (*Nasalis larvatus*), and which also provides a breeding place for marine life and birds. To increase the people's awareness of the great value of their natural environment, the Tarakan government constructed a limited number of boardwalks for local residents and visitors to enable them to walk through the forest. The number of entrants to the reserve is limited at any given time in order not to disturb the local forest habitat.

The protection of a mangrove forest is only a small part of the city's efforts to look after the environment while, at the same time, promoting economic development. The city's Local Agenda 21 clearly shows Tarakan's strategy toward sustainable local development. Also, the city has attempted to maintain the island's biodiversity, especially by identifying, protecting, and, where possible, cultivating endangered plant species. The city administration is determined to increase the amount of forested land on the island by at least 150%, and to increase the people's awareness on the importance of environmental protection, especially the younger generation, through information dissemination in public schools and other venues. The city also passed a local regulation banning the trade of mangrove wood and other protected species.

Development of Human and Social Capital

Serious attention to human resource development is also apparent. While most resource-rich districts in East Kalimantan Province spend their newly and substantially enlarged budgets on lavish government buildings and facilities as well as other (often extravagant) physical projects, Tarakan has instead spent its modestly enlarged budget on improvements in education and health facilities. The mayor continues to work in an unassuming office and lives in a modest official residence, at least by resource-rich East Kalimantan standards.

The local government of Tarakan has not only improved the physical facilities of public schools (elementary, middle, and high schools) and built a campus for a local university—which includes a seven-story library and education information center—but has also attempted to improve the welfare and caliber of the teachers as well as the quality of the curriculum. The local university invites education experts not only from Jakarta and other centers of education in the country but also from Malaysia, Philippines, and the United States (Santosa 2003). It has already introduced full-day schools while most Indonesian schools only have half-day teaching sessions. An incidental consequence of this is the provision of healthy lunches for the students. It has also introduced more experimental or active learning exercises for students in an Indonesian education system that is still dominated by conventional methods of teaching, where teachers speak and students listen or take notes. Relatively more classes are taught in English to equip Tarakan's younger generation to face an increasingly globalized world. Overall, the city administration now allocates approximately 30% of its annual budget to education.

Interviews with the mayor also suggest that the city administration is fully aware that education is not limited to classrooms, schools, or campuses. The city also pays serious attention to improving public facilities, such as community centers, public parks, and sport centers. While local sport clubs are admittedly still playing in lower divisions of a few sport leagues in the country, the city administration proudly offers facilities that meet international standards. Moreover, the mayor believes that community centers, public parks, and sports facilities—still a rarity in the Indonesian urban landscape in general—are a good investment for strengthening social and communal bonds among the citizens. Strong social capital is indeed one of the bases for sustainable development.

These serious considerations of environmental as well as social aspects of local development top the administration's continued efforts to develop the local economy and improve its people's welfare. Investment procedures have been eased, as long as new investments do not create significant negative environmental impacts. Traditional economic facilities, such as public markets, fishports and harbors, and local roads are continually being improved. Regular visitors to the island can see rapid economic growth through the physical changes taking place with the addition of new hotels, stores, and shopping centers.

Institutional Reform

The city administration is also attempting to address the issue of energy. It believes the lack of energy supply in the city is not only due to bad management and inadequate technology used by the national energy company, but also because of shifts in people's attitude to consumption, which tends to be wasteful because energy is relatively cheap. The local government has issued a policy to increase local electricity basic rates and endeavor to change people's attitudes about the consumption of energy. The additional income gained from these pricing measures is used to improve the energy supply on the island so that economic development is not hindered through shortages.

Managed Migration

The progress made in Tarakan has attracted migrants to work and live there. As a part of a unified country, Tarakan certainly cannot stop such a population flow. To control the in-migration and mitigate its negative impact, the city administration has introduced tough population regulations, requiring new settlers to have permanent jobs within 6 months of their arrival or be asked to return home using the cash deposit required of new entrants who request residential permits. Similarly, strict law enforcement is also applied to maintain the cleanliness and orderliness of the city. In initiating and implementing this population management approach, Tarakan learned from a similar approach by the city of Balikpapan—an example that shows that such a transfer of experience, knowledge, and expertise does occur among autonomous local governments.

Innovation and Change

Importantly, the innovative changes in Tarakan are mostly initiated locally, with the mayor taking a dominant role and with minimum external support from the central Government or aid donor agencies. In personal conversations, the mayor acknowledged that external support might be needed to further foster the progress that has been made mostly through internal resources. The seven-story library and education information center in the new campus of Borneo University, for example, urgently needs to be filled with current books and other sources of knowledge, for which the local government needs support. However, the mayor also believes in being self-sufficient as much as possible. To strengthen the long-term financial capacity of Takaran, the local government has, since 2001, set aside approximately 10% of its budget for future reserves, which also functions as an emergency budget.

The brief description of developments in Tarakan above provides some evidence that the decentralization policy has created many opportunities for local governments to improve their services to the people, while also making local development more balanced. However, in the case of Tarakan (as well as in the following two cases), there is clearly a very strong dependency on strong, local one-person leadership. From a sustainability viewpoint, this dependency on one-person leadership certainly cannot be seen as sustainable. Yet, learning from the history of development worldwide, there is often a need for such a strong leadership in the early stages of development. If a charismatic leader is able to nurture future leaders, then progress can be continued.

Managing Rapid Urbanization in Sleman, the Special Region of Yogyakarta[18]

Sleman Regency abuts Yogyakarta in southern Java. It has an area of about 575 km² with a total population in 2003 of 850,000 people. Some parts of the local government area have become urbanized as a result of the rapid expansion of Yogyakarta urban region. The agriculture sector still contributes approximately 19% to the district's total economy (Giannie 2003).

GOOD PRACTICE	
Good Governance	✓
Urban Management	✓
Infrastructure/Service Provision	✓
Financing and Cost Recovery	✓
Sustainability	✓
Innovation and Change	✓
Leveraging ODA	✓

Sleman is acknowledged as having one of the most progressive local governments in Indonesia. It has achieved a number of awards in recognition of its focus on achieving excellence in good governance, economic development, and financial management. Several urban development good practices were adopted by the local government that have significantly contributed to sustainability, as discussed in the following sections.

Center of Learning

Sleman is unique, in that it not only houses one of the largest and finest universities in Indonesia—Gajah Mada University—but also is the home of no less than 35 other large and small universities. This makes Sleman, rather than Yogyakarta, more deserving of the title of Indonesia's "City of Education." Sleman has become an education cluster that has enabled it to develop a degree of competitiveness and specialization in knowledge and learning not found elsewhere in Indonesia.

The university campuses and their activities naturally attract economic development through multiplier effects—private dormitories or rented rooms for students, restaurants, photocopy service centers, bookstores, and various other retail outlets and facilities. Four subdistricts within the regency directly adjacent to Yogyakarta are already fully urbanized, predominantly but not exclusively with education-related facilities (Giannie 2003). The educational level of Sleman residents can be assumed to be relatively high compared to those in the average district in the country. This certainly poses another challenge for the regency government, as the citizens tend to be more rationally critical. This has provided an impetus for various good governance measures to be introduced.

Good Governance

Sleman is acknowledged in Indonesia as a leader in good governance. The district has adopted good practice administrative procedures under its *bupati* (mayor) for the past 5 years. The Government, assisted by the USAID's performance-based budgeting training program, has adopted asset- and accrual-based accounting and valued the entire region's public assets. The asset appraisal process took some time to complete because the location of many utility services was not known, the result of poor plan record keeping. In 2003, it took the initiative to prepare and present publicly an annual financial report. An independent professional audit of this report was conducted to ensure that it complied with national accountancy standards. The audited financial report is considered a very important instrument in the operation of corporate governance. The report meets a number of objectives as follows:

- a manifestation of public accountability and transparency – of how far the Regent and the local government have carried out their respective authorities;
- an internal performance evaluation – to determine how well the government institutions of Sleman have implemented policies based on the regency's political documents and regulations issued by the higher governments;
- an analytical instrument –- enabling other parties outside the local government to participate in local economics and investment considerations;
- a managerial controlling instrument – to determine the level of achievement of the central management in implementing the local political decisions and operational policies; and

- a regional planning instrument – that considers all aspects of strengths, weaknesses, threats, and opportunities.

These five aspects are contained in Sleman's financial report that comprises the regency's balance sheet report on the regency's revenues and expenditures, report on the regency's cash flow, and other related explanations.

Sleman became the first district in the country to report the summary of its annual budget and its implementation publicly through local newspapers. Although the same practices have been implemented by some other district governments, many other local governments are still content to report only to the local councils. Council finances are reported by journalists in newspapers, but the balance sheets are not reported. Sleman and a few other districts are pioneering transparency, which is demanded by a local population that is increasingly better informed and educated about matters of local government. Such a climate not only elicits a positive reception from the population but has also been seen as improving the environment for private investment. In various appraisals of investment opportunities among districts in Indonesia by independent bodies, Sleman has always performed well, although it is not necessarily the highest on the list.

Urban Management

Urban problems have become apparent for the kabupaten administration. Because most urban problems, such as transportation, waste, drainage, and water supply, are shared with two other districts, the city of Yogyakarta and the Regency of Bantul, Sleman has taken a leadership role in developing stronger and more institutionalized cooperation with the two districts to cope with inter-district urban problems. The three districts have established a joint secretariat "Kartamantul" (from the names Yogyakarta, Sleman, and Bantul), which has successfully dealt with the problems of solid waste collection and processing, wastewater management, public transportation management, and many other issues. While it was somewhat dormant in the years prior to decentralization, this entirely local initiative now provides the local governments with greater opportunity to deal with their own problems. More recently, it has obtained external support from development partners, in particular the GTZ Urban Quality program.

The above activities show that Sleman approaches sustainable local development through two main strategies: externally though leadership in cooperation with adjacent districts to solve common problems, and internally by implementing principles of good governance, such as transparency, participation, efficiency, and effectiveness.

The district has undertaken extensive mapping of social, environmental, and economic resources under a project known as AAA. This project has involved assistance from the Swiss Government to establish a geographic information system, linked to cadastral maps prepared for the region. The district has used the maps to analyze complex information and undertake detailed planning, monitoring, and evaluation of environmental impacts resulting from development. It has also shared information and has collaborated on projects with other districts in the province.

Investment in Strategic Infrastructure

Sleman has invested in building infrastructure and facilities, such as the Kebonagung-Kaliprogo bridge, roads, a sports and recreation center with road access, regional government office building, modeling school, Tambakboyo dam for water conservation and recreation, and Gamping market, and relocating the informal sector *(Pedagang Kaki Lima/PKL)* center. These investments have been important in developing a clean and efficient physical environment.

Sleman has been able to build unique strategic infrastructure to give it a competitive advantage over other regions in Indonesia in tourism, education, and specialized food industries. The large number of education establishments in the municipality has led to an informal industry cluster that the district is seeking to develop by encouraging international universities to establish campuses in the district. There is a growing synergy emerging between businesses, leading to an increased interest in development, innovation, and new small business activities. The extension of these networks into wider regional and global networks is considered important to the long-term development of the economy.

The district has invested extensively in the education of staff and government agencies, which have developed a high level of competency and expertise in addressing a wide range of development problems. The district has also focused on developing international linkages to identify opportunities for leveraging resources and cost-sharing arrangements. It has developed a high level of community consultation, which commands trust and respect from the community.

Community Improvement Program, Jembrana, Bali

With an annual budget of about $1.1 million (2004), Jembrana is the poorest regency in the Bali Province. Covering a land area of approximately 84,180 km^2, the regency had a population in 2003 of 222,000 people. It remains rural in nature although it is located along the main road connecting Bali's capital city of Denpasar and the harbor city of Gilimanuk, which functions as the island's gateway to the adjacent island of Java. Some urban activities exist along the main road, but are not very notable except in and around the town of Negara, the district's capital. While the kabupaten has beautiful beaches and other potential tourism features, tourism has not played

GOOD PRACTICE	
Good Governance	✓
Urban Management	
Infrastructure/Service Provision	
Financing and Cost Recovery	✓
Sustainability	✓
Innovation and Change	✓
Leveraging ODA	

a significant role in the lives of its people, unlike in the other parts of Bali.

Strategic Planning

The district administration sees the main issue as not only improving agricultural production, but more fundamentally eradicating poverty and developing local human resources. In 2001, the proportion of poor people was 19.4%, but it is widely believed that many people live only slightly above the poverty line, making them vulnerable to economic upheavals. Human resource development in Jembrana has been hindered by poor education and health facilities. In such circumstances, it is difficult to develop the local economy in sustainable ways. This situation has molded the strategy taken by the district's administration under the leadership of I Gede Winasa (2000–2005 and 2005–2010) as the *bupati* (regent).[19] Regent Winasa applies a business management approach to the problems that he and his staff face, especially by introducing efficiency and effectiveness in the government and related works (Winasa 2005).

Urban Management

With a limited budget, ways had to be found to finance poverty eradication and human resource development. The local government structure has been streamlined by merging some local agencies (*dinas*). The use of government assets has been evaluated to take full advantage of them. A "one-roof" government service has been introduced to modernize the bureaucracy for various civil undertakings and economic investment and to create some savings in the government budget.

Learning Community

The drive for efficiency also includes rationalization in the number of public schools. Some public schools had few students, making them inefficient, while at the same time giving the students poor quality education. Closing down some of these schools and transferring the students to nearby schools has reduced the operating budget for schools. This created an opportunity for improvement in the remaining schools, including increasing teachers' salaries as well as teaching quality. The kabupaten has initiated a pilot project of full-day "special schools," which are aimed at introducing more active learning without lessening traditional student discipline; two such schools have been established in Jembrana.

As poor as the regency is, Jembrana has provided free education for students in public schools. It also provides scholarships for students from low-income families to attend private schools. Free education and scholarships have increased school attendance in Jembrana quite significantly (Prasojo et al. 2004). Interestingly, the funding for such long-term investment also comes from the efficiency efforts within the local government budget. One indication that such a measure is effective is that in recent years Jembrana students have performed much better on the average than those from other districts in Bali Province in most recent national tests, even achieving best performances on occasion.

Health Audit

In the health sector, efficiency has been improved by evaluating the various components of health cost. One innovation has been the reduction in the costs of drugs without reducing the quality of services. Instead, the savings from unnecessary drug expenses have been used for improving the quality of health services, including the provision of health insurance for all Jembrana citizens.

While the above education and health improvement measures are aimed at long-term development goals, measures to support the livelihood of the people on a short-term basis have also been taken. These measures include revolving funds for fishers and farmers through a community approach to ensure that the money indeed revolves. Community monitoring tends to be more effective than government monitoring because community groups are fully aware that if the money does not revolve, some members will not receive financing for their working capital. The Government then complements such tough measures with capacity building so that the borrowing farmers and fishers will not default on their credit.

KEY LESSONS LEARNED

Indonesia has taken up the opportunity provided by the late 1990s crisis to build a more sustainable basis for development through democratization and decentralization and, to some extent, privatization. The ensuing strengthening of local governments is crucial in view of the challenges posed by continuous urbanization. Indeed, democratization—including the implementation of good local governance—and decentralization could be seen as one of the prerequisites for successful urbanization.

The three local good practices outlined above, as well as a number of other local good practices that are not presented in this short chapter, provide the following lessons:

- By transferring authority and necessary resources to the city/local governments, decentralization has provided opportunities for city/local governments to pay much more thorough attention to problems faced at the local level than could any central government.
- The Tarakan case highlights the real possibility of balancing economic, social, and environmental considerations in development—something that has been frequently said but rarely consistently applied in many rapidly growing economies.
- The Sleman case demonstrates that intergovernment cooperation can work to benefit all parties involved and shows that implementation of good governance principles can have positive outcomes for local governments.
- The Jembrana case shares lessons of efficiency and effectiveness while, at the same time, illustrating that it is possible to combine short-term objectives with long-term goals, even by a poor local government.

In the three selected good practices—as well as in some other case not reported here—local leadership has been an imperative factor to success. However, to sustain good practice in the longer term, there should be a more concerted effort to reduce dependency on particular local leaders and to transform personalized leadership into a more systemic or institutional course of actions.

STRATEGIES TO ENHANCE SUSTAINABLE URBAN REGION DEVELOPMENT

In the case of Tarakan and Jembrana, external support has been minimal; however, not all cities or districts are able to start reform initiatives on their own. Sleman received external support in the form of capacity-building programs, such as ADB's Sustainable Capacity Building for Decentralization, and technical assistance, such as that related to the WB's Urban Sector Development Reform Project and more especially GTZ's Urban Quality Support to the Kartamantul joint secretariat. External support is important in many cases to start up local initiatives for improvement. However, in such cases, external assistance needs to be designed based on local ownership and project sustainability.

Ownership of the initiatives has to be kept as local as possible (with local governments or communities). Many good projects in the past failed to be sustained because the ownership of the initiatives was too tightly attached to development partners or central government departments. Local political and popular support from local leadership and the community is crucial to the success of the initiatives.

Local contributions (financial or in-kind, including human resources) should be gradually increased during the projects or programs so that the activities can be sustained after external support ends. Even the poorest communities or cities can contribute something. Charity approaches only generate dependency. Similarly, the external support has to be flexible and adjust from time to time with the dynamics of the local conditions. Rigid project design from development partners or central government is a recipe for unsustainability.

CONCLUSION

Indonesia has less than 5 years' experience in fostering regional development under decentralization. The progress on decentralization has been rapid, but there have been enormous problems that will take many years to solve. Coupled with the need for institutional reforms associated with decentralization is the high level of urbanization. Developing and managing land, housing, infrastructure, and community services for an expected 80 million people that will be added to the populations of Indonesian cities in the next 25 years will be a great challenge. The lack of institutional capacity and resistance to change, shortage of skills in local government agencies, and deficiencies in the decentralization laws are major factors contributing to the slowness in implementing many aspects of decentralization and improving the management of cities. These issues have been well documented by the Indonesian Government, development partners, and NGOs.

Few in Indonesia anticipated the difficulties that have been experienced with the implementation of the decentralization laws. The slow pace of change has caused disillusionment; however, the case studies presented here show that success stories are beginning to emerge. Enhancing the competitiveness of urban regions will be important to the development of a strong Indonesia, but will take time, patience, and a concerted effort across all levels of government, and involve developing new modalities and systems to implement and finance urban development projects and programs.

Finally, it is apparent that there is an overwhelming need for a substantial program of capacity building for local government institutions in Indonesia. Unless this is done as a matter of priority, urban governance and management, investment attractiveness, and the competitiveness of Indonesian cities will fall behind those of many other Asian cities. The resources available for such a program are significant and beyond the capacity of the central Government to fund. All levels of government in Indonesia should, therefore, identify smart ways to unlock, develop, and leverage institutional and private capital and assets and maximize the multiplier effect of investments needed to strengthen the capacity of urban institutions and the business sector. This calls for institutional cultural change that will not occur overnight. Unless urban institutions are reformed, the ability of most Indonesian cities to support and attract development and investment will be very limited. The consequences will be a further widening of income disparities and the poverty gap.

Notes

[1] The number of islands in Indonesia varies from one source to another; however, it is generally agreed that not more than half of them are inhabited.

[2] For most Indonesians, the national language, *Bahasa* Indonesia, is their second language after their own particular local language. The fact that Indonesia's founding fathers chose Indonesian as the national language instead of Javanese, which is spoken by more than 50% of Indonesians, has been seen as an advantage in the continuous and often-thorny attempt to unify this diverse nation.

[3] These transformations are not independent of each other (one does affect the other) but none of them is dependent on any other.

[4] The term "big bang" decentralization has been widely used to connote the radical transfer of wide-ranging government responsibilities from the national to local governments and appears in a number of reports and publications.

[5] However, it is important to note that if certain conditions are met, the private sector can contribute to providing decent housing for the urban poor.

[6] For further information about rural-to-urban migration as a consequence of regional unrest in the 1950s and 1960s, see Vickers (2005).

[7] There are districts that legally allow "contravention" of an existing spatial plan as long as the "violators" pay some kind of penalty. Such a local regulation has become a source of local income, while at the same time effectively making the local spatial plan useless.

[8] The sources for the population figures are *Profil Kabupaten dan Kota* (The Profiles of Kabupaten and Cities), Jakarta: Kompas, volumes 1, 2, 3, and 4.

The population growth figures are collected from BPS Statistik Indonesia 2001 (Jakarta), www.prospecktus.its.ac.id/sby.html (Surabaya), www.kompas.com December 6, 2004 (Bandung), www.sumut.bps.go.id (Medan), www.pilkada.partai-golkar.or.id (Bekasi), BPS Palembang Dalam Angka (Palembang), www.semarang.go.id/draft-rpjp.htm (Semarang), www. kotatangerang.go.id (Tangerang), www.depok.go.id (Depok), www.makassar.go.id (Makassar), www.perhubungan. pemkot-malang.go.id (Malang), and www.kotabogor.go.id (Bogor). All were accessed on 27 February 2006.

[9] McGee (1989), in which he adopted the Indonesian words of desa (village) and kota (city); when put together this term explains the phenomenon.

[10] Part of this case study used information from an internal report to ADB (2005) Catalysts for Sustainable Urban and Regional Development in Southeast Asia: A Study of Best Practice Approaches, Centre for Developing Cities, University of Canberra. www.cities.canberra.edu.au

[11] Poverty Reduction Strategy, by Sri Mulyani Indrawati.

[12] It is important to note that in Indonesia exist a number of national agencies dealing with the multidimensional issues of urban development. Most notable are the Ministry of Public Works (which is responsible for infrastructure development as well as spatial planning), Ministry of Home Affairs (which oversees urban governance matters), and National Planning Agency (Bappenas, which is in charge of development planning). However, in the decentralization era, there is no longer a formal linkage between Bappenas and the Bappedas (regional/local planning agencies) as there was in the past.

[13] *Keputusan Presiden* 7/1998 is a presidential decree that relates to processes used for infrastructure development in Indonesia. Under this decree the Government sets regulations concerning cooperation between government and private sectors in the development and management of infrastructure. It also includes a mechanism for the implementation of infrastructure projects.

[14] See World Bank Public Private Infrastructure Advisory Facilities http://wbln0018. worldbank.org/ppiaf/activity.nsf/0/a5f00937729cb84d85256c3600690d66

[15] Adapted from the categories by the CIDA-Bappenas-Hicling mapping project as quoted in CLGI and URDI. 2004. *Initiatives for Strengthening Local Government Capacity*. Jakarta.

[16] The word *tarakan* in the local language, Tidung, literally means "a place to stay and eat," especially for travelers.

[17] Assuming 1 US$ = Rp. 9,500.

[18] Part of this case study used information from an internal report to ADB (2005), *Catalysts for Sustainable Urban and Regional Development in Southeast Asia: A Study of Best Practice Approaches*, Centre for Developing Cities, University of Canberra.

[19] I Gede Winasa of Jembrana and Jusuf Serang Kasim of Tarakan were originally medical doctors.

8. Lao People's Democratic Republic

RICHARD MABBITT

INTRODUCTION

The Lao People's Democratic Republic (Lao PDR) was created when the Royal Lao Government was overthrown following a popular revolution in 1975. During 1975–1986, the country was run under a strict command economy. Since then, there has been a slow transition to a socialist market economy, including the adoption of the Lao PDR Constitution in 1991. The changes to the economy have led to increased urbanization, which is placing pressure on local governments to meet the growing demand for improved urban services to encourage industrial development and new investment opportunities. Table 8.1 shows relevant national statistics.

This chapter explores the issues affecting sustainable urban region development in the Lao PDR. The case studies have been chosen to illustrate different aspects of urban and regional development planning at three scales. In the Vientiane case study, attention is focused on participatory village improvements. The Luang Prabang case study looks at the achievements and problems of urban upgrading and heritage management projects working alongside each other in a medium-sized secondary town. The third study examines the broad objectives of the international East-West Economic Corridor and how it is affecting the development of the country's second city, Savannakhet, and its hinterland.

COUNTRY CONTEXT

Physical and Demographic Background

The Lao PDR is a landlocked country with an area of 236,800 square kilometers (km^2). It shares borders with Cambodia, Myanmar, Thailand, Viet Nam, and

Table 8.1: Country Development Profile, Lao PDR

Human Development Index rank of 177 countries (2003)^	133
GDP growth (annual %, 2004)	6.00
GNI per capita, Atlas method (current $, 2004)	390
GNI, Atlas method (current $ billion, 2004)	2.2
GDP per capita PPP ($, 2003)^	1,759
GDP PPP ($ billion, 2003)^	10.0
Population growth (annual 2005-2010 %)#	2.16
Population, total (million, 2005)##	5.92
Urban population, total (million, 2005)#	1.28
Urban population percent of total population (2005)#	22
Population largest city: Vientiane (2005, million)	0.78
Population growth: 1 capital cities or agglomerations > 750,000 inhabitants 2000#	
- Est. average growth of capital cities or urban agglomerations 2005-2015 (%)	51
- Number of capital cities or urban agglomerations with growth > 50%, 2005-2015	1
- Number of capital cities or urban agglomerations with growth > 30%, 2005-2015	1
Sanitation, % of urban population with access to improved sanitation (2002)**	61
Water, % of urban population with access to improved water sources (2002)**	66
Slum population, % of urban population (2001)**	66
Slum population in urban areas (2001, million)**	0.70
Poverty, % of urban population below national poverty line (1998)**	26.9
Aid (Net ODA received, $ million, 2003)^	298.6
Aid as a share of country income (Net ODA/GNI; 2003 %)*	16.1
Aid per capita (current $, 2003)^	52.8

GDP = gross domestic product, GNI = gross national income, ODA = official development assistance, PPP = purchasing power parity.
Sources: See Footnote Table 3.1, World Bank (2005); Organisation for Economic Co-operation and Development (2003); United Nations (2004, 2005).

Yunnan Province of the People's Republic of China (PRC). Mountains cover approximately 70% of the land area is covered by mountains. Forests, which were once estimated to cover two thirds of the country, have diminished significantly in the last 30 years. The Mekong River traverses the entire length of the country from north to south. Some 1,865 kilometers (km) of its total length of 4,000 km is within the Lao PDR or on its border with Thailand and Myanmar.

The preliminary results of the 2005 national census show a total population of 5.6 million (National Statistical Center 2005). The annual growth rate of the country as a whole in 1995–2005 was 2.05%. This is lower than many of the assessments made between censuses by the Government and international agencies.

Majority of the population lives in rural areas, and different estimates put the urban population as between 17% and 22% of the total (see the section on Measuring Urbanization). The capital city, Vientiane, and many major urban areas are located in the western, less mountainous parts of the country adjacent to the Mekong River. Vientiane is an administrative prefecture[1] comprising nine districts. In official documents (the basis for some estimates in Table 8.1), the population of the city is given as that of the prefecture. However, this is misleading as the contiguous urban area is only a small part of the prefecture and several districts are predominantly rural. The main urban area is limited to four districts, which have a combined population of about 340,000. In addition, parts of the urban area are in adjacent districts. Detailed village data from the 2005 census were not available at the time of writing, but based on aggregations of village populations undertaken by the author for the Vientiane Urban Infrastructure and Services Project (GHK International 2000) in 2000, the current population of these areas is estimated at about 60,000–70,000. This gives a total population of the Vientiane urban area of about 400,000.

Economic Setting

The economy of the Lao PDR is primarily based on agriculture and natural resources. Hydroelectric power is the primary foreign income earner (mostly from Thailand) and tourism is increasingly important. Real GDP growth was estimated to be 6.0% in 2004. There was 11.4% growth in the industrial sector, driven by an expansion in mining. The largest sector, agriculture, recorded growth of 3.5%. Although rice still accounts for majority of agricultural production, the production of cash crops has been increasing. The services sector grew by 7.3%, partly reflecting a recovery in tourist arrivals. Preliminary estimates indicate that the post-tsunami impact on tourism in Thailand has not had significant spillover effects in the Lao PDR (ADB 2005a).

With its membership in the ASEAN, and its commitment to further trade liberalization along the guidelines of the ASEAN Free Trade Agreement, and the World Trade Organization, the Lao PDR is striving for stronger economic integration into markets of the Greater Mekong Subregion (GMS). However, with a small population, minimal "monetarization" of the rural economy, and low demand for diversified products, the opportunity for internal market expansion appears limited. Continuing market research is needed to identify the country's competitive advantages and develop strategies to exploit these while offering incentives for greater involvement of farmers, traders, and investors in regional market operations.

URBANIZATION ISSUES

The Lao PDR's economic development, albeit slow, is most noticeable in urban areas as they try to gain increasing access to national and international markets. Improved roads, better and more reliable power networks, and digital telecommunication are supporting this economic growth. Significant achievements have been made in urban areas through a number of large-scale infrastructure developments. At the same time, however, inadequate institutional, legal, and regulatory frameworks hinder the efficient provision and management of urban services.

The improvements have not benefited all. Critical of previous initiatives, the United Nations Development Programme (UNDP) reported (UNDP 2002) that:

> "Despite more than a decade of high economic growth, following the introduction of the NEM and market oriented reforms, annual GDP per capita is just $350.[2] Many of the benefits deriving from economic growth and sociopolitical reform have yet to reach a significant proportion of the population. Despite enormous capital investment in infrastructure, many households, particularly those in rural areas, lack access to basic health and education services, as well as essential household amenities, such as clean water, sanitation facilities and electricity."

The Lao PDR has so far escaped serious urban environmental pollution. The Norwegian Agency for Development Cooperation (NORAD) and the United Nations Environment Programme (UNEP) (NORAD and UNEP 2001) report that "Since the towns are still small, population densities are

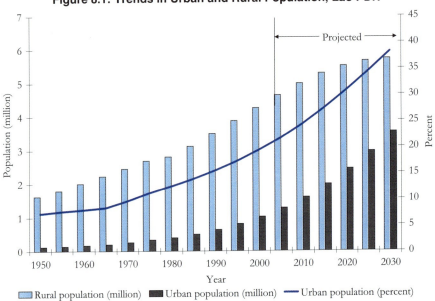

Figure 8.1: Trends in Urban and Rural Population, Lao PDR

low, private car ownership is minimal, and industrial activity is only emerging in a few of the largest towns. The ambient effects of industrial activities are minor and localized." But the situation is changing and pressure for development that has the potential to damage the environment is increasing.

Measuring Urbanization

The analysis of urbanization in the Lao PDR is hampered by the lack of accurate data and ambiguity over the definition of urban. Official figures from the National Statistics Center (NSC) are based on five criteria for determining if a village can be considered urban. Under this system, a village is classified as urban if at least three of five conditions apply. The criteria are a market in the village, a road for motor vehicles to get access to the village, district or provincial government offices in the village, the majority of households in the village electrified, and a tap water supply in service for the majority of households.

Using this definition, urban villages had a population of 781,753 in 1995, which was 17% of the total population. In the population update carried out by the NSC in 2000, there were 962 urban villages with a population of 985,352, representing 20% of the total population. While this definition provides a guide to the status of villages and shows growth of 26% in the "urban" population since 1995, it is not an entirely accurate indication of truly urban areas. A village can be classified as urban but be located on its own and not part of a greater settlement or urban area. The average size of individual villages in the Lao PDR is about 500 people. In urban areas, however, villages have an average population of about 1,000.

Thus, it is difficult to assess the rate and scale of urbanization in the Lao PDR. In looking at trends, further uncertainty concerning the consistency and accuracy of data over time arises. While the trends shown in Table 8.1 and Figure 8.1 probably represent a reasonable overview of the urbanization process, the projections are at best an educated guess.

The dramatic urbanization process shown in Figure 8.2 is particularly open to question with empirical evidence on the ground suggesting a steadier growth trajectory. The urban population of the Lao PDR is expected to increase from 1.28 million in 2005 to about 3.5 million—or 38% of the total population—by 2030. During the ADB Vientiane Urban Infrastructure and Services Project (VUISP) project in 2000, anecdotal reports suggested that rapid urban-rural migration was occurring, but this was not borne out by comparison of village population records. Growth on the urban fringes was seen to be moderate but not exceptional, and some was clearly due to an outward migration of residents to the suburbs from city center locations. There is also a marked seasonal migration of workers. Managers of garment factories, for instance, reported that many staff returned to their rural villages for several months during harvest periods.

Detailed population growth estimates in the Lao PDR have been difficult to determine due to the lack of time-series data collected using consistent methodologies. Since the national census in 1995, NSC has provided updates of the population based on a sampling of village records. In the absence of other sources, these have been used by various projects and practitioners in preparing estimates of growth rates. The outcome has been widely varying rate estimates. For instance, the recent urban sector strategy (MCTPC 2004) quoted a comparison undertaken by the Urban Research Institute, which showed growth of urban areas ranging from -7% to more than 25%. Changes in boundaries and differences in collection methods and urban definitions can probably explain these anomalies.

In the preliminary results from the 2005 census, most provinces show growth similar to the national rate (Savannakhet at 2.07%, Champasack at 1.89%), but some show quite significant variations (Luang Prabang at 1.06% and Luang Namtha at 2.40%). The situation is the same at the district level, with many districts showing a rate of about 2.0%, although again Namtha District is high at 2.4%. It should be noted that these are preliminary results, and definitive rates will only be possible when the data have been checked and verified. Detailed analysis of urban areas must also wait until data are available by village.

National Regional Development and Decentralization Policies

Regional Planning

The Government of the Lao PDR identifies three broad regions—northern, central, and southern—in its official publications. In the past, these regions have been used primarily for statistical purposes and have not been widely adopted for planning. Indeed, there has been little recognizable regional planning until recently. Previous national 5-year plans have been notable for their lack of geographic context and have tended to simply be policy statements and lists of proposed projects. The regions are large and not homogeneous; more rational and coherent alternatives have been suggested by various observers. For instance, the national program Participatory Poverty Assessment (PPA) (ADB 2001a) put forward four regions based on geographical and ethnic criteria, while the Small Towns Development Strategy (ADB 2001b) identified five regions based on physical and developmental characteristics and connectivity. However, neither of these has been adopted and the three regions prevail.

At the time of writing, the draft of the Five-Year Plan 2006–2010 was in preparation and not publicly available. However, it is understood that the Plan will use a more region-based approach than in the past and that it will contain clear goals and objectives for the three broad regions mentioned above: in the north, a focus on infrastructure provision to realize the potentials for agriculture and tourism; in the central region, the expansion of commodity capacities and the development of high-end technologies; and in the south, accelerated development based on natural resources, agriculture, and tourism. The south illustrates the heterogeneous nature of the regions. While the southwest is a well-developed area with rich agricultural land and good infrastructure centered on the secondary town of Pakse, the southeast is mountainous, lacking in infrastructure, and has only small urban centers. There is clearly a need to distinguish between these two areas for strategic planning purposes.

National development priorities are also now set out in the Government's National Growth and Poverty Eradication Strategy (NGPES) (GOL PDR 2003). This was formally adopted in 2003 following a lengthy roundtable process. NGPES is complementary to the Five-Year Plan and it is expected that the two will be combined in future years. While NGPES recognizes the need for a regional approach, it does not have a geographical focus other than in identifying the 72 poorest districts in the country. The basis for highlighting these districts, and by implication the strategy as a whole, is the data collected under PPA, which used a small sample size (in some districts only one or two villages) and may provide a less-than-accurate picture of the distribution of poverty. The need to update and expand the poverty database will be addressed by an imminent project jointly funded by the Swedish International Development Agency, World Bank, and ADB. Another shortcoming of NGPES is the lack of acknowledgment of the role of urban centers. The strategy has a strong rural focus reflecting the nature of poverty in the Lao PDR and almost entirely ignores the fact that urban centers will be the engines for economic growth to help lift the country out of least-developed-country status.

A regional approach to development is also implicit in the Government's involvement in several multicountry initiatives. These include the Lao-Cambodia-Viet Nam Development Triangle, the Lao-Thailand-Cambodia Emerald Triangle, and the Ayeyawaddy-Chao Phraya Economic Cooperation Strategy. These are all primarily partnership agreements to foster trade and border development. On the whole, however, the contribution from the Government has been reactive rather than proactive. There are no comprehensive planning strategies for the Lao components of these areas, leaving the country vulnerable to being exploited by stronger partners, who have already formulated and implemented clear plans and strategies.

There has been little international assistance for regional planning. The exception to this is ADB's recent focus on the northern region, reflecting its position as the poorest of the three regions.

Urban Plan Preparation in the Lao PDR

The responsibility for preparing plans for urban areas lies with the URI, which has prepared 81 urban master plans—61 of these since 1995. Although the older ones need updating, they still provide a basis for guiding growth and are used by local authorities in regulating development permits. This task has been undertaken largely without the help of any international assistance—technical or financial. The output is remarkable because it has been achieved without the benefit of any appropriate digital mapping or geographic information system technology.

Decentralization

A process of decentralization of government functions has been put in train in the Lao PDR. This started on 11 March 2000, with the Prime Minister's Instruction 01/PM. The stated objectives of this are that provincial governments will become strategic development units, district governments will become budgetary and planning units, and village councils will become implementing units. The decentralization process took a significant step forward when the Local Administration Law was passed in 2003 (President's Office 2003). This law sets out the rights and duties of provincial, district, municipal, and village authorities. It thereby establishes the framework for local decision making and, to some extent, local budgeting, but these will require the issuance of further decrees and instructions to actually empower them.

As described above, plans for urban areas are produced centrally. District authorities are responsible for the day-to-day administration of rural and urban areas within their boundaries, which includes the processing of planning and building permits in accordance with the master plans. In most cases, there is no separate authority for managing the main urban areas. The exceptions are Vientiane and the secondary towns (Luang Prabang, Savannakhet, Pakse, and Thakhek), which have operational Urban Development Administration Authorities (UDAAs) responsible for a range of functions. UDAAs have also recently been established in some other provincial capitals.

UNDP is supporting the decentralization process through its Governance and Public Administration Reform (GPAR) project. This is being done on a number of fronts, including the National Assembly and the legal sector, but the key areas are local administration organization, financial management, and procedures. Pilot projects concern participatory planning at the village level and implementation of the new *khum ban* (village clusters) approach. (Department of Planning and Investment 2005). GPAR is also addressing the issue of municipalities. This follows the Government's commitment to pursue the establishment of municipal authorities, initially in Vientiane and Luang Prabang, and later in other provincial capitals (Prime Minister's Office 2005).

Regional Economic Governance and Intergovernmental Financial Relations

The planning and development of the Lao PDR has been driven from the center since the socialist regime came into power in 1975. Most administrative functions and decisions currently operate from central Government through line ministries at the provincial and district levels. While provincial authorities enjoy some decision-making powers, there is little autonomy at the district level. There are no regional authorities in the Lao PDR.

As mentioned above, the system of national 5-year plans prevails as the major tool guiding the country's growth. Although the philosophy of the 5-year plans system is one of consensus building with inputs from the provinces and districts, the principal decisions are taken and targets are set centrally. The Committee for Planning and Investment (CPI) oversees the review and combination of proposed policies, programs, and projects included in the draft 5-year plans for consideration and approval by the National Assembly.

While the process of decentralizing administration is well underway, similar processes for revenue raising and budget control are not far advanced. Significant hurdles may remain, therefore, because provisions of the Local Administrative Law appear to conflict with already existing legislation, such as the Budget Law.

The creation of UDAAs, the designation of the Savan-Seno Special Economic Zone in Savannakhet (see below), and the move toward the establishment of municipalities are expected to spearhead the financial decentralization process.

The Role of International Aid in Supporting Regional Development

The Lao PDR benefits from a wide range of development assistance from multilateral and bilateral agencies. In 2003, the country received just under $300 million in net official development assistance (ODA). Total external debt currently stands at about $3 billion. Although this is 170% of GDP and, therefore, an apparently heavy burden, more than half is with the Russian Federation and is currently not being serviced.

Aid is received across all sectors. Over the past decade, ADB has been the lead agency in the urban sector. The World Bank, Danish International Development Assistance, Japan International Cooperation Agency (JICA), and Agence Française de Développement (AFD) are also active in infrastructure and environmental planning and management, and the Australian Agency for International Development (AusAID) in land titling. Support for regional development is mostly implicit rather than specifically addressed. The exceptions to this are ADB's GMS initiatives and recent ADB technical assistance projects for the northern region and for a national urban sector strategy. ADB has also supported the decentralization process through the establishment of UDAAs, but the bulk of the work on decentralization is being done by UNDP through its GPAR program.

The international aid program in the Lao PDR is characterized by a very clear matrix of donor activities by sector. There are some overlaps, but it is generally well understood which of the agencies is involved and which ones are taking the lead in the different sectors. This provides a transparent rationale for investment and results in minimal duplication.

GOOD PRACTICE CASE STUDIES

The case studies described here have been chosen to illustrate different aspects of urban and regional development planning at three scales. The Vientiane case study focuses on participatory village improvements. The Luang Prabang case study looks at the achievements and problems of urban upgrading and heritage management projects. The third case study examines the broad objectives of the international East-West Economic Corridor and its impacts on the country's second city, Savannakhet. The locations of the case studies are shown in Figure 8.2.

Vientiane Urban Region Village improvements

Location and Characteristics of the Region

Vientiane is the dominant and capital city of the Lao PDR. Although the city is located on the western boundary of the country, the shape of the Lao PDR is such that the capital is situated at a point that is geographically quite central. The area immediately west, north, and east of the city functions as a region based on the capital, which is a much smaller area than the official "central" region. This region is characterized by mostly

GOOD PRACTICE	
Good Governance	
Urban Management	✓
Infrastructure/Service Provision	✓
Financing and Cost Recovery	✓
Sustainability	✓
Innovation and Change	
Leveraging ODA	

Figure 8.2: Map Showing Location of the Case Studies

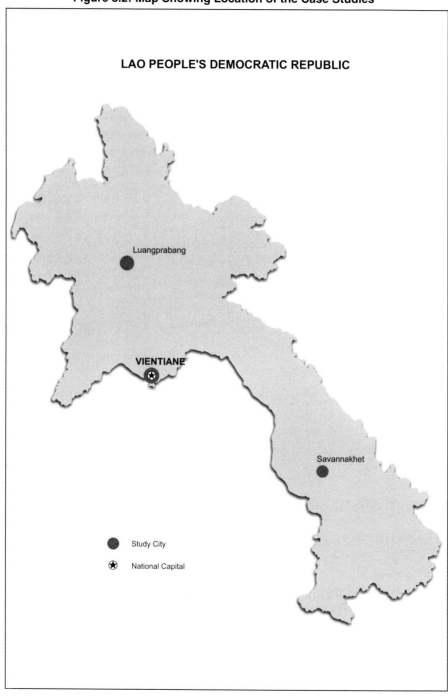

flat, intensively farmed land, many small urban settlements and, compared to the rest of the country, a relatively extensive road network.

The region described above equates approximately to the combination of the administrative areas of Vientiane Prefecture and Vientiane Province, plus the westernmost district of Borikhamxay Province. This represents an area with a population of about 1.1 million.[3] The average annual population growth in Vientiane Prefecture in 1995–2005 was 2.79%.

Economic Base of the Region

Vientiane is essentially a market town servicing an extensive agricultural hinterland, and is the conduit through which a considerable quantity of imported goods finds their way to customers in the city and the surrounding area. Much of the industrial production centered on Vientiane is for national domestic consumption, such as pharmaceuticals, beer and soft drinks, steel fabrication works, and a range of construction material companies. Garment manufacture is the only significant export earner in the city. The service industry constitutes a major proportion of the city's economy.

The industrial survey undertaken as part of the ADB's VUISP project in 2000 highlighted four major concerns for formal sector businesses: (a) the lack of skilled labor, (b) poor state of local infrastructure (e.g., roads, drains), (c) ambiguous government rules and regulations, and (d) lack of finance. Since 2000, infrastructure has largely been addressed through ADB, JICA, and other development partner projects, and finances are improving through significant foreign investment, notably by entrepreneurs from the PRC, Thailand, and Malaysia. The Government continues to issue many new laws and regulations, so improvement in consistency in government regulations is ongoing. The shortage of skilled labor remains a problem.

Village Area Improvements Project

VUISP was designed in 2000 under an ADB Project Preparation Technical Assistance (PPTA) that identified a range of urban improvements with the main focus on roads, drainage, and solid waste collection. These were mostly secondary network elements designed to complement the primary infrastructure built under a previous loan project. It also included capacity-building project components in the areas of urban management and road safety. PPTA was the basis of an ADB loan for just over $30 million approved in 2001. AFD separately funded the capacity-building element.

After completing the primary drainage infrastructure under the previous project, flooding continued to occur in Vientiane away from the main drainage network. Stagnant, often polluted, water continued to lie in open roadside channels due to an incomplete primary network and mostly unimproved secondary and tertiary networks. In response to this, strategic areas for the project undertaken in 2000 were identified as five low-lying locations where flooding was most frequent and extensive. In line with the recommendations in PPTA, the road and drainage improvements were divided into two components: citywide projects and village area improvement (VAI) projects. It is the latter component that is the subject of this case study.

Prior to 2000, the benefits of physical interventions in Vientiane were compromised by the absence of parallel interventions at the tertiary or village level to complement citywide infrastructure and service improvements. This absence of adequate tertiary-level infrastructure and services to support the primary and secondary networks was highlighted in public responses recorded under the PPA carried out as part of VUISP. The village area improvement component sought to address this through a demand-led, village-by-village approach to tertiary-level infrastructure improvement. PPA indicated that environmental improvements, particularly drainage improvements, were the most pressing demands of the urban poor.

The urban area covered by the project included 100 villages with about 162,000 residents within the original boundary of the Vientiane Urban Development and Administration Authority (VUDAA). Its jurisdiction has since been expanded to 189 villages. With insufficient funds to cover all 100 villages, using a selection process to prioritize the villages was necessary. Criteria used included current environmental and public health conditions, the quality and coverage of existing infrastructure, incidence and severity of flooding experienced, quality of access and availability of reasonable access throughout the year, proximity to the trunk infrastructure from which they can be served, and socioeconomic conditions. The last of these incorporated an assessment of the prevalence of the urban poor based on the results of the PPA, which was the first comprehensive study of poverty in an urban area in the Lao PDR (ADB 2000).

The result of the selection process was a long list of villages ranked in order of priority. The first 50 were initially included in the project. Ultimately, four of these villages chose not to participate because they were due to benefit directly from improvements under the citywide projects. These were replaced by four other villages from the long list.

The main stages and key activities in the consultation, design, and contract processes are shown in Table 8.2 below. (Note: Table 8.2 is a summary; many more detailed activities are involved in the process.)

The VAI program was undertaken in phases. The first phase involved only six villages and all were completed by January 2005, while the second

Table 8.2: Stages of the Village Area Improvement Process

Stage	Key Activities
Coordination with village head	• Meet with village head for organizing orientation meeting in the village. • Introduction and orientation of VAI program. • Set up village committee. • Assist village committee in developing outline village proposals.
Outline village proposals	• Village committee submits outline village proposals.
Village project, commitment and selection	• Engineers visit the sites together with village committee. • Reconnaissance/walkout survey for developing scope of work for surveys. • Present preliminary designs and cost estimates to village committee and villagers. • Villagers and village committee to review options and select the preferred options of the village within the budget. • Draft village agreement on village contributions. • Village agreement signing ceremony.
Detailed design	• Develop contract packages. • Develop payment schedule. • Prepare bidding documents and technical specifications. • Present final designs and cost estimates to village committee. • Village committee confirms that designs meet their requirements.
Bidding process and contract award	• Bid opening and evaluation. • Negotiation with reasonable lowest-priced bidder. • Contract signing ceremony between contractor, VUDAA, and village committee.
Construction supervision	• Notice to commencement of contract works. • Mobilization. • Construction supervision in coordination with village committee. • Issue of completion certificate.

VAI = village area improvement, VUDAA = Vientiane Urban Development and Administration Authority.

phase involved 20 villages. The third phase includes 24 villages, including the four late additions to make up the target of 50 villages. In developing the village proposals into contract packages, the engineering team aimed at a contract value per village of about $75,000. Under the VAI agreements, the villages contribute 10% of the cost of the contracts, the project loan covers 62%, and the Government meets the remaining 28%. In the initial concept, the villages' 10% was intended to be in cash or labor. To date, however, all contributions have been made in cash. During the final phase of villages, the project team aims to explore ways to use village labor, with nine villages having specifically expressed interest in this.

All the physical works carried out under the VAI program have been roads (including a small bridge) and drains. This is a close reflection of the community priorities identified during VAI village meetings. It also reflects the fact that villages in low-lying, flood-prone areas ranked highly. From discussions with villagers and their representatives, the mud and dust created by unsealed roads were clearly near the top of their list of concerns. Initial village meetings did not include the project's engineers so the villagers were not steered toward these proposals in any way. Other potential project components were mentioned in these meetings; however, it seems probable that villagers primarily associate VUDAA with roads and drains and that they may have been somewhat blinkered to other possibilities.

Solid waste collection was generally not raised as a priority issue in village meetings. This is no doubt partly due to the fact that there were other ongoing solid waste pr ojects in Vientiane of which the villagers were aware. However, the VAI program did include a program on sanitation and environmental health awareness, which covered solid waste handling issues.

Village Contributions

With each successive phase, the project team has developed and refined the VAI process. This has been partly based on improvements identified by the team, and is also a reflection of villagers' increasing willingness to participate. For instance, the schedules for collecting the village contribution have been amended to achieve better payment performance to contractors. In the initial group of six villages, payments were scheduled in four installments over 12 months. However, works were generally completed before the final sums were collected and it proved difficult to collect outstanding payments, particularly where any works defects were pending. In the second phase, four equal installments were scheduled over 6 months. In the third phase, the 6-month payment period was maintained, but with the proviso that 40% of the total amount due from the village was to be collected prior to the commencement of the contract.

While there was understandable resistance and skepticism among villagers at the start of the project, village committees have reported that residents are ready and willing to contribute now they have seen the success of the earlier projects in other villages. Indeed, one village in the final phase collected the total village contribution well before the contract started. The speed of collection appears to be influenced also by the relative levels of commitment and management skills of the village chiefs. In the collection of the village contributions, village chiefs and their committees have been pragmatic in determining the amount to be paid by individual households. Most have adopted a sliding scale on the basis of ability to pay, with the poorest households being exempt. Where there are relatively wealthy businesses or households in a village, they have been asked to pay, or have voluntarily paid, many times the average payments.

The inconsistent and delayed collections in the early phases caused problems for the contractors and for VUDAA. Contractors were aggrieved at the delays, while VUDAA's administration was unable to cope with ad hoc payments. A result of the contractors' concerns was that they increased their bids for subsequent contracts specifically to allow for costs of expected payment delays. The problems with payments likely deterred some contractors from bidding, probably including some of the better quality firms.

Community Liaison

An important part of the project operation is the involvement of the Lao Women's Union (LWU) in the role of monitoring and community facilitation. As well as the active participation of village LWU representatives in village meetings, two LWU appointees were assigned full-time to the project. A reflection of the importance given to this role by LWU is the fact that one of the people assigned to the project was the then vice-president of LWU.

One of the initial tasks of LWU was to explain to villagers how to participate. There has been only one previous attempt at community participation in urban improvements in Vientiane, by the United Nations Development Programme (UNDP) in the Sihom area, which was on a small and localized scale. LWU ran a series of workshops on community participation as well as providing a conduit for day-to-day liaison between residents and the project. This was important for dialogue in both directions. It enabled the villagers to voice their opinions and be heard by VUDAA and the project team, thereby overcoming a general community reluctance to confront government authorities. It also helped the engineers on the project team to communicate more effectively with residents. This also resulted in the engineers' adopting a more flexible approach to infrastructure design. LWU was also closely involved in setting up VAI committees in each village and in ensuring that women and the poor were appropriately represented on these committees. Close cooperation between LWU and the VAI team was also an important element in dealing with resettlement and other minor impacts.

Initial village meetings followed a standard format. This included a general introduction to the aims of the project, followed by discussion and agreement on priorities. To ascertain priorities, the meetings were divided into three groups: women, men, and the village committee. The results of each group were then compared and combined.

As mentioned above, participatory village-level urban infrastructure provision on this scale has not been achieved previously in the Lao PDR. The project has, therefore, been a learning process for all concerned, and its success is testament to the effective collaboration between the engineering and social development professionals, community advisors, and village representatives. The project's accomplishments are reflected in the fact that it has been mentioned in the National Assembly as an example of good participatory planning, which is one of the Government's areas of focus in its move toward decentralized planning. Its popular success is also borne out by demand. Many villages currently not in the scheme have approached the project's national project director with requests to be included.

Taking Forward the Lessons Learned

Many lessons learned during the VAI process should be used to inform the design of future projects. Many lessons were taken on board and adjustments made as the project moved from one phase to the next, while other lessons required going beyond those adjustments and were able to be made while the project was ongoing. Some key lessons and observations are described below.

One very noticeable result of the scheme is the level of interest shown by residents in the work of the contractors. This "ownership" has led to many reports by villagers to their committees about the quality of completed works. Some of these instances led to contractors being required to remedy defects. At the same time, it was necessary to explain to the local residents that the standards of road and drain construction were not the same as those for main roads in the city.

Some shortcomings of the VAI scheme could have been avoided if the VAI component was a separate project rather than an "add-on" to the much larger citywide component. The way the project was set up allowed insufficient time for the professional team to explore alternative design and construction options in the villages. An example of this is the road construction material. The double bituminous surface treatment used in all village roads may not be as sustainable as concrete construction. The latter is generally more expensive, but there could have been scope for reducing costs by utilizing existing road substructures. Alternative options for contracting arrangements should be investigated. For instance, future maintenance of roads and drains might be more sustainable if villages were able to contract VUDAA to do this.

The funding structure of the project may have contributed to the contractors' payment problems referred to above. Under the loan agreement with ADB, the Government was required to contribute 28% of the project cost in cash. The high demand on the Government's cash resources led to delays in payments of their contributions to contractors' fees. An outcome of these payment problems was that better contractors chose not to bid for contracts and the quality of work suffered.

The learning process during the VAI project was ad hoc. According to the VAI team, community development consultant members of the team felt they would have benefited from more structured training, including study tours to see how the process was undertaken elsewhere. Despite this, the knowledge and skills that have been developed represent a significant resource. Unfortunately, there are doubts about how well this resource will be utilized in the future. VUDAA and the Government should make sure that these skills are disseminated and applied elsewhere. The ongoing ADB Small Towns Development Sector Project, which also includes a village improvements component, represents one such opportunity.

While there is plenty of room for improvement, including widening the scope and type of work entailed, the VAI projects have already made a significant impact on the environments in the villages concerned.

Luang Prabang Urban Improvements and Heritage Conservation

Location and Characteristics of the Region

Luang Prabang is the ancient capital of the 14th century kingdom known as Lan Xang ("a million elephants"), which included what is now the northern part of the Lao PDR and also much of northeastern Thailand. It remained a royal residential town until 1975.

Today, Luang Prabang is an administrative district and the main urban center of the province of the same name.

GOOD PRACTICE	
Good Governance	
Urban Management	✓
Infrastructure/Service Provision	✓
Financing and Cost Recovery	
Sustainability	
Innovation and Change	✓
Leveraging ODA	

Located in the heart of the northern, mountainous part of the Lao PDR, it is considered by some to be the regional center for the north. Inasmuch as it has the only international airport north of the capital Vientiane, it fulfills the role of a regional transport hub. However, the difficult terrain and tenuous road system throughout this northern third of the country mean that the town has only limited ground-level connection with most of the surrounding areas. As with Vientiane, therefore, the actual region is probably smaller than the one suggested on paper. Nevertheless, Luang Prabang serves as a focal point, as well as a jump-off point, for tourism, which is a key component of the region's economic growth.

In the Government's 2020 Vision, developed in a roundtable process between 2000 and 2002, (UNDP/GOL 2002) Luang Prabang was identified as a "pole for the north." However, the main development zone in the northern part of the country is now expected to be along Road No. 3, which is being improved to provide an international economic corridor from Thailand to Yunnan in the PRC. Towns on or close to this route, such as Luang Namtha and Oudomxay, will likely become the principal economic centers of the region. It is understood that in the Five-Year Plan, which was being prepared when this chapter was being written, the emphasis for the northern region is on development in Luang Namtha.

In the preliminary results from the 2005 National Census, the population of Luang Prabang Province is given as about 405,000 with the "urban" district population as 77,500. However, the district includes 132 villages of which only 58 are within the general urban area. An estimate of the urban area population using village records in 2003 was about 41,000 (ADB 2003). The average annual population growth rate for the district from 1995–2005 was 2.05%.

The urban area of Luang Prabang is situated on the bank of the Mekong River at its confluence with the Nam Khan River. The historic core of the town is located on the peninsula created by the two rivers. This area includes a large number of temples from different centuries along with many surviving vernacular buildings. The temples in particular represent some of the most sophisticated Buddhist architecture in the country (MIC 2003). Overlaid on this is the architectural legacy of the French rule of the 19th and 20th centuries in the form of numerous elegant colonial style buildings of various scale and forms. The overall result is a rich fusion of local and colonial townscapes that is unique in the Lao PDR and of international significance. Its importance was recognized by the United Nations Educational, Scientific and Cultural Organization (UNESCO) and the town was added to the World Heritage List in 1995.

Economic Base of the Region

The underlying economic base of the Luang Prabang region is agriculture as is common for most of the Lao PDR. This includes a wide variety of vegetables and fruits as well as groundnuts. A number of nontimber forest products, including mulberry, sugar palm, and incense bark, are also being developed. Two of the local products are also processed in factories in the region. These are sesame and Job's Tears (a grass that produces beads used in ethnic jewelry). There is little other industrial activity in the region.

Luang Prabang is the country's principal tourist destination. Since its inauguration as a World Heritage Site, the town has seen significant development of its tourism industry. According to official sources, the number of tourist visitors to the town rose from 19,463 in 1996 to 165,222 in 2000

(Tourism Authority 2000). The SARS crisis in Asia led to a dip in arrivals in subsequent years, but the Department for Planning and Investment in Luang Prabang reports that the number of tourists has significantly increased again since then. They estimate that in 2004 the number of tourists was in excess of 250,000, but this has not yet been verified.

According to the national PPA, Luang Prabang has some of the poorest districts in the country, making it one of the poorest provinces.

Urban Improvements and Heritage Conservation

A range of infrastructure improvements were designed for the urban area through the ADB's Secondary Towns Urban Development Project (STUDP) (which also included Pakse, Savannaket, and Takhek) and implemented during the ensuing loan project in 1998–2003. The physical works included roads and drains, a road bridge over the Nam Dong on the southern side of the town, bank protection work on the Nam Khan, and an office building for UDAA. The total cost of the improvement works in Luang Prabang, excluding the office building, was just under $4 million. The project also included some technical assistance for solid waste management (under UNDP and NORAD), and capacity-building components.

The establishment of discrete urban authorities in all four towns was one of the covenants attached to the loan from ADB. UDAAs were inaugurated under the Prime Minister's Decree in 1997 (Prime Minister's Office 1997). Much of the capacity building provided under the loan was targeted at local staff in UDAAs. In support of this, ADB also funded additional projects dealing with the organization and strengthening of UDAAs. A key part of this support was the identification and development of local revenue-raising mechanisms and financial management (also specific items in the loan covenant). While these first steps toward the decentralization of urban responsibilities were taking place and the infrastructure improvements were being planned and constructed in Luang Prabang, the protection and management of the World Heritage Site were also being addressed by another organization, La Maison du Patrimoine (MdP), supported by UNESCO and AFD. These two agencies operated side by side for 5 years. They were not always in concert, but the outcome is probably the most successful of the four ADB STUDP projects.

MdP was established following the World Heritage listing and has been supported by two phases of funding from AFD. The first phase, from 1998 to 2001 and costing $2.2 million, focused on pilot research, some civil works, training, and planning. The second phase, worth about $6.6 million, commenced in July 2001 and is due to be completed in 2006. This phase has four components and includes the preparation of a detailed preservation plan

(MdP 2002), building conservation, improvements to the urban infrastructure networks, and institutional support. MdP's responsibilities fall into two work streams. The first is an ongoing role in managing and monitoring development in the heritage zone in accordance with the conservation regulations, which involves giving advice to residents, commenting on building applications, and training local staff. The second is ad hoc activities in coordinating and running specific conservation and improvement projects.

Complementary or Competing Projects?

In the early days of the heritage project, there was a widespread lack of understanding of what MdP was trying to achieve among local government offices, international agencies, and the public alike. This led to problems of conflicting ideas and approaches. No doubt this was partly because MdP was still establishing itself and its advisers and staff were probably not entirely clear themselves on what were realistic targets. At the same time, there was a lack of communication and an element of elitism in the approach taken by the heritage camp. As a result, local officials and residents were unclear about who and what UNESCO and MdP were. Moreover, there was ambiguity about who the intended beneficiaries of the town's preservation were. The situation would certainly have benefited from a more comprehensive and effective public information exercise.

The problems encountered stemmed from two areas of activity—the urban infrastructure improvements proposed under the secondary towns project and the construction of buildings and extensions by residents in the heritage zone. Both areas of conflict were probably inevitable as the program for work by UDAA was being designed and implemented while the heritage plans were still in gestation. In addition, there had been little enforcement of any kind of building code on householders in Luang Prabang (or anywhere else in the Lao PDR) up to that time. The zoning and building codes tended to be quite complex, going far beyond the level of detail of any existing regulations. This meant that it was not only the general public who found them difficult to understand but the local officials as well. The technical capacities of provincial, district, and UDAA staff in the Lao PDR was, and still is, generally low. Very few qualified urban planners or architects work outside Vientiane.

The more or less simultaneous birth of the two new authorities—UDAA and MdP—in Luang Prabang was also a cause for confusion. Up to that point, the district authority (primarily the local Department of the Ministry of Communications, Transport Post and Construction [or DCTPC]) was responsible for day-to-day matters, such as construction permits and maintenance of urban services. In all four secondary towns, the introduction of UDAAs resulted in a division of roles between UDAAs and DCTPCs. This division was not always clear, especially because in their infancy UDAAs did not have the resources to fulfill their assigned tasks.

To some extent, the UDAAs' position was also undermined by the attitude of some parties in government, who felt UDAAs were simply project implementation units for the ADB project. In Luang Prabang, the establishment of MdP added another element to an already confused situation. It is not surprising, therefore, that there was a period characterized by overlap, duplication, and conflict between the agencies. Today, the three authorities have established an effective working relationship with clear lines of consultation and cooperation. Nevertheless, ambiguities still remain and these will probably not be fully resolved until the establishment of a formal municipality in Luang Prabang.

Friction between UDAA and MdP arose because of disagreements over the design and, in some cases, the principles behind the designs of the urban infrastructure works. The issues related mostly to road widths, drainage dimensions, footpath design and materials, riverbank protection, and the treatment of natural drainage ponds. The apparent incompatibility of the two programs was the subject of a masters thesis by J. Touber (2001) (now of the Earth Institute at Columbia University) written in 2001. At that time, Touber saw the divergent objectives and approaches of the agencies as irreconcilable. Thankfully, events have demonstrated that this was probably an overly pessimistic viewpoint.

UDAA's original designs were based on established Government standards and on optimum engineering solutions. MdP, on the other hand, was concerned about appearance and environmental impacts. Both sides can probably be criticized for their initial stances; the engineering team for being unimaginative and inflexible, and the heritage experts for being unrealistic in their approach to conservation. However, at the end of the day, compromise positions were reached that, in most cases, satisfied both parties. The culmination of this, as evidenced by the result on the ground, is a notable example of how the upgrading of physical services can be achieved within an historic urban environment. The achievement is also notable because this is a "living heritage" area. The approaches required in the busy town of Luang Prabang are quite different from the more-established techniques for preserving unoccupied heritage sites.

The scaling down of some UDAA's projects resulted in cost savings, which were used to fund additional works. This was despite the fact that the materials used in the heritage area, such as bricks for footways, were more expensive than those originally planned. This suggests that there may be scope to reduce the dimensions of roads in other urban settings, and particularly in areas of built heritage.

Sustainability

While the results of the physical interventions in Luang Prabang are impressive, there are questions about the sustainability and efficacy of the achievements. The first concern is over the future of MdP, and the second is how far the investment in the urban area benefits the surrounding areas.

The combined success of the Luang Prabang projects would certainly not have been achieved without the strong hand of MdP. Working through the official powers exercised by the local authorities, MdP managed to enforce a building code far stricter than anything else operating in the Lao PDR. To sustain this level of control, MdP will have to continue its operations in some form or other. Although it has been supported financially by two phases of grant from AFD, there is no guarantee that there will be subsequent phases. A third phase is apparently being considered, but has yet to be approved.

The question mark hanging over long-term sustainability is recognized by AFD itself. In its own journal, it identifies the funding issue and risks of losing control over illegal construction (Leroux 2002). The new Heritage Law, passed on 10 December 2005, gives MdP a legal mandate through the Ministry of Culture. However, there is no parallel financing plan for its continued existence. There is talk of a tourist tax but no detailed studies have yet been undertaken on its feasibility. A related concern is the maintenance of the improvements undertaken by MdP. The responsibility for this lies with the villages themselves, and only time will tell as to whether they are willing and able to undertake and fund this work.

The preservation of the heritage area has come at a substantial cost ($8.6 million from AFD alone), and some may ask for whom this has been undertaken. There has been significant investment by the private sector, with most of the investors from outside Luang Prabang and many from overseas. In the central heritage area, new hotel ventures, restaurants, and shops selling artifacts have displaced the local businesses. Very little of the income generated is going directly into the hands of Luang Prabang people. This position is compounded by the fact that the type of visitor is changing. Whereas it used to be mostly independent travelers using local travel services and paying for accommodation on site, tourists are increasingly arriving as part of tours arranged and bought at their overseas points of origin.

A number of ongoing and planned projects in the rural areas around Luang Prabang may facilitate the economic benefits of the heritage scheme filtering out to these parts. Some have the specific aim of attracting tourists to stay longer in the province and spend money outside the main urban area, such as ecotourism schemes under the European Union (EU) micro-project development project (European Commission 2005), and the assistance provided by UNDP under its GPAR program to districts in identifying potential tourism activities. Others will help local communities to better manage their resources and opportunities, such as the participatory village planning being undertaken by GPAR (Department of Planning and Investment 2005), and a proposed project to assist farmers close to the urban area to better service the needs of the town under the EU's Asia-Urbs program.

A third phase of AFD funding likely includes a plan for the urban periphery. Inevitably, it will be some time before any tangible benefits from these projects can be identified and evaluated.

The achievements in Luang Prabang have received international acclaim and MdP plays host to a continuous stream of official visitors from historic towns and cities throughout Asia eager to see how it has been done. Its fame and attraction also mean that there is no shortage of interest from development partners wanting to work in the region. While this effective leverage of international assistance must be welcomed, it must also be carefully targeted. It should be remembered that the provincial authority is still struggling to meet the Government's poverty reduction targets.

Savannakhet and the East-West Economic Corridor

Location and Characteristics of the Region

Savannakhet is the largest and most populous province in the Lao PDR. In the preliminary results of the 2005 National Census, the population is given as about 800,000. This compares to 690,000 in the Vientiane Prefecture, and 600,000 in Champasack, while all other provinces have populations of 400,000 or less. The province is located in the central part of the country and is one of four provinces that span the width of the country, having borders with both Thailand and Viet Nam. The western edge of the province follows the Mekong River. From the lowland plains along the Mekong, the topography rises to the mountainous areas in the east, adjacent to Viet Nam.

GOOD PRACTICE	
Good Governance	✓
Urban Management	
Infrastructure/Service Provision	✓
Financing and Cost Recovery	
Sustainability	
Innovation and Change	✓
Leveraging ODA	✓

The provincial capital is officially referred to as Khantabouly, which is the name of its district. However, it is also popularly known as Savannakhet. In 2003, the urban area was estimated to have a population of 63,634 making it the second most populous in the country (Mabbitt 2003). From the same source, the combined population for urban centers in the province with a population over 5,000 was 101,864, which is also second only to Vientiane. District boundaries changed between 1995 and 2005, so a population growth rate for the district cannot be derived from data thus far available from the 2005 census. The average annual growth rate of the province over this period, however, was 2.07%, which is close to the national rate.

Economic Base of the Region

The major economic activities in the region are rice farming and animal husbandry. Savannakhet Province is the largest rice-producing province in the country. The agriculture sector accounts for 80% of gross provincial product (GPP). It also has the largest number of industry-handicraft establishments of any province, although these are mostly small establishments. The industrial sector accounts for 25% of GPP. Most industry-handicraft establishments are in the sectors of wood products, garments, and food processing. Gold and copper mining started in 2004 (see below). The service sector is also significant. The major commercial activities are retail and wholesale establishments, reflecting the commodity flows crossing the Mekong River and along National Road No. 9. Many small-scale hotels and restaurants are also concentrated in the urban areas.

International Corridor and Urban Development

Savannakhet Province is within the East-West Economic Corridor (EWEC), which is one of the 11 "flagship projects" of the GMS program. The move to set up the GMS was led by ADB, and was formally established in 1992. At the GMS 1998 ministerial meeting, a commitment was made to support economic corridors. The principle behind the creation of corridors is that investments in priority infrastructure sectors, such as transport, energy, telecommunications, and tourism would focus on the same geographic space to maximize development impact while minimizing development costs (ADB 2005b).

The benefits expected from EWEC include better access to raw materials, regional development of remote border areas, growth of secondary towns, poverty reduction, greater cross-border trade, more efficient use of economic space, increased investment in agro-industries, and industrial zones and tourism (ADB 2002). EWEC runs from the Andaman Sea in the west to the South China Sea in the east, incorporating parts of the Lao PDR, Myanmar, Thailand, and Viet Nam. The main axis of the corridor is a 1,500-km road from Mawlamyine in Myanmar to Da Nang in Viet Nam. The Lao PDR section of this axis is Road No. 9, which dissects Savannakhet Province and connects Savannakhet town on the Mekong with Dansavanh on the Viet Nam border.

The EWEC initiative will require road, rail, water transport, and air transport linkages. A bridge crossing the Mekong River from Mukdahan in Thailand to Savannakhet in the Lao PDR is being constructed through loan financing from the Japan Bank for International Cooperation. This bridge is expected to be completed in 2006, and will be a crucial part of the infrastructure for the transition of the Lao PDR from a landlocked to a "land-linked" territory. Sections of the EWEC in the Lao PDR are being upgraded with financial assistance from JICA and ADB.

A pre-investment study for EWEC was completed in 2001 under ADB technical assistance (ADB 2001c). The study developed a framework for cooperation and development in agro-industry, infrastructure, trade and investment, tourism, and industrial estates, and recommended 74 projects, including policy and institutional development initiatives. The combined total cost of proposed projects for EWEC is about $364 million. The Government has proposed the inclusion of a project to improve the Savannakhet airport in the program. This project will make Savannakhet airport a subregional airport for Thailand as well as for the Lao PDR, and allow it to accommodate medium-sized aircraft. The EWEC proposal has been fully endorsed by the governments of the four countries concerned. In support of the infrastructure programs, several "soft" policy initiatives have also been instigated. An accord was signed in 1999 to facilitate the movement of people and goods between the Lao PDR, Thailand, and Viet Nam. Travel time along the corridor will also be reduced through the adoption of one-stop customs procedures.

Many national projects also stem from the EWEC program. In the Lao PDR, the most significant of these is the Savan-Seno Special Economic Zone (SASEZ). The intended establishment of SASEZ was declared in 2002; and in 2003, it was formally enacted through two Prime Minister's Decrees, Nos. 148 and 177 (Prime Minister's Office 2004a). SASEZ has been set up to take advantage of the favorable location of this zone at the central crossroads of the GMS, and to attract and promote foreign and domestic investments in compliance with the general investment policies of the Government. The overriding objectives are to foster production, export, and services growth, and to create opportunities for learning experiences in the fields of business management and administration and the use of new technology, as well as for promoting industrial, trade, and service relationships with the regional and international communities.

SASEZ is composed of two separate sites both located along National Road No. 9 in Savannakhet Province. Site A has an area of 300 hectares (ha) and is located on the northern edge of the Savannakhet urban area next to the

Mekong Bridge. Site B has an area of about 20 ha at Seno, at the junction between National Road No. 13 and National Road No. 9, some 30 km east of Savannakhet. Operations are now at the stage of land clearing and resettlement of the people occupying the land. SASEZ will be competing with similar investment promotion schemes in northeastern Thailand, but the Lao sites may have an advantage in attracting international investors through the export quotas enjoyed by the Government of the Lao PDR. It remains to be seen how soon this conceptual framework can be translated into actual investments.

Another EWEC initiative is the newly established Border Trade Zone at Danesavanh at the border with Viet Nam. This is in a relatively large area of 28 km^2. The zone is designed to become a commercial center for the Lao PDR and a stopping point for local and foreign tourists. Construction activities have begun to create the necessary facilities. Incentives to investors include land fee exemption for the first 11 years, tax-free for the first 7 years and 50% tax discount for the next 5 years. Across the border in Viet Nam, the newly created border town of Lao Bao is even larger than the one on the Lao PDR side.

A major new investment has been made in EWEC in recent years in the form of a gold and copper mining concession located at Sepon in the eastern part of Savannakhet Province. The gold mining company, owned by a joint venture between Oxiana N.L (Australia) and Lane Xang Minerals (Vientiane), has a total concession area of 1,947 km^2. Work on the gold mine started in 2002, with the first gold sent to Australia for refining in 2003. Copper production started in November 2004. The gold and copper mining operations employ about 3,000 people. Some of these are trained workers and specialists from elsewhere, but more than 1,500 local residents are employed. This is having a direct impact on incomes in the area, with average per capita incomes rising from $64 in 2001 to $300 in 2004 (Vientiane Times 2004). The company has also undertaken to initiate and fund livelihood projects. Silk production, mulberry tree cultivation, and pig-breeding schemes are already underway.

Impact and Sustainability

In the context of this book, the question to be asked is what the EWEC has done for this part of the Lao PDR? How has the big, broad idea of the multinational corridor affected the urban and rural areas of Savannakhet Province, and are the impacts sustainable?

Savannakhet has long been considered the second city of the Lao PDR. However, anecdotal evidence suggests that Pakse has now overtaken Savannakhet as the country's fastest- growing commercial center outside Vientiane. Although there are no GDP figures for urban areas, the change in importance is reflected in statistics gathered for the expenditure and consumption survey undertaken by the National Statistics Office in 2002/2003 (National Statistical Centre 2004). The total investment in constructing residential, agricultural, and business buildings in Champasack Province in 2002–2003 was 25% higher than that in Savannakhet, despite having a smaller population and area.

This situation is also illustrated by the closure in recent years of the airport at Savannakhet due to insufficient passenger numbers. Pakse's recent growth can probably be largely explained by the presence of its new bridge over the Mekong completed in 2000. Although both banks of the river there are within Lao PDR territory, the bridge has also given the town direct road access to the Thai border about 40 km away. The expectation is that the bridge at Savannakhet will have an even more marked impact on the economy of the town and province, as it is part of a major corridor, rather than the less-established route that goes through Pakse. Once the bridge is completed, the direct road link from Savannakhet to Bangkok will be shorter than the one from Vientiane.

Savannakhet was one of the four secondary towns in ADB's STUDP (see Luang Prabang case study). Under the project, urban infrastructure upgrading to the value of about $4.5 million (not including a new office building for UDAA) was completed in 2003. The individual improvement projects were as effective as they had been in the other towns, but the overall impact of STUDP was less noticeable in Savannakhet due to the scale of the town's infrastructure networks. The town's development has been guided by a somewhat overextensive road system, planned and laid out in the 1980s and early 1990s. In total there are about 200 km of road in the main urban area. This layout has encouraged urban sprawl at a very low density. Although the suburban areas are being slowly filled, the town still has the feel of a road system waiting for a city.

A product of this overgrown road network is a very expensive improvement and maintenance bill, a cost that UDAA alone cannot afford. The provincial government has recently funded the surfacing and sealing of 47 km of roads in the urban area with an eye to hosting two impending major national events in the city—the national games and party conference. As is common with other UDAAs, the one in Savannakhet is under-resourced and its revenues from building permits, event permits, and septic and solid waste collection do not match its outgoings. In 2005, the central Government provided about $50,000 equivalent to support UDAA's activities. There is also a direct local contribution; residents were asked to pay 20% of the cost of road improvements in 2005.

With the expected spin-off from EWEC in general, and the bridge in particular, the prospects for Savannakhet urban area are good. There is a chance that the anticipated increase in economic activity and transport movements will help rekindle growth in the area. However, proactive action needs to be taken to ensure that the town is best placed to capitalize on the opportunities. This includes preparation of urban development plans for the whole urban area, including the bridge and its approaches. The town has already suffered a shift in the center of gravity in terms of its retail operations with the construction of a new Chinese-funded market center on the northern edge of the urban area in the late 1990s. This took business away from the historic core and traditional retail center. In the development framework prepared for the town in STUDP, the need to address this negative affect on the heritage area was identified. To date, however, nothing has been done to revitalize it. The advent of the bridge and the proposed SASEZ will create an additional pull northwards; therefore, a comprehensive plan to guide the growth of the whole area is needed.

The same is true for other parts of the region. Proactive planning should be undertaken to ensure that opportunities are not missed. However, as pointed out by the recent study into urban and rural linkages (Kammeier et al. 2005), "The creation of industry and service-based border towns in a hitherto remote area may not take off as quickly as the promotion brochures suggest…it will take a number of years to see a thriving border town where so far there is not much more than some infrastructure provision and very limited investment."

At the macro level of EWEC, it is not easy to identify tangible results and assess sustainability. Also, it is probably too early to expect to see any major impacts. The next few years will show whether the GMS initiatives have really benefited the local communities in the Lao part of the corridor.

LESSONS LEARNED

General

It would probably be wrong to claim that the case studies presented in this chapter represent "good practice." However, they do provide lessons on what can be achieved using the approaches and procedures described and, to a certain extent, what cannot. Sustainability is probably the objective that international and bilateral donors talk about the most but achieve the least. It is not surprising, therefore, that the sustainability of the three case studies is far from clear-cut. One benchmark of sustainability is replicability. In this respect, these projects will score differently because replicability is likely directly inversely proportional to the scale of the projects.

A factor affecting the sustainability of these and other projects is that lessons are mostly not learned. There is generally a very poor level of information exchange between agencies and practitioners in urban and regional development. This holds true for international agencies, national and local governments, and consultants. There is a clear need, therefore, for better transfer of information and knowledge. In the Lao PDR, the Government still suffers badly from compartmentalization with little communication between and within sectors. International advisers should lead the way in improving integration and continuity. Consultants should be encouraged to compare notes more readily; there is a role here for development partners to facilitate and coordinate this.

A prime example of this can be seen in Vientiane. At the time of writing, ADB's Small Towns Development Sector Project (STDSP) was just embarking on works in the first tranche of four small towns. The projects in the towns include a village-upgrading component very similar to the VAI scheme described in the Vientiane case study. As explained in the case study, the VUISP team learned many lessons in developing and refining their VAI scheme, which should be passed on to the STDSP team. The VUISP team is keen to propagate their procedures, but thus far have not been asked to do so.

Another overriding issue for urban and regional planning that these case studies have highlighted is the division between "spatial" and "economic" planning, common in many countries with socialist/communist regimes in their past or present. In the Lao PDR, all strategic economic and development planning is undertaken by or for CPI, which is part of the Prime Minister's Office. It is the General Planning Department in CPI that prepares the national socioeconomic development plans.

On the other hand, the Ministry of Communications, Transport, Posts and Construction (MCTPC) undertakes all spatial planning. Urban plans, infrastructure plans, and urban sector strategies all come within their domain. The problem lies in the fact that these two sets of outputs rarely come together. In interviews carried out for this chapter, it was apparent that senior officers in CPI were unaware of key studies and plans undertaken for MCTPC, including the Small Towns Development Strategy and the recent Urban Sector Strategy and Investment Plan, both of which included broad-reaching recommendations for the whole country.

This situation is compounded by the fact that "soft" outputs from primarily "hard" technical assistance projects, such as ADB's urban projects, are often overlooked or not followed through. For example, plans for urban areas and recommendations on the planning system were presented to MCTPC and ADB as part of the projects for Vientiane, the secondary towns, and the small towns. The fate of these reports has been to disappear onto shelves, never to be seen by other agencies either in or outside the Government. This must surely undermine the impact, effectiveness, and probably the sustainability of these major interventions.

Overall, existing policy and action are having only minor and gradual impacts on the conditions found in both urban and rural parts of the Lao PDR. There is no clear overall strategy for intervention and the traditional top-down processes will not lead to truly responsive solutions. In particular they will not, on their own, achieve significant or effective impacts on the livelihoods of the poor in these towns and their surrounding hinterlands. There is a need to review and improve existing procedures and to build on initial experiences in community-based procedures.

Lessons from the Specific Case Studies

Many lessons learned are incorporated in the text of the case studies. Some key issues are summarized below.

The key finding in the Vientiane case study is that small-scale projects supported at the village level are a feasible and effective approach to urban upgrading. Overall project design needs to be considered, as the VAI scheme would probably have been more efficient if it had been a discrete project rather than part of a much bigger package. These small-scale interventions are highly replicable and, if properly managed, they should be generally sustainable.

In common with many developing countries, there is a tendency in the Lao PDR to view the environment and the cultural heritage as discrete sectors to be taken care of by their respective government departments. In fact, the protection of environmental and cultural heritage resources can only be achieved through an integrated approach involving all development sectors. The situation in Luang Prabang today shows what can be achieved when urban improvements and conservation are tackled together. However, this has required very close control by an agency heavily dependent on international staff and support. There is uncertainty as to how sustainable this will be. The Luang Prabang case also raises the question as to how widespread the benefits of urban heritage preservation will be. By intensively supporting a small, exclusive heritage zone, there is a possible danger of accentuating the urban/rural divide.

EWEC demonstrates that multinational regional planning initiatives can bear fruit. The parts of the Lao PDR on and close to this corridor look set to benefit significantly from the initiative. At the same time, complementary local initiatives should be enacted to capitalize on the potential benefits. If these are not in place, there is a danger that the advantages will be enjoyed elsewhere, mostly outside the country. The Lao PDR should have clear spatial and economic strategies established to be in a position to balance the moves of its more powerful neighbors.

STRATEGIES TO ENHANCE SUSTAINABLE URBAN REGION DEVELOPMENT

Action to enhance sustainable urban region development in the Lao PDR will need to focus on improving strategic planning and on the development of inclusive, participatory local planning. In response to this, a strategy is outlined below with the two components development management and community planning (Table 8.3).

Development management involves addressing the need for improved planning and management at all levels and in all sectors leading to better-targeted interventions. Most activities of development management are already taking place; therefore, the objective must be to improve the institutional approach with a view to achieving responsive urban and regional management—responsive, that is, to the issues of urban and regional development and particularly to the needs of the poor.

A key aspect of this will be establishing a clear hierarchy of planning authorities. To this end, the clarification of the roles of UDAAs and municipalities needs to be given priority. This needs to be supported by extensive

Table 8.3: Strategy Components

	OBJECTIVES	TOOLS	PRODUCTS	OUTCOMES
Development Management	Sustainable development through responsive urban and regional management	Strategic planning Institutional awareness and capacity building – planning and financial management techniques, including community involvement	Strategies for growth Strategic transport plans Economic strategies Tourism strategies Regional Strategy Responsive town plans	*Urban area and regional improvements:* Primary regional and local infrastructure Secondary infrastructure Community services Strengthened town economies Benefits to rural hinterlands
Community Planning	Sustainable development through empowering the poor	Decentralization Demand-led infrastructure planning Consensus building and partnerships Microfinance strategies	Community-led village improvement programs Village groups (self-help groups, joint-liability groups) Village-led procurement Improved access to credit Subsidies to the poor to ensure access to services	*Village improvements:* Tertiary infrastructure Community facilities Improved economic stability Enhanced advocacy capacity Sustainable improvements

capacity building in the provinces and districts. Strategic regional plans must also be put in place to guide growth and investment. Development management will have some direct effects on the lives of the people in poor communities, but it will have mainly an indirect impact on poverty.

Community planning involves addressing the urgent need for improvements in the living conditions of the poor, utilizing the knowledge and skills of the poor themselves. There is little coordinated community planning taking place in the Lao PDR and efforts should be made to build on the VUISP experiences in Vientiane and the GPAR work in Luang Prabang. The objective is to facilitate the involvement of under-serviced communities in determining their own priorities, thereby empowering the poor. The outcomes of community planning should have a direct impact on poverty.

The two elements differ in one key aspect. That is, that development management already happens within an established framework of policy and action, while community planning does not. Some nongovernment organizations may claim that it is taking place, but there is no coordinated, nationwide program. The needs are, therefore, fundamentally different. In development management, the aim is to improve existing processes and enhance capacities for coordinated and responsive management. In community planning, the aim is to introduce new methodologies and develop mechanisms for integrating community involvement into the process of local area improvement. While the two elements will need to be addressed separately, the ultimate aim must be to combine them into a seamless system for managing sustainable growth and improving the livelihoods of the population.

Notes

[1] The terms "prefecture" and "municipality" have both been used when describing the grouping of nine districts comprising the Vientiane City administrative area. However, as yet there are no administrative entities known as "municipality" in the Lao PDR. For this reason, prefecture is the preferred term here.

[2] GDP per capita was $350 in 2002, and increased to $375 by 2003.

[3] Extracted from 2005 National Census, Preliminary Results.

9. Malaysia

BELINDA YUEN, SUPIAN AHMAD, AND CHIN SIONG HO

INTRODUCTION

During the past 15 years, Malaysia has experienced rapid urbanization and its economy has undergone major changes. These changes have led to a significant influx of rural people and migrants to urban centers, bringing about pressure on local and state governments to provide land for development and infrastructure and housing for growing urban populations. The latest national statistics are shown in Table 9.1.

Table 9.1: Country Development Profile, Malaysia

Human Development Index rank of 177 countries (2003)^	61
GDP growth (annual %, 2004)	7.06
GNI per capita, Atlas method (current $, 2004)	4,650
GNI, Atlas method (current $ billion, 2004)	117.1
GDP per capita PPP ($, 2003) ^	9,512
GDP PPP ($ billion, 2003) ^	235.7
Population growth (annual 2005–2010, %) #	1.66
Population, total (million, 2005) #	25.33
Urban population, total (million, 2005) #	16.48
Urban population percent of total population (2005) #	65
Population largest city: Kuala Lumpur (2005, million)	1.39
Population growth: 16 capital cities or agglomerations > 750,000 inhabitants 2000#	
- Est. average growth of capital cities or urban agglomerations 2005–2015 (%)	28
- Number of capital cities or urban agglomerations with growth > 50%, 2005–2015	1
- Number of capital cities or urban agglomerations with growth over 30%, 2005–2015	4
Sanitation, % of urban population with access to improved sanitation (2002)**	96
Water, % of urban population with access to improved water sources (2002)**	96
Slum population, % of urban population (2001)**	2
Slum population in urban areas (2001, million)**	0.26
Poverty, % of urban population below national poverty line (2001)**	n.a.
Aid (Net ODA received, $ million, 2003)^	109.1
Aid as a share of Country Income (Net ODA/GNI, 2003 %)*	0.1
Aid per capita (current $, 2003)^	4.4

GDP = gross domestic product, GNI = gross national income, ODA = official development assistance, PPP = purchasing power parity.
Sources: See Footnote Table 3.1; World Bank (2005); OECD (2003); United Nations (2004, 2005).

This chapter examines trends and issues concerned with urbanization in Malaysia. It presents three case studies demonstrating sustainable aspects of urban region development: Planning of Petaling Jaya satellite new town; Putrajaya Wetland Lake development; and innovation and change involving the Cyberjaya Multimedia Super Corridor. The chapter then discusses lessons learned and sustainable urban strategies for the future.

COUNTRY CONTEXT

Political Structure

Malaysia consists of two distinct land regions: Peninsula Malaysia, which shares common land borders with Thailand and Singapore; and the eastern states of Sabah and Sarawak in northwestern Borneo, where it shares a common land boundary with Brunei Darussalam and Indonesia. There are 11 states in Peninsula Malaysia—Perlis, Kedah, Penang, Perak, Selangor, Negri Sembilan, Melaka, Johor, Pahang, Trengganu, and Kelantan.

Population and Urbanization

Malaysia is a multicultural and multiracial society of about 25 million people where ethnic Malays, Chinese, and Indians live together in relative harmony. According to Agus (2002, p. 130), the tempo of urbanization for all ethnic groups in Malaysia during 1970–1980 was faster than in 1957–1970, but the Malays had the fastest rate of urbanization. The increasing relocation of *bumiputras* (bumiputra means the "sons of the soil" and it refers to the indigenous people of Malaysia) to cities resulted in a reduced Chinese majority in the urban areas.[1] During 1980–1990, urban population increased by 3.1.million. Of this increase, 10.3% was due to net migration, 52.3% from natural increase, and 37.4% from net urban boundary adjustments. As Figure 9.1 illustrates, the trend is that the rural population is on the decline and will enter negative growth after 2010. The rural population by 2030 is projected to decline to 7.9 million compared with 27.3 million people in urban areas.

GOOD PRACTICE CASE STUDIES

The chosen good practice study cases are Petaling Jaya, Putrajaya, and Cyberjaya. All three are located in Kelang Valley in the state of Selangor, which is

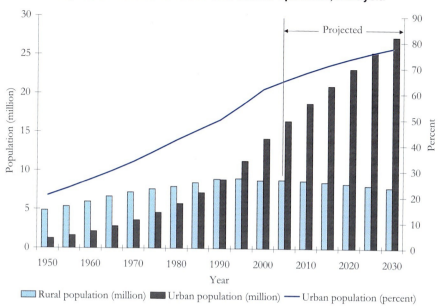

Figure 9.1: Trends in Urban and Rural Population, Malaysia

the fastest-growing region in Malaysia. They are pioneer model projects and represent milestones in the country's sustainable urban development.

Petaling Jaya is the earliest satellite new town, planned in the 1950s to alleviate the increasing congestion of the capital city, Kuala Lumpur. It has a total area of 51.4 square kilometers (km$^{2)}$ and gained the status of a municipality in 1977. It has developed into an important city in the urban conurbation of Kuala Lumpur with a population of about half a million people governed by Petaling Jaya Municipality. Local Agenda 21 was successfully implemented there in 2000.

Putrajaya is the new administrative seat of the Malaysian Government, following the Government's decision in June 1993 to relocate the federal administrative capital from Kuala Lumpur to the district of Sepang in Selangor. The relocation is part of the decentralization effort as well as a means to alleviate traffic congestion in Kuala Lumpur and ensure its continued development as Malaysia's premier business hub. Putrajaya is a model city planned with "great respect for the environment" (Putrajaya Malaysia tourist information pamphlet). The city plans to embrace two main themes: city in a garden and "intelligent city."

The construction of Putrajaya commenced in October 1996. By 2005, it had about 80,000 inhabitants, with modern and "smart" public amenities and infrastructure. Putrajaya is equipped with a good inter- and intra-city transport system, including monorail and water taxis, a broadband global

Figure 9.2: Map Showing Location of the Case Studies

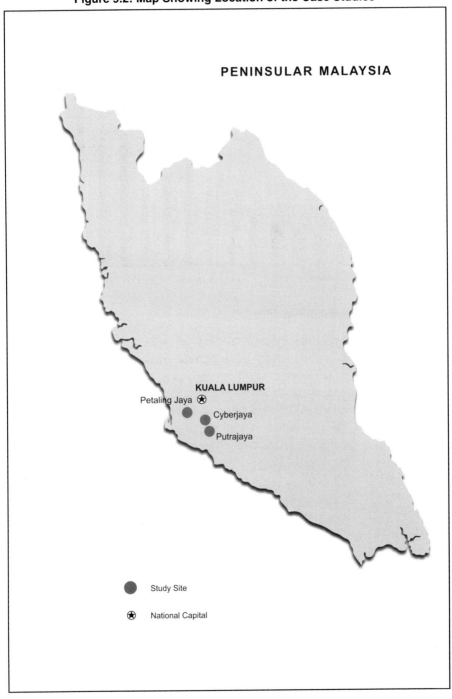

multimedia communication platform, and a common utility tunnel for services, hospitals, and schools. About 38% of the land is being developed into parkland. Putrajaya has the largest man-made wetland in Malaysia with a total area of about 160 hectares (ha), which is used for recreational activities as well as scientific and biological research.

Cyberjaya is the multimedia super corridor (MSC) city dedicated to multimedia companies. It is the national information technology (IT) hub of Malaysia. It is adjacent to Putrajaya and is surrounded by other MSC clusters such as "tele-suburbs," a high-tech park, and cyber-village and airport city. The development started in 1996 with seven flagship applications and 50 world-class companies. Cyberjaya exemplifies a planned city open to innovation and change and seems ready to take advantage of the opportunity of global IT development.

Petaling Jaya: Local Agenda 21 Implementation

Background

Along with many other countries in the world, Malaysia has implemented Local Agenda 21. Agenda 21 is a comprehensive plan of action developed at the Rio Earth Summit in 1992 to be taken globally, nationally, and locally by organizations of the United Nations System, governments, and major groups in every area in which humans impact on the environment.

GOOD PRACTICE	
Good Governance	✓
Urban Management	
Infrastructure/Service Provision	✓
Financing and Cost Recovery	
Sustainability	✓
Innovation and Change	✓
Leveraging ODA	

Local Agenda 21 has been used as a program for cooperation between local authorities, communities, and the private sector to plan and manage their built and natural environments toward sustainable development.

It can be described as a local action plan aiming at sustainable development in the 21st century. Petaling Jaya Municipal Council carried out a Local Agenda 21 Pilot Project for 2 years starting in early 2000 (Lee 2001).² It was selected due to its commitment, geographical location, capacity, and existence as a community-based organization in promoting community development.

Petaling Jaya is a satellite town of the federal capital, Kuala Lumpur. It is located in the district of Petaling, State of Selangor. It was established in 1952 with an area of 19.9 km² and was originally planned to accommodate 70,000 people to help relieve the problem of congestion in Kuala Lumpur and provide new homes and job opportunities. Petaling Jaya experienced rapid urbanization as more people from rural areas migrated to the town, leading to the development of Sungai Way and Subang districts and more than 50 other

Table 9.2: Land Use, Petaling Jaya

Land Use	Proportion (%)
Housing	52.1
Industry	14.3
Commerce	6.4
Public facilities	4.5
Open space and recreation	8.8
Institutions	0.3
Infrastructure	9.2
Others	4.4
Total	100

Source: Petaling Jaya Municipal Council.

new areas within the jurisdiction of the municipality.[3] With the growth of the town, the Petaling Jaya Town Authority was upgraded to the Petaling Jaya Municipal Council in 1977. Petaling Jaya has since expanded to about five times its original size, covering an area of about 97.2 km^2, with a population of 486,040 (2005).

The Petaling Jaya Municipality is Malaysia's first and largest industrial area. It acts as one of the center hubs of Klang Valley (comprising Kuala Lumpur, Petaling Jaya, Shah Alam, Subang Jaya, and surrounding areas) for industry. Table 9.2 shows the major land use of the municipality. Housing and industry are the two major land uses, constituting about two thirds of the municipality's total land area.

Implementation of Local Agenda 21

The state of Selangor, one of the most developed states in Peninsular Malaysia, was the first to draft a sustainable development strategy toward a more developed state by 2005. The Petaling Jaya Municipal Council (MPPJ) adopted the Selangor Sustainable Development Strategies and Selangor Agenda 21 as a guide in formulating its action plans, publicity program, courses, and training for the Local Agenda 21 Petaling Jaya program.

The broad Local Agenda 21 initiatives, national policies, Selangor Agenda 21, and the local authority's policies were all compiled and presented to the community at large for their feedback and consideration. The Local Agenda 21 Petaling Jaya pilot project (2000–2002) planning process, following the United Nations Development Program (UNDP), aims to (Ministry of Housing et al. 2002, 28):

(i) balance economic, community, and environmental interests and considerations into projects, processes, and strategies;

(ii) fully engage a wide local stakeholders' group to get a range of views and interests, particularly those who will benefit from or be affected by the outcome of the planning process; and
(iii) create mechanisms and strategies that can be maintained over the long term to address various issues in an in-depth and sustained manner.

There are six main stages in the Local Agenda 21 Petaling Jaya planning process:

(i) formulation of a community vision and the aspirations of stakeholders;
(ii) formation of partnership (local authority, community, and businesses);
(iii) community input (community-based issues, local knowledge);
(iv) drafting of action plan (formalized agreed objectives, targets, commitments);
(v) implementation and monitoring (stakeholders monitor activities); and
(vi) evaluation and feedback (medium- and long-term review).

A total of 150 participants representing 80 organizations participated in the formulation of the community vision during a 2-day workshop in 2000. They included representatives from nongovernment organizations (NGOs), resident associations, schools, the private sector, and government agencies. The adopted community vision states:

> *The MPPJ, communities, and other agencies in Petaling Jaya give our commitment to solve the identified issues through greater participation, consultation, and awareness-raising process in building a comfortable, harmonious and healthy city within the sustainable environment. (MPPJ, 2000, p. 4)*

Following the establishment of the community vision as a common direction and mandate, a Local Agenda 21 Petaling Jaya Committee was set up with the mayor of MPPJ as the chairperson.[4] The Local Agenda 21 Committee consists of 37 members, comprising representatives from NGOs, community-building organizations, religious institutions, the private sector, government agencies, and the MPPJ. A especially formulated Local Agenda 21 Petaling Jaya logo and slogan "Petaling Jaya: Toward Sustainable Development" was used to create public awareness shared identity and enhance ownership.

A second workshop was organized to disseminate the common vision to a large number of residents and stakeholders to obtain their feedback and reach a consensus. In the second workshop, the participants identified three neighborhood areas—SS 21, SS 22, and PJS 2—in Petaling Jaya to be the Local Agenda 21 PJ pilot project sites. Since 2000, six working committees[5] have been set up. Three of them were formed according to major themes of the common vision, i.e., safety, social integration, and environment. The other three working committees were established according to the geographical locations of the selected neighborhoods (SS 21, SS 22, and PJS 2). The working committees then formed three action plan committees:

- Social Integration Working Committee (SS 21) – strengthening the relationship of the neighborhood;
- Environment Working Committee (SS 22) – domestic waste management; and
- Safety Working Committee (PJS 2) – petty crime prevention and vandalism action plan.

Discussions were held to improve participation in the Local Agenda 21 action plan formulation, using such techniques as logical framework analysis, SWOT analysis, and card systems. The aim was to ensure that all action plans had been formulated through effective roundtable and multi-stakeholder discussions. Table 9.3 gives an illustration of the detailed activities and programs implemented under the respective action plans.

From the pilot program implementation, shown above, residents were found to be more concerned with daily pressing problems such as recycling, safety, vandalism, and service quality, rather than global environmental issues such as global warming and biodiversity. The working committee for the action plans showed a tendency to emphasize local rather than global matters. This emphasis continued into the current phases of Local Agenda 21 PJ implementation.[6] Another interesting finding was that a heightened neighborhood spirit can be fostered through innovative initiatives and community-based activities, such as neighborhood competitions, recycling campaigns, and ecological projects.[7]

Lessons Learned

The experience from the pilot projects as shared by MPPJ Petaling Jaya Local Agenda 21 Officer, Lee Lih Shyan, demonstrates several key learning elements in Local Agenda 21 implementation. These concern capacity building, institutional and mechanism arrangements, leadership, and information accessibility.

Capacity building of the stakeholders should be a continuous process to promote stakeholder understanding of sustainable development. As demonstrated by the Local Agenda 21 Petaling Jaya pilot project implementa-

Table 9.3: Programs Implemented under Working Committees

Working Committee	Programs
Environment	a) Briefing of recycling project in schools b) Demonstration of kitchen and garden waste composting c) Distribution of brochure on recycling d) Establishment of community recycling e) Awareness and training program f) Natural and organic food carnival with NGO
Social Integration	a) Family day b) Best neighborhood competition c) Consultation with disabled people d) Festive season celebration
Safety	a) Safety and security guidebook b) Neighborhood watch scheme c) Fire hydrant adoption scheme d) Exhibition on anti-vandalism
Other initiatives	a) Section 17 town center beautification and cleanliness activities b) Advertising and billboard to promote LA21 c) Publication of publicity materials d) Website creation: www.mppj.gov.my/la21 e) Stakeholder training f) Operation of community ICT center at section 17 through partnership with MPPJ, PIKOM, and PJCC g) Consultation process on planning and development projects (town park, traffic control, etc.)

ICT = information and communications technology, LA = Local Agenda, MPPJ = Petaling Jaya Municipal Council, NGO = nongovernment organization, PIKOM = Persatuan Industri Komputer dan Mutimedia Malaysia or Association of the Computer and Multimedia Industries of Malaysia.
Source: Petaling Jaya Municipal Council 2005.

tion, this is best achieved through awareness and education programs such as training, workshops, and group discussions or seminars. The participation of professionals and experts, academicians, NGOs, and local authorities help promote stakeholders' understanding of the problems faced by the authorities as well as the general public.

At the local authority level, institutional arrangements, such as the setting up of multidisciplinary departments, multi-stakeholders' groups, and multisectoral committees, are useful in leading to better understanding and consistency of policies about sustainable development. The participation of local leaders in Local Agenda 21 pilot projects is another critical success factor because they have the ability to influence, educate, and initiate ideas in the community to promote Local Agenda 21 implementation. To enhance participation and dissemination of information to a wide group, information and communications technology (ICT) is employed as an effective tool to facilitate effective communication. A high penetration rate of ICT among the community members will further enhance participation, transparency, equity, responsiveness, and efficiency in the local delivery service system and planning process.

The successful implementation of Local Agenda Petaling Jaya 21 pilot projects has led to current key ecological projects, such as Kelana Jaya lake rehabilitation scheme, Stream Keepers Handbook project, and Sungei Penchala Rehabilitation program.

The implementation of these projects illustrates the confidence and strong partnership with various stakeholders as well as funding and support from local groups and international agencies, such as the Danish International Development Agency, Canadian International Development Agency, and UNDP-Global Environment Facility (UNDP-GEF). Specifically, these projects aim at improving the quality of water from the current standard IV to standard IIB that is suitable for recreational purposes. Strong partnership spirit and active participation can be seen from the involvement of the Section 19 Resident Association in monitoring water quality, launching the State Irrigation and Drainage project of "One State-One River Pilot Scheme," and launching environmental brigades by the Malaysian Department of Environment. They demonstrate the workability of community-based participation and development.

Putrajaya, Model City of Sustainable Development

Background

Putrajaya is the country's largest urban development project on a greenfield site, set to be a model city of sustainable development. It is 25 km from Kuala Lumpur City and 20 km from Kuala Lumpur International Airport. It is situated within the southern growth corridor and MSC, 5 km from Cyberjaya. It has an area of 4,931 ha (about one third

GOOD PRACTICE	
Good Governance	
Urban Management	
Infrastructure/Service Provision	
Financing and Cost Recovery	
Sustainability	✓
Innovation and Change	✓
Leveraging ODA	

the size of Kuala Lumpur) with a target population of 330,000 (2010) and daytime population of 500,000 (Table 9.4). To accommodate this population, a total of 67,000 detached and row housing and condominiums are planned, with 3.8 million m^2 of government and 3.4 million m^2 of commercial land use in eight precincts.

In terms of land use distribution, as an administrative center, Putrajaya has a high percentage of government institutional (53%) and commercial land use (29%), followed by a relatively high percentage of green area (38%). Government use; mixed development; and civic, cultural, commercial, sports, and recreational precincts are located in the core area, while the residential areas and diplomatic enclave are on the periphery. A large tract of greenery is important to ensure the implementation of the garden city concept where landscaping and water bodies are prominent components.

Table 9.4: Population and Area of Putrajaya

Area	4,931 hectares
Land use	
- Government	53.0%
- Commercial	29.0%
- Residential	25.8%
- Civic and cultural	0.2%
- Public facilities	10.1%
- Utility and infrastructure	18.2%
- Green area	37.5%
Planned population	330,000
Daytime population	500,000
Government	3.8 million m^2
Commercial	3.4 million m^2
Planned housing units	67,000 units

Source: Putrajaya Holding 2005.

The intention is to build a city that reflects the natural and cultural heritage of the country with the capacity and amenities to meet the challenges of the millennium (Perbadanan Putrajaya and Putrajaya Holdings Sdn Bhd 1999, p. 13). Its residents can look forward to a diverse range of entertainment, sports, leisure, and recreational activities, both indoor and outdoor. Businesses can locate or invest in a wide range of commercial products from an A grade office to business parks, hotel developments, or other leisure/entertainment/retail and waterfront projects. Approved businesses/industries will also receive and enjoy various incentives.

The city development is in two phases over a period of 15 years. Phase 1 (1996–2000) and Phase 2 (2000–2010). Putrajaya Holdings Sdn Bhd, the developer of the township, was incorporated in 1995; Perbadanan Putrajaya was incorporated (1996) as the body to administer and manage Putrajaya.

Table 9.5 shows the development position of Putrajaya in 2003, with a population of about 40,000 people, which was to double to 80,000 by end 2005 with an additional 9,700 housing units. Population growth depends greatly on the speed of construction of the government buildings, which is the main source of employment in the city's initial stage of development.

In 2003, more than 2 million m² or half of the government buildings were completed/under construction. In addition, about 20,000 houses were completed/under construction. The housing was built largely for public servants and their families.

Table 9.5: Existing Putrajaya Population and Status (2003)

Planning Information	Size (Status)
Resident population	40,000
Government office worker	13,200
Government offices	802,319 m² (completed)
	1,203,694.3 m² (under construction)
Commercial spaces	28,110 m² (completed)
	148,645 m² (under construction)
Housing units	9,711 units (completed)
	10,991 units (under construction)

Source: Putrajaya Holding 2005.

An already completed development is the Putrajaya Lake and Wetlands, which is in the heart of the city and is a critical component of the project. Built to demonstrate the benefits of incorporating the wetlands ecosystem into an urban area, Putrajaya Wetlands is next discussed as a good practice case in sustainability. The key environment-friendly solution of constructing the wetlands is to treat catchment water before it enters the Putrajaya Lake, thus ensuring that the water in Putrajaya Lake remains clean and unpolluted. The 197 ha Putrajaya Wetlands is one of the largest freshwater wetlands in the tropics (Perbadanan Putrajaya and Putrajaya Holdings Sdn Bhd 1999). It is Malaysia's first such project and represents a milestone in its urban development.

Implementation of Putrajaya Wetlands

Central to the development objective of Putrajaya as a model city of sustainable development is the concept of a "city in a garden." The planners incorporated nature through greening programs and creating Putrajaya Lake as an integral part of the urban development concept. The 400 ha Putrajaya Lake, created by damming the two rivers, River Chuau and River Bisa, forms the centerpiece and distinctive identity of the new city.

Studies of the Putrajaya catchment revealed the presence of increased pollutant levels in the lake's water from upstream sources and outside the city's development boundary. Sustaining the long-term urban development of the wetlands is proposed with the aim "to create a self-sustaining and balanced ecosystem in Putrajaya" (Perbadanan Putrajaya and Putrajaya Holdings Sdn Bhd 1999, p. 37). Wetlands are defined as "land inundated with temporary or permanent water that is usually slow moving or stationary, shallow, either fresh, brackish or saline, where the inundation determines the types and productivity of soils and the plant and animal communities" (Ramsar Convention 1971, cited in Perbadanan Putrajaya and Putrajaya Holdings Sdn Bhd 1999, p. 21).

Putrajaya Lake is a constructed wetland with human-made systems that involve altering the existing terrain to simulate natural wetland conditions. This is primarily designed to replicate observations that wetlands purify water by removing organic compounds and oxidizing ammonia, reducing nitrates, and removing phosphorous. The mechanisms are complex and involve bacteria oxidation, filtration, sedimentation, and chemical precipitation.

Among the goals of the wetland development are to construct a self-sustaining, balanced lake and tropical wetland ecosystem to guarantee the high quality of the lake water, and to develop a natural habitat of public conservation of indigenous wetland flora and fauna. Research and knowledge of the role of natural wetlands in water resource management, especially controlling water pollution have helped construct this man-made wetland that replicates an environment-friendly ecosystem. Even so, given its size, the fast-track nature of the project, catchment management, and the presence of numerous inlets, several key challenges in its development confront even its innovative lake design.[8]

The Putrajaya Wetlands has been constructed to remove pollutants from the catchment before it enters the lake. A series of wetlands is to be constructed to filter and cleanse the water that enters the lake. As with many other development projects, the Putrajaya Wetlands showcase predominantly Malaysian resources. They are a product of a dedicated team of Malaysian scientists in various disciplines working together to combine international

Table 9.6: Principal Features of Putrajaya Lake and Putrajaya Wetlands

A. Putrajaya Lake

Catchment area	Water level	Surface area	Storage volume	Average depth	Average catchment inflow	Average retention time
50.9 km²	RL 21 m	400 hectares	26.5 million m³	6.6 m	200 million liters/day	132 days

B. Putrajaya Wetlands (Area in ha)

Total area	Planted area	Open water	Weirs and islands	Zone of intermittent inundation	Maintenance tracks
197.2	77.7	76.8	9.6	23.7	9.4

ha = hectare, m = meter, m³ = cubic meter.
Source: Perbadanan Putrajaya and Putrajaya Holdings Sdn Bhd, 1999, 16 and 34.

and local research to provide an acceptable solution to meet system design criteria, including minimum lake design standards for phosphorus, nitrogen, suspended solids, and bacteria. It is an innovative design, especially the multicell and multi-stage approach layout. This design strategy ensures the better distribution of flow across wetlands and maximizes shallow areas required for successful growth of aquatic plants in the filtration and cleansing function. This approach also permits cost-effective maintenance of the lake.

A total of 24 wetlands cells are being created based on the height of the water level and classified as upper, central, and lower cells. Within each cell, the water depth varies from 0.5 meters (m) to 3 m to allow downstream flow direction. Each wetland cell is designed to create zones of wetland and intermittent inundation. Aquatic plants are established in the wetland zones where the primary role is filtration by intercepting pollutants. The wetland zones are permanently flooded. The zone of intermittent inundation on the lower slope of the inundated area is flooded only during high flows.

Putrajaya Wetland Lake is composed of three control levels, namely, normal water level, weir overflow level, and major flood level. The detention storage level is between normal water level and weir overflow level only. Orifice control is used to increase the wetland retention time and control the release of floodwater during flooding.[9] Beyond design and construction, the quality of the water is continuously monitored and managed by the wetlands management department.

The Putrajaya wetlands management has also implemented an extensive public education program to foster greater community awareness and participation in environmental conservation. With the wetlands construction, Putrajaya Lake and its environs have "altered from a terrestrial plantation [of oil palm and rubber] into a marsh of aquatic plants (in the wetlands itself) and banks of riparian and littoral vegetation" (Perbadanan Putrajaya and Putrajaya Holdings Sdn Bhd, 1999, p. 107). It has become an important part of the green corridor linking Putrajaya to the surrounding forest reserves.

Lessons Learned

The Putrajaya Wetlands project illustrates the benefits of incorporating wetland ecosystems into urban development. It demonstrates how a country with vision, determination, and planning may draw inspiration from nature to solve an urban problem, which is not just of local but also of global significance. As the former Malaysian prime minister said: "We call upon the global community to target at least 30% of the earth's terrestrial area to be greened by the year 2000…The greening of the world will hopefully inspire a new spirit of international cooperation and partnership in which global resources are fairly shared. If successful, we would have solved, at least partially, an important environmental problem" (Perbadanan Putrajaya and Putrajaya Holdings Sdn Bhd 1999, p. 11).

Wetlands, whether natural or man-made, can be planned as an integral part of a city's urban greening and further harnessed as an environmental-friendly solution to improve water quality and urban aesthetics, with a wider role for ecotourism, public education, and scientific research. This, as the Malaysian case demonstrates, clearly requires careful planning at the design, construction, and management phases, and engagement of the entire community. Herein lies the challenge as well as opportunity for harmonious coexistence of humans and the environment. The Malaysian case of wetlands in urban planning holds relevance for other cities in other countries seeking to improve the quality of life and water resource management in urban areas.

Cyberjaya Multimedia Super Corridor, Innovation and Change

Background

The Cyberjaya intelligent city is located at the center of a rapidly expanding technology region, the MSC. This technology region is Malaysia's first development initiative to move the economy from traditional manufacturing to a knowledge economy. The MSC, to be developed in three phases during 1996–2020, is located to the south of

GOOD PRACTICE	
Good Governance	✓
Urban Management	
Infrastructure/Service Provision	
Financing and Cost Recovery	
Sustainability	✓
Innovation and Change	✓
Leveraging ODA	

the Kuala Lumpur Metropolitan Area. Covering an area of 15 km by 50 km, the corridor stretches from Kuala Lumpur City Center in the north to the Kuala Lumpur International Airport in the south, with Cyberjaya and Putrajaya, the new administrative capital, in the middle. By 2020, there will be 12 intelligent cities. The Multimedia Development Corporation (MDC) is especially set up and empowered by an act of Parliament to spearhead MSC development. The MSC is set to offer an attractive physical, legal, and financial environment for both indigenous and foreign ICT companies to create products and services for the global market. In addition to good infrastructure, the MSC provides cyber laws to protect the intellectual property of ICT firms. Both local and foreign firms are eligible to apply and receive MSC status,[10] special incentives that include tax-free status for up to 10 years, duty-free imports of equipment, and unrestricted employment of foreign ICT workers (MDC 2004).

Implementation of Cyberjaya

Cyberjaya, at the center of MSC, acts as the main catalyst for the region's economic and ICT growth. It is the first intelligent garden city planned and developed by Malaysian planners. The development of the 2,894 ha site started in 1997 and was officially launched on 8 July 1999. Due for completion in 2011, total project cost is expected to be in the region of $5.3 billion.

The township is planned with easy access to the nearby cities of Kuala Lumpur and Shah Alam. The Express Rail Link, for example, connects Cyberjaya to the center of Kuala Lumpur. Several planning zones facilitate phased development.[11] The central area of Cyberjaya, called the flagship zones and covering almost half of the total land area, is made up of enterprise, commercial, and residential zones. The rest of the technology township is allocated for public facilities, green areas, and recreational areas. Unlike many other technology-based townships, Cyberjaya is a self-contained area with emphasis on eco-friendly, low-density development that preserves nature and maintains a good landscape for an excellent quality of life.[12]

The development of MSC is supported by a high-capacity, digital telecommunications infrastructure designed to meet international standards in aspects of capacity, reliability, and pricing.[13] As a technology township, Cyberjaya is to be provided with a broad range of the latest technology infrastructure, including

- international and national fiber-optic backbone with multiple internet service providers;
- broadband connectivity to all buildings;
- wireless WiFi hot-spot service at most public areas;
- equal availability of cheap, dark-fiber fiber-optic connectivity to all internet service providers, telcos and other service providers regardless of size;
- local online e-commerce portal; and,
- "smart" homes and schools.

Some provisions, for example, smart schools, will be benchmarked and tracked against international developments. As an intelligent city, one of the salient features of Cyberjaya development is the establishment of the city command center (CCC). The CCC acts as a central monitoring hub to monitor, manage, and implement key services. It is considered as the "brain" of the city, providing single management of traffic, utilities, community facilities, municipal services, and public amenities through integration of systems and services in three major areas: advanced traffic management, integrated utility management, interactive community service, and municipal and public amenities.

The CCC can be accessed through a variety of means, including the customer service counter at the CCC building, telephone service, interactive voice response system, interactive television, personal computers at home and office, and mobile data terminals and kiosks in public areas. The development of Cyberjaya and MSC showcases how innovation and change in ICT are integrated with eco-friendly urban development to enhance the quality of life.[14]

To attract and encourage ICT development, the Malaysian Government through the MDC, backed by the Bill of Guarantees, offers the following commitments to companies:

- provide a world-class physical and information infrastructure;
- allow unrestricted employment of local and foreign ICT workers;
- ensure freedom of ownership by exempting companies with MSC status from local ownership requirements;
- give freedom to source capital globally for MSC infrastructure and right to borrow funds globally;
- provide competitive financial incentives, including Pioneer Status (100% tax exemption) for up to 10 years or an investment tax allowance for up to 5 years, and no duties on the importation of multimedia equipment;
- become a regional leader in intellectual property protection and cyber laws;
- ensure no censorship of the internet;
- provide globally competitive telecommunication tariffs;
- tender key MSC infrastructure contracts to leading companies willing to use the MSC as their regional hub; and
- provide a high-powered agency to act as an effective one-stop super shop.

Unlike many industrial development strategies elsewhere, the above constitutes probably one of the most innovative strategies put forward to promote the MSC as a center of ICT industries. The Bill of Guarantees and incentives are not only competitive in comparison with other technology regions but are lucrative as well to make this technology region a business attraction for local as well as global companies.[15]

Within 2 years of development, several facilities were completed, including the Multimedia University, Lim Kok Wing University College of Creative Technology, Century Square office blocks, the MDC headquarters, Cyberview Lodge Resort and Spa, several Enterprise Buildings, a smart school, the transport terminal, Cyberpark, the central incubator, and the Street Mall. Several other facilities, including a sports complex, Tele-Medicine Centre, and an 18-hole golf course are expected to be completed in the near future.

The township currently houses about 10,000 people with an anticipated population of 120,000 (2010). Table 9.7 shows the current number of MSC companies by sectors. These include large technology companies such as NTT Japan and TMNet, both operating from their own premises. Other world-leading companies, such as DHL, HSBC, Shell, BMW, EDS, Motorola, Ericsson, and Nokia, have also established their companies within single tenancy buildings. As well, other smaller companies operate from office buildings for multiple tenancies, including the Century Square. Facilities to be owned or rented have been built to cater to the differing needs of ICT industries. The target is to locate about 500 IT companies in Cyberjaya by 2020.

Lessons Learned

Diversifying the economic base and promoting ICT growth is never an easy task. Focused start-up efforts are useful to catalyze development and enhance confidence, especially when such development is new and unfamiliar. The country and its population need time to build up the ICT and knowledge capacity. The Cyberjaya development manifests what might be achieved

Table 9.7: MSC Companies according to Sectors

Sectors	Number
Software Development/Business Application	339
Software Development, Engineering and Specialized Application	238
Internet Business-E-commerce services/Solution Providers	117
Content Development	113
Internet-based Business/Web hosting/Online publishing	110
Hardware/Electronics Design	109
Education and Training	85
Internet Based Business – Application Service Provider	71
Wireless/Mobile Technology	58
Shared Services/Outsourcing	55
Systems Integration	40
Telecommunications/Networking	45
Computer/Systems Security	30
Production/Post-production/Animation	26
Computer/Engineering Design	17
Incubator	17
Consultancy	16
Bio Informatics/Life Sciences	8

Source: MDC 2004.

by fusing technology, vision, and determination to make that leap. As a trailblazer and long-term investment, the technology township is carefully planned with a large budget from the start.

The importance of government commitment and support to every aspect of the city's development and success has to be underscored. Its implementation necessitates capacity in ICT infrastructure, including the promotion of ICT education and culture for young and old, at home, work, and play, which requires broad changes in workforce planning, resources channeling, and simultaneous updates on the impacts of ICT and other new innovations. With comprehensive and up-to-date technological innovations, infrastructure, laws, schools, and software, Cyberjaya is set to showcase how technology and development may improve the quality of life in a sustainable development model, and illuminate the development path for the remaining proposed intelligent cities in the years ahead.

STRATEGIES TO ENHANCE SUSTAINABLE URBAN DEVELOPMENT

The Malaysian Government has continuously given attention to avoiding environmental degradation from overdevelopment while seeking innovative ideas to build sustainable cities. The three case studies showcase some of those efforts: community participation in Local Agenda 21 PJ, innovative construction of Putrajaya wetlands, and the building of a new Cyberjaya intelligent garden city to achieve the broader goal of urban development and sustainability. They are primarily aimed at making cities work better for all who live, work, do business, and play in them. They provide examples of the public-led national processes and approaches that are being implemented at various levels—from local to metropolitan and regional—to meet existing concerns and challenges.

As with many other Asian countries, Malaysia is rapidly urbanizing. Beyond meeting the services that are required of all city governments, some key challenges facing Malaysian urban development concern the increased size of cities in terms of both their population and land consumption, which, if not properly managed, will have far-reaching negative environmental impact. Examples include the massive land conversion of oil palm plantations into mixed housing development (a form of unsustainable "greenfield development"), low-density urban suburbs, illegal hillside development, and encroachment of wetlands, especially in the form of waterfront or riverfront development.

There is a growing awareness that these will not remain isolated local issues. The Federal Town and Country Planning Department and respective local authorities have initiated broad policy strategies and a legal framework in the form of development plans, development guidelines, and planning standards to arrest such undesirable development and their adverse environmental impact. However, these problems will prevail and continue unless stringent monitoring mechanisms by the local authorities and respective government authorities are adopted. In other words, while there is commitment to sustainable development as set out in the National Vision Policy, a more holistic approach to sustainable development planning is necessary in preparing development plans at the structure plan and local plan levels. Even though the sustainable development debate may be in full swing globally, the alternatives are at an initial stage in Malaysia. A wide dissemination and stocktaking of urban good practices in sustainable development will hopefully entrench their sharing and sharpen the practice.

What is most important is that there is no turning back in regard to sustainable development. Recent efforts of government agencies, especially by the Federal Town and Country Planning Department and local authorities to develop innovative models of city building—Putrajaya and Cyberjaya—have led the way in demonstrating the urban possibilities in utilizing ecological solutions and ICT. Partnership between the different levels of government and inclusion appear to be yet another immediate strategic area of policy action. Active and effective participation at the neighborhood level involving different stakeholders (as in the case of Petaling Jaya Local Agenda 21) offers new directions for consolidating community-based action. It presents relevant options for achieving not just economic sustainability but also social justice and equity, which are important in identifying urban solutions that are tailored as closely as possible to people's needs.

Notes

[1] The relocation is a part of the Government's New Economic Policy to promote greater growth and equality among the various ethnic groups in the country. See Economic Planning Unit (2004) and www.epu.jpm.my for further discussion of the policy and details of Malaysia's Vision Policy and 5-year development plans.

[2] Petaling Jaya, Miri, Kuantan, and Kubang Kerian are among the pioneer local authorities implementing Local Agenda 21.

[3] Following a boundary realignment exercise in early 1997, parts of Petaling Jaya, such as Subang Jaya, Sunway, Puchong, and USJ, have been placed under the jurisdiction of the newly formed Subang Jaya Municipal Council.

[4] The functions of the Local Agenda 21 Petaling Jaya Committee included facilitating the implementation of the Local Agenda 21 pilot project; steering the direction of the Local Agenda 21 pilot project; formulating an action plan and implementation strategies; coordinating, implementing, and monitoring the implementation of the

Local Agenda 21 pilot project; and reporting the project progress to the full council, and national, technical, and steering committees.

[5] The functions of the working committees include awareness-raising activities via dialogue, research and campaigning at the local level; formulating action plans and implementation strategies; coordinating, implementing and monitoring the progress of Local Agenda 21 Pilot Project, and reporting progress to Local Agenda 21 Petaling Jaya Committee.

[6] See www.mppj.gov.my/la21 for more details.

[7] The key ecological projects are the restoration of Kelana Jaya Lake, Sungei Penchala, and the production of a stream keeper's handbook. While the pilot projects were funded by MPPJ and the Malaysian Government, these later ecological projects enjoy international funding from Danish International Development Agency, Canadian International Development Agency, and United Nations Development Program - Global Environment Facility.

[8] See Perbadanan Putrajaya and Putrajaya Holdings Sdn Bhd (1999), Chapter 4, for further discussion of how a vision becomes reality.

[9] See Perbadanan Putrajaya and Putrajaya Holdings Sdn Bhd (1999), Chapter 6, for details of these innovations in the wetland design.

[10] Companies with strong value-added activities, which are providers or heavy users of multimedia products and services, are eligible for MSC status, which then entitle them to certain privileges and incentives offered under the Bill of Guarantees.

[11] There are two phases of development, with phase 1 comprising approximately 1,460 hectares.

[12] See Setia Haruman Sdn Berhad webpage (www.setiaharuman.com/msc/intro.htm, accessed on 11 Jan 2006) for more information. Setia Haruman Sdn Berhad is the master developer of the Cyberjaya Flagship Zone.

[13] The main features of the telecommunications infrastructure include, first, a fiber-optic backbone with 2.5–10 gigabits per second capacity; second, high-capacity links to international centers; third, open standards; fourth, high-speed switching and multiple protocols including ATM; fifth, best-in-class performance guarantees; sixth, competitive telecommunications pricing; and seventh, integration into new transportation projects.

[14] See MDC (2003) for more details.

[15] Especially the income tax allowance as sourcing of capital is fundamental to emerging indigenous companies in the ICT sector.

10. Pakistan

MURTAZA HAIDER AND IRTEZA HAIDER

INTRODUCTION

The current state of towns and cities in Pakistan is at complete odds with the rich heritage of urban planning that flourished in the subcontinent for more than a millennium. Cities once known for manicured gardens and exquisite fountains today reek of unmanaged solid waste and sewage. Due to resource constraints, sanitation and water supply have not been given top priority for the disenfranchised urban poor in Pakistan, who face poverty, disease, and lack of opportunity. This chapter explores issues related to urbanization.[1] It provides three case studies that demonstrate good practice in sustainable urban development in Pakistan related to water supply, solid waste management, and sanitation.[2] Table 10.1 shows some development statistics for Pakistan.

COUNTRY CONTEXT

Pakistan in the early 1950s was primarily rural, with only a handful of small to mid-sized cities. The population was estimated at 34 million in 1951; it is estimated at 160 million in 2005. The current urban population is about 56 million. The proportion of urban population increased from 17% in 1951 to 35% in 2005.

Since its inception as an independent state in 1947, Pakistan has experienced dramatic changes in economy and demographics. The agriculture sector, which contributed more than 53% of gross domestic product (GDP) in 1949–1950, declined to 24% of GDP in 2004 (Zaidi 2005). Over the same period, manufacturing increased from 8% to 26%, and services and trade increased from 25% to 51%. Whereas the share of agriculture in the national GDP halved over the last 5 decades, the agricultural labor force has declined less, from 65% in 1951 to 48% in 2003 (Zaidi 2005).

Urbanization Issues

Pakistan has experienced a large increase in population over the last 5 decades, with the population growth rate in urban and rural areas differing

Table 10.1: Country Development Profile, Pakistan

Human Development Index rank of 177 countries (2003)^	135
GDP growth (annual %, 2004)	6.38
GNI per capita, Atlas method (current $, 2004)	600
GNI, Atlas method (current $ billion, 2004)	90.7
GDP per capita PPP ($, 2003)^	2,097
GDP PPP ($ billion, 2003)^	311.3
Population growth (annual, 2005–2010, %)#	2.41
Population, total (million, 2005)#	161.15
Urban Population, total (million, 2005)#	56.08
Urban Population percent of total population (2005)#	35
Population Largest City: Karachi (2005, million)	11.82
Population Growth: 26 capital cities or centers with > 750,000 (2000)#	
- Est. average growth of capital cities or urban agglomerations 2005–2015 (%)	40
- No. of capital cities or urban agglomerations with growth > 50%, 2005–2015	1
- No. of capital cities or urban agglomerations with growth > 30%, 2005–2015	26
Sanitation, % of urban population with access to improved sanitation (2002)**	92
Water, % of urban population with access to improved water sources (2002)**	95
Slum population, % of urban population (2001)**	74
Slum population in urban areas (million, 2001)**	35.63
Poverty, % of urban population below national poverty line (1999)**	24.2
Aid (Net ODA received; ($ million, 2003)^	1,068.4
Aid as share of country income (Net ODA/GNI, 2003, %)*	1.5
Aid per capita (current $, 2003)^	7.20

GDP = gross domestic product, GNI = gross national income, ODA = official development assistance, PPP = purchasing power parity.
Sources: See Footnote Table 3.1, World Bank (2005); OECD (2003); United Nations (2004, 2005).

considerably. The population growth rate averaged about 2.5% per year for rural areas and about 3.5% per year for urban areas. The urban population in Baluchistan Province has been increasing at a rate of 5.1%, which is much higher than those of other provinces. However, the population base of

Table 10.2: Heterogeneity in the Rate of Urbanization in Pakistan

Area	1981 Urban (%)	1998 Urban (%)	Growth Rate Rural (%)	Growth Rate Urban (%)
Pakistan	29.1	33.1	2.3	3.5
NWFP	15.1	16.9	2.7	3.5
Punjab	27.6	31.3	2.3	3.4
Sindh	43.4	48.8	2.2	3.5
Baluchistan	15.5	23.9	1.9	5.1
Islamabad	60.1	65.7	4.3	5.8

NWFP = North-West Frontier Province.
Source: Population Census 1998.

Baluchistan is very small and does not affect the national growth rate of urban populations. Table 10.2 shows population growth rates in various provinces.

Over the next 25 years, the urban population is expected to increase significantly (Figure 10.1). By 2030, the urban population is expected to have grown by 80 million, reaching 135 million, or 50% of the total population.

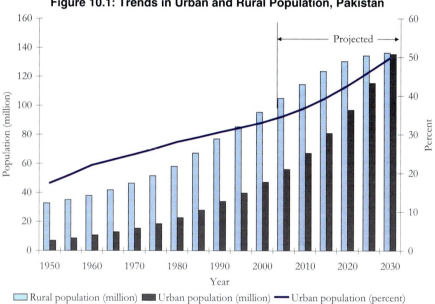

Figure 10.1: Trends in Urban and Rural Population, Pakistan

Underestimating the Urban Population

Defining what is urban is controversial. The definition carries huge ramifications for the political balance of the country. It has been argued in the past that there has been a systematic underestimating of the urban population. Pakistan has traditionally been governed by the rural elite, which has drawn its economic and political power from the large workforce that also serves as a captive electorate. The argument goes that the true representation of urban population will shift the electoral balance from the rural electorates to urban centers. The shift of the political center of gravity to urban centers could diminish the influence of rural politicians.

Behind the controversy is an ad hoc land classification system that has been used in the past to designate areas as urban or rural. Until 1972, an area was designated as urban by the census if it had a population of at least 5,000 inhabitants or if an area, regardless of its population, enjoyed the administrative designation of a municipal corporation, municipal committee, town committee, or a cantonment board (Ali 2003). The local census commissioner also had the discretion of declaring an area urban if it displayed certain "urban characteristics." The nonfarming labor force characteristics of an area were also considered in declaring a place as urban.[3] The definition for urban changed in the 1981 census and only areas designated as municipal corporations, municipal committees, or cantonment boards were considered urban areas.

This seriously underestimated the urban population in the 1981 census. At least 1,462 communities with population exceeding 5,000 were classified as rural under the new classification system (Ali 2003). Because administrative boundaries were used to define urban areas, the population of Lahore—the second largest city with a population exceeding 5 million—was underestimated by at least 1 million. If the populations of small towns that are congruent to the administrative boundaries of Lahore and enjoy strong economic linkages with Lahore were added to the population of Lahore, the estimated population of the city would swell to 7 million.

High-density peri-urban areas showing urban characteristics have been emerging in South Asia. This phenomenon has been termed "ruralopolis" (Qadeer 2000). These areas exhibit characteristics that are similar to those of urban areas. Indicators of housing quality, labor force characteristics, educational attainment, and the travel behavior of the inhabitants of such "rural" areas are similar to those of low- to middle-income communities in designated urban areas. Characterizing such areas as rural serves only to maintain the political status quo.

Housing and Land Policies

Pakistan faces an acute housing shortage. The current estimate of the housing backlog is about 6 million (Government of Pakistan 2005). The annual construction of housing is about 300,000 units whereas the estimated demand is about 570,000 units.

The housing backlog presents only a partial view of the housing crisis. Another aspect is the housing affordability crisis for low-income households. The poor do not have access to financial institutions to borrow funds to build homes. The very poor segments of society occupy abandoned land alongside large open sewers and railway/highway corridors. These informal settlements lack adequate housing amenities, such as latrines and potable water. In addition, the municipalities seldom extend municipal services to squatter settlements. Many low-income, nonsquatter settlements also remain deprived of water supply and sanitation facilities.

In the absence of a financing mechanism that targets the very poor, the housing crisis continues. In the last few decades, a land "mafia" has developed and has been devouring public land under varying guises. The urban development authorities have been transferring state-owned land at nominal prices to housing schemes, which are often managed by the military or civil elite. Such housing schemes develop the land and transfer parcels to their members who, in turn, sell the developed land in open markets where land prices are very high.

In the absence of a land speculation tax and proper fiscal cadastre, money made in land market speculation generates little tax revenue. The land development industry has systematically transferred wealth to a privileged few, who have benefited from exclusive access to state-owned land. Government policies have encouraged such schemes in the name of promoting the housing industry (Jacobsen et al. 2002). The fact remains that the housing needs of low- and middle-income households have remained largely unmet, resulting in huge housing backlogs.

Infrastructure Deficit

Municipal infrastructure is, in general, in very poor shape. Underfunding of municipal governments by the national Government and poor attention to revenue collection over the decades have weakened the capacity of municipal governments to fund, build, and maintain infrastructure. In the absence of capital grants, new infrastructure required to cope with the needs of rapidly growing urban populations has not been planned or built (Zaidi 2005).

These factors paint a disturbing picture of municipal service delivery. Only 63% of the overall population has access to potable water (Shah 2003). The situation is more acute in rural areas, where only 53% of the population has ready access to water compared with 83% in urban areas. Access to sanitation facilities is worse: only 39% of the total population has access to proper sanitation facilities, of which only 27% is in the rural areas and 59% in cities (Shah 2003).[4] Furthermore, overall, less than 1% of wastewater is treated and only 40% of the solid waste is disposed of properly.

The quality of municipal services is not uniform throughout the country. For example, the 1998 census revealed that only 28% of the population had in-house access to tap water (Table 10.3), 42% relied on hand pumps, and another 5% obtained drinking water from wells. A comparison of water supply across the provinces reveals huge disparities in coverage. For instance, only 42% of the population in Baluchistan had sources of drinking water inside the house and 36% relied on ponds and other sources

Table 10.3: Sources of Drinking Water in Pakistan (%)

Area	Outside the House					Inside the House		
	Tap Water	Hand Pump	Well	Pond	Others	Tap Water	Hand Pump	Well
Pakistan	4.2	5.1	5.1	2.9	7.8	28.1	42.1	4.9
NWFP	12.3	1.2	8.4	4.0	18.8	27.2	9.7	18.4
Punjab	2.2	5.3	2.2	1.1	2.5	24.3	60.4	2.0
Sindh	4.5	7.2	6.1	3.2	10.1	47.2	29.3	2.4
Baluchistan	4.3	2.1	16.1	16.7	19.0	25.3	2.4	14.1
Islamabad	6.1	1.9	18.3	0.5	3.1	57.3	5.0	7.9

NWFP = North-West Frontier Province.
Source: Population Census 1998.

of drinking water. In Punjab, 87% of the population had drinking water outlets inside the house.

National Regional Development and Decentralization Policies

Pakistan began implementing a major devolution plan in 2000, which has produced a new breed of local leadership under the military-led government of General Pervez Musharraf, who also holds the civilian office of the President of Pakistan. Some studies have viewed the current devolution exercise in Pakistan as a success; others have seen it as the military's attempt to prolong its rule in Pakistan.

Since its independence in 1947, Pakistan has been governed by civil or military dictatorships. Military rule has been interrupted by a few short periods of civilian rule where the military governed by proxy. After dismantling the elected political bodies at the national and provincial levels, the military regimes have always felt the need to produce a new breed of politicians who would owe their allegiance to the armed forces rather than to the political party or civil society. In this regard, the first military rule under General Ayub Khan in 1959 introduced the Basic Democracies System of local governments (Government of Sindh 2004). This system disappeared with the fall of General Ayub's military regime, as it did not enjoy grassroots support.

The civilian government following General Ayub's regime embarked on a devolution program and promulgated the People's Local Government Ordinance of 1975. However, the civilian government did not hold local government elections, which the Constitution mandated. The next military regime of General Zia-ul-Haq, which took power in 1977, stayed in office for 8 years before it eventually held nonparty-based local government elections. With the demise of General Zia-ul-Haq in 1988, the local government system he introduced also faded away.

It is interesting to note that civilian governments have also tried to undermine local governments. This was done by diverting funds for local development from the local governments to the members of national and provincial assemblies. The government of Prime Minister Muhammad Khan Junejo in 1986 and that of Prime Minister Benazir Bhutto in 1989 allocated development funds to the elected members of national and provincial assemblies and, in the process, weakened the local government institutions.

The current military regime overthrew the civilian government in October 1999. Within a year of its control of government, the regime began a decentralization and devolution program, which has proven to be the most ambitious of all devolution programs to date. Unlike the previous devolution programs, the new plan enjoys the protection of the Constitution.

Under the new system, local governments have been set up in urban and rural areas. A new generation of more than 126,000 municipal councilors was elected in the first elections held in August 2001 (Manning et al. 2005). The devolution plan involves "devolution of political power, decentralization of administrative authority, decentralization of management functions, diffusion of power authority nexus, and distribution of resources at different levels" (Government of Sindh 2004). The injection of new blood into the political establishment in Pakistan has brought about some changes. The devolution plan has reserved 33% of seats for women. As a result, nearly 25% of the new councilors elected in 2001 were women. Although this number is less than the constitutionally mandated target, the new order has certainly given a voice to women, who have for the most part remained disenfranchised in the Pakistani political system.

Review of the Devolution Program

The initial results of the decentralization and devolution program are mixed. The devolution plan has been successful in bringing women into the political process and at the same time creating a higher degree of awareness of local issues in the political setup. International and bilateral development partners have run training schools for women councilors to prepare them for municipal governance. The impact of women's involvement in policy making at the grassroots level will be felt in time. Nevertheless, this scale of women's involvement in decision making in Pakistan is unprecedented.

Critics view the devolution plan as another attempt by Pakistan's armed forces to discredit political institutions and to create a new breed of political cronies (International Crisis Group 2005). The International Crisis Group documented gross electoral irregularities, which facilitated the government-backed candidates to win their seats in an essentially non-party-based local government election.

The devolution plan also provides for community involvement. The plan mandates constituting citizen community boards (CCB) to work in parallel with the elected representatives. In fact, CCBs can recommend projects to be financed by the development budget on an 80:20 principle, where the community bears 20% of the proposed budget. Some communities have taken advantage of the opportunity by proposing projects to improve water supply and sanitation. Other communities have spent funds on projects that were not urgent in nature. For instance, one community in Lodhran District used the funds to build a wall around a graveyard.[5]

Detractors of the devolution plan point out its financial shortcomings. For instance, the plan has transferred responsibility of municipal service delivery—such as water supply, sanitation, primary education, and basic health—to the local governments. However, the devolution plan falls short of building institutional, financial, and technical capacity of local governments. Thus, the local governments have assumed the mandate without the resources required. The lack of technical expertise at the union council and *tehsil* level of government limits their ability to plan and deliver municipal services. The local governments are financially dependent on provincial and federal governments, which subject the local governments to potential exploitation by the higher tiers of government.

Municipal finances in Pakistan are a financial conundrum. The lack of local revenue is due to poorly managed and enforced property taxation. A study conducted by the United Kingdom's Department for International Development (DFID) found that own-sources of revenue in municipal governments varied between 0% and 8%. The ad hoc transfer of funds from the higher levels of government to local government restricted the latter's capacity to plan and deliver municipal services.

The devolution plan tried to maintain the status quo by upholding "revenue adequacy" to keep municipal service delivery at the pre-devolution level (Manning et al. 2005). As such, the plan was not innovative when it came to municipal finances and it did not provide for formula-based and stable sources of funding (Kardar 2003). In fact, some stable local sources of revenue, such as the import duty on out-of-district goods (*octroi*), were withdrawn from the local governments. That local governments cannot levy new taxes, which exclude direct revenues, does not bode well for them. In addition, a significant portion of their budget is spent on recurring expenditures. The local government in Peshawar, for example, spent 86% of its budget on salaries and utility bills (Zaidi 2005). This left insufficient funds either to maintain the existing level of services or to expand services to areas not yet covered.

The Role of International Aid in Supporting Regional Development

Development banks and bilateral development partners have been involved in supporting regional development in Pakistan. The Asian Development Bank (ADB) has supported regional and urban development projects in the past. In the Water Supply, Sanitation, and Waste Management Sector, ADB invested a total of $600 million up to 2003 while another $620 million was undergoing approval (Shah 2003). A recently completed project worth $72 million in Rawalpindi District focused on improving water supply and sanitation. ADB has also invested funds in support of the devolution plan in Pakistan. For the period 2003–2007, ADB is providing $23 million for local government performance enhancement (Shah 2003). Numerous bilateral donors, such as DFID and the Canadian International Development Agency (CIDA), are also supporting the devolution plan. CIDA, for instance, is operating a devolution support program, which is operating in districts in Punjab.[6]

GOOD PRACTICE CASE STUDIES

Three case studies that highlight projects dealing with water supply, sanitation, and solid waste management are presented in the following section. These case studies underscore the role of community-based organizations (CBOs) that have stepped in to furnish the basic municipal services, which municipal authorities have failed to provide. The role of international donors that have provided the seed funding for the projects is also highlighted. These good practice case studies serve as successful examples of community mobilization, partnership with local authorities, and use of donor assistance to provide municipal services.

The selection of the good practice case studies was prompted by the deplorable state of water supply and sanitation in Pakistan and the communities' response to take the lead in addressing their needs. Most communities do not have access to proper sanitation facilities. Only 13.5% of rural communities have access to any such amenities in Pakistan (Bajwa 2005). The situation is only marginally better in urban areas. Research has suggested that accessibility of municipal services and infrastructure does not perfectly correlate with income (Brook and Irwin 2003). The case of inadequate water supply in high-income urban areas in Pakistan suggests that access to basic infrastructure faces inherent structural constraints, which adds to the complexity of these issues.

The three case studies highlight the need for government and CBOs to work together. The three projects succeeded because they did not try to eliminate

Figure 10.2: Map Showing Location of the Case Studies

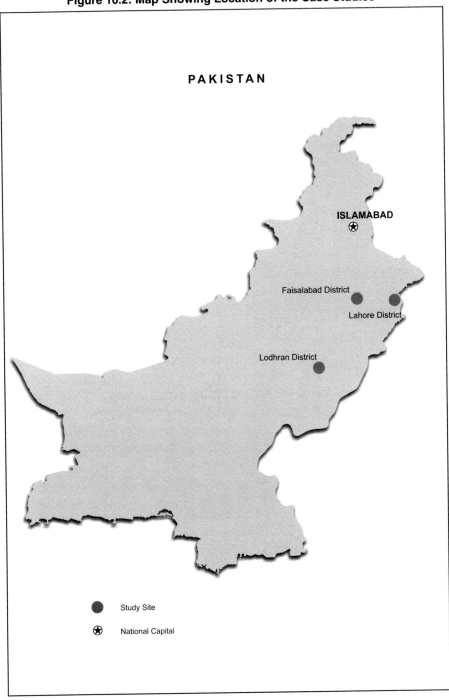

or replace the role of the state (municipal governments), but instead collaborated with them. The very recognition that the state has the mandate and is most likely to develop the capacity to deliver region-wide solutions has helped the community-based initiatives in the three good practice case studies.

The demographic makeup of the communities being discussed in the following sections is presented in Table 10.4. The case studies are based in Faisalabad, Lahore, and Lodhran districts.

Lodhran Pilot Project

The Lodhran Pilot Project (LPP) is a community-based sanitation program, which started in the urban areas in Lodhran District. LPP is a local nongovernment organization (NGO) headed by Jahangeer Khan Tareen, who is a local philanthropist and a politician. LPP was influenced by the self-help philosophy pioneered in Pakistan by Akhtar Hameed Khan in Orangi, Karachi. The Orangi Pilot Project (OPP) was the first large-scale community-based sanitation project developed in a low-income neighborhood in Karachi.

GOOD PRACTICE	
Good Governance	
Urban Management	✓
Infrastructure/Service Provision	✓
Financing and Cost Recovery	✓
Sustainability	
Innovation and Change	
Leveraging ODA	✓

Lodhran is an evolving district in Punjab. The provision of sanitation facilities is largely poor throughout the district. LPP followed the OPP approach where the sanitation project was divided between internal and external works. The internal development, which was self-financed by the community, paid for the construction of in-house latrines and the laying of drains in the lanes. The external works—financed and developed by the local government—linked the neighborhood drains with the trunk sewers. In its initial phase, LPP completed 18 projects in Lodhran district costing $143,000, of which $45,000 was contributed by the community. Within Lodhran City, which is the urban part of Lodhran Tehsil and has an estimated population of 75,000, 6.7 kilometers (km) of sewer lines were laid by LPP.

LPP serves as an excellent example of the synergies resulting from the combined efforts of the community and the local governments. Donor support helped develop the organizational and technical capacity of LPP.

Characteristics of the Region

Lodhran District comprises three *tehsils*: Lodhran, Dunyapur, and Karor Pacca. The district has a population of 1.17 million and an area of 1,790 square

Table 10.4: Demographic Makeup and Infrastructure Provision in Selected Districts

Area	Ave. Annual G.R.	Population Density	Urban %	Ave. HH Size	Literacy Rate	Rooms Per HH/Unit	Housing Structure		
							Formal (%)	Semi-formal (%)	Informal (%)
Faisalabad District	2.5	962	42.7	7.2	51.9	2.3	69.8	14.0	16.1
Lahore District	3.5	3,566	82.4	7.1	64.7	2.4	92.3	3.4	4.3
Lodhran District	2.7	422	14.5	7.2	29.9	2.1	33.7	10.7	55.6
Rural									
Faisalabad District	1.8			7.1	42.5	2.3	60.5	14.1	25.4
Lahore District	4.1			7.3	41.7	2.0	84.6	5.7	9.7
Lodhran District	2.4			7.2	26.8	2.1	30.2	11.3	58.5
Urban									
Faisalabad District	3.7			7.3	64.2	2.4	82.8	14.0	3.3
Lahore District	3.3			7.1	69.2	2.4	93.9	2.9	3.2
Lodhran District	5.0			7.5	47.7	2.4	55.1	6.8	38.1

Area	Kitchen			Bath Room			Lavatory		
	Private (%)	Shared (%)	None (%)	Private (%)	Shared (%)	None (%)	Private (%)	Shared (%)	None (%)
Faisalabad District	27.4	12.9	59.6	38.2	26.3	35.5	33.5	24.4	42.1
Lahore District	44.2	19.9	35.9	47.8	36.7	15.5	48.8	38.2	13.0
Lodhran District	22.5	7.4	70.2	19.4	9.0	71.6	15.7	7.5	76.9
Rural									
Faisalabad District	23.3	9.9	66.8	31.3	16.9	51.8	21.6	12.3	66.2
Lahore District	28.0	12.9	59.2	31.3	23.4	45.3	29.0	22.2	48.8
Lodhran District	20.9	6.6	72.5	15.3	6.5	78.3	10.1	4.5	85.4
Urban									
Faisalabad District	33.2	17.2	49.7	47.7	39.3	13.0	50.0	41.3	8.7
Lahore District	47.5	21.4	31.1	51.2	39.5	9.4	52.9	41.5	5.6
Lodhran District	32.0	12.2	55.9	45.3	24.7	30.0	50.1	25.9	23.9

Area	Source of Drinking Water							
	Outside House					Inside House		
	Tap Water (%)	Hand Pump (%)	Well (%)	Pond (%)	Other (%)	Tap Water (%)	Hand Pump (%)	Well (%)
Faisalabad District	2.4	3.5	0.1	0.2	1.8	28.1	63.6	0.3
Lahore District	2.2	1.3	0.1	0.0	0.7	75.2	20.4	0.3
Lodhran District	1.5	9.4	0.2	1.7	4.0	13.3	69.7	0.2
Rural								
Faisalabad District	1.1	5.1	0.2	0.4	2.3	15.3	75.7	0.2
Lahore District	1.1	4.9	0.2	0.0	1.2	26.1	65.8	0.6
Lodhran District	1.4	10.5	0.2	2.0	4.4	10.8	70.6	0.2
Urban								
Faisalabad District	4.1	1.3	0.0	0.0	1.2	45.9	46.9	0.5
Lahore District	2.4	0.5	0.0	0.0	0.6	85.2	11.0	0.2
Lodhran District	2.3	2.8	0.0	0.0	1.7	28.9	64.1	0.1

Ave. = average, G.R. = growth rate, HH = household.
Source: Population and Housing Census. 1998.

kilometers (km^2). The gross population density is about 422 persons/km^2. The locality is composed of 11 urban and 62 rural union councils. The economy is primarily agrarian. Lodhran District represents 0.2% of the total area of Pakistan and 0.8% of its population.

A sewerage system was laid many years ago. The lack of maintenance and repair of the system, however, resulted in clogging, silting, and overflowing. Eventually, sewer lines stopped functioning. The result was that rubbish and sewage filled the streets, which increased the incidence of disease among women and children, in particular. The local governments did not have the resources to serve the communities where these conditions existed, or to extend the sewerage system to newer communities. These conditions were the same for both urban and rural areas.

The local government in Lodhran does not have a master plan for the district.[7] The Population Health and Engineering Department, a provincial institution, provided some informal drawings of the infrastructure to the *tehsil* municipal administration (TMA). The plans for housing and physical planning, however, were not implemented.

Lodhran TMA has a total budget of $1.2 million equivalent. TMA spends 73% of its budget on development of roads and *solings*,[8] water supply and sewerage, and drainage projects. The remaining budget is for salaries, utility bills, and the operation and maintenance costs of sanitation. The main sources of revenue are urban immovable property tax, tax on the sale and purchase of livestock, grants in lieu of the abolished *octroi*, and from the province or multilateral donors.

Description of the Project

In March 1999, a local community leader, Mr. Tareen, invited Akhtar Hameed Khan to visit Lodhran and analyze the region's potential for a community-based sanitation project. Dr. Khan visited Lodhran in 1999. Dr. Khan encouraged Mr. Tareen to register an NGO and initiate the work. Dr. Khan also deputed the late Hafeez Arain to the project.

Mr. Arain, an expert in community mobilization, relocated to Lodhran and initiated outreach efforts in the community. Mr. Arain's dedication to Dr. Khan, coupled with his commitment to the downtrodden, was legendary. His devotion and sincerity—his biggest strengths—enabled Mr. Arain to influence communities in Lodhran, Faisalabad, and Karachi.

Leadership at the community level played an important role in LPP. The vision and initiative of Mr. Tareen were instrumental in making LPP a success. Mr. Tareen realized from the beginning that OPP had developed a workable model for Pakistan that brought the community together with development partners and the local governments in extending sanitation services to the poor neighborhoods. Later, CIDA, the Natural Resources Systems Programme, United Nations Development Programme (UNDP), and the World Bank also supported the LPP-launched sanitation schemes.

LPP is also a good example of collaboration between the local government and the CBOs. TMA has seconded a municipal engineer and a community "mobilizer" to LPP. The seconded expert has formed the critical link between TMA and LPP. Because of this link, the community, CBO, and TMA were always updated on each stakeholder's progress. In 2005, TMA in Dunyapur allocated 25% of its development budget for projects initiated by CBOs (or CBBs). This arrangement also eliminated the mistrust between the community and the local government. CBBs have extended LPP's work into solid waste management in Teshil Dunyapur, where households pay the equivalent of $0.50 monthly for the service.

LPP operates on the OPP philosophy, which divides the project into internal and external development. Internal development refers to building a sanitary latrine and a modified septic tank in the house and construction of primary and secondary sewer lines. The local community finances, develops, and maintains the internal development. External development refers to constructing main sewer lines and connecting these to the trunk sewers, and the final disposal and treatment of sewage. TMA finances and manages the external development.

LPP mobilizes the community and helps it constitute a sanitation committee. In rural areas, these committees are called village sanitation committees. LPP's experts survey the area, prepare cost estimates for the project, and develop technical details, including surveying. LPP trains the local volunteers and monitors project implementation. The sanitation committee appoints lane managers, collects local contributions, procures construction materials, manages internal development, and maintains the infrastructure over the long term. TMA connects the components to the municipal sewers, manages disposal and treatment plants, and paves the streets and lanes where sewer pipes have been laid.

LPP-run projects have transcended the district boundaries of Lodhran. At present, LPP is operating in Lodhran, Khanpur (District Rahim Yar Khan), and Melsi (District Vehari). In 2003, the World Bank took notice of LPP, which at that time had successfully operated for 4 years and was carrying out sanitation projects in 30 communities. In 2005, the World Bank and Japan Social Development Fund injected $1.1 million in LPP to extend the project to an additional 100 villages. LPP is expanding the project using the same principle of internal and external development. The expansion will help improve sanitation for 20,000 households at an average cost of $25/household. World Bank's support also includes funding for workshops to educate communities, develop curriculum in community-based sanitation, and train 150 associate engineers and 400 municipal councilors.

LPP has made certain technical innovations in the laying of sewer lines and connecting primary sewer lines to outlets from houses. Community participation has eliminated intermediaries, resulting in huge savings. LPP has also relied on the use of a geographical information system (GIS) to map and plan infrastructure development. The streamlining of activities between LPP and TMA resulted in synergies that would have not happened if the two worked in isolation or, worse, worked against each other.

The long-term success of donor-assisted projects in Pakistan depends on the sustained interest of development partners, whose priorities are dictated by the geo-politics of the region. CBOs and the local governments have to generate own-source revenue to guarantee their long-term success. While LPP continues with successfully implementing sanitation projects in mostly rural and some urban areas of Punjab Province, the longevity of LPP is not certain. To sustain itself over the long run, LPP should generate sufficient local funds to mobilize communities for internal development. Similarly, own-source revenue is required for TMAs to fund external development.

LPP is considered a good practice model in rural/urban sanitation because it mobilizes communities, partners with local authorities, and uses donor assistance to provide municipal services. LPP exemplifies the demand-responsive approach, where the need for improved service is established, which is followed by an expression of interest and an assessment of the willingness to pay by the community.

Community-based Water Supply and Sanitation Services in Faisalabad

In Faisalabad, numerous low-income communities—home to blue-collar labor—lacked proper water supply and sanitation. Local community leaders lobbied the politicians for years for improved municipal services. In return, they only received empty promises. Meanwhile, the size and density of communities had increased.

GOOD PRACTICE	
Good Governance	
Urban Management	✓
Infrastructure/Service Provision	✓
Financing and Cost Recovery	✓
Sustainability	
Innovation and Change	✓
Leveraging ODA	✓

The lack of sanitation resulted in streets filled with sewage and other wastes. These unhygienic conditions were more than just an eyesore. Poor sanitary conditions resulted in higher disease incidence. Women and children who spend the most time in the unhygienic environment suffered the most. The community relied on donkey carts to supply water to the households.

A few local leaders in the community of Daddiwala, Faisalabad, tried to attract the attention of politicians to their plight. Their NGO, Anjuman Samaji Behbood (ASB), aimed to promote social welfare in the localities it served. However, for years, ASB confined its role to lobbying politicians.

Eventually, ASB transformed itself to become an agent of change and has helped launch a community-driven water supply and sanitation program that has equipped 10,000 households in 85 communities. These households have spent the equivalent of $0.72 million for better water supply and sanitation facilities.

Characteristics of the Region

Faisalabad is a sprawling metropolis with a population of 2 million (1998 Census). The city evolved from a primarily agrarian economy to a more diversified economy where manufacturing and textile production saw a huge increase. The emergence of the textile industry attracted job seekers from rural areas and other towns to Faisalabad. The city grew rapidly and became the third largest city in Pakistan.

The population in Faisalabad has been growing at a rate of 2.5% annually (Table 10.4). The annual growth rate of urban areas—at 3.7%—is twice that of rural areas. According to the 1998 census, 43% of Faisalabad District was categorized as urban. Three quarters of the rural households obtained water from a hand pump located in the house. In urban areas, nearly half of the housing units obtained water from a municipal tap located in the house, and most of the remainder drew water from a hand pump located in the house.

The rural part of Faisalabad consists of numerous villages. The urbanization that followed industry was mostly unplanned. Communities in the rural parts of Faisalabad lacked water supply and sanitation facilities. Because of the high water table, communities relied on hand pumps to draw water. The high water table also caused waterlogging on agricultural land.

Description of the Project

In Faisalabad, ASB is based in the Dhuddiwala neighborhood, which could be characterized as an urbanized village. ASB's community-based water supply and sanitation project in Faisalabad is another spin-off from OPP. Akhtar Hameed Khan inspired Nazeer Ahmad Wattoo (ASB leader in Faisalabad) and other volunteers and shared his philosophy of community mobilization and community-based development.

Before joining hands with OPP, ASB had been lobbying the political leadership for better municipal services in vain. OPP invited Mr. Wattoo for a visit in 1988. He returned with the idea of self-help and community-based solutions. Over the next 6 years, OPP trained ASB in community mobilization.

Mr. Hafeez Arain played a critical role in the success of ASB's projects. He relocated to Faisalabad to take up the challenge of restoring the community's trust in ASB because years of association with political parties had tainted its reputation.

OPP assisted ASP launch a microfinance project in Faisalabad similar to OPP's microcredit program in Karachi. Mr. Arain invited the community to submit applications for five microcredit schemes for a total value of $1,670 equivalent. Three projects were chosen after due consideration. The success of these projects was instrumental in building the community's trust in ASB. It was only then that Mr. Wattoo and Mr. Arain started to mobilize the community for a self-financed water supply scheme.

ASB's first project was based in Hasanpura, a community that suffered from waterlogging. Residents of Hasanpura (about 1,000 households) used hand pumps to obtain water. The local authorities, however, used eight deep tube wells to lower the water table, rendering most of the residents' hand pumps useless. The residents had to rely on private vendors, who used donkey carts to supply water. Poor-quality water was responsible for the high disease incidence in the community. ASB estimated the total cost of illness and loss of business due to poor water quality to be more than $150,000/year.

ASB initiated work on the project in 1994 by conducting infrastructure surveys, GIS mapping, establishing linkages with the Water and Sanitation Authority, Faisalabad Development Authority, and Faisalabad Municipal Corporation. ASB followed OPP's philosophy of dividing the project into internal and external development. FDA's main water pipe ran only 335 meters away from the community. The municipal authorities initially declined ASB's request to link the community water supply scheme with the municipal network. For community mobilization, ASB identified notable persons in the region and approached them with their plan. ASB held meetings with the community and formed lane committees to undertake the construction work. A lane supervisor was appointed to manage each lane committee.

A water supply committee was formed in November 1995. The lane committees collected funds from each lane, purchased construction materials, arranged for labor, and laid pipes in the lanes and connected them to individual houses. OPP continued providing technical help. Once the network within the community was completed, it was linked with FDA's water mains. Each lane paid for the installation of pipes within their respective lanes.

The collaboration between ASB and FDA is another example of public-community partnership. Such collaboration reduces project costs significantly. According to ASB, community-based projects could be 60% lower in cost because they eliminate the intermediaries and their mark-ups, and the community volunteers its services for the operation and maintenance of the infrastructure. On average, each household in Hasanpura paid the equivalent of $53 to install the infrastructure.

A drainage and sanitation scheme, which was based on OPP's planning approach, followed. The result was that sewage and garbage disappeared from the streets. As the streets became clean, a significant decline in disease incidence was observed. The community's health improved and it became an attractive place for both residents and businesses. An additional benefit of this scheme was the relocation of small businesses into the community, which brought jobs and increased prosperity.

Challenges Faced in Project Implementation

Unlike LPP, where the municipal authorities were involved from the beginning, ASB's first project in Hasanpura struggled to win the trust of the municipal authorities. In addition, not everyone in the community bought into the community-based development paradigm. Local politicians tried to dissuade the community from joining ASB's projects. A local provincial member of Parliament lied to the community about a bogus government-funded water supply project, which would supposedly provide free water connections to the community. However, community leaders discovered the hoax. This added to the credibility of ASB.

ASB was also successful in dispute resolution. In August 1996, some 65 households established unauthorized and unpaid connections. ASB challenged these households in the courts and complained to the municipal authorities about the unauthorized connections. The authorities decided in ASB's favor, and the households paid fines and other fees for their connections. By June 1999, 30% of the households in Hasanpura were connected to the network.

Role of Development Partners

The role of development partners was very critical in the successful implementation of ASB's water supply and drainage schemes. The community was willing to finance internal development only and not the cost of linking with the main water line. WaterAid, a United Kingdom-based development agency, offered a revolving loan of $3,330 that made the project feasible.

DFID has been instrumental in building capacity of local governments in Faisalabad. It launched four pilot initiatives under the Faisalabad Area Upgrading Project (FAUP) in 1994–1995 to upgrade the quality of life of slum dwellers in Faisalabad. FAUP also offered technical expertise in planning, design, and implementation of primary and secondary water/sewerage infrastructure. At present, an adequate research and operational unit called the Strategic Policy Unit is working in Faisalabad.[10] FAUP played an important role in convincing municipal authorities to allow the community's water supply network to tap the municipal water supply network.

ASB has received numerous requests for technical assistance from TMAs in neighboring areas wanting to adopt ASB's model to empower communities. ASB's innovative use of GIS to map the existing infrastructure and the spatial distribution of communities that required services also helped convince the local government to connect the community water supply infrastructure to the municipality's water mains.

Solid Waste Management in Lahore

GOOD PRACTICE	
Good Governance	
Urban Management	
Infrastructure/Service Provision	
Financing and Cost Recovery	
Sustainability	
Innovation and Change	
Leveraging ODA	

Solid waste in Pakistan is largely unmanaged. According to the national conservation strategy, Pakistan generates an estimated 48,000 tons (t) of solid waste per day, of which almost 20,000 t are generated in urban areas. In worst cases, solid waste is left to litter or decompose on streets and empty lots. Even solid waste collected by the municipal authorities is dumped and burned in open areas. Although solid waste directorates do exist in most large urban centers, the service they offer is irregular, inefficient, and inadequate. Moreover, the final disposal of waste involves either dumping in non-engineered landfills or burning, which further pollutes the environment.

Lahore, with a population of about 7 million, is the second largest city in Pakistan. Housing conditions in Lahore are far superior to those in Lodhran and Faisalabad. Most housing units (92%) in Lahore are categorized as formal housing, yet 36% of these lack a proper kitchen facility (Table 10.4). Only 15% of housing units are without a bathroom and 13% lack a lavatory. Most households (78%) obtain water from municipal taps, while others obtain water from hand pumps. Thus, Lahore benefits from good water supply.

Waste Busters is a private company that collects solid waste in Lahore. The company operates in the middle- to high-income neighborhoods in urban centers where it charges a market price for collecting waste. Waste Busters sorts and recycles the waste, and produces organic fertilizers for sale to farmers.

This case study is different from the previous two case studies for the following reasons. First, Waste Busters operates largely in urban centers where water supply and drainage facilities have been provided by the municipal authorities. Second, it operates in communities that exhibit willingness to pay for improved solid waste management. Because of its success, Waste Busters has been able to win long-term contracts from numerous local governments in Pakistan to collect, dispose of, and recycle solid waste. It uses a differential fee structure, based on the income level in the neighborhood.

This project highlights the need for entrepreneurial leadership. Waste Busters and other similar waste management companies occupy the waste management niche in Pakistan. But, in the absence of imaginative entrepreneurs, the demand for solid waste management services remains unmet. Entrepreneurs such as Waste Busters manager, Asif Farooki, have turned waste into profit while at the same time have cleaned up the cities and helped curb the spread of disease.

Description of the Project

Averaging about 0.5–0.7 kilograms (kg) per capita/day, the rate of waste generation is significantly lower in Pakistan than those in developed countries. Yet, managing solid waste in Pakistan remains a formidable challenge for municipal authorities. Municipal authorities in Karachi, the largest city in Pakistan, recover only 50% of the 7,000 t of solid waste generated every day.[11]

Despite the large municipal workforce dedicated to the solid waste management operations in Lahore, solid waste remains a huge problem. The Lahore Municipal Corporation (LMC) and two cantonment boards struggle to keep the streets clean.[12] Lahore generates 4,750 t of solid waste/day, of which almost 10% is estimated to be recyclable. Even where waste is collected by the municipal authorities, it is disposed of in an ad hoc manner, causing harmful pollution. Most solid waste (almost 60%) is vegetable and fruit residue, along with dust, dirt, and remnants of construction.[13]

LMC's budget for solid waste management is about $8 million. With the advent of the devolution plan, the City District Government of Lahore (CDGL) has assumed responsibilities for waste management. Since devolution, the new city has grown by 1,350 km^2 to almost 1,800 km^2. Its budget for solid waste management, however, has remained the same.[14] At present, CDGL spends roughly $1.10/person annually on solid waste management.

Even with these paltry funds, there have been accusations of mismanagement (Dogar 2001).

Waste Busters started its operations in the cantonment areas of Lahore in 1996. Initially, garbage was collected on donkey carts. Later, small-sized pickups replaced donkey carts. Nowadays, Waste Busters uses large trucks for transporting waste more expediently. Waste Busters works in collaboration with the municipal authorities from whom it has leased land for its operations.

CDGL has contracted out waste management to Waste Busters in three union councils for $72,000/month. As part of the decentralization plan, CDGL will continue with privatizing these services, which have proven to be run more efficiently by the private sector.

Waste Busters has installed a composting and a biogas (methane) generation plant in Lahore at a cost of about $500,000.[15] The plant has a processing capacity of 500 t/day (10% of the waste generated in Lahore). It can also generate 150 t of organic fertilizer and 1,000 cubic meters (m^3) of methane. The organic fertilizer is sold to farmers at $0.05/kg. Waste Busters has planned a similar plant for the federal capital, Islamabad.

Waste Busters distributes to households large bags for storing waste, which are collected every day and transported to the waste management sites where solid waste is sorted, composted, or dumped in a landfill.

Waste Busters has received numerous international awards for its approach to solid waste management. UNDP awarded the TUGI Award to Waste Busters in 2003 for practicing sustainable development. Waste Busters' project in Gujarat was selected by the United Nations Centre for Human Settlements (UN-HABITAT) as good practice in solid waste management. Its work is being replicated in many cities in Pakistan and in other countries. In Pakistan, Waste Busters has franchised its operations to local entrepreneurs in different cities. Commercial enterprises have approached Waste Busters to sponsor waste management programs. For instance, Tetrapak, which specializes in dairy products and packages milk in small cartons, retained Waste Busters to collect used Tetrapak packaging for recycling. Other corporations have initiated promotional campaigns for environmentally sustainable solid waste management with Waste Busters. Waste Busters' successful approach provides evidence in support of public-private partnerships.

The donor community also has played a role in solid waste management. The recycling plants, vehicles, and the hiring of a large number of workers require huge capital investments. Waste Busters and other similar establishments have been unable to convince commercial banks to invest in waste management. Development partners have provided the start-up capital or loans.

KEY LESSONS LEARNED

Community-based Solutions are Preferred

The three case studies are examples of successful community involvement in municipal service delivery. The local governments were unable to offer vital municipal services. Each community realized a need, formed a leadership structure, either self-financed or obtained loans from a donor, developed an infrastructure, and started delivering the services. The merits of community-based initiatives have been recognized globally. The Copenhagen Convention, a project involving the world's leading economists and offering solutions for the most pressing challenges, also endorses community-based solutions. CBOs check corruption and excessive pricing by eliminating intermediaries and by encouraging the community to invest labor, time, and expertise.

The case studies highlight the need for the Government and CBOs to work together. The projects succeeded because they did not try to eliminate or replace the state (municipal governments), but instead worked with it. In neighborhood-level sanitation, the local government offered assistance to connect local sewer lines to the trunk sewers. In the case of water supply, the community laid out the internal network, which the local government linked up with the municipal water supply network. The formula of neighborhood-level development by CBO and the external development by the local government was partially behind the success of these projects. In addition, since the community took responsibility for maintaining the neighborhood infrastructure, these projects experience longevity that has eluded numerous other pilot projects.

The Role of Leadership in CBO-led Initiatives

The three case studies highlight the important role played by community leaders in the success of these projects. The pioneering role and intellectual leadership of Akhtar Hameed Khan of OPP is evident in the Faisalabad water supply project and Lodhran's sanitation project. Even after his death, Dr. Khan, through his writings, continues to inspire community workers. Dr. Khan influenced Mr. Wattoo, the force behind the Faisalabad project, and Jahangeer Khan Tareen, who founded LPP.

Along with the intellectual leadership is the crucial role of community mobilizers whose job is to win the trust of the community and mobilize them toward a common goal. In this regard, the key role of the late Hafeez Arain of OPP needs to be recognized. Mr. Arain worked tirelessly in communities across Pakistan. He earned their confidence before he proposed any plans for infrastructure development. Mr. Arain laid the foundation of trust in Lodhran and in Faisalabad that allowed local leaders, such as Mr. Wattoo and Mr. Tareen, to proceed with the development.

In the case of solid waste management in Lahore, a local entrepreneur, Asif Farooki, provided the leadership role in a slightly different capacity. The project was based in a middle-income community demonstrating willingness to pay for an improved service. Mr. Farooki provided the entrepreneurial leadership to offer a service that the municipal authorities failed to provide.

CBOs Need Technical Help

While CBOs have undertaken municipal infrastructure projects with little or no training, technically sound designs will further reduce operating costs and prevent communities from erecting infrastructure that fails to deliver. In the case of Lodhran, the engineering staff on deputation from the municipal government provided technical expertise to the community, resulting in a public-community partnership that drove projects to success.

Comprehensiveness

The community-based initiatives are inherently local. They often focus on one municipal service, such as water supply or sanitation. Healthy, prosperous, and dynamic communities have varying needs for *all* types of infrastructure. Communities with poor sanitation may also need an improved water supply. Similarly, a community with proper drainage will also require an adequate solid waste program, so that the solid waste does not clog the municipal drains. In Lahore, the solid waste program did not complement the newly built drainage system; thus, solid waste ended up in drains and the city flooded in the very first shower of the monsoon season in 2004.

Role of Donor Agencies

Two schools of thought concerning development partner assistance are prevalent in Pakistan. Dr. Khan's vision precludes grants to the poor for community-based development projects. He argued that the community should finance its own development. The other school of thought argues that in very poor communities, development partners can provide the seed funding on a cost-sharing basis toward the capital costs of the projects. The role of WaterAid in Faisalabad in extending loans to the community is one such example. In Lodhran, the World Bank joined the initiative after seeing the successful implementation of the sanitation project.

Since September 2001, donor interest in Pakistan has reached new heights. During the Afghan war in the late 1970s and mid-1980s, the international donor community showed a similar interest in financing development projects in Pakistan. But this was only temporary. Some development partners, such as the United States Agency for International Development (USAID), shut down their offices in Pakistan when their interest in Afghanistan diminished in the mid-1980s. With the renewed interest in Afghanistan today, USAID and other partners have returned. Multilateral donors, such as the World Bank, have extended loans on very favorable terms since September 2001. Once the dust settles on the "war on terror," the interest of development partners and their investments in Pakistan may diminish yet again. This has serious repercussions for longevity of donor-assisted projects in the country.

Linking Community Infrastructure with Municipal Networks

In community-based initiatives, infrastructure is developed locally for the neighborhood and the services are extended to the same community. However, the local initiatives have to be integrated with the regional networks of water supply and sewerage systems. The network service operators, often the local governments, need to charge the marginal costs of extending the services to the community. This has caused confusion in Faisalabad, where the local community did not realize that it also had to pay the network operator to provide water through the water mains. The communities should be educated about the local as well as regional operating costs associated with municipal service delivery.

STRATEGIES TO ENHANCE SUSTAINABLE URBAN REGION DEVELOPMENT

When it comes to infrastructure development in Pakistan, the private banking sector is missing from the picture. There is great potential for commercial banks to make a meaningful contribution in reducing poverty while creating a new client base. The Grameen Bank in Bangladesh established the viability of microcredit in that country. OPP-run microcredit programs have done the same. With lower-than-average default rates, poor consumers have proven themselves to be creditworthy and bankable. Realizing the potential of microcredit, the Pakistan Government has initiated a microcredit facility: the Khushhali Bank. However, the bank's coverage is rather limited, expecting to reach only 600,000 households by 2006. With millions of households needing assistance, no one bank can service this demand. There is an opportunity for the commercial banks to participate in development finance.

Akhtar Hameed Khan's OPP pioneered the community-based development culture in Pakistan in the late 1970s. What is not widely known is the role of the private banking sector in the creation of OPP. Agha Hasan Abedi, who headed the Bank of Credit and Commerce International, financed the creation of OPP and supported Dr. Khan's initial setup in Pakistan. Agha Hasan Abedi saw value in investing in the country's poorest people. What he envisioned in the early 1980s has been reproduced globally. In fact, the latest in financial thought proposes targeting the largest market segment—those in the world who live on less than $2 a day (Prahalad 2006).

The poor purchase all services they consume, often paying more than the market price. Development finance in developing countries needs to become mainstreamed. The commercial banks should consider extending loans to self-organizing communities that are ready to invest in their own future. The scale of the development challenge is such that it cannot be left to multilateral and bilateral development partners whose funding is already stretched. The commercial banks have to step in and realize the potential involved in banking the poor.

There are no simple answers for the role of development partners in offering financial assistance to communities. However, the likelihood of long-term survival is higher for projects where assistance is restricted to capital costs and where the community pays operating and maintenance costs.

Municipal finance in Pakistan, as in many other developing countries, needs to be reengineered. Local governments rely on transfer of payments from higher tiers of government. They lack own-source revenue and sources of buoyant taxes. This needs to be changed. While small communities may not have a sufficient tax base, large municipalities could generate funds from efficient pricing of services they deliver and by direct taxation. Metropolitan areas, such as Lahore (population: more than 5 million) and Karachi (population: 11 million) have a critical mass to sustain their operations from local taxes. In addition, large municipalities possessing high-value assets should be permitted to float bonds and debentures in open markets to finance urban development.

There is a dire need for capacity building in local governments. Municipal governments have inadequate technical experts, such as engineers and planners. Thus, they continue to struggle in delivering the mandate they have assumed under the devolution plan. Similarly, there is a need to extend technical assistance to CBOs while they plan local infrastructure development. The central Government could create a national agency with the mandate to assist CBOs in this regard. Given the lack of trained technical staff at the local government level, it may not yet be feasible to deputize local government staff to CBOs.

These case studies have highlighted the strengths of public-community partnerships, which are inherently different from public-private partnerships.

The latter involve a private, for-profit enterprise that builds the infrastructure and provides service at a price that also includes the profits for the private enterprise, which is essentially acting as an intermediary between the community and the Government. A public-community partnership eliminates the intermediary and places the community in the driving seat. This approach reduced project costs by almost 60% in Faisalabad.

The successes outlined in the three case studies point to the synergies that can be attained when stakeholders—NGO, community, and local government—pool their resources. The important lesson learned is that NGOs and CBOs do not eliminate or replace the state, but in fact work with it for large-scale implementation of community-led initiatives.

Revising the engineering and planning curricula to include community-based infrastructure development is also needed. Those who are employed in the field also lack experience in community-based infrastructure development. This creates an opportunity for the institutes of higher learning to step in and design new programs for students and practitioners.

Some agencies dealing with municipal services, such as water supply, sanitation, and transportation, continue to be under the control of provincial governments. The devolution plan did not bring these agencies under the purview of local governments. This has created some administrative and operational confusion. While the local governments have the mandate to deliver municipal services, the state apparatus bearing the technical expertise and financial resources continues to be under provincial control. Needless to say, this shortcoming should be addressed at the earliest opportunity by bringing such entities under the ambit of local governments.

Efficient planning and service delivery cannot happen without location-specific data. Such information has not been made available in the past in Pakistan. The donor community has financed numerous surveys in Pakistan on municipal service delivery, literacy, and gender-related development. Often such data sets have remained with the international consultants and have not been made available to local planners and policy makers. A paradigm shift is in order when it comes to making data available for informed policy making.

Only recently, the Population Census Organization in Pakistan started publishing district-wide reports with details on development indicators at the neighborhood level. In addition, different state agencies have started to generate GIS databases with spatial details at the local level. A databank that pools information from the various entities of government and development partners could play a major role in improved decision making by becoming a data depository, which would also disseminate information to various stakeholders. In the absence of such a databank, many agencies will waste precious development funds by duplicating data collection. The databank would support research, planning, and execution of municipal services so that informed, timely, and relevant decisions can be made to improve the lives of millions of poor in Pakistan.

Notes

[1] This chapter is dedicated to the memory of Hafeez Arain, hero of community development in Pakistan. He worked tirelessly in spreading the vision of Akhtar Hameed Khan.

[2] The authors acknowledge the considerable support given by persons involved in the case study projects and the community members who shared their experiences about the projects.

[3] Interview with M. Saeed, Census Commissioner at the Population Census Organization. December 2005.

[4] These data differ significantly from the United Nations data shown in Table 10.1 for percent of the population with access to improved urban water supply and improved sanitation.

[5] Najeeb Aslam Qureshi. 2005. *A Success Story of Citizen Community Boards at Tehsil Dunyapur*. Mr. Qureshi is the Tehsil Municipal Officer in Dunyapur.

[6] Details of CIDA supported projects are listed on the site www.pakdevolution.com.

[7] Interview with Ashraf Gill, Assistant Tehsil Officer (Infrastructure and Services) in TMA Lodhran.

[8] *Solings* are street pavements of brick masonry generally laid with cement and sand mortar both in rural and peri-urban settlements.

[9] The SPU's website URL is www.spu.com.pk. SPU operates out of the DCO's office in Faisalabad and is assisting the devolution program.

[10] Sadiq Ibrahim Khan. 2004. ISLAMABAD: Upgradation of solid waste management need of hour. 6 February. Available: www.dawn.com/2004/02/06/local20.htm.

[11] www.tve.org/ho/doc.cfm?aid=640. Accessed on 11 November 2005.

[12] Cantonment boards are military garrisons. Although these areas remain under the control of the director general of Military Land and Cantonments in the Ministry of Defense, cantonments have essentially become residential areas. There are more than 40 cantonments in Pakistan.

[13] Hammad Naqi Khan, Director, Freshwater and Toxics Programme WWF-Pakistan.

[14] Babar Dogar. 2001. Solid waste disposal a great challenge. *The Nation*. 24 November. Available: www.nation.com.pk/daily/241101/national/lhr1.htm.

[15] Anonymous. 2003. Pakistan's first biogas plant opens tomorrow. *Daily Dawn*. 22 April. Available: www.dawn.com/2003/04/22/local60.htm.

11. The Philippines
JOEL V. MANGAHAS[1]

INTRODUCTION

This chapter examines the policies, programs, and practices on sustainable regional development in the Philippines and presents strategies to address identified issues and challenges. The paper commences with an overview of economic, social, and urban trends in the Philippines, which leads to a discussion on urbanization and sustainable development issues. Three case studies of good practice of urban city region development as experienced by Bacolod, Naga, and Iloilo are presented, followed by a discussion on key lessons learned and strategies to enhance urban region development. Table 11.1 shows relevant national statistics.

Table 11.1: Country Development Profile, Philippines

Human Development Index rank of 177 countries (2003)^	84
GDP growth (annual %, 2004)	6.15
GNI per capita, Atlas method (current $, 2004)	1,170
GNI, Atlas method (current $ billion, 2004)	96.9
GDP per capita PPP ($, 2003)^	4,321
GDP PPP ($ billion, 2003)^	352.2
Population growth (annual 2005–2010 %) #	1.59
Population, total (million, 2005)#	82.81
Urban population, total (million, 2005)#	51.82
Urban population % of total population (2005)#	63
Population largest city: Metro Manila (million, 2005)	10.68
Population growth: 42 capital cities or agglomerations >750,000 inhabitants 2000#	
- Est. average growth of capital cities or urban agglomerations 2005–2015 (%)	28
- Number of capital cities or urban agglomerations with growth > 50%, 2005–2015	0
- Number of capital cities or urban agglomerations with growth > 30%, 2005–2015	13
Sanitation, % of urban population with access to improved sanitation (2002)**	81
Water, % of urban population with access to improved water sources (2002)**	90
Slum population, % of urban population (2001)**	44
Slum population in urban areas (million, 2001)**	20.18
Poverty, % of urban population below national poverty line (1997)**	21.5
Aid (Net ODA received; $ million, 2003)^	737.2
Aid as share of country income (Net ODA/GNI, %, 2003)*	0.9
Aid per capita (current $, 2003)^	9.10

GDP = gross domestic product, GNI = gross national income, ODA = official development assistance, PPP = purchasing power parity.
Sources: See Footnote Table 3.1, World Bank (2005); Organisation for Economic Co-operation and Development (2003); United Nations (2004, 2005).

COUNTRY CONTEXT

Urbanization Issues

The rapid pace of urbanization in the Philippines poses a wide range of challenges.

The country's population growth rate—which is one of the highest in the world—places serious strains on the economy.[2] In 2005, the population was 82.8 million, of which 51.8 million or 63% lived in urban areas. Metropolitan Manila is the most densely populated urban area with 10.7 million. In 2000, there were 42 capital cities or urban agglomerations. From 2005 to 2015, the estimated average growth of capital cities or urban agglomerations is 28%. By 2030, the urban population is estimated to reach 85 million or approximately 70% of the total population (Figure 11.1). About 20% of the urban population is below the national poverty line (UN Millennium Indicators Database 1997).

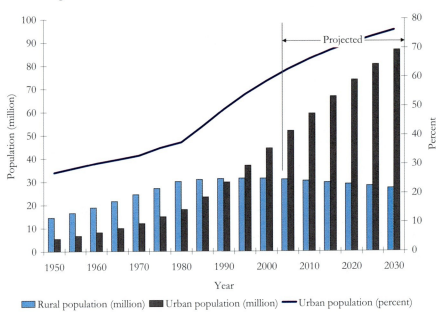

Figure 11.1: Trends in Urban and Rural Population, Philippines

Economic Performance

In the early 1950s, the Philippines was second only to Japan in terms of economic performance. Over the past 3 decades, the country's economy slid behind many Asian economies. Gross domestic product (GDP) grew at an average of only 3%, compared with 8% in the People's Republic of China (PRC); 6% in the Republic of Korea, Singapore, Malaysia, and Thailand; and 5% in Indonesia over the last 30 years (Wallace Report 2004).

Growth has been primarily consumption-led and consumer-driven. Out of the 2003 GDP, 70% was personal consumption. As percentage of GDP, services increased from 40% in 1985 to 53% in 2003.[3] Between 1985 and 2003, manufacturing declined from 35% to 32% while agriculture dropped from 25% to 14%. The country's debt burden accounts for 71% of GDP. However, the GDP annual percentage growth is increasing, now slightly over 6%.

Investment trends in 1986–2001 showed a general decline in key industries, such as manufacturing, food processing, electrical and transport machinery, and fabricated metal products. Investments in textile, plastic, and metal basic industries continued to show resiliency.[4] The country also has one of the highest unemployment rates in Asia,[5] at 7.4% in October 2005.

Gross Regional Domestic Product

The National Capital Region (NCR) accounts for 30% of GDP while the adjacent Southern Tagalog Region or Region 4 contributes 16%. The other 14 regions together account for 54% of GDP. Interestingly, the Autonomous Region in Muslim Mindanao (ARMM) contributes less than 1% of GDP.[6]

Debt and Revenue Trends

In 2003, total debt of the national Government reached about $55 billion with debt service payments on interest alone amounting to $4 billion.[7] During 1999–2003, total national debt increased by 89%, from about $35 billion to nearly $70 billion. Domestic debt increased from $18 billion to $35 billion, representing a 74% increase over a 5-year period, while foreign debt increased from $15 billion to $35 billion. Overall debt service payments increased from $3.7 billion to $8.5 billion, a 129% increase. Debt service expenditures as a percentage of the national annual budget increased from 30% in 1999 to 44% in 2003. Debt service as percentage of government revenues is more alarming, increasing from 42.9% in 1999 to 75% in 2004. Without significant improvements in revenue collection efficiency, national debt is projected to reach $110 billion by 2008 and debt service payment to reach $18 billion.[8]

National revenue effort[9] has been declining since 1998. Prior to the Asian financial crisis in 1997, it was 19%, but dropped to 13% in 2003. Low revenues and increasing debt levels are squeezing resources for development, including those intended for regional development. The Government's fiscal woes mean that fewer financial resources can be expected for local and regional development projects.

Investment Trends

In 2001–2004, a total of $6 billion in foreign direct investment (FDI) was approved by the four investment promotion agencies, namely, the Board of Investments (BOI), Philippine Economic Zone Authority (PEZA), Subic Bay Metropolitan Authority (SBMA), and Clark Development Corporation (CDC).[10] BOI and PEZA approved 48% and 46% of the total FDI in 2001 and 2004, respectively. CDC approved 5%, while the SBMA processed only 1% of these FDIs. FDI inflows to the country are focused on manufacturing, electricity, services, transportation, and communications. Call centers and business outsourcing industries are increasing.

In contrast to the increasing trend in FDI inflows in most members of the Association of Southeast Asian Nations over the past 20 years, the Philippines has experienced a declining trend. From an annual average of $1,343 million in 1992–1997, total FDI inflows fell to $319 million in 2003.[11]

There are regional differences in FDI inflows into the country. Three of the 16 regions each have 8–13% of total FDI. These are also the regions with relatively low levels of poverty incidence. Eleven of the 16 regions have less than 1% share each of total FDI and poverty incidence in these regions is relatively high. Regions that are more affluent experience a higher level of such urban problems as increased levels of in-migration, informal settlers, pollution, and crime relative to other less affluent regions.

Banking System

Banking institutions are important sources of finance for development. The *Bangko Sentral ng Pilipinas,* the country's independent central bank, supervises a total of 19,003 financial institutions[12] consisting of 7,593 banks (4,344 universal and commercial banks; 1,264 thrift banks; and 1,985 cooperative and rural banks) and 11,400 nonbank institutions, such as investment houses, credit card companies, security dealers, and other financial institutions.

Banks are concentrated in cities and wealthier regions. Bank density ratio (number of banks per city/municipality) is highest in the NCR with about 155 banks per city/municipality,[13] followed by Central Luzon with six. Bank density ratios in the ARMM and the Cordillera Administrative Region are zero and one, respectively. About 75% of the country's banks are concentrated in six regions with low- to medium-levels of poverty incidence. Eleven regions compete for the capital and investments provided by the remaining 25% of the total number of banks. NCR, with the lowest poverty incidence, has 35% of the total number of banks. Five regions with very high poverty incidence have a combined 8% share of the total number of banks.

Infrastructure

The 2004–2010 Medium-Term Philippine Development Plan (MTPDP) recognizes the lack of public investment in infrastructure.[14] In 1998–2002, infrastructure expenditure was only 3% of GDP. The cost of electricity is one of the highest in Asia. Transportation systems depend heavily on the road network that caters to 90% and 50% of passenger and freight movement, respectively. The road network consists of provincial roads (13%), city and municipal roads (11%), and mostly unpaved barangay or village roads (60%). About 1,400 ports complement the road network but only 25 of them are considered major. The telecommunications sector has been deregulated, paving the way for multiple ventures in this sector. The private sector undertakes 90% of telecommunications projects.

Poverty Trends

As is evident in the above discussion, regional development in the Philippines is uneven. In 2000, the NCR's per capita income was more than twice the national average and almost six times that of the Bicol Region or Region 5. NCR has the highest regional share of GDP at 36%, with Southern Tagalog (or Region 4) the second highest at 14%. Table 11.2 shows poverty incidence in the Philippines, ranked by region. Table 11.3 also provides comparison of regions in terms of revenues and poverty incidence.

Table 11.2: Poverty Incidence in the Philippines, Ranked by Regions, 1997 and 2000 (%)

Rank	Region	1997	2000	Rank	Region	1997	2000
1	ARMM	50	57	9	Region VII	29.8	32.3
2	Region V	46.9	49	10	Region XI	31.1	31.5
3	Region XII	45.3	48.4	11	CAR	35.9	31.1
4	Caraga	44.7	42.9	12	Region I	31.4	29.6
5	Region IX	31.9	38.3	13	Region II	27.1	24.8
6	Region VI	37.2	37.8	14	Region IV	22.8	20.8
7	Region VIII	39.9	37.8	15	Region III	13.9	17
8	Region X	37.8	32.9	16	NCR	4.8	5.7

Note: Highest rank indicates highest poverty incidence.
ARMM = Autonomous Region in Muslim Mindanao, CAR = Cordillera Administrative Region, NCR = National Capital Region.
Source: National Statistics Coordination Board.

Table 11.3: IRA Share, HDI, Local Taxes and Poverty Incidence, 2000

	IRA Share	HDI	Local Revenue	IRA Share vis-à-vis Poverty Incidence
Better Performing Regions	Regions IV, VI, III, and NCR	NCR, Regions III, IV, and II	NCR, Regions IV, VI, and III	NCR, Region III, Region IV
Poor Performing Regions	CAR, Region XII, Caraga, and ARMM	ARMM, Regions V, XII, and Caraga	ARMM, Caraga, Region XII, and II	ARMM, Region XII, Caraga

ARMM = Autonomous Region in Muslim Mindanao, CAR = Cordillera Administrative Region, HDI = Human Development Index, IRA = internal revenue allotment, NCR = National Capital Region.
Source: Brillantes and Tiu Sonco 2005.

National Regional Development and Decentralization Policies

National Regional Development

Regional development has been enshrined in the policy and administrative agenda of every political leadership since the 1960s. President Gloria Macapagal-Arroyo, upon her assumption into office in 2001,[15] promptly declared the need to address regional development issues, such as reducing regional disparities, strengthening cities and urban areas, promoting peace and development in Mindanao, and stepping up tourism development (Mercado 2002).

Major strategies for regional development as mentioned in the National Framework for Regional Development of the National Economic Development Authority (NEDA) include national dispersion through regional deconcentration, enhancement of the urban-rural linkages, resource- and area-based development, effective mechanisms for regional development administration, and delivery of minimum desirable levels of welfare (NEDA 1998).

The 2004–2010 MTPDP provides the broad guidelines in implementing the 10-point agenda of the President released after her election in May 2004. Her administration promises to create 10 million new jobs, increase exports in the short term, develop 2 million hectares (ha) of land for agribusiness, and increase exports from $38 billion to $50 billion in the next 2 years. The plan calls for the development and rationalization of key infrastructure and utilities, promotion and development of identified tourism areas, and the provision of microfinance for small and medium-size enterprises.

In terms of regional development, MTPDP aims to maximize physical planning as a development tool for job creation, and to develop maritime basins and major rivers as transport and trading areas. It calls for congruence of development plans within the archipelagic economy of the country and the need to conserve its fragile island ecosystem. The development agenda also calls for decongesting NCR or Metropolitan Manila by "developing new centers for government, business and housing in each of Luzon, Visayas, and Mindanao," establishing commuter links between Metropolitan Manila and the north and south regional areas, and the development of other transport hubs, such as airports and ports in identified areas in the country (SONA 2004). Specific items in the agenda likewise aim to link Northern Luzon to the Taipei,China-Southern PRC-Hong Kong, China growth triangle and to establish special export outlets to the southern PRC.

Decentralization and Legislative Framework

The Local Government Code (LGC) of 1991 not only provides the legal mandate for government decentralization, but also contributes to the policy framework for regional planning and development, which is part of the functions and responsibilities devolved to local governments. LGC encourages local governments to group themselves, develop alliances, and form partnerships with civil society in managing development. It also recognizes the potential of metropolitan arrangements consisting of clusters of local government units (LGUs). The LGC further broadens opportunities for increased revenue generation of LGUs through more defined delineation of taxation powers and authority to venture into alternative sources of financing.

LGC devolves to LGUs the responsibility for the delivery of basic services—agriculture, health, social services, environment, and public works—that was formerly the responsibility of the national Government. In addition, LGC provides opportunities for LGUs, civil society, and businesses to work together and make choices that serve their collective interests.

LGC provides for the transfers of national income to LGUs through the internal revenue allotment (IRA) to finance the delivery of public services, particularly the devolved functions. IRA represents 40% of internal taxes collected by the national Government from the third preceding year's collection. IRA is first distributed by levels of LGU: provinces (23%), cities (23%), municipalities (34%), and barangays (20%). IRA share at each level is then distributed to individual LGUs using weighting factors: population (50%), land area (25%), and equal sharing (25%).

LGC expands the financial resources available to LGUs by (i) broadening their revenue-generating and taxation powers; (ii) providing them with a specific share from the national resources extracted in their area, such as charges for mining, fisheries, and forestry; and (iii) increasing their share from the national taxes, i.e., IRA. Moreover, LGC provides better opportunities for entrepreneurial leadership and corporate governance.

In 1995, the Special Economic Zone Act (SEZA) was signed into law to disperse the benefits of industrialization from Metropolitan Manila. SEZA aims to "encourage, promote, induce, and accelerate a sound and balanced industrial, economic, and social development of the country through the establishment of special economic zones in suitable and strategic locations in the country and through measures that shall effectively attract legitimate and productive foreign investments." By law, each economic zone is to be provided with transportation, telecommunications, and other facilities needed to link the zone with industries and employment opportunities for its own inhabitants and those of nearby towns and cities. Enterprises within the zones are granted fiscal incentives.

Regional Planning, Economic Governance, and Financing Regional Development

Regional Planning and Management

The 1987 Constitution provides for establishing regional development councils (RDC) or other similar bodies composed of local government officials, regional heads of departments and other government offices, and representatives from nongovernment organizations (NGOs) in the regions for purposes of administrative decentralization to strengthen the autonomy of the units therein and to accelerate the economic and social growth and development of the units in the regions (Sec. 14, Art. X, 1987 Philippine Constitution).

In practice, regional development planning has been fairly consistent over the years in terms of process. RDCs go through the established planning, programming, and budgeting process.[16] This involves preparing the regional development plans, regional development investment plans, and annual investment plans, as well as the review and endorsement of the proposed budget of the agency regional offices to the agency central offices for consideration in the final agency budget proposed to Congress.

Regional planning is indicated through the regional development plan, regional development investment plan, and regional physical framework plan. There is a need, however, to integrate these plans horizontally and to integrate them vertically with the national plan (Sec. 14, Art. X, 1987 Philippine Constitution).

Regional Economic Governance

Regional economic governance essentially favors a policy of consolidation rather than fragmentation of administrative regions and key areas in the country. This manifested in the MTPDP 2000–2004, which delineated nine regional groupings (out of 16 administrative regions) that cut across and overlap with the existing administrative regional delineations. These new regional groupings were based on the extent of existing and potential economic interaction, level of development, cultural and ethnic factors, and natural resources features like watersheds and river basins (Mercado 2002).

The President also appoints seven Presidential Assistants for Regional Concerns to advise her on regional development concerns. These are "liaison officers" of the Office of the President under the administrative supervision of the Executive Secretary (Mercado 2002).

The recent regional groupings seem to convey the importance of enhancing cooperation and connections rather than fragmentation among regions and key areas in the country. They seek to foster greater inter- and intraregional connections that have been more or less diminished by the practice of dividing the country into as many regions as possible for the sake of administrative convenience.

Regional development in the country, however, cannot escape from the problem of continuing income and human development disparities that necessarily call for greater inflow of labor and capital from richer to poorer regions. In addition, greater dispersion of concentrated development is needed to sustain development that is being threatened by increased migration of the rural population to relatively developed regions and urban areas in the country.

Financing Regional Development

IRAs to LGUs is the most dominant form of intergovernmental transfers. It is a block unconditional grant, giving an LGU-wide discretion as to its utilization. Each LGU is required to set aside no less than 20% of its IRA to local development projects contained in its local development plan.

LGUs are authorized to borrow for financing development, i.e., access alternative financing mechanisms, such as bond flotation and build-operate-transfer (BOT) arrangements. The legislative branch of the Government through the Priority Development Assistance Fund (PDAF) is also another source of funding for LGU projects. Such funding is highly political and less strategic, and may finance development programs or projects inconsistent with the local development plans or unresponsive to local needs.

Foreign development assistance from multilateral institutions to LGUs has to be approved by and channeled through the national Government, which can make lending adjustments on the interest rates to LGUs that may be high and unattractive.[17] LGU access to the banking system has been limited. Commercial banks have not been keen on transacting with LGUs because there is no established system for evaluating their credit worthiness. To a certain extent, national development banks and even commercial banks extend loans to LGUs, with the IRA as the key indicator for obtaining the loan portfolio (Manasan and Chatterjee 2003).

The Municipal Finance Corporation (MFC) was formed in 2003 from an earlier LGU funding body. MFC aims to develop a viable and sustainable financing system that will enable LGUs, in the era of decentralization, to have greater access to financing their investment needs at competitive terms (Executive Order No. 41). The chairperson of the Board of Directors of MFC is the Finance Secretary.

In 1998, the Development Bank of the Philippines and the Bankers Association of the Philippines formed the LGU Guarantee Corporation (LGUGC) to help raise money in capital markets.[18] LGUGC is the leading private institution in developing primary and secondary markets for LGU debt instruments. It provides financial guarantees for LGUs' credit instruments, thus enhancing the sourcing of funds in the capital market.[19] Its total assets in 2004 stood at only $6.7 million, which meant it was only good for a guarantee of up to $55 million of LGU borrowings. The Asian Development Bank (ADB), through the Asian Development Fund, recently infused about $1.3 million of capital investments, thereby taking a 25% stake in LGUGC.[20] ADB's investment in LGUGC marks the first time it has assumed risk on subsovereign commercial obligations without a national Government guarantee. Borrowing from private credit markets provides a good option for LGUs keen to invest in revenue-generating projects with a long payback period.[21]

In the absence of an independent credit rating agency, LGUGC performs credit screening and evaluates credit ratings before it provides guarantees to LGUs issuing bonds or debt instruments. In rating an LGU, LGUGC adopts internationally accepted standards for due diligence requirements of private financial institutions.[22] The bond market at the local level is at the fledgling stage. Only a few LGUs have experienced bond flotation and the results have been uneven. LGUs are perceived to be high credit risks (Manasan and Chatterjee 2003).

The Role of International Aid and Loans in Supporting Regional Development

Official development assistance (ODA) loan commitments declined from $13 billion in 2000 to $10.9 billion in 2003.[23] In 2003, the Government of Japan was the biggest source of ODA, accounting for $7 billion or 62% of total ODA.[24] Other major sources were ADB and the World Bank, which contributed $1.6 billion (14%) and $1.4 billion (13%), respectively, of total

ODA loans in 2004.[25] Eleven percent of the total ODA portfolios came from Australia, Austria, PRC, Danish International Development Agency, European Investment Bank, France, Germany, International Fund for Agricultural Development, Republic of Korea, Kuwait, NORDIC (Denmark, Finland, Iceland, Norway, and Sweden) Development Fund, Organization of Petroleum Exporting Countries, Spain, and United Kingdom.

There is still substantial national government control over ODA as a source of development financing. During 2000–2003, the number of national government-implemented projects increased from 48% to 57%.

In 2000 and 2003, 17% and 18%, respectively, of ODA-funded projects had direct LGU participation. These projects have encountered problems, including the weak capacity of LGUs in putting up the required counterpart funds as well as in project development and management. The national Government usually provides budget covers for ODA-funded projects at the local level. In addition, LGU priorities are often unpredictable because of the political cycles (i.e., 3-year terms of local chief executives). Another issue is the poor compliance of LGUs with ODA requirements.

Paradoxically, regions that most need ODA usually have the least access. In 2003, for example, the NCR alone had a 15% share of total ODA commitments while the four poorest regions (Regions 5, 12, Caraga, and ARMM) together received only 10% of total ODA commitments.[26]

Impediments to Urban Region Development

In the Philippines, while both national Government and local governments pursue local and regional development, their efforts are hardly coordinated, resulting in the duplication and dissipation of scarce resources. Several factors work against effective coordination of central and local government units.

Disparate Planning and Budgeting Process at the National and Local Levels

There is a weak link between the planning and budgeting processes at the national and local government levels. Planning and budgeting processes at the national level are dominated by sectoral bias and have very weak spatial and physical orientation.

There has to be a coherent planning exercise at the regional level congruent with the spatial and physical dimensions of national and medium-term development plans. There is an apparent limited integration of regional and LGU plans. National line agencies implement and fund agency regional plans and programs, which usually do not reflect LGU programs and projects. LGUs implement their local plans, programs, and projects using local funds, unable to maximize resources and optimize results and benefits in the region.

A recent study noted that there appears to be a break in the planning chain from local government levels to the regional level, and then to the national level (Government of the Philippines, World Bank, and ADB 2003). The break occurs between the provincial and regional levels. It is noteworthy that national and regional planning processes are supervised by NEDA while LGU planning is supervised by the Department of Interior and Local Government, which has administrative supervision over all LGUs, and the Department of Finance through the Bureau of Local Government Finance.[27]

National and local development plans are weighed down by a number of factors. First, they often lack coherence and are hardly forward-looking. Sectoral plans tend to be fragmented and not closely linked to each other. Planning horizons tend to be short and dictated by 3-year political cycles of elections and potential changes in political leaderships. Second, plans are far from being knowledge based. Planning processes can be haphazardly executed over very tight schedules. Lack of information, objective criteria, and measurable parameters open frequent opportunities for discretion and arbitrariness. As such, the quality of plans is severely compromised, which has negative consequences for implementation and, more importantly, in directing development. Third, physical planning at the local level is a matter of concern. The comprehensive land-use plans of LGUs tend to be parochial and limited in coverage. The plans are not linked to or directed at promoting economic development from a regional or broader perspective. Maximizing the benefits of physical infrastructure, for instance, requires that it be established to its optimal size and may therefore cover more than one political jurisdiction. Fourth, plans are not linked to budgets. Fifth, there is a weak institutional mechanism for planning processes to take into account information on past performance and citizens' feedback. Finally, there is lack of accountability in the entire planning process.

Lack of Orientation to Compete in Global Economy

Individual LGUs hardly contemplate competing in the global economy. Most local development plans are supply-driven, inward-looking, and limited to encouraging businesses that cater to local consumption needs or, at best, attracting industries producing relatively low-value and small-scale products for export. Ironically, the national Government shares the same orientation and is neither providing the required strategic direction nor the enabling policy and institutional environment. The national Government has not provided leadership in developing basic infrastructure for efficient and cost-effective movement of goods and products within the country.

The Special Economic Zone Act and the creation of hundreds of economic zones in the country, for instance, have not helped in developing national/local industries that can compete in the world market, but instead have made LGUs compete with each other to host foreign locators, and impeded LGUs' ability to harness their competitive advantages and develop competitive alliances. Specialization of products and services—critical to sustainable growth—has been stifled by this mode of development.

There is a strong service orientation but very weak investment orientation in local development planning, even in the case of metropolitan planning as advocated by NEDA. NEDA's metropolitan concept has been observed to be primarily service oriented, dealing with traffic congestion, infrastructure, and other urban services (Robredo 1998). It is, however, seen as an instrument for promoting investment.

Weak System of Intergovernmental Transfers

Most LGUs rely on IRAs to finance their operations. The existing system of intergovernmental transfers does not facilitate the development of integrated and well-coordinated plans and programs across the different tiers of government. The IRA formula has also been criticized for being inequitable, inefficient, and incapable of promoting local tax effort. Provinces and cities each get 23% share of IRA. The cities, however, have more taxes and a richer tax base than do provinces. Among individual LGUs, it has also been observed that poor or low-income class LGUs tend to get lower shares than high-income class LGUs. The equal sharing component of IRA encourages greater local government fragmentation and discourages local government mergers that could lead to more efficient provision of local goods and services. Finally, there are indications that IRA tends to substitute or decrease local tax efforts. For LGUs not inclined to put up new projects or improve their services, the IRA is enough to meet their operational requirements.

In spite of the authority of LGUs to incur debts and raise equity, many LGUs seldom utilize the credit market for development financing. Most LGUs prefer to secure grants and donations. The PDAF is among the most popular sources of funding for many local projects. Such projects do not pass through local or regional development councils, bypassing prioritization procedures and possibly crowding out crucial projects.

A major factor constraining LGUs from borrowing is their lack of technical capability to formulate development plans and package project proposals for acquiring loans or other types of financing, such as BOT programs. Many LGUs do not have updated local development plans, and many development plans are not supported by sound financing programs. There is limited knowledge of the policy implications and general technical content of the different means of credit financing. For small and medium-sized LGUs, budgets are not available for preparing project feasibility studies.

In addition to the internal constraints of LGUs are legal and administrative constraints from the national Government. One major constraint is the debt cap on LGU borrowing under Section 324 of the LGC. It limits the annual appropriation for debt service to 20% of the regular income of an LGU, thus hindering the local government from implementing even self-liquidating and/or self-supporting projects that require sizeable capital outlay.

The Commission on Audit and Central Bank regulations requiring LGUs to maintain their deposits with government financial institutions constitute another restriction. This requirement effectively disallows private financial institutions from availing of the IRA mechanism that serves as collateral for LGU and weakens the power of LGUs to negotiate or search for the cheapest borrowing rate.

The bond market is an alternative source of capital financing for LGUs, but such offerings are seen as high credit risk. The private sector sees LGU management, operations, and financial record-keeping as weak. In addition, LGUs and private financial institutions use different financial and accounting systems. Investors are wary that long-term credit obligations will not be honored should there be a change in administration. This problem is compounded by the absence of an independent LGU credit rating agency and the lack of a secondary market for LGU bonds.

Inadequate Infrastructure

The low capital outlay and infrastructure spending by local governments do not augur well for local and regional development. Infrastructure affects both supply of and demand for goods and services, reducing the cost of production and facilitating access to markets. It also improves the delivery of and access to social services. Moreover, the presence of key infrastructure is a major factor for the formation of industry clusters.

Infrastructure in the Philippines has been focused on the NCR, hindering local and regional development elsewhere. The special economic zones were created across the country in an effort to promote and encourage economic and social development around the country. According to the SEZA, "each ecozone shall be provided with transportation, telecommunications, and other facilities needed to generate linkage with industries and employment opportunities for its own inhabitants and those of nearby towns and cities." However, it appears that the majority of these ecozones are located in the Southern Tagalog Region, which is adjacent to Metro Manila. Of the total 150 ecozones in 2002, 63 of them, or 42%, were in Southern Tagalog, followed by the NCR with 13%, and by Central Luzon and Central Visayas with 9% each.

As expected, the share in approved investments (both foreign and domestic) is dominated by the four regions hosting the majority of the ecozones. Export processing zones and industrial estates, which are the predecessors of ecozones, generate little employment and have very weak forward and backward linkage with the rest of the regional economy (Lamberte et al. 1993). Thus, in terms of the avowed goal of spreading economic and social development and promoting local and regional development, ecozones leave much to be desired.

Inadequate Credit and Financial Services

Another major constraint to local and regional development, particularly in rural areas, is the inadequate flow of capital and credit to both agricultural and off-farm business, despite Central Bank and Government efforts to provide policy and practical support to agriculture and small enterprises. This can be attributed to two major factors. The first is the lack or inadequate presence of financial institutions, such as thrift banks, rural banks, development banks, and nonbank microfinance institutions that are able to cater to the unique requirements of agricultural and small borrowers and savers. The second is the increased uncertainty and risk involved in lending to and investing in these sectors. The problems with land tenure and uncertainty in the resolution of property rights brought about by the poor implementation of the agrarian reform law have been a big disincentive to bank lending. In the case of small enterprises, information asymmetry is the major problem.

Weak Human Capital Development

To prepare human resources adequately for higher levels of productivity, regional disparities in access to and quality of education should be addressed. The Philippine Progress Report on the Millennium Development Goals noted that, while regional disparities are not very evident in elementary participation rates, there are differences between the public and private schools in terms of achievement level at the elementary and secondary levels (United Nations Resident Coordinator 2004). The Report also highlighted the gross disparity in the functional literacy rates of women in urban and rural areas and cited the lack of educational opportunities, access to schools, and the tendency of some parents to discourage their daughters from attending school, as possible reasons.

Environmental Degradation

Metro Manila and other urban centers in the Philippines already exhibit many problems associated with unmanaged urbanization, such as pollution, inadequate water supply, weak sewerage infrastructure and waste disposal, high unemployment and crime rates, presence of squatter colonies, and traffic congestion. Population growth and urban migration have also resulted in the premature conversion of productive agricultural lands for residential and other urban uses. Lack of economic opportunities and poverty in the countryside leads to low productivity and destructive activities that threaten the already fragile ecosystem. The devastating typhoons and numerous landslide and flooding incidents in the recent past attest to the environmental degradation that besets the country.

Policy and Institutional Deficiencies

Regional economic development is further challenged by many other policy gaps and institutional constraints. The agrarian reform program, although well-meaning, subdivided farm production to the extent that economies of scale have been significantly distorted. Agriculture has, therefore, become an unattractive sector, contributing to increased rural unemployment.

There is also much to be desired in terms of the country's land information and management system. With the entire country divided into thousands of land parcels, titling and recording are problematic. Transfer of deeds and titles is extremely difficult and unnecessarily increases delays and transaction costs, thus impeding business development. Significant percentages of total land parcels are either untitled, disputed, or undervalued. LGUs have not adjusted the valuation of real properties in recent years for political reasons. This contributes to the lack of capacity of LGUs to raise revenue other than IRA. The highly politicized bureaucracy and corrupt activities similarly affect sustainable regional economic growth.

GOOD PRACTICE CASE STUDIES

Despite constraints to regional development, some cities in the country have begun laying down the foundations for good governance and undertaking initiatives to improve service delivery systems that improve living conditions. Bacolod was selected as a case study because it won the medium-sized cities category in the 2004 Philippine Cities Competitive Report (PCCR) conducted by the Asian Institute of Management. Naga, which was a runner-up

Figure 11.2: Map Showing Location of the Case Studies

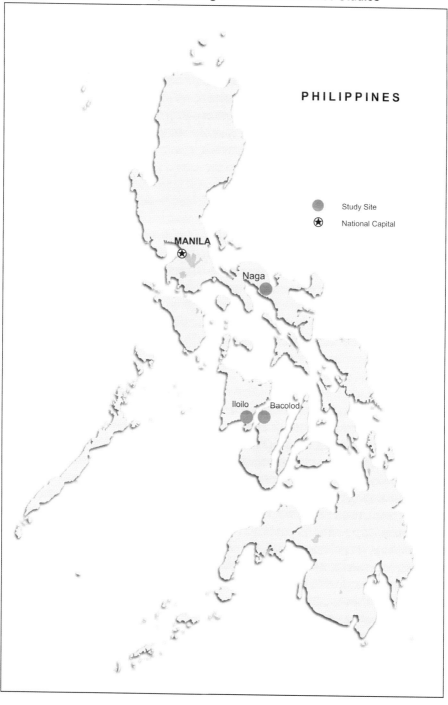

in the study, was selected in view of the numerous awards and recognition it has received from national and international agencies. Iloilo, the third case study, is also one of the leading cities in the country, and its critical role in establishing a local area network partnership with adjacent municipalities deserves attention. Table 11.4 provides data on the three case study sites and other cities in the country.

Table 11.4: Comparative Data on Case Study Sites and other Cities

City	Population 2000 Census	Population growth rate (%)	Income Class	IRA (P Mn)[a] 2003	Local Revenue (P Mn)[a] 2003	land area (km^2)
Naga	137,810	1.72[28]	1st	178	532	84.48
Bacolod	429,076	1.39	1st	370	284	161.45
Iloilo	365,820	1.93	1st	310	394	56
Quezon City	2,173,831	1.92	Special	1,473	4,669	153.60
Manila	1,581,082	(0.97)	Special	1,100	3,911	38.3
Cebu	718,821	1.77	1st	608	1,215	291.25
San Fernando, La Union	102,082	2.09[29]	3rd	165	82	100
Marikina	391,170	1.96	1st	307	805	21.50
Davao	1,147,116	2.83	1st	1,395	783	2,443.6
Calbayog	147,187	1.83[30]	1st	383	32	903
Cagayan De Oro	461,877	1.63	1st	474	550	488.86

IRA = internal revenue allotment, km^2 = square kilometers, mn = million.
[a] US$ 1.0 = approximately P55 in 2003.
Sources: www.census.gov.ph/census2000/index.html; www.census.gov.ph/census2000/index.html (1995–2000 annual growth rate); www.nscb.gov.ph/activestats/psgc/listcity.asp; BLGF; 2003 SIE Report; LGU Websites; Provincial annual growth rates.

Bacolod City

Bacolod City is the capital of Negros Occidental Province in Region 6 or Western Visayas. It is a medium-size city with a low annual population growth rate of about 1% compared to the national average of 2%. It is the seat of the provincial government and a center of commerce, trade, industry, and cultural activities. The city consists

GOOD PRACTICE	
Good Governance	✓
Urban Management	✓
Infrastructure/Service Provision	✓
Financing and Cost Recovery	
Sustainability	✓
Innovation and Change	
Leveraging ODA	

of 61 barangays with a total land area of around 18,000 ha, of which 56.4% is classified as agricultural land. Sugar is the main agricultural product of

Bacolod City as it is for the entire province, supplying 50% of the country's sugar requirements. The city is also well-known for its handicrafts and cottage industries, such as wood carving, ceramics, pottery, and novelty candles. Bacolod, together with the entire Region 6, is one of the country's steady sources of fishery and aquaculture products.

Initiatives and Gains

Bacolod City ranked first among mid-size cities in the 2004 PCCR. Bacolod City topped in three out of seven drivers of change identified by the PCCR: (1) human resources and training; (2) infrastructure; and (3) quality of life.[31] Through partnerships and cooperation between and among the different stakeholders, Bacolod has been able to sustain modest economic growth and significantly improve the quality of life for its citizens in recent years. Notwithstanding the wide-ranging improvements that need to be put in place for Bacolod to harness its full potential, the city has shown encouraging initiatives and positive results worth noting for purposes of replication by similarly situated localities and providing inputs in crafting a viable framework for regional development.

Trained Human Resources. Bacolod has a well-educated labor force. Bacolod is consistently one of the top performers in the National Elementary Assessment Test and National Secondary Assessment Test administered by the Department of Education. The city's educational system is unique in its institutionalized system of on-the-job training programs for students, which has been made possible through effective partnerships between local industries and educational institutions. Businesses allow trainees from schools and other institutions, and provide ample opportunities for students to develop practical skills needed for actual work situations. Bacolod has two universities, 11 colleges, and 23 vocational schools.[32] Efforts have been undertaken to make the school curricula responsive to the needs of local businesses as well as demands for specialized services, both domestic and abroad (e.g., call center, nursing, caregiver, and maritime professions).

Educational and training institutions have been tapped to advance and sustain various initiatives, such as community-based solid waste management, fire prevention, rescue operations, disaster preparedness, and crime prevention. In support of the National Civic Welfare Training Service, college students are sent on field training and social immersion wherein they are asked to serve their communities as part of their schooling and learning experience.

The Technical Education for Skills Development Authority, in collaboration with the National Federation of Sugar Cane Planters, co-manages a vocational school for the children of sugar planters who intend to develop skills in automotive repair, as diesel mechanics, and other technical rural subjects. The city government works closely with civil society organizations in providing scholarships, training programs, and special projects for the elderly, unemployed adults, out-of-school youth, and physically challenged residents.

Good Infrastructure Base. Bacolod has a relatively well-developed infrastructure base. It has seaports and airports within the city limits and nearby areas that serve domestic and international clients. Bacolod is 45 minutes away by sea from bigger and busier Iloilo City. An airport following international standards will be built by the city government about 60 km from the city center under a BOT scheme. Bacolod has a well-managed road network with extensive drainage systems, wide streets, and well-maintained footpaths. With assistance from Japan International Cooperation Agency, Bacolod has a traffic management plan that identifies directions for road expansion and widening, building of bridges, and improving the mass transport system. Communication facilities are likewise well developed. Together with landline networks, the city has adequate cell sites that ensure stable and high-speed internet connections. The city also has a steady supply of water and electricity.

Livable City. Bacolod has been identified as an ideal place to reside in due to its clean air, healthy population, low incidence of crime, and easy access to basic amenities and leisure activities. Bacolod belongs to the *Cleanest and Greenest City Hall of Fame*.[33] The city government, citizens, and private groups cooperate in maintaining the cleanliness of the whole city and the preservation of public domains, such as median islands, parks, and gardens.[34]

The solid waste management program implemented by the city government is well received and well supported by the citizens. Garbage is collected daily in commercial and urban residential areas, and weekly in rural residential areas. The city government provides refuse bins and compost pits in selected locations. Waste segregation and recycling are part of the program. The city also regularly sprays anti-pollutants and insecticides to prevent diseases.

The city has one of the lowest maternal and infant mortality rates and one of the highest numbers of hospital beds among mid-size cities nationwide. The city government highly prioritizes maternal health care and family planning. The 61 barangays all have easy access to basic health services.

The crime rate is low with the city police force being cited as the best in Region 6. This can be attributed to a monthly financial assistance of about $10,000 extended by the office of the city mayor, which is drawn from the monthly donation of some $20,000 by the Philippine Gaming Corporation to the city government. The financial assistance is used to augment the meager budget of the police force for operating and maintenance expenses. With more money for fuel and maintenance of patrol cars, police visibility and effectiveness have been enhanced.

Governance. Participatory approaches and consultative processes are increasingly becoming very familiar in managing the city's affairs. The LGC has not only provided the basic legal mandate for devolving power and authority to subnational administrative units, but it also opened opportunities for citizens' empowerment by their gaining access to and representation in government decision-making bodies and discharge of official functions. LGC provides the enabling policy environment to promote good governance. The partnerships and linkages that have evolved in Bacolod are attributable to the LGC, and have been reinforced by local ordinances, such as the Investment Code (1996 and 2002) establishing a multisectoral local investment board and providing tax incentives to investors.

Citizens' feedback on public services has also been welcomed and used to improve service delivery. This feedback, coupled with benchmarking of good practices by other LGUs, prompted the city government to institutionalize a one-stop shop for processing business license applications and payment of local taxes and fees. The concept resulted in a modest but steady increase in non-IRA revenues.

Practicing the principles of transparency and public accountability, the incumbent local chief executive delivers his annual State of the City Address wherein he publicly announces his administrative agenda and reports his accomplishments in measurable terms. He openly encourages his constituents to hold his administration to account for the services and changes that he has promised to deliver. Local business associations and civil society organizations have been very cooperative and active in working with the city government to advance and sustain a number of initiatives that improve the quality of life.

Economic Activities and Opportunities. Issuance of business permits/licenses is increasing as more residents are employed. Business taxes and real property taxes accounted for an average of 43% and 47%, respectively, of the total local tax collections in 2004. Real property tax collections increased by PhP20.4M from 2001 to 2002, PhP7.9M from 2002 to 2003 and PhP4.9M from 2003 to 2004 or approximately PhP33.2M for four years from 2001 to 2004.[35] Tourist arrivals have been increasing. The number of banks increased from 47 in 1998 to 56 in 2003. There is an increasing trend in real estate business. Repatriated earnings from overseas Filipino workers and relatives are also increasing.

Bacolod and Iloilo provide good educational institutions for residents of Western Visayas, thus avoiding the high costs of tuition and living in Metro Manila and Metro Cebu. Western Visayas is known for its mango and sugar production. Rich aquatic resources and white sand beaches are the other competitive advantages of the region. The city is a jump-off point to various ecotourism destinations in the Western Visayas. Bacolod offers opportunities for food processing and manufacturing of the region's produce. It also serves as an alternative place for conventions and permanent residence to the crowded and nearby Iloilo.

Challenges and Future Directions

Economic Development and Revenue Generation. Bacolod needs to increase its capacity to promote sustainable local economic development to generate more revenues and become less dependent on the IRA. As of 2004, IRA and local sources were 54% and 46%, respectively. IRA dependency has decreased and improved by 5% from 2001 to 2004.[36]

The city's revenue-generating capacity can be improved by implementing a strategic and coherent business model and providing the enabling policy and appropriate institutional environment. The efficiency of tax and revenue collection should also be strengthened. Increases in applications for new businesses and commercial activities have not been matched by increases in total annual tax collections.

Economic activities have been largely limited to domestic consumption. Sugar production—the key industry in Bacolod and the rest of Negros Occidental Province—has remained the same for many decades, and has not adopted new methods of production to increase yield and quality or to make the price competitive in the world market. Investment programs need to be more effective to attract foreign investments for new ventures. The city government, like most local governments in the country, is yet to think globally in the context of the new economic order and orient its way of doing things accordingly.

The Local Investment Ordinance of Bacolod—passed in 1996, reinstated, and amended in 2002—has provided tax incentives to investors and established the Local Investment Board. This policy instrument needs to be reviewed because potential revenues of the city are undermined due to tax cuts and exemptions. Besides, these do not necessarily attract investors to bring their business to Bacolod. Investors give more weight to the availability and costs of inputs, security of investments, and profit margins.

The city can generate more revenue by rationalizing its land information system and real property valuation, and linking them to an efficient revenue collection system. Land titling is problematic. Some titles either have conflicting information, are missing, unrecorded, or not updated. Real property valuation is not regularly updated and reconciled with tax records. Valuation is significantly below the market value and adjusting it to higher rates has not been included in the administrative agenda in view of the perceived political risks and resistance from influential and landed residents. Accurate and updated tax maps are critical to revenue generation.

Development Planning and Management. The comprehensive land-use plan (CLUP) serves as the blueprint for city development. The Philippine Regional Municipal Development Project provided support to Bacolod in digitizing land information, which became the bases for land classification and setting development priorities. CLUP, together with the annual investment plans, however, need to be more information-based, inclusive, and forward looking. An effective national and regional development framework can be helpful and provide the needed guidance. Existing policy guidelines from the national Government are similarly in disarray. Development planning lacks careful analysis and strategic direction. Plans are usually reduced to an enumeration of activities that are not linked to budgets and directed at achieving the desired outcomes.

Weaknesses in development plans and the lack of career opportunities and performance culture further subject development administration to extreme pressures of political patronage and partisan politics. Development priorities have been largely influenced by the local chief executive and the dominant political party in the city council.[37] It has been difficult to pursue and sustain development initiatives in the long term.

Knowledge Management. Information is essential to enhancing productivity and competitiveness. Basic data about the city is nonetheless either incomplete or inaccurate or both. Official records on revenues and other development indices are sometimes conflicting even when generated by the same office. Variations in the reported figures can become greater and more confusing as more offices get involved in gathering and generating the information. There are no economic development indices at the level of cities and municipalities. In the absence of adequate and reliable information, development planning and management are severely compromised.

Naga City

Naga is 500 km southeast of the NCR. Although an established center of commerce in the Bicol Region,[38] Naga's performance before the mid-1980s was poor. The city government's overspending in a time of scarce revenue prompted the Department of Finance to downgrade the city's status in 1988. The prevalence of illegal gambling and other vices

GOOD PRACTICE	
Good Governance	✓
Urban Management	✓
Infrastructure/Service Provision	✓
Financing and Cost Recovery	✓
Sustainability	✓
Innovation and Change	✓
Leveraging ODA	✓

worsened the quality of life in the city. The election of 29-year old Jesse Robredo as city mayor in 1988 ushered in inspiring governance practices that, in just 3 years, helped the city regain its premier status. Through transparent and participatory governance, the city government has rebuilt its credibility. With over 100 international, national, and regional awards in best governance practices, Naga City is also now one of the country's brightest economic spots.

As Bicol's center for commerce, finance, trade, and services, Naga plays a crucial role in regional development. It serves as an industrial hub for Metro Naga and the Legaspi-Iriga-Daet growth corridors and is being groomed to be a major link to Metro Manila and other metropolitan areas in the country.[39] The dynamism of Naga's economy is evident in its 6.5% average annual growth rate, the presence of two business districts and several new growth zones, and an average family income that is 126% and 42% higher than the national and regional averages, respectively (Robredo 2003). Without appropriate intervention to reduce regional poverty (Bicol houses the largest number of poor families in the country) and accelerate regional growth (a mere 2.7% contribution to the gross regional domestic product compared to Metro Manila's 30%), Naga's economic gains are not sustainable in the long run.

Initiatives and Gains

Economic Governance. Strengthening partnerships with the organized sectors and eliciting people's participation are key governance practices (Robredo 2003). The city government shows a strong drive for economic growth and poverty reduction. It uses a pragmatic governance approach providing key directions for the local economy and empowering the private sector in spurring economic development.[40] It practices strategic planning that goes beyond the confines of the city's immediate concerns. To sustain economic and service-delivery partnerships, it provides technical, livelihood, and job-placement services that benefit not only its constituents but also those of other local governments.

Improving Local Government Capability. To enhance its capability to manage economic development, the city government reorganized its bureaucracy based on aptitude and competence, implemented an award-winning Productivity Improvement Program, activated the Merit and Promotions Board to eliminate patronage, empowered employees to propose innovations, and improved systems and procedures (Robredo 1999). Naga's economic recovery lies in working with people with very good credentials.[41]

Metro Naga. The city government initiated the formation of the Metro Naga Development Council (MNDC) or Metro Naga, which comprises Naga

City and 14 towns of Camarines Sur, Bicol's largest province, accounting for 33% of the regional population. Unlike other metropolitan groupings in the Philippines, Metro Naga is a cooperative undertaking among local governments exercising their new prerogatives in the era of enhanced local autonomy. It operates on the principles of complementing limited resources and pooling investment potentials and comparative advantages. It relies on enhanced urban-rural linkages (Robredo 1999) and practices metro-wide planning to ensure balanced growth and sustainable development. It earned formal legal status in 1993 (Mercado and Ubaldo 2002; Robredo 2005). Some key features of MNDC are:

- *Council structure to facilitate economic cooperation.* MNDC established a plan to formulate programs through the coordination of mayors and governors. It consists of 15 mayors and representatives of the provincial government, and representatives of NEDA, the private sector, and NGOs.
- *Metro-wide planning and role definitions.* A Metro Naga Development Program serves as a framework for defining the roles of LGUs. An agreement empowers each LGU to implement a complementary development program within its area. Naga is the trade, financial, education, and services center. One town is the industrial center. The other towns are key sites for manufacturing, food processing, and other industries.
- *Organizational machinery.* The city government created a separate office that initiates and manages MNDC activities. Led by an Executive Director who supervises the project formulation, implementation, and support-service units, this office is crucial in sustaining LGU interests in the economic and service-delivery partnership.[42]
- *Pooling of resources and services for Metro-wide service delivery.* LGUs contribute 2% of their economic development fund to a common fund. During 1993–1997, this fund reached about $400,000 (half of it came from Naga City). Other initiatives include setting up a Metro Naga equipment pool and emergency rescue network, construction of 50 km of farm-to-market roads, and 500 water systems and extension of livelihood assistance to Metro Naga constituents.
- *Pooling investment potentials and comparative advantages.* Metro Naga capitalizes on its competitive advantages: the city's image as one of the fastest-growing local economies in the country, the presence of four special economic zones, two of the country's richest fishing grounds, and a market of over half a million people. Investment-promotion activities are guided by the objectives of economic diversification, employment generation, and poverty reduction.

Partnerships with the Private Sector. The city government encourages private-sector partnerships by eliminating vices, reducing the costs of public works construction, practicing transparency in its operations, and implementing other confidence-building measures. It partnered with the private sector even before the enactment of the LGC of 1991. In 1989, private firms, through a build-operate-lease agreement, converted a kilometer-long eyesore into a commercial strip. Partnerships with the private sector resulted in the development of four new satellite markets that decongested and, in turn, made the old business district dynamic again.

Participatory and Inclusive Governance. The city government fosters and institutionalizes community consensus and ownership of development priorities. Through the Empowerment Ordinance (95-092), accredited NGOs were organized into a People's Council that sits in every legislative committee and local special body mandated under the LGC. Through its award-winning *i*-governance program, the city government published the *Naga Citizen's Charter* which provides step-by-step procedures for availing of its 150 frontline services. It also set up an award-winning website (www.naga.gov.ph) that updates citizens on the city's finances, policies, and activities.

Local Policies and Initiatives. By virtue of Ordinance No. 97-114, the city government grants incentives to investors in preferred investments. The ordinance aims to generate jobs for Metro Naga constituents and promote balanced growth. The Investment Promotions and Action Center implements the objectives set by the city's investment board, markets Metro Naga as an investment site, facilitates joint venture projects with local and external investors, and provides assistance to investors.

Economic Planning and Analysis. The mayor helped change planning practices; from a "shotgun" approach in formulating annual plans, to a planning process that has become more participatory and focused on what the city and its people need.[43] A needs inventory ensured the formulation of feasible projects. Plans became long-term policies defying the limitations of 3-year political cycles, e.g., the city's 1990 zoning ordinance guided city development until year 2000. For planning purposes, the city was viewed as a system whose sustainability also depended on conditions beyond its immediate geographic environment.

Financing Development. Less than 60% of the city's income is from the national Government; the rest is from local revenues. City government income rose from $0.5 million in 1988 to about $6.0 million in 2001. Borrowing from banks, mixed public-private financing, and grants are the forms of development financing. Bond flotation is not widely practiced.

Presence of a Competent and Willing Catalyst. The city government served as a regional development catalyst by spearheading the formation of an economic region out of disparate political units in the province. Its readiness as a catalyst springs from the realization that the sustainability of the city also rests on the development of neighboring towns. Its enhanced financial and administrative capability enabled it to absorb most of the burdens of sustaining the needed LGU partnerships for the economic region. The presence of a strong political leader and skilled development manager and the city's good reputation served it well in speeding up the process of regional development.

Institutionalization of Good Governance. The Naga experience strongly demonstrates the imperatives of promoting participation, accountability, transparency, and predictability in managing state and societal affairs. Realizing that it cannot pursue development objectives by itself and that quality of public decisions will be ensured by meaningful stakeholder engagement, the political leadership developed partnerships with nongovernment actors in development management. Stakeholders were given permanent seats in decision-making bodies and the public has been adequately informed about government transactions, particularly finances.

Naga citizens were empowered by the institutionalization of the so-called Citizens Charter, which clearly enumerates the services provided by the city government as well as the responsible persons and offices for the delivery of a particular service, including the maximum time required to deliver the service. This initiative has tremendously strengthened public accountability and improves the efficiency and responsiveness of service delivery.

Challenges and Future Directions

Strengthening Economic Partnerships. An ongoing conflict between the provincial and city leadership threatens the gains of Metro Naga and reveals the urgent task of achieving greater cohesiveness among politically fragmented LGUs. The potential for conflict to short-circuit the development process reveals the precariousness of a politically driven arrangement. Surmounting this challenge will surely involve pooling resources, investment potentials, and comparative advantages that, in turn, boost regional competitiveness. A key direction is to put in place stronger public-private partnerships for managing the next stages of the development process.

Accelerating Economic Development in the Region. The city is an island of prosperity in the sea of want"[44]. More than 60% of the Metro Naga population live below the poverty line. Investments are still heavily concentrated in the city. Diffusing economic opportunities and key infrastructure, such as seaports, to other towns in Metro Naga is a major step to reduce poverty. Strategies for developing Metro Naga must also complement the strategies prescribed by NEDA for developing the wider Bicol administrative region. These include increasing revenue collections and agricultural productivity, developing human capital, and providing infrastructure support.[45]

Financing Regional Projects. Accessing low-interest financing for major projects is a significant problem for hastening regional development. Borrowing directly from multilateral agencies is constrained by a centralized financing system and, of course, by the existing practice of multilateral agencies to channel loans through national offices. A comprehensive valuation of the assets of the city and Metro Naga member LGUs should be undertaken to generate a reliable credit rating that would both serve as a guide for credit risks and investment opportunities.

Developing Linkages. The absence of very good seaport and rail facilities explains why the region has been unable to sell its local products outside the regional market.[46] Campaigns to develop national and international linkages must be launched to surmount the geographic and infrastructural disadvantage. Overseas Filipino workers can be tapped to sell Metro Naga as an investment site and tourism destination. Developing its information and communications technology infrastructure would enable Metro Naga to ride on the booming global services industry. The high cost of power and frequent outages in the region, however, must be addressed as well (AIM 2003).

Iloilo City

Iloilo City is the capital of the Province of Ilolilo and is also located in Region 6. It has a small land area of only 56 km². It has an annual population growth rate of nearly 2% and is a highly urbanized city consisting of 180 barangays.

Iloilo is strategically located at the center of the Philippines with an excellent port, airport, extensive infrastruc-

GOOD PRACTICE	
Good Governance	✓
Urban Management	✓
Infrastructure/Service Provision	✓
Financing and Cost Recovery	
Sustainability	✓
Innovation and Change	
Leveraging ODA	✓

ture, modern telecommunications systems, and reliable utilities. It serves as the hub of trade, commerce, industry, information, and services in the region. The main industry is agriculture—cultivating rice, corn, coconuts, bananas, mangos, coffee, and sugarcane. It also has rich fishing grounds and cottage industries, including weaving, pottery, processing of marine products, and cut flowers. Museo Iloilo, which displays its cultural heritage, Fort San Pedro waterfront promenade, and the Dinagyang festival are among the tourist attractions in the city.

Initiatives and Gains

The establishment of the Metropolitan Iloilo Development Council (MIDC) is one of the key development initiatives of Iloilo City and its adjacent four municipalities within a 15 km radius, namely, Oton in the south, San Miguel in the northwest, and Pavia and Leganes in the north. MIDC was created as a mechanism to promote inter- and intra-LGU cooperation in the pursuit of well-planned and coordinated local and regional development toward national development objectives. It helps reduce unwanted competition between cities and municipalities, which oftentimes dissipates the impact on regional and national development. MIDC formulates spatial development strategies and governance arrangements. It is particularly concerned with (i) development planning; (ii) transport and traffic engineering and management; (iii) environmental sanitation and waste management and disposal; (iv) flood control and sewerage management; (v) urban renewal, land use, and zoning and shelter services; (vi) networking of economic support infrastructure; (vii) public safety, maintenance of peace and order, and disaster management; and (viii) trade and investment promotion.

With Iloilo City serving as the center for residential, commercial, financial, and industrial activities in the region, each participating municipality has a distinct area of specialization: (i) Pavia is the agro-industrial center; (ii) Leganes concentrates on heavy industry; (iii) Oton is best suited as a residential area; and (iv) San Miguel concentrates on agricultural production.

It took the proponents and advocates of Metro Iloilo nearly 10 years of discussion and consultation before the MIDC was formally approved in February 2001. The mayors of the five participating LGUs comprise the Executive Council of MIDC, which provides overall supervision and policy direction. An advisory board contributes policy and technical advice to the Executive Council while an MIDC secretariat coordinates the administrative work of the Council. Six project steering committees have been organized to plan and coordinate services that have metro-wide impact, namely: (i) environmental management, (ii) land-use planning and management, (iii) public safety and security, (iv) infrastructure development, (v) basic services delivery, and (vi) economic promotion. In addition, a technical working group supports each steering committee.

With a view of applying a coherent urban development plan, Iloilo City together with its four satellite municipalities formulated a regional growth management strategy through the preparation of the Metro Iloilo Land Use Framework (MILUF) plan. It serves as the overall policy framework for sustainable Metro Iloilo development programs and projects. Iloilo City has learned not to fast-track metropolitanization. The preparation of the MILUF followed a six-step land-use planning process, as follows:

(i) review of existing municipal and city comprehensive land-use plans;
(ii) information, analysis, and mapping—which required data gathering, comprehensive review of reports, plans, and strategies—and preparation and integration of land-use maps in the region;
(iii) sectoral consultations and reports on social development, economic development, infrastructure development, environmental development, and local administration;
(iv) public consultation (phase I) to review initial data and maps and develop framework for the plan, develop regional growth options for Metro Iloilo, and draft MILUF vision, mission, goals, and strategies;
(v) prepare draft metropolitan plan containing the goals, objectives, and framework; and
(vi) public consultation (phase II) and approval.

The spatial expansion of Iloilo City to the north (toward the municipalities of Leganes and Pavia) is supported by an extensive road network connecting the city to other locations in Panay Island. Recent infrastructure projects include the coastal road, providing a second link to the municipality of Leganes and adjacent municipalities of Zaraga and Dumangas in the north as well as to the Iloilo International Port Complex. The municipality of Leganes has initiated a large-scale multipurpose land development, providing opportunities for an attractive industrial and residential zone. Reclamation of about 200 ha of seashore along the Guimaras Strait for industrial use is being considered under a BOT scheme.[47]

Challenges and Future Directions

Transport and Traffic Management. Iloilo City and the adjoining municipalities need to expand further and improve the road network as well as to address the worsening traffic problem effectively. Roads are narrow and inadequate to accommodate the increasing number of vehicles. The number of provincial buses and public utility vehicles going through the city and the location of the bus terminals in the city proper further clog the overcrowded roads. The plan is to relocate the bus terminals outside the city proper.[48] The effectiveness of the fledgling metropolitan arrangement in redesigning the road network will be put to the test.

Waste Management. Another task ahead for MIDC is to establish an environmental friendly and common solid waste management system. Iloilo City is facing serious constraints in disposing waste. The current disposal site is no longer viable in view of the mounting protests from concerned residents. An alternative site in the municipality of Oton is being considered, but agreeing on a landfill site through cost-sharing arrangements is expected to be contentious.

Flood Control and Sewerage System. A comprehensive flood control system for Metro Iloilo is deemed necessary to address the perennial flooding that significantly affects social and economic activities, particularly in Iloilo City and the municipality of Pavia. A cooperative arrangement is being considered that will involve dredging adjoining bodies of water and constructing a network of floodways. An equally important challenge is the establishment of a comprehensive sewerage system to minimize the effects on the underground water aquifer.[49] It is in this context that large-scale and integrated physical planning for the whole metropolis must be undertaken.

Urban Infrastructure and Economic Promotion. The proposed construction of an international standard airport in lieu of the present one located in Iloilo City will require collaboration between the province of Iloilo and Iloilo City. The current airport facilities cannot accommodate large aircraft and expansion is constrained by limited land availability. Alternative sites in the municipalities of Cabatuan and Santa Barbara, adjacent to the municipality of Pavia, are being considered. Other concerns requiring collaborative effort are in the areas of public safety, maintenance of peace and order, disaster management, and trade and investment promotion.

Key Lessons Learned

Responsible leadership is critical in providing direction and mobilizing resources to bring about results. Reform initiatives would not have been possible without the vision and commitment of local chief executives. The case studies also underscore the value of engaging nonstate actors and the private sector in public decision making and the management of state affairs. Their involvement does not only help improve the quality of public policies but also improves the delivery of basic services. Citizens' empowerment and engagement in public management were part of the administrative agenda of the three city governments.

People's participation and ownership during the establishment of metropolitan arrangements in Naga and Iloilo demonstrate that LGUs are keen and committed to partnering with each other to pursue shared development goals. All three cities underscore the active role of civil society in undertaking numerous development projects with the local governments.

Policy instruments, such as the LGC of 1991 and city ordinances, open avenues not only for citizen participation, but also for encouraging private sector development. Strict enforcement of the rule of law is common to the three cities. They have also prioritized and invested in developing human capital. Although there is much to be desired in terms of infrastructure, the three cities are relatively accessible for commerce and trade.

There is, however, a need to reorient the thinking and approach to promoting economic development, which is largely inward looking and consumption driven. Too often, progress is equated with the presence of a popular shopping mall and food chains, expansion of housing subdivisions, and more bus terminals. Local governments are yet to promote private investments focusing on high value-adding industries or export-oriented and import-substitution strategies.

ENHANCING SUSTAINABLE URBAN REGION DEVELOPMENT

Provide Enabling Policy Instruments and Institutional Environment. The existing regional development framework and statutes tend to restrict business opportunities and weigh down economic efficiency. SEZA, for instance, identifies more than a hundred ecozones nationwide, which results in localities competing with each other to attract business locators. Another example is the negative externality to economies of scale in agricultural production brought about by CARP. Many LGUs also extend tax incentives to investors, but such are not really key factors in attracting investments. The excessive and increasing number of LGUs in the country also impedes resource allocation and utilization.

Address Issue of Fiscal Sustainability and Intergovernment Fiscal Transfers. National and local governments need to enhance their revenue-generating and collection capacities. This will require simplification and rationalization of tax policies and tax administration. Leakages in collections must be effectively stopped.

Run LGUs Like Corporations. Local capacities for development financing remain weak. Being asset rich and cash poor, local government capacities for asset management should be built. LGUs should make their assets work for them, which would tremendously improve their revenue-generating capacities and ability to finance development. LGUs should be able to participate in credit rating systems just like private corporations. At present, they are still largely dependent on revenue transfers, which are inadequate for financing economic projects with big returns. Joint LGU initiatives to raise financing for regional projects are uncommon but should be promoted when appropriate. Development financing and building the credit worthiness of city governments have not been fully explored. Asset valuation for credit rating purposes is not widely practiced although this could widen avenues for accessing low-interest financing. At present, the borrowing capacity of local governments is measured by development and commercial banks in terms of the size of the IRA.

Increase Effort to Attract Foreign Investments. Attracting foreign direct investment has proven to be very difficult for the three cities, despite initiatives to provide liberal investment incentives. Such investment comes in trickles, if at all. Two key factors may explain this. First, issues such as high cost of doing business, leakages, and peace and security affect investment opportunities. Second, there is concentration of government and private investments, infrastructure facilities, and business opportunities in better-off regions. Well-coordinated national, regional, and local initiatives are needed to deal with the problems of decreasing foreign direct investment inflows in the country and concentrated development.

Adopt a More Regional Planning Outlook. LGUs across regions become more economically competitive when they pool their resources. Most local governments may have to change their governance paradigm. They need to realize that addressing poverty, joblessness, and other complex issues that transcend political and geographical jurisdictions requires stronger partnerships and collaboration. Hence, they need to adopt a more regional development outlook. Planning and programming that transcend the regional and national levels would be far more effective if based on information provided by the LGUs.

Notes

[1] With research inputs from Prof. Simeon Ilago, Dr. Romulo Miral, Mr. Jose Tiu Sonco, Mr. Julius Dumangas, and Ms. Ely Cureg.
[2] See www.census.gov.ph/data/quickstat.
[3] The changing structure of the country's economic output since 1985 is very evident in the key indicators published by the Asian Development Bank. See www.adb.org/Documents/Books/Key_Indicators/ 2004/pdf/PHI.pdf.
[4] localweb.neda.gov.ph/~ioneda/cgi-bin/st2.cgi?   /eds/db/national/finvest/peza_investments_a.sc.
[5] Thailand (2.8875), Malaysia (3.465), and Republic of Korea (3.625).
[6] These performance figures are very consistent across the years (1990–2003, the most recent data).
[7] The main source of data for these computations is the Department of Budget and Management's annual Budget of Expenditures and Sources of Financing, a document accompanying the President's Executive Budget submitted to the House of Representatives.
[8] These projections are based on past revenue performance and actual average increases in debt service burdens. It is highly possible that actual figures in 2008 will be much higher.

[9] Revenue effort is the ratio of annual revenue collections over the gross domestic product.
[10] Total foreign direct investment (FDI) and percentage contribution of the four investment promotion agencies to the total approved FDIs for 2001–2004 were computed based on data from the Board of Investments, as compiled by the Philippine Institute of Development Studies. See dirp.pids.gov.ph/cgi-bin/sg? fdi_agency.tbl.
[11] See www.undp.org.ph/news/readnews.asp? id=108.
[12] See www.bsp.gov.ph/statistics/sipbs/table1a.htm.
[13] Bank density ratios can also be used as indicators of dynamism of regional and local economies.
[14] www.neda.gov.ph/ads/mtpdp/MTPDP2004-2010/MTPDP%202004-2010%20NEDA%20v11-12.pdf
[15] The incumbent was installed into office in 2001, following impeachment charges against then President Joseph Estrada.
[16] Regional Development Council (RDC) members initially consisted of the heads of regional offices of the national government with sectoral functions, and elected local government and congressional district officials. The regional office of the National Economic Development Authority provided technical assistance and acted as secretariat to the RDC.
[17] An interview with Mayor Jesse Robredo of Naga City revealed that the city government borrowed from a bank to finance the construction of the Metro Naga Coliseum. At 11% interest, the loan was much lower than the lending extended by the World Bank or the Department of Finance's Municipal Development Fund.
[18] The Development Bank of the Philippines and Bankers Association of the Philippines are the original incorporators of LGU Guarantee Corporation, owning 51% and 49%, respectively. www.mb.com.ph/BSNS2004122224934.html.
[19] www.lgugc.com/about.htm.
[20] www.manilatimes.net/national/2005/jan/22/yehey/business/20050122bus2.html.
[21] www.adb.org/Documents/Speeches/2005/sp2005005.asp.
[22] www.mb.com.ph/BSNS2004122224934.html.
[23] www.neda.gov.ph/progs_prj/12th%20oda/12th_odamain.htm.
[24] www.neda.gov.ph/progs_prj/12th%20oda/12th_odamain.htm.
[25] www.neda.gov.ph/progs_prj/12th%20oda/12th_odamain.htm.
[26] ibid.
[27] To date, local treasurers are appointed by and under the administrative supervision and control of the Department of Finance.
[28] Ibid.
[29] Provincial annual growth rate.
[30] Ibid.
[31] The other four drivers of change are: (1) cost of doing business, (2) dynamism of local economy, (3) linkages and accessibility, (4) responsiveness of the local government unit.

[32] Within a 30-kilometer radius from the city center of Bacolod, other schools also participate in the program: two colleges and two vocational schools in Talisay City; one college and three vocational schools in Silay City; one college and one vocational school in Bago City; and one college in Murcia.

[33] This is an award given by the national Government.

[34] Bacolod served as an example and inspiration to Marikina City in the late 1990s by having a clean and healthy environment. Marikina put up large billboards praising Bacolod for its gains and encouraging the residents of Marikina to support the city government's campaign for cleanliness. Marikina is a leading small-size city in the country and one of the cleanest and greenest cities.

[35] Based on Bureau of Local Government Finance Data.

[36] IRA dependency of Bacolod City is 59% and 54% for the years 2001 and 2004, respectively, based on Bureau of Local Government Finance data.

[37] The incumbent mayor belongs to the opposition party. Thirteen out of the 14 members in the city council belong to the rival party.

[38] Bicol is one of the five poorest of the country's 16 administrative regions based on recent statistics.

[39] The Regional Physical Framework Plan identifies Naga City as the regional center for commerce, finance, trade, and public/private services [*Naga City Statistical Profile*].

[40] Willy Prilles, Executive Director of the Naga City School Board and coordinator of the I-Governance program. *Fieldwork Study/Interview in Naga*, February 2005.

[41] Statement of Mayor Jesse Robredo. *Field study/interview in Naga*, February 2005.

[42] Ibid.

[43] Statement of Juan Villegas, City Planning and Development Officer. *Field study/interview in Naga*, February 2005.

[44] While Naga's land area is only 0.48% and 2.9% of Bicol's land area and population, respectively, 21% of investments in the region are concentrated in the city. An estimated 51% of all enterprises in the whole province of Camarines Sur are concentrated in the city (Robredo 2003).

[45] See www.neda5.net/MTRDP/chap2.htm (2005).

[46] Statement of Mr. Beda Priela of the Metro Naga Chamber of Commerce and Industry. *Field study/interview in Naga*, February 2005.

[47] http://chymera00.blogspot.com/2005/12/metro-iloilo-development-council.html.

[48] Ibid.

[49] Ibid.

12. Sri Lanka

BASIL VAN HOREN AND SISIRA PINNAWALA

INTRODUCTION

Sri Lanka is an island country that has been affected significantly in recent years by natural disasters and civil unrest. The uncertainty created by these events has made it difficult for Sri Lanka to attract foreign investment for the development of new industries, which is a factor contributing to its low level and rate of urbanization However, like other Asian countries, Sri Lanka is expected to experience increasing urbanization in the future. National statistics are shown in Table 12.1.

This chapter examines issues concerned with urbanization in Sri Lanka. It presents three cases studies based on projects located in the Colombo Core Urban Area that demonstrate sustainable aspects of urban region development.[1] The case studies examined are the neighborhood health and environment improvement project (Green Star Homes Project) and the Clean Settlements Program, both in the Colombo Municipal Council (CMC) area, and a community-based solid waste management program in Dehiwala Mount Lavinia Municipality to the south of Colombo City. The applications of lessons learned from these projects are presented in the final part of the chapter.

COUNTRY CONTEXT

History

The history of Sri Lanka dates back over 3,000 years. During the early stages, indigenous Sinhalese and Tamil kings controlled various separate, and often competing, kingdoms on the island. In the early years of human settlement, the most important settlements on the island were Anuradhapura and Polonnaruwa, each of which had their own local governments and dated back to the 3rd century BC (de Silva 1981; Codrington 2000). Chinese, Arab, and Persian traders were active in the vicinity of Colombo as early as the 5th century AD Arab traders dominated the seas around the island. There is a belief among

Table 12.1: Country Development Profile, Sri Lanka

Human Development Index (HDI) rank of 177 countries (2003)^	93
GDP growth (annual %; 2004)	6.00
GNI per capita, Atlas method (current $; 2004)	1,010
GNI, Atlas method (current $ billion; 2004)	19.6
GDP per capita PPP ($; 2003)^	3,778
GDP PPP ($ billion; 2003)^	72.7
Population growth (annual 2005-2010 %)#	0.69
Population, total (million; 2005)#	19.37
Urban population, total (million; 2005)#	4.07
Urban population percent of total population (2005)#	21
Population largest city: Colombo (2005; million)	0.65
Population growth: 8 capital cities or agglomerations > 750,000 inhabitants 2000#	
- Est. average growth of capital cities or urban agglomerations 2005–2015 (%)	13
- Number of capital cities or urban agglomerations with growth >50%, 2005–2015	0
- Number of capital cities or urban agglomerations with growth > 30%, 2005–2015	1
Sanitation, % of urban population with access to improved sanitation (2002)**	98
Water, % of urban population with access to improved water sources (2002)**	99
Slum population, % of urban population (2001)**	14
Slum population in urban areas (2001, million)**	0.60
Poverty, % of urban population below national poverty line (1996)**	15.0
Aid (Net ODA received; $ million; 2003)^	671.9
Aid as a share of country income (Net ODA/GNI; 2003 %)*	3.7
Aid per capita (current $; 2003)^	35.0

GDP = gross domestic product, GNI = gross national income, ODA = official development assistance, PPP = purchasing power parity.
Sources: See Footnote Table 3.1, World Bank (2005); Organisation for Economic Co-operation and Development (2003); United Nations (2004, 2005).

Sri Lankan Muslims that their ancestors established themselves in the early part of the 8th century in Colombo, Galle, Baberyn, Jaffna, Trincomalee, Puttalam, and Kudiramalai (Hulugalle 1965).

Sri Lanka was under colonial rule, variously from the Portuguese, Dutch, and British from 1505 until 1948. Ceylon (Sri Lanka) achieved independence from the British in 1948.

Politics and Government

Tensions between ethnic groups and a civil war lasting more than 2 decades have dominsted politics in Sri Lanka since independence. Public administration after independence was led by a group of westernized elite persons who replaced the colonial rulers. This group was brought together to form the first post-independence government by the United National Party (UNP), which pursued anticommunist intercommunal policies. In spite of the intercommunal orientation of UNP and the liberal political ideology of the elite leadership (Pinnawala 2004), one of the first acts of this government led to the disenfranchisement of Tamils of Indian origin in 1948. This began the process of diminishing the political and economic status of the country's Tamil population (van Horen 2002).

By the early 1980s, militant groups were operating in Tamil areas of the country. Their actions were limited to the consolidation of their position in the Tamil community and engaging in low-level violent actions. In July 1983, riots broke out throughout the country. At the end of the rioting, approximately 3,000 Tamils had been killed and more than 100,000 had fled to India (Hoole et al. 1989; Singer 1990). This was a turning point for many Tamils, who were thereafter convinced that only a totally separate state— *Tamil Eelam*—could protect them. Since then, Sri Lanka has become a country troubled by civil unrest, making it difficult to provide stable government and a secure environment for investment and development.

In December 2001, a new Government, led by the United National Front came to office. The Government gave high priority to a political settlement to the civil conflict plaguing the country and signed a memorandum of understanding (MOU) with the Liberation Tigers of Tamil Eelam (LTTE) to end hostilities, with the Government of Norway working as mediator. With this MOU, popularly known as the Peace Agreement, the Government and LTTE agreed to formally cease hostilities, restore normality to the country, and provide an environment for direct talks between the two parties. Although the peace process is fragile, its gradual progress has raised hopes for sociopolitical and economic stability (ADB 2002a; ADB 2004a).

Although the Government was able to stabilize the economy, which was contracting under the previous administration, dialogue with the LTTE did not work as expected after the peace agreement due to changes in the Government and political environment. However, discussions between the two parties continue.

The instability as a result of hostilities with LTTE has made it extremely difficult to maintain stable government; many local government systems became inoperable. Hundreds of thousands of people have been displaced, seeking refuge in urban centers around the country and overseas. The ability of local governments to provide and maintain basic services, sound financial management, and well-managed development has been severely curtailed. Despite early attempts to encourage decentralization, the national security situation and political structure had led to the maintenance of a strongly centralized government system. As a result, local governments, especially municipalities, have not been able to provide key strategic infrastructure, leadership, and governance needed to support regional and local economic development. The weakness of local government to provide even basic support to communities became very apparent after the tragedy of the December 2004 tsunami.

Decentralization

A policy of political decentralization was initiated in 1965 by a UNP government in coalition with the Federal Party, the main Tamil political group, partly in an attempt to establish more efficient structures of government, but mainly to address Tamil demands for autonomy. District development councils (DDCs) were established and granted some administrative powers, although real political authority was not granted to the districts. J. R. Jayawardhene, who came to power as Prime Minister in 1977 and installed himself President, had scant respect for these councils and appointed ministers, called district ministers, from his party to oversee development work of the districts. Even though the Tamil leaders were not happy with the operations of DDCs—especially their weakened positions as a result of the above move by Jayawardhene—they took part in the DDC elections held in 1983.

The local elections were a disaster and led to a period of civil unrest. In 1987, as a result of the Indian intervention, Sri Lanka amended its Constitution and established eight provincial councils with substantial political and financial autonomy. These were created to bridge the gap between government structures at the national and local levels, and to facilitate the process of decentralization (van Horen 2002).

In addition to devolution of political power through provincial councils, another form of decentralization was undertaken, mainly of development and service activities of the national Government. Decentralized district coordinating committees (DCCs)—not to be confused with the now-defunct DDCs, which were elected bodies—were established and headed by the chief government administrator in the district (known as the district secretary). DCCs coordinate work of national agencies working in the provinces (technically known as line agencies) and are also responsible for planning and policy formulation, determining district priorities and overall coordination of public sector activities. The implementation of plans and policies ideally involves these government bodies as well as *pradeshiya* and *gramodaya mandalayas*—subnational public authorities entrusted with wider functions and responsibilities than local government bodies, covering regulatory, service-oriented, and development activities.

Despite progress made on decentralization, many challenges remain. Administrative decentralization is limited, with control over many local government functions remaining with central Government (Asian Resource

Centre 2002). Many layers of public administration and overlapping responsibilities between governments lead to inefficiencies in the delivery of public services. The national budget situation creates enormous financial management difficulties for local governments, which are often short of funds to meet salary payments and provide basic services. Most local governments are poorly equipped to provide even a basic level of services due to weak management structures and lack of skilled personnel. Revenue generation at the local government level is constrained by regulation of local taxation systems, poor asset appraisal and valuation, and the failure of the land administration system. A significant proportion of local taxes are never collected because the status of ownership remains unclear or local governments are unwilling to impose penalties for not paying taxes.

Population and Urbanization

The current population is approximately 19 million, with an annual population growth rate of 1.1%. Population data, by district, are shown in Table 12.2.

The urban population is distributed throughout 134 cities and towns. Colombo accounts for about 20%. Urban populations are expected to grow from 4 million to 6.5 million by 2030, at which time 30% of the population is expected to be living in urban centers (Figure 12.1).

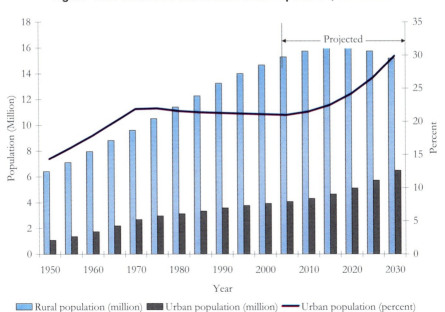

Figure 12.1: Trends in Urban and Rural Population, Sri Lanka

Table 12.2: Population Data by District, 1981 and 2001[2]

	District	Population 1981	Population 2001	Average Annual Rate of Growth (%) 1981–2001	Population Density (per km^2) 1981	Population Density (per km^2) 2001
1.	Colombo	1,699,241	2,234,289	1.3	2,605	3,305
2.	Gampaha	1,390,862	2,066,096	1.9	994	1,541
3.	Kalutara	829,704	1,060,800	1.2	516	673
4.	Kandy	1,048,317	1,272,463	1.0	554	664
5.	Matale	357,354	442,427	1.1	180	227
6.	Nuwara Biya	603,577	700,083	0.7	354	410
7.	Galle	814,531	990,539	1.0	487	613
8.	Matara	643,786	761,236	0.8	516	599
9.	Hambantota	424,344	525,370	1.1	164	210
10.	Jaffna	738,788	490,621	-2.0	795	528
11.	Mannar	106,235	151,577	1.7	53	81
12.	Vavuniya	95,428	149,835	2.2	36	81
13.	Mullathivu	77,189	121,667	2.2	39	50
14.	Killinochchi	91,764	127,263	1.6	80	106
15.	Batticaloa	330,333	486,447	1.9	134	186
16.	Ampara	388,970	589,344	2.0	86	140
17.	Trincomalee	255,948	340,158	1.4	98	135
18.	Kurunegala	1,211,801	1,452,369	0.9	254	314
19.	Puttalam	492,533	705,342	1.8	165	245
20.	Anuradhapura	587,929	746,466	1.2	82	112
21.	Polonnaruwa	261,563	359,197	1.6	77	117
22.	Badulla	640,952	774,555	0.9	227	274
23.	Monaragala	273,570	396,173	1.8	49	72
24.	Ratnapura	797,087	1,008,164	1.2	246	312
25.	Kegalle	684,944	779,774	0.6	412	463
	Total, Sri Lanka	14,846,750	18,732,255	1.1	230	299

km^2 = square kilometer.
Source: 2001 Census of Population and Housing, Department of Census and Statistics, Sri Lanka.

Urbanization has affected almost every part of the country since independence, with urbanization rates rising sharply prior to the conflict in the north. Thereafter, urbanization levels stabilized and fell slightly until the Peace Agreement in 2002. Sri Lanka has not experienced the levels of urbanization that have occurred in other Asian countries. This is partly explained by the high levels of migration to the Middle East, mainly by females employed as domestic workers and to refugee camps in India. Migration rates are projected to rise in future, especially with the growing demands for employment in new manufacturing areas located in and close to the capital.

Urbanization has been greatest in the southwest, especially in Colombo. Middle-sized towns with populations of 20,000–50,000, however, are the fastest-growing component of the urban sector. The urban poor lack access to basic amenities and endure poor-quality physical environment. Few own their dwellings, and those in the lowest-income categories do not have their own shelter; many share accommodation, mostly in urban shack settlements (Gunatilleke and Perera 1988).

Economic and Social Development

The Economy

The year 1977 marked an important turning point in the economic direction of the country. Sri Lanka adopted an economic strategy of liberalization in which markets were opened to foreign investment through tax, tariff, trade, and fiscal reforms. Simultaneously, the Government centralized political control around the presidency. However, it took many years for structural changes to occur in the economy because many state-owned enterprises (*parastatals*) were poorly managed during the socialist period of government.

In recent years, the structure of the economy has significantly changed as the result of neoliberalist policies. The gross domestic product (GDP) in 2003 was $72 billion, with a GDP per capita of $3,778. The share of primary industries (agriculture, forestry, and fisheries) to GDP fell from 23% in 1995 to 19.1% in 2003. During the same period, the manufacturing contribution went from 15.7% to 26.2%. Manufacturing in 2003 contributed 78% of total exports estimated at $5.3 billion (USAID 2004). Services now contribute more than 54% of GDP and are the fastest-growing sector. However, the economy is still experiencing many structural problems that significantly slowed the growth rate over the last decade.

Like the Philippines, remittances to Sri Lanka make a significant contribution to export earnings. In 2002, private remittances to Sri Lanka have exceeded foreign direct investment and comprised about 15–20% of export earnings, or 5% of the gross national product (Sriskandarajah 2002). Labor migration due to the conflict has left many Sri Lankans displaced with no local livelihood, spawning the migration of household members abroad (Hyndman 2003; Brun 2002).

Economically, Sri Lanka suffered a 1.4% contraction of GDP in 2001 due in part to external factors, such as falling export demand from the global slowdown, and internal factors, such as poor agricultural yields caused by continuing drought. Continuing political instability in 2001 further damaged the ailing macroeconomy, reflected most directly in the unsustainable fiscal deficit of nearly 10% of GDP. This substantially limited the Government's development resources and undermined prospects for future growth and private investment. The 2004 tsunami also has had a devastating impact on some sectors of the economy, especially the fishing industry.

Paralysis in decision making caused capital expenditures to decline to less than 5% of GDP and even impaired counterpart funding for foreign-financed projects (ADB 2002a). The LTTE attack on the country's only international airport in Colombo caused tourism and shipping to plummet in the last half of 2001, with power cuts of up to 8 hours daily affecting production levels. The new Government, elected in December 2001, responded to these developments in its first budget, announced in March 2002. It focused on bringing back fiscal discipline with a deficit target of 8.5% of GDP, excluding privatization proceeds and foreign grants, mainly through revenue reforms. The economic program initiated by the UNP Government, however, did not continue due to the dissolution of Parliament in November 2003, leading to a new general election in April 2004.

The effectiveness of Sri Lanka's plans for economic recovery, in addition to the economic direction the budgets will adopt, will largely depend on the progress of the peace process. Cessation of hostilities and continued peace would help keep defense expenditures under control and help the Government achieve its ambitious fiscal targets. A permanent peace agreement between the Government and LTTE would also allow higher levels of rehabilitation work in the north and east to commence.

Since 1997, every Sri Lankan budget has basically followed the same economic fundamentals and committed to undertake reforms to put the country on a path toward sustainable growth. The reforms have generally been in line with the ongoing policy dialogue in the infrastructure and finance sectors and may even be accelerating. ADB has indicated its support for the Government's reform agenda through the lending and nonlending pipeline (ADB 2004a).

Employment

The employment structure of Sri Lanka has changed significantly over the last decade. The proportion of labor in agriculture fell from 37.4 % in 1996 to 34.1% in 2004; in manufacturing, it has risen from 14.6 % to 16.7%, and in services, from 48.0% to 49.2 % (Department of Statistics 2005). The national labor force in 2004 was approximately 8 million, of which 1 million comprised the urban labor force.

Little information on employment and skills needs in urban areas is available. The nation has experienced significant skills loss through migration

(Lowell and Findlay 2001), which is undermining the capacity of institutions, especially local governments, to provide essential public services. There is a significant lack of skills in the field of urban management, especially those related to the implementation of urban development and infrastructure projects, asset appraisal and management, and urban finance (ADB 1997).

Urban unemployment is about 8.8% but this disguises a very large number of people who are underemployed, mainly in the informal sector. Majority of the urban poor work in the informal sector as self-employed income earners or as casual laborers (ADB 2004a). Most of them have no productive assets and depend only on their labor and skills to survive. Importantly, the income flow in the urban sector is irregular and seasonal, with employment in low-paying industries subject to unpredictable changes (Gunatilleke and Perera 1988; Ali and Sirivardana 1996). The proportion of youth in the informal sector is about 30%, compared with 40% for the employed population as a whole (Department of National Planning 2002).

Social Development

The health infrastructure is well developed, covering all parts of the country, with well-organized health and nutrition facilities and service networks island-wide that the poor can access. These services include preventative health care, treatment in outpatient facilities, and curative care in hospitals. Social indicators show a total fertility rate (births per woman) of 1.9, a maternal mortality rate (per 100,000 births) of 92, and an infant mortality rate (per 1,000 live births) of 16 (WHO 2004). Life expectancy at birth is 73 years (UNICEF 2003). However, more than one fifth of the total population is undernourished. The high prevalence of underweight children below 5 years of age is a source of concern, although it decreased from 38% in 1993 to 29% in 2000 (ADB 2004a).

The population below the poverty line is 22.7% (Sri Lanka Census Department 2002). Extreme poverty, measured as the proportion of the population living on less than $1 a day, is the lowest (6.6%) among South Asian countries.

In terms of access to resources, in 2002, the population using improved drinking water sources was 78% and access to adequate sanitation was 91% (UNICEF 2003). In these respects, Sri Lanka has made good progress toward achieving the Millennium Development Goals and targets.

The adult literacy rate is currently 91.4%, and primary school enrollment is universal. Children of the urban poor can attend government schools, which are generally among the better-equipped schools in the country and compare favorably with rural counterparts. Poverty does not present an insurmountable barrier to education because students are given free textbooks, subsidized transport, free school uniforms, and a food stamp for a mid-day meal (Ali and Sirivardana 1996; Gunatilleke and Perera 1988).

Under the current economic policy framework, the Government will continue economic restructuring and reform to put the economy on a more efficient footing. The reform focus will be on commercializing state-owned enterprises, creating a balance between the private sector and public interests, and improving the institutional framework to reap larger benefits from technology transfers and trade. Regional inequality has increased and in some provinces, poverty levels have also increased, despite overall improvements in living conditions (ADB 2004a).

National Transportation Network and Urban Infrastructure

The 2004 tsunami devastated large parts of the country's coastal infrastructure (roads, railway, power, telecommunications, water supply, fishing ports).The overall loss of assets has been estimated at 4.4% of GDP, with reconstruction costs rising to $1.5 billion, or 7% of GDP (ADB 2004). However, not only the loss of infrastructure from the disaster poses significant challenges to the development of the country. Much of the country's infrastructure has been damaged or neglected as the result of civil unrest, political instability, and poor economic management over many years.

Sri Lanka has among the highest density of roads in Asia. However, poor maintenance has resulted in a degraded urban and rural road network across the country. The World Bank-funded Road Sector Assistance Project will help lower transportation cost across the country by improving 620 km of national roads by reducing the poor condition of national highways from 52% in 2005 to 35% in 2010 (World Bank 2005). This project is closely coordinated with ADB and the Japan Bank for International Cooperation. While developing the national road network is a high priority for the country, improving local urban roads networks is plagued by a lack of funds for maintenance. Improved revenue-raising and tax collections, as well as community partnership approaches, are required to improve the quality of urban and rural roads.

The establishment of a Road Maintenance Trust Fund, which is a financing mechanism to manage budgetary allocations to national and provincial roads, will be important to maintaining the national road network. The Government will increase annual maintenance expenditure from $13 million in 2005, to $30 million in 2006, and $46 million in 2010 (World Bank 2005).

While the level of urbanization in Sri Lanka is low compared to that of other Asian countries, urban settlements face similar infrastructure and maintenance problems as other cities in the region. Data on urban infrastructure are poor. According to the UN indicators shown in Table 12.1, most urban populations have access to basic water supply and sanitation services, but the quality is poor or intermittent. Other statistical data suggest that more than 12% of urban populations have inadequate water and sanitation services. Drainage systems in low-lying areas are poorly maintained, giving rise to health problems in poor urban communities.

The problems associated with urbanization are most prominent in the Greater Colombo Area, where 43% of the population lives in slums and shanty settlements lacking proper basic facilities, such as water supply, lighting, and toilets. The situation of the shanty settlements around Colombo is serious because they are located in areas unsuited for residential purposes, such as inside canal banks, road reservations, and flood-prone areas (ADB 2000). Most of these settlements lack basic facilities, have poor road access, few community facilities, and improvized housing structures. Less than 25% of wastewater in the Colombo Municipal Council area is treated. More than 900 tons of solid waste daily are collected and disposed of through open dumping without any sanitary consideration.

Conditions in the small- and medium-sized (secondary) towns outside Greater Colombo are not much different. Improvement and expansion of water supply, sanitation, stormwater drainage, and solid waste collection and disposal are considered priority investment areas by urban local governments; however, most lack the capacity and means of funding improvements in urban infrastructure. There is a tendency to give priority to improvement of roads and transportation and development of bus terminals because these are seen to generate greater economic opportunities (ADB 2000). Smaller towns lack good telecommunication infrastructure, which is a significant impediment to urban development.

Sustainability and Urban Development

Like those in other Asian countries, many urban settlements in Sri Lanka are developing in ways that are not sustainable. Land planning, management, and administration are weak. Urban household density in Colombo is in the order of 17 persons/ha and more than 550,000 live in slum communities, with the poorest of slum dwellers occupying 2.18 perches (55 square meters [m^2]) of land per household (Gunesekera 2003). Although these are much lower than densities in other South Asian cities, such as Mumbai (24 m^2 per dwelling), these are still high and result in poor living conditions for more than 25% of the city's population.

Groundwater pollution through industrial and domestic sewage contamination has made much of the capital city's water supply unfit for drinking

(IGES 2005). There has been a rapid fall in the groundwater table, with rising levels of salinity resulting from excessive drawdown. More than 22% of households in Colombo lack basic sanitation services. Air-pollution levels in the capital and other cities continue to rise due to the failure to enforce conditions on environmental emission by manufacturing industries and large numbers of two-stroke vehicles operating in the city. Similar environmental problems are emerging in other Sri Lankan cities.

The 2004 Asian tsunami had a devastating impact on Sri Lanka's coastal communities and the country's economy. The livelihood and homes of more than 450,000 people were affected by the disaster, with more than 27,000 lives lost. The estimated overall damage is $1 billion, much of it in housing, tourism, fisheries, and transportation (World Bank 2005).

Poverty

While absolute poverty in the rural sector appeared to remain unchanged during 1969–1985, available data for urban areas show a significant reduction in urban poverty. According to the Labor Force Socio-economic Survey (LFSS), the levels of poverty are understood in terms of four basic categories (Gunatilleke and Perera 1988). Nationwide estimates of poverty derived from the 1985/1986 LFSS indicate that 50% of households were poor in terms of nutritional deficiency and 24% were nutritionally at risk. In terms of minimum per capita food expenditure, the incidence of poverty is estimated at 22.7% (Sri Lanka Census Department 2002). Urban poverty is about 15%, but has been on the decline according to both a consumer finance survey and LFSS data.

A poverty reduction partnership agreement between the Government and ADB was made in 2002. The poverty reduction partnership agreement is fully consistent with the Government's poverty reduction strategy as well as the relief, rehabilitation, and reconciliation framework. The Government and ADB agreed that the impact of ADB's assistance on poverty reduction would be stronger if policy and institutional reforms improved the economic and sector investment environment. Poverty reduction is currently focused on a number of economic sectors, including agriculture and natural resources, energy, private sector development, social sectors, transport, and governance (ADB 2004a).

In this regard, the public assistance program for the disabled and destitute is important. A monthly subsistence allowance is given to those who cannot work due to poor health, old age, or disability, and to those families who have lost their sole income-earning member. This program is being evaluated by the Government and will likely be restructured (Ali and Sirivardana 1996; Gunatilleke and Perera 1988).

International Development Assistance

Official development assistance (ODA) plays a major role in the development of Sri Lanka. ODA in 2003 was $671.9 million, equivalent to 3.7% of GDP. This compares with 9.1% in 1990. Sri Lanka is heavily dependent on foreign assistance to support the development of several strategic projects to develop the economy.

At a conference in Tokyo in 2003, the International Monetary Fund, World Bank, ADB, the Government of Japan, the European Union, and the Government of the United States pledged a total of $4.5 billion to support strategic development projects related to the poverty reduction strategy program laid out in the "Regaining Sri Lanka," a Government action paper, and studies commissioned by the donor community that, together, provide a basic framework for economic revival. While implementation of previous aid projects has been inconsistent, the Government believes it can improve this record by streamlining tender processes and improving project management skills.

ADB has funded several important projects to support the development of the urban sector: Capacity Building in Urban Infrastructure Management, Local Government Infrastructure Improvement Project, and Basic Social Infrastructure Development. The World Bank has supported projects for Improving the Rural and Urban Investment Climate, Community Development and Livelihood Improvement *Gemi Diriya*, and road sector assistance projects. United Nations (UN) agencies and bilateral development partners have a wide range of development projects supporting the urban sector in Sri Lanka.

GOOD PRACTICE CASE STUDIES

The case studies are from projects initiated to deal with environmental and health-related problems. They all are local government authority-community partnerships using community action plans to varying degrees. Two are projects that are facilitated by the same voluntary organization.

According to a survey carried out by the Sustainable Township Program, low-income settlements in Colombo do not have access to most basic municipal services. About 56% of households rely on common water taps and, on average, there are 40–100 households per tap. About 67% of households in low-income settlements either share or do not have access to toilets. In the case of garbage collection, 66% of low-income communities do not have access to municipal waste collection services and throw garbage into nearby canals, drains, or reservation lands. In most low-income settlements (about 70%), paved roads and improved storm and wastewater drains have not been constructed (Prema kumara, undated).

Figure 12.2: Map Showing Location of the Case Studies

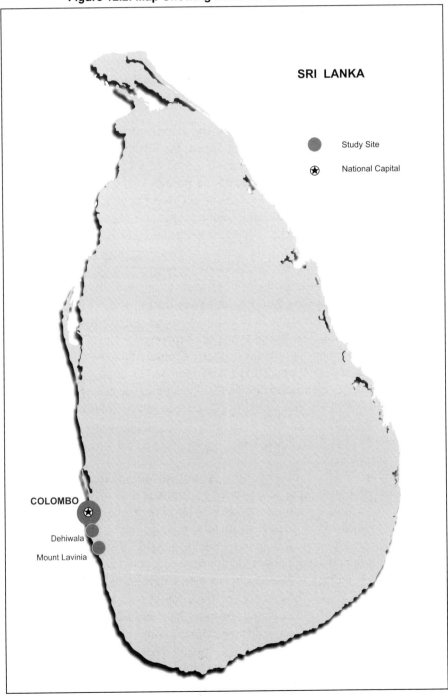

Community-based Solid Waste Management in Low-income Settlements in Dehiwala Mount Lavinia Municipality

One of the major problems in Sri Lanka is inefficiency in collection and disposal of waste in urban areas. There is a scarcity of land for dumping or landfill sites. Waste management is still a function of the local authorities, many of whom have been unable to deal with health and sanitation issues that are aggravated by environmental pollution

GOOD PRACTICE	
Good Governance	✓
Urban Management	✓
Infrastructure/Service Provision	✓
Financing and Cost Recovery	
Sustainability	✓
Innovation and Change	✓
Leveraging ODA	

from urban waste. Formulation of a sustainable waste management system has become a priority for local and central government agencies involved in urban development in Sri Lanka. This case study examines the community-based solid waste management work of the Dehiwala Mount Lavinia, which is the second biggest urban concentration in the country.

Dehiwala Mount Lavinia is part of the Colombo Core Area (CCA) and lies to the south of Colombo City. The area served by the Dehiwala Mount Lavinia Municipal Council (DMMC) generates about 150 metric tons of solid waste per day. The municipal council collects about 75% of the waste. Many under-serviced communities in the municipal area either do not receive waste disposal services or have only limited access to such services. Limited institutional and material resources—mainly caused by budgetary problems and the lack of suitable land for waste disposal—are some of the major constraints the council faces in the provision of an effective waste disposal service to the community. Community-based waste collection, therefore, is not only important as an attempt at urban governance good practice but also to relieve the burden on the council.

The DMMC composting project is part of the Sustainable Colombo Core Area Project funded by the United Nations Development Programme (UNDP) and implemented by the UN Human Settlements Programme (Prema kumara 2000). The municipal administration started its first community-based waste management project in 1999 in a shanty community called Badowita. The objective was to get the community to carry out compost production from domestic garbage. The project was a three-way partnership that brought together the community, the municipal council, and an NGO called Sevanatha. Sevanatha was selected for its experience in urban good practice activities and its familiarity with waste management work using compost bins (Prema kumara 2000). Project design was participatory and facilitation and implementation was by the NGO. There had been previous efforts, for example, in Colombo City (Jayaratne 1996); however, this project differs in its enterprise component.

The compost project was started in two communities as pilot projects. One was in a shanty settlement called Badowita. Majority of the settlers are from families living along canal banks in Colombo, relocated in 1993–1994 as part of the Greater Colombo Canal Improvement Project. According to 2001 population data, the settlement had about 1,400 households (UNHS 2002) composed of about 4,500 persons. The other pilot project was in Udyana, a middle-income area close to the city center. The municipal ward is also called Udyana. This is a smaller community consisting of about 200 families, of which about 13% are illiterate. As Badowita is a shanty community, the people living there do not own land; the land is owned by the Sri Lanka Land Reclamation and Development Corporation, a government agency. The shanty community is also known for its high crime rate, mainly drug and alcohol related.

Strategy

The approach to planning and implementation was participatory and evolved in three stages. In the first stage, DMMC formed a task force concerned with solid waste management and prepared a strategic action plan for solid waste problems, a community action planning program with Sevanatha. During the first 2 months in 1999, brainstorming sessions were organized for city stakeholders, including the electoral ward members in the DMMC.

During the implementation stage, Sevanatha carried out a needs assessment and an assessment of aspirations through informal meetings, discussions, and interviews of members of the households. Also, formal meetings with the officials of community-based organizations (CBOs) were held to explain the need for waste separation and the associated benefits.

Women were given training on how to segregate waste at source and compost the organic waste in barrels (to be provided). Initially, 50 families from each community were selected for compost bin distribution.

In addition, neighborhood cleaning programs, art and photograph exhibitions for young people, and health programs were introduced to encourage the participatory families to take part. The following are the main outcomes of the community-based solid waste management program of the *Dehiwala* Municipal Council:

- an action plan developed by the stakeholders with the participation of the target community (community action plan);

- an institutional setup (community development society, etc.) linking the community with the other stakeholders to foster communication and coordination of activities;
- clear division of responsibilities for each stakeholder (household, small group, core group, local authority); and
- availability of funds from donors.

The compost was intended for use by community members in their home gardens. To deal with nonbiodegradable waste, the project adopted a commercial approach. A recycling center to buy nonbiodegradable waste from households was established with funding support from JICA and assistance from the Municipal Council. The community development council of the community now successfully operates it.

Achievements and Problems

The project was successful in organizing and changing the waste disposal behavior of households. Within a year, 40% of the households in the low-income settlement and 60% of the households in the middle-income area were using compost bins. In addition, less waste was being discarded along the roadside. Composting is now an income-generating activity in Badowita. This low-income settlement today has a waste collection center constructed with funding support from JICA and the municipal council. The center office was constructed by the community on a labor and resource-sharing basis on land provided by the Land Reclamation and Development Board. The center buys waste from the households for composting.

The community, through its strong federation of CBOs, was able to mobilize support from the Urban Settlements Improvement Project and the Sri Lankan Land Reclamation and Development Corporation of the Ministry of Housing, the JICA volunteer program, Sevanatha, and the Sustainable Sri Lankan Cities Program to make this participatory approach a success as well as a reality.

A working group represented by the above stakeholders developed a strategy and action plan to manage the solid waste generated in the settlement. The waste collection center is managed and operated by the community's federation of CBOs as an income-generating activity with a percentage of profits from the resale of recyclable items going toward community development projects. The federation earned the equivalent of $17,500 over a 5-month period in 2001–2002 and boasts a litter-free internal road network and a garbage-free canal (UNHS 2002).

The project in Badowita is considered sustainable; it has a strong link to the University of Sri Lanka, which will continue supporting and monitoring the community. The project model is also considered transferable (ADB 2002b). The area had a very strong and active community leadership, active community development society, and supplementary support from external agencies.

The Integrated Program of Action to Improve Health and Environment Management in the Colombo Municipal Area (Green Star Homes Project)

There are more than 1,600 underserved settlements (slums and shanties) in Colombo City, housing about 51% of the total residential population. Although a major feature in the cityscape, they are relatively small— 75% of them have fewer than 50 housing units. Large settlements with more than 500 units account for only about

GOOD PRACTICE	
Good Governance	✓
Urban Management	✓
Infrastructure/Service Provision	✓
Financing and Cost Recovery	
Sustainability	
Innovation and Change	
Leveraging ODA	

0.7% of the urban poor settlements in Colombo. One of the major problems in these settlements is disease caused by poor sanitary conditions. During the monsoon periods in April–June and September–November, dengue and other mosquito-borne diseases become a major health problem. In 2004, there were 4,347 officially recorded dengue cases, including 22 deaths, a 40% increase from 2003 (Gunarathna 2004). The CMC spends more than $50,000 in material and another $160,000 for wages annually in mosquito control alone,[3] but officials admit that the budget is seriously inadequate (Gunarathna 2004). However, there has not been an increase in the budget, due mainly to public lethargy and a sectoral approach to tackling the problem.

The Integrated Program of Action to Improve Health and Environment Management in the Colombo Municipal Area was initiated as a response to the problem. Better known as the Green Star Homes Project, this project was inaugurated in July 2001. It is supported by the Sustainable Cities Program of UNDP, which has partnered with the Colombo Municipality, a consortium of leading private sector companies, and a group of nongovernment orgranizations (NGOs) operating in Colombo.[4] The program is probably the largest community mobilization and participation effort undertaken by CMC. It is the first mosquito breeding-site elimination project launched to counteract the fast-spreading and deadly dengue epidemic. Three hundred CMC staff, including doctors, nurses, midwives, laborers, public health volunteers, members of the Leo Club, and schoolchildren contributed to its success.

Strategy

The activity began with the formation of a working group, which included personnel representing relevant CMC divisions, private sector entities, and NGOs. The strategy developed by the working group was two-pronged. The first step was to carry out a campaign to destroy all mosquito-breeding places by direct intervention of CMC and the other groups to obtain community cooperation to clean their home environments and keep them mosquito-free. As the latter required creating awareness at the neighborhood and household levels, special promotional material was designed. One of the major tools to acquire community cooperation was called Green Star Sticker certification, which was in the form of a sticker that can be displayed at the site, often on the front wall of the house.

To receive the Green Star Certificate, households had to ensure that no mosquito breeding places would be found on their premises. This would require the householders to remove overgrown bushes and hedges, and maintain clean road frontages, drains, and gutters. Announcements in all three national languages were placed at various vantage points. The project also took into account the leading role that women play in keeping the environment clean and eliminating the mosquito breeding areas around their houses and settlements. Initially, only the CMC wards that had dengue cases in that year were chosen. In the second round, the CMC wards that had dengue patients in the previous years were chosen, while in the third round, areas with no history of dengue were included.

The project, although called a community partnership, did not use community participation strategies in the implementation. There was neither a community action plan nor community mobilization. The working group was the decision maker and there was no inclusion of stakeholders. Stakeholders only shared the tasks and responsibilities and, in the case of the private sector, part of the cost as determined at the working group level.

Achievements

In its first phase, 45,410 households were checked, and 10,316 houses and institutions received certification. More than 1,000 notices under the Mosquito-borne Diseases Regulations were issued to unhygienic households and 675 were fined within 3 years for noncompliance under the Mosquito-borne Diseases Regulations of the city. There was an immediate favorable response from the community. The suspected cases reported during the monsoon period of the first year of operation fell from 80 cases in July to zero in November (ADB 2004b).

Clean Settlements Program in the Colombo Municipal Council Area

The Clean Settlement Program was started as a pilot project in 1992 by the Colombo Environment Improvement Project, with the assistance of the Metropolitan Environmental Improvement Program (MEIP) of UNDP. The project was part of the community empowerment component of its community-based environmental management action. The

GOOD PRACTICE	
Good Governance	✓
Urban Management	✓
Infrastructure/Service Provision	✓
Financing and Cost Recovery	✓
Sustainability	
Innovation and Change	✓
Leveraging ODA	

cornerstone of the MEIP approach in Colombo was the preparation of the Environmental Management Strategy (EMS). The objective of the EMS was to provide a citywide strategic framework within which public and private agencies and community groups could implement planned environmental improvement and investment activities. The first pilot project was in two under-serviced settlements, Gajabapura-Bo-Sevana and Stadiumgama. These two communities had been already earmarked for upgrading. The NGO Sevanatha was the implementing agency in the pilot projects. In 1996, the program was extended to another area, Jayagathpura in the Moratuwa Municipal, south of Colombo. Later, the operational responsibilities of the project were taken over by the Ministry of Housing and Urban Development, which runs it at present.

Strategy

The entire project plan was formulated through a participatory process that brought the community, the municipal council, and other stakeholders into constant dialogue. As the first step, Sevanatha organized a community workshop that brought together selected members, health officials from the municipality, and housing officers from the National Housing Development Authority. The workshop's objective was to allow the community and the local authorities to jointly identify problems and develop a community action plan.

The action plan gave the responsibilities of the activities of the project to the community development society of the beneficiary community. In the pilot projects, Sevanatha served as the facilitator in community mobilization work and linking local government and other agencies with the community development society. The action plan contained both long- and short-term solutions to environmental problems of the community. The short-term solutions were to be executed by the community without external assistance. Examples included repair of damaged common toilets, water taps, and drains.

Long-term solutions or permanent remedies were to be done by the communities in partnership with external key players and using outside assistance.

As part of institutional development and community mobilization, a savings and credit scheme for women was established. A community center equipped with a reading room and sanitary toilets was built for community use. Many families also improved their homes, facilitated through the availability of information and frequent contact with representatives of Sevanatha and local and state agencies. These were followed by environmental improvement activities, such as garbage disposal and neighborhood cleanups. There were also campaigns aimed at raising public awareness, which included meetings, simple newsletters, and music and drama classes for children. MEIP also undertook a public awareness-raising campaign using meetings, simple newsletters, and music and drama classes for children. The newsletter, called *Thorathuru Malla,* meaning "Information Basket," now reaches about 400 organizations throughout the country.

Achievements

The Clean Settlements Project has evolved into a stand-alone project funded by the World Bank. It has been scaled up and, as stated earlier, is currently run by the Ministry of Housing Construction and Public Utilities. It has secured an International Development Association grant and receives funds from other donors, such as the Norwegian Agency for Development Cooperation.

As a result of the cumulative impacts of the various waste-related CMC initiatives, the daily tonnage of garbage in Colombo has been reduced from 780 to 680 a year. This is an indication of the positive impacts of building partnerships with the community. Wayside dumps in Colombo City have been reduced to 300, with the introduction of individual plastic bins for household waste (ADB 2004b). The process and the partnerships forged under the pilot projects have made a substantial impact by changing a government-controlled environmental service delivery process into a community-managed process. The Clean Settlements project has been successful in providing a platform for low-income settlements to plan and manage their own environment.

Lessons from the Case Studies

Lack of or Inadequate Inter-Institutional/Organizational Cooperation. This is primarily a question of priorities, logistics, and coordination. Given the existence of a multitude of institutions in Sri Lanka, it is not always easy to arrive at a consensus in a short time. Each agency has its own development priorities and often wants to accelerate its pace of achievement. As a result, approaches to problem solving are sectoral and compartmentalized. For example, in many cases, officials from both the energy and industry sectors in the Government and in the private sector have seen environment issues as a delaying factor. Many months of often painstaking consultation were required to develop strategies that majority of the stakeholders could embrace. Generating cooperation of stakeholders is not the main problem. The problem is sustainability, that is, long-term maintenance of the efficient mobilization and cooperation that is achieved by these actions.

Difficulties with Partnerships. In the case study areas where this partnership was attempted, some groups were evidently not comfortable working together. Some factors that led to these problems were organizational and institutional cultures and work ethics. Transparency of actions and efficient communication leading to efficient action (means, ends, relations, and realization of objectives) have been often found to be areas of conflict. On the one hand, the private sector was concerned with results and efficiency of actions. On the other hand, the public sector, which functions under the constraints of an institutional culture burdened by a plethora of restrictive regulations, was more interested in proper procedures. The result was that the two groups in the Dehiwala Mount Lavinia Municipality case study found it difficult to find common areas of action (Sevanatha et al. 2004).

Community Consultation and Involvement to Build Trust and Identify Priorities. The common misconception in officialdom is that a community, especially in underserved areas, lacks the organizational capacity and resourcefulness to become involved in environment-related activities and services that do not bring direct economic gains. The success of the cases discussed, at least in the short term, shows that this is not the case; these communities can be effectively mobilized if a correct approach is used and awareness is created.

Lack of Real Devolution along Agency Lines. Some problems faced by the programs were due to local government agencies being given tasks to perform without real authority. There are limitations constraining financial and budgetary work that impede local authorities from investing in innovative and locality-specific action. Furthermore, crosscutting power and authority is a feature in Sri Lankan devolution where one agency oversteps the activities and authority of other agencies. National-level agencies, therefore, often come into conflict with local governmental authorities, which delays work. There are also problems of local authorities not generating enough income to fund their work, making them dependent on donor agency support. This affects the continuity of many programs especially if adequate levels of community participation are not achieved. Local politics and politicians are also part of this; politics affects CDC work (Russel 1999).

Combining Household Environmental Management with Income-generating Activities. This can be done through activities based directly on environmental management, such as recycling, or through programs that create community-based enterprises, enabling household members to simultaneously earn an income and to obtain essentials, such as food, clean water, and building materials; economic provisions, such as credit mechanisms, help.

Community Participation and Partnerships of Stakeholders are not only Structural, Technical, Financial, and Institutional Issues. Behavioral aspects also need to be considered. Urban solid waste management is primarily about changing behavior. Therefore, capacity building at every level (household, community, municipal, and national) is necessary to facilitate behavioral changes of interest groups. Another behavioral/attitude change needed is in terms of the relationship/partnership between the private sector and government agencies. In case study areas where this partnership was attempted, the two groups were evidently not comfortable working together. There was mutual suspicion and distrust (Sevanatha et al. 2001).

Women Are Key Players in Household Garbage Management. This may be because solid waste generated in poor households is mainly from kitchens. This makes women the most important partner in waste management actions in underserved communities. The fact that in these communities women are the greater contributors to household budgets is another important factor.

Financial Management Continues to be a Problem with Many Urban Development Projects. Management and delays in the disbursement of government funds to be available for timely inputs into projects were a problem common to all case studies. Management of funds, especially disbursement of government counterpart funds to projects, was unsatisfactory. A common complaint of the donor agencies in Sri Lanka is the high levels of underutilization of funds and wastage of funds. There are a number of reasons for this--with corruption and delays caused by outdated regulations and other institutional bottlenecks being the most cited. The problem is linked to lack of institutional capacity—especially poor budget, planning, and financial management systems—and the lack of political will to devolve power and responsibility.

STRATEGIES FOR ENHANCING SUSTAINABLE URBAN DEVELOPMENT

Three strategic thrusts are needed to support sustainable urban development in Sri Lanka. The first is a focus on partnership building (UN-HABITAT

1998), which brings together four actors—the public and private sectors, NGOs, and local communities. The second is a commitment to decentralization. The third is capacity building to support decentralization and strong local government. This includes institutional and individual capacity building to maximize the utilization of the nation's human resources and to encourage more community-based (bottom up) approaches to development.

Development Partnerships

The Millennium Development Goals and the Johannesburg Earth Summit (2002) identified the importance of developing partnerships to support economic and social development. The strategic thrust on the development of partnerships in Sri Lanka is not driven so much by developmental ideologies but more by the shortage of financial and skilled human resources the country is experiencing. While the private sector is a potential source of funding, the NGO sector has the added advantage of possessing the necessary skills and capacities for work in the areas of community mobilization and participatory development actions, something lacking in the public and private sector agencies.

A major problem experienced with many urban development projects in Sri Lanka, especially those supported by overseas funding, is that their sustainability is undermined by the lack of funds beyond the life of the project. This problem can be partially overcome through engaging in partnerships, especially with the business sector. The major benefit of partnership building is that the participation of various stakeholder groups often leads to cooperative action and long-term commitment to projects. The Sri Lankan urban development experience shows that success comes when these partnerships are established across multiple sectors, comprising institutions and community groups. For example, MEIP was successful (Sohail and Boldwin 2004) because it managed to obtain the widest possible involvement of stakeholders (UN-HABITAT 1998) and achieve institutional integration by establishing an apex body (Sohail and Boldwin 2004). This project, which is now being adopted elsewhere, demonstrated effective partnership building leading to integrated sector and institutional efforts in planning and interdisciplinary input into project work.

A critical element of stakeholder participation is the need to achieve and maintain a sense of project ownership. For different stakeholders, ownership means different things, ranging from involvement in decision making to immediate material benefits generated by development actions. The case studies show that community-based environmental improvement programs in Sri Lanka have generated economic benefits along with household and environmental improvements. This strategic linkage is based on the assumption that many poor households have pressing economic needs that are fundamental to their immediate survival.

Material benefits are particularly important in getting community support for partnership building. Partnership building has had a modicum of success in Sri Lanka's urban development projects. Institutional and ideological issues create barriers to establish effective partnerships. These issues, in turn, lead to suspicion and mistrust, which has led to the breakdown of many partnerships between the private and the public sectors on urban development activities in Colombo (Riley and Wakely 2003; Sevanatha et al. 2001). To overcome some of these problems, change management programs should be introduced in all development projects involving institutional partnerships. Change management can improve trust building and openness in urban partnerships. The failure to change institutional, business, and community attitudes; beliefs; customs; and habits is the reason many urban partnerships in Sri Lanka continue to fail.

Decentralization of Government

If the political-administrative decentralization system is to work effectively, each DDC should have complete control of all funds allocated to that district; however, this conflicts with the spirit of political devolution through provincial councils. The result is that devolution has been undermined. In some cases, this has led to conflict between provincial councils and the central Government, especially when two opposing parties control the Government and the provincial councils. The lack of proper devolution has affected the working of the local bodies as noted in the case studies.

The effective decentralization of the administrative decision-making process requires a highly skilled cadre of staff with management and professional expertise. Officers and personnel possessing the ability to perform "superior" services should be transferable between any district and region. All middle- and junior-level personnel agreeing to serve in a particular district or region should be integrated with or brought together into a separate district or regional service to be set up in each administrative district or region. These officers would be expected to serve in a single district or region during their careers. To operate a two-tier public personnel management system, each service should temporarily release an adequate number of officers to fill positions in various districts for specific periods. However, a number of issues have to be dealt with if the system were to work efficiently.

To be in line with the current trends of devolution, provincial and regional services need to be placed under provincial administration. This will require substantial effort in changing the mind-set of the administrators, who prefer a national service that carries better prospects and opportunities and a greater sense of power and authority. To match the national service and to attract personnel, the provincial councils will need an allocation of funds, necessitating additional sources of income. The success of this will, therefore, depend on careful and long-term planning of training and addressing financial issues.

Training and organizational support for decentralization is critical. Since the required skilled workforce is in short supply, immediate steps need to be taken to train an adequate number of persons who have the relevant skills. Public service training should be accorded the highest priority at the policy-making levels. A national training policy that would set goals and determine priorities for the public service training effort must be formulated. Strengthening the capacities of district training units attached to the district secretariats is also critical. This will ensure the availability of adequate trainers at the district level. Mini-libraries should also be set up at these training units.

In addition, training activities undertaken by the different agencies should be coordinated and rationalized to avoid duplication of effort and waste scarce training resources. A coordinating mechanism should undertake such an exercise because even apex training institutions cannot undertake all the training required. Government organizations need to ensure adequate training, designing of curricula, and monitoring the performance of such training. While providing additional and more competent cadres, immediate action should be taken to strengthen the existing institutional capacities and streamline the present operations systems at all subnational levels.

Building Institutional Capacity to Support Decentralization

Sri Lanka must adopt six key ingredients or pillars to build institutional capacity. The long-term impact of any capacity-building intervention on poverty reduction is dependent on the extent to which poor urban communities' productive asset portfolios are built, as well as the capacity for their management. Five categories of assets or resources need to be put in place during the capacity-building process to ensure the continuity of capacity building. These are building up physical assets, building up natural assets, strengthening human capital, strengthening social capital, and building up a viable local economic base. In addition, the extent to which capacity building makes a positive impact in reforming governance institutions needs to be assessed (Figure 12.3).

By combining case study methods for evaluating capacity-building practice (Laquian 1983; Skinner 1987) and innovative techniques for evaluating urban poverty reduction interventions (Scoones 1998; Moser 1998; Grosh

Figure 12.3: Six Pillars of Institutional Capacity Building

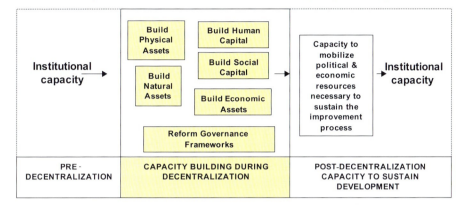

and Glewwe 2000), the extent to which capacity building has been built up in these five categories of assets and has contributed to reform the institutional framework at the six levels noted above can be examined.

As an illustration, the pre- and post-decentralization ingredients of institutional capacity in poor areas are analyzed to evaluate the extent to which institutional capacity was built as part of the capacity-building process, as well as an identification of factors supporting and constraining the building of these assets.

1. Building Physical Assets

A foundation for improving low-income settlements is the physical infrastructure that is either improved or put in place. This includes water and sanitation; garbage removal; a transportation system (roads, lanes, and footpaths); stormwater drainage; electricity; health and education facilities; community halls; and recreation facilities (Laquian 1983; Skinner et al. 1987; Mukhija 2001; Abbott 2002a). The improvement of infrastructure will also contribute to the success of good-practice activities. The community-based waste management case study in Dehiwala Mount Lavinia and the communities that are part of the Clean Cities case study in Colombo both show that improvement in housing conditions made people more conscious of proper waste disposal practices simply because people did not want garbage lying around their newly improved houses. This, in turn, worked as an incentive for members of the community to take part in the project activities.

2. Building Natural Assets

Building natural assets involves restoring and rehabilitating damaged physical environments as well as putting in place preventative measures designed to avoid future environmental damage. Capacity-building initiatives are often weak in environmental management, with service delivery seldom being linked to longer-term environmental monitoring and education programs. At least four dimensions require attention in this regard. First, capacity building should include rehabilitation of damaged natural resources. Second, measures need to be put in place to ensure the prevention of future damage to those natural resources. Third, there should be a focus on environmental education of settlement residents. Fourth, given the limited capacity of local governments, community monitoring of environmental conditions is an important longer-term consideration (van Horen 2001).

Integrating these dimensions within a community-based approach to environmental management moves beyond attempts that place an excessive reliance on legal mechanisms to police development in environmentally sensitive areas. Rather, environmental management should reflect an attempt to involve low-income residents of low-income settlements in the planning and development process as stewards of the environment (Berkes et al. 2000; Grierson 2000; Curthoys 2002).

Capacity building of government agency officials, community leaders, and community members was a built-in component of both the Clean Settlement Program case study and community-based waste management case study. This was not present in the Green Star Homes Project, in which the educational and awareness components were disseminated through public media and other formal means, such as posters. There was no close community interaction as in the other two cases. Green Star Homes Project did show that initial progress failed to maintain the momentum generated, which can be attributed to inadequate attention to capacity building.

3. Building Human Capital

Building human capital encompasses ensuring settlement residents' health status, which determines capacity to work, and strengthening knowledge and skills. Human capital development is closely linked to economic and social infrastructure provision. Social services, such as education, ensure that people gain skills and knowledge, while economic infrastructure, such as water, transport, electricity, and health care, ensure that they are able to use these skills and knowledge productively.

Raising levels of knowledge and skills makes a crucial difference in the urban poor's ability to overcome poverty insofar as higher levels of knowledge and skills mean an increase in returns to labor (Moser 1998; Mitlin 2003). While meeting basic health and safety needs is necessary, it is not a sufficient prerequisite for building longer-term improvement processes (Laquian 1983; Skinner et al. 1987; Durrand-Lasserve and Pajoni 1993).

Health levels play a crucial role in the ability of the poor to work—health being positively correlated with people's capacity to work.

4. Building Social Capital

Social capital involves the development of networks, associations, social interaction, and community engagement for some form of mutual benefit. Network building was successfully carried out in the compost project (Case Study 1) and the Clean Cities project (Case Study 3). Of course, both programs benefited from these communities having preexisting and well-established community-level organizations. There is a danger that these organizations become enmeshed in local politics, often as the result of local loyalties, particularly where political leaders come from within the community and other relationships. In Sri Lanka, a politician who is influential and proactive can often overcome the lethargy of bureaucracy by drawing on political connections (patronage relationships). Such relationships were not uncommon in the case study areas. Network building of the Green Star Homes Project was not a success, especially as regards networking with private sector stakeholders.

5. Strengthening the Local Economic Base

Building economic assets involves strengthening the productive base of the community, which includes ensuring land tenure security, improving housing quality, strengthening microenterprises, providing access to credit, and increasing income-earning opportunities. A prerequisite to ensure the continuity of the improvement process is the economic viability of capacity-building initiatives. In capacity building, capital costs are commonly treated as outright grants to end-users, given the low-income levels of informal settlement residents. Internationally, one major shortcoming of capacity building has been the limited ability to recover the operating costs of ongoing service provision.

Recent experience in water and sanitation projects provides some insights on economically sustainable approaches. Although cost recovery is not one of the major objectives of the community-based waste management case study, it has a cost-recovery component in the form of the waste collection center, which has managed to establish its own office through community contracting. Projects with the best cost-recovery records are those in which residents play a primary role both in initiating projects and in making key decisions regarding affordable service levels, cost recovery, and ongoing management. Capacity-building literature has long argued that the prerequisites for successful cost recovery are affordable standards of service provision, effective development management systems, and meaningful participation of settlement residents in decision making (Laquian 1983; Payne 1984; Skinner et al 1987; Devas and Rakodi 1993; Kessides 2002).

Financial constraints on utility providers and users need to be removed. For instance, this could include providing credit to households for initial connection costs, offering poor households flexible bill payment options, and targeting one-off subsidies for the households most in need. Also, officially imposed service standards need to be adjusted to better reflect affordability and needs of poor households (Kessides 2002). Private companies could provide services, including water, electricity, and telephones, and residents could pay the consumption costs for these services.

6. Reform of Governance Framework

Building on the seminal works on governance in developing countries (Sivaramakrishnan and Green 1986; World Bank 1989), the theoretical work on urban governance is well-developed (Friedmann 1999; Friere and Stren 2001). Most empirical research on governance focuses on performance in terms of service delivery and management—in which performance is generally poor (Ruble et al. 2002; Laquian 2005). Analyses of governance institutions in developing countries reveal that they are too rigid and are insufficiently adaptive to changing imperatives at the micro- or metropolitan levels (McCarney 1996). Thus, they are poorly equipped to manage poverty reduction interventions, such as urban improvement initiatives, effectively. Consequently, even after capacity building has taken place, governance institutions typically fail to facilitate the effective integration of low-income settlements into the urban fabric or ensure the continuity of the settlement improvement process.

The six areas noted above are critical for ensuring the longer-term continuation of the process and the subsequent improvement in urban areas. Attributes of capacity building that form each of these pillars are presented in Table 12.3. This is particularly important in the context of decentralization. Some countries in Asia have decentralized power to the local level, but have not built capacity at this level, with the consequence that local government is unable to deal with issues at the local government level. Not every single item noted in the table needs to be addressed, but all six areas do need to be engaged.

If institutional capacity is *not* developed, then it is only a matter of 2 or 3 years before the infrastructure starts falling apart and the community will be no better off than before the development intervention began. Similarly, a local government that lacks the capacity at the local level does not have the capacity to engage with, and deal with issues that have been devolved to the local level.

Table 12.3: Attributes of Institutional Capacity Building

Building Physical Assets	• Water: access to potable water. • Sanitation: sewerage disposal system for each household. • Garbage removal: garbage removed from settlement on regular basis. • Storm water drainage: adequate to prevent damage to housing and infrastructure. • Flood protection: in areas susceptible to flooding. • Roads, lanes, and footpaths: adequate circulation system. • Electricity: public lighting, community facilities, and household access to electricity. • Health facilities: buildings from which health services can be delivered. • Education facilities: buildings for schools. • Community facilities: buildings for community meetings and community activities. • Housing: good quality construction and materials. • Economic viability: no outstanding debt, consumption costs paid. • Flexible bill payment: given reliance on irregular informal sector incomes. • Service standards: must reflect affordability levels.
Building Natural Assets	• Rehabilitation of damaged natural resources. • Protection of existing environment. • Community education in respect of environmental protection. • Community monitoring of environmental conditions.
Building Human Capital	• Health of settlement residents. • Build knowledge and skill levels to ensure livelihood opportunities. • Organizational skills of area leadership. Areas of competence and how they are used.
Building Relational Assets	• Level and effectiveness of social organization within area. • Internal networks: build strong relationships between organizations within slum. • Nature of relationship between slum-based organizations and external organizations. • Extent of dependence on external NGOs and support agencies. • Effectiveness of networks (in facilitating delivery and management of services). • Nature of collaboration between service providers, NGOs, and communities.
Building Economic Assets	• Access to credit: ensure women and microenterprise access to credit. • Increase the number of microenterprises and their income-generating potential. • Security of tenure: range from certificate of ownership to legal title. • Housing: extent to which land or rooms are rented out as means of earning income.
Reform of Governance Framework	• Upgrading should contribute to policy reform. • Upgrading should contribute to reform of regulations in respect of informal settlements and slums. • Upgrading should be replicated in other parts of the city. • Adaptive regulatory system: regulatory framework must be flexible so as to be able to adapt to on-the-ground changes, thereby ensuring its relevance to the poor.

CONCLUSION

Sri Lanka has undergone a long and difficult period of development since it obtained independence from Britain in 1948. Two decades of conflict with the LTTE and the devastating effect of the 2004 tsunami have slowed economic development of the nation and resulted in hundreds of thousands of people being displaced and homeless. The Peace Agreement with LTTE in 2002 provided a fragile but important respite for the country to develop a more sustainable future.

The level of urbanization in Sri Lanka is lower than those in most Asian countries; however, many urban areas of the country are experiencing serious environmental and urban development problems. With further improvements expected in the economy in future, urbanization rates are projected to rise. This will present a significant challenge to national and local governments in trying to ensure that urban and regional development is sustainable. Most local governments do not have the capability to manage and provide basic services to meet the needs of communities and/or support local economic development. The general failure of central Government to fully embrace decentralization also presents significant challenges to the development of the country.

In the context of decentralization, building institutional capacity is critical to ensure that the longer-term development process continues. If institutional capacity is built and the six areas noted earlier are addressed, then the long-term improvement process has a good chance of continuing. If the six areas are addressed and skills and knowledge are developed within local governments and poor communities, then both local governments and poor communities will be able to work toward a more sustainable future.

Notes

[1] Colombo core urban area, alternatively called Colombo core area or Colombo urban area, consists of the municipal council areas of Colombo City, the City of Sri Jayewardenepura (capital city), and Dehiwala Mount Lavinia. The total land area is about 7,500 hectares.

[2] See: www.statistics.gov.lk/population/tables.pdf.

[3] One third of Colombo Municipal Council (CMC)'s annual budget is spent on waste collection (Jayaratne 1996). According to CMC Chief Medical Officer, Pradeep Kariyawasam, the disease outbreak control programs of the council cost about $250,000 annually.

[4] The Sustainable Cities Program has been operating in Sri Lanka since the early 1990s and, along with the CMC, is one of the main sources of project funding.

13. Thailand

CHAMNIERN VORRATNCHAIPHAN AND DAVID VILLENEUVE

INTRODUCTION

Thailand has grown impressively in recent decades, particularly in comparison with its neighbors in the Greater Mekong Subregion (GMS). However, growth was interrupted by the 1997 financial crisis, which badly affected the economy and increased poverty across the nation. The past few years have seen the economy rebound and poverty rates falling again, particularly in urban areas. Table 13.1 presents recent national development statistics.

COUNTRY CONTEXT

Economic and Social Trends in Thailand

In many ways, Thailand has become the economic gateway to the GMS. With its ranking of 73rd in the Human Development Index, and 21st out of 88 in the Human Poverty Ranking (2003), Thailand is economically more advanced than most of its neighbors and constitutes the subregion's most developed and largest market. It is an important source of expertise, economic knowledge, and capital resources in the region. It also serves as a communication and transportation hub, and an entry point from which many potential foreign investors view the GMS. In spite of its impressive growth, poverty remains a key issue, particularly in the northeastern region bordering the Lao People's Democratic Republic, and border areas adjacent to Cambodia to the east and Myanmar to the west.

Thailand considers that it "will achieve most, if not all, of the Millennium Development Goals (MDGs) well in advance of the global targets set for 2015." Since 1990, poverty has been reduced by two thirds, the proportion of underweight children has fallen by half, and universal access to primary school education is likely to be achieved within a few years (National Economic and Social Development Board [NESDB] 2004). Building on its achievements, the country has introduced the concept of "MDG Plus" as a set of tailor-made and ambitious development targets going well beyond the international MDG targets.

Table 13.1: Country Development Profile, Thailand

Human Development Index (HDI) rank of 177 countries (2003)^	73
GDP growth (annual %, 2004)	6.05
GNI per capita, Atlas method (current $, 2004)	2,540
GNI, Atlas method (current $ billion, 2004)	158.7
GDP per capita PPP ($, 2003)^	7,595
GDP PPP ($ billion, 2003)^	471.0
Population growth (annual 2005–2010 %) #	0.87
Population, total (million, 2005)#	64.08
Urban population, total (million, 2005)#	20.82
Urban population percent of total population (2005)#	33
Population largest city: Bangkok (million, 2005)	6.60
Population Growth: 9 capital cities or agglomerations > 750,000 inhabitants (2000)#	
- Est. average growth of capital cities or urban agglomerations 2005–2015 (%)	16
- Number of capital cities or urban agglomerations with growth > 50%, 2005–2015	0
- Number of capital cities or urban agglomerations with growth > 30%, 2005–2015	0
Sanitation, % of urban population with access to improved sanitation (2002)**	97
Water, % of urban population with access to potable water (2002)**	95
Slum population, % of urban population (2001)**	2
Slum population in urban areas (million, 2001)**	0.25
Poverty, % of urban population below national poverty line (1992)**	10.2
Aid (Net ODA received ($ million, 2003)^	-966.3
Aid as a share of country income (Net ODA/GNI 2003 %)*	-0.7
Aid per capita (current $, 2003)^	-15.6

GDP = gross domestic product, GNI = gross national income, ODA = official development assistance, PPP = purchasing power parity.
Sources: See Footnote Table 3.1,; World Bank (2005); Organisation for Economic Co-operation and Development (2003); United Nations (2004, 2005).

While substantial progress has been made in reducing poverty since the early 1980s, the 1997 Asian financial crisis dealt a blow that was felt throughout all income groups, with the poorest being the most affected. Government sources estimate that the incidence of poverty increased from about 11.4% in 1996 to 15.9% in 2001 (NESDB 2003a). However, with the return to stronger economic growth over the past few years, poverty has fallen significantly. It is the rural areas, particularly in the northeast, that are not likely to have gained as much from economic growth as the greater Bangkok area and other urban areas.

Urban and rural poverty in 1993 were relatively evenly distributed. But by 2002, the incidence of urban poverty had dropped to 4.0% while rural poverty was at 12.6%, resulting in an overall national poverty rate of 9.8% (Table 13.2). However, when applying the $1 per day criterion, in 2000 only 1.9% of the population was below this threshold.

Urban Trends

Urban growth

Thailand is estimated to be about 43% urbanized by 2006, and will have 50% of the population living in urban areas by the year 2015 (NESDB 1998). Figure 13.1 illustrates past and projected changes in urban populations to 2030. Thailand is experiencing a slower rural-urban transition than other countries in the region. While the return to higher economic growth may see more rural to urban migration, urbanization pressures are being tempered by overall low rates of natural population increase.

Previous projections showed Thailand's population at over 50% urbanized by 2008; however, the economic crisis of 1997 substantially slowed the pace of urbanization. Much of this urban growth is occurring at the expense of

Table 13.2: Population Statistics, Thailand[1]

Total area (km^2)	513,225
Total population (million)	
1980*	46.7
1995	59.4
2000	62.4
2003	63.9
2015*	66.3
Population Density (persons/km^2)	
1995	116
2000	122
2003	123
Population annual change (%)	
1995	1.2
2000	1
2001–2015*	0.6
Urban population as percentage of total population	
1990	32.7
2000	38.1
2006	40
2006**	43
2015**	50
Urban population % annual growth rate 1990–2003	5.3
Population (%) below the national poverty line (2002)	
Total	9.8
Urban	4.0
Rural	12.6

km^2 = square kilometers.
Unless otherwise noted, the source is *Key Indicators 2004*. Manila: Asian Development Bank.
* Source: *2003 World Development Indicators*. Washington, DC: World Bank.
** Source: PSUT Project. The Future of Thai Urbanization: New Drivers, New Patterns.

adjacent arable lands being transformed into peri-urban zones. This growth on the urban fringes means that 70% of Thais live within 75 kilometers (km) of an urban area of at least 50,000 inhabitants (NESDB/ADB 2003b). Given the relatively good road network and readily available public transportation, major urban areas are now easily accessible to the majority of the Thai population.

Urban policies

While Thailand does not pursue an overall urban strategy, various government agencies set a number of explicit and implied urban policy guidelines that affect the urban system. Thai policy for the past several decades has not promoted urbanization. Rather, it has sought to maintain a balance, resulting in a cautious approach to urbanization. Since 2000, there has been increased concern about urban areas in terms of such issues as housing and planning for mega infrastructure investment projects (NESDB/ADB 2005).

Challenges of peri-urban growth

The main direction of urbanization is in the peri-urban areas, which still largely fall within the "rural-focused" administration of the Tambon administrative organizations (TAOs). Many of these local authorities are ill-equipped to manage the new demands for the timely provision of necessary infrastructure

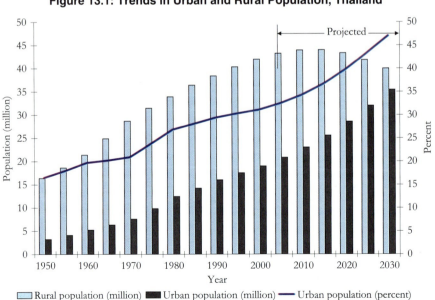

Figure 13.1: Trends in Urban and Rural Population, Thailand

as well as other services. An emerging challenge is how local jurisdictions can cooperate effectively to manage urban growth and address strategic issues in a coordinated manner. For example, in "Samut Prakarn and Pathum Thani and other Bangkok vicinity provinces, there are TAOs located next to the Bangkok metropolis that have to grapple with the expansion forces of a mega-city of 11 million persons, but do so equipped only with the organization, staffing, and resources of a rural district administration" (Archer, 2001).

Poverty

While Thailand has made significant strides in reducing poverty, poor and below-average health conditions still exist in the northeast, remote highland areas of the north, and the three predominantly Muslim southernmost provinces. When considering poverty from a rural-urban perspective under the Planning for Sustainable Urbanization in Thailand (PSUT) Project, it was noted that geographic income disparity in Thailand is mainly rural-urban rather than interregional. "To a significant extent, lower incomes in regions such as the northeast have been explained by lower levels of urbanization" (NESDB/ADB 2003b).

The mean household income in Bangkok is about 3.4 times higher than the nation as a whole and eight times more than in the poorest provinces in the northeast. Still, about 1.3 million of the estimated 2 million people nationwide living in substandard housing are in Bangkok. The geographic structure of slum areas is changing rapidly with the decrease of slum areas in the urban core and the rapid rise of new slums in the urban fringe areas, typically near the industrial areas in the north and east of Bangkok. Additionally, slums are starting to emerge around the edges of major secondary cities.

Environment

Ongoing environmental degradation and increasing pollution detract from the quality of life of urban Thai people. Urban environmental concerns are also spreading well beyond Bangkok to the broader Bangkok region and other urban areas. There is also a lack of capacity and often initiative to undertake the needed analysis, mobilization, and action to tackle these emerging problems. With the ongoing focus on economic development at the local level, this situation can be expected to worsen. Of critical importance are problems associated with wastewater, air quality, and solid waste. Public health is increasingly threatened by declining environmental conditions, especially air pollution in urban centers, leading to increased public and private health care costs. For example, 39% of Bangkok residents suffer from respiratory diseases, a rate that is seven times higher than in rural areas (NESDB/ADB 2005).

Only about 60% of urban solid waste is disposed of to a high standard, with even a smaller proportion being properly handled in the urban fringe areas (NESDB/ADB 2005). In the area of wastewater, while vast sums have been spent on treatment plants in cities throughout the country, virtually none are operational. Linked to the underperformance of city planning is the neglect of managing the built environment in most Thai municipalities, severely affecting quality of life and overall public health and safety.

Public participation in decision making

There has not been a strong tradition of public participation in the decision-making process at any level. However, with the advent of the new Constitution in 1997, there are explicit provisions for public input into the local decision-making process, especially in managing the local environment and resources. While there is now a strong constitutional and legal basis for civic participation, the reality is much weaker. On the positive side, through the recent "SML" program, community-level planning is being introduced for the first time as a means of better integrating grassroots input into the development process. However, coordination within the municipal development plans is not being encouraged as funding is going directly to villages, bypassing the local administrative planning process.

Efficiency of local authorities: With the adoption of the 1997 Constitution, Thailand began an ambitious decentralization process made possible by the adoption of the Decentralization Act (1999) and subsequent Decentralization Plan (2001). As part of this decentralization process, the total number of municipalities dramatically increased from 149 to 1,129 and former "sanitary districts" were upgraded, thereby creating a major demand for well-qualified local managers and staff. While there are signs of change, very few localities are led by a clear vision and supporting strategies. Municipalities still have difficulty in attracting and retaining a critical mass of high quality, appropriately skilled persons, due to arrangements in the national civil service commission. Typically, officers working in local governments are rotated to other assignments every 3–4 years as part of the promotion process and to facilitate sharing of experience.

Fragmented urban areas

Many urban/urbanizing areas are fragmented into multiple jurisdictions. With the devolution of authority and financial resources to the subdistricts in 1994, there has been little interest by these units to merge with adjacent municipalities as the urban areas expand to "engulf" them, thereby creating a situation of uncoordinated urban service delivery. Additionally, local authorities of different designations (i.e., municipality and TAO) are not permitted to share budgets.

City/urban planning

Planning is an area where Thai urban areas tend to perform very poorly. Part of the issue is that the development and spatial planning processes are still largely carried out by two separate levels, with development planning carried out at the local level and local spatial planning conducted by a national-based agency through its provincial offices. The result is that town planning has had almost no effect on shaping Thai urban form and land use. Essentially, Thai cities remain "self-organizing" systems rather than planned. At the development planning level, emphasis is still predominantly placed on economic development with few attempts at true integration of the other development aspects.

Decentralization process under threat

Because of local inefficiency and corruption, recent changes threaten the ongoing decentralization process. Whether these remain a reaction to individual circumstances or part of an overall attempt to recentralize power has yet to be determined. To date, only 172 of the 245 functions specified for devolution in the master plan have been or are in the process of being devolved (NESDB/ADB 2003b), and the rate of devolution has declined over the past 2 years. The nine policy measures to improve local revenue mobilization, approved by the Cabinet in 1994, have made slow progress toward legal enactment. More recently, the decentralization of education has been postponed and possibly reversed in response to a large protest by teachers, citing their concerns at being placed under local government direction rather than under the central ministry.

Urban finance

Local governments prepare and execute their own budgets through annual plans, but they still remain subject to central government direction and provincial oversight. A significant share of local expenditure is still centrally mandated, with the largest percentage being assigned to personnel expenses (representing about 30% of local budgets). Central regulations govern staffing, salaries, and benefits. Major bureaucratic reforms are being proposed to eventually restructure this highly centralized civil service to one where local governments have considerable authority over personnel management.

While the Constitution has mandated a reallocation of a percentage share of the national revenue to the local level, there are neither specific formulae nor criteria. Whether this will in reality provide additional funds at the urban level is yet to be determined; it currently appears that the *tambons* (subdistricts) and provinces have been the main beneficiaries of redistribution. Most urban governments generally still lack sufficient revenues to undertake needed capital works projects. With the recent introduction of strategic and 3-year rolling plans of operation by municipalities, there is now a better opportunity to undertake a longer-term development perspective and to secure funding on a program rather than on individual project basis. However, few municipalities have access to commercial loans from which to finance major infrastructure works and must still rely upon allocations from the central Government.

Multiple actors in service delivery

In spite of the ongoing decentralization process, state enterprises still play a very important role in the delivery of urban services, such as water, electricity, expressways, and wastewater. Up to about 58% of infrastructure spending related to urbanization is by national-scale state enterprises (NESDB 1997).

The changing urban structure of slum settlements

In Bangkok and its surroundings, urban development has generated many slums. They increased from 50 in 1968 to 1,020 in 1985 (Pornchockchai, 1985) and to 1,208 by 2000, containing 243,204 households in Bangkok and its peri-urban areas (NHA, 2002).

Starting in the 1980s, low-income settlements in Bangkok have shifted increasingly to the peri-urban areas. Using aerial photos taken in 1974 and 1984, the National Housing Authority estimated that 150 slums with approximately 30,750 households had disappeared from Bangkok proper and the land changed to other uses during that period. Moreover, between 1984 and 1988, another 107 slums had disappeared (Khan 1994). During the same period, new settlements appeared in the peri-urban areas and expanded into the adjacent provinces. Low-income settlements increased by 84% in the outer zone of Bangkok during 1990–1993 alone (Pacific Consultants International 1997).

Factors pushing low-income residents from the city center originated in the first economic bubble of 1988–1990 and continued through to the second boom ending in the 1997 Asian financial crisis. These factors were related to new urban development projects, such as expressways, office complexes, and shopping centers, and were reflected in the property market in Bangkok where prices of prime land in the city center and suburbs increased up to tenfold (Phongpaichit and Baker 1998).

Related to this, the income of Bangkok citizens has become more skewed. A few became extremely rich as a result of the economic boom and inflation of urban land prices, resulting in the average income of the top 10% of the nation's households tripling between 1981 and 1994. The incomes of the bottom 10% barely changed during the same period, such that the gap between the top and bottom widened from 17 times to 37 times. A combination of rapidly rising land prices and enormous redevelopment pressures, coupled with the widening gap between the rich and the poor during these boom years (until 1995), saw many lower income groups unable to compete for access to land in good locations for their housing and livelihood needs[2] (Phongpaichit and Baker 1998).

This shift in the growth of slums to the suburban areas was typically not a voluntary one. A survey on evictions in 1988 showed that 28% of slum communities were in various stages of eviction and about 71.5% expressed fear of the threat of eviction. From 1981 to 1985, approximately 16 slum communities were demolished each year to make way for new developments (NHA2002). In 1994, the National Housing Authority reported that only 50% of total slum households in Bangkok had some security of land tenure (NHA 2002). This lack of secure land tenure resulted in an unwillingness of residents to improve their living conditions, thereby contributing to further decline in the quality of life for people living in these communities.

To help redress the affordability of housing not only in Bangkok but throughout the country, the Government introduced three mega schemes that offer to subsidize the provision of 1.4 million houses for the poor in the country: (1) Baan Mankong, 300,000 secure housing units for slum dwellers; (2) Baan Uah A Thon, 600,000 housing units for the poor; and (3) Baan Knockdown, 500,000 prefabricated houses. Qualifying persons will pay about $12–37 per month for these units. The total cost of the three schemes is about $10 billion. The minister claims that these projects will be operated with a "combination of socialist goals for housing provision and the capitalist means of investment for profit." The projects are expected to help drive the national economy in terms of employment, construction, and finance mobilization. The Baan Mankong project has a process different from the other two in that it relies on a demand-driven approach and consensus decisions. People of Baan Mankong can choose their own design, costs, location, and neighborhood.

The concern is that this mega approach to housing and development will create significant problems in the future. The social and environmental impacts may be to create more, rather than reduce the number of, slum communities.

This approach could lead to the mismanagement of land use by not providing proper and effective infrastructure, or for its long-term maintenance.

NGO participation

The role of civil society groups is limited, but growing slowly. However, the recent government policy to go directly to the community level (urban and rural through the village fund program) effectively bypasses both the local governments and nongovernment organizations (NGOs) that previously had active roles as partners in promoting public participation at that level. Reducing their role has had the effect of building greater dependency on the central Government and reducing the self-sufficiency of communities.

Private sector participation: Typically, the private sector is involved at the national level in implementing mega projects. However, the sector has not been fully utilized nor promoted at the subnational level due to a lack of a policy framework to involve them in local planning and development.

National Regional Development and Decentralization Policies

National regional development policies

For the last half century, the national Government in Thailand viewed cities and the associated urbanization process rather cautiously, often considering them agents of spatial inequality. This careful attitude toward urbanization comes through strongly in all nine 5-year plans produced by the Government to date as well as in policies and programs administered by the Ministry of Interior—for instance, in rural development programming that stressed self-sufficiency. The result is that compared to other policy approaches in East Asia, Thailand has had a rural bias.

For many decades, successive governments have been concerned about the primacy of Bangkok and attempted to disperse secondary and tertiary activities. They have sought to create a more balanced urban system through the promotion of special economic zones, regional cities development, and border towns (NESDB/ADB 2003a).

More recently, national policy has shifted from focusing on urban areas or places to projects and issues, and the provision of mega infrastructure projects under six thematic areas. As part of its strategy to reduce poverty and in keeping with the change in investment orientation to a project/issue approach, the Government is implementing a "1 million houses" project through the Community Organization Development Institute in the Ministry of Human Security.

Regional integration of development priorities was supported by a Cabinet resolution requiring all provinces to adopt the concept of Integrated Provincial Administration (IPA). Under this, each province is required to establish its own management strategies and targets correlated with those of the country as a whole. Each province is also required to integrate its approach within a cluster of provinces so as to work together and share resources to set common development strategies and subsequent cocoordinated actions. An example of such a grouping is the Upper North Region Cluster involving nine provinces.

The IPA Committee[3] (IPAC) independently (of the central Government) sets down development indicators in detail. This is an attempt to place importance on the integrated development of economic, social, environmental, and administrative factors. Annual monitoring and evaluating of the results are to be carried out via the network of the Ministry of Interior monitoring system and the Office of the Public Sector Development Commission. Through this network, information and results concerning provincial development can be assessed on an ongoing basis.

Decentralization policies
There is no precedent in Thailand for autonomous local governance. In 1932, the system of absolute monarchy was modified to a constitutional monarchy. The major feature of this system of governance has been a very strong central Government, with its focus of operation in Bangkok. Unlike most of its neighboring countries, Thailand was not colonized by any Western power; therefore, while other Asian countries have developed or been influenced by a western approach to local self-government, Thailand has not. As a result, the unitary form of government has proceeded largely unchanged for the last 7 decades. While the concept of decentralization was being legally pursued in the form of minor constitutional changes (1978) and through stated government policy (NESDB 5-year plans), there is a substantial difference between the legally prescribed frameworks and the reality as it exists in the administrative implementation of the laws and policies.

With the adoption of the new Constitution in October 1997, a major step was taken toward effective decentralization.[4] For example, Section 79 states:

The State shall promote and encourage public participation in the preservation, maintenance, and balanced exploitation of natural resources and biological diversity and in the promotion, maintenance, and protection of the quality of the environment in accordance with the persistent development principle as well as the control and elimination of pollution affecting public health, sanitary conditions, welfare, and quality of life.

Organic laws were subsequently enacted, among them the Decentralization Act (1999), which structured the planning and implementation of decentralization to the local level as well as assigning responsibility to the National Decentralization Committee for elaborating a Decentralization Plan (2001), with the Office of Decentralization as the secretariat. This framework formed the guiding strategy for the formulation of the ninth National Economic and Social Development Plan (2002–2006) as well as the forthcoming 10th plan.

Reallocation of functions
The Decentralization Plan was set up in two phases: 4 years and 6 years. The first 4 years (2001–2004) dealt primarily with reclassification and allocation of service responsibilities among different levels of government, outlining reform of key central administrative systems regarding intergovernmental relations and proposing a planning framework. Policy was elaborated for reform of regional administration concerning public service provisions as well as revitalizing laws and regulations concerning local service performance standards. Important objectives that would affect changes in the budgeting and accounting systems were also established. Civil service reform policies have been elaborated and are in the process of being implemented. The second phase (2005–2010) looks to continue the reclassification and devolution of public service responsibilities, finance, and personnel administration to a full-scale operation. The target is to have all local services fully devolved to local authorities (Suwanmala 2000).

Under the plan, six areas of public services are to be devolved to local governments: construction and maintenance of local infrastructure, social welfare, public safety, local economic development, natural resource and environmental management, and promotion of culture.

Financial reallocation
Concurrent with increased devolution of services to local authorities, the Decentralization Act provides financial decentralization benchmarks where a specified percentage of the national revenue must be allocated to local authorities. By 2007, this will amount to 35%, which represents a significant increase since fiscal year 1999, when local governments received only an estimated 9% of national revenues.[5] This has attracted significant public attention. For fiscal year 2004, the national Government transferred 22% of the mandated 27%, which was in contravention of the Decentralization Act. An explanation was presented from the Finance Committee to the effect that the ratio was less than had been mandated because two major services (i.e., education and public health) had not been transferred, so the budget remained at the central level.

Transfer of staff

Major reforms are underway to eventually transfer the highly centralized civil service to one where local governments have considerable authority over personnel management. By 2003, 4,100 people had been transferred[6] from senior levels of the administration to the local level,[7] representing less than 1% of the 1.2 million national civil servants. Most transfers involved five departments in the Department of Public Works and the Ministry of Interior's Accelerated Rural Development Department.

Thus, the transfer of staff has not followed the transfer of functions as stipulated in the decentralization legislation. The strategy of the Office of the Civil Service Commission for transferring remaining staff prioritizes voluntary transfers, although mandatory transfers and compensated retrenchment are still options. The commission has set up a public sector personnel development and deployment center as a hub for training and deploying central staff to positions in local government. Provincial personnel transfer centers are evaluating the staffing implications of devolved authority for local governments.

In light of the new and expanding responsibilities, many localities are expressing the view that the shortfall in personnel is still increasing in relative terms. This situation is worsened by the limited access to financial resources to hire additional human resources from either the government or private sector. In response, many local governments want to increase the capability and capacity of their existing personnel rather than wait for an increase in staff or financial resources.

Regional economic governance and intergovernment financial relations

Even with the ongoing decentralization process, Thailand's central Government is still highly involved—either directly through line agencies or indirectly through state enterprises—in regulating, planning, and funding many local services. A significant share of local expenditures thus remains centrally mandated, with the largest portion devoted to personnel expenses (representing 30% of local budgets, on average). Subnational revenues include locally collected tax and nontax revenues, as well as centrally collected taxes and shared taxes.

Central government and local sources of revenues are both available to local governments. However, in Thailand, as in many other developing countries, local government authorities have limited tax resources at their disposal. By law, they can now levy seven taxes locally: on house and rent, land development, signboards, animal slaughter, gasoline, tobacco, and entertainment. Shared taxes include value-added tax and sales tax, special business tax, natural resource tax, excise taxes, and vehicle tax, all of which accrue to local governments. In addition, local authorities are authorized to collect license fees, fines, and user charges and permit fees.

In 2001, locally collected revenues accounted for only 11–12% of subnational revenues, while shared revenues accounted for about 54%, including about 18% from the value-added tax. The recent Property Tax Act—which combines the land and building tax and the land development tax—could provide subnational governments with more local revenue. Some shared taxes are not truly unconditional. Specific grants are mostly for capital expenditures, with one type earmarked for education and other types being less restricted and not so heavily conditional. Some "general" transfers are subject to conditions (World Bank 2005). For major capital improvements, such as bridges and drainage systems, there is usually a capital cost-sharing arrangement between central and local governments. With the delivery of services being either directly provided or regulated by the central Government, local administration is often assigned the maintenance of such projects upon completion.

Through a detailed approval procedure of projects and subsequent budgets, the central Government retains considerable regulation of major decisions by local government administration for spending on development services. The Ministry of Interior and Bureau of Budget must approve any budget or project amendments proposed by local government prior to implementation. This process applies to both regulation of development and the revenue structure of local government.

Regarding intergovernmental transfers, the effect of the constraints imposed by the central Government is that local administration cannot determine accurate funding levels (revenues) to support local government services. This is mainly due to delays in establishing the criteria for distributing the allocations from the central to the local governments.

Local governments may borrow domestically and internationally, with prior authorization from the Cabinet, and issue debt securities and borrow from official, external bilateral creditors for development projects. In practice, local debt financing is somewhat limited, including that from domestic capital markets. The primary source of borrowing has been local development funds managed by the Ministry of Interior. Subnational governments have more recently borrowed from commercial banks and public revolving funds.

The Role of International Aid in supporting Regional Development

Thailand is moving from being a recipient country to being a donor, with a focus on providing assistance to its immediate neighbors. In terms of its bilateral arrangements, several donors are either downscaling or ending their direct cooperation. Major interventions are now coming from such agencies as the World Bank, Asian Development Bank (ADB), and United Nations agencies. An example is the World Bank's assistance, focusing on working in partnership with the Royal Thai Government, other donors, the private sector, and civil society to support the country's efforts to reduce poverty, improve the business environment, protect the environment, and promote public sector management and governance. ADB has recently supported the PSUT project.

GOOD PRACTICE CASE STUDIES

Three case studies have been selected from three regions (Figure 13.2), representing three levels of municipal government. Each municipality was the winner in its class of municipality for the 2005 Sustainable City Award for Thai municipalities. A panel of representatives from the National Municipal League of Thailand, the central Government, NGOs, and key experts selected the winners. The appraisal of the entrants was based on criteria related to aspects of good governance, sustainability, and innovative urban management practices, as well as submission of documentation. The initiation of this award has not only raised awareness among municipalities; it has seen increased "competition" where they genuinely strive not only to perform well but also to have these efforts recognized. As a result, several municipalities are now discussing possible application to the Dubai International Award for Best Practices to Improve the Living Environment.

Muang Klaeng Municipality: Sustainable City Initiative

The good practice from this municipality, winner of the 2005 "Sustainable City" award for *Tambon* class municipality (the smallest level municipality), focuses on aspects of citizen and private sector mobilization and participation to rehabilitate the primary river in the municipality. The river serves not only consumption needs but also plays an important economic and social role.

GOOD PRACTICE	
Good Governance	✓
Urban Management	✓
Infrastructure/Service Provision	
Financing and Cost Recovery	
Sustainability	✓
Innovation and Change	
Leveraging ODA	

Location and characteristics of the region
The municipality is located in Rayong Province in the east-central region of the country. The municipal jurisdiction covers 14.5 km^2 with a registered population of 18,843 (2005 estimate) residing in eight communities (*chumchon*). The growth rate of the registered population is about 1% per annum. Klaeng is an old town, previously famous as a trading place in the region. It still functions more as an important rural service node than an urban center.

Figure 13.2: Map Showing the Location of the Case Studies

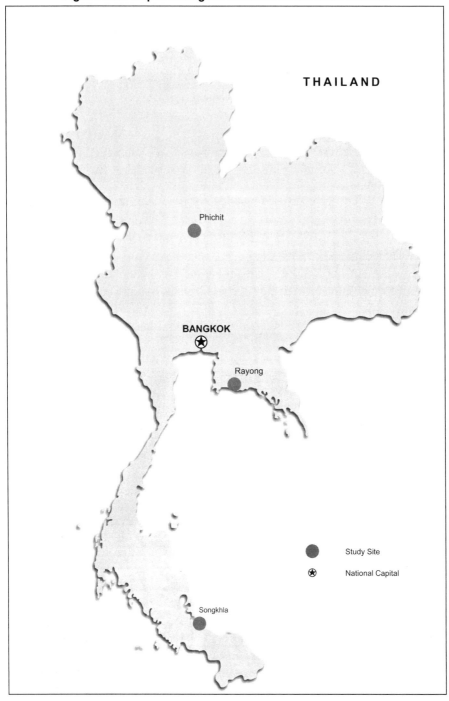

Land use in the municipality is made up of agriculture and rural areas, 54%; low density residential, 22%; moderate density residential, 8%; high density/core commercial, 4.5%; open space, recreation, and environmental protection, 4.3%; institutional uses, 1%; public areas, 2.5%; major highways, 0.2%; industrial, 1.4%; academic institutions, 0.9%; and religious establishments, 1.2%. The major occupations of the residents are listed as agriculture (rubber plantation, fruit orchard); fisheries; livestock; and industrial (para-wood furniture factory, flour processing, and motorcycle helmet manufacturing).

A small, unregistered population of migrants from northeastern Thailand and Myanmar work in the para-wood processing and furniture industry. Priority development issues identified by the municipality concern public health. Notably, the municipal leaders have worked to keep the town "small and beautiful." Part of this initiative has seen the municipality become one of the first Thai local governments to achieve the ISO 14001 certification (environmental management standards).

Good practice: conservation of Pra Sae River

The Pra Sae River is a major resource of Klaeng for transportation, consumption (domestic, agricultural, and commercial), and food (through fisheries). With increased urbanization, waste discharged directly into the river and upstream pollutants from agriculture and other uses entering the system, the overall quality and viability of this important resource are being threatened. Rather than waiting for a national response to local requests for action, the mayor initiated an operation to begin managing and rehabilitating this important resource.

In 2002, Klaeng Municipality, in cooperation with Makut College and a local private company, implemented a project called Nak Sueb Sai Nam (River Spy to conserve Pra Sae River). With private sector support, the project activities included the mobilization of six youth groups, who monitored water quality along the river within the municipal area. Consequently, the municipality scaled up pollution control and protection by focusing on steps to rehabilitate the river environment and ecosystem, including a mangrove replanting program.

A key component was the promotion of people's participation in and increased awareness of river conservation. This involved a wider set of participants beyond the municipal boundaries to include other districts and players in the surrounding jurisdictions. The "River Spy" program was extended to youth groups from 18 schools, with the intention of mobilizing young people and increasing their awareness early to help them develop as leaders in promoting more sustainable practices.

Within the program, the municipality implemented related activities to conserve and rehabilitate the river (e.g., canal dredging, increasing the quantity of aquatic animals, campaigns to promote the use of grease traps by street vendors and residents). To track the effectiveness of the actions, the municipality monitored the water quality every 3 months. Complementary to these activities, it introduced a process of fermenting organic waste with microorganisms that helped the water treatment process.

To build public awareness, the municipality published the *Rak Nam Pra Sae Newsletter* to disseminate news and information about activities concerning river conservation to the public. The newsletter has now been produced for 3 years with close support from two private companies, Apina Industrial Company and National Starch and Chemical (Thailand) Company.

The activities have markedly improved the river water quality and the quantity of aquatic animals, and enhanced the scenic view along the river, creating additional tourism activities and income-generating opportunities for local fishers. At present, there are 25 monitoring stations along the river involving three additional districts, all in Rayong Province.

The success of the work is largely attributable to the initiative demonstrated by the mayor (Somchai Jareeyajarun), who has been pursuing a vision for the municipality, and going from analysis to action. A unique aspect of the plan is that the mayor is looking well beyond his own tenure and has a true vision of the future for the municipality. With his leadership qualities, he is able to mobilize government officers, the key community stakeholders, and the private sector to take action on a priority basis. This is also reflected in related matters, such as the achievement of the ISO certification and general willingness to participate in such global-scale activities as projects related to climate change. To minimize administrative costs, the municipality has intentionally avoided seeking an upgrading to a higher municipality classification, for which it is entitled—the belief being that they are able to better manage what they have with a streamlined operation and greater involvement of citizens and businesses.

Phichit Municipality: Waste Recycling

Phichit Municipality was the winner of the 2005 "Sustainable City" Award for Muang Class Municipality (medium-level municipality). The good practice from this municipality focused on creating projects that linked improving the environment with generating income for the people. Three projects were identified under this theme: paper recycling

GOOD PRACTICE	
Good Governance	✓
Urban Management	✓
Infrastructure/Service Provision	
Financing and Cost Recovery	
Sustainability	✓
Innovation and Change	✓
Leveraging ODA	

for income generation, creating a "waste bank," and producing fertilizer pellets from organic waste.

Location and characteristics of the region
The municipality is the capital of Phichit Province in the north central region of the country, 345 km north of Bangkok. The municipal jurisdiction covers 12.017 square kilometers (km^2) with a registered population of approximately 25,000 in 2005, residing in 15 communities, and 8,242 households. The resultant density is relatively high at 2,093 persons per km^2. The population growth rate from 2002 to 2003 was only 0.02%. With an average working age income of $800 per year, income generation is a very important challenge for residents. To formulate its 3-year development plan, the municipality undertook an extensive public input process that involved questionnaires and public hearings to identify people's needs and opinions as well as to prioritize key problems. Local people and experts were subsequently invited to help formulate the municipal development plan. Phichit Municipality now has a strategy to improve working methods and procedures for delivery of municipal services to the public.

Saving Paper Project (halving the amount of waste paper)
One activity emphasized by the municipality was improving the workplace through well-organized service delivery in all aspects. This activity sought to increase satisfaction levels of the people using municipal services and to introduce approaches that would help generate income for municipal staff by recycling paper products.

The paper recycling project involved municipal staff collecting used paper from offices to form a waste paper "bank," which was subsequently processed into pulp and formed into a variety of moulds and dried in sunlight. The product was eventually used as decorative paper. Currently, officers and staff of the Public Health and Environment Department are providing their own time to fabricate products from recycled paper as a secondary occupation. The results and lessons learned from this project have not only brought the municipal staff kudos due to their innovative products created from waste materials but also additional income, with the most important aspect being the building up of expertise and maximizing resource utilization in an organization.

Paak Tang Community Waste Bank
Concern about waste management in Phichit Municipality has been growing, partly because of its growing expense. The municipality developed a way to minimize costs for waste management while also minimizing the quantity of waste produced. The goal was to minimize the quantity of waste in the municipal area by promoting domestic and community waste separation at the source.

The Paak Tang Community Waste Bank was established at the end of 2000 and was an entry point for the separation and recycling of materials of value from domestic waste. Seed money to run this activity was borrowed from the Local Public Health Volunteer Fund as well as capital raised through the efforts of the municipal executives.

The Waste Bank is run like other waste recycling shops but rather than being a private enterprise, it is managed by a community committee. In practice, it is organized like a bank where members have waste "bankbooks" for depositing/selling their recycled materials to the waste bank. Presently, there are more than 80 members, mostly children and adolescents. The cash flow is more than $2,500 per month, involving 4–8 tons of recycled materials. The Waste Bank has also established a low-price grocery for community members and others where other community produce can also be sold. The bank offers many advantages to the local people as a source of income for households, providing money for children that can be spent on their education, and as a depot for people who buy recycling materials from households and subsequently sell them to this bank. From the profit, the bank can also allocate funds to organize social and sporting activities for the community, which help create a more livable and harmonious populace.

Using Waste to Make Fertilizer Pellets
Based on the achievements gained from the Waste Bank, the mayor of Phichit Municipality sought to minimize organic waste from the fresh food market. There resulted a joint collaboration between the municipality, the Provincial Administrative Organization, and the Regional Environmental Office for utilizing organic waste.

With input from a local university, the initiative involved the composting of organic waste to produce fertilizer pellets. The municipal composting plant is the first such instrumentality in Thailand. The process to make fertilizer pellets involved collecting organic waste from fresh food markets and households, which was then chopped up and mixed with molasses in a composting chamber. As an alternative to molasses, they now use fruit peels (such as banana, papaya, and pineapple). An anaerobic process carries out the initial composting with further composting undertaken on an aerobic basis. In this step, additional ingredients are added, such as ash, to augment nutrient composition, depending on the composition of the plants. After further blending, the output is finally formed into pellets, which are sun dried, packaged, and distributed back to community leaders either for use or resale by the community. People interested in this product can also trade their organic waste for fertilizer pellets as a further source of income.

While the end results for the above projects are admirable, the initiatives represent stand-alone work and are not really integrated as part of an overall management system at the local level. In essence, the success of the work rests with the mayor (Prakasit Yuwawet) and is more the result of a "one-man-show" with the support of only a few key staff members rather than a concentrated effort at overall teamwork. Due to the desire to produce concrete success, the mayor used a combination of proven good practices (paper recycling and waste banks), with a search for alternate and innovative approaches that involved academic research (fertilizer pellets).

Songkhla Municipality: Waste Management and Education

Songkhla Municipality was the winner of the 2005 "Sustainable City" Award for Nakorn Class Municipality (the largest-level municipality), the good practice from this municipality focused on aspects of citizen and private sector mobilization and participation. The aims were to undertake better solid waste management practices to extend the life of the landfill, to promote education and reading, and to enhance key tourist attractions.

GOOD PRACTICE	
Good Governance	✓
Urban Management	✓
Infrastructure/Service Provision	
Financing and Cost Recovery	
Sustainability	✓
Innovation and Change	
Leveraging ODA	

Location and characteristics of the region

The municipality is the capital of Songkhla Province in the southern region of the country, 950 km south of Bangkok. It is situated on a peninsula between Thaleh Sap (an inland estuary) and the Gulf of Thailand. The municipal jurisdiction covers a very compact 9.27 km^2 with a population of 83,000 registered and 15,000 nonregistered persons living in 18,298 households at a density of over 10,500 persons per km^2. The municipality is composed of 30 communities, most of which are slum or squatter settlements. Songkhla's function must also be considered in regard to Had Yai—for which Songkhla is the provincial administrative center. Had Yai is the region's economic hub, where the wealthier population tends to live.

Songkhla has very little land on which to expand or develop. Surrounded on three sides by water and steep hillsides on the fourth, Songkhla must intensify its urban development. Additionally, all land is typically owned by government agencies that in turn lease the land, resulting in very few direct landowners. Under these constraints, Songkhla is one of the very few municipalities to adopt a "specific plan" to guide its land use and development. Because of its limited land, the municipality has paid considerable attention to acquiring open spaces; there are approximately 13 square meters of green area per person (primarily in the hillsides), one of the highest such ratios in Thailand.

Government administration is the main activity of the municipality; tourism and fishing are the main sources of revenue for many residents. While the locality is predominantly Buddhist, large communities adhere to other beliefs, with good integration of the differing religious groups, in spite of such crowded living conditions. In recognition of Samila beach as an important domestic tourist destination, considerable efforts have previously been made to clean up the area and persuade the beach vendors to conform to certain standards of layout and operation. Considerable energy has gone into mobilizing communal participation, including efforts by the executive to hold forums in all communities, with representatives from all of them becoming involved in the local planning process, leading to an impressive 29 events per year.

Solid Waste Management
Songkhla Municipality is one of the larger cities in southern Thailand. As in other cities, solid waste management remains one of the most challenging problems. The quantity of waste generated is 81–85 tons per day, which is categorized as 60% wet/organic garbage and 40% dry. Previously, most solid waste in the municipality was treated through sanitary landfill. Hazardous waste was transferred for incineration to Had Yai Municipality.

Based on the volume and weight of waste being disposed of each day, it would take less than 20 years to use up the landfill's capacity. Given the scarcity of land available to Songkhla, maximizing the life of such facilities is imperative. Therefore, to prolong the life of the landfill, Songkhla Municipality undertook to take old waste from the landfill site for processing at a waste separation plant for subsequent separation and production of usable compost.

The process involved extracting and sifting waste that had been buried for more than 10 years and separating metal, plastic, glass, and other nonbiodegradable materials, which were either recycled or returned to the landfill site. The remaining mixture of dirt and organic waste was used as material for creating compost. This was supplemented with collected sewerage and processed using an anaerobic fermentation procedure, which was dried in sunlight. Tree branches and other similar matter were chopped and mixed with dirt, organic waste, and sludge. After further processing, the materials were further sifted and sorted for eventual use as fertilizer in municipal areas as well as for sale to the public.

Mobile Library
Education has a high priority in Songkhla. One initiative is the establishment of a symbol and mechanism of learning at Samila beach to remind

people that "Knowledge creates man, man creates the nation, and knowledge is power...to create nation and man." To put this into effect, a mobile library was established on the city beach to supplement the implementation of the city's learning strategy. This promotes reading among city people and visitors to Songkhla. The mobile library was converted from containers donated by the Southern Informal Education Center. The municipality designed and decorated the library and provided more than 1,000 up-to-date books and magazines. The library also provided a lending service and mats to allow people to sit on the beach, along with toys and games for children.

The mobile library rotates its service between Samila beach and other communities, with 10 days in each locale, operating on Tuesdays to Sundays from 1100 to 1900 hours.

As in the other case studies above, the success of this work is largely attributable to the initiative of the mayor, in this case, Uthit Chuchauy, who has sought to find a workable integration of the social, economic, and environmental development outcomes. However, unlike smaller municipalities, success also depends on achieving good teamwork from a core group of municipal officers at the senior level, whereby results can be incorporated as part of the overall planning and development system in the municipality. This overall teamwork approach under strong leadership is vital in such a complex work setting. The above good practices must also be considered in light of the previous development initiatives that focused on improving the built environment, ensuring that both public and private activities are well-structured and organized, and where land use is well planned and implemented (unlike many other municipalities). The commitment of the mayor to the processes of planning and participation is very clear and is the key to the success of such initiatives.

Key Lessons Learned

Leadership is one of the common features that emerge from the three case study municipalities. In Thai municipalities, good governance needs good, strong, and persevering leaders who also demonstrate their leadership, beyond providing management inputs, by their decisiveness and ability to see projects through and to monitor and follow up the results. This involves mobilizing resources (financial, human, and material) at all levels. For the cases cited, this mobilization of resources occurred irrespective of political allegiance. The attributes of the mayor were crucial in all cases. The mayors had a desire to learn and be innovative. The learning was not necessarily an academic process but involved a practical mentality, which seeks specific solutions and alternatives.

How this leadership takes form varies from locality to locality. In the case of Phichit, it resulted in specific actions that were demonstrable, practical, and offered visual improvement. In Klaeng, the focus was on decision making and mobilization of people. In Songkhla, the main aspect was the ability to integrate a range of development issues. One key characteristic common to all the case studies was that they all moved beyond awareness building to mobilization of people in various communities.

The main urban management quality that emerges in these cases is respect for people and community. While this is much easier to realize in smaller centers, the principles are observable in all cases, including the much larger center of Songkhla. These effective decision makers typically listen first and subsequently involve and motivate people in the processes.

Specific "management processes" cannot truly be defined in these cases but each generally worked under strategic principles of moving from vision, through analysis, into action. This involved each mayor seeing beyond his tenure and looking to the future, which is a very different way of looking at issues by many mayors in many parts of the world.

In the case of Songkhla, the examples of good practice demonstrate the impacts of considering issues beyond economic concerns and attempting to undertake a more integrated and holistic approach to managing the area.

While such leaders are effective in their own jurisdictions, their impact on the overall urban situation is frequently limited by many factors pointed out in previous sections. Urban-wide effectiveness is hampered mostly by a lack of willingness to cooperate on common issues by adjoining jurisdictions. Some may see the need for a "legal" solution; however, the results of these case studies support the argument for a capacity-building solution that builds on local leadership regardless of the enabling environment.

STRATEGIES TO ENHANCE SUSTAINABLE URBAN REGION DEVELOPMENT

Many strategic options can be pursued to address the urbanization issues identified earlier. Following is a small selection of strategies that emerge from the results of the case studies.

Building local leadership. While the above good practices identified a number of tangible activities, the solutions to urban issues being faced in these communities are not necessarily technical in nature but concern managerial and leadership qualities. Therefore, one of the key strategies is to focus on building leadership capacity at all levels (elected and senior staff) within the municipal and subdistrict organizations that are being confronted by growing urban issues. These capacity-building inputs must nurture local leadership while promoting innovation, with the further aim of involving the affected communities. There must be a concentrated effort to "break the mould" of creating "administrators." Centrally produced administrators can no longer effectively cope with the emerging complex urban situations occurring in and around Thai cities. There is a need for innovative and strategically oriented leaders. Such training has been conducted on a pilot basis under the Department of Environmental Quality, which supported a training project for local officials in "strategy management" approaches that introduced the use of such tools as the balanced scorecard and strategy mapping techniques.

Such a capacity-building strategy can be supported by enhancing technical and professional capacity at the provincial level. The provincial level is where the capacity-building role changes from undertaking planning and project implementation activities, to providing the needed inputs according to local requirements and demands.

Overcoming the fragmentation of urban areas. To gain a more sustainable approach to Thai urban region development, there needs to be a means to overcome the fragmentation of urban areas. This could be achieved either through supporting and facilitating local government cooperation led by the central municipality, or possibly through an aggressive replotting of municipal boundaries to encompass urbanizing areas. This would expand municipal jurisdiction on a legal basis. It requires a national urban development strategy that moves away from viewing urbanization based on jurisdictional boundaries, and considers it from a more functional perspective.

To be truly effective, urban policy must look beyond the immediate municipal jurisdictions and increasingly pay attention to the planning and development of the urban fringe areas that have become the main urban growth areas. These locales lack the capacity, infrastructure, and resources to effectively manage this development. Such a perspective would build up local capacities and support local authorities entering into agreements for local cooperation toward achieving impacts at the regional level. An example for such an approach in the Thai context can be drawn from the emerging work of the integrated provincial administration clusters, which seek to coordinate provincial development activities at a functional region scale that recognizes the commonalities and synergies to be gained from coordination. However, to implement this at the local level, some legal obstacles, such as the prohibition of different classes of local government from sharing budgets on development projects, need to be overcome.

Integration of physical and development planning. To support development at the city-region scale, development and physical planning must be integrated at the local level, freeing up the provincial agencies to provide technical and professional support to the local process. Such planning should also provide regional frameworks that involve local input to help guide the local planning process.

Supporting decentralization. The ongoing decentralization process must continue to be supported and efforts to recentralize power countered. With greater local capacity, one of the main arguments against fiscal decentralization will be overcome. In addition, greater access to and mobilization of local resources are needed, whereby there is a more direct link between taxes paid and services provided at the local level. An example would be the introduction of a local tax based on capital value of land.

CONCLUSION

Given Thailand's generally slow urbanization rate and available wealth for infrastructure investment, there is an opportunity to take a rational view to implementing strategies without having to deal with crisis situations of rapid urbanization and limited resources. The above strategies will need to be placed within an overarching initiative that looks to clarify and redefine the roles of all three levels of government. Such a redefinition will need to see the central level shift from direct implementation of development projects to one of facilitating the local development process. While strengthening its coordinating role, the provincial level will need to adapt to become more professionally and technically competent to provide direct support to the local level on a needs basis, leaving local level personnel to truly become the planners and implementers of development initiatives.

Such a reorientation will need supporting mechanisms, guidelines, and frameworks to facilitate the needed cooperation not only at the local level, but also between the various government levels and agencies. While various new forms of planning and development innovation are often good, there is also the potential to make use of existing planning systems and processes by seeking to strengthen them through building "innovative leadership" rather than introducing "innovative technology."

Notes

[1] There are considerable differences between the population and urbanization data from United Nations sources in the Country Profile Table 13.1 and Figure 13.1, and the data from these sources. They reflect definitional issues about what is classified as urban. These problems are most acute in peri-urban areas.

[2] Most low-income households spend approximately 12% of their income on housing (and about 51% on food). (Source: Somsook Boonyabancha. *Community Ennoblement Through Savings and Integrated Credit Schemes as a Strategy for Dealing with Poverty Alleviation*).

[3] Mae Hong Son Province appointed its Integrated Provincial Administration Committee on 19 November 2003; the governor is chairman and the chief of the provincial office is secretary. There are 56 members in total from 44 chiefs of central and regional agencies located in the province, 6 local mayors (from Mae Hong Son Provincial Administrative Organization and municipalities), 3 private enterprise representatives, and 3 nongovernment organizations and civil society representatives.

[4] Specifically sections 56, 78, 79, 282–284, and 290 of the 1997 Constitution.

[5] Ministry of Interior Information.

[6] Government civil servants are transferred to local authorities. They will be under local authorities. Their payment would not be less than their current salary. Other benefits would be the same as centrl government's civil service commission.

[7] Civil Service Commission. 2003.

14. Viet Nam

NGUYEN TO LANG

INTRODUCTION

Viet Nam is a long, narrow country with an area of 331,000 km² and a population in 2005 of approximately 83.6 million. Ravaged by more than 30 years of war and civil conflict since the 1940s, it remains one of the least-urbanized countries in Asia. However, the advent of *doi moi* (renovation) in 1986 triggered the transformation of the nation's economy and accelerated a process of rapid urbanization, much of which is not sustainable. Relevant national statistics are presented in Table 14.1.

Table 14.1: Country Development Profile, Viet Nam

Human Development Index (HDI) rank of 177 countries (2003)^	108
GDP growth (annual %, 2004)	7.50
GNI per capita, Atlas method (current $, 2004)	550
GNI, Atlas method (current $ billion, 2004)	45.1
GDP per capita PPP ($, 2003)^	2,490
GDP PPP ($ billion, 2003)^	202.5
Population growth (annual 2005–2010 %) #	1.28
Population, total (million, 2005)#	83.59
Urban population, total (million, 2005)#	22.34
Urban population percent of total population (2005)#	27
Population largest city: Ho Chi Minh City (2005, million)	5.03
Population growth: 23 capital cities or agglomerations > 750,000 inhabitants 2000#	
- Est. average growth of capital cities or urban agglomerations 2005–2015 (%)	30
- Number of capital cities or urban agglomerations with growth > 50%, 2005–2015	0
- Number of capital cities or urban agglomerations with growth > 30%, 2005–2015	8
Sanitation, % of urban population with access to improved sanitation (2002)**	84
Water, % of urban population with access to improved water sources (2002)**	93
Slum population, % of urban population (2001)**	47
Slum population in urban areas (2001, million)**	9.20
Poverty, % of urban population below national poverty line (1993)**	25.9
Aid (Net ODA received, $ million, 2003)^	1,768.6
Aid as share of country income (Net ODA/GNI, 2003, %)*	4.5
Aid per capita (current $, 2003)^	21.8

GDP = gross domestic product, GNI = gross national income, ODA = official development assistance, PPP = purchasing power parity.
Sources: See Footnote Table 3.1, World Bank (2005); Organisation for Economic Co-operation and Development (2003); United Nations (2004, 2005).

This chapter examines urbanization in Viet Nam and some of the difficulties it poses for sustainability of urban development. Three case studies are presented: Institutional Building in Urban Upgrading in Phu Thuong Ward, Hanoi; Environmental Improvement of Nhieu Loc-Thi Nghe Basin, Ho Chi Minh City; and Urban Upgrading, Environmental Impact Assessment in Van Mieu Ward, Nam Dinh City, Nam Dinh Province. Lessons from the case studies and strategies to improve approaches toward sustainable urbanization are presented in the final part of the chapter.

COUNTRY CONTEXT

National Development Indicators

The modern Socialist Republic of Viet Nam was formed with the reunification of the southern and northern parts of the country at the end of the Viet Nam War in April 1975. The transformation of Viet Nam to a socialist market economy since doi moi has been rapid. Ranked as one of the poorest countries in the world in the 1980s, it now ranks 124th out of 177 countries in GDP per capita (DESA-UN 2005). Since 1986, GDP per capita has increased from less than $100 to $2,490. In the two major cities—Hanoi and Ho Chi Minh City—GDP per capita has increased much faster than GDP per capita in other cities. More than 50% of the country's industrial output is from these two major cities.

The poverty rate remains high. In 2002, the general national poverty rate was 28.9%. This has fallen to 25% and is projected to decline further to 15% in 2010 (Hong Khanh 2005). In rural areas and mountainous provinces, such as Lai Chau, the poverty rate in 2002 was 77%. The urban poverty rate is well below that of rural areas. In the larger cities, the latest figures on poverty rates (set at under $2 per capita income per day) are Ho Chi Minh City (2%), Danang (4%), Hanoi (5%), and Haiphong (12%) (Asian Development Bank [ADB] 2002). The high demand for labor and the growing industrialization of cities are factors contributing to the low level of urban poverty.

National economic policy has focused on the development of manufacturing industry, services, agriculture, tourism, and retail sales. The annual growth (GDP) in 2004 was about 7.5%, due to sound economic management and generally low inflation. The forecast for average inflation in 2005 was 6.0% (World Bank 2005a). The employment structure of the economy is expected to change significantly between the present and 2020. Employment in the manufacturing and service sectors is expected to increase to 41% and 49%, respectively, with a 10% reduction in the agriculture sector.

National government economic policy supports the development of six sectors: state, collective, private, private capitalist, state capitalist economies, and foreign investment. A range of incentives and new laws has been provided to encourage the development of new enterprises and private citizens to invest in these sectors. Under the national economic strategy, the country is divided into six economic regions and three focused economic zones. Each region has the power to mobilize resources for development, including an open economic mechanism, to develop infrastructure and other services to support investment in agriculture, manufacturing, and tourism development to meet the growing demands of domestic and international markets. The national Government has given high priority to supporting the development of focused economic zones, and facilitates and invests appropriately in these.

The Government continues to reform the national finance and monetary system to ensure more equitable distribution of public revenues. This includes the adoption of a more unified and simpler sector taxation system, completion of the decentralization procedures relating to financial management in regions and cities, and the promotion of creativity and innovation in local authorities and industries to enhance the decentralization process.

The rapid growth and transformation of the economy have placed enormous pressure on Viet Nam's urban systems. With much of its infrastructure severely damaged by war, the focus of government policy has been to restore and develop the capacity of urban services to support industrialization, especially modern industrial estates and transportation facilities located on the periphery of cities. Unfortunately, the lack of attention paid to urban management, poor plan implementation, and lack of development control have resulted in the development of cities that lack structure and basic services—especially housing, water supply, and transport—to meet the growing needs of rapidly growing urban populations. Consequently, environmental conditions in Vietnamese cities began to deteriorate rapidly throughout the 1990s.

The first urban settlements in Viet Nam were built more than 2,000 years ago. Hanoi and Ho Chi Minh City (formerly Saigon) have a history as trading centers dating back 1,000 years. French colonial interests in the 18th and 19th centuries led to the development of expanded urban trading centers, but the economy was still backward and largely based on subsistence agriculture. After independence in 1945, the urban centers developed gradually but were severely disrupted and, in some cases, damaged by the ravages of war. Since reunification in 1975, the country has developed rapidly and urban centers have developed in all respects (Nguyen 2002).

About 27% of the population or 22.34 million people (World Bank 2005b) live in urban centers composed of a few major cities and many towns. Viet Nam has an urban network of 716 cities and towns (Tran 2004). Urban areas include the national capital city, Hanoi, and the capitals or centers of regions, provinces, and districts. The definition of urban in Viet Nam is any settlement with more than 4,000 people and where the percentage of non agriculture sector employment is greater than 65%. Urban areas are classified into six categories: special city and categories I, II, III, IV, and V (Government of Viet Nam 2001).

Table 14.2 gives the names of the regional centers. Two cities dominate the country—Hanoi (population: 3 million) and Ho Chi Minh City (5 million). In addition to these cities are 15 cities with populations exceeding 250,000 and 74 with populations of more than 50,000.

Besides these urban areas, there are also centers of general or sectoral economic development importance (industrial, agricultural, tourism, mining regions, etc.), and special administrative economic zones (special economic zones, concentrated industrial areas, etc.), many of which lie outside, but are part of, urban conurbations. About 90 industrial parks, 22 new towns, and 18 border gate economic zones are included in the national urban system (Tran 2004).

Prior to doi moi, there was a lack of clarity on policies related to rural and urban development. Less than 18% of the population was urbanized. Since the rate of urbanization was low, the process was not seen as creating significant difficulties for a nontechnological society. Development planning was highly centralized, based largely on eastern European ideas grounded in planned economies and physical master planning.

Post-renovation, the urbanization process has been influenced by open-door market economic policies, the overhaul of policies relating to land and housing, and greater state support for urban planning, which stimulated urban growth in the whole country. These changes instigated calls for greater decentralization and transfer of economic development and infrastructure development responsibilities to provincial and municipal government systems. Viet Nam lags well behind other Asian countries in this respect.

Viet Nam's Urban Development Strategy

Viet Nam was one of the Asian countries least affected by the 1997 financial crisis. The collapse of property markets in cities, such as Bangkok and Jakarta, and the growing concern about the dominance and vulnerability of Ho Chi Minh City and Hanoi as the country's centers of manufacturing led the Government of Viet Nam to place a stronger emphasis on regional development, especially decentralization policies.

In 1998, the Prime Minister (MoC 1999) outlined the framework for a Vietnamese Urban Development Strategy to be fully implemented by 2020.

For the planning and management of the urban development system, the country has 10 regions (Nguyen 2003). Table 14.2 explains the numbered regions and indicates the major city in each region.

Table 14.2: Regions and Regional Centers in Viet Nam

No.	National Urban Systems Region	Regional Center
1	North focal region of Red River, including Hanoi	Hanoi
2	South focal region and Dong Nam Bo	Ho Chi Minh City
3	Central focal Region and Trung Trung Bo	Da Nang
4	Plateau region of Mekong River	Can Tho
5	Nam Trung Bo	Nha Trang
6	Tay Nguyen (highlands in the central region)	Tay Nguyen
7	Bac Trung Bo	Vinh
8	Viet Bac	Thai Nguyen
9	Tay Bac and midland of Viet Tri City	Bac Bo
10	Rest of Tay Bac	Hoa Binh

Each region has a special policy for development based on its specific characteristics in regard to the natural environment and socioeconomic conditions. The policies for decentralization empower regional and local governments to provide a wide range of urban and rural services. For example, the Construction Law (2003) allows provinces, districts, and commune-level authorities to approve planning projects within their areas (National Assembly 2003). These policies cater to all sectors—private sector, nongovernment organizations (NGOs), and state sector—to be engaged in the decision-making process. However, due to weaknesses in institutional capacity, many authorities are not able to fulfill their tasks successfully and continue to rely on central Government to plan and deliver essential services.

The 2020 Urban Development Strategy provides the basis for managing urbanization in Viet Nam. The directions outlined by the strategy are summarized below:

- Urban development is to be more equitably distributed and related to the development levels of the labor force nationwide. Effort should be concentrated on developing technical and professional skills to promote the development of dynamic and specialized urban centers that are much more capable of responding to changes in markets and reduced levels of government support.
- A hierarchy of large-, medium-, and small-sized cities is to be developed, recognizing the need to create the balance of development

between regions and combining the process of promoting urbanization with new rural development.
- The functions of municipalities are to be outlined in law according to an urban system at the national, regional, and local levels, with set targets related to economic, demographic, social development, and environmental protection defined according to the grade and type of government.
- Policies and mechanisms suitable to local circumstances are to be created, allowing cities and regions to mobilize resources for urban development and to ensure orderly urban development and control in accordance with urban planning and legal regulations.
- Urban planning and construction must be more strategic and provide for appropriate short- and long-term development. Local governments need to be better managed and organized to improve the protection and conservation of varying environmental habitats, maintain urban ecological balance, and protect urban areas from natural disasters and environmental pollution and industrial accidents.
- Feasible plans, programs, or projects that will continue to fund improved capacity and socioeconomic conditions in local municipalities are to be made. Economic and technological resources should be used to create the driving forces for urban development based on city size. Economic development should be structured based on the natural and socioeconomic advantages of the urban region concerned.

The strategy also provides for minimizing the use of agricultural land for urban purposes, especially land for cultivating rice, by maximizing the use of vacant or underutilized urban land, and encouraging the use of hilly land. It is intended that all urban development must include the simultaneous provision of complementary social facilities and physical infrastructure.

Urbanization Development Issues

Population Growth and Urbanization

Table 14.3 shows national and urban population statistics, together with estimates of annual percentage growth rates for 5-year intervals since 1951. Urban population growth rates have varied significantly over this period. During the Viet Nam War, urban centers—particularly those in the south—grew as rural populations fled to the relative safety of cities. By the late 1980s, with declining economic conditions, urbanization rates fell dramatically to less than 1% in 1989. By the mid-1990s, the impact of the doi moi economic reforms led to a rapid influx of direct foreign investment—especially into new manufacturing industries located in large industrial estates on the outskirts of the country's two major cities. This led to a second wave of urbanization, which has continued to rise, except for a small fall following the Asian financial crisis.

Table 14.3: Population Growth and Urbanization in Viet Nam, 1951–2005

Year	National Population ('000)	Annual Growth Rate (%)	Urban Population ('000)	Annual Urban Population Growth Rate (%)	Urban Population (% of Total Population)
1951	23,061	0.5	2,306	1.5	10.0
1955	25,074	2.1	2,748	4.4	11.0
1960	30,172	3.7	4,527	10.0	15.0
1965	34,929	2.9	6,008	5.7	17.0
1970	41,063	3.2	8,517	7.0	20.7
1975	47,638	2.8	10,242	3.7	21.5
1980	53,722	1.8	10,301	2.0	19.2
1985	59,872	2.1	11,360	2.3	19.0
1989	64,376	1.0	12,740	0.6	19.8
1999	76,325	1.9	18,000	4.1	24.0
2004	82,100	1.5	21,000	3.3	25.8
2005	83,590	1.8	22,340	6.4	27.0

Sources: Viet Nam Annual Statistical Directory and World Bank 2005b (for 2005).

Urbanization rates of more than 5%/year have significant implications for the country. The 2005 urban population was 22.3 million (27.0%) and is predicted to reach 26.2 million (29.4%) by 2010 and 35.8 million (36.0%) by 2020. By 2030, the population of Viet Nam's cities is expected to reach 47 million, or more than double their current size (Figure 14.1). By then, almost 50.0% of Viet Nam's population is expected to live in urban centers.

Land under urban development is expected to reach 2,430 km^2 (0.74% of Viet Nam's total land area) with 80 m^2 per capita by 2010. This is projected to increase to 4,600 km^2 or 1.4% of Viet Nam's total land area, with an average of 100 m^2 per capita by 2020. The population of urban centers is growing at 1.15 million a year, with almost 100 km^2 of mainly rural farmland being converted into urban use annually (Tran 2004). By 2030, the absolute growth of urban populations can be expected to rise to over 1.7 million a year, with an expected conversion of land into urban purposes increasing to 170–200 km^2 a year as densities in newly developed urban areas fall in line with the trends in other Asian countries.

Rapid urbanization poses a major threat to the loss of land for food production in Viet Nam. The conversion of agricultural land for

Figure 14.1: Trends in Urban and Rural Population, Viet Nam

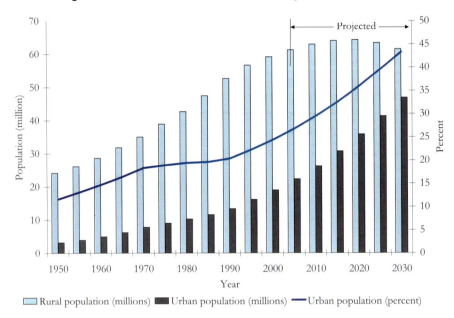

Rural population (millions) ■ Urban population (millions) — Urban population (percent)

Source: DESA-UN. 2005.

residential and industrial purposes is also having a major impact on the natural environment and rural landscape. Land clearance and industrial development are evident on the outskirts of large cities, along major trunk roads, and in provincial towns. According to a report by the Ministry of Natural Resources and Environment (MONRE 2005), there are 192 major industrial zones and clusters in 13 provinces, which resulted in 292.14 km^2 of land being converted into urban use since 1990, of which 84% was previously used for agriculture. (Land Tenure, Administration, and Management)

Although the state officially owns land, the management of land tenure and administration is inefficient. Improvements are being made to accelerate the issue of leases for development. Most land transactions in urban areas take place informally and are based on records of ownership established in the French colonial era. Many areas on the periphery of cities are developed for residential purposes without approval, often with the knowledge of public officials.

The uncertainty in land tenure and administration creates uncertainty in land markets, which leads to high levels of speculation, differential land prices—especially between land with development approval and land sold informally—and an unwillingness among residents in slum areas to invest in improvements to their dwellings and local infrastructure. The Government has undertaken reforms to the land management and administration systems, but not to the same extent as in the Lao People's Democratic Republic (Lao PDR) and Cambodia.

Urban Infrastructure

Urban infrastructure in all Vietnamese cities is inadequate and generally well below the standard of more industrialized and developed countries. The development of social infrastructure in residential areas is also inadequate and, in many cases, poorly planned. The spontaneous way in which infrastructure is provided results in leapfrogging of development, with new residential and peri-urban areas often waiting many years for physical and social infrastructure to be provided.

The general status of infrastructure in urban areas can be described as follows:

- Transportation networks and services in urban and suburban areas are still poorly developed. The failure to plan and protect road reserves impedes the connection, efficiency, and convenience of movement between urban and rural areas, as well as access to recreation and entertainment activities. In big cities, public transport provides a very small proportion of passenger trips, with high motorcycle ownership levels contributing to traffic congestion. Land area dedicated to transportation use is very small, especially parking spaces, which accounts for less than 5% of the total. Improvement to the arterial road networks is expensive; housing and commercial developments have not been set back from the road and are instead built up to the edge of road reserves. Improvements to roads can involve substantial demolition with high levels of compensation demanded. This is despite most dwellings being constructed without a building permit.
- More than 93% of urban areas have access to potable water (World Bank 2005b). However, the reliability of water supply remains a problem, with most cities having reached capacity limits on distribution and in need of major augmentation to supply sources. Poor rural catchment management has led to the contamination of urban water supply sources. The often sporadic and uncontrolled nature of urban development has made the improvement of water supply for domestic and industrial use difficult. System loss of water is high, due to the aging infrastructure and poor quality construction and supervision of

new infrastructure. Theft of water remains a problem, especially in larger cities.
- More than 84% of urban populations have access to basic sanitation services; however, this falls to less than 50% in poor districts of major cities (World Bank 2005b). Only 41% of urban areas have reticulated sewerage. The sewerage system relies heavily on local systems, which cause waterlogging and environmental pollution of local wells. The high density of development and the incremental additions to dwellings make the planning of sanitation services difficult, often leading to an overload of sanitation systems.
- Electricity supply is much improved although provision is still unstable. Consumption is low at only 107 kilowatt hours (kWh) per capita (MoC 1999). As incomes rise, there has been a growing trend toward air conditioning in modern dwellings, which adds to the demand for electricity. The Government is taking steps to improve the supply of electricity; however, the lack of planning and protection of infrastructure corridors from encroachment by housing and other forms of development creates significant problems for authorities responsible for improving the quality of electricity supply in inner urban areas. Many inner city areas rely on overhead cable supply that is old and often in a dangerous condition, which can lead to localized blackouts.

Urban planning and management generally lag behind the development process. Under pressure to meet the demand for urban infrastructure services, quantity is often forgone at the expense of quick provision of services with little or no consideration given to future changes in demand. The institutional structures and method of delivery and management of services are still largely unreformed. The lack of an efficient land administration system and measures to manage land, housing, and construction activities, combined with the lack of integration between government agencies and different localities, undermines the capacity of many cities to adopt more sustainable approaches to urban development.

Residential Development

Viet Nam has one of the highest urban residential housing and population densities in Asia. Historically, the pattern of development was determined by the property tax system, which was levied on the width of street frontage and the desire by landowners to maximize yields from land development. The pattern of urban development outside the more formally and mainly colonial planned areas of cities is one of very narrow streets, with plot frontages ranging from

2.5 meters (m) to 5 m, many less than 35 m^2 in area and ranging from two to five storeys in height. The total area of housing stock in urban areas is estimated at 80 million m^2. This corresponds to 5.8 m^2 per capita (MoC 1999).

The lack of planning, failure of developers to fully service new residential areas, and ineffective control over building construction have led to uncertainty in land markets and high levels of speculation. The slum population in urban areas in 2001 was 9.2 million, accounting for 47% of urban population (World Bank 2005b). With little provision given to public open space and the needs of modern transport access, conditions in many Vietnamese cities and towns are overcrowded and congested. Improving the conditions of many inner city areas has been a major challenge, particularly for road, housing, and waterway systems.

Urban Governance and Policies

The weakness and unwillingness of local governments in Viet Nam to take control of urban development has led to much indecision on how to address serious urban development problems. There have been tensions in central and local governments about:

- conservative versus more innovative approaches to addressing urban problems;
- upgrading versus redevelopment and new building involving clearance;
- benefits of urban development to society, community, and the private sector, and the extent to which developers should contribute to the provision of community infrastructure and services;
- demand for urban services and financial capacity and willingness of governments, business, and communities to pay for these;
- urban development and protection of agricultural land; and
- urban development and environmental protection.

Most local governments have a poor understanding of the nature and causes of urbanization. Some municipalities understand urbanization simply as a process of migration to towns resulting from overcrowding in the countryside. Few appreciate that urbanization is being driven by major structural changes in the economy and by powerful forces resulting from globalization and foreign direct investment. Many local governments lack the necessary skills to develop appropriate policies responsive to the development of a market economy. There are still strong ideological differences in national and local governments over the extent to which the state should control development or hand over greater responsibility for urban development to the private sector.

Urban Environmental Management

The increasing industrialization of Vietnamese cities has led to increased environmental management problems. The levels of air and water pollution in all cities continue to increase as do problems with urban sanitation and waste management. Industrial pollution is causing damage to waterways and estuaries. In many low-lying cities in the Red River and Mekong River deltas, canals have become heavily polluted by urban wastes. The pace of urbanization has proved overwhelming for local governments, leaving most unable or unwilling to enforce environmental controls and provisions to ensure proper treatment of wastes and emissions.

Motorcycles have become the dominant form of transport in cities. Motorcycle ownership rates in Viet Nam are the highest in Asia: one motorcycle per five urban inhabitants. The rise in this form of transport has led to an overall increase in traffic congestion and vehicle emissions.

The Role of International Aid in Supporting Regional Development

Viet Nam is a significant recipient of official development assistance (ODA) involving grants loans and other forms of credit from international development banks. In 2003, the money received from international aid (net ODA) was $1,768.6 million, or $21.8 per capita. Aid as a share of country income (net ODA/gross national income) was 4.5% (World Bank 2005b). ODA is used for technical assistance, especially for urban development and decentralization programs and budget support. ODA is channeled from the central Government to programs at the provincial, district, and ward levels. The primary ODA agencies are the World Bank and ADB, and bilateral agencies, such as the Australian Agency for International Development, Canadian International Development Agency, Danish International Development Assistance, Finnish International Development Agency, Swedish International Development Cooperation Agency, Korean International Development Agency, and Japan International Cooperation Agency.

ODA committed for 2006 is $3,747.9 million. This assistance will be mainly used for fulfilling the basic reform of state enterprises and alleviating poverty. The biggest bilateral donors are Japan ($835.6 million), France ($397.7 million), PRC ($200 million), Germany ($114.7 million), and Republic of Korea ($105 million). ADB is committed to support Viet Nam to the sum of $539 million, while the World Bank and United Nations Development Programme (UNDP) have committed $750 million and $69.1 million in aid, respectively (Hong Phuc 2005).

Since 1993, the World Bank has committed $5 billion to support more than 40 development projects to help the Government reduce poverty by providing technical expertise and financing for agriculture, infrastructure, health programs, schools, and other essential needs. The projects have been conducted both for the rural and urban poor (World Bank 2005a). In World Bank projects, Viet Nam authorities manage the implementation, which requires cooperation of different groups, including communities and civil societies. The criteria of the World Bank, including social and environmental standards, must be met.

Assistance from ADB is utilized mainly for promoting pro-poor economic growth, inclusive social development, and good governance. ADB guidance is concentrated largely into private sector development, regional cooperation, and environmental sustainability, especially in the Central Region, where the incidence of poverty remains high. ADB has also helped Viet Nam modernize and expand its economic infrastructure as well as provided support in the field of industrial and technical standards, and small- and medium-sized enterprise development. Cumulative ADB lending to Viet Nam, as of end of 2004, was about $3.2 billion in agriculture and natural resources, transport and communications, energy, finance, water supply, sanitation, waste management, education, law, economic management, public policy, health, nutrition, social protection, industry, and nonfuel minerals (ADB 2005).

GOOD PRACTICE CASE STUDIES

Three case studies of good practices in sustainable urban development are presented: institutional building in urban upgrading in Phu Thuong ward, Hanoi; environmental improvement of Nhieu Loc—Thi Nghe Basin, Ho Chi Minh City; and urban upgrading in Van Mieu Ward, Nam Dinh City, Nam Dinh Province. The first two cases are located in the country's two largest cultural and socioeconomic centers. These projects used innovative approaches in solving urban development problems and resulted in sustainable development. The third case study—similar to the first but carried out in a second-category city—demonstrates the value of engaging communities in the design and implementation of a program involving local area urban improvement. Figure 14.2 shows the location of the case studies.

The three case studies emphasize the importance of good governance, urban management, better infrastructure, and service provision, and programs designed to ensure social and environmental sustainability. They illustrate the importance of learning from trial and error in working toward the development of good practices in Viet Nam.

Figure 14.2: Map Showing Location of the Case Studies

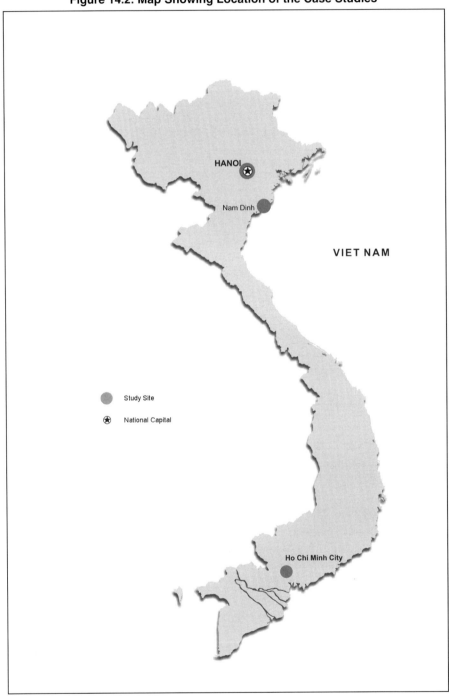

Institutional Building in Urban Upgrading in Phu Thuong Ward, Hanoi

Background

This case study on Phu Thuong Ward, Hanoi investigates the improvement of governance and institutional capacity building in urban upgrading in an area undergoing transition from rural to urban development. The area was the subject of a pilot study of a UNDP project on Strengthening the Capacity of Urban Planning and Development in

GOOD PRACTICE	
Good Governance	✓
Urban Management	✓
Infrastructure/Service Provision	✓
Financing and Cost Recovery	
Sustainability	✓
Innovation and Change	
Leveraging ODA	✓

Hanoi. The study commenced in 1997 and was completed in 2000; results of the study helped improve the situation of the ward markedly.

Phu Thuong is a traditional village famous for growing flowers and other ornamental plants, especially for the Lunar New Year, which is the biggest traditional festival in Viet Nam. Phu Thuong Ward is located in Tay Ho District, at the northern end of a series of "flower villages," 9 km northwest of Hanoi City center between National Highway No. 23 and the south bank of the Red River. Hanoi's famous West Lake is located on the northwestern edge of the ward.

Phu Thuong has experienced spontaneous residential urbanization on the fringes of the city. The ward became classified as an urban ward on 1 January 1996, although three quarters of the households were engaged in agriculture and related activities. The ward covers an area of 609.5 hectares (ha). The encroachment of urbanization has raised debate about the loss of valuable land devoted to rice farming, an industry with a traditional identity.

In September 1998, the population of Phu Thuong was about 10,200 living in 2,238 households. The ward was recently divided into nine residential clusters, each composed of 265–300 households. By 2003, the population of Phu Thuong had increased to 12,480 living in 2,740 households, an average growth rate of 1.8%/year (Phu Thuong 2004).

Before 1998, the residents living in the ward had no running water; 88% of the households used wells while the remainder relied on other sources of water. Water from well sources did not meet basic health standards. An estimated 67% of wastewater was discharged untreated directly into ponds, lakes, or gardens (VIE/95/050 1998). In addition, storm water and drainage were combined with sewerage and irrigation systems in the ward. Waste removal vehicles collected 54% of waste, with 23% disposed of in local dumps in the ward and the remaining 23% disposed of in residents' yards. The lack of an adequate sewerage system led to human waste being used to fertilize flower gardens and rice fields. Such waste management practices were beginning to seriously exacerbate water pollution in local ponds, lakes, and gardens (VIE/95/050 1998) and affect the health of residents.

Air pollution increased from using poor-quality coal for cooking and heating, and from vehicle emissions. Lack of development control led to some roads and lanes being constructed at widths of 1.5–2 meters, leaving little room for emergency vehicles and air circulation. The need to reduce emissions from motorcycles and newly emerging industrial enterprises has been identified but not yet addressed.

Prior to 1998, Phu Thuong had few buildings and faculties for cultural, sport, or recreation activities. There was only one kindergarten, one primary school, one secondary school, and a technical college for more than 4,000 children. With the exception of the secondary school, most structures were temporary one-storey buildings on small land areas (VIE/95/050 1998). Health facilities were also lacking—only one clinic with a small staff (one doctor, three nurses, and another clinic staff) to service 10,000 residents. The ward had 2,830 houses, of which 86% were temporary single-storey dwellings, 12% were two-storey, 1.3% were three-storey, and only one four-storey and one five-storey house, respectively (0.70%).

The labor force in the agriculture sector of the ward numbered approximately 1,600 persons, with the remainder employed in the other sectors, such as business and a mix of business and agriculture (HAU 1998). The economic structure of Phu Thuong Ward has changed largely because cultivated land has been lost due to new housing construction. In the near future, all land formerly used for rice cultivation is anticipated to be used for flower growing. As the household economy in the ward changes significantly, there has been an increasing shift toward developing microenterprises. In recent years, small-scale services (including packaging enterprises, food processing for markets, tailors, hair salons, electrical repairers, and small stores) have developed rapidly (Phu Thuong 2004). In 2004, monthly income of households averaged Viet Nam dong (D)250,000–350,000 (about $25–35).

Many problems are associated with land and housing management, construction, and tenure, including the inflexible and complicated nature of administrative procedures related to development. The ward has not been able to monitor and control construction activities effectively due to weaknesses in the capabilities of local government administration and unwillingness of public officials to enforce laws related to development.

Capacity-building Project

The Strengthening the Capacity of Urban Planning and Development pilot project (VIE/95/050 1998) provided the basis for supporting the upgrade of Phu Thuong Ward and improving institutional capacity and management of service delivery. UNDP provided technical assistance as well as financial support to the ward and the city. The project organized seminars and training activities, conducted surveys, and provided proposals for the ward, which were supported by the city government and other bodies. A number of elements for the project needed to be put in place to ensure the longer-term continuity of the settlement improvement process. These included building physical assets, restoring natural assets, building on human capital, building social capital, building economic assets, and reforming governance institutions.

Physical assets include infrastructure and services for water and sanitation, garbage removal, storm water drainage, electricity, health and education projects, and community and recreation facilities.

Sustainable Impacts of the Project

Infrastructure and Environmental Improvements. After the upgrading (1998–2004), the infrastructure in the ward improved significantly. Most residents of Phu Thuong now have access to reticulated drinking water and electricity, while 85% of sewage is now discharged into the ward's sewerage system, which has been linked to the city urban sewerage system. Domestic waste and farm water no longer run over the roads and are not allowed to pool, thereby reducing the odorous and unhygienic conditions that once prevailed in the area. In 2003, the storm water drainage system was upgraded. However, old systems are still in use.

Since 2003, 81% of garbage generated by households, public buildings, and industrial enterprises is regularly collected and transferred to the city disposal sites. Following the upgrading of the solid waste management system and the widening of roads, waste collection trucks can reach each household. The transportation system has been significantly improved with support of the Government and contributions from citizens. Most roads have been surfaced with asphalt and connect reasonably well to the central and southern areas of the city. A bus route to Phu Thuong from the city center has also been established.

Housing construction is based on planning approval, and households are encouraged to fulfill necessary procedures before building. By 2002, the housing stock had been significantly improved. Single-storey houses had decreased to only 30%; two- and three-storey houses had increased to

65%, and higher than four-storey houses accounted for 5% of all dwellings. Playgrounds for children and cultural facilities were constructed. Religious buildings were upgraded. Since 2002, Phu Thuong has achieved improved education results, with nearly 99% of children in the ward currently attending schools. Besides the Government's investment, educational dissemination has mobilized capital resources from residents and social organizations; at present, all ward schools are regarded as high-quality schools (HAU 2004).

Environmental Management and Public Health. In 2002, both the Hanoi and ward people's committees (WPCs) developed and implemented an improved health care program for the prevention of diseases, as well as for providing information on food safety and advice on reducing the threat of HIV/AIDS. Programs to prevent malnutrition for 764 children under 5 years of age were initiated, resulting in a reduction of malnourishment (by 2%) since 2001. During upgrading, the WPCs encouraged residents to build toilets using appropriate techniques. At present, the proportion of households using waterborne toilets has increased to 72% while the number with latrines has decreased to 20%; only 8% use temporary latrines (Do 2005).

The 1993 Environmental Protection Law provides for the protection of the environment and charges local governments and residents with the responsibility for improving environmental management. WPCs play an important role in raising community awareness about environmental protection. Every Saturday, all residents participate in cleaning the ward. In addition, residents contribute funds to help improve the quality of lanes and the storm water drainage system. The ward authority has organized numerous environment protection training courses with the help of the city and district authorities and social organizations. By 2003, the majority of households used gas and electricity to meet their energy needs while the proportion using leaves and straw decreased to 20%. Pollution caused by industrial production is not seen as a problem as there are no major industrial enterprises in the ward (Phu Thuong 2004).

Human Capital Development. Building human and social capital has been an integral part of the upgrading of Phu Thuong Ward. Human capital development is closely linked to economic and social infrastructure provision. Upgrading has involved improvement in educational and health care facilities, and strengthening internal social organizations within the ward. Importantly, particular attention has been paid to the needs of the poorest households in the ward. The WPC has cooperated with many agencies and associations in its drive to control the population growth rate using advanced methods. It has taken an active interest in family planning and, consequently, the natural population growth rate has remained relatively stable at about 1.6–1.7%. The ward has also established a Board of Poverty Reduction and

Alleviation, collaborating with many other agencies to create opportunities to borrow capital. Moreover, to prepare laborers to work on the contiguous Ciputra residential development—a new housing and office development plan that will house 50,000 residents when it is completed in 2010—the ward has organized technical training courses for workers.

The ward has also collaborated with the Fatherland Front and other organizations to deal with residential complaints and provide households with information related to economic, social, cultural, and security matters. The residents receive all available information because it is announced publicly.

Governance. In Viet Nam, the ward is the smallest local authority governance system within the organizational structure of the Communist Party, people's committees, people's councils, and other groups, such as trade unions, youth unions, women's unions, and veterans unions. Since 2003, the Phu Thuong Ward People's Committee has been streamlined and is composed of 15 people. The chairperson is responsible for all activities of the WPC and is directly responsible for personnel, socioeconomic development strategy, finance planning, land use, and urban development. The vice-chair, as well as being the head of the finance board, is responsible for cultural and social issues.

After upgrading, the tasks of all members were clearly defined. Technical assistance from the donor and the guidelines of the city government and district authorities have enabled the ward to strengthen its capacity to mobilize participation, partnerships, and involvement in planning, monitoring, and evaluation of all residents, groups, and organizations in the community.

Economic Development. The pressure on land for urban development in Phu Thuong is bringing about a structural change in the ward's economy. By 2003, the area of cultivated land in the ward was 80 ha, of which 65 ha were used for flower growing and 15 ha for rice cultivation. Rice farming activities are slowly declining and will eventually disappear while flower growing has become more specialized. Phu Thuong no longer just produces flowers—it has also established a small-sized flower industry cluster with a range of value-adding industries that serve markets beyond Hanoi. Flower- and ornamental tree-growing techniques have been improved, leading to better quality and increased quantity. Income from flowers is high, amounting to $600,000 per year. Consequently, the number of poor households in the ward decreased significantly—from 180 poor households in 1996 to 20 in 2003 (Phu Thuong 2004).

Housing is an important asset as it can be used to generate rental income as well as providing opportunities for home-based enterprises (Moser 1998; Gilbert 2000 in Do 2005). Many Phu Thuong households rent out their housing space to students or laborers from other regions. Land management is also very important in Phu Thuong because tenure security can enable private investments in housing.

Phu Thuong has become a high-density urban area of Hanoi and its economic structure has changed dramatically. Urban upgrading, institutional and human capacity building, and improved local governance have enabled the ward to improve its economic situation, become more specialized, and be responsive to change. However, to provide the basis for a sustainable economy in the future, the ward has to focus much harder on encouraging business to use local labor and to encourage households to develop private business services. In addition, the ward needs to provide better information on markets and new technology, and learn from the experience of other regions especially in terms of flower marketing and establishing small business enterprises and cooperatives.

Environmental Improvement of Nhieu Loc-Thi Nghe Basin, Ho Chi Minh City

Background

This case study presents Viet Nam's largest urban environmental improvement project, covering the Nhieu Loc-Thi Nghe Basin canal of Ho Chi Minh City (HCMC). The project, which commenced in 2000, is co-funded by the World Bank and Ho Chi Minh People's Committee. The program has involved upgrading the urban environment along the Nhieu Loc-Thi Nghe Basin canal, separating sewerage and storm-water drainage, reducing the impact of flooding, promoting economic development, and improving the efficiency of public institutions involved in the management of infrastructure systems in the basin.

Nhieu Loc-Thi Nghe Basin is one of five drainage catchments in the urban area of HCMC. The Nhieu Loc-Thi Nghe Basin covers an area of 33 km^2, and incorporates the center of HCMC and seven districts partially or totally, and parts of the districts of Phu Nhuan, Tan Binh, Binh Thanh, and Go Vap. The population in the Nhieu Loc-Thi Nghe Basin is approximately 1.2 million people, or about 14% of the city's population (World Bank 2001a). A significant proportion is poor.

The Nhieu Loc-Thi Nghe canal, which runs the length of the basin, is a combined sewerage/drainage system. It is the main drain and collector for untreated wastewater into which some 280 km of the city's sewers discharge. The canal poses a serious threat to public health (World Bank 2001a) with biochemical oxygen demand of 150–200 milligrams per liter, fecal coliforms measuring about 8,000 units per milliliter, and dissolved oxygen almost zero (CDM 2000a). Only 73% of people living in the basin have piped water connections and only 64% have in-house toilets. Housing densities in the basin are 12,600–55,000 persons/km^2 (World Bank 2001a), creating conditions of excessive overcrowding.

Extensive flooding occurs along the canal during the monsoon season, with raw sewage overflowing into the public areas, roads and sidewalks, and the ground floor of homes and other structures within the basin. The capacity of the Nhieu Loc-Thi Nghe Canal has diminished over the years because of deposits of sewage sludge, solid waste, debris, and sediments from soil erosion in the basin. The drainage system is old and has insufficient capacity to serve the currently developed urban area.

Project Activities

Concerns were expressed about the problems associated with the Nhieu Loc-Thi Nghe Canal in 1985, when the first attempts were made by the local government (HCMC People's Committee) to clear and improve a 100 m section in the central area of the city. Work stopped because of difficulties in persuading inhabitants to move. In 1991, the HCMC People's Committee began formulating a program to relocate residents, build housing, and improve the canal. At first, lack of funds prevented work from being done. In 1995, the HCMC People's Committee embarked on a program to sell public houses to raise $40 million to ensure sufficient starting capital to commence the project. The first phase started in 1996, with 500 m of canal improvement and 1,000 houses constructed for relocated residents.

After the success of the first phase, the World Bank agreed to support a second phase with a $166 million loan, supplemented by $34 million from the Government. The second phase was intended to extend and improve on the approaches used during the first stage of the project. Many lessons were learned during the first phase in relation to design, funding, project management, consultation, and compensation claims. Some of these will be discussed later.

The second phase of the project was essentially designed as a wastewater environmental engineering and housing resettlement project (World Bank 2001a). The design of the wastewater component entailed intensive efforts to minimize project impacts. Scheduled for completion in 2009, this phase aims to reduce flooding, improve the quality of the environment, improve public health and well-being, promote economic development, and strengthen the institutional capacity of the urban drainage company to manage the costs for wastewater services.

The three components of this phase are wastewater, drainage, and technical assistance. Works related to wastewater include the construction of

8.4 km wastewater interceptors, combined storm overflow and canal flushing chambers, outfall to the Saigon River, and wastewater pumping stations (World Bank 2001b). Works related to drainage include the replacement and extension of 72 km of combined primary and secondary sewers and storm-water drains; dredging sludge and related strengthening of 18 km of canal embankments; field investigation, design, and rehabilitation of 54 km of pre-1954 secondary combined sewers; and the extension of about 270 km of tertiary sewers (with less than 0.40 m diameter) to connect 30% of the basin's mainly low-income houses that are not currently linked to the system (World Bank 2001a). Technical assistance involved consultants contracted for detailed design, construction, management, and institutional strengthening.

Phase two has three stages: preconstruction, construction, and operation and maintenance. The preconstruction stage involved relocation and resettlement of an estimated 40,000 people (Wust et al. 2002). Preliminary calculations indicated the clearing of 11,400 houses, with new apartments for 8,000 households at a cost of $51 million.

Efforts to minimize noise and dust levels, which affected residents during the land clearing and construction stage, were also made. Moreover, the bid specifications restricted working hours and methods that could be employed. Up to 1.1 million m^3 of material arising from canal dredging and excavation activities required disposal; however, the use of the material in landfills is clearly beneficial to the environment.

At the operation and maintenance stage, trash racks will be incorporated in the combined sewer network to prevent waste from blocking the system and polluting the canal. When completed, most works will be located underground. Strengthening the maintenance arrangements, including the introduction of management contracting of facilities, is the most important measure.

Sustainable Impacts of the Project

The first phase and completed sections of the second phase of the project have resulted in significant improvements in the quality of the waterway system in HCMC. A research project conducted by the head of the Department of Science and Cooperation Management of the HCMC Institute for Economic Research, Du Phuoc Tan, showed that most households (87% of those surveyed) believed their living environment was far better than in their previous residences (Vietnamese Style 2005). While some residents expressed discontent over issues related to compensation and the quality of housing provided, this has been a small price to pay for achievements gained.

There had been extensive public involvement and consultation to engender improved public understanding of the project and its potential benefits. The consultations, together with a survey questionnaire designed for households affected by the project, provided important inputs into the project objectives, design, and implementation features of resettlement, compensation programs, and rehabilitation measures. The regular flooding that occurs in Nhieu Loc-Thi Nghe Canal and the noxious condition of the canal have given the project a high public profile and elicited regular calls by the media for government action to address these issues. Consequently, there is very strong public support for the project.

A Resettlement and Compensation Policy, which will apply to the entire project, and a detailed Resettlement Action Plan for the wastewater component have been prepared. The Resettlement Action Plan policy details resettlement principles and an eligibility/entitlements framework. The policy applies to both the wastewater and drainage components. According to the policy, all people likely to be affected are eligible for compensation, which varies according to the type of loss. Modes of compensation include cash, "land for land," or "apartment for land/house," or a combination of the above (CDM 2000b).

Specific task forces established by the city have received operative support in the field by the WPC, which coordinated information/consultation meetings and provided assistance during the implementation of the Resettlement Action Plan. The project management unit is responsible for internal monitoring. The project is also monitored by an external monitoring agency, the HCMC Institute of Social Sciences. The WPC first deals with any complaints or grievances regarding compensation, relocation, or unaccounted losses. If no amicable solution can be reached, project-affected families may appeal to the District Resettlement Committee, the project steering committee, or the City Court.

International development agencies and the World Bank are financing 90% of the wastewater and drainage components of the second phase, with the exception of tertiary sewers, which will be jointly financed by the city government (80%) and the district authorities and beneficiaries (20%). In the case of poor families, the entire 20% will be borne by the district authority. As part of the feasibility studies, 1,000 beneficiary households throughout the project area were surveyed to determine their socioeconomic characteristics, priorities among a range of infrastructure improvements, and willingness to pay for different improvements (World Bank 2001a).

The project will contribute to poverty reduction. Public health and environmental conditions along the canal have improved significantly.

Relocated residents from the canal banks have been compensated and provided with new apartment accommodation or accommodation elsewhere. Not all residents are satisfied; some have reportedly sold the accommodation provided in order to move to more traditional housing. There have been attempts to develop microenterprises, which are contributing to the growth of employment and raising income levels. The canals have also provided welcome open space to poorer communities and are being used for recreational activities.

The HCMC People's Committee has benefited from the project by strengthening the capacity of the organization's staff to design, construct, and maintain water and wastewater management systems. Prior to project implementation, the magnitude of the problems simply overwhelmed the ability of government to deal with them. The project will also assist in developing more efficient institutions to sustainably manage drainage and wastewater services. There is still room to further enhance capacity building and institutional learning so that the Urban Drainage Company is fully able to address the many urban wastewater management problems facing the city. However, in the interim, the establishment of the Urban Drainage Company has strengthened the capacity and capability in HCMC to pursue future programs and to provide assistance to other local governments in Viet Nam facing similar environmental wastewater problems.

The second phase of the Nhieu Loc-Thi Nghe Canal project is already bringing major improvements to the urban areas in HCMC. By reducing flooding and improving water quality in the canal, the project will bring general benefits to the city's economy as a whole, and private benefits to individual households. In particular, it will improve the health of women and children, who have the greatest exposure to unsanitary conditions. The community has benefited through reduced odors and waste management costs, greater access to public open space, better services, and increased property values.

The Nhieu Loc-Thi Nghe Canal project has been an important learning experience for the Government and community of HCMC in the art of creating and implementing a project to improve the quality of the urban environment with a sustainable development outcome. While many benefits have been derived from the project, these have had social, financial, and administrative costs. Not everyone—especially the very poor—had benefited from the project. Weaknesses in governance, urban and project management, land administration, and handling of compensation have delayed and added to the costs and complaints about the implementation of the project. These must be accepted as part of the learning process for what is Viet Nam's largest urban environmental improvement project. Learning to plan, construct, and manage projects of this size has been a real challenge to the institutional capacity of the Government.

Urban Upgrading, Environmental Impact Assessment in Van Mieu Ward, Nam Dinh City, Nam Dinh Province

Background

This case study examines an urban upgrading project in Van Mieu Ward, Nam Dinh City, Nam Dinh Province, about 100 km south of Hanoi. The Van Mieu Ward urban upgrading project was selected as one of four projects funded under the World Bank Urban Upgrading Project. The other three projects are located in HCMC, Can Tho, and Hai Phong. The projects selected all include urban areas with poor environmental conditions and high levels of poverty. The project was implemented in the third quarter of 2004 and is scheduled to be completed by the end of 2006. The objectives of the urban upgrading project are to:

GOOD PRACTICE	
Good Governance	✓
Urban Management	✓
Infrastructure/Service Provision	✓
Financing and Cost Recovery	
Sustainability	✓
Innovation and Change	
Leveraging ODA	

- improve basic tertiary infrastructure and other services in low-income areas through partnerships between communities and local governments, and through capacity building for participatory planning and management;
- provide and/or rehabilitate primary and secondary infrastructure networks to connect to the tertiary infrastructure in low-income areas;
- provide affordable housing and/or serviced plots to low-income families that have to be resettled as a result of upgrading; and
- provide technical assistance to improve land administration processes in the project cities (World Bank Project Document 2004).

Van Mieu Ward is located at the west-southern part of Nam Dinh City. It has an area of 37.7 ha, with a population of 12,186 in 2,797 households. The population density is more than 320 persons/ha, Each household has an average floor area of 29.8 m^2 (7.5 m^2/person). In recent years, the population of the ward has declined by about 1.2 %/year due to out-migration to Hanoi.

The economic development of Nam Dinh City has been very slow compared to that in other parts of Viet Nam. The city's economy lacks competitiveness and has been unable to attract investment in new economic enterprises.

The textile and garment industry has played a crucial role in the economy of Nam Dinh City and the ward; however, this industry lacks the infrastructure and business capabilities to compete with more modern industries located in the industrial estates around Hanoi. Other industries important to the economy are meat processing, seafood, fruits and drinks, and wood, along with the manufacturing of woolen carpets, jute fiber products, boat building, and handicrafts. In 2003, the estimated income of 78.5% of the population was less than $25/month (SW 2003).

The economic decline of Nam Dinh City has been exacerbated by the paucity of basic infrastructure, lack of maintenance, and poor condition of housing and the urban environment, especially in Van Mieu Ward. An estimated 23.8% of houses in the ward front onto a road no wider than 5 m, making emergency vehicle access difficult. The proximity of buildings to one another poses major fire, health, and security hazards. Only 30% of the structures are made of robust materials.

While most houses have access to potable water and electricity, the quality of supply is not good. In addition, sanitation conditions are basic, with only three public toilets servicing about 600 families in the ward. Flooding and surface water drainage creates a safety and health hazard for the area. Most inhabitants in the project area have solid waste collected by the Urban Environmental Company. However, the dirty streets pose serious environmental and health risks to the community.

Van Mieu Ward is typical of many residential districts in smaller towns and cities of Viet Nam. Few of the economic benefits seen in the national economy and larger cities have trickled down to regional towns struggling to come to grips with market reforms, reduced national government support for projects, and the responsibilities imposed on local governments under decentralization. These conditions provided a good opportunity for the World Bank to test and evaluate approaches toward urban environmental improvements in smaller regional towns and cities. The Van Mieu Ward project is a learning and innovation experience to show how to develop approaches that provide a model for achieving more sustainable urban development outcomes in smaller cities.

Upgrading Project

The urban upgrading project has been implemented at a decentralized level by city authorities in four cities of Viet Nam. Under the People's Committee of Nam Dinh Province, a multidisciplinary project management unit reports to the province-level project steering committee, which is composed of representatives of relevant departments and utility companies. The steering committee provides overall guidance, ensures consistency, and coordinates with other projects.

As with the three other projects, the Nam Dinh project has six components:

- tertiary infrastructure upgrading and service improvements,
- complementary primary and secondary infrastructure,
- resettlement housing,
- land and housing management,
- housing improvement loan program, and
- capacity building.

Together with the other projects, a seventh component will be financing the development of a national urban upgrading program, which the Ministry of Construction will manage.

The Nam Dinh project was implemented in two phases. Phase One covered the Van Mieu Ward. Objectives of the urban upgrading project in Van Mieu were to mobilize active participation of communities on financial contributions, project preparation, and implementation; minimize resettlement and land acquisition; coordinate synchronously the various sectors; and implement a project based on suitable technical standards.

Sustainable Impacts of the Project

Although only two thirds through the first phase, the project has had some positive impacts:

- *Roads*: Access to some houses has improved and traffic flows enhanced.
- *Street Lighting*: There is improved security and safety and a decrease in accidents due to better street lighting.
- *Water Supply*: Household connections and supply to the area are improving.
- *Sewerage and Drainage*: There has been reduced flooding and remarkably improved living conditions, hygiene, and overall health of the people.
- *Solid Waste Collection and Public Toilets*: Hygiene and environmental conditions are improving.
- *Social Works*: Overall improvement is being made to the social infrastructure in such institutions as schools.

Three alternative strategies were considered for Phase One. The first strategy was related to the master plan, the detailed area plan, and planning and engineering standards. For low-income residential areas, some standards required adjustment following site surveys and public opinion polls. The second strategy considered was minimizing resettlement and compensation effects by applying more functional standards. The third was a compromise of the two. Communities, local authorities, city departments, and provincial authorities agreed on this last alternative. The project's principle of incremental upgrading is being followed and appropriate technical standards that are affordable to the city and community are being applied.

The city was already familiar with community participation programs by virtue of an earlier Swiss-financed project. The city already had a community consultancy department and volunteers available in all wards. Capacity of all people in Van Mieu Ward had been built. Community groups had been formed, trained, and motivated to plan and comanage. These groups are aware of and understand urban environmental problems and their solutions. The design of tertiary infrastructure was developed using participatory methods that were agreed on by the communities in the ward. The communities agreed to pay D280,000 ($17.50) per household over a period of 3 years (World Bank 2004). The community also contributed to the maintenance of access roads and alleys as well as the branch sewers.

Urban authorities are more confident and capable of planning and managing appropriate solutions to urban environmental problems. Environmental assessments were carried out in consultation with affected communities and others, with the final reports made available to the public. In phase one, two types of environmental assessments were prepared, depending on the type of infrastructure interventions: for primary and secondary infrastructure and housing construction for resettled populations, environmental impact assessment reports, and environmental management plans; and for tertiary infrastructure, which emphasized a participatory approach to identifying environmental solutions at the community level, plans of community environmental management (World Bank 2004).

Professional planners considered and solved local environmental problems and local needs to make urban planning more appropriate and to improve methods of urban environmental planning and management at the project outset. In this regard, provincial and city planners are seen as being capable of analyzing local environmental planning needs. Appropriate cost-recovery mechanisms were also developed to ensure sustainability of urban services.

The environmental and planning issues of the ward have been studied and implemented through cooperation between all sectors and government bodies at all levels of the province as well as between the provincial authorities, the central Government, and international agencies.

Lessons Learned from the Case Studies

Many urban development practices in Viet Nam are not sustainable. The nation is struggling to meet the demand for new and improved urban infrastructure, housing, and transportation and to improve urban management by local and provincial governments. Environmental problems are proving increasingly challenging and expensive to address. However, despite these difficulties, there is growing awareness at all levels of government that urban development and management practices must change. It is hoped that the lessons gained from the three case studies can be replicated throughout the country.

The upgrading of Phu Thuong Ward case study in Hanoi has been an important learning experience for local government working with local communities on integrated planning for areas undergoing urbanization. The process of engaging the community in the planning, delivery, and ongoing maintenance of physical infrastructure and social services led to substantial improvements in the quality of life for most ward residents.

The importance of institutional capacity building has been critical in ensuring the longer-term continuity of the improvements made to the ward. Phu Thuong has been very effective in building relevant knowledge and skills among residents, strengthening community social organization and the knowledge and skills base, building a local economic base, and reforming governance institutions to ensure a supportive legal and regulatory context for the ongoing improvement of this residential area.

The case study of Nhieu Loc–Thi Nghe Basin Canal, HCMC, focused on a major urban environmental improvement program that is ongoing. The decision to sell public housing to raise capital to start the project was controversial, reversing strong socialist ideology; however, this decision enabled the local government to raise capital to undertake important environmental improvements that have had significant health and economic benefits, thereby promising greater sustainability.

That case study provides important opportunities for learning lessons on the need for good implementation arrangements at all levels of government, from national to local. The role of NGOs and special interest groups has added value to the project, with NGOs acting as an intermediate agent encouraging direct participation in the tertiary sewer component to promote better health and quality of life from the project.

This case study also illustrates the premise that to achieve sustainable development outcomes for cities facing serious environmental problems, bold initiatives and often difficult and expensive interventions—spearheaded by the Government—need to be undertaken. It further shows that a massive relocation of people may be necessary if the health of people and quality of urban environments are to be improved. However, in choosing to act, innovative ways must be found to minimize the negative impacts.

The Van Mieu Ward, Nam Dinh City case study shows that better mechanisms for coordination between various stakeholders are a prerequisite for effective project implementation. The project demonstrates the advantages of improved cooperation with other projects involved in implementing ventures in the same area, avoiding the overlap that occurs between agencies with so many projects and, hopefully, optimizing the effectiveness of physical infrastructure in the city.

This case study points to the advantages of engaging communities in constructing social infrastructure. The project design minimized the need for resettlement. The lowest-cost options for upgrading infrastructure should be sought to allow greater coverage with limited resources. Land use and the impact of existing activities in the surrounding areas have to be properly considered in the project design. Environmental matters have to be integrated in all steps of the project.

Construction standards, regulations, and instructions concerning dimensions have to be followed and adjusted to suit the local circumstances. Subsequent operation and maintenance arrangements for upgraded infrastructure by the responsible agencies also need attention. In this case, experienced civil works contractors and supervision consultants with local knowledge were engaged to ensure a high-quality construction.

Project ownership by the beneficiary community is an essential prerequisite that can only be achieved through effective community empowerment—politically, economically, and socially. Schemes based on community participation take time and the timing of community participation in decision making is critical for effectiveness. Community participation is a key factor in urban upgrading projects.

STRATEGIES TO ENHANCE SUSTAINABLE URBAN DEVELOPMENT

The basic principles outlined in the Urban Development Strategy (MoC 1999) provide a basis for Viet Nam to move toward a more sustainable urban system. There are many problems in implementation of the strategy. However, it has had an important impact by raising the consciousness of politicians and government officials of the need to pay greater attention to managing urbanization in the future if Viet Nam is to avoid many of the problems facing the more urbanized nations of Asia.

Strategies to achieve more sustainable urban development in Viet Nam must be realistic and achievable within manageable time frames. Viet Nam is a poor country, and the standards and targets applied in more advanced countries of Asia are not achievable, given the state of the nation's development. The following strategies to improve the sustainability of urban development are suggested.

Housing and Land Management

Land Tenure. To ensure more efficient management and operation of land and property markets, policies are needed for the reform of the land administration and management system, along the lines taking place in the Lao PDR and Cambodia. Improvements in terms of land registration and the length of tenure are needed. There is also the need to develop financial markets that enable land to be used as collateral for private individuals and business to raise capital for investments to support development and improved living environments.

Housing. Policies that improve the recognition and protection of property rights and provide a more stable basis of tenure are needed. The establishment of a mortgage market for residential property in Viet Nam is also needed. Policies and standards for housing construction should aim to achieve a minimum of 18–20 m^2 per capita in 2020 to reduce overcrowding and improve livability in urban areas.

Urban Infrastructure and Utility Services

Transportation. More land needs to be set aside in new and redevelopment projects to increase the capacity of the road and river transportation networks and parking spaces. Total land use allocated for transport purposes in larger cities should be increased to 20–30%. For large cities, urban public transport using bus and rail systems should be developed and integrated at ground, underground, and elevated levels. Also, greater use of water transport should be made. Policies should be introduced at the national and local government levels to reduce private motorcycle and car usage in favor of public transport systems meeting 30–50% of travel demand.

Water Supply. National targets and support programs are needed to achieve 90% supply of running water to the urban populations by 2010 and 100% by 2020 (based on a target of 180 liters per capita in 2020). Measures to ensure sustainable use of water in dwellings, commercial premises, and factories should be introduced to ensure more efficient use and recycling of water. Developers should be responsible for providing all services and utilities to new urban areas.

Drainage, Sewerage, and Urban Hygiene. Upgrading and completion of the system of urban sewerage, including sewers, treatment, and pumping stations, to ensure all urban areas have a basic minimum standard of service by 2025. Local sewerage and package treatment systems should be constructed in favor of building large systems that will take many years to construct. In new towns, the sewerage system needs to be separated from the drainage system.

Solid Waste Management. Local governments should introduce recycling of domestic and industrial wastes, especially in large industrial estates and public utilities, such as power stations and wastewater treatment facilities.

Electricity Supply. The target for the supply of electricity should be set at 1,000 kWh per capita per year in major cities by 2020, 700 kWh per capita per year in the regional cities, 350 kWh per capita per year in medium-sized towns, and 250 kWh per capita per year in small-sized towns. Currently, all municipalities have public lighting systems.

Telecommunications. Modernization of the telecommunication network is ongoing, increasing the numbers of persons using telephones to over 100 machines per 1,000 people since 2000.

Protecting Environment, Landscape, and Ecological System. Upgrading and new urban development must incorporate the need to preserve cultural values and national traditions. Natural areas of ecological significance should be protected, managed and, where necessary, rehabilitated. Urban open space provisions in newly developed areas should be increased to at least 20 m²/person. Urban development must be coordinated closely with security, national defense, and social safety. There must be greater enforcement of laws on building construction and control of urban development to ensure public safety and compliance with plans.

Urban Management

Allocation and Organization of Key Zones in Municipalities. Existing and new industrial zones need to be better integrated with residential areas to avoid long and often dangerous commuting to industrial employment centers on the outskirts of cities.

Socioeconomic Development Strategies. Strategies on reducing unemployment, attracting investment, and reducing poverty need to be more focused. More investment in urban infrastructure is essential because it has a great multiplier effect on employment growth and investment.

Policies and Measures for Urban Development toward Poverty Reduction. Management effectiveness of urban policies and mechanisms designed to reduce poverty needs to be strengthened. Preferential policies for investments, which help reduce urban poverty and stimulate microbusiness, need to be developed. Improvements in housing and land policies for social stability and urban human resource development are also needed.

Completion of Legal Documents for Urban Planning Management. Improvements in the legal framework on urban planning and construction management are needed. Reforms to construction planning and design that incorporate public participation in updating standards are necessary, as is the need to update standards and qualifications of urban construction workers.

Strengthening Urban Development Plan Implementation Management. Publicizing and disseminating urban development plans in various formats are required for easy access and implementation by civil society. Urban development and construction plans should be integrated in a way that attracts more investment in big cities and key economic zones.

CONCLUSION

Urbanization is creating many challenges for Viet Nam. Less than 30% of the population is in urban areas but the urban population is expected to double over the next 25 years. The current approach to dealing with urbanization is not sustainable. Public authorities have not yet come to grips with the extent of urbanization and how to manage the forces behind it. Sustainable urban development is not a widely understood concept. There is a need for public institutions to learn how to develop solutions and practices that result in improved urban development outcomes, recognizing that this will require a switch of policy and priorities for the development of sustainable cities (Nguyen 2005). This is going to take time.

Viet Nam is slowly adjusting to the realities and problems of urban development. The national Government has proposed many strategies, policies, and solutions to improve urban environments and to reduce poverty. Under decentralization, local governments are moving toward developing and implementing more sustainable urban development policies and practices. However, there are major weaknesses in policy frameworks, approaches, and institutional capacity. The three case studies in this chapter provide insights into ways local governments in Viet Nam are seeking to adopt more sustainable approaches toward urban management and development.

15. Global Good Practices in Sustainable Urban Region Development

BRIAN ROBERTS
HUGH SCHWARTZ JOHNNY CARLINE
AND LYNDA KING JOHN ORANGE
AND PETER CUMMING BELINDA
YUEN JOE RAVETZ

A search on the Internet on the topic of good practice in sustainable urban development will yield more than 9 million hits. Literally, hundreds of examples of good practices are to be found, illustrating ways that local governments, businesses, and communities have gone about improving development practices and achieved more sustainable development outcomes. There are also many databases of good practice in sustainable urban and regional development. These include the United Nations (UN)-HABITAT Database of Best Practice,[1] Better e-Europe practices,[2] MOST[3], EPA Gateway to International Best Practices & Innovations[4], and many others. However, many examples of best practice included in these databases can no longer be considered best practice because practices are constantly changing.

In putting together the ideas for this book, the Asian Development Bank and Cities Alliance felt it would be useful to provide small case studies (vignettes) of cities considered global leaders in developing and applying good practice in sustainable urban region development. The intent was to provide a benchmark for approaches to good practices, which cities in Asian countries could aim to achieve, recognizing the need to consider cultural, governance, legal, and level of development factors in applying these to specific countries.

Many cities around the world are applying global good practices to achieve more sustainable urban region development. Selecting five case studies was very difficult. It was decided to select case studies of cities from each continent that demonstrate a high level of commitment and performance in achieving sustainable urban region development.

The cities selected for the case studies are Curitiba, Vancouver, Brisbane, Singapore, and Manchester. Curitiba, Brazil was selected as it is internationally acknowledged as a leader in the application of sustainable development good practice. Vancouver, Canada is internationally recognized for its work in relation to applying the concept of the ecological footprint to urban development. Brisbane, Australia has been internationally recognized as one of the world's most livable cities and for its innovation in public sector management. Singapore has been an international leader in sustainable urban design, housing development, logistics, and recycling. Manchester, England was selected because it was the first city in the world to experience rapid urbanization resulting from industrialization. The city has gone through many transformations in response to environmental, economic, and social threats, and has emerged to become one of the most sustainable cities in Europe.

The case studies for each city are presented as vignettes. They are designed to demonstrate different applications of good practice in sustainable urban region development. These range from management and planning of transportation systems, urban governance and management, resource leveraging, and environmental improvements to economic development. The case studies present only a few examples of applications of good practices. More examples could be found by perusing the range of publications or visiting websites for the respective cities.

CURITIBA, BRAZIL: AN UNLIKELY BUT STRIKING SUCCESS OF URBAN REVITALIZATION

Hugh Schwartz

Curitiba, the capital of the then eminently agricultural Brazilian State of Paraná, must not have seemed a likely place for major urban renewal in the mid-20th century, with farmlands and nearly 2,000 miles of rivers and streams within city limits. The laid-back provincial capital was known primarily for small lumber mills, yerba mate (green tea) processing plants, and the first public university in the country. Coffee was relatively new to the state, but by

1960, two thirds of Brazil's production and a third of the world's output came from Paraná. The coffee boom brought increased prosperity to Curitiba, but also more congestion and pollution. The population of the 300-year-old city exploded, increasing 7% annually in the 1950s, with the 1960s rate nearly as high. The city's infrastructure, modest to begin with, was severely strained. Municipal leaders voiced concern and talk turned to considerations of urban renewal. At that point, several years of frosts led to a sharp reduction in the output of labor-intensive coffee and a migration of nearly a third of the state's rural population, many to Curitiba. The city's population continued to increase at nearly 6% a year, and the small communities on the outskirts of the city grew even more rapidly. Although Brazil was experiencing its most rapid rate of economic growth, Paraná was in crisis and the state's 1960s programs of road and electric power expansion and lending for agriculture and industry were not having the desired effect.

History of Urban Renewal

The urban renewal of Curitiba began with the *Plano Direktor* (Master Plan), approved in 1966, and the establishment of the Curitiba Research and Planning Institute (IPPUC). The Master Plan provided only a set of guidelines but, unlike similar efforts in many cities, the local counterpart involved in preparing those guidelines continued to be active in expounding its visions of urban restructuring, in elaborating them at IPPUC, and in helping to implement them. Involving the planners in the implementation of urban renewal, in particular, through the establishment of IPPUC and oversight entities, was critical to the sustainability of urban planning. Continuity was also a key to success.

Full-fledged implementation began in 1971, with the naming of architect-urban planner, former IPPUC Director Jaime Lerner, to be mayor, and continued with his involvement or that of his close colleagues through 1982 and again in 1989–2005. In the generation since urban renewal was initiated, per capita income in the city has risen from just below the national average to nearly 70% above it, even while the city received an extraordinary influx of migrants from other regions of the country. If one takes into account the entire Curitiba Metropolitan Region, the increase in per capita income would be smaller.

The sustainability of what was achieved also rested on other factors, most notably the emphasis given to providing a solid economic base for the restructuring. The latter, sometimes overlooked in urban renewal projects, was aided by the promotion of what was being done, which stressed the quality of life as well as what was offered to prospective investors in financial terms. The result has been an extraordinary private response to public initiatives, numerous factories, and billions of dollars of investment from outside the city, primarily from abroad. Also of importance in assuring sustainability was the attention to environmental matters and the achievement of good governance. The latter was important in part to offset the uneven nature of public participation in the Curitiba experience.

Townhall-type open meetings were held to discuss the proposed master plan during the period of military dictatorship, although transparency regarding urban renewal deliberations subsequent to this was low. Input from the neighborhoods was not much considered until the late 1990s. While this may have contributed to the eventually declining margins of public support for the Lerner Group, this has been abated not only by recognition of the socioeconomic gains for most in the city and the many social action programs aimed at target groups who did not benefit significantly from increased prosperity, but also by the lackluster performance of the highly touted neighborhood participatory urban restructuring of Porto Alegre, Brazil. However, several of the more serious criticisms of Curitiba's urban renewal were eventually taken into account. From the outset, attention was paid to the various interest groups, informally as well as by their membership in municipal commissions, which led to modification of some of the planners' proposals. This has been criticized as corporatism, but the continuing support of the interest groups was important to get the urban restructuring underway.

Renewal Innovations

Curitiba's urban renewal has been characterized by a number of innovations. The most recognized are in public transport, where the city has been a model for medium-sized cities. The changes have involved traffic flows, the mode of transport, and the design of vehicles. Financial and ecological considerations led to a decision against a subway or a light rail system in favor of bus transportation, with public infrastructure (including several routes with dedicated, exclusive bus lanes) and public regulations. The actual transportation operations are, however, in the hands of private companies. Dedicated lanes, combined with passenger loading platforms and vehicle design modifications have greatly reduced travel time and the capital expenditures required for equipment.

Two dozen terminals have been located around the city, sharply reducing the proportion of those going from one extremity of the city to another, and through the downtown area. This has alleviated congestion and contributed to the preservation of the historic district. Although per capita ownership of automobiles is among the highest of Brazilian cities, nearly 75% of daily commuters use public transport. Variations of Curitiba's transport system have been adopted by cities around the world.

A second group of innovations has been with respect to the environment. The former approach to flood control was expensive and did not prevent periodic inundations. This was replaced by one that has virtually eliminated the problem and, at the same time, has vastly expanded recreational space, such that it now greatly exceeds UN per capita recommendations. Several hundred thousand trees have been planted and garbage collection programs instituted that contribute to the separation of different types of garbage and obtain refuse collected from difficult-to-reach areas; however, neither of these is as widespread as claimed. Abandoned quarries, which were dangerous as well as being eyesores, have been transformed into magnificent public sites. Efforts have also been made to protect river basins in the greater metropolitan region, although the latter achievements have not been uniform.

One of the very first major innovations was the revitalization of the historic downtown area at a time when such districts in most Brazilian cities were in rapid decline. The five most important blocks of Curitiba's commercial area were transformed—dramatically and controversially—into an attractive pedestrian mall, extended since then, and less controversially, to 20 blocks. This was accompanied by the restoration of many historic buildings, the rehabilitation of former industrial and commercial sites for cultural purposes, and the establishment of a major new shopping center, as well as the initiation of an increased number of fairs and special events, making for a unique urban atmosphere and helping maintain much of the focus of *Curitibanos* on the city center.

An important aspect of Curitiba's success has rested in the city's accomplishments in infrastructure and the provision of services even as the population in the city tripled. This has been both in regard to the aspects already mentioned, and with respect to access to electricity, clean water, sewerage, education, and public health facilities. However, the key to sustainability may well have been the attention given to increasing the economic base, as noted above. From the outset, architects and urban planners sought a separate industrial district, though to an extent for esthetic reasons. As the migration due to the coffee crisis grew, it was decided that an industrial district larger, greener, and with more infrastructure than perhaps any in the world be established; this at a time when many Latin American industrial parks were proving to be white elephants. The Curitiba Industrial City was located within the city limits and, despite the tax incentives, provided revenue that helped fund what was accomplished in the city and alleviated what might otherwise have become a disaster in terms of unemployment.

The success of Curitiba—though sometimes exaggerated—has given the city and the State of Paraná important leverage with international aid agencies. Loans, even for new types of projects, have been readily available.

In the words of one prominent foreign development executive: "In Paraná, they get things done." One aspect that has not progressed as rapidly as might be desired in this metropolitan area of now nearly 3 million people is the integration of urban planning for the suburban communities with that of the city itself—although this has improved since 1995.

GREATER VANCOUVER REGIONAL DISTRICT SUSTAINABLE REGION INITIATIVE: TURNING IDEAS INTO ACTION

Johnny Carline and Lynda King

One major challenge facing all governments today is how to achieve sustainable regional development—development that meets both the vocal present day and unspoken future generation's desire for economic prosperity, community well-being, and environmental health.

This case study describes the Greater Vancouver Regional District (GVRD) Sustainable Region Initiative (SRI). The SRI provides not only a framework for planning for and reporting on sustainable regional development but also for turning ideas into action—for identifying and implementing "best sustainable practices." The SRI contributes to improved urban management, effective and efficient infrastructure and services, and social and environmental sustainability in the Greater Vancouver region.

Greater Vancouver and the GVRD

The Greater Vancouver region is the third largest urban region in Canada, with a population of 2.1 million, and Canada's fastest-growing metropolitan region. It stretches over approximately 4,500 square kilometers (km^2) in the southwestern part of the country. The region consistently ranks as one of the world's best places to live. Contributing to the quality of life in Greater Vancouver is the stunning natural setting combined with extensive public green space and the overall high quality of air and water.

The Greater Vancouver region is the last non-amalgamated large urban region in Canada. The GVRD was formed in 1967 to provide coordination and planning function for the many municipalities that make up the Greater Vancouver region. Today, the GVRD is a federation of 22 local jurisdictions. In 2005, the GVRD had a budget of $366.7 million.

The GVRD governance model focuses on cooperation among municipalities to achieve a high level of service delivery. The GVRD's Board of Directors is composed of elected representatives—mayors and councilors—from the member municipalities, on a representation by population basis. Because the GVRD serves as a collective voice and a decision-making body on a variety of issues, the system is structured so that each member municipality has a voice in how the GVRD is run.

In operation, this nonhierarchical partnership works through municipalities delivering services to the taxpayer while the regional district provides services mostly to municipalities. The GVRD's responsibilities include:

- essential utility services for participating municipalities that are most economical and effective to provide on a regional basis: potable water, sewage collection and treatment, and solid waste disposal and recycling
- regional parks and greenways
- affordable rental housing
- labor relations services for participating municipalities
- strategic growth management planning
- air quality management and pollution control
- strategic and financial oversight of Greater Vancouver Transportation Authority (TransLink), and
- electoral area administration, Sasamat Volunteer Fire Department, and management of the 9-1-1 emergency phone system.

One of the major challenges facing the GVRD is how to ensure sustainable regional development while providing efficient and affordable regional services and a coordinating and planning function for a large number of local municipalities. Like others around the world, the GVRD is seeking ways to ensure that regional development plans and actions support greater economic prosperity, community well-being, and environmental health.

Sustainable Region Initiative

Launched in 2001, the SRI is a vision for the region and the organization, a management philosophy, and an overarching organizational framework. The SRI is used to integrate all GVRD corporate activities, regionally mandated plans, and partnership initiatives and align them with the principles of sustainability, recognizing and reflecting the integrated nature of urban systems.

The conceptualization and implementation of the SRI has been a dynamic process, beginning with corporate implementation, adjusting policies and business practices, redefining business cases to incorporate sustainability, engaging staff, and reporting on progress. Success in this area supported the political buy-in necessary to align these plans with sustainability principles and to begin to expand the SRI to the broader regional community.

Figure 15.1: The SRI Framework

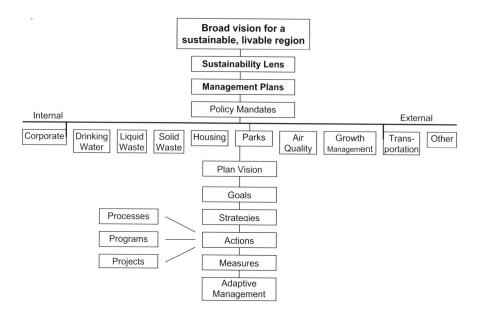

Planning and Reporting

Under the SRI, the GVRD is revising all management plans as they come up for renewal, including plans on growth management, air quality, liquid waste, solid waste and recycling, drinking water, and regional parks.

The SRI Framework for Regional Mandates is premised on the concept that the region comprises a system of systems that are in part represented by GVRD mandates and in part represented by other areas of interest. As such, the SRI Framework for Regional Mandates creates a set of integrated management plans that reflect the integrated systems of a sustainable urban region.

For GVRD mandates, the SRI Framework sets out a template for developing management plans according to the principles of sustainability. The Framework establishes links between the regional vision, sustainability principles, and the execution of individual plans. It also establishes links across regionally mandated plans and links to other initiatives beyond regional mandates that are executed by other agencies.

Each management plan identifies actions that contribute to a sustainable region through social, economic, and environmental considerations; links to the goals of other GVRD management plans; performance measures to track implementation progress; and adaptive management considerations on how the plan might respond to new and emerging issues so as to build in resiliency and opportunities for continuous improvement.

The GVRD is also committed to reporting on how its plans and actions contribute to the sustainable development of the region. In 2003, the GVRD launched its first sustainability report—a report card intended to stimulate open dialog about progress toward sustainability. The performance categories reflect the GVRD's main responsibilities, including its regional mandates and services. The report is guided by the Sustainability Reporting Guidelines of the Global Reporting Initiative (GRI) as well as the Sector Supplement for Public Agencies. The report and a GVRD-GRI comparative index are available online.

Turning Ideas into Action

The SRI provides not only a framework for planning for and reporting on sustainable regional development but also for turning ideas into action—for identifying and implementing best sustainable practices.

Four examples of the GVRD's best sustainable practices are: (i) integrated greenways and utility corridors; (ii) Surrey transfer station; (iii) sanitary sewer overflow facility; and (iv) conservation at wastewater treatment plants.

Integrated Greenways and Utility Corridors

Integrating greenways and utility corridors is an innovative approach to sustainability incorporating recreation, habitat protection, public transportation, and utility functions.

A new recreational greenway was recently created in two Greater Vancouver municipalities by projects that combined installation of sewer pipes with plans to connect natural open spaces for people and animals. The project also involved resurfacing utility access roads for cyclists and walkers and replacing culverts to allow free movement of fish.

Successful integrated utility and greenway planning required collaboration between the GVRD and the community. The cooperative approach saved money and other resources.

Sewer alignment was evaluated based on social, environmental, technical, and financial factors. Meetings held with interested groups included the local municipality, community committees, and the federal government department responsible for fisheries. Open houses were held in local municipalities to outline the proposal before public gatherings.

The partnership approach resulted in an off-channel fish habitat being developed with design by the federal government responsible for fisheries, construction on land donated by the local municipality, channel design by the GVRD, and trees bought and planted by a local community committee.

Integrated planning saved GVRD money, protected environmentally sensitive areas through carefully developed trails, and helped support environmental stewardship by encouraging community organizations, such as schools, to adopt streams near the greenway.

Surrey Transfer Station

On 28 April 2004, the GVRD's Surrey transfer station (STS) located in Surrey, BC, opened to the public on schedule and under budget. The facility was designed and constructed employing the Leadership in Energy and Environmental Design (LEED™) Green Building Rating System for guidance and received Silver certification in 2005. The LEED™ Rating System is a set of standards developed by the United States Green Building Council and evaluates building performance in six categories: sustainable sites, water efficiency, energy and atmosphere, materials and resources, indoor environmental quality, and innovation and design processes.

Construction of a waste management facility was a key component of the project. As the agency responsible for managing the region's waste, the GVRD both advocates and facilitates waste reduction through their regional recycling programs, of which the STS is a key component. These programs accommodate the diversion of construction debris from the waste stream. Over 80% of the STS project's potential waste was recycled and a further 15% was recovered as marketable fuel. In total, over 95% of the construction debris from the STS was diverted from disposal. The native trees that could be salvaged from the site were replanted, and those that could not be replanted were chipped on site for use as mulch.

The 5,600 square meter facility was designed to serve 2,021 waste flow projections with minimal impact on its neighbors and was constructed on a remediated site in an industrial area of Surrey. Design input was solicited early on from a committee that represented community associations, property and business owners, and the host municipality. This committee met regularly throughout the design and construction phases and continues to meet to monitor the ongoing operations and maintenance of the facility.

Sanitary Sewer Overflow Facility

To manage sanitary sewer overflows caused by excessive infiltration and inflow of storm water into sewers during major storm events, the GVRD built an innovative sanitary sewer overflow storage facility, among the first of its kind in North America.

The system operates automatically to divert sanitary sewer overflows into the storage facility during major storms, and to return stored flows back to the pump station after the storm. The energy efficient design allows for over 60% of the tank to be drained by gravity. The innovative vacuum flush system uses retained wastewater for flushing, and has a circular tank design that requires less concrete than the standard rectangular tank with tipping bucket. This innovative system eliminates the use of potable water to flush the tank.

Sustainable design features also include the use of sustainable materials, such as a high volume recycled fly ash concrete mix, natural landscaping to reduce surface runoff and reuse of existing soils, and extensive consultation with the surrounding farming community and the local municipality, incorporating their issues and concerns into the design.

Conservation at Wastewater Treatment Plants

By working together, GVRD staff at the Annacis and Lulu wastewater treatment plants developed an innovative, award-winning plan to simultaneously save money and protect the environment. The initiative won the 2002 Federation of Canadian Municipalities Sustainable Community Award for excellence in municipal service delivery.

Faced with high natural gas bills for the plant, operations and maintenance staff came up with a way to reduce natural gas consumption and cut the flaring of digester gas produced in the wastewater treatment process. While some digester gas was already being recycled within the plant to fuel boilers and engines that produce electricity, staff thought more could be done.

Utilizing a computerized data acquisition and control system, new computer logic was developed and initiated to optimize and balance gas feeds to the plant's hot water boilers and cogeneration units. The changes resulted in $60,000 savings during the cold winter months, and a big cut in the flaring of greenhouse gases. Additional savings of $130,000 are expected.

Other conservation methods are being worked on to further reduce digester gas flaring and cut natural gas consumption. Measures include optimizing generator heat recovery to use more of the waste heat.

Challenged to find better, more sustainable practices in their day-to-day work, staff at GVRD wastewater treatment plants found ways to reduce potable water consumption at the plants by over 50% in less than 2 years by substituting groundwater where appropriate, and installing water-efficient fixtures and other aids to save enough drinking water to supply the daily needs of 8,000 people. The Reclamation Pilot Plant under construction will further reduce the wastewater treatment plants' consumption of potable water by using reclaimed effluent instead of municipal water for various applications.

Conclusion

The SRI provides not only a framework for planning and reporting on sustainable regional development but also for turning ideas into action—for identifying and implementing best sustainable practices. The SRI is fundamentally an innovative change management strategy for both the organization and the region. Working with government, industry and business, and nongovernment organizations (NGOs) and community groups, the GVRD is using the SRI to improve urban management in Greater Vancouver, deliver effective and efficient regional infrastructure and services in a sustainable manner, and build a broad partnership committed to ensuring that Greater Vancouver is one of the most sustainable regions in the world as well as one of the most livable.

INNOVATION: KEY TO SUSTAINABLE URBAN DEVELOPMENT IN SINGAPORE

Belinda Yuen

Singapore is a small island economy at the southern end of the Malay Peninsula, which is heavily dependent on the import and export of goods and services to support its development. Since its independence in 1965, Singapore has worked hard to make the most efficient use of the region's limited natural resources and to capitalize on its strategic location as a world transport hub, and knowledge and financial center. The planning, design, and management of the urban environments are much admired by other Asian nations. Singapore has been a leader in the development of improved housing, environmental management, transportation, and innovation. The following outlines three good practice examples of approaches to sustainable urban development that have relevance to other Asian cities.

From Slums to Quality Living

Affordable housing provision for the growing urban population remains a challenge to many cities. Among Asian cities, Singapore is often held up as a success story in affordable housing delivery (Castells et al. 1990; Doling

1999). Singapore's shelter provision since the 1960s has been nothing short of phenomenal. Nearly all (99%) squatter settlements have been cleared. Most (84%) of Singapore's 3.2 million residents are provided with security of tenure, including home ownership (92%) in state-provided housing. More than 850,000 public housing units in 23 new towns have been constructed, and the worst of the housing shortages have been resolved. The statistics bear witness to the realization of access to housing.

A central focus of Singapore's public housing program is to provide good affordable housing for all who lack it, in particular, poor families. This has encouraged the formulation of policies aimed at transparent housing allocation, reducing housing cost, and easing access to owner occupancy in public housing for lower-income residents (Yuen 2005). Mortgage finance assistance, including the innovative use of homebuyers' central provident fund (CPF) savings has increased the ability of householders to accelerate their purchase of housing. CPF savings are essentially accumulated funds from the worker's pay-as-you-go social security scheme to which both employer and employee make mandatory contributions of a certain percentage of the employee's monthly contractual wage (Low and Aw 1997). At the heart of these policies is an inclusive housing delivery system that recognizes the needs of varying income earners and family sizes.

At the outset, the Government has participated in and taken a major and responsible role in organizing the conditions for public housing development and consumption. It set up a national housing authority, the Housing and Development Board (HDB), in 1960 and vested it with wide legal, land, and financial powers to implement the public housing program. While this may not be the only institutional framework for housing delivery, Singapore, in centralizing all public housing functions under a single authority, has circumvented the problems of bureaucratic fragmentation often associated with multiagency implementation. Through this program, poor quality, overcrowded housing and temporary self-help housing in unimproved squatter settlements have been progressively cleared and replaced by high-rise accommodation and improved services in public housing estates and new towns. With an emphasis on comprehensive service development, the new towns enhance the quality of life. The thrust is not just on providing dwelling units but also developing a good housing environment and community in the new towns (Teo and Phillips 1989; Yuen et al. forthcoming).

Moving with Speed

Over the past 4 decades, Singapore has moved from a practice of little or no systematic transport planning to problem-driven transport planning to vision-driven transport planning (Chin 1998). Since the 1990s, the vision has been to develop Singapore into a tropical city of excellence with world-class infrastructure and facilities (Urban Redevelopment Authority 1991). In transport terms, the objective has been to achieve an effective land transport system that is integrated, efficient, cost-effective, and at the same time meets the needs of the population, economy, and environment (Land Transport Authority 1996). To this end, the city has implemented a multipronged approach, comprising:

- integration of land use and transport planning, including regional centers and mixed-use development to minimize the need to travel
- expansion of the road network and maximization of road capacity through intelligent transport systems to increase transport network capacity
- demand management of road usage through restraint measures on vehicle ownership and usage to alleviate traffic congestion, and
- provision of quality public transport choices, including the development of mass rapid transit, light rail and integrated, seamless public transport travel to offer alternatives to the private car.

Singapore has introduced various innovations toward solving urban mobility problems in the market economy, for example, the car quota system (1990, certificate of entitlement and bidding system for car purchase), area licensing scheme (1975, which allows holders to pay to enter restricted zones in the city), and electronic road pricing (1998, electronic system of road usage charge based on pay-as-you-use principle). In the case of the car quota scheme, the primary idea is, as Thomson (1978, p. 292) explains, that the Government decides on the maximum number of cars to be owned on the island and issues no more than that number of licenses while the market determines the cost of owning the car. Registration fees, taxes, and fiscal disincentives have increased the cost of owning and operating a private car in Singapore to among the highest in the world. Basically, the Singapore prescription is to make people pay for the convenience of their cars, which consume and emit greater energy per person than other transport modes. Given the success in keeping traffic moving in Singapore (Doli 1993; *The Straits Times*, 26 November 2002), the Singapore experience shows the importance of an integrated transport policy approach to solving the problem of urban traffic congestion.

Bringing Nature into Urban Singapore

The rapid growth of cities and the increasing concentration of people in urban areas have accentuated the need to make the city a pleasant place in which to live and work and to visit. As early as 1967, under a postindependence policy of balanced economic and urban growth, Singapore set in motion a greening program to transform Singapore into a garden city—a city with nature in mind (Urban Redevelopment Authority 1991). The aim is to make rapidly urbanizing Singapore a better place to live.

A surfeit of urban problems (rapid population growth, housing shortage, unemployment, and inadequate urban infrastructure) led to extensive clearance and loss of the country's natural vegetation. During 1967–1982, Singapore's built-up area expanded by 80% with substantial increases in land allocated to industry, transport, public utilities and telecommunications, housing, and commerce. This stirred up the sensibilities for an urban greening program that eventually saw the careful introduction of various forms of greenery into the city-state: green buffers between new towns; parks and gardens; park connectors; roadside trees and shrubs; creepers and climbers on lamp posts, walls, overhead pedestrian bridges and other concrete surfaces; and rooftop gardens (Yuen 1996; Oi 1998). Beyond the creation of new parks, there is an increasing emphasis on the preservation of existing natural areas, such as hills, wooded areas, riverbanks, mangrove swamps, and coral reefs. The groundswell opinion is that these areas would yield environmentally pleasant, identifiable, and empathetic places to strengthen a local sense of belonging (Yuen 2005).

As a declared objective of the Government, Singapore's garden city development is assiduously pursued as a state project and accorded institutional, financial, and legislative support. It is embodied in the national policy of keeping Singapore "clean and green" and every effort is made to engage community participation in the beautification. An important process in the garden city implementation is the coordinating framework of the country's planning system of development plans and development control. Under this framework, provision for greenery is secured and codified into planning standards—such as for communal open space provision in private condominium development, buffer and roadside planting, neighborhood parks, and open space provision in residential areas, for implementation at the start of development planning. Three main strategies have been proposed to enhance greenery in the urban environment:

- having more parks and gardens
- carefully tending the natural foliage, and
- bringing the natural environment closer to the urban areas.

The approach is to provide "seamless greenery" through a network of park connectors and, most recently, "vertical greenery" on rooftops of tall buildings (Yuen and Wong 2005). By adopting an integrated approach to the environment and development, Singapore's long-range development plan, the Concept Plan, has demonstrated that the environment need not suffer because of strong economic growth and urbanization. The task of creating a garden city is framed in the larger and more holistic perspective of developing Singapore into a dynamic, distinctive, and delightful global city (Motha and Yuen 1998). This has provided a reference point for individual and national participation in greening.

At the microlevel of implementation, building stakeholding and continuous maintenance are important aspects of the greening process, especially in sustaining and giving meaning to development. The challenge is not only to understand and respond to the changing patterns of urban living but also to continually encourage community involvement and support of the greening effort. In this regard, the Adopt-the-Park community program and the installation of fruit trees in public housing parks and gardens are some schemes that encourage schools, residents, and other community groups and organizations to feel a greater sense of ownership and to participate in the garden city initiative. Even though the plan to transform Singapore into a garden city is largely government-led, several NGOs have increasingly argued for greater nature conservation to preserve the country's biodiversity.

Their voices have been heard through the *Singapore Green Plan: Towards a Model Green City*, by the Ministry of Environment in 1992, and presented to the 1992 Earth Summit in Rio de Janeiro. This plan reviews all areas of environmental concern and charts the policy directions and key strategies for preserving, protecting, and enhancing Singapore's environment, including a proposal to set aside 5% of the country's land—forests, swamps, marine environments, and other areas of ecological merit—for nature conservation. The Singapore Green Plan, recently updated for 2012, shows that cities do not need to accept concrete jungles and unsustainable urban growth as inevitable. Other options are possible with forward planning.

BRISBANE: SUSTAINABILITY THROUGH IMPROVED CITY MANAGEMENT

John Orange, Peter Cumming, and Brian Roberts

Brisbane, located in the southeast of the State of Queensland, is unique in Australia because it has a single metropolitan government covering the entire urban area of the city. In all other Australian states, the capital cities, such as Sydney and Melbourne, are divided into multiple, smaller local government areas. This unique state came about through a 1924 Act of State Parliament that aggregated 20 small local governments into one metropolitan government. Brisbane City covers an area of 1,220 km^2. It is the largest local government in Australia with a population of 900,000 residents. The Brisbane City Council employs 6,200 people, has a 2005 budget of $1.1 billion, and manages assets worth around $9.3 billion.

For many years, Brisbane lord mayors and councilors have recognized the importance of fostering and developing closer links with Asia and Pacific neighbors as a means of developing trade and investment in the city. The city has had a succession of mayors over 20 years who have provided strong vision and leadership, and who understood the need for city government to be efficient, effective, and competitive. Planning has played a key role in the city's development. Brisbane City Council's 2010 vision includes a regional and world city theme that seeks to both reinforce and promote Brisbane as part of the region of southeast Queensland nationally and as part of the Asia and Pacific region. The city is possibly one of the best-run local governments in Australia. It is the only city in Australia with a Standard and Poor's credit rating (AA+), which is a reflection of the sound approach it has taken to financial management.

The importance of creating a livable city has been central to the policies and plans of the City Council. Brisbane ranks in the top 10 of the world's most livable cities. Over the past 20 years, the city has embarked upon major projects and programs to clean up the Brisbane River; to develop an intermodal transport hub and industrial area, with the co-location of transport infrastructure involving the city airport and port; to redevelop large parts of the inner city, including improvement of urban design of urban areas; to improve city management and cost recovery; and to provide public infrastructure services. In 1995, the city council underwent a major restructure to introduce a purchaser-provider model of public sector management.

This vignette describes two elements of good practice urban management implemented by Brisbane City Council to improve the sustainability and development of the city. The first involves a case study of the purchaser-provider model, which separates the functions of council into purchasers and providers of services. The second case study involves infrastructure charges plans (ICPs), which were introduced as part of a user-pays policy on the provision of infrastructure to new development areas or areas undergoing urban renewal.

Purchaser-Provider Model of Service Delivery

Over the past decade, Australia has followed international trends in delegating greater financial and administrative responsibilities to local government for the delivery of public services. Australia's version was the National

Competition Policy (NCP), which came to life as an agreement between the state governments and the federal Government in 1995. It was designed to lower costs and to improve the quality of public sector service delivery. In 2000, the federal Government introduced a goods and service tax (GST) with all revenues being passed to the state and territory governments. The GST replaced a range of taxes and charges that created inequalities and undermined business and institutional competitiveness between the states.

To respond to this top-down reform agenda, Brisbane City found itself needing to review not only its business activities but also all of its functional activities. This drove the city to introduce a clearer segregation of responsibilities, roles, and functions of its operational areas. Prior to 1996, most service delivery activities were embedded within policy and regulatory arms of the organization. NCP argued that policy and regulation should be distinct and separate from service delivery and that service delivery functions should be made competitive and business-like. The means of doing this, after looking at approaches in Denmark, Netherlands, New Zealand, and Sweden (Orange 2004) was the adoption of a purchaser-provider model[5] for the delivery of urban services.

The adoption of the purchaser-provider model introduced many changes. Under the Brisbane City Council's internal reform process, politicians have had to develop corporate governance skills and bureaucrats have been segregated into policy, regulatory, administration, and service provision functions. The chart below (Fig. 15.2) identifies the purchaser or policy divisions of the council, the regulatory, customer and community divisions (program providers) and its commercial and business divisions (the business units, commercial service providers and subsidiaries).

The purchasers own the assets, secure any rights, are the source of funding, and negotiate contracts for service delivery with program providers and providers. The difference between program providers and providers is that the former are not set up as a business in a competitive or reporting sense because they largely deal with a regulatory enforcement, community engagement, and customer service channels. Providers are the segregated business units involved in activities that deliver services procured from them by the purchasers. They are accountable for the quality, timeliness, and prices of their services through negotiated agreements.

Brisbane City Council's organizational structure is set up under the purchaser-provider model. Under this model, purchasers procure products and services on behalf of stakeholders (largely the Brisbane community) from providers, who deliver these to agreed specifications or standards of service at competitive prices. Providers are of four types: commercial providers, program providers, business units, and subsidiary companies.

Figure 15.2: Brisbane's Purchaser-provider Model

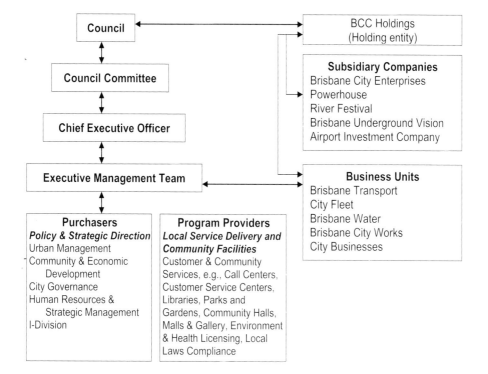

Lessons Learned

Through an appropriate segregation of the various functions and decision-making areas, Brisbane City was able to provide clarity of purpose and ownership by staff; clearly identify accountabilities; apply improved oversight and monitoring; and, as a consequence, reduce duplication, streamline processes, and improve efficiency and service levels. These benefits were neither instantaneous nor easily achieved. Brisbane City Council is still on its journey of reform and improvement, some 9 years after it started. There have been blind alleys—some internal shared service areas have been reaggregated back into the purchaser group. Some businesses have failed and have been closed or sold. The governance structure is complex and senior managers can be responsible to a number of masters.

Beneath the single governing purchaser-provider principle, Brisbane City Council has adopted a pragmatic approach in selecting its service delivery models. Political management of the past 10 years has decided that some assets and activities are essential to the delivery of local government services should be retained within public ownership. For Brisbane, this means that essential assets and activities—such as water supply, public transport, wastewater management, public venues, parks and designated green space, and a regulatory policy and compliance activities—will not be outsourced or privatized under the current political administration. Within this constraint, Brisbane has selected the following array of service delivery methods:

Table 15.1: Service Delivery Methods

Internal service provider	→	Revenue collection, accounting, HR and IR, IT support, legal services.
Business-like activity	→	Cemeteries, design, vegetation and pest control, building and maintenance, supply services.
Business units	→	Water and wastewater, transport, civil works, fleet.
Outsourced	→	Refuse collection, landfill management, building certification, printing services.
100%-owned company	→	Consulting and product sales, an entertainment venue, the annual river festival, an investment company.
Minority equity ownership	→	Bulk water storage company, Brisbane Airport.

HR = human resources, IR = information resources, IT = information technology.

Through international research and Brisbane's practical experience, the Council has recognized that service delivery choices are driven by different forms of motivation. Clear evidence shows that where fiscal concerns exist, external service delivery choices (such as contracting out and privatization) are most often favored. Where the fiscal situation is such that it allows a focus on matters other than financial, such as service delivery improvements and internal efficiency, internal reform options (like internal service providers and business units) are often preferred. As a rule, internal reforms create more complex governance arrangements while external reforms are simpler but more traumatic in terms of organizational change.

Infrastructure Charges Plans

In 1997, the Queensland State Government introduced the Integrated Planning Act. This law required local governments to adopt an integrated approach to multisector planning and development assessment. It also provided for headworks charges to be introduced as part of a full user-pays approach to the provision, and improvement of citywide infrastructure. Headworks are major infrastructure investments, such as plant, equipment, or structures for water supply, floodways, and sewers. Previously, the city council carried the costs of providing or upgrading headworks. Since 2000, the Brisbane City Council has progressively introduced infrastructure charges plans[6] to ensure a more equitable and sustainable approach to the provision of major infrastructure and urban services.

Infrastructure charges are based on the notion of the user pays where infrastructure provides a direct, private benefit to an immediate user. Infrastructure charges are not used to provide funding for community facilities, such as schools, public hospitals, and national highways. Central to the user-pays notion is the principle of fair apportionment. This implies that the infrastructure charges levy imposed by local government on a developer must be apportioned in relation to the total development of an area. This means that a developer only pays a levy on his proportion of the costs of infrastructure head works in relation to the total cost of providing infrastructure to a new development area.

Infrastructure charges provide a mechanism for charging for land and capital costs of supplying essential development infrastructure. Brisbane City levies contributions toward land and capital works for the following network of development infrastructure items:

Water Supply	Major reticulation mains
	Minor reticulation mains
	Water treatment
Sewerage	Major reticulation mains
	Minor reticulation mains
	Sewerage treatment
Waterways	Major relief drainage
	Minor relief drainage
Transport	Major roads
	Minor roads
	Public transport facilities
	Off-road pedestrian facilities
Community Purposes	Acquisition of new public recreation land
	Improvements to existing public recreation land
	New Farm River Walk
	Land for multipurpose community centers

The council levies infrastructure charges to achieve design standards of service. Setting the design standard of service is basically a policy issue set out in the City Plan. The charges for the capital cost of infrastructure are calculated to meet the life-cycle costs of the infrastructure network according to the design standard of service. The life-cycle costs are defined as the total cost (in present-day terms) of the development to the infrastructure network (including operating and maintenance costs) over a period of 30 years or longer if the council determines.

An ICP describes how charges will be applied. It forms part of the City Plan. ICPs have been prepared for different areas of the city because the contribution costs to the provision of infrastructure vary according to location, ground conditions, and ease of servicing parts of the city. The City has prepared 12 ICPs for newly developing areas and areas undergoing renewal.

ICPs identify development infrastructure items making up the network, states the desired development of services for the network, and evaluates alternative ways of funding infrastructure items. ICPs must provide information on:

- the need for the works, services, and facilities
- the amount to be funded by infrastructure charges
- the schedule of works, including timing of provision and costs
- the method by which infrastructure charges are calculated
- the boundaries to which the infrastructure charges plan applies
- the description of each type of lot or parcel of land, work or use to which charges apply, and
- the rate of charges.

These charges, called infrastructure charge units (ICUs), apply when a subdivision or reconfiguring a lot or material change of use occurs. ICUs are adjusted in the budget each financial year. The 2005/2006 infrastructure charge units value is about $1.10. The infrastructure charge payable for each system is calculated according to the formula below. An example of the application of infrastructure charges for the Bulimba Industrial Area can be found at the footnoted website.[7]

$$\text{Total Infrastructure Charge} = \left(\begin{array}{c} \text{Amount of proposed} \\ \text{development} \\ \text{x total applicable} \\ \text{infrastructure} \\ \text{charge rate} \end{array} \right) - \left(\begin{array}{c} \text{Amount of existing} \\ \text{development} \\ \text{x total applicable} \\ \text{infrastructure} \\ \text{credit rate} \end{array} \right) \times \text{value of ICU}$$

For large-scale urban development or redevelopment projects, the council normally enters into an infrastructure charges agreement with a developer. Under these agreements, instead of the council or a public utility agency providing major infrastructure to service a new development area, the developer enters into an agreement to provide trunk infrastructure, such as a new road or water supply to a new development area. This often has significant cost savings to the council because the work can be undertaken in conjunction with the provision of other infrastructure services to a new development area. This procedure is known as an infrastructure agreement, and may involve the government paying a share of development costs that cannot be apportioned to the developer under an ICP.

Fair apportionment is an important principle to follow when calculating infrastructure charges. Central to this principle is that a clear link can be made between infrastructure items and the user. The user is only levied for their fair share of the development infrastructure items. In calculating charges, issues that need to be addressed include

- areas to be serviced by the development infrastructure system
- development infrastructure items
- proportion of cost to be funded by the charges plan
- index to be used to adjust charges to reflect current costs, for example, an inflationary indicator
- existing infrastructure with spare capacity and estimated depreciated value
- new infrastructure required and estimated present value
- service catchments
- existing demand for each service catchment
- future demand for each service catchment; demand may vary depending on user, e.g., industrial versus residential
- future demand in present value terms
- an apportionment charge for both new and existing infrastructure, and
- the annual review of the charges plan and infrastructure supply and charges rates.

An important element of ICP is benchmark development sequencing (BDS). BDS identifies the preferred pathway to supply infrastructure to a new development area. Benchmark development sequencing plans will indicate the phasing of development for an area for 5 years and provide some estimate of the schedule of works that will be undertaken during that period. The council used BDS to ensure progressive expansion of the infrastructure network in priority development areas to avoid leapfrogging of development.

ICPs and BDS plans have particular relevance for cities in Southeast Asia, where the cost of providing and funding external infrastructure works often lies with local governments. Unless local governments in Southeast Asia move toward developers paying for the extension of major infrastructure, the backlog of infrastructure service provision will continue to rise. The Brisbane City Council has been able to substantially reduce its capital outlays on extending infrastructure to newly developing areas, thus freeing up capital for other priority capital works projects in the city.

Conclusion

The introduction of the purchaser-provider model and ICPs has created significant improvements in the efficiency and operation of the Council. The reforms to urban management have led Brisbane City to become a leader and innovator in developing sustainable urban systems. The institutional reforms have achieved a great deal, but these have been underpinned by other factors such as the city's size, strong leadership, good governance and urban management, and a commitment to city building. However, it has taken 9 years to implement reforms, some of which are ongoing. Some things have not been successful, but in attempting to try new and innovative approaches to urban management practices, the Council has learned which practices are sustainable and which are not. The significance of staff resistance and the time involved in embedding change to institutional arrangements should not be underestimated. However, the city's commitment to sustainability, especially in planning and urban management, has paid off and ensured that Brisbane is one of the most livable cities in the world.[8]

GREATER MANCHESTER, UK: POST-INDUSTRIAL SUSTAINABILITY?

Joe Ravetz

As one of the birthplaces of the industrial revolution, Manchester suffered extreme levels of pollution, followed by 50 years of decline and restructuring. From the challenges of unemployment, ill health, obsolescence, and dereliction, the city is now reinventing itself as a globalized hub for creative and knowledge-based industries. It has also pioneered the "new urbanism" and urban environmental management in the UK, and is a major hub for sustainability research and development.

This case study is a contrast to most Asian cities—the dynamic and problematic conurbation of Greater Manchester (GM) in northern England. At the center, the City of Manchester is an icon for style and sports, and a thriving center for finance, media, education, and culture. The City of Manchester is surrounded by the suburbs and ex-urbs of GM—that is, a sprawling conurbation of 2.5 million people in a large urban core and a ring of satellites. A further 1.5 million people live in the surrounding area within a 1-hour journey, including Liverpool and smaller cities. To the east and

Global Good Practices in Sustainable Urban Region Development 427

Figure 15.3: Map of Greater Manchester

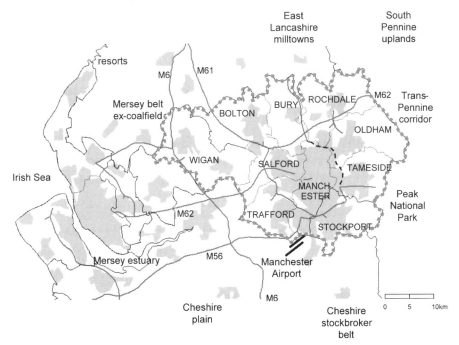

north are rolling hills surrounding an extended urban fringe, and to the west and south is mainly farmland with a patchwork of small towns and large suburbs. GM sits at a national crossroads, halfway between Scotland and London, and is also the gateway to the "peripheral" North West region, and a playground for wealthy commuters and tourists. Its governance is divided among 10 autonomous municipalities, and many vital functions are devolved to the regional level.

Some vital statistics on growth trends are shown below to serve as a guide to sources of future pressures.

Urbanization Past and Future

Manchester a century ago was the 10th largest city in the world, and the classic industrial "shock city" of free trade and enterprise. At various times, it was the site of the world's first railway station, first free public library, first retail cooperative, first trade union congress, and first programmable computer. There emerged a unique combination of factors—access to iron and coal, and a seaport for the British trading empire; a damp climate suitable for textile processing; and the nonconformist churches with their promotion of

Table 15.2: Growth Trend, Greater Manchester

Parameter	Growth per year (%)
"World's best" airport, 60,000 trips per day	8
Gross domestic product, $51.6 billion	2.5
Total waste arising, 11 million tons per year	2
About 1 million cars: 6 million trips per day	2
About 1 million houses, 100,000 buildings	1.2
Carbon dioxide emissions: 32 million tons per year	0.7
Population 2.5 million people	0.2
Urban area 55,000 hectares: 43% of total	0.15
700,000 bus trips per day, 70,000 local rail trips	0.1
8,000 kilometers (km) of roads	
152 km of motorways	
350 km of railways	
10 autonomous local authorities	
land area, 1,286 square kilometers	

technical learning and innovation by the "working classes" (Hall 1998). A journey from east to west crosses many layers of this history, from the birth of the textile industry in the Pennine Valleys to the sunrise business parks surrounding the airport.

Current trends are indicative of the prospects for many such city-regions in the developed world:

- globalization – increasing integration of investment, production, trade, and consumption into global systems (Townroe 1996)
- connexity– new forms of networks and communities enabled by information and communications technology, media, and international travel (Mulgan 1996)
- exclusion – new patterns of alienation, dependency, and segmentation for large sections of the population;
- post-fordism – dissolution of former economic and political structures in favor of more complex and fluid patterns (Amin 1996). New interactions between production and consumption, between local and global, etc., exist.

For several centuries manufacturing activity was the basis of the industrial city—local and imported materials were processed to produce goods to send along water or railway corridors. Economic "advantage" could be defined in terms of the city-region's location and resources as a "'material processor." That model is now in transition to a more postindustrial "city of flows" (Castells 1997). The city-region now functions more as a node in a global "hyper grid"—networks of motorways and airports for movement of people and goods, and networks of satellites and wires for movement of information and capital. Many patterns of urban activity and urban form are turning inside out, as the growth nodes of production and consumption migrate to the urban fringe or "edge city"—retail, leisure, and business parks with easy links to the hyper grid. City functions now center on services and consumption, and its cultural "cachet" or branding now competes in a global hierarchy.

There are many paradoxes in such a transition in GM. For instance, 19th, 20th, and 21st century cultures and economies are side by side and are often in conflict. While production and consumption are globalized, there is a countertrend of "localization"—a new kind of "place advantage" gained through cultural amenity and attraction to mobile consumption and production (Dicken 1996). In physical terms, edge cities are "counter-urbanized," while historic centers are "re-urbanized" and industrial areas "regenerated." In social terms, uneven development creates clusters of unemployment and exclusion. In environmental terms, the bulk of resources travel through the hyper grid, which is increasingly privatized and deregulated, and where environmental management presents an even greater challenge than before.

Economic and Social Trends

A city-region such as GM displays both vulnerability and opportunity in the global hierarchy. With an industrial base that is partly obsolete, and partly booming with hi-tech and tertiary activities, it is a major hub to a peripheral region and at the same time saddled with socioeconomic decline and dependency. The combined effect is the trend of segmentation—a "sunrise" high-tech economy with global markets is surrounded by large areas on the threshold of dependency and decline.

In parallel are equally fundamental social dynamics. Demographic trends are changing age structure, gender balance, family structure, disposable time and income, and household organization. Cultural trends see a shift from former one-nation patterns toward self-identity and empowerment, and its counterpart of alienation and disorder. Former cultures of governance and welfare provision are replaced by one of "enabling" in partnership with other organizations. The civic body is "splintering" both culturally and physically into countless fragments (Graham and Marvin 2001).

Generally, there is a prospect of an aging population, with rising disposable income and leisure time, chasing volatile employment and a diversifying set of lifestyle activities. Such trends may accelerate. Many visions of the future, even without "surprises," such as terrorism or sudden climate change, suggest structural conflict between cultures and corporate interests (Castells 1997). Cities and urban systems have a continuing role not only as economic producers and consumers, but as arenas for creative conflict between the local and global, and between the corporate and the civic worlds.

Environmental Trends

Environmental quality in GM shows the legacy of 200 years of heavy industry, and Manchester is still the "pollution capital" of the United Kingdom (UK). The surrounding uplands are well over their "critical loads" for acidity, river quality is only now less than toxic, and a tenth of urban land is potentially contaminated and unstable. A quarter of all households drink lead in their water, half are seriously disturbed by noise, and there is a 3% annual growth trend in household waste.

In the longer run, environmental dynamics that could enhance pollution hazards, whether actual or perceived, exist. Economic growth will tend to increase material throughput, other things being equal, with new and more complex substances and processes. There will also be ever-tighter standards for health and amenities, and better evidence on environmental pathways, processes, and impacts.

The result can be seen in the environmental history of the city-region, as the "urban environment transition" or phase model (Ravetz 2006). In its first industrial phase, 150 years ago, the combined hazards of work, housing, diet, and pollution resulted in an average life expectancy of 40 years. In a second phase, the fossil fuels used in heating and transport dominated urban air pollution. In a third phase, many impacts are displaced to a global level, and other hazards now emerge as the more insidious effects of carcinogens, trace metals, and genetic engineering. While life expectancies have doubled, public concerns on risks have multiplied (Beck 1991). The risks of production have now shifted to those of consumption—transport, noise, waste, food chains, obesity, and mental health. And in the modern risk society, social divisions are as sharp as ever. Pollution mapping shows the poor breathing the emissions of the rich: health mapping shows a 7-year life span difference between poor and rich areas—95% of all major industrial polluters are in poor areas. An increasing proportion of the environmental burden of affluence is exported to poor countries overseas via resource extraction and climate emissions, even while the UK becomes gradually cleaner and greener.

With the general shift of urban activity from production to consumption, environmental management has likewise shifted from the "dilute and disperse" approach of the industrial revolution to integrated pollution control for all media, as in the integrated pollution control system of the UK (Environment Agency 1996). More recently, environmental management has emerged as a driver for business opportunity and competitiveness, as in the principle of "eco-modernization" (Weale 1993). Taking this one step further, "integrated chain management" coordinates all materials and processes (Wolters 1997). The end goal is "de-materialization," or de-linking of economic growth from material throughput, and this is the general goal of the UK strategy on "sustainable consumption and production" (Jackson and Michaelis 2003).

Sustainability Profile and Initiatives

Manchester-GM is often quoted as an international good practice, even while it is not obviously as green, socially responsible, or well-organized as some cities in the Nordic or Latin American countries. However, it does have a certain case to demonstrate, from which other cities might learn: this was documented in City-Region 2020—Integrated Planning for a Sustainable Environment," a large-scale feasibility study and history of the future (Ravetz 2000).

The case is basically that where GM is treading now, many other cities are likely to follow. If in 50 years, a typical Asian city has a mature industrial system and urban form, a settled social structure, and a need to reinvent its form and function for changing global markets, then it is likely to experience a similar challenge of "sustainable" restructuring and regeneration.

Arguably, this is a result of the unique history and trajectory of GM, where the gross physical problems of industrial pollution and unsanitary housing have, for the most part, been overcome. What remains is a kind of showpiece for the contradictions of postindustrial or late capitalism. Environmental impacts are largely displaced overseas; the physical urban form is congested and segmented; urban governance is weak but still operates with only subtle forms of corruption; the economy has enough diversity to provide at least for the middle classes; and public services are increasingly corporatized but still mostly function for most of the population. What remains is the gap between aspirations and reality, as below.

GM can also offer a long history of initiatives and campaigns, building on a long history of urban reform and idealism. GM first quoted the word "sustainability" in the Global Forum 94 event, intended as the follow up to the Rio Summit. These are some current examples:

- At the municipality scale is Manchester Green City, a raft of local policies, including purchasing renewable energy, active curbside recycling, and large-scale urban tree planting. On a proactive front,

the website www.Manchesterismyplanet.com is a current campaign and pledge system, which over 6 months has engaged 10,000 citizens and numerous organizations.
- There is more critical mass at the regional level, much of which is promoted through NGOs, such as Sustainability North West. Responsibility North West is a networking and promotions scheme for business corporate social responsibility, while the Climate Change Charter for the North West builds capacity and offers assessment tools for larger organizations. "Enworks" promotes environmental management among small and medium-size enterprises and "Enviro-link" promotes environmental technologies.
- Most large corporate bodies have sustainability appraisals and mission statements: these include many of the largest polluters in the region, e.g., Shell UK, Manchester Airport, and British Nuclear Fuels.
- Most public policies are subject to sustainability assessment and evaluation, and there is active experimentation in toolkits for "integrated appraisal." On close inspection, many of these are broad enough to quote the principles and then to proceed with the original plans, showing that the real issue is not the appraisal method but the definition of options, boundaries, trends, and responsibilities (Ravetz et al. 2004).

A pragmatic view of urban sustainability in GM sees much rhetoric about public transport, but 86% of all journeys go by car; much research on climate change, but an airport that doubles in size every 10 years; many policies on fostering local communities, but where 10% of local shops close every year. Possibly the largest single success is outside the urban policy agenda—the 25% per year growth of organic production and ethical food trading, with its "responsible capitalism" model for global supply chains.

Generally, the Manchester-GM model of urban sustainability is a demonstration of such contradictions, not only in physical facts but also in the discourse of the actors involved. Because the added value of urban sustainability involves local and global issues in the short and long term, this is also a source of confusion and contradiction. This is highlighted by some of the current sustainability headline themes, which can be seen to mix communications, aspirations, strategies, and tactics in a postmodern display of mediums and messages.

- "Sustainable consumption and production" is promoted by the UK Department of Environment, Food and Rural Affairs, while its more powerful neighbor, the Department of Trade and Industry, continues on a business-oriented material growth trajectory.

- "Sustainable economic development" and "sustainable regeneration" are widely sounded. On close inspection, the definition means the lowest-cost strategy that leads to economic recovery while reducing public sector funding.
- "Sustainable communities" are promoted at the city level with the agenda for social inclusion and avoidance of dependency. The same title is promoted at the national level, as a plan to relieve housing shortages in the London hinterland and revive failed housing markets in the North.

The urban development trajectory of GM over 200 years can now be observed in only 20 years in some Asian cities, and this enormous acceleration can create its own problems. However, the overlapping of different cultures, economies, spatial patterns, and environmental problems in GM can be seen from both sides. It creates the problems of weak governance, segmented societies, and fragmented urban form. But it also provides a melting pot for diversity, innovation, and new forms of networks. Other cities with greatly accelerated growth may also be able to turn such problems into opportunities.

LESSONS FOR URBAN SUSTAINABILITY

Many lessons related to sustainability can be learned from these global good practice case studies. The first is the important role that leadership has played in developing vision and winning commitment to tackle the difficult and often expensive plans to solve environmental and economic problems. Without Lerner's vision for Curitiba, the city would never have achieved the success it has in addressing serious environmental, land-use, and transportation problems. Without strong governance, leadership, and innovation, a modern Singapore city-state would never have solved its environmental and housing problems, or transformed its economy to provide a more sustainable basis for development in the future.

Second, the emergence of a crisis or threat has been a major factor in initiating actions to ensure survival of the city's economy. The social and environmental conditions in Manchester required action to improve public health and the quality of the environment in the 19th century, while redevelopment and economic restructuring were necessary to rebuild the economy when the impacts of globalization and change of materials used in clothing manufacturing undermined the competitiveness of the city's economy. Singapore, as its standard of living increased, was likewise able to transform its economy to become one of Asia's leading service centers. In Brisbane, the implication of the National Competition Policy forced a complete change in the mode of service delivery.

Third, the willingness of communities to embrace change, often reluctantly, has led to innovation in public administration, urban management, and environmental design. The establishment of the purchaser-provider model in Brisbane has led to a highly competitive and efficient local government, which outperforms most other local governments in Australia. The program, designed to encourage community engagement in Curitiba, has led to changes in behavior and support for environmental and waste management programs. The integrated greenways and utility corridor and the successes of the wastewater treatment plants in Vancouver came about because of staff initiatives, coming up with innovative approaches to old issues.

Fourth, all the cities have sought to leverage resources through various forms of partnerships to build infrastructure and provide housing and community facilities. In Curitiba, the multiple uses of facilities have reduced operational costs, enabling capital to be used for other priority projects. The Vancouver approach to sustainability has involved the engagement of many partners and municipal, business, and community organizations. The approach was to "turn ideas into action" using top-down leadership-driven and bottom-up staff engagement processes.

Fifth, the planning and integration of transportation services has led to greater efficiency in vehicle and passenger movement in the cities. Sound planning has led to the development of intermodal facilities and mixed-use developments that have created vibrancy and convenience not present in many urban developments. The integration of residential, social, cultural, and educational landuses with commerce, research, and specialized integrated low-intensity manufacturing highlights the importance of building urban places in which people feel comfortable to visit, work, and live. The focus on integrated development has had a significant impact on improving the quality of life in all five cities.

Sixth, the importance of urban planning, enforcement of construction laws and environmental policies, and attention to asset management and maintenance have enabled the cities to maintain efficient urban systems, a high quality of visual amenity and livability. The focus on livability is present in all aspects of urban planning and management.

Finally, a significant amount of trial and error has occurred in the five cities to refine and develop approaches to good practice. Mistakes have been made and some things have worked better than others. However, the willingness to change, commit to new ideas, try alternatives, and test options make these cities different. These cities have understood that risks must be accepted if changes in community behavior, technology, governance, and approaches to urban management that benefit sustainability are to occur.

The most sobering lesson gained from all these case studies is from Manchester. The effect that more than 200 years of industrial and urban development has had on the landscape on the city and region has been devastating. Restoring the environmental capital of the region will take years. It is important that Asian cities appreciate the inheritance that current approaches to urban management and development practices might leave on their landscapes if these do not change.

Other valuable lessons can be learned from studies of these five cities. The practices, which have been presented in the vignettes, can be applied to many Asian cities. The important lesson learned from these global city examples is the need for commitment to sustainability.

Notes

[1] Habitat Best practices Database: www.bestpractices.org/
[2] Regional development in the Europe knowledge society: www.beepregional.org/
[3] MOST Clearing House, Best Practices: www.unesco.org/most/bpsites.htm
[4] EPA Gateway: www.epa.gov/innovation/international/urban.htm#databases
[5] www.brisbane.qld.gov.au/BCCWR/about_council/documents/publications_annual_report_accountable_organisation.pdf?xml=/BCC:PDFHITXML:357179652:svDocNum=
[6] Infrastructure Charges Plan: www.brisbane.qld.gov.au/BCC:STANDARD:357179652:pc=PC_1765
[7] Bulimba Industrial Area ICP: www.brisbane.qld.gov.au/bccwr/building_and_development/documents/bulimba_industrial_infrastructure_charges_plan.pdf
[8] Economist Intelligence Unit Survey: theage.com.au/articles/2004/02/06/1075854028808.html

16. Lessons and Strategies for Sustainable Urban Futures

BRIAN ROBERTS AND
TREVOR KANALEY

Asia's future is urban. It is in developing sustainable cities. Urbanization is both driven by and supports economic growth. The economy of the PRC is doubling in size every 10 years; India is doubling in size every 13 years. The spatial patterns of land use in Asia are changing rapidly with growing concentrations of people and economic activity. Over the next 25 years to 2030, Asia's urban population is set to increase by about 1,100 million people or 70%. While the precise figures of urban and economic growth may be debatable, the scale of the transformation makes any imprecision irrelevant.

The challenge for urban governance in Asia is to accommodate rapidly increasing populations while facilitating improvements in the welfare of cities' inhabitants—raising living standards, services, and urban amenity over time. A particular challenge is to manage effectively the envelopment of rural areas on the rapidly expanding periphery of cities while developing synergies between urban areas and their rural hinterlands to the benefit of both urban and rural people. For improvements in urban welfare to be sustainable, they need to be achieved in a way that recognizes the interdependence of social, economic, and environmental systems, avoids damaging shocks, allows for an acceptable level of equity between the city's inhabitants, and provides a stable platform for the well-being of future generations.

Sustainable urban development in Asia will require major changes to the way cities are developed and managed. The growth of cities combined with existing management practices has resulted in large imbalances between demand and supply in the provision of infrastructure and services necessary for sustainable urban development. Cities have been swamped by growth and have responded after the event, trying to catch up in infrastructure and service provision. Without change and with the continuing growth of cities, these shortfalls in supply will inevitably widen. While thresholds are unclear, widening infrastructure and service shortfalls will result in further degradation of the physical and social environment—negative externalities, which will slow and, in some cases, possibly reverse, economic development and improvements in welfare.

Development on this scale will always involve elements of chaos. Nevertheless, good city governance is able to accommodate and exploit change and achieve acceptable outcomes. A "new" urban governance needs to be developed in Asian countries where, as far as possible, cities actively guide urban development and the provision of infrastructure and services, rather than simply respond to problems and shortfalls. This will require a focus on strategic planning, financial viability, and delivery of sustainable outcomes. Urban systems are continually undergoing change by external and internal forces. Urban management and communities must monitor change, assess risks, and be open to the opportunities that change presents. The five global case studies demonstrate the importance of local governments' constantly focusing on innovation and change, and on continually improving their performance. Many Asian cities tend to be very receptive to new technologies, but are less innovative when it comes to institutional reforms and approaches to change management.

There is no easy solution to strengthening city governance in Asia and improving the way cities are developed and managed. For this to be achieved, country-enabling environments that encourage proactive city governments and authorities need to be developed. Such frameworks need to be complemented by capacity building and institutional strengthening of city governments and authorities so they are able to exploit fully the policy "space" available to them. It will also involve the development of a culture of city building in city leaders, institutions, and communities based on citywide vision and concerns, proactive local government, and local initiative through participation and partnerships between different community groups. This will take concerted action over many years to develop, with incremental steps, learning from mistakes.

While there is no simple template for successful urban development and arrangements will vary between countries, this chapter attempts to draw out common themes from the analysis of urban development in Asia and the case studies. The chapter then focuses on strengthening the enabling environment for urban governance and on improving local government performance. The role of international development partners in urban development in Asia is also considered and some suggestions made for improving their performance.

COMMON THEMES

Diversity

The 12 countries in Asia considered in this book—Bangladesh, Cambodia, PRC, India, Indonesia, Lao People's Democratic Republic (Lao PDR), Malaysia, Pakistan, Philippines, Sri Lanka, Thailand, and Viet Nam—display great physical, social, economic, and political diversity. While their cities face many common issues and problems, their differences are as great as their similarities. These differences need to be taken into account in developing country- and city-specific policies and activities and in prescribing Asia-wide frameworks and solutions. What applies here may not apply there. Strategies and programs for sustainable urban futures have to be carefully tailored to particular country circumstances and to the unique characteristics of the particular city-region.

At the country level, there are major differences across virtually all indicators and in the enabling environments for urban development and management. Bangladesh, Cambodia, Lao PDR, Pakistan, and Viet Nam are the poorest countries considered here but have the highest rates of urbanization, with their urban populations estimated to increase by over 100% during 2005–2030. Malaysia is the wealthiest country, and its urbanization rate is estimated to be 66% over this period. Decentralization is much further developed in countries, such as India, Indonesia, and Philippines, than in Viet Nam or Cambodia. Moreover, while the PRC and India have decentralized systems, the guiding role of the central Government in the PRC is far more pervasive than in India. Slums and squatter settlements are more prevalent in India, Pakistan, and Philippines than in the PRC or Viet Nam, reflecting their histories and the role of central governments in controlling rural-urban migration and urban development.

Within countries, regional variations can be as wide as those between countries. There are major disparities in the economic performance of urban regions, and foreign investment is concentrated in a small number of "international" cities. This is particularly apparent in the PRC, with major income and employment differentials between the high-income, trade-oriented coastal cities and the inland cities based on underperforming state enterprises. It is also apparent in Thailand, with growth concentrated in the greater Bangkok urban agglomeration.

Within cities in Asia, there is also often great diversity in people's incomes; cultural, religious, and ethnic backgrounds; and in people's priorities and preferences. Consumption patterns vary widely. In virtually all Asian cities, there is an emerging middle class that, in some respects, lives more comfortably than their counterparts in developed countries, demanding services of all kinds and improved urban amenity. There is also a much larger group of poorly skilled workers struggling to find and maintain regular employment in low-paid jobs, often in the informal economy, highly vulnerable to the economic cycle, with low levels of consumption. Urban policies have to be cognizant of the widely disparate groups that comprise the urban community and incorporate and balance the various interests involved. Urban development is a political as well as an economic process, and priorities and trade-offs will vary between countries, between and within cities, and over time as circumstances change.

There Will be Winners and Losers

In a globalizing world of trade and capital and labor market mobility, the economic performance of cities and their ability to generate employment and income are increasingly dependent on the cities' comparative advantage nationally and globally. This has led to an increased emphasis on the competitiveness of cities and their role in fostering investment, private sector development, and employment. An important focus of city governance is now necessarily on improving the attractiveness of the city to businesses by reducing unnecessary obstacles to productivity and by providing necessary infrastructure and services. Actions of government can provide incentives (and disincentives) to business development through the efficacy of the regulatory environment, flexibility of labor force rules and regulations, efficiency and transparency of taxation and user charges, and political stability and accountability. All these are related to good governance.

While a focus on governance and locational competitiveness is important, it is but one factor affecting the location and investment decisions of firms. Other factors include agglomeration economies, resource endowment, etc. There will always be cities that, regardless of the efficiency of governance, are unable to compete in attracting businesses and investment. Over the long term, there may be a tendency to equalization, as the unemployed move to more attractive locations or prices fall sufficiently—including for labor to raise returns on investment (or the costs of other locations rise due to the negative effects of agglomeration, such as congestion). However, depressed cities and regions will remain a problem for national and city governments. Regional disparities in the PRC are one example of this problem.

A focus on locational competitiveness and city governance should not mask the need for appropriate national policies to meet the challenge of depressed cities and regions. The design of such policies will vary depending on the underlying causes of poor economic performance but may include measures, such as central government assistance with minimum levels of service provision or with key catalytic infrastructure, such as transport facilities. Policy development in this area is particularly difficult. The experience of countries worldwide with growth center and regional development policies has been at best mixed and the time frame for returns on investments has often been much longer than initially estimated. A starting point for such policies is ensuring that firms meet the full economic costs of locating and operating in rapidly expanding urban centers. Agglomeration economies are overwhelming when the benefits of agglomeration directly lift firms' bottom lines but the costs are largely unpriced and outside market forces.

Need for Policy Consistency

Policy defines the objectives of government action and the broad means to their achievement. It provides the basis for governments to develop and implement projects and programs. Policies affecting the development of cities are formulated at the national, provincial, and local levels. The integration of policy, when so many agencies and different levels of government are involved, is difficult and leads to inconsistencies and inefficiencies in policy implementation. Policy development frameworks and processes in many Asian cities need strengthening if desired outcomes are to be achieved.

Historically, the development of many Asian countries has been driven by strong, directive, national policy agendas. Since the 1990s, however, there has been a movement toward more of a guiding, less-intrusive national policy role and the decentralization of government activities to provincial and local governments. A challenge for governments in Asia is to develop consistent, effective policy frameworks for urban development within governments and across the different tiers of government. A reading of the case studies suggests that in some cases, policies—including decentralization policies—are giving mixed signals, pulling and pushing in different directions.

An example of conflicting frameworks in many Asian countries is policies for land markets and policies encouraging improved local government performance. There are close interrelationships between the efficient operation of land markets, land titling, and secure property rights that are often a national concern, and land taxes, local economic development, and land-use planning, which are usually matters for regional and local governments.

Land titling and secure property rights underpin the efficient operation of land markets and facilitate investment and local economic development. Land markets cannot operate efficiently when prospective purchasers or lessees are not sure as to the rights they are buying—there can be no fair price.

Even if land is obtained, it is then difficult to use as collateral to obtain finance because the lending institution is unsure of its rights in case of default. Unclear titling and ownership also affect regional and local governments, restricting their ability to value land and levy land taxes, leading to under-collection of taxes and legal disputes over taxes levied. Similarly, local land-use planning and land development procedures are complicated and restricted by unclear property rights. Land development becomes time consuming and is often impeded by the illegal occupation of land. This is particularly a problem in the rapidly growing, peri-urban areas of Asian cities.

The benefits of capacity building at the provincial and local government levels in such areas as land taxation, local economic development, and land-use planning will always be undermined by inadequacies in land titling and land markets. The policy frameworks need to be brought into line so that they are mutually reinforcing.

Comprehensive land reform to develop efficient land markets involves complex political, legislative, and administrative issues at all levels of government. It will not be achieved quickly and it may be necessary at the city level to develop "quasi markets," such as in special development zones, to attract investment. Such interim approaches may be unavoidable for provincial and local governments but are a poor substitute for the far broader benefits of national, efficiently functioning land markets.

The case studies clearly illustrate the damaging effects of poorly functioning land markets and inadequate land titling on local economic development and the performance of local government. Well-managed land markets are a primary factor contributing to the success of urban development in Hong Kong, China; Malaysia; and Singapore. Recent improvements to Thai land administration and management systems have contributed significantly to stabilizing property markets in Bangkok, following the 1997 Asian financial crisis. The case study on the reform of property taxation in Andhra Pradesh, India shows the relationship between land titling and properly administered land valuation systems and the successful collection of property taxes by local government authorities.

Policy consistency is also an issue in cities in Asia where multiple local governments usually exist. Left to themselves, there will inevitably be differences in approaches to land development, building standards, land-use planning, environmental standards and management, infrastructure provision, and property taxes and user charges. While some differences may be desirable, they can also be damaging to the development of sustainable cities and the management of citywide issues. Problems can include substandard construction of buildings, economic rent-seeking from land speculation, nonviable extension of infrastructure services into peri-urban areas, shortfalls in the quantity and quality of infrastructure services, and citywide environmental problems. A challenge for central governments in Asia is to set broad policy directions for city building, for regional and local governments to work within. This policy framework should emphasize effective citywide strategic planning and coordination and balance the need for consistent citywide policies with the benefits of local initiatives and innovation.

Mixed Results from Decentralization

Decentralization is being pursued by virtually all national governments in Asia to varying degrees and with mixed results. Decentralization is pursued by central governments because it provides for the more effective identification of local needs and for local resource mobilization to meet them. Empowering local communities is an instrument for achieving more effective and efficient service delivery. While the situation varies between countries, there is a general lack of clarity and confidence in local authorities as to their roles and powers under decentralization. Relatively few local governments appear to understand or utilize the opportunities that decentralization has made available to them. There is often uncertainty on the part of local authorities, a lack of capacity to develop and finance appropriate policies and programs and possibly a level of caution about central government's real expectations. These problems are particularly acute in countries, such as Cambodia and the Lao PDR, moving from centrally planned economies and with severe local resource constraints, and in Indonesia and the Philippines, which have undertaken radical decentralization reforms. While some tentative "feeling the way" is prudent, inaction can become entrenched and the benefits of decentralization lost.

Few regional or local government administrations appear to understand that decentralization calls for greater autonomy and responsibility for policy development and a reduced dependence on central government for resources and other advice. Respective roles and responsibilities for developing and implementing policy have often been clouded by a lack of clarity in legislation defining the financial and administrative responsibilities of the various levels of government. This was the case in Indonesia with the initial decentralization legislation that gave provincial and local governments much the same powers. Policy on regional development can also be ambiguous, with central government both wishing to decentralize and wanting control. Some central government involvement is necessary in strategic planning, coordination, resource mobilization, establishment of minimum service standards, and in major infrastructure projects of national importance, but it should facilitate— rather than substitute for—local development efforts.

At the city level, the role and importance of regional and urban development policy are poorly understood. Even with decentralization, many institutions continue to look to central and provincial governments for advice and direction on policy development. Local efforts are inhibited by limited skills and experience in policy development and analysis and by poor information and data. Implementing policy also has problems, with significant weaknesses in program and project design and implementation and financial management and control. The weakness of policy development and execution frameworks in Asian cities significantly undermines the effectiveness of decentralization efforts.

There appears to be a critical need for central governments to clarify their decentralization policies and expectations of local government. This goes beyond legislation and government directives to an ongoing dialogue with local government as a partner in development and appropriate training and technical assistance. Clear, consistent enabling environments and policy frameworks are central to such efforts.

Importance of Leadership

Probably the clearest message from the case studies is the importance of local leadership in achieving results. The role and importance of leadership are prevalent in virtually all the case studies, in particular the Chittagong Service Delivery and Resource Mobilization Project in Bangladesh, issue of municipal bonds by the Ahmedabad Municipal Corporation in India, Naga Metropolitan Development Council in the Philippines, Muang Klaeng Pra Sae River Rehabilitation Project in Thailand, and the Tarakan balanced approach toward urban development in East Kalimantan, Indonesia. Without strong political and community leadership, none of these projects and activities would have been initiated or driven through to successful completion.

Local leadership plays a critical role in identifying issues, engaging the community, defining priorities for action and approaches and solutions, and in mobilizing resources to achieve outcomes. The sources of leadership range from individual action—an individual sees a problem and initiates a solution—to community, nongovernment, and private sector groups, to formal political processes. Its impacts can range from small local interventions to citywide initiatives. Leadership is successful if it can involve the community and galvanize action. Leadership explains why some cities in Asia are proactive, progressive, and better able to accommodate change than others. To some extent, leadership is able to substitute for weak institutional capacity by providing drive, networks, and direction.

The case studies demonstrate different styles of leadership. Political leadership and commitment to change are important; however, academic, business, and institutional leadership is also important. As part of capacity building, there is a role for programs aimed at strengthening local leadership and sharing information on successful initiatives.

Strengthening Urban Management

Improved urban management is essential to the sustainable development of Asian cities, including the provision of land, infrastructure, community services, logistics, communications, and environmental management. Successful urban management is multisector and involves multidisciplinary engagement in activities related to urban policy development, planning and administration, finance, development, operations, and maintenance of cities. It also involves creating enabling mechanisms to facilitate engagement between governments, business, and communities in building and maintaining better cities. Many Asian cities lack an urban management framework and the institutional and coordination arrangements that allow effective, citywide strategic planning, community participation, and infrastructure and service provision.

Problems of Coordination

Coordination of policy, planning, and service provision is a major problem for Asian cities. Decentralization, the rapidly expanding size of cities, the number of governments at various levels involved in city governance, and the range of special-purpose authorities providing city infrastructure and services have all contributed to the need for effective formal and informal frameworks of coordination. Coordination is necessary vertically between central and local governments and special-purpose authorities, and horizontally between subnational governments and institutions. Cities are rarely governed at the city or city-region level and, even if they are, there are also usually numerous local authorities. Some infrastructure and services may not be able to be efficiently provided by smaller local authorities. Duplication of infrastructure can be a problem. Some infrastructure requires citywide provision and other infrastructure in a city is a small part of a much larger national network.

Coordination is inevitably problematic. Cities are large complex systems, with many stakeholders with varying interests. Local authority boundaries are important in minimizing coordination problems, as are clear understanding of jurisdictions and functions. Frameworks of coordination need to be established to facilitate the resolution of cross-border issues, such as environment and transport problems, and to manage interactions with rural areas.

They are also important for citywide infrastructure and service provision in areas, such as strategic planning, financing and cost recovery, and quality and reliability of service provision. Central governments and other more senior levels of government play an important role in establishing and implementing coordination frameworks. They must practice what they preach in order to establish a culture of coordination.

Improvements to coordination and decision-making processes do not occur organically. Analysis and monitoring can improve their structure, efficiency, and effectiveness. This could potentially be a productive area for assistance with urban management.

Institutional Strengthening and Capacity Building

Capacity building of city governments and local institutions is central to meeting the challenge of growing cities in Asia. Underperformance in the provision of city infrastructure and services is the inevitable consequence of weak institutions. Local institutions are generally lacking in human, financial, and technical resources and in systems for strategic planning, policy development, management, and financial budgeting and control. Strengthening local governments and local institutions will take time, resources, and concerted effort. Strategies for achieving stronger city institutions are essential to achieving sustainable improvements and should be the first priority for assistance for urban development.

The pace of urbanization in Asia and of decentralization of governance has left many regional/local institutions ill prepared to conduct the business of government. The bureaucratic nature of operation, complexity of organization structures, and overlapping of agency functions hamper the efficiency and effectiveness of many institutions. There is often strong resistance to institutional reforms and to the introduction of technologies and systems that threaten job security, hierarchies, and established workplace practices. There is a lack of strategic planning and a poorly developed culture of consultation on matters of public interest and concern. Institutions have poor customer and client orientation. Many institutions have little experience of developing partnerships with community groups or private enterprise and no experience of business development. Financial management is poor, with little focus on developing the local revenue base. Many of these issues are local, but central government assistance is necessary to guide and encourage reforms, including through staff development and training programs and assistance with systems development. Improvement in the performance of local governments and regional state-owned enterprises is vital to enhancing the competitiveness and sustainability of cities in Asia.

Human capital underpins the sustainability of the projects presented in the case studies. Most local governments in Asia, especially those outside the larger cities, lack the critical mass of skills, competencies, and technologies needed to create and manage efficient institutions. In some countries, like Indonesia and the Philippines, there is a huge loss of intellectual capital caused by the migration of skilled people from the country. While many of these people continue to contribute to the development of the country through remittances, these countries are deprived of critical human capital needed to support their development. Increasingly, efforts are needed to develop a large pool of urban development and management skills and expertise to meet the growing pressures of urbanization.

Stakeholder Participation, Network Building, and Partnerships

Developing sustainable cities within decentralized governance frameworks relies on developing processes at the local level for defining and fulfilling local needs and for holding local authorities accountable for their performance in both meeting needs and balancing competing priorities. Such processes require stakeholder participation and the building of broad networks and partnerships involving all elements of civil society—government and government agencies, communities, nongovernment and local community organizations, and private sector interests and organizations. The case studies virtually all relied for their success on building frameworks for active stakeholder participation. To be effective, stakeholder participation requires involving these groups in strategic planning as well as activity design, financing, and implementation. This is resource intensive and trust building is continuous and time consuming. It is critical for city development to mobilize all of the assets of the city—its intellectual, physical, and financial capital—and to develop partnerships and strategic alliances between the various interest groups. Transparent systems and processes for stakeholder participation, network building, and partnerships are not generally well developed in Asian cities, and this acts to undermine the development of cities.

Local economic development is a particular area for network building and partnerships. Much regional business tends to be parochial in nature with a focus restricted to the local market. Networks and partnerships are critical for regional businesses and organizations to build up the marketing, information, and supply chain networks necessary for business expansion and for cities to develop broader trade and investment opportunities. Networks, strategic alliances, and innovative public-private and community-based partnerships can be critical elements of strategic infrastructure for regions and cities to diversify and develop growing, often more service-based economies.

The building up of networks, however, takes time and is difficult, particularly as there can be cultural, social, and religious barriers to overcome. Few local governments appear to appreciate their role in creating an investment and business climate for encouraging development.

Reforming City Planning

Most countries in Asia have put considerable resources into economic and spatial planning processes at the regional and city levels over the last 50 years. While the details and results have varied between countries, these have generally borne little relationship to forces in the real economy and to the range of factors affecting the investment decisions of firms or to realistic projections of resource mobilization by urban governments. They have often been little more than "wish lists."

Plans have failed for many reasons. Neither the resources nor the mechanisms have been in place for implementation. There have been weak linkages between planning and budgeting, and the integration of sector strategies has been frustrated by the "silo mentality" of agencies. The approach to development has often been supply rather than demand driven, with a focus on outputs rather than outcomes. There has also been a lack of understanding or analysis of what strategic, catalytic infrastructure a region needs to build to develop a competitive and more sustainable economy.

In countries with more directed economies, such as the PRC and Viet Nam, more has been achieved in allocating investment and in restricting rural-urban migration, but at the cost of efficient, flexible resource allocation. The high efficiency cost of rigid central planning has been a factor leading to the growing liberalization of these economies. Land-use planning involving zoning has been similarly unsuccessful and proven difficult to enforce. It has crumbled in the face of rapid urbanization, inefficient land and housing markets, pressures to attract firms and create employment, and been widely subject to corruption.

Decentralization, globalization, the transition to more market-oriented economies, and the failure of existing processes are causing a revision of city planning processes for Asian cities. Uncontrolled forces have created chaos on the urban periphery of many cities, with the envelopment of productive agricultural land, difficulties of access to employment and services, and substandard, often illegal housing and disputes over land tenure. These costs fall disproportionately on the poor. The cost of infrastructure provision has been increased as it follows development. Local economic development has been set back because the lack of infrastructure inhibits access and it is difficult to obtain services.

Land use and the form of urban structure significantly influence economic development and welfare in cities, and the costs of infrastructure and service provision. The issue is how to get the benefits of guiding urban land use without the high costs of regulations that are difficult to enforce, bureaucratic, open to corruption, and act as a disincentive to local economic development. While some regulation is necessary and unavoidable, cities are attempting to rebalance city planning and shift the focus to rolling, anticipatory approaches where urban form is shaped by the provision of trunk infrastructure, zoning is simplified, and market-based approaches using prices are used to control such matters as environmental emissions. In this model, the public sector is less concerned with directly providing services, such as infrastructure, land, and housing, and focuses instead on developing an enabling role through partnerships with the private sector and community groups that support the supply of such services.

The extent to which city planning has adjusted to very rapid urban development in Asia varies between cities but is generally poor. Reforms are not progressing fast enough to accommodate the projected rapid future economic and population growth and rapidly increasing demands for urban infrastructure and services. City planning is another area where research, experience sharing, and technical assistance and training will be necessary to achieve better approaches and outcomes.

Financial Sustainability and Weaknesses in Financial Management

Ultimately, local financial sustainability and political autonomy can only be achieved if the costs of providing infrastructure and services are paid by users either directly through tariffs and user charges or indirectly through local taxes, possibly supplemented by formula-driven, general-purpose grants from more centralized governments.

Local financial sustainability is poorly developed in Asian countries. While there is considerable variation from country to country, local institutions are generally reliant on revenue-sharing arrangements with the central government for the major part of their revenues. This has tended to create a culture within local authorities of resources being mainly a matter for central governments. There is little alignment between local authority functions and revenue-raising capacity and little incentive to fully exploit the local tax base or user charges. Access of local authorities to loan funds and capital markets is often restricted by central governments—both in total and as to appropriate investments—and little attention has been paid to their asset base, creditworthiness, and capacity to pay. As a result, local authorities tend to be only "semifinancial" and most would fail to meet the requirements of credit rating agencies in the absence of central government guarantees. New financial frameworks are essential if more proactive urban governments are to be developed, capable of addressing the major underinvestment in infrastructure and services.

Another challenge facing the sustainable development of cities in Asia is the inadequacy of financial management. This has many aspects. Some relate to the enabling environment for financial management created by central government; others reflect poor leadership, inadequate skills, and systems within the local authorities themselves. Systems for financial management and control—including accounting and audit, management and accountability, monitoring, risk management, asset management, cash flow management, billing and collections, and debt management—are poorly developed. Corruption is a significant problem. Local tax collections are low, and the systems are inefficient.

Several case studies provide examples of good practice approaches to urban financial management. Sleman in Indonesia is an excellent example of the local government introducing performance-based budgeting and sound financial management. This municipality provides a benchmark for sound financial management for local governments in Indonesia. The Ahmedabad and Andhra Pradesh case studies from India illustrate the need for improved financial management and the importance of establishing credit ratings for cities. Credit rating of local governments is a good practice being adopted in many developed countries, as illustrated in the Brisbane case study. However, in Asian countries, it is a relatively new concept but essential to improving the overall financial management of local governments. The Phnom Penh Planning for All Project demonstrates the willingness of poor communities to invest in improved urban services.

Cost recovery and affordability remain significant problems for providing infrastructure in Asian cities. The case studies demonstrate that where there are high levels of engagement and a clear understanding of benefits by communities from the provision of infrastructure, there is a willingness to pay. Problems with the financing of infrastructure are with both cost-recovery mechanisms and the lack of enabling mechanisms for local governments to gain access to markets for capital. In some cases, the borrowing limits set by central governments relate to their grant allocations to local government, providing little incentive for local governments to be better financial managers and to improve cash flow through traditional revenue sources or other innovative means.

Weaknesses in financial management are a factor inhibiting central governments from decentralizing greater financial autonomy to local government and leading to the mixed results from decentralization discussed earlier.

Strengthening of enabling environments and assistance for capacity building of city institutions in all areas of financial management and control are necessary if financial sustainability is to be attained.

Mobilization of Regional Capital Stocks

Local governments' ability to provide infrastructure and services is dependent on its ability to mobilize resources and service its repayment responsibilities. An important factor in mobilizing resources is the city's asset base. The value and quality of all aspects of the capital base in most cities in Asia, however, are generally unknown. This inhibits the ability of local authorities to leverage assets and mobilize funds for strategic investments. With few exceptions, local governments do not know what land or other assets they hold or their value; nor have they prepared a balance sheet suitable to establish a credit rating. The extent of private investment and of capital held by regional banks is also generally unknown. Little attention appears to have been paid to mobilizing local savings for local capital needs. Private capital through domestic savings often flows out of cities to the larger "international" cities because of the lack of bankable investments. A large proportion of land and housing is not part of the formal property market due to weaknesses in the administration of land titling, which inhibits its use as collateral. There is, therefore, a situation in which regions are capital rich and cash poor, with few mechanisms for mobilizing capital into funds for investment.

These problems, along with the deficiencies in financial sustainability and financial management noted above, have been a major contributor to backlogs in infrastructure and service provision. Frameworks need to be put in place for local authorities to mobilize capital, provide infrastructure and services, and take responsibility for payments.

THE ENABLING ENVIRONMENT AND THE PERFORMANCE OF CITIES

National governments in Asia have a strong interest in urban development because economically dynamic cities are central to economic growth and to improvements in standards of living and poverty reduction. In general, rapid urbanization and economic growth in Asia have increased the political and administrative pressures for national governments to decentralize government decision making and service delivery to subnational, more local government, and, in the case of such utilities as electricity supply, to special-purpose authorities.

Urban governance comprises the totality of national government, regional government, local government, and special-purpose authority policies and programs directed at managing or providing infrastructure and services in cities. Urban governance in Asia, as elsewhere, is a complex mix of interventions. Each of the 12 Asian countries considered in this book has a unique set of arrangements. Nowhere is city governance in all its aspects and local government synonymous and this is further complicated by most cities' comprising many local government areas. The results are overlapping boundaries, unclear jurisdictions, and problems of coordination that inhibit strategic planning and the development of citywide policies and approaches. Compounding such problems is the weak institutional capacity of local government, including major discrepancies between nominal functions and tax base and revenue-raising capacities.

National governments largely set the framework in which provincial and local governments operate; increasingly, central controls are being balanced with greater local responsibility, allowing real local-level decision-making. Even with decentralization, national governments can be expected to continue to play an active role in urban governance, selectively intervening in areas considered to be of national interest or priority, setting national standards for service delivery, providing technical assistance for institutional strengthening and capacity building, monitoring local authority performance, intervening where local governments are deemed to have failed, and providing incentives for effective coordination, improved service delivery, and financial performance.

While details vary from country to country in Asia, national government laws, policies, regulations, financial arrangements, and directives set the enabling environment through which urban governance is established and operates. They establish what must be done, what can be done, what cannot be done, and by whom. They establish the policy and program space within which local governments have the flexibility to operate. Parts of this enabling environment are directly related to local government (such as legislation establishing local government, local government revenue-sharing arrangements, and employment regulations governing local authorities); others are national policies that indirectly affect local government activities (examples vary but often include land titling and land markets, housing policies, poverty reduction programs, heritage protection, and resettlement guidelines); still other parts of the enabling environment comprise legislation and regulations establishing and controlling the operations of special-purpose authorities. The national government enabling environment for urban governance and its associated incentives structure is a key factor influencing the performance of local authorities and of urban areas.

The role of national governments is also critical in facilitating coordination between the various levels of government and with special-purpose authorities.

The structure and operation of the enabling environment are central to the functioning of urban governance and to the provision of infrastructure and services. Importantly, the impact of the enabling environment is more than laws and regulations; it also plays an important role in setting the culture of operation of local authorities. At one end of the spectrum, the enabling environment can encourage the development of performance-based cities with a focus on locational competitiveness, results, performance benchmarks, incentives for achievement, and efficiency of service provision; at the other extreme, it can lead to a culture of stifling, unproductive, administrative process and inefficiency. Decentralization can only yield improved performance in infrastructure and service delivery if it is associated with a culture of performance improvement, often supported by incentives. Generally, the enabling environment is less important the stronger the leadership, capacity, and resources of the local government; governments with stronger leadership are better able to find and exploit policy, program, and administrative flexibility.

While there is no ideal system of city governance—the arrangements in each country are always a work in progress evolving to reflect the country's history, politics, culture, and stage of development—there are some universal features of effective, proactive systems of city governance and administration. Importantly, these features are all the responsibility in the first instance of national government, which creates the enabling environment for city governance. The following features provide a useful yardstick for assessing governance systems in Asia and a starting point for any efforts to improve the efficiency of urban governance.

- **The functions of government**. Central, regional, and local governments and special-purpose authorities have clearly defined functions, minimizing areas of overlapping responsibilities.
- **Geographic boundaries**. Regional and local governments and special-purpose authorities have boundaries, which effectively balance the need for efficiency of service delivery with appropriate community representation. Too much government can be as big a problem as too little.
- **City region governance**. There are frameworks in place that provide for whole of city and urban region issues to be analyzed and addressed across administrative boundaries in areas, such as economic development, strategic planning, rural-urban linkages, the envelopment of peri-urban areas, and infrastructure and service provision.

- **Coordination and consultation arrangements.** Frameworks for formally undertaking coordination and consultation are widely understood and effectively utilized by all levels of government; these are supplemented by extensive informal consultation.
- **Financial relations.** The framework for intergovernmental financial relations supports the financial sustainability of cities and local governments by broadly aligning the tax bases and revenue-raising capabilities of governments and authorities (including any intergovernmental revenue-sharing arrangements and general- and specific-purpose transfers from more central governments) with their functional responsibilities; such frameworks support financial independence and a proactive approach to service delivery by rewarding the appropriate exploitation of tax bases and of user charges/cost recovery.
- **Capital requirements.** Central government frameworks encourage access to loan funds and capital markets by local authorities at market terms and conditions within the constraints of prudent financial management by local authorities and within the requirements of overall macroeconomic management; such frameworks encourage local authorities to operate as market entities, balancing capital requirements with risk and capacity to pay considerations, and prudent financial management is rewarded by increased access to capital.
- **Performance-based management.** Management and financial frameworks are structured to emphasize results and performance against benchmarks, including through the use of incentives.
- **Accountability.** Decision-making processes and audit and reporting systems emphasize transparency, performance, and community consultation and involvement.

The various frameworks of decentralized governance in Asian countries can be assessed against these features. While there is much information on urban development and on local government, relatively little attention has been paid to comprehensively assessing the enabling environments in countries for city governance and on its impacts on city performance. While this architecture varies widely across the region, it has generally encouraged weak, fragmented urban governance, major problems of planning and coordination in cities, and problems of resource mobilization and infrastructure and service provision. The country chapters provide ample examples of these problems.

The tendency to date has been for central governments and international development partners to focus on the local level and on capacity problems of local government while giving insufficient attention to the enabling environment. While local government has major capacity problems that need to be addressed, this is the microeconomic equivalent of trying to develop an efficient textiles industry behind a high tariff wall and being surprised that the result is not a sustainable industry! Periodic reviews of the enabling environment in countries are an essential component to developing a culture of proactive city governance and to improving the performance of cities. Enabling environments should not be static. Rather they should be viewed as policy instruments to phase the development of responsive, effective city governance.

STRENGTHENING LOCAL GOVERNMENT

While the enabling environment defines the space within which local government operates and plays a major role in developing the culture of local government, major efforts across Asia are required to strengthen and build the capacity of local government itself. Local government must be capable of exploiting fully the policy and program opportunities made available to it. The enabling environment and the capacity of local government are closely related. The stronger the ability of local government, the more national governments are likely to increase the role and responsibilities of local government and vice versa.

Local government plays a central role in the welfare and amenity of urban communities. It does this in many ways. Local government directly affects local economic development and employment through its impacts on locational competitiveness and the local investment climate.[1] It affects the costs of establishing and operating business enterprises and their profitability. An important objective of local government should be to improve the income and employment effects of urbanization by reducing barriers to productivity growth. Local government also plays an important role in protecting the poor and most disadvantaged members of the community, affects the supply and availability of infrastructure and services, and guides and regulates the social, environmental, and spatial effects of growth. Virtually all the case studies were dependent in one way or another for their success on local government.

The challenge for local government in Asia, as elsewhere, is to increase the welfare of citizens. To fulfill its responsibilities, it requires the capacity to assess community needs, plan strategically for future community development, set priorities, balance numerous and sometimes competing interests, and provide infrastructure and services. Local government needs to approach these roles flexibly—to plan ahead, manage risk, and focus on outcomes. Its roles will vary depending upon circumstances. In some cases, it will be a provider of services or regulator of activities and in others, indirectly guide development or act as an enabler of service provision.

In the 12 countries considered in this book, the operation of local government in cities is made more difficult by the rapid pace of population and economic growth. During the 10 years 2005–2015, the populations in 219 of these 12 countries' major cities[2] are projected to grow by more than 30% and many will grow faster. The capacity of local government has to change fundamentally and increase if it is to meet this challenge of urban growth.

The outlook is further complicated by the fact that many urban services require major investments in capital facilities, such as electricity generation and distribution capacity, water treatment works and distribution pipelines, and sewerage capacity. Such investments have a long life and maintenance requirements and there are long planning and construction lead times before services are brought on line. Even if there are concerted attempts to strengthen local government now, Asian cities will inevitably continue to struggle to keep up with service provision as population growth overtakes planning and design capacity, and in view of the time necessary for construction and service augmentation.

The management, mobilization, and application of resources to meet the challenge of rapid urban growth will be major factors determining the successful evolution in Asia from rural to urban societies. While economic growth and urbanization increase income, a central issue for local government is how to capture an adequate share of this income to finance the supply and maintenance of necessary infrastructure and services. A related issue is how best to finance and provide these services as effectively and efficiently as possible, whether directly by government, through public-private partnerships, or indirectly through creating markets to encourage the private or community sector provision of such services. Different approaches will suit different circumstances, but what is important is that such services are efficiently provided and that local government fulfills an enabling role to achieve this end.

Strengthening local government and improving its performance requires action across the wide range of areas of local government management and operation. Priorities will vary depending on the particular capabilities of the local government concerned. Programs for strengthening local government are primarily the responsibility of the local authority itself. However, left to themselves, this will result in the more proactive and progressive authorities moving further ahead in overall performance and other authorities being left behind. National programs sponsored by central governments in Asia are probably essential if the overall performance of their local government system is to improve. As part of efforts to strengthen local government, attention also needs to be paid to the development of local area information, maps and statistics, and to networks and processes for sharing information, including the wide dissemination of information on successes and failures.

Areas for local government capacity building and institution strengthening cover the ambit of local government activities. Priorities will depend on the particular authority, its needs, and circumstances. Areas include:

- **civic and local government leadership,** including probity, transparency, and accountability in decision making;
- **the involvement of civil society,** including consultation and involvement of communities, community organizations, and the private sector in planning and decision making, and in partnerships in infrastructure and service provision;
- **human resource development and training,** to improve the skills and technical capacities of local authority staff;
- **policy development and policy instruments,** to strengthen the capacity of local authorities to develop policy, make strategic choices and establish priorities for action, and to canvass the policy instruments available to local authorities—civic guidance, regulations and codes, fines, taxes, user charges—and their applicability and efficiency in different circumstances;
- **local government management systems,** to support strategic planning, risk management, and policy and program development;
- **local government information systems,** reliable, recent data and maps that are the starting point for environmental management and strategic planning, and for property taxes, tariff collections, and environmental taxes and charges;
- **financial management policies and systems,** to strengthen local government revenue raising and expenditure controls while providing for necessary audit and review;
- **capital and asset management policies and systems,** to improve local authority access to capital markets, and ability to mobilize resources and assess financial risk;
- **environmental management,** including priority setting, cost-effective technologies, establishment of appropriate environmental standards and instruments for their achievement, and monitoring arrangements;
- **land-use planning and land management**;
- **modalities of service provision,** including local government business operations and the involvement of the private sector in infrastructure provision and service delivery; and
- **benchmarking,** the establishment of standards for assessing local authority performance.

Cities, if they are to become more competitive and able to provide necessary infrastructure and services in this decentralized environment, will need to become much smarter and more efficient in the way they are governed. This will not simply evolve. It will require the progressive development of an enabling environment that provides policy and program space for local governments and encourages a culture of innovation and change; it will also require substantial investment in institutional development and capacity building, including management and staff training and systems development. It will involve the development of proactive local governments partnering with community groups and leveraging capital and resources with the private sector to deliver the services that those increasingly affluent communities have come to expect. It will also involve paying greater attention to environmental and social development issues. Present decentralization efforts are the first small step in empowering city governments and management in Asia.

THE ROLE OF INTERNATIONAL DEVELOPMENT INSTITUTIONS

International development institutions have been engaged in activities in Asian cities over many years. They include the multilateral development banks—the World Bank, Asian Development Bank, United Nations agencies, and donor country aid agencies. These institutions have a long involvement in sectors, such as electricity, water supply, health, education, and transport that in one way or another involve urban areas. They have also developed programs and projects with a specifically cities focus in areas, such as municipal capacity building, municipal finance, housing and slum upgrading, sanitation, and solid waste management. Many case studies considered in this book would not have been initiated and undertaken without financial and technical assistance from international development institutions. This section does not attempt to assess existing strategies or to analyze program and project performance but to make some brief, general observations on the role of international development institutions in urban development in Asia.

A common problem for the international development agencies is that cities are not a sector in their parlance; these institutions are usually structured to provide assistance on a sectoral basis. While they have more or less well-developed practices for accommodating such crosscutting issues as women in development, cities also do not sit comfortably within a crosscutting issues framework. City-regions are more analogous with nation states—they have a distinct economy, engage in trade, face issues of competition and comparative advantage, and have labor and capital markets. Like a nation state, they are a distinct spatial entity around which issues of economic development, infrastructure provision, environmental sustainability, community welfare, and poverty have to be managed. Also like nation states, there are complex governance arrangements, numerous cross-border issues, and matters for inter jurisdictional management.

The international development agencies have struggled to develop institutional arrangements for urban development that foster the analysis and development of integrated programs for cities as unique spatial entities and economies. The level of comparability between urban regions is about the same as that between nation states. They require similar levels of information and analysis to understand development processes; yet information and depth of analysis on city economies remain poorly developed compared to the wealth of information on nation states. The economies of large cities, like Jakarta and Bangkok, are much larger than those of smaller nation states, such as Cambodia and Lao PDR, but our understanding of what is taking place and how to improve city performance is much less developed. An important role for international development agencies is to assist in developing the information base on cities along with analytical frameworks for making this information relevant to governments and decision makers.

The international development institutions as a whole provide very modest additional resources for investment in urban development in Asia. Precise figures are difficult to obtain because of differences about what is classified as an urban development activity. They probably provide about 3–5% of total urban development investments, although this can be much higher in some smaller, poorer countries in the region. On the whole, urban projects have been assessed by these institutions as reasonably successful in delivering infrastructure and services, but sustainability has been a recurring issue. Broader benefits for urban development through systemic policy reforms and the transfer of knowledge and approaches—intellectual capital—which flow through and influences future urban development activities, have proven elusive. The overall influence of the international development institutions on city development and performance in Asia can be important but needs to be kept in perspective; it is dwarfed by that of national and local governments.

Critical to the role of an international development agency is the process of consultation and dialogue with partner governments that acts to bring the government's and agency's perspectives on needs, objectives, and activities into alignment. While there are cases where one-off activities without broader benefits are justified in their own right, there is a compelling case for international development institutions to focus as far as possible on investments with broader systemic benefits to national or citywide frameworks or that showcase new technologies or approaches likely to be replicated in other locations. This implies that they should focus on their catalytic role as facilitators and enablers rather than as providers of infrastructure and services, and include specific processes for capturing multiplier benefits in program and project designs.

The objective of improving the performance of cities so that cities can themselves mobilize resources, provide necessary infrastructure and services, and contribute to improvements in standards of living and reductions in poverty underpins the involvement of international development agencies in urban development. This is the same objective as that of national governments in establishing the enabling environment for city governance and in decentralizing governance and service provision. Central to achieving this objective is facilitating markets—broadening and deepening capital, land, and housing markets; strengthening local economic development; and capacity building/institutional strengthening of city governments and institutions. These areas should be the focus of assistance to urban areas. Assistance with infrastructure and service provision needs to be assessed in terms of its catalytic impacts and contribution to sustainable improvements in city performance. With facilitating markets, it is important to avoid the creation of new quasi-market intermediaries that themselves become new barriers to developing efficiently functioning markets.

The development banks and, to a lesser extent, other international development agencies, have addressed issues associated with the growth of cities by developing urban strategies to guide their lending and program activities. These have become increasingly sophisticated over time as their operational experience expanded. Nevertheless, the development and management of urban programs have remained a difficult area for the international development agencies and their level of commitment to urban development has waxed and waned along with that of partner governments. The audience for the urban strategies of international development institutions is multi-layered; these strategies are written for their own management and staff and for the broader professional and consulting community. It is less clear to what extent these documents are embraced by partner governments as strategies for action. There is a real risk of engaging with those "in the club" rather than building broad support within partner governments for strengthening urban development frameworks and improving the performance of cities.

The starting point for a successful urban strategy is developing a robust case, in dialogue with partner governments, that national development is based on the development of sustainable cities and that investing scarce resources through an urban framework will have higher, more sustainable development returns than using sectoral frameworks alone. This needs to be followed by developing urban country strategies with interested governments, which analyze individual country circumstances—the enabling environment for urban governance and the capacities of local governments and institutions—and establish agreed priorities for action. Process is critical if strategies are to be translated into action. Country urban strategies are in many ways more important than generalized urban strategies because they are able to reflect the wide differences in urban development in Asian countries and suggest approaches specifically tailored to country situations.

In developing and implementing an urban strategy, it is important to recognize that there are barriers to moving away from sectoral approaches, not least of which is that it is often administratively simpler and cheaper to work within a "provider" sectoral model. These are usually well established and, even at the project level, the development and supervision costs of a single sector activity, say, in augmenting urban water supply, will usually be lower than for a similarly sized, multiagency urban capacity building project that might have management, finance, and infrastructure components. To be successful, urban development activities tend to be relatively high cost and long term because they focus on systemic citywide issues and capacity building rather than focusing directly on increasing infrastructure or service provision. If well designed, the benefits can be high but generating performance benefits quickly is more difficult and this can be a problem for the relatively short-term, performance-based management systems that many international development agencies favor.

There are three main areas for involvement by the international development institutions in urban development:

- **Global Issues.** The multilateral development institutions have a natural advantage in addressing cross-border issues of global environmental sustainability. Global issues, such as climate change and greenhouse gas emissions, are closely tied to economic development, the growth of cities, and the use of resource intensive technologies. As noted in Chapter 2, the scale of development and production and consumption patterns in Asian cities are major factors contributing to the global growth of greenhouse gases. Multilateral institutions are able to take a global view, undertake cross-country analyses, and put forward programs of action for addressing such issues. They provide a forum where the allocation of costs can be discussed. Looking ahead, issues of production and consumption patterns in Asian cities, transport technologies and modes, technologies for electricity generation, the efficiency of energy use, application of less resource-intensive technologies, and modalities for financing activities in this area are likely to be at the cutting edge of multilateral development institutions' involvement in Asian cities.

- **Country Urban Strategies.** As discussed earlier, the enabling environment in each country is a critical factor in the development and performance of cities. International development institutions are well placed to work with governments in Asia on strengthening national enabling environments. While each country's situation is unique, knowledge of international practices and approaches can supplement national efforts to strengthen the enabling environment and improve the performance of cities and the operation of urban governance. The involvement of international development agencies in this area can be via technical assistance with analysis and policy formulation; it can potentially lead to policy-based assistance and very broad-based countrywide programs of city development.
- **City Projects and Programs.** These will remain a mainstay of assistance through international development institutions for urban development. They will still involve single city and multicity activities but their focus will change. The pressure for cities to generate employment and services for rapidly expanding populations will see the focus of these activities move toward improving city performance, local economic development, and deepening and broadening markets. Such projects and programs will increasingly need to focus on the institutions of urban governance, and on issues of capacity building and institutional strengthening. Their sustainability will largely depend on successfully balancing the complexity of interventions and reforms with capacity building of authorities. Capacity building takes time.

PATHWAYS TO SUSTAINABLE URBAN FUTURES

There are many perspectives on urban sustainability. Some see it as an environment and development issue. Others emphasize the protection of culture and heritage values. Others see it as a social issue with aspects of equity, fairness, and responsibility in meeting the needs of future generations. Still, others focus on resource use and the better leveraging of resources, closing the waste loop, building better knowledge, leadership, and governance and planning. The path to sustainability involves all these things. It does not provide for simply protecting and maintaining the status quo for future generations. This is neither desirable nor achievable.

Sustainability is concerned with change; managing risks, tensions, shocks, disruption, and other forces that threaten to undermine life systems—physical, social, and economic. It is also about generating change and building on change to renew systems and improve peoples' welfare.

The challenge of creating sustainable futures for Asian cities is how to promote a culture of city building that embraces change and proactively seeks to improve people's living standards and welfare, while minimizing and managing its associated problems. This is difficult because there is a strong inertia in existing practices and change can involve conflict with respected values, traditions, culture, beliefs, and institutions.

Achieving greater sustainability of urban development will be difficult. In the longer term, it will require a significant shift in societal values, behavior, and consumption and production patterns. Such changes will not occur quickly. Powerful forces are at play in Asian cities, as elsewhere, that are resistant to such changes and that shape consumer behavior and aspirations, and drive production and distribution systems and governments. Much of the machinery, technology, and institutions for maintaining everyday life in Asian cities will inevitably remain much the same for years to come. Some infrastructure and systems will take several generations to be replaced by more sustainable systems, practices, and processes. Identifying ways to make existing systems and practices more sustainable is one of the most significant challenges facing Asian cities.

The challenge of urbanization and sustainability in Asia is enormous. Accommodating the needs for housing, infrastructure, and employment for the 1.1 billion people expected to be added to cities by 2030 will require major changes to the development and management of cities. As stated in Chapter 1, the scale of urbanization is unprecedented in human history. For many, when considering the magnitude of the needs and problems facing Asian cities, there is a tendency to despair. But history shows that cities have a remarkable ability for resilience when faced with problems and adversity that threaten their existence. Asian cities are slowly developing pathways to achieving more sustainable development outcomes, but now is the time to accelerate change to achieve these ends. To do this will require governments, and particularly central governments, to provide the leadership to radically strengthen city governance and its ability to mobilize resources and provide infrastructure and services.

There are three main pillars to strengthening city governance and accelerating the sustainable development of cities in Asia. All are important to success.

The first pillar involves *improving the enabling environments,* the framework of institutions, policies, incentive structures, and reporting requirements for urban governance. It will also involve further developing and deepening financial, land, and property markets. This is essential to allow urban governance to operate effectively and set cities on pathways toward more sustainable urban futures.

The second pillar in building more sustainable urban futures for Asian cities is ensuring that *decentralization and devolution* are made to work. Central governments have neither the resources nor local knowledge to provide local infrastructure and services and this is recognized in the movement toward decentralization across the region. This is not going to change. Urban governance and particularly local governments have to have clear, unencumbered responsibilities and be provided with the ability to finance and provide citywide infrastructure and services. To date, decentralization has had only mixed success and been held back by problems in the enabling environment and with the capacities of local governments and institutions.

The third pillar in moving toward more sustainable urban futures is continuing programs of technical assistance and training for improving *urban governance and management.* These need to be fast-tracked and should be particularly directed toward local government. Their focus should be on improving the competitiveness of cities and the management of cities on a performance-results basis. Major investments are required in leadership development and human resource development programs for local authority politicians, management, and staff. Institutional strengthening through the development and implementation of performance-based systems of management and control is essential to improving urban governance.

Overall, a shift in priorities for assistance is required. The priority should be on developing the enabling environment and performance-based institutions, with less direct attention to infrastructure and service provision. Dynamic, performance-based local governments are central to meeting the development challenge of rapidly increasing urban populations with rising standards of living.

Putting these three pillars in place is essential to moving more quickly to achieving sustainable development outcomes for cities in Asia. This book has demonstrated the importance of enabling environments and good local governance and management in achieving sustainable development outcomes. The roles of leadership, learning, networks, community participation and involvement, and leveraging resources have been critical to the success of the case studies.

As a conclusion, the city of Manchester is revisited. Manchester was a mother city of the industrial revolution. Many problems associated with overcrowding, poor housing, environmental pollution, transport congestion, education, health, and poverty in Asian cities today can be read in the pages of the history of Manchester. It is a city that has experienced many crises; polluted by its industrial wastes, destroyed by war, and its traditional industries devastated by globalization, technological change, and changes to markets for its products. Through more than 200 years of urbanization and industrialization, the city has learned to deal with these crises and has reinvented itself and improved its amenity and governance practices to become a leader in sustainable urban development in Europe.

But Manchester has left an awful legacy for future generations. As the author of the Manchester case study has written that after 200 years of heavy industry, "Manchester is still the 'pollution capital' of the United Kingdom. The surrounding uplands are well over their 'critical loads' for acidity, river quality is only now less than toxic, and a tenth of urban land is potentially contaminated and unstable. A quarter of all households drink lead in their water, half are seriously disturbed by noise, and there is a 3% annual growth trend in household waste."

Unless Asian cities begin to change their development path, they risk creating a legacy of the type that the inhabitants of Greater Manchester face today. That inheritance has left a mortgage, which future generations of the city will be paying for another 100 years or more. Those responsible for the development and management of cities in Asia would be irresponsible not to learn from other cities' experience. Now is the time to act and set new pathways to ensure the future sustainable development of Asian cities.

Notes

[1] The paper by David Dollar, Anqing Shi, Shuilin Wang, and Lixin Colin Xu, *Improving City Competitiveness through the Investment Climate: Ranking 23 Chinese Cities* (World Bank 2003), provides an analysis of city competitiveness in the People's Republic of China (PRC) and a review of the literature on the PRC and other Asian countries. They characterize the investment climate as having the following elements: infrastructure, domestic entry and exit barriers, skills and technology endowment, labor market flexibility, international integration, private sector participation, informal payments, tax burdens, court efficiency, and finance. While the paper does not focus specifically on local government, the performance of local governments affects virtually all of these elements and the competitiveness rankings of the cities analyzed.

[2] Capital cities or urban agglomerations with 750,000 or more inhabitants in 2000.

References

Abbott, J. 2002. An Analysis of Informal Settlement Upgrading and Critique of Existing Methodological Approaches. *Habitat International* 26: 303–315.

ADB. 1997.. *Policies for Improving Urban Management. Loan 1572-INO: Capacity Building in Urban Infrastructure Management*. Manila.

———. 2000a. *Vientiane Urban Infrastructure and Services Project, Final Report*. Manila.

———. 2000b. *Vientiane Urban Infrastructure and Services Project, Vientiane Participatory Poverty Assessment*. Manila.

———. 2001a. *A Participatory Poverty Assessment, Lao PDR*. Manila.

———. 2001b. *Pre-Investment Study for GMS East-West Economic Corridor*. Manila.

———. 2001c. *Small Towns Development Project, Small Towns Development Strategy*. Manila.

———. 2001d. *Poverty Reduction Partnership Agreement between ADB and Lao PDR Vientiane*. Manila.

———. 2002. *Provincial Poverty Rates 2002*. Manila.

———. 2002a. *Country Strategy and Program Update (2003-2005): Sri Lanka*. Manila.

———. 2002a. *Connecting Nations, Linking People, The Greater Mekong Subregion Economic Cooperation Program*. Manila.

———. 2002b. *Annex*. Proceedings of the Regional Consultation Workshop on Water in Asian Cities – The Role of Civil Society, 14–16 October 2002. Manila.

———. 2002b. *Connecting Nations, Linking People. The Greater Mekong Subregion Economic Cooperation Program*. Manila.

———. 2003. *Lao Urban Data Book*. Manila.

———. 2003. *Sri Lanka Urban Development Sector Study*. Manila.

———. 2004. *Key Indicators 2004*. Manila.

———. 2004. *Key Indicators of Developing Asian and Pacific Countries: Philippines*. Available: http://www.adb.org/Documents/Books/Key_Indicators/2004/pdf/PHI.pdf

———. 2004a. *Country Strategy and Program Update (2005-2006): Sri Lanka*. Manila.

———. 2004a. *The Mekong Region, an Economic Over*view. Manila.

———. 2004b. Promoting Service Delivery by the Colombo Municipal Council through Effective Partnerships. Paper presented at the *Regional Seminar and Learning Event, Local Governance and Pro-Poor Service Delivery*, 10–12 Feb. Available: http://www.fukuoka.unhabitat.org/out/siryo/project_b/12/srl.casestudies2002-e.html

———. 2004b. *Urban Indicators for Measuring Cities*. Manila.

———. 2005. Catalysts for Sustainable Urban and Regional Development in Southeast Asia: A Study of Best Practice Approaches. Internal Report. Centre for Developing Cities. Canberra: University of Canberra. Available: www.cities.canberra.edu.au

———. 2005. Fact Sheet, Viet Nam and ADB. Manila. Available: http://www.adb.org/documents/fact sheets

———. 2005a. *Country Strategy and Program Update 2006-2008, Lao People's Democratic Republic.* Manila.

———. 2005b. *GMS Flagship Program, East-West Economic Corridor. Executive Summary.* Manila.

ADB, World Bank, and Japan Bank for International Cooperation. 2005. *Connecting East Asia: A New Framework for Infrastructure.* Washington, DC.

Agus, M.R. 2002. Malaysia. In *Housing Policy Systems in South and East Asia*, edited by M.R. Agus, J. Doling, and D.S. Lee. New York: Palgrave Macmillan.

Ali S.M., and S. Sirivardana. 1996. Towards a New Paradigm for Poverty Eradication in South Asia. *International Journal of Social Science* 14(8): 207-218.

Ali, R. 2003. Underestimating Urbanisation. In *Continuity and Change: Socio-political and Institutional Dynamics in Pakistan*, edited by S.A. Zaidi. Karachi: City Press.

Amin, A, and N. Thrift. 1995. Globalization, Institutional Thickness and the Local Economy. In *Managing Cities: the New Urban Context,* edited by P. Healey et al. Chichester: Wiley.

Arcadis, Aldbar Ltd. 2001. *Small Towns Development Project, Small Towns Development Strategy.* Manila.

Archer, R W. 2001. *Decentralization of Town Planning to Local Government.* Prepared for the Urban Planning and Management Project (UPMP) a joint GTZ/MOI Cooperation.

Arroyo, G. Executive Order No. 252 Transferring the Assets, Functions, Funds, Personnel and Records of the Municipal Development Fund Office to an Affiliate Corporation of the Land Bank of the Philippines and for Other Purposes. Available: http://www.ops.gov.ph/records/eo_no252.htm

Asia Focus. 2005. *China: an Evolving Housing Market.* San Francisco: Federal Reserve Bank of San Francisco.

Asian Institute of Management (AIM). 2003. *Pinoy Cities of the Future: A Competitiveness Ranking of 50 Philippine Cities.* Makati City: AIM Policy Center.

Asian Resource Center for Decentralization. 2002. *Decentralization & Power Shift An Imperative For Good Governance A Sourcebook on Decentralization Experiences in Asia, Volume I*, edited by Alex B. Brillantes, Jr. and Nora G. Cuachon. Manila: University of the Philippines.

Astillero, N., and J. Mangahas. 2002. *Assessment of Capacity Building Needs of Biodiversity and Protected Areas Management Board in the Philippines.* Manila: Department of Environment and Natural Resources, and United Nations Development Programme.

Atkins China, Ltd. 2003. Sustainable Development Strategic Planning of a Comprehensive Transport System in Shenzhen. Draft Final Report. Shenzhen City:

Shenzhen Transport Bureau (A confidential draft report on the World Bank TC4 Project)

Azad, A. K. 2003. Micro-credit in Bangladesh. In *Banglapedia*, Volume 6, edited by S. Islam. Dhaka: Asiatic Society of Bangladesh. p477–479.

Bagchi, A. 1994. *Intergovernmental Fiscal Relations: The Case of India and Indonesia.* Mimeo.

Bajwa, R. 2005. *Successful Approaches to Improving Wastewater Management and Sanitation in Pakistan.* National Rural Support Program. p1–13.

Bangko Sentral ng Pilipinas. 2004. Bank Density Ratio of the Philippine Banking System. Available: http://www.bsp.gov.ph/statistics/sipbs/table2.htm

——. 2004. *Financial Institutions under BSP Supervision and Regulation.* Available: http://www.bsp.gov.ph/statistics/sipbs/table1a.htm

Bangkok Metropolitan Administration (BMA). 2001. *Bangkok State of Environment 2001.* Bangkok.

——. 2003. *Progress Report on City Planning of Bangkok Project - 2nd revision* (in Thai). Bangkok Metropolitan Administration. Bangkok

Bangladesh Bureau of Statistics. (BBS). 2005. *Statistical Pocketbook. Bangladesh 2003.* Dhaka.

BAPA. 2005. Bangladesh Paribesh Anddolon (BAPA). Bangladesh Environment Movement Brochure.

Beck, U. 1995. *Ecological Politics in an Age of Risk.* Cambridge: Polity Press.

Berkes, F., J. Colding, and C. Folke. 2000. Rediscovery of Traditional Ecological Knowledge as Adaptive Management. *Ecological Applications* 10(5): 1,251–1,262.

Borja, J., and M. Castells. 1997. *Local and Global: the Management of Cities in the Information Age.* London: Earthscan Publications Ltd.

Bounchanh Sinthavong. 2005. *Environment - Challenges Facing Vientiane.* Seoul Mayors' Forum. Seoul .

BPS Statistik Indonesia. 2001. The sources for the population figures are *Profil Kabupaten dan Kota* (The Profiles of Kabupatens and Cities), Jakarta: Kompas, volumes 1,2,3 and 4, while the population growth figures are collected from BPS Statistik Indonesia 2001 (Jakarta), www.prospecktus .its.ac.id/sby.html (Surabaya), www.kompas.com December 6, 2004 (Bandung), www.sumut. bps.go.id (Medan), www.pilkada.partai-golkar.or.id (Bekasi), BPS Palembang Dalam Angka (Palembang), www.semarang.go.id/draft-rpjp.htm (Semarang), www. kotatangerang.go.id (Tangerang), www.depok.go.id (Depok), www.makassar.go.id (Makassar), www.perhubungan.pemkot-malang.go.id (Malang), and www.kotabogor.go.id (Bogor).

Brillantes, A Jr., and J. Tiu Sonco. 2005. *Policy Paper on Strengthening Devolution through Meaningful Financial Decentralization: Improving Fiscal Transfers to LGUs.* Manila: Local Government Development Foundation.

Brisbane City Council. 2006. *Infrastructure Charges Plans.* Available: http://www. brisbane.qld.gov.au/BCC:STANDARD:464923556:pc=PC_1765

Brook, P.J., and T.C. Irwin. 2003. *Infrastructure for Poor People: Public Policy for Private Provision.* Washington, DC: World Bank.

Brun, C. 2002. *Finding a Place: Local Integration and Protracted Displacement in Sri Lanka*. Dr. Polit. thesis. Department of Geography. Trondheim: Norwegian University of Science and Technology.

Camp Dresser & McKee International Inc (CDM). 2000a. *Ho Chi Minh City Environmental Sanitation Project (Nhieu Loc - Thi Nghe Basin). Environmental Impact Assessment Executive Summary Final Report.*

———. 2000b. *Ho Chi Minh City Environmental Sanitation Project (Nhieu Loc - Thi Nghe Basin). Resettlement Action Plan.*

Campanella, Thomas, Ming Zhang, Tunney Lee, and Nien Dak Sze. 2002. The Pearl River Delta: an Evolving Region. In *Building a Competitive Pearl River Delta Region, Cooperation, Coordination and Planning*, edited by Anthony Gar-on Yeh, Yok-shiu Lee, Tunney Lee, and Nien Dak Sze. Centre of Urban Planning and Environmental Management. Hong Kong, China: University of Hong Kong. p9-26.

Castells, M, L Goh, R Kwok, L K Toh. 1988. *Economic Development and Housing Policy in the Asian Pacific Rim: A Comparative Study of Hong Kong, Singapore and Shenzhen Special Economic Zone*. Monograph 37. Berkeley: Institute of Urban and Regional Development.

Central Party Politbureau. 2004. Instruction No. Na09/CPPB, Establishment of Villages and Village Development Groups. Vientiane: Government of Lao PDR

Centre for Environmental Technologies (CETEC). 2005a. *An Approach for Pilot Community Action Plan for Stream/Pond Conservation and Sustainable Use of Biodiversity - The Sungei Penchala (Stream) and Tasik Taman Jaya (Pond)*. Petaling Jaya.

———. 2005b. *The Malaysian Stream Keepers Handbook - Practical Guide to a stream and pond care*. Petaling Jaya.

Centre for Policy Dialogue(CPD). 2001. *Report of the Task Force on Urban Governance*. National Policy Forum 2001. Dhaka.

Chin, H.C. 1998. Urban Transport Planning in Singapore. In *Singapore Planning: From Plan to Implementation*, edited by B Yuen. Singapore: Singapore Institute of Planners.

China Daily Online. 2004. Shenyang Cleans Up its Act. 31 December.

———. 2006. Housing Prices Up 9.9% in Major Chinese Cities. 1 January.

China in Brief. 2005. *Opening to the Outside World: Special Economic Zones and Open Coastal Cities*. Beijing: September 30, 2005. Available: http://www.china.org.cn/e-china/openingup/sez.htm

Chowdhury, A.B.M. 2005. Committed to Develop Chittagong as the Environment Friendly Megacity of the Region. Lecture at the PRO-ACT Second Euro-Asian Seminar in Lyon, France, 20–22 November.

Clark, TA & Tsai, T. 2005. The Agricultural Consequences of Compact Urban Development: The Case of Asian Cities pp 63 – 71. In Jenks, M, Burgess, R (eds) *Compact Cities: Sustainable Urban Forms for Developing Countries*. London: Spon Press.

Codrington, H W. 2000. A *Short History of Sri Lanka*. *Available*: http://www.lakdiva.com/codrington (accessed December 2001)

Committee for Planning and Cooperation. 2002. *Macroeconomic Policy Support for Socio-Economic Development in Lao PDR*. Tokyo: Japan International Cooperation Agency. Committee for Planning and Investment. 2005. *Northern Region Development Strategy*. Vientiane: Government of Lao PDR.

Curthoys, L.P. 2002. Mary's Point Western Hemispheric Shorebird Reserve: A Case Study in Community Leadership and Successful Protected Area Management. *Environments* 30(2): 43–62.

De Silva, K M. 1981. A *History of Sri Lanka*. New Delhi: Oxford University Press.

De Soto, H. 2000. *The Mystery of Capital: Why Capitalism Triumphs in the West and Fails Everywhere Else*. New York: Basic Books.

Department of National Planning. 2002. *Employment and Unemployment of Youth in Sri Lanka*. Colombo.

Department of Planning and Investment, Luang Prabang Province. 2005. *Participatory Kum-ban Planning Guidelines (Draft)*.

——. 2005. *Participatory Village Development Planning Manual*. Luang Prabang: Governance and Public Administration Reform (GPAR) project.

Desoto, H. 2000. *The Mystery of Capital: Why Capitalism Triumphs in the West and Fails Everywhere Else*. London: Bantam Press.

Devas, N., and C. Rakodi. 1993. Planning and Managing Urban Development. In *Managing Fast Growing Cities*, edited by N. Devas and C. Rakodi. Essex: Longman. p41–62.

Dicken, P. 1998. *Global Shift: Transforming the World Economy*. London: Paul Chapman.

Do, H., T.L.Nguyen, L.Q. Nguyen, T.H. Pham, V.H. Ngo, and B. Van Horen. 2005. Building Institutional Capacity in Urban Upgrading in Phu Thuong Ward, Hanoi, Vietnam. (forthcoming)

Doli, J. 1993. Keeping the Traffic Moving: The Singapore Experience. *International Journal of Public Sector Management* 6(1): 4–10.

Doling, J. 1999. Housing Policies and the Little Tigers: How do they Compare with Other Industrialized Countries? *Housing Studies* 14(2): 229–250.

Durand-Lasserve, A., and R. Pajoni. 1993. *Managing the Access of the Poor to Urban Land: New Approaches for Regularization Policies in the Developing Countries*. Mexico City: World Bank - UNDP – UNCHS.

Economic Commission for Asia and the Pacific (ESCAP). 1995. *Development and Environmental Management in Shenyang City, China. A Case Study under the Integrating Environmental Considerations into the Economic Decision-making Process* project. Bangkok.

Economic Planning Unit. 2004. *Development Planning in Malaysia*. Kuala Lumpur.

Energy Information Administration. 2005. *International Energy Outlook 2005*. Office of Integrated Analysis and Forecasting, U.S. Department of Energy. Table A9.

European Commission. 2005. *Micro-project Development through Local Communities, Mid-term Internal Evaluation*. Brussels.

Evans, P. 2002. *Livable Cities? Urban Struggles for Livelihood and Sustainability*. Berkley: University of California Press.

Firman, T. 1997. Land Conversion and Urban Development in Northern Region of West Java, Indonesia. *Urban Studies*. 34(7): 1027–1046.
Forbes, D., and M. Lindfield. 1997. *Urbanisation in Asia: Lessons Learned and Innovative Responses*. Canberra: AusAID. Available: http://www.ausaid.gov.au/publications/pdf/urban_asia.pdf
Friedmann, J. 1999. The Common Good: Assessing the Performance of Cities. In *Urban and Regional Governance in the Asia Pacific*, edited by John Friedmann. Vancouver: UBC Institute of Asian Research. p1–16.
Friere, M., and R. Stren. 2001. The *Challenges of Urban Government, Policies and Practices*. Washington, DC: World Bank Institute.
Fu-Chen Lo, and Peter J. Marcotullio. 2001. *Globalization and the Sustainability of Cities in the Asia Pacific Region*. Tokyo: United Nations University Press.
GED, Planning Commission. 2005. *Unlocking the Potential: National Strategy for Accelerated Poverty Reduction (PRSP)*. Dhaka: General Economics Division, Planning Commission. Government of Bangladesh.
GHK International. 2000a. *Vientiane Urban Infrastructure and Services Project, Final Report*. Manila: ADB.
———. 2000b. *Vientiane Urban Infrastructure and Services Project, Vientiane Participatory Poverty Assessment*. Manila: ADB.
———. 2000c. *Vientiane Urban Infrastructure and Services Project, Land Use Planning Report*. Manila: ADB.
Governance and Public Administration Reform (GPAR) Project. 2004. GPAR Luang Prabang News. Issue Quarter 2. Luang Prabang.
Government of India. 2004. Report of the Twelfth Finance Commission. New Delhi
———. 2005. *Toolkits for Implementing the Jawaharlal Nehru*. New Delhi: National Urban Renewal Mission.
Government of Lao PDR. 2003. *National Growth and Poverty Eradication Strategy*. Vientiane.
Government of Lao PDR. 2005a. *Promotion Policies for Foreign Direct Investment in Lao PDR* Department of Planning and Investment, Savannakhet Province
Government of Lao PDR. 2005b. *Savan-Seno the Trade and Service Hub of the East-West Economic Corridor* Savan-Seno Special Economic Zone Authority
Government of Malaysia. 1971. *Second Malaysia Plan (1971-75)*. Kuala Lumpur.
———. 1976. *Third Malaysia Plan (1976-80)*. Kuala Lumpur.
———. 1981. *Fourth Malaysia Plan (1981-85)*. Kuala Lumpur.
———. 1986. *Fifth Malaysia Plan (1986-90)*. Government Printers. Kuala Lumpur
———. 1991. *Sixth Malaysia Plan (1991-95)*. Kuala Lumpur.
———. 1996. *Seventh Malaysia Plan (1996-2000*. Kuala Lumpur.
———. 2001. *Eighth Malaysia Plan (2001-05)*. Kuala Lumpur.
———. 2003. The Mid-Term Review of the Eight Malaysia Plan. Kuala Lumpur.
———. 2005. *National Physical Plan*. Kuala Lumpur: Federal Department of Town and Country Planning.
Government of Pakistan. 2005. Environment and housing. In *Economic Survey of Pakistan*. Government of Pakistan. Islamabad. p205–212.

Government of Sindh. 2004. *About Local Government in Pakistan.*
Government of Sri Lanka. 2002. *Regaining Sri Lanka: Vision and Strategy for Accelerated Development.* Available: www. poverty2.forumone.com/files/Sri_Lanka_PRSP.pdf
Government of the Philippines, World Bank, and ADB. 2003. *Philippines: Improving Government Performance: Discipline, Efficiency and Equity in Managing Public Resources.* Manila: Southeast Asia Department, ADB.
Government of Viet Nam (Gov). 2001. Decree 72/2001/ND-CP on Urban Classifications and Levels of Management, 5 October 2001.
Graham, S., and S. Marvin. 2001. *Splintering Urbanism: Networked Infrastructures, Technological Mobilities and the Urban Condition.* London: Routledge.
Greater Vancouver Regional District. 2006. *Sustainable Region Initiative: Turning Ideas into Action.* Available: http://www.gvrd.bc.ca/sustainability/
Grierson, J. 2000. Vocational Training for Self-employment- Learning from Enterprise Development Best Practice. *Small Enterprise Development* 11(3): 25–35.
Grosh, M., and P. Glewwe. 2000. *Designing Household Survey Questionnaires for Developing Countries: Lessons from 15 Years of the Living Standards Measurement Study.* Volumes 1, 2, and 3. Washington, DC: World Bank.
Gunaratna, Ajitha. 2004. *Dengue Outbreak in Sri Lanka Highlights Deteriorating Public Health Services.* World Socialist Website, 16 June. Available: http://www.wsws.org/articles/2004/jun2004/deng-j16.shtml
Gunatilleke, G., and M. Perera. 1988. Urban Poverty in Sri Lanka: Critical Issues and Policy Measures. *Asian Development Review.* Nagoya.
Gunesekera, D. 2003. *Housing for Slum Communities, LSE Management.* Available: http://www.google.com.au/search?hl=en&q=population+slum+communities+colombo&btnG=Search&meta=
Hall, P. 1998. *Cities in Civilization - Culture, Innovation and Urban Order.* London: Weidenfeld & Nicolson.
Hall, P. 1999. *Cities in Civilization: Culture, Innovation and Urban Order.* London: Orion Publishing Co.
Hanoi Architectural University (HAU). 1998. *Pilot Study: Spatial Planning of Phu Thuong Ward - Tay Ho District.* Hanoi.
———. 2004. *Report on the Survey Results of Existing Situations of Phu Thuong Ward - Tay Ho District.* Hanoi.
Healey, P. 1998.. Building Institutional Capacity through Collaborative Approaches to Urban Planning. *Environment and Planning* A.30: 1,531–1,546.
Hong Khanh. 2005. *The Country will Have More Than Four Million Poor Households According to the New Standard.* 30 June 2005. Available: http://www.vnexpress.vn
Hong Phuc. 2005. *ODA for Vietnam Reaches a New Record.* 7 December 2005. Available: http://vietnamnet.com.vn
Hoole, R., D. Somasundarum, and R. Thiringama. 1989. *The Broken Palmyra: the Tamil Crisis in Sri Lanka – an Inside Account.* Claremont: Sri Lanka Studies Institute.

Hulugalle, H.A.J. 1965. *Centenary Volume of the Colombo Municipal Council 1865-1965*. Colombo: Colombo Municipal Council.
Human Settlements Foundation (HSF). 1988. Swept Under the Carpet of Affluence: Evictions in Bangkok. In *Forced Evictions and Housing Right Abuses in Asia – Second Report (1996-1997)*, edited by K. Fernandes. p145–148. Karachi: City Press.
Hyndman, J. 2003. *The Canadian Geographer* 47.
Institute for Global Environmental Strategies (IGES). 2005, *Sustainable Groundwater Management of Asian Cities. Part II the State of Ground Water Resources and Management Case Studies*. Tokyo. Available: www.iges.or.jp/en/fw/pdf/report01/part1.pdf
International Crisis Group. 2005. Pakistan's Local Polls: Shoring Up Military Rule. *Asia Briefing* No. 43. International Crisis Group. Brussels.
International Labour Organization (ILO), and Urban and Regional Development Institute (URDI). 2005. *Municipal Policies and Actions on the Informal Economy in Selected Indonesian Cities*. Jakarta: URDI.
Irazabal, C. 2005. *City Making and Urban Government in the Americas: Curitiba and Portland*. Aldershot, England: Ashgate.
Islam, H. 2005. Annual Report of the Executive Director. Shakti Foundation. Dhaka
Islam, N. 2004. An Urban Governance Strategy for Urban Development. In *Bangladesh in the New Millennium: A University of Dhaka Study*, edited by Abul Kalam. Dhaka: University of Dhaka. p235–248.
———. *Dhaka Now: Contemporary Urban Development*. Dhaka: Bangladesh Geographical Society.
Jackson, T., and L. Michaelis. 2003. *Policies for Sustainable Consumption*. London: Sustainable Development Commission. Available: www.sdc.gov.uk
Jacobsen, K., S.H. Khan, and A. Alexander. 2002. Building a Foundation: Poverty, Development, and Housing in Pakistan. *Harvard International Review* 23(4): 20–24.
Jayaratne K A. 1996. *Community Participation in Urban Solid Waste Management Case Study of Siddharthapura Low Income Settlement*. Colombo. Available: http://www.sandeeonline.org/publications/bibliographies/pdf/Economics%20of%20SWM.pdf
———. 2004. Role of Civil Society Organizations in Promoting Responsive and Accountable Local Government for Improved Service Delivery in Colombo. Paper presented at the *Regional Seminar and Learning Event – Local Governance and Pro-poor Service Delivery*, Feb 10-12, 2004, Manila. Available: http://www.adb.org/Governance/Pro_poor/Civil_society/PDF/role_civil_society.pdf
Jenks, M., and R. Burgess. 2000. *Compact Cities: Sustainable Urban Forms for Developing Countries*. London: Spon Press.
Kammeier, D., et al. 2005. *Regional Study on Rural, Urban and Sub-regional Linkages in the Greater Mekong Sub-Region* (Viet Nam, Lao PDR, Cambodia)
Kardar, S.H. 2003. Pakistan. In *Local Government Finance and Bond Market*, edited by Y-H Kim. p1-214.

Kessides, C. 2002. A Framework of Economic Policies for Urban Upgrading. Paper presented at the *World Bank Workshop on Scaling Up Urban Upgrading in Latin America*. Available: http://wbln0018.worldbank.org/External/Urban/ UrbanDev.nsf/Urban+Slums+&+Upgrading.

Khan, A.M.M. 1982. Rural-urban Migration and Urbanization in Bangladesh. *Geographical Review* 72 (A): 79–94.

Khan, S.A. 1994. Attributes of Informal Settlements Affecting their Vulnerability to Eviction: A Study of Bangkok. *Environment and Urbanization* 6: 25–39.

Konsortium Perang Besar. 1995. *Perancangan Pembangunan Pusat Pentadbiran Persekutuan Putrajaya*. Kuala Lumpur.

KRI International, International Development Center of Japan, Pacific Consultants International. 2001a. *The Study on the Integrated Regional Development Plan for the Savannakhet and Khammouane Region*. Final Report. Tokyo: Japan International Cooperation Agency.

———. 2001b. *The Study on the Integrated Regional Development Plan for the Savannakhet and Khammouane Region, Development Vision and Cooperation Programs for the Cross Border Region*. Tokyo: Japan International Cooperation Agency.

KRI International, Nippon Koei. 2001. *The Study on Special Economic Zone Development in Border Area of Savannakhet Province*. Tokyo: Japan International Cooperation Agency.

Kuala Lumpur City Hall. 2004. *Kuala Lumpur Structure Plan 2020, A World Class City*. Kuala Lumpur.

La Maison du Patrimoine (MdP). 2002. Minutes of Meeting between MdP and UDAA on incompatibilities between Secondary Towns Project and heritage protection. Luang Prabang.

———. 2002. *Plan de Sauvegarde et de Mise en Valeur*. Luang Prabang: UNESCO.

Lam, Kin-che, and Shu Tao. 1996. Environmental Quality and Pollution Control. In *Shanghai: Transformation and Modernization under China's Open Policy*, edited by Yeung Yue-man and Sung Yun-ming. Hong Kong, China: Chinese University Press.

Lamberte, M. 2001. *Financing for Micro-enterprises, Small and Medium-sized Business and Poor Households in the Philippines*. Available: http://www.unescap.org/drpad/publication/fin_2206/part7.pdf

Land Transport Authority, Singapore. 1996. *A World Class Land Transport System*. White Paper presented to Parliament. 2 Jan.

Laquian, A. 1983. *Basic Housing: Policies for Urban Sites, Services and Shelter in Developing Countries*. Ottawa: International Development Research Centre.

———. 2005. *Beyond Metropolis: the Planning and Governance of Asia's Mega-urban Regions*. Baltimore: John Hopkins University Press.

Laquian, A.B.J. 2005. *Beyond Metropolis: The Planning and Governance of Asia's Mega-Urban Regions*. Baltimore: Johns Hopkins University Press.

Laquian, Aprodicio. 2002. Urban Governance: Some Lessons Learned. In *Democratic Governance and Urban Sustainability*, edited by Joseph S. Tulchin,

Diana H. Varat, and Blair A. Ruble. Washington, DC: Woodrow Wilson International Center for Scholars. p97–125.

———. 2005. *Beyond Metropolis: The Planning and Governance of Asia's Mega-Urban Regions.* Baltimore: Johns Hopkins University Press.

Leroux, H. 2002. Luang Prabang, World Heritage. *Villes en Developpement*, Issue No.55.

LGU Guarantee Corporation Vision, Mission and Company Profile Available: http://www.lgugc.com/about.htm

Liang Yu. 2003. Room at the Top. *Shanghai Star.* 18 September.

Llanto, G., R. Manasan, M. Lamberte, and J. Laya. 1998. *Local Government Units' Access to the Private Capital Markets.* Makati City: Philippine Institute of Development Studies.

Local Case Study Team. 2000. *Cultural Heritage Management and Tourism, A Case Study on Luang Prabang.* Luang Prabang: UNESCO.

Lomborg, Bjorn (ed). 2004. *Global Crises, Global Solutions.* Cambridge, UK: Cambridge University Press.

Low, L., and T.C. Aw. 1997. *Housing a Healthy, Educated and Wealthy Nation through the CPF.* Singapore: Times Academic Press.

Lowell, B.L, and A.M. Findlay. 2001. *Migration of Highly Skilled Persons from Developing Countries: Impact and Policy Responses - Synthesis Report.* Geneva: International Labour Organization..

Mabbitt, R. 2002. *Secondary Towns Urban Development Project, Resettlement Post Evaluation Survey.* Vientiane: Ministry of Communications, Transport, Posts and Construction.

———. 2003. *Lao Urban Data Book.* Manila: ADB.

Manasan, R., and Jasharuhiya. 2003. Regional Development. In *The Philippine Economy: Development, Policies, and Challenges*, edited by A. Balisacan and H. Hill. New York: Oxford University Press.

Manning, N, D. Porter, J. Charlton, M. Cyan, and Z. Hasnain. 2005. *Devolution in Pakistan - Preparing for Service Delivery Improvements.* Washington, DC: World Bank.

Mayfield, James. 2005. Answers to the Most Frequently Asked Questions about China's Environmental Sector. *The China Business Review Online.* 2 September.

McGee, T. 1989. 'Urbanisasi' or 'Desakota'? Evolving Pattern of Urbanization in Asia. In *Urbanization in Asia: Spatial Dimension and Policy Issues*, edited by F.J. Costa. Honolulu: University of Hawaii Press.

Mercado, R. 2002. Regional Development in the Philippines: A Review of Experience, State of the Art and Agenda for Research and Action. *Discussion Paper Series* No. 2002-0. Philippine Makati City: Institute of Development Studies.

Mercado, R., and R. Anlocotan. 2002. Metro Iloilo: A Struggle for Acceptance and Organization. In *Managing Urbanization under a Decentralized Governance Framework Vol.1*, edited by R. Manasan.. Makati City: Philippine Institute of Development Studies. p235–245.

Mercado, R and V. Ubaldo. 2002. Metro Naga: A Continuing Challenge of Local Autonomy and Sustainability. In *Managing Urbanization under a Decentralized Governance Framework Vol. 1*, edited by R. Manasan. Makati City: Philippine Institute of Development Studies. p221–234.

Ministry of Communications, Transport, Posts and Construction (MCTPC). 2004. *Northern and Central Regions Water Supply and Urban Development Project (2004) National Urban Sector Strategy and Investment Plan, Interim Report*. Vientiane.

Ministry of Construction (MoC). 1999. *Orientation of Urban Planning and Development of Vietnam up to 2020*. Hanoi: Construction Publishing House.

Ministry of Environment, Singapore. 1992. *Singapore Green Plan: Towards a Model Green City*. Singapore.

Ministry of Housing, et al. 2002. *An Implementation Guide and Case Studies- Local Agenda 21*. Kuala Lumpur.

Ministry of Information and Culture. 2003. *Periodic Reporting Exercise on the Application of the World Heritage Convention*. Luang Prabang: UNESCO.

Ministry of Natural Resources and Environment (MONRE). 2005. Report on the Use of Agricultural Land for the Construction of Industrial Zones and the Living Standards of Those from Whom Land was Recovered. In ADB. 2005. *Summary Report on Industrial and Commercial Land Markets and their Impact on the Poor Making Market Work Better for the Poor*. Manila.

Ministry of Planning. 2005. *Achieving the Cambodia Millennium Development Goals*. Phnom Penh.

——. 2005. *National Population Policy: What Does It Mean for Planning?* Phnom Penh.

Ministry of Urban Development. 1992. *The Constitution (seventy-fourth) Amendment on Municipalities*. New Delhi: Government of India Press.

Motha, P., and B. Yuen. 1998. *Singapore Real Property Guide*. Singapore University Press.

Mulgan, G. 1997. *Connexity*. London: Calder & Boyars.

Multimedia Development Corporation (MDC). 2003. *Cyberjaya Community Updates. Cyber News*. Cyberjaya.

——. 2004. *MSC Impact Survey 2004*. Cyberjaya.

——. 2005. *MSC Cybercities, Facts and Figures*. MDC. Cyberjaya.

Naga City Investment Board. 2005. *Naga City Investment Profile*. Naga City.

Naga City Planning and Development Office. 2004. *Naga City Statistical Profile*. Naga City.

National Assembly. 1994. *Environmental Protection Law*. Hanoi: National Politics Publishing House.

——. 2003. *Construction Law*. Hanoi: National Politics Publishing House.

National Economic and Social Development Board (NESDB) and World Bank. 1997. *Urban Development Under the 8th and 9th Plans: Report of Assessment Mission*. Bangkok.

National Economic and Social Development Board and ADB. 1998. *Assessment Mission*. Manila

———. 2003a. Planning for Sustainable Urbanization in Thailand (PSUT) Project. *The Future of Thai Urbanization: New Drivers, New Patterns*. Manila.

———. 2003b. Planning for Sustainable Urbanization in Thailand Project. *Towards an Operational Definition of Urban Sustainability in Thailand*. Bangkok.

National Economic and Social Development Board. 2004. *Thailand Millennium Development Goals Report*. Bangkok.

National Economic Development Authority. Economic Indicators Online. Available: http://localweb.neda.gov.ph/~ioneda/

———. 12th Annual ODA Portfolio Review. Available: http://www.neda.gov.ph/progs_prj/12th%20oda/12th_odamain.htm.

———. 1998. *National Framework for Regional Development*. Pasig City.

———. Investment Indicators of Regions. Regional Economics Indicators. Available: http://localweb.neda.gov.ph/~ioneda/regional.html

———. Medium-Term Philippine Development Plan 2004-201. Available: http://www.neda.gov.ph/../ads/mtpdp/MTPDP2004-2010/MTPDP%2020042010%20NEDA%20v11-12.pdf

———. Report on the Outcome of the 11th Annual ODA Portfolio Review. In Previous ODA Portfolio Reviews . Available: http://www.neda.gov.ph/progs_prj/12th%20oda/12th_odamain.htm.

National Economic Development Authority-Region V. *Ensuring Sustained Growth and Equity*. Available: http://www.neda.net/MTRDP/chap2.HTM

National Housing Authority (NHA). 2002. *Housing Development Program for Slum and Urban poor for National Economic and Social Development Plan IX (2002-2006)* (mimeo in Thai). Bangkok. (As cited in Viratkapan V. 2005.)

National Statistical Center. 2004. *The Households of Lao PDR, Social and Economic Indicators*. LECS 3. Vientiane: Government Publications Center.

National Statistical Center. 2005. *Initial Summary Results of 2005 National Census of Population*. Vientiane: Government of Lao PDR

National Statistics Office. 2005. *QuickStat*. Available: http://www.census.gov.ph/data/quickstat

New York Times. 2003. China's Leader Calls for Democratic Changes (by Joseph Kahn). 1 October.

———. 2005. 10 October.

———. 2005. China Builds Its Dreams, and Some Fear a Bubble. 16 October.

———. 2005. US Offers Plans for Open Markets in China. 16 October.

Nguyen, T.L. 2002. Urbanization Patterns and Urban Problems in Vietnam. *Journal of the Korean Regional Development Association* 14(3): 81–92.

———. 2003. Regional Classifications in Vietnam for Urban and Rural Development. Paper presented at the *7th International Congress of Asian Planning Schools Association*, Hanoi.

———. 2005. Urbanization in Vietnam, Features and Developing Trends in the Early 21st Century. Paper Presented at the *Urban Sector Strategy Review – Expert Group Meeting*, 28–29 July 2005. Manila: ADB.

Noledo, J.N. 1992. *The Omnibus Election Code of the Philippines as Amended.* National Book Store. Quezon City.

Norwegian Agency for International Cooperation (NORAD), and United Nations Environment Programme (UNEP). 2001. *State of the Environment Report, Lao PDR.*

O'Sullivan and Graham. 1996. *Secondary Towns Urban Development Project, Final Report.* Manila: ADB.

OECD. 2003. Development Assistance Committee, Recipient Aid Charts.

Oi, K.H. 1998. Park Connectors. In *Planning Singapore: From Plan to Implementation*, edited by B. Yuen. Singapore Institute of Planners.

Om Prakash Mathur. 1996. Property Tax Policy and Local Governance. In *Fiscal Polices, Public Policy and Governance*, edited by Parthasarathi Shome. New Delhi: National Institute of Public Finance and Policy.

——. 2005. India's Urban Transition. Paper presented at a Conference on Urban Sector Strategy Review: Expert Group Meeting, organized by ADB, July 2005.

Om Prakash Mathur and Sanjukta Ray. 2003. *Financing Municipal Services: Reaching out to Capital Markets.* New Delhi: National Institute of Public Finance and Policy.

Orange, J. 2004. Governance Responses to Decentralization. In *Decentralization and Good Urban Governance,* edited by A. Brillantes, A. Simeon, L. Celenia, and P. Bootes. Centre for Local and Regional Governments. Manila: University the Philippines. p215–228.

Organisation for Economic Co-operation and Development (OECD). 2003. Development Assistance Committee, Recipient Aid Charts.

Pacific Consultants International. 1997. *The Study on Urban Environmental Improvement Program in Bangkok Metropolitan Area*: *Sector Plans and Technical Studies* (volume 3). Japan International Cooperation Agency. Bangkok.

Pascual, A. 2005. Remarks at the Signing Ceremony of ADB's support to the LGU Guarantee Corporation. Available: http://www.adb.org/Documents/Speeches/2005/sp2005005.asp

Parveen, S. 2004. *Report on Impact of Monitoring & Evaluation, Shakti Foundation for Disadvantaged Women.* Dhaka: Shakti Foundation.

People's Daily Online. 2002. China to Accelerate its Urbanization Pace. 6 December.

——. 2003. Dream to Buy Own Housing in China Comes True. 21 August.

——. 2004. China's Population to Reach 800 to 900 Million by 2020. 6 September.

——. 2005. ADB Shifts Focus of Road Projects to China's Central, Southwest Regions. 25 March.

People's Republic of China. 1994. *China's Agenda 21, White Paper on China's Population, Environment and Development in the 21st Century, Beijing:* Executive Committee of the State Council. Available: web@acca21.org.cn

Perbadanan Putrajaya. 1997. Putrajaya, Review of Masterplan (unpublished).

Perbadanan Putrajaya and Putrajaya Holding Sdn Bhd. 1999. *Putrajaya Wetlands.* Petaling Jaya.

Pernia, E. M., and P.F. Quising. 2003. Economic Openness and Regional Development in the Philippines. *ERD Working Paper* No. 34. Manila: ADB. Available: http://www.adb.org/Documents/ERD/Working_Papers/wp034.pdf

Petaling Jaya Municipal Council (MPPJ). 2000. *Local Agenda 21 Petaling Jaya.* Petaling Jaya.
——. 2005a. *A Smart Partnership in Urban Governance, PJCC.* Petaling Jaya Municipal Council and University of Malaya.
——. 2005b. *Local Agenda 21 Petaling Jaya – Petaling Jaya towards Sustainable Development.* Petaling Jaya.
Philippine Economic Zone Authority. 2002. *PEZA New Registered and Expansion/ Additional Investments.* Available: http://localweb.neda.gov.ph/~ioneda/cgi-bin/st2.cgi?/eds/db/national/finvest/peza_investments_a.sc
Phongpaichit, P. and Baker, C. 1998. *Thailand's Boom and Bust.* Chiangmai. Silkworm Books. Thailand
Phu Thuong People's Committee. 2004. *Report on the Synthesis of Activities of Phu Thuong Ward in the period of 1999–2004.* Hanoi.
Pihakberkuasa Perancangan tempatan Putrajaya dan Pihakberkuasa Perancangan tempatan daerah Sepang. 1995. Rancangan Struktur Putrajaya dan Sebahagian Sepang (1995) Warta: GN Selangor 1530 Jld 48 tambahan 1 bertarikh 1 November.
Population and Housing Census. 2000. *Population Distribution by Local Authority Areas and Mukim.* Putrajaya: Department of Statistics.
Pornchockchai, S. 1985. *1020 Bangkok Slums – Evidence, Analysis, Critics.* Bangkok: School of Urban Community Research and Action.
Prahalad, C.K. 2006. *The Fortune at the Bottom of the Pyramid: Eradicating Poverty through Profits.* Philadelphia: Wharton School Publishing.
President's Office. 2003. Decree (No.60 PO) on the Promulgation of the Law on Local Administration Government of Lao PDR
Prime Minister's Office. 1997. Decree PM177 Organization of Urban Development and Administration Authorities, Government of Lao PDR
——. 2001. Decree PM 01 (on decentralization) Government of Lao PDR
——. 2004a. Draft Decree on Local and Central Government Responsibilities and Grassroots Development (Prime Minister Decree on Decentralization) PACSA. Government of Lao PDR
——. 2004b. Compilation of Decrees concerning the Savan-Seno Special Economic Zone. Savan-Seno Special Economic Zone Authority
——. 2005. Instruction No.01/PACSA Action Plan for Municipality Development Government of Lao PDR
Qadeer, M. 2000. Ruralopolises: The Spatial Organization and Residential Land Economy of High Density Rural Regions in South Asia. *Urban Studies* 37(9): 1,583–1,603.
Ravetz, J. 2006. Environment in Transition in an Industrial City-Region: Analysis and Experience: In: *The Urban Environmental Transition*, edited by G. Granahan and P. Marcotullio. London: Earthscan Publications, with the association with the International Institute for Environment & Development.
Ravetz, J., H. Coccossis, R. Schleicher-Tappeser, and P. Steele. 2004. Evaluation of Regional Sustainable Development – Transitions and Prospects. *Journal of Environmental Assessment Planning & Management* 6(4).

Riley, Elizabeth, and Patrick Wakely. 2003. *Communication for Sustainable Urban Livelihoods (CSUL), Final Research Report.* Development Planning Unit. University College London. Available: www.ucl.ac.uk/dpu/research/urban_mgmt/proj_csul.htm

Riskin, Carl. 2000. *Decentralization in China's Transition.* New York: East Asian Institute.

Robredo, J. 1999. *The Naga City Experience. Asian Cities in the 21st Century: Contemporary Approaches to Municipal Management.* p30-41. Available: http://www.adb.org/Documents/Conference/Asian_Cities_1/vol1roman.pdf

Robredo, J. 2003. *Making Local Governance Work: The Naga City Model.* Naga City: City Publications Group and the City Development Information Office.

Royal Government of Cambodia. 2005. *Strategic Framework for Decentralisation and De-concentration Reforms.* Phnom Penh.(In Khmer and English)

Royal Government of Cambodia: SEILA Programme. 2005. *Planning Activities and Budget of SEILA Programme.* Phnom Penh. (In Khmer Language)

——. 2005. Newsletter, SEILA: Supporting Decentralisation and De-concentration Policies and to Strengthen Good Governance and Local Development. Phnom Penh. (In Khmer Language)

Rural Bankers Association of the Philippines. *Commercial, Thrift Banks Violate Agri Loan Rule.* Available: http://www.rbap.org/article/articleview/2397/1/20

Schwartz, H. 2004. *Urban Renewal, Municipal Revitalization: The Case of Curitiba, Brazil.* Falls Church, VA: Higher Education Publications.

Shah, M.A. 2003. *ADB's Involvement in Water Supply and Sanitation Sector in Pakistan.* Manila: ADB.

Shiu Sin-por, and Yang Chun. 2002. A Study on Developing the Hong Kong Shenzhen Border Zone. In *Building a Competitive Pearl River Delta Region, Cooperation, Coordination and Planning,* edited by Anthony Gar-on Yeh, Yok-shiu Lee, Tunney Lee, and Nien Dak Sze. Centre of Urban Planning and Environmental Management. Hong Kong, China: University of Hong Kong. p245–269.

SMERU. 2005. *Developing a Poverty Map for Indonesia: A Tool for Better Targeting in Poverty Reduction and Social Protection Programs. Book 1 Technical Report.* SMERU Research Institute. Jakarta: University of Indonesia.. Available: http://www.smeru.or.id/report/research/povetymapping1/

Smith, R. V. *Industry Cluster Analysis: Inspiring a Common Strategy for Community Development.* Available: http://www.extension.psu.edu/workforce/Briefs/NDclustAnal.pdf

Soetandyo Wignosubroto, et.al. 2005. *Pasang Surut Otonomi Daerah: Sketsa Perjalanan 100 Tahun.* Jakarta: Institute for Local Development and Yayasan Tifa.

Sohail, M., and A.N. Baldwin. 2004. Community-partnered Contracts in Developing Countries. *Engineering Sustainability* (157)4: 193–202.

Soil and Water Ltd., Finland, in association with Duongthanh Water and Environment Ltd., Vietnam. 2003. *Vietnam Urban Upgrading Project. Final Environmental Impact Assessment, Nam Dinh City Sub-Project.* Report No. E817, Vol.16 (SW).

Sri Lanka Census Department. 2002. *Official Poverty Line for Sri Lanka.* Available: http://www.statistics.gov.lk/poverty/OfficialPovertyLineBuletin.pdf

Statistics General Department. *Vietnam Annual Statistical Directory.* Hanoi: Statistics Publishing House.

Stoop, P. 2004. *Decentralization Report Summary, Vientiane.* Governance and Public Administration Reform (GPAR) Project.

Suryanarayan, V. 2001. Land of the Displaced. *Frontline* 18(12).

Suwanmala, C. 2000. *Overview of Decentralization in Thailand.* Copenhagen: Danish International Development Agency.

Taubman, Wolfgang. 2002. Urban Administration, Urban Development and Migrant Enclaves: the Case of Guangzhou. In *Resource Management, Urbanization and Governance in Hong Kong and the Zhujiang Delta*, edited by Kwan-jiu Wong and Jianfa Shen. Hong Kong, China: Chinese University Press.

Teo, S. E., and D.R. Phillips. 1989. Attitudes Towards Service Provision in Public Housing Estates and New Towns in Singapore. *Singapore Journal of Tropical Geography* 10(1): 74–94.

Thakur, R., and O. Wiggen. 2004. *South Asia in the World: Problem Solving Perspectives on Security, Sustainable Development and Good Governance.* Tokyo: United Nations University Press.

The Manila Bulletin. *ADB Poised to take 25% Equity Ownership in LGU Guarantee Corp.* Available: http://www.mb.com.ph/BSNS2004122224934.html

The Manila Times. *ADB Invests in Guarantee Firm to Boost LGU Borrowing.* Available: http://www.manilatimes.net/national/2005/jan/22/yehey/business/20050122bus2.html

The World Fact Book. 2003. *China.*

Thomson, M.J. 1978. *Great Cities and their Traffic.* Hammondsworth: Penguin.

Tolley, George S. 1991. *Housing Reform in China, an Economic Analysis.* Washington, DC: World Bank.

Touber, J. 2001. *La Mise en Valeur du Patrimoine et ses Effets dans un Pays en Développement : le Cas de Luang Prabang, Laos.* MA Thesis.

Tourism Authority of Lao PDR. 2000. *Statistical Report on Tourism in Lao PDR.* Vientiane: Government of Lao PDR.

Townroe, P. 1996. Urban Sustainability & Social Cohesion. In: *Sustainability, the Environment & Urbanization*, edited by C. Pugh. London: Earthscan Publications Ltd.

Tran, N.C. 2004. Vietnamese Urban Development Strategy from Vision to Growth and Poverty Reduction. Paper presented at the *City Development Strategies Conference.* Hanoi.

Tran, T.H. 2002. *New Solution to Planning Procedure in Vietnam.* Hanoi: Department of Architecture and Planning Management, Ministry of Construction.

Treñas, J P. 2004. Metropolitan Arrangement in the Philippines: the Case of Metro Iloilo Development Council. In *Decentralization and Good Urban Governance*, edited by A. Brillantes, Jr. et al. p177–198 .

Tuan Chyau and Linda Fung-yee Ng. 2002. From Cross Border Manufacturing Operations to Regional Economic Integration: Evolution of Hong Kong's Economy and the Guangdong Factor. In *Building a Competitive Pearl River Delta Region, Cooperation, Coordination and Planning*, edited by Anthony Gar-on Yeh, Yok-shiu Lee, Tunney Lee, and Nien Dak Sze. Centre of Urban Planning and Environmental Management. Hong Kong, China: University of Hong Kong. p81–97.

Turner M., O. Podger, M. Sumardjono, and W. Tirthayasa. 2003. *Decentralisation in Indonesia: Redesigning the State.* Canberra: Asia Pacific Press.

U.S. Department of State. 2004. *Background Note: Philippines.* Available: http://www.state.gov/r/pa/ei/bgn/2794.htm

UNDP. 2005. *Human Development Report, 2005.* Available: http://hdr.undp.org/statistics/

UNDP. 2006. Glossary Best Practice. Available: http://www.undp.org/eo/ADR/glossary.htm

UN-HABITAT. 1998. *Metropolitan Environmental Improvement Programme, Colombo, Sri Lanka.* Available: http://database.bestpractices.org/bp_display_best_practice.php?best_practice_id=741

United Nations. 2002. *Development Assistance Framework, Lao PDR.* Vientiane: United Nations.

United Nations. 2004. *Cities and Sustainable Development: Lessons and Experiences from Asia and the Pacific.* New York: United Nations.

United Nations. 2004. *World Urbanization Prospects, the 2003 Revision.* Population Division, Department of Economic and Social Affairs. New York.

United Nations. 2004. *World Urbanization Prospects: The 2003 Revision..* New York: United Nations

United Nations Children's Fund (UNICEF). 2003. *Sri Lanka: Basic Indicators.* Available: http://www.unicef.org/infobycountry/sri_lanka_sri_lanka_statistics.html

United Nations Development Programme (Philippines). *RP Has One of Lowest FDI Inflows in ASEAN—UNCTAD.* UNDP Philippines Latest News. Available: http://www.undp.org.ph/news/readnews.asp?id=108

United Nations Development Programme (UNDP). 2005. *Human Development Report, 2005.* Available: http://hdr.undp.org/statistics/

United Nations Development Programme (UNDP). 2005. *The World Human Development Report 2005.* New York. Available: http://hdr.undp.org/statistics

United Nations Development Programme (UNDP), and Government of Lao PDR (GOL). 2002. Macro-economic Policy and Reform Framework Discussion Paper for the Policy Dialogue Meeting. Roundtable Process. Vientiane: Government of Lao PDR.

United Nations Development Programme (UNDP), and Urban and Regional Development Institute (URDI). 2004. *The Role of Civil Society in Supporting the Informal Economy.* Jakarta: URDI.

United Nations Resident Coordinator (Philippines). 2004. *Philippines Progress Report on the Millennium Development Goals.* Manila.

United Nations Secretariat. 2003. *World Population Prospects: The 2002 Revision and World Urbanization Prospects: The 2003 Revision.* Available: http://esa.un.org/unup

United States Agency for International Development (USAID). 2004. *Country Profile.* Available: http://www.usaid.gov/lk/country_profile/economy.html

Urban Redevelopment Authority. 1991. *Living the Next Lap.* Singapore.

Vickers, A. 2005. *A History of Modern Indonesia.* Cambridge: Cambridge University Press.

VIE/95/050 Project. 1998. *Report on the Survey Results of Existing Situations of Phu Thuong Ward - Tay Ho District.* Hanoi.

Vientiane Times. 2005. 4 November.

Vietnam Style. 2005. *Vietnam in Close Up: Nhieu Loc - Thi Nghe Canal.* 5 Dec. Available: http://vn-style.com.

Viratkapan, V. 1999. Relocation of Slum and Squatter Housing Settlements under Eviction in the Greater Bangkok Area: Case Studies of Three Relocation Settlements (unpublished Special Study). Bangkok: Asian Institute of Technology.

———. 2005. *Factors Contributing to the Development Performance of Slum Relocation Projects in Bangkok, Thailand.*

Wallace, P. 2004. The Wallace Report. Unpublished. U.P-NCPAG Library.
Available: http://www.nscb.gov.ph/ru6/iloilo_city.htm
http://www.iloilocity.cjb.net/
http://www.census.gov.ph/data/pressrelease/2002/pr02105tx.html

Weale, A. 1993. *The New Politics of Pollution.* Manchester: Manchester University Press.

Westfall, M.S., De Villa.V. 2001. *Urban Indicators for Managing Cities.* Manila: ADB.

Winasa, I. Gede. 2005. Kabupaten Jembrana: Peningkatan Kesejahteraan Masyarakat (Kabupaten Jembrana: Improvement of People's Welfare). In *Pembangunan Kota Indonesia dalam Abad 21: Pengalaman Pembangunan Perkotaan di Indonesia* (Urban Development in 21st Century Indonesia: Experiences in Urban Development in Indonesia). Volume 2. Jakarta: Urban and Regional Development Institute.

Wolters, T., P. James, and M. Bowman. 1997. Stepping Stones for Integrated Chain Management in the Firm. *Business Strategy & Environment* 6(3):121–132.

World Bank. 1995. *Better Urban Services: Finding the Right Incentives.* New York: Oxford University Press.

World Bank. 2003. Cities in Transition: Urban Sector Review in an Era of Decentralization in Indonesia. *Dissemination Paper* No. 7. Washington, DC.

World Bank. 2003. *World Development Indicators 2003.* Washington, DC.

World Bank. 2003. *World Development Report 2003. Sustainable Development in a Dynamic World: Transforming Institutions, Growth, and Quality of Life.* New York: Oxford University Press.

World Bank. 2005. *Report to the 25 September Development Committee Meeting, Infrastructure and the World Bank: A Progress Report.* Washington, DC. p6, 9.

World Bank. 2005. *World Development Indicators 2005*. Washington, DC. Available: http://www.worldbank.org/data/wdi2005/index.html.
World Bank. 2005a. *Decentralization in Southeast Asia*. Available: http://web.worldbank.org/wbsite/external/countries/southasiaext
——. 2005a. *World Development Indicators 2005*. Washington, DC.
——. 2005b. *East Asia Decentralizes: Making Local Government Work in East Asia*. Washington, DC.
——. 2005b. *Sri Lanka Needs US$1.5 billion For Tsunami Recovery and Reconstruction*. News Release No:2005/308/SAR. Available: http://www.worldbank.lk
——. 2006. *Global Economic Prospects - Economic Implications of Remittances and Migration*. Washington, DC.
World Bank (WB). 2001a. Appraisal Document for the Ho Chi Minh City Environmental Sanitation (Nhieu Loc – Thi Nghe Basin) Project. Report No. 21030-VN.
——. 2001b. *Ho Chi Minh City Environmental Sanitation (Nhieu Loc-Thi Nghe Basin) Project*. Available: http://web.worldbank.org
——. 2004. *Vietnam –Urban Upgrading Project Vol. 1*. Available: http://www-wds.worldbank.org/servlet/WDSContentServer/WDSP/IB
——. 2005a. *Vietnam*. Available: http://web.worldbank.org/wbsite/external/countries/eastasiapacificext/vietnamextn
——. 2005b. *World Development Indicators 2005*. Available: http://www.worldbank.org/data/wdi2005/index.html
World Commission on Environment and Development (WCED). 1987. *Our Common Future* (the Brundtland Commission Report). Oxford: Oxford University Press.
World Health Organization (WHO). 2004. *Country Health Profile-Sri Lanka*. Available: http://w3.whose.org/EN/section313/section1524.html
World Population Prospects: *The 2002 Revision and World Urbanization Prospects: The 2003 Revision*. Washington, DC: World Bank.
World Population Prospects (WPP). 2005. *The 2002 Revision and World Urbanization Prospects: The (2003) Revision*. Available: http://esa.un.org/unup
World Resources Institute. 1996. *World Resources 1996-97 – A guide to the Global Environment, Part 1 – The Urban Environment*. Oxford University Press. p4
——. *World Resources 2005 – The Wealth of the Poor, Managing Ecosystems to Fight Poverty*. Washington, DC. p16.
Wust, S., J-Cl. Bolay, and Thai Thi Ngoc Du. 2002. Metropolisation and the Ecological Crisis: Precarious Settlements in Ho Chi Minh City, Vietnam. *Review of Environment and Urbanization* 14(2): 211–22.
Yeh, Anthony Gar-on. 2002. Further Cooperation between Hong Kong and the Pearl River Delta in Creating a More Competitive Region. In *Building a Competitive Pearl River Delta Region, Cooperation, Coordination and Planning*, edited by Anthony Gar-on Yeh, Yok-shiu Lee, Tunney Lee, and Nien Dak Sze. Centre of Urban Planning and Environmental Management. Hong Kong, China: University of Hong Kong. p319–345.
Yeh, Anthony Gar-on, and Xia Li. 1996. An Integrated Remote Sensing and GIS Approach in the Monitoring and Evaluation of Rapid Urban Growth for

Sustainable Development in the Pearl River Delta, China. *International Planning Studies* 2(2): 195–222.

Yepes, Tito. 2004. *Expenditure on Infrastructure in East Asia Region, 2006–2010*. Available: http://siteresources.worldbank.org

Yuen, B. 1996. Creating the Garden City: The Singapore Experience. *Urban Studies* 33(1): 955–970.

———. 2005. Searching for Place Identity in Singapore. *Habitat International* 29(2): 197–214.

Yuen, B. 2005. Squatters no More: Singapore Social Housing. Paper presented at *the World Bank Third Urban Research Symposium: Land Development, Urban Policy and Poverty Reduction,* April, Brasilia, Brazil.

Yuen, B, A. Yeh, S.J. Appold, G. Earl, J. Ting, and L.K. Kwee. High-rise Living in Singapore Public Housing. *Urban Studies*. (forthcoming)

Yuen, B, and N.H. Wong. 2005. Resident Perceptions and Expectations of Rooftop Gardens in Singapore. *Landscape and Urban Planning* 73(4): 263–276.

Zaidi, S.A. 2005. *Issues in Pakistan's Economy*. Karachi: Oxford University Press.

Index

Action plan, 91, 163, 227-230, 242-243, 321, 324-325, 327-328, 391
Adaptive management, 410
Administrative leadership, 144-145
Adopt-the-park community program, 418
Ahmedabad municipal corporation, 140, 144, 146, 444
Andhra Pradesh, 9, 141, 147-150, 153-154, 442, 450
Area licensing scheme, 416
Arterial road networks, 377
ASEAN, 71, 191
Asian Development Bank (ADB), 3, 26, 67, 74, 84, 114, 170, 253, 282, 305, 343, 354, 370, 403, 458
Asset and accrual-based accounting, 179
Asset appraisal, 179, 313, 317
Asset management, 36, 169, 304, 434, 450, 457

Baan mankong project, 349
Bacolod, 10, 23, 273, 288, 290-295, 307
Balanced development, 9, 155, 173
Baluchistan, 246-247, 249-250
Bandung, 22-23, 162, 187
Bangkok, 18-19, 28, 216, 342, 345, 348-351, 359, 361, 372, 439, 442, 459
Bangladesh, 6, 9, 14-15, 19, 23, 32-33, 41, 43-45, 47-51, 53-54, 56, 58-59, 61-69, 268, 439, 444
Bangladesh environment movement, 9, 58, 63
Bangladesh planning commission, 51, 66
Banking, 107, 151, 268-269, 276, 281
Battambang, 9, 71, 75, 80, 83, 86-90, 99
Beijing, 106-107, 109-112, 118, 128, 130
Benchmark development sequencing, 425

Bond market, 282, 286
Bonds, 9, 135, 140-141, 143, 146-147, 153-154, 167, 176, 269, 282, 286, 444
Brisbane, 8, 11, 404, 418-423, 425-426, 434-435, 450
Brisbane city council, 419-422, 425
Budgeting, 36, 171, 179, 196, 280, 283, 352, 446, 448, 450
Buses, 126, 302

Cambodia, 6, 9, 14-15, 19, 32, 39, 41, 71-76, 78-80, 83-86, 90-91, 93-95, 98-100, 189, 195, 341, 377, 399, 439, 443, 459
Capacity building, 4-5, 76-77, 79, 96, 165, 169-171, 183-184, 186, 200, 208, 220-221, 230, 269, 321, 331-332, 334-339, 364-365, 383, 385, 388, 392-393, 395, 397, 438, 442, 445-446, 451-452, 457-458, 460-462
Capacity of governments, 37
Capital markets, 17, 28, 35-36, 282, 354, 449, 454, 457-458
Change management, 333, 414, 438
Chittagong city corporation, 58, 60, 66
Chittagong, 9, 43, 46-47, 49-50, 52-53, 56, 58-64, 66, 444
Cities in Indonesia, 161-162
Citizen community boards, 252, 271
City command center, 238
City management, 5, 17, 83, 418-419
City region 2020 - integrated planning for a sustainable environment, 431
City size, 15-16, 374
City/urban planning, 347
City-regions, 110, 112, 428, 458
Clean settlements program, 10, 309, 328

Coimbatore, 22-23
Colombo municipal council, 309, 319, 328, 340
Community, 5, 8-10, 21, 29, 34, 36, 38, 40, 68, 79, 83-85, 92-97, 109, 120-121, 125, 134, 157, 167, 170-171, 176, 181-183, 185, 202, 204-206, 219-221, 227-232, 236-239, 241-242, 252-253, 255, 257-263, 265-271, 291, 298, 309, 311, 318-319, 321, 323-333, 335-339, 346, 350, 358-360, 364, 367, 379, 385-387, 392, 394, 396-398, 408-409, 411-415, 417-418, 420-421, 423, 434-435, 438, 440, 444-447, 449, 453-460, 464
Community building, 229
Community consultancy, 396
Community contribution, 92-93
Community development management, 83, 95
Community development schemes, 121
Community liaison, 204
Community mobilization, 253, 257, 260-261, 326-329, 332
Community organization development institute, 350
Community waste bank, 359-360
Community-based organization, 134, 227, 253, 324
Community-based sanitation, 10, 255, 257, 259
Community-based solid waste management, 10, 291, 309, 323-324
Community-based solutions, 261, 266
Community-based water supply and sanitation services, 259
Competitiveness, 3, 5, 17, 36, 178, 185-186, 295, 299, 393, 420, 431, 433, 440, 446, 453, 455, 464-465
Complexity of governance, 37
Composting, 231, 265, 323, 325, 360
Concentrated urban development, 107
Conservation at wastewater treatment plants, 411, 413

Conservation of agricultural areas, 129, 131
Conservation of pra sae river, 357
Conservation of the environment, 175
Consumption patterns, 19-20, 32, 439, 461
Coordinated regional planning, 129
Coordination, 37-38, 40, 53, 80, 82, 128-129, 202, 277, 283, 297, 312, 325, 329, 346, 365, 398, 408, 443, 445-446, 452-454
Copenhagen convention, 266
Corruption, 29, 36-37, 76, 98, 145, 149, 153, 266, 331, 347, 431, 448-450
Cost recovery, 7, 9-11, 29, 36, 58, 61, 63, 80, 84, 86, 88, 90, 92, 118, 122, 127, 141, 147, 152, 173, 178, 182, 198, 206, 212, 227, 232, 237, 255, 259, 263, 290, 295, 300, 323, 326, 328, 337, 355, 358, 361, 383, 393, 396, 419, 446, 450, 454
Credit rating, 28, 146, 154, 282, 286, 300, 304, 419, 450-451
Credit scheme, 329, 367
Credit-rating information, 154
Cross-border, 123, 213, 445, 459, 461
Cultural heritage, 118, 130, 219, 233, 300
Curitiba, 8, 11, 404-407, 433-434
Cyberjaya multimedia super corridor, 10, 224, 237
Cyberjaya-, 10, 224, 227, 232, 237-243

Dana alokasi khusus, 167
Dana alokasi umum, 167
Decentralization, 4-5, 7, 35, 38-41, 47, 49-50, 71, 75-77, 79, 83, 86-87, 89-91, 95, 111-113, 152, 155-158, 161, 163-164, 166-167, 169-171, 174, 178, 180, 184-187, 194, 196-198, 208, 220, 225, 250-251, 265, 278-280, 282, 311-312, 332-335, 338, 340, 346-348, 350-353, 366, 371-373, 380, 394, 401, 439, 441, 443-446, 448, 450, 452-453, 458, 464

Decentralization policies, 4, 7, 40, 163, 194, 250, 278, 350-351, 372, 441, 444
Deconcentration, 75-77, 79, 83, 86-87, 89, 95, 166, 278
Dehiwala mount lavinia municipality, 309, 323, 330
Democratization, 155-158, 166, 183-184
Densification, 129-130
Desakota, 162
Development issues, 5, 273, 278, 357, 364, 374, 458
Development management, 83, 95, 220-221, 299, 337, 446
Development planning, 51-52, 77, 79, 170-171, 187, 189, 198, 218, 224, 242, 280, 285, 295, 301, 347, 365, 372, 417
Development policy, 89, 104, 444
Devolution program, 250-251, 271
Dhaka, 19, 43-44, 46-47, 49-50, 53-56, 58-59, 62-65, 67-69
Disaster management, 59-60, 301, 303
Dr. akhtar hameed khan, 255, 257, 260, 266, 269, 271

East-west economic corridor, 9, 189, 198, 212-213
Ecological sustainability, 20-21, 115
Economic base, 17, 39, 54, 146, 200, 207, 213, 240, 334, 337, 397, 405, 407
Economic development, 1, 3, 15, 21, 37, 51, 72-73, 79, 90, 101, 107, 112, 118, 155, 161, 165, 167, 169-170, 174-175, 177-179, 191, 218, 278, 284, 288, 294-297, 299, 302, 304, 306, 312, 340, 345, 347, 352, 372, 374, 387-389, 393, 404, 421, 433, 438, 441-442, 447-449, 453, 455, 458, 460-462
Economic governance, 113, 167, 197, 280, 296, 353
Economic growth, 1, 3, 6, 15, 18-20, 26, 30-31, 38, 72-73, 85, 98, 104, 109, 115, 119, 147, 152-153, 159-160, 173-176, 192, 195, 206, 288, 291, 296, 342-343, 381, 405, 418, 430-431, 437, 451, 456
Economic output, 19, 305
Economic planning, 66, 157, 218, 242, 298
Ecozone, 286-287, 304
Education, 1, 10, 13, 30, 53-54, 59-60, 76, 79, 93, 96, 105, 114-115, 117, 122, 124, 129, 136, 144, 163, 167, 176-179, 181-183, 192, 231, 236-237, 240-241, 248, 252, 287, 291, 293, 297, 318, 335-336, 339, 341, 347, 352, 354, 360-363, 381, 385-386, 407, 426, 458, 464
Educational institutions, 60, 291, 293
Electricity consumption, 26, 32, 169
Embrace change, 434
Enabling policy instruments, 304
Environmental degradation, 2, 34, 64, 241, 288, 345
Environmental impact assessment, 370, 393, 396
Environmental improvement, 2-4, 10, 56, 132, 152, 201, 328-329, 332-333, 370, 381, 385, 388, 392, 394, 397, 404
Environmental issues, 31, 128, 230
Environmental management and public health, 386
Environmental pollution, 107, 117, 128-129, 131-133, 192, 323, 374, 378, 464
Environmental protection, 59, 64-65, 129, 132, 167, 173, 175, 339, 357, 374, 379, 386
Environmental sustainability, 2, 7, 9-11, 66, 78, 85, 89, 93, 133-134, 173, 381, 408, 459, 461

Faisalabad, 10, 255-257, 259-261, 263, 266-268, 270-271
Federal town and country planning department, 241-242

Financial management, 331, 449
Financial performance, 28, 36, 452
Financial reallocation, 352
Financial services, 287
Fiscal sustainability, 304
Foreign investments, 3, 18, 108, 122, 168, 200, 280, 294, 305, 309, 315, 371, 375, 439
Fragmentation of urban areas, 365
Fukuoka, 22

Garbage collection, 321, 407
Garbage disposal, 59, 152, 329
GDP, 14-15, 18-19, 26-27, 32, 35, 43-44, 72, 102, 105-106, 109, 113, 122, 129, 132, 136, 143, 148, 156, 162, 168, 190-192, 197, 215, 221, 223, 245-246, 273-275, 277, 310, 315-316, 318, 321, 342, 369-370
General allocation fund, 167
Global environment facility, 232, 243
Global good practice, 8-9, 403-404, 433
Global sustainability, 18, 20
Globalization, 17, 115, 379, 428, 433, 448, 464
Good governance, 7-11, 53, 55, 58, 61, 63, 66, 76, 80, 82, 86, 90-91, 118, 122, 127, 141, 147, 152, 154-155, 170, 173, 178-180, 182, 184, 198, 206, 212, 227, 232, 237, 255, 259, 263, 288, 290, 293, 295, 299-300, 323, 326, 328, 355, 358, 361, 363, 381, 383, 393, 406, 426, 440
Good practice 5-9, 11, 24, 40, 41, 43, 50, 56, 58, 61, 63, 68, 80, 86, 88, 90, 95, 96, 101, 115, 117-119, 122, 127, 129, 133-134, 140-141, 147, 152, 156, 171, 173, 178-179, 182, 184, 198, 206, 212, 217, 224, 227, 232, 234, 237, 242, 245, 253, 255, 259, 263, 265, 273, 288, 290, 293, 295, 300, 321, 323, 326, 328, 335, 355, 357-358, 361, 363, 364, 381, 383, 393, 403, 404, 414, 419, 431, 434, 450

Governance, 2, 4-5, 7-11, 13, 17, 27, 31, 33-40, 43, 50, 53-56, 58, 61, 63, 66, 68, 76, 80, 82, 86, 90-91, 96, 110, 112-113, 118, 122, 127, 134, 140-141, 147, 152-158, 164, 166-167, 170, 173, 178-180, 182, 184, 186-187, 196-198, 206, 212, 227, 232, 237, 251, 255, 259, 263, 279-280, 288, 290, 293, 295-296, 298-301, 305, 307, 312, 320, 323, 326, 328, 334-335, 338-339, 351, 353, 355, 358, 361, 363, 379, 381, 383, 385, 387-388, 392-393, 397, 404, 406, 408, 420-422, 426-427, 429, 431, 433, 435, 437-438, 440, 445-447, 452-455, 459-465
Grameen bank, 58, 62, 268
Greater Manchester, 426-428, 465
Greater Vancouver regional district, 408
Green star certificate, 327
Greenfield site, 232
Gross domestic product (GDP), 14-15, 19, 27, 32, 43-44, 72, 102, 105, 136, 156, 162, 190, 223, 245-246, 273-274, 306, 310, 315, 342, 369, 428
Gross regional domestic product, 275, 296
Growth pole strategy for kratie, 9, 90
Guangzhou, 22-23, 105, 108-109, 111, 126

HCMC people's committee, 389, 392
HDI, 72, 102, 278, 310, 342, 369
Health, 5, 10, 13, 21, 24, 30-31, 33-34, 53-54, 56, 59-60, 62, 76, 79, 105-106, 114-115, 117, 120, 128-129, 136-137, 141, 143, 163, 167, 174, 176, 182-183, 192, 201, 203, 252, 257, 262, 267, 279, 292, 309, 317, 319-321, 323-324, 326, 328, 335-337, 339, 345-346, 351-352, 357, 359-360, 381, 383-386, 388-389, 391-392, 394-395,

Index 491

397, 407-409, 421, 426, 430, 433, 458, 464
Health and environment management, 10, 326
Health audit, 183
Health infrastructure, 317
Health service, 13, 31, 60, 105, 183, 292, 339
Heritage conservation, 9, 206, 208
High-tech parks, 111
Hong Kong, 41, 102, 122-123, 125-127, 279, 442
Household size, 21, 25
Housing, 2, 8, 11, 21-22, 24-25, 28, 30-31, 33-34, 52-54, 56, 64, 67-68, 82, 85, 89, 94, 99, 105-110, 113-114, 117, 119-124, 129-132, 134-135, 137, 139-140, 152-153, 158-159, 161, 165, 185-186, 223, 228, 232-234, 241, 248-249, 256-257, 260, 263, 279, 304, 314, 319-320, 325-326, 328-329, 335, 337, 339, 344-345, 348-349, 367, 371-372, 377-379, 384-385, 387-390, 392-397, 399, 401, 404, 409-410, 414-415, 417-418, 430-431, 433-434, 448-449, 451-452, 458, 460, 463-464
Housing and development, 349, 415
Housing and land policies, 248, 401
Housing environment, 415
Housing reform, 106, 109, 114, 119, 121, 130
Housing resettlement, 389
Hukou system, 104
Human capital development, 287, 336, 386
Human capital, 71, 300, 334-336, 339, 385-386, 447
Human resource development, 5, 67-68, 174-175, 182, 401, 457, 464
Hyper grid, 429

Iloilo city, 10, 292, 300-303
Implementation, 3, 10, 48, 51-52, 55, 67, 76-77, 79-80, 83, 94-95, 100, 164-165, 180, 184-185, 187, 196, 210, 227-234, 238, 241-243, 258, 262-263, 267, 270, 284, 287, 297, 312, 317, 321, 323-324, 327, 351-352, 354, 363, 365-366, 371, 381, 391-392, 395, 397-398, 401, 405, 409-410, 415, 417-418, 441, 444, 447-448, 464
Inclusive governance, 298
Income, 15, 17-18, 21-22, 24-25, 30, 32-33, 44, 54, 56, 61-62, 72-73, 86, 94, 102, 105, 108-109, 113-114, 136-137, 140, 143-144, 146, 149, 156, 162-163, 167-168, 177, 183, 186, 190-191, 211, 215, 223, 243, 246, 248-249, 253, 255, 259, 263-264, 267, 273, 277, 279, 281, 285-286, 290, 296, 298, 310, 315, 317, 320-321, 323-325, 329-331, 334-339, 342, 345, 348-349, 358-360, 367, 369-370, 378, 380, 384, 387, 390, 392-394, 396, 405, 415, 429, 439-440, 455-456
India, 6, 9, 14-16, 19, 22-23, 26, 32, 35, 41, 64, 135-140, 143, 146-148, 151-154, 311, 314, 437, 439, 442, 444, 450
Indonesia, 7, 9, 14-16, 19, 22-23, 26, 32, 35, 39, 41, 100, 138, 155-164, 167-171, 173, 178-181, 183, 185-187, 224, 275, 439, 443-444, 447, 450
Industrial city, 407, 428
Industrial revolution, 426, 430, 464
Information and communications technology, 231, 300, 428
Infrastructure, 1-2, 4-11, 13, 17-18, 20, 22, 24-29, 31, 33-38, 48, 54, 58-61, 63, 67-68, 71, 74-76, 78, 80, 84-86, 88, 90-94, 99, 108, 110, 112, 114-115, 117-118, 122, 127, 135, 137, 139-141, 143-144, 147, 152-154, 158-159, 161, 164-166, 168-170, 173-174, 178, 181-182,

185, 187, 191-193, 195, 198, 200-201, 204, 206, 208-210, 212-214, 216-218, 220, 223, 225, 227-228, 232-233, 237-239, 241, 243, 249, 253, 255-259, 261-263, 266-271, 277-278, 284-286, 288, 290-292, 295, 299-305, 311, 316-319, 321, 323, 326, 328, 335-336, 338-339, 344, 348, 350, 352, 355, 358, 361, 365-366, 371-372, 374, 377-379, 381, 383, 385-386, 388, 391, 393-400, 405-408, 414, 416-417, 419, 422-426, 434-435, 437-438, 440-443, 445-461, 463-465
Infrastructure and environmental improvements, 385
Infrastructure and maintenance, 26, 34, 318
Infrastructure charge units, 424
Infrastructure charges, 419, 422-425, 435
Infrastructure charges plan, 419, 422, 424, 435
Infrastructure deficit, 249
Inner city areas, 16, 107, 109-110, 118-120, 129, 134, 159, 378-379
Inner city development, 107, 120
Inner city redevelopment, 108, 120, 130
Innovation, 1, 7-11, 18, 58, 61, 63, 78, 80, 85-86, 89-90, 93, 97, 110-111, 115, 118, 122, 127, 129, 131, 141, 147, 152-153, 173, 177-178, 181-183, 198, 206, 212, 224, 227, 232, 237, 239, 241, 243, 255, 259, 263, 290, 295-296, 300, 323, 326, 328, 355, 358, 361, 365-366, 371, 383, 393-394, 403-404, 406-407, 412, 414, 416, 428, 433-435, 438, 443, 458
Innovative ways, 398
Institutional building, 10, 370, 381, 383
Institutional capacity, 33, 165, 185, 331, 334-335, 338-340, 373, 383, 385, 389 393, 397, 401, 444, 452
Institutional development, 4-5, 56, 68, 214, 329, 458

Institutional reform, 56, 177, 185, 320, 426, 438, 446
Institutional weaknesses, 33, 35
Integrated greenways, 411, 434
Integrated greenways and utility corridors, 411
Integrated planning, 397, 412, 422, 431
Integrated planning act, 422
Integrated provincial administration committee, 367
Integrated transport policy, 416
Integration of land use, 302, 416
Integration of physical and development planning, 365
Intergovernment fiscal transfers, 304
Intergovernmental financial relations, 113, 167, 197
Intergovernmental transfers, 137, 141, 281, 285, 354
International aid, 170, 197-198, 253, 282, 354, 380, 407
International crisis group, 251
International development agencies, 3-4, 391, 458-462
International donors, 98, 253
Investment, 2-3, 5-6, 17-18, 24-29, 33, 35-36, 38, 47, 52, 73-77, 89, 93, 97, 107-108, 110, 115, 117, 122-123, 127-128, 132, 135, 141, 143, 146, 153-154, 161-162, 168-170, 174-176, 179-183, 186, 189, 192, 196-198, 200, 208, 211-218, 221, 239, 241, 265, 268, 275-277, 280, 282-283, 285, 287, 293-295, 297-301, 303-307, 309, 311, 315-316, 319-321, 328, 344, 349-350, 366, 371, 375, 379, 386, 388, 393, 399-401, 405, 419, 421-422, 428, 439-442, 447-451, 455-456, 458-459, 464-465
Investment funds, 28-29

Jacobsen, *et al.* 2002, 249
Jaime lerner, 405
Jembrana, 9, 155, 171, 173, 181-184, 187

Khmer rouge, 71, 74-76, 82, 86, 91, 95, 98
Kota, 161, 166, 186-187
Kuala lumpur, 22-23, 223, 225, 227-228, 232, 237-238

La maison du patrimoine, 208
Lahore, 10, 248, 255-256, 263-265, 267, 269
Land, 1, 13, 16, 19, 21-25, 28, 31-32, 34-36, 41, 56, 59, 67, 73, 75, 78-79, 83, 85-87, 89-90, 92-94, 98-99, 103-104, 108-112, 117, 123-125, 127-128, 130-131, 133-137, 139-141, 148, 150, 152-153, 159-161, 163, 165, 173, 175, 181, 185, 190, 195, 198, 200, 214-215, 223-224, 227-228, 232-234, 238, 241, 247-249, 260, 265, 278-279, 287-288, 290, 294-295, 300-303, 307, 313, 319, 321, 323-325, 337, 339-340, 344, 347-350, 353-354, 357, 361-363, 366, 372, 374-379, 383-384, 387, 390-393, 395, 398-399, 401, 412, 415-418, 423-424, 428, 430, 433, 437, 441-442, 445, 448-449, 451-452, 457, 460, 463, 465
Land management, 56, 78, 87, 89, 99, 128, 377, 387, 399, 457
Land tenure, 16, 24, 31, 34, 75, 79, 287, 337, 349, 376, 399, 448
Land-use control legislation, 67
Lao people's democratic republic (Lao PDR), 7, 14-15, 32, 41, 71, 189, 341, 377, 439
Law 22/1999, 157, 166, 174
Law 32/2004, 157, 166
Leadership, 2, 8-9, 40, 50, 55, 58-59, 65-66, 82, 84, 98, 144-146, 154, 173, 178, 180, 182, 184-185, 230, 250, 257, 261, 264, 266-267, 278-279, 284, 299, 303, 311, 326, 339, 358, 363-366, 412, 419, 426, 433-434, 444-445, 450, 453, 457, 462-464

Leadership in energy and environmental design, 412
Learning, 176, 178, 182-183, 204, 206, 214, 230, 270, 291, 362-363, 381, 392, 394, 397, 428, 438, 464
Learning community, 182
Legacy of 200 years of heavy industry, 430
Lessons, 7, 61, 65, 71, 94, 96, 153, 155, 183-184, 205, 217-219, 224, 230, 236, 240, 266, 273, 303, 309, 329, 359, 363, 370, 389, 397, 421, 433, 435, 437, 439, 441, 443, 445, 447, 449, 451, 453, 455, 457, 459, 461, 463, 465
Leverage resources, 434
Leveraging international development assistance, 7, 79
LGU guarantee corporation, 282, 306
Liaodong peninsula, 9, 101, 108, 117-118, 127-129, 131
Light rail transit (LRT), 126
Linkages, 73-74, 97-98, 100, 108, 110, 123, 125, 161, 181, 214, 217, 248, 261, 278, 293, 297, 300, 306, 448, 453
Livable city, 292, 419
Local agenda 21, 10, 175, 225, 227-231, 241-243
Local authorities, 4, 35-36, 39, 50, 76-78, 82, 88-91, 95, 113, 196, 211, 227, 231, 242, 253, 259, 261, 323, 328, 330, 344, 346-347, 352-353, 365, 367, 371, 396, 428, 443, 445, 447, 449-454, 457
Local governance, 76, 156-157, 166, 173, 184, 351, 388, 464
Local leadership, 50, 184-185, 250, 364-365, 444-445
Local needs, 83, 281, 396, 443, 447
Local policies, 4, 298, 431
Location, 11, 17, 29, 34, 36, 53, 57, 80-81, 85, 90, 107, 116-117, 122, 129, 142, 150, 172, 179, 193, 198-199, 201, 206, 212, 214, 226-227, 230, 254, 280, 289, 292,

302, 322, 349, 355-356, 359, 361, 381-382, 414, 419, 424, 428, 440, 459
Lodhran, 10, 252, 255-258, 263, 266-267, 271
Low-cost housing, 25
Luang prabang urban improvements, 9, 206

Maintenance, 2, 4, 25-27, 29, 33-34, 53, 59, 92-93, 106, 109, 115, 120, 134, 139, 148, 168-169, 205, 209, 211, 216, 235-236, 257, 262, 269, 292-293, 301, 303, 311, 318, 330, 350-352, 354, 390, 394, 396-398, 412-413, 418, 422-423, 434, 445-456
Malaysia, 7, 10, 14-15, 19, 23, 32-33, 35, 41, 84, 176, 200, 223-225, 227-228, 231, 234, 237, 241-242, 275, 305, 439, 442
Managed migration, 177
Management of funds, 331
Manchester green city, 431
Mangrove, 175, 357, 417
Mangrove forest, 175
Mapping, 162, 181, 187, 196, 261, 302, 365, 430
MDGs, 63, 71, 341
Methods of valuation, 149
Metropolitan development, 119-120, 444
Metropolitan Iloilo development council, 301
Metropolitan manila, 274, 279-280
Microcredit, 9, 43, 58, 61-63, 85, 261, 268
Millennium development goals, 71, 163, 287, 317, 332, 341
Mobile library, 362-363
Mohammad yunus, 61
Morbidity, 34, 60
Mortgage finance assistance, 415
Motor vehicle pollution reduction, 64
MSC, 227, 232, 237-240, 243
Muang klaeng municipality, 10, 355

Multimedia university, 239
Mumbai, 22-23, 136, 138-139, 319
Municipal bonds, 9, 141, 146, 154, 444
Municipal finance, 252, 269

Naga city, 10, 295-297, 306-307
Nanjing: revitalizing the inner city, 9, 118
National accountancy standards, 179
National development planning, 51
National regional development, 163, 194, 250, 278
National regional development policies, 350
National urban renewal mission, 9, 151
Natural assets, 334-335, 339, 385
Natural Resources management, 79
Networks of motorways, 429
NGO participation, 350
Nhicu loc-thi nghe canal, 10, 388-389, 391-392
Non government organizations (NGO), 56, 58, 62-63, 68, 78-79, 88, 91-92, 94-95, 134, 185, 229, 231, 255, 257, 260, 270, 280, 297-298, 323, 326-328, 332, 339, 350, 355, 373, 397, 414, 418, 432

Official development assistance, 11, 44, 72, 102, 114, 136, 156, 190, 197, 223, 246, 273, 282, 310, 321, 342, 369, 380
One-window service, 77, 86-89, 95, 98
Ownership, 24, 89, 91, 93-97, 126, 158, 164, 185, 193, 205, 229, 239, 298, 303, 313, 332, 339, 376, 380, 398, 406, 415-416, 418, 421-422, 442

Parks and open spaces, 120, 133-134
Participatory land use planning (PLUP), 78-79, 90-91, 95, 98
Partnership building, 331-333
Partnerships, 2, 29, 40, 68, 77, 154, 220, 265, 269, 279, 291, 293, 296,

298-299, 305, 321, 329-333, 387, 393, 434, 438, 446-447, 449, 456-457
Pearl river delta, 108-109, 111, 122-125, 127
Pearl river delta regional plan, 125
People's republic of china, 2, 9, 14-15, 23, 32, 41, 101-102, 138, 190, 275, 465
Performance-based budgeting, 36, 179, 450
Peri-urban development, 13
Peri-urban growth, 344
Petaling jaya, 10, 224-225, 227-232, 242-243
Phase model, 430
Phichit municipality, 10, 358-360
Philippine cities competitive report, 288
Philippines, 7, 10, 14-15, 19, 22-24, 32, 35, 39, 41, 124, 176, 273-274, 276-277, 282-284, 286, 288, 297, 300, 306, 315, 439, 443-444, 447
Phnom penh, 9, 19, 71-75, 80, 82-86, 90, 94, 98-99, 450
Phu thuong ward, Hanoi, 370, 381, 383
Physical assets, 143, 334-335, 339, 385
Plan record keeping, 179
Planned urban region development, 66
Planning and integration of transportation services, 434
Policy, 2-3, 6, 24, 38-39, 47, 51-52, 54-56, 65-66, 73, 77, 80, 82-85, 87, 89-91, 93-95, 99, 101-102, 104-105, 107, 117, 123, 133, 137, 147-148, 152, 161, 164-166, 171, 177-178, 194, 214, 219, 221, 242, 251, 263, 270, 278-280, 284, 286-288, 293-295, 301, 303-304, 312, 316, 318, 320, 334, 339, 344, 347, 350 352, 365, 370-371, 373, 381, 391, 401, 410, 416-423, 432, 434, 438, 441-446, 452-453, 455, 457-459, 462
Pollution, 1, 19, 24, 31, 33-34, 54, 59, 63-64, 75, 106-107, 117, 128-129, 131-133, 139, 161, 192, 235, 264, 276, 288, 319-320, 323, 345, 351, 357, 374, 378, 380, 384, 386, 405, 409, 426, 430-431, 464-465
Pollution mapping, 430
Polycentric metropolis, 125
Population, 1-2, 13-16, 18-23, 25, 29-30, 32, 37, 41, 44-47, 49-50, 55, 58, 60, 63, 66-67, 71-80, 82, 84-86, 88-91, 95, 97-99, 101-103, 105-107, 110-111, 114, 118, 122, 127-129, 131, 136, 138-139, 143, 152, 154-156, 159-164, 166-167, 171, 173-174, 177-178, 180-181, 185-187, 190-194, 200, 207, 212-213, 216, 221, 223-225, 228, 232-234, 240-241, 245-250, 255-257, 260, 263, 269-271, 273-274, 279, 281, 288, 290, 292, 297, 299-300, 307, 310-311, 313-315, 317, 319, 324, 326, 340, 342-344, 355, 357, 359, 361, 367, 369, 371-372, 374-376, 378-379, 383, 386, 388, 393-394, 396, 399, 401, 405, 407-408, 414, 416-417, 419, 428-429, 431, 437, 439, 449, 456, 462, 464
Population and urbanization, 224, 313, 367
Population densities, 21-22, 192, 378
Population growth, 14-16, 21, 25, 37, 44, 46, 72, 82, 85, 97-98, 102-103, 136, 156, 159-160, 173, 187, 190, 194, 200, 207, 213, 223, 233, 245-247, 273-274, 288, 290, 300, 310, 313, 342, 359, 369, 374-375, 386, 417, 449, 456
Post-industrial sustainability, 426
Poverty, 1, 3, 18, 20, 26, 30-32, 34, 44, 51, 54, 56, 58, 61-63, 66, 68, 72-73, 79, 83, 85, 95, 97, 99, 100, 102, 114-115, 119, 136-137, 139-140, 152, 156, 161-163, 168, 170-171, 182, 186-187, 190, 194-195, 201, 212-213, 221, 223, 245-246, 268, 273-274, 276-278, 288, 296-297,

299, 305, 310, 317-318, 320-321, 334, 336, 338, 341-343, 345, 350, 355, 367, 369-370, 380-381, 386, 391, 393, 400-401, 451-452, 459-460, 464
Poverty reduction, 3, 26, 31, 51, 54, 56, 66, 68, 79, 83, 100, 114-115, 119, 137, 140, 163, 171, 187, 212-213, 296-297, 320-321, 334, 338, 386, 391, 400, 451-452
Pra sae river, 357, 444
Private sector, 2, 7, 17, 26, 28-29, 35, 40, 59, 65, 68, 76, 88, 91-92, 153, 158-159, 163, 169, 186-187, 211, 227, 229, 265, 277, 286, 296-298, 303, 318, 320, 326-327, 330-332, 337, 350, 353, 355, 357-358, 361, 373, 379, 381, 440, 444, 447, 449, 457-458, 465
Private sector participation, 350, 465
Privatization, 84, 91, 156, 159, 184, 316, 422
Processes of governance, 37
Project implementation, 100, 210, 258, 262, 365, 392, 398
Promoting ICT, 240
Property tax payment, 151
Property taxation, 9, 141, 147, 150, 154, 252, 442
Property taxes, 36, 144-145, 147-151, 167, 293, 442, 457
Public health, 21, 34, 128, 136-137, 143, 201, 326, 345-346, 351-352, 357, 359-360, 386, 388-389, 391, 407, 433
Public information, 96, 209
Public participation, 76-77, 83, 93, 346, 350-351, 401, 406
Public-community partnership, 262, 267, 269-270
Pudong new zone, 108
Purchaser provider model, 419-421, 426, 434
Purchaser-provider model of service delivery, 419

Putrajaya, 10, 224-225, 227, 232-237, 241-243
Putrajaya lake, 234-236
Putrajaya wetlands, 234-236, 241

Quality of life, 1-2, 237-239, 241, 263, 291, 293, 296, 345-346, 349, 351, 397, 405, 408, 415, 434

Rapid urbanization, 8-9, 14, 43, 46, 102, 106, 155-156, 158, 160, 168, 178, 223, 227, 366, 369, 375, 404, 448, 451
Regional development, 11, 38, 48, 51-52, 69, 107, 110-111, 117-118, 163, 168, 170, 185, 187, 189, 194, 197-198, 213, 220, 250, 253, 273, 275-278, 280-283, 285-288, 291, 295-296, 298-301, 304-306, 340, 350, 354, 372, 380, 403, 408-409, 411, 414, 435, 443
Regional development policies, 107, 111, 350
Regional economic governance, 113, 167, 197, 280, 353
Regional planning, 51-52, 66, 68, 118, 129, 180, 194-195, 218-219, 279-280, 284, 305
Regional structure in Bangladesh, 48
Relocation and resettlement, 390
Requirement for infrastructure investments, 27
Residential development, 378, 387
Resource-intensive technologies, 19, 33
Responsible capitalism, 432
Restructuring, 68, 145, 318, 405-406, 426, 431, 433
Revenue generation, 169, 279, 294-295, 313
Rural development, 13, 48, 50, 53, 66, 73, 78, 117, 350, 353, 374
Rural linkages, 217
Ruralopolis, 248
Rural-urban linkages, 97-98, 100, 453
Rust belt industries, 101, 118, 127, 130

Sanitary sewer overflow facility, 412
Sanitation, 5, 10, 25-27, 30-33, 44, 54, 72, 92, 102, 106, 109, 117, 121, 128, 136-137, 156, 190, 192, 203, 223, 245-246, 248-249, 252-253, 255, 257-262, 266-267, 270-271, 273, 301, 310, 317, 319-320, 323, 335, 337, 339, 342, 369, 378, 380-381, 385, 394, 458
Savannakhet, 9, 189, 194, 196-198, 212-216
Savan-seno special economic zone, 197, 214
Saving paper project, 359
Secondary towns urban development project, 208
Sewers, 3, 248, 255, 258, 266, 388, 390-391, 396, 399, 412, 422
Shakti foundation, 9, 58, 61-63
Shanghai, 102, 105-106, 108-113, 118, 129
Shelter, 5, 13, 25, 35, 62, 162, 170, 301, 315, 415
Shenyang, 106, 109, 127-132
Shenyang city, 106, 109, 127, 131
Shenzhen, 9, 101, 108-109, 117-118, 121-127, 133
Singapore, 8, 11, 24-25, 41, 174, 224, 275, 404, 414-418, 433, 442
Singapore green plan, 418
Sleman, 9, 155, 161, 164, 171, 173, 178-181, 184, 450
Slum settlements, 83, 94, 348
Slums, 31, 54, 56, 61, 63, 107, 139, 152, 162, 319, 326, 339, 345, 348-349, 414, 439
Small towns development, 194, 206, 218
Social capital, 115, 175-176, 334-335, 337, 385-386
Social indicators, 317
Social transformation, 1, 29
Social trends, 341, 429
Solid waste management, 10, 26, 33, 54, 56, 113, 143, 208, 245, 253, 258, 263-265, 267, 271, 291-292, 302, 309, 323-324, 331, 361-362, 385, 400, 458
Songkhla municipality, 10, 361-362
Spatial concentration of people, 1, 31, 33
Spatial imbalance, 46, 103
Special economic zones, 108, 110-111, 280, 286, 297, 350, 372
Special-purpose transfers, 167
Sri lanka, 7, 10, 14-15, 19, 32, 41, 124, 309-321, 323-325, 329-334, 337, 340, 439
Stakeholder participation, 332, 447
Stakeholders, 6, 67, 79, 82, 87-88, 91, 93, 95, 97, 157-158, 163, 165, 171, 174, 229-232, 242, 270, 291, 299, 324-325, 327-328, 330-332, 337, 358, 398, 420, 445
Strategic development planning, 79
Strategic infrastructure, 181, 311, 447
Strategic planning, 5, 40, 80, 83, 122, 182, 195, 220, 296, 438, 443, 445-447, 452-453, 457
Strategies, 3, 7, 43, 65, 68, 71, 96, 98, 151, 155, 164-165, 180, 184, 191, 195, 218-220, 224, 228-229, 239, 241-243, 268, 273, 278, 299-302, 304, 327, 330-331, 346, 351, 364, 366, 370, 395, 398-401, 410, 417-418, 432, 437, 439, 446, 448, 458, 460-462
Strategies to enhance sustainable urban development, 43, 65, 241, 398
Strategy for national urban development, 164
Stream keepers handbook, 232
Sungei penchala rehabilitation program, 232
Surrey transfer station, 411-412
Sustainability, 2-4, 6-11, 13, 18, 20-21, 24-25, 36-37, 40, 58, 61, 63, 66, 78, 80, 85-86, 89-90, 93, 98-99, 101-103, 115, 117-118, 122, 124, 127, 133-134, 141, 147, 152, 159,

170, 173, 178, 182, 185, 198, 206, 211-212, 215, 217-218, 227, 232, 234, 237, 241-242, 255, 259, 263, 290, 295, 298-300, 304, 319, 323, 326, 328, 330, 332, 355, 358, 361, 370, 381, 383, 393, 396-397, 399, 405-411, 418-419, 426, 431-435, 446-447, 449, 451, 454, 459, 461-463
Sustainability principles, 409-410
Sustainable capacity building for decentralization, 170, 184
Sustainable city initiative, 10, 355
Sustainable communities, 433
Sustainable consumption and production, 431-432
Sustainable development, 1, 5, 21, 24, 34, 56, 65, 74, 101, 107, 117, 127, 133, 171, 176, 220, 227-232, 234, 241-242, 265, 273, 297, 381, 392, 397, 403-404, 411, 445, 450, 460, 463-465
Sustainable regeneration, 433
Sustainable region initiative, 408-409
Sustainable regional development, 11, 273, 408-409, 411, 414
Sustainable township program, 321
Sustainable urban development, 6-7, 41, 43, 65, 68, 71, 96-97, 101, 114, 154, 225, 241, 245, 331, 381, 394, 398, 401, 403, 414, 437, 465

Tambons, 348
Tarakan, east Kalimantan, 155, 173
Task force, 89, 99, 324, 391
Tax powers, 136-137
Thailand, 7, 10, 14-15, 19, 23, 28, 32-33, 41, 71, 86, 189-191, 195, 200, 206-207, 212-215, 224, 275, 305, 341-346, 350-351, 353-355, 357-358, 360-362, 366, 439, 444
The lodhran pilot project, 255
The people's republic of china (PRC), 2, 9, 14-15, 23, 32, 41, 101-102, 138, 190, 275, 465

The PRC's agenda, 101-102
Tianjin, 105-106, 108
Traditional village, 383
Transferability of good practice, 6
Transport planning, 127, 133, 415-416
Transport strategy, 126
Transportation, 5, 28, 53, 73, 86, 125, 129, 180, 243, 270, 276-277, 280, 286, 318-320, 335, 341, 344, 357, 371, 377, 385, 397, 399, 404, 406, 409-411, 414, 433-434

Urban atmosphere, 407
Urban concentration, 47, 323
Urban credit program, 61-62
Urban development, 1, 3-8, 13, 24, 35, 37, 39-41, 43, 52-54, 56, 65-68, 71, 74-75, 77, 96-97, 99, 101, 104, 107, 114, 129, 135-137, 139-140, 152, 154, 158, 161, 163-165, 178, 186-187, 196, 201-202, 208, 213, 217, 225, 232, 234, 236, 239, 241, 245, 249, 253, 269, 301, 317, 319, 323, 328, 331-333, 340, 348, 361, 365, 370, 372-375, 377-381, 383, 387, 394, 397-401, 403-404, 414, 424, 433-435, 437-442, 444, 446-447, 451, 454, 458-463, 465
Urban development administration authorities, 196
Urban environment transition, 430
Urban environmental management, 380, 426
Urban finance, 34, 347
Urban governance, 2, 4-5, 17, 33-39, 54-56, 68, 134, 186-187, 323, 338, 379, 404, 431, 437-438, 452-454, 462-464
Urban greening program, 417
Urban growth, 2, 14, 17, 22, 27, 34, 37-38, 43, 46, 69, 76, 107, 139, 155, 343-345, 365, 372, 417-418, 456
Urban hygiene, 399
Urban improvements, 9, 200, 204, 206, 208, 219

Index

Urban infrastructure, 2, 8, 25, 27-29, 71, 75-76, 117-118, 135, 137, 140-141, 152, 161, 164-165, 191, 193, 204, 209-210, 216, 303, 318-319, 321, 377-378, 397, 399-400, 417, 449

Urban management, 4, 6-11, 43, 58, 61, 63, 77, 80, 83, 86-87, 90-91, 96, 118, 122, 127, 134, 141, 147, 152, 165, 173, 178, 180, 182, 198, 200, 206, 212, 227, 232, 237, 255, 259, 263, 290, 295, 300, 317, 323, 326, 328, 355, 358, 361, 364, 371, 381, 383, 393, 397, 400-401, 408, 414, 419, 421, 426, 434-435, 438, 445-446

Urban planning, 24, 38, 53-55, 63, 67, 87, 89, 99, 128, 237, 245, 347, 372, 374, 378, 383, 385, 396, 401, 405, 408, 434

Urban policies, 4, 134, 344, 400, 440

Urban population, 2, 13-15, 18, 21, 23, 25, 29-30, 32, 37, 44-47, 55, 72, 74-75, 98, 101-103, 106-107, 136, 138-139, 152, 154, 156, 159-160, 190, 192-193, 223-225, 245-249, 273-274, 310, 313, 319, 342-344, 369, 371, 374-376, 378-379, 399, 401, 414, 437, 439, 464

Urban public transport, 399

Urban redevelopment authority, 416-417

Urban renewal, 9, 140, 151, 301, 404-406, 419

Urban-rural migration, 193

Urban trends, 273, 343

Urban upgrading, 10, 189, 198, 219, 370, 381, 383, 388, 393-395, 398

Urbanization, 1-6, 8-9, 13-16, 18-19, 21, 29-31, 33, 38, 40-41, 43-46, 54, 66-67, 71-75, 80, 82, 99, 101-102, 104-107, 115, 133, 138, 151, 155-156, 158-162, 164, 166, 168, 178, 184-185, 189-191, 193, 223-224, 227, 245-246, 260, 273-274, 288, 309, 313-315, 318-319, 340, 343-345, 348, 350, 357, 364-367, 369-370, 372-375, 373-375, 379-380, 383, 397-398, 401, 404, 418, 427, 437, 439, 446-448, 451, 455-456, 463, 464

Urbanization trends, 14

USAID, 55-56, 179, 268, 315

Valuation, 36, 115, 133, 141, 145-146, 149-150, 166, 169, 179, 181, 202, 229, 288, 294, 300, 304, 313, 387, 432, 442

Van mieu ward, nam dinh city, 370, 381, 393, 398

Vientiane, 9, 19, 189-191, 193, 196-198, 200-204, 206, 209, 212-213, 215-216, 218-219, 221

Vientiane urban development and administration authority, 201-202

Viet Nam, 7, 10, 14-15, 19, 32, 35, 39, 41, 71, 100, 189, 195, 212-215, 369-376, 378-381, 383-384, 387-388, 392-394, 397-399, 401, 439, 448

Vietnamese urban development strategy, 372

Village area improvements, 9, 200

Vision for Curitiba, 433

Waste busters, 263-265

Waste disposal behavior, 325

Waste management, 10, 26, 33, 54, 56, 113, 139, 143, 161, 208, 230, 245, 253, 258, 263-265, 267, 271, 291-292, 301-302, 309, 323-324, 331, 335-337, 359, 361-362, 380-381, 384-385, 392, 400, 412, 434, 458

Waste recycling, 10, 358, 360

Waste to make fertilizer pellets, 360

Wastewater, 34, 106, 128, 180, 249, 319, 321, 345-346, 348, 383, 388-392, 400, 411, 413-414, 422, 434

WaterAid, 262, 267
Water for the poor, 61
Wetland, 69, 224, 227, 234-237, 241, 243
White paper on china's population, 101

World heritage list, 207-208
World leadership awards, 82, 84, 98

Yangtze river delta, 108, 111
Youth groups, 357